CAMBRIDGE GRAMMAR OF ENGLISH

A COMPREHENSIVE GUIDE

Spoken and Written English Grammar and Usage

RONALD CARTER
MICHAEL McCARTHY

CAMBRIDGE
UNIVERSITY PRESS

CAMBRIDGE UNIVERSITY PRESS
Cambridge, New York, Melbourne, Madrid, Cape Town, Singapore, São Paulo

Cambridge University Press
The Edinburgh Building, Cambridge CB2 2RU, UK

www.cambridge.org
Information on this title: www.cambridge.org/9780521588664

First published 2006
Reprinted 2006

Printed in Singapore by KHL Printing Co Pte Ltd

A catalogue record for this publication is available from the British Library

ISBN-13 978-0-521-58846-1 Paperback
ISBN-10 0-521-58846-4 Paperback

ISBN-13 978-0-521-58166-0 Hardcover
ISBN-10 0-521-58166-4 Hardcover

ISBN-13 978-0-521-67439-3 Paperback and CD ROM
ISBN-10 0-521-67439-5 Paperback and CD ROM

ISBN-13 978-0-521-85767-3 Hardcover and CD ROM
ISBN-10 0-521-85767-8 Hardcover and CD ROM

ISBN-13 978-0-521-58845-4 Network CD ROM
ISBN-10 0-521-58845-6 Network CD ROM

The Authors

Professor Ronald Carter is Professor of Modern English Language in the School of English Studies, University of Nottingham. He has published extensively in the fields of language education, applied linguistics and literary-linguistic studies. He is co-author of *Exploring Spoken English* and *Exploring Grammar in Context*, and co-editor of *The Cambridge Guide to Teaching English to Speakers of Other Languages* for Cambridge ELT.

Professor Michael McCarthy is Emeritus Professor of Applied Linguistics in the School of English Studies, University of Nottingham. He has also published extensively on corpora, vocabulary and discourse. He is the co-author of several of the *Vocabulary in Use* titles, *Exploring Spoken English* and *Exploring Grammar in Context* as well as a number of applied linguistics titles for Cambridge ELT.

The Cambridge Grammar Reference Panel

The Cambridge Grammar Reference Panel is a group of eminent and experienced applied linguists and teachers of English who have collaborated with the publisher and authors in the development of the *Cambridge Grammar of English*.

The panel members have contributed to workshops, commented on draft chapters and generously offered their time, advice and support during various stages of the project.

Professor Karin Aijmer, Gothenburg University
Dr Franz Andres Morrissey, University of Bern
Dra. Pilar Aguado Giménez, Universidad de Murcia
Dr Jean Hudson, Malmö University
Professor Susan Hunston, University of Birmingham
Dr Anne O'Keeffe, Mary Immaculate College, University of Limerick
Ms Marilyn Lewis, University of Auckland
Mr Keith Mitchell, Edinburgh University
Professor Sophia Papaefthymiou-Lytra, University of Athens
Professor Svetlana Ter-Minasova, Moscow State University
Professor Masanori Toyota, Kansaigaidai University

Ms Geraldine Mark, Project manager, UK

To Jane and Jeanne

Acknowledgements

AUTHORS' ACKNOWLEDGEMENTS

In relation to a huge book such as this one, which has been some seven years in the writing, many colleagues and other scholars have been influential in our thinking and have directly or indirectly influenced the content and wording of the grammar as it is now published. Some names deserve a special expression of our gratitude.

First and foremost we thank the Cambridge Grammar Reference Panel, whose names are listed on the preceding page. Without the input and inspiration of the panel, the book would have lacked much in terms of accuracy, organisation and detail. In particular we thank Karin Aijmer, Franz Andres Morrissey, Susan Hunston, Marilyn Lewis, Keith Mitchell and Anne O'Keeffe for their most thorough and meticulously detailed reports on the various versions of the manuscript and their suggestions, always an improvement on our attempts, for revision. Special thanks also go to Jean Hudson, who began as our research assistant for the project and taught us a great deal about searching corpora, and who later became a member of the Cambridge Grammar Reference Panel in its initial stages.

Cambridge University Press has given us outstanding and unfailing support from the outset. First and foremost, thanks must go to Colin Hayes, Group Director of ELT at the Press from 1988 to 2003, whose vision and willingness to back this project effectively started the whole enterprise. It was Colin, along with Jeanne McCarten, to whom we also owe a huge debt, who saw the significance of developments in corpus linguistics and their implications for English Language Teaching and, as a result, was prepared to make the commitment on behalf of CUP to the building of the CANCODE spoken corpus and the commissioning of this grammar. In its latter phase of development, we have enjoyed continued support and unstinting commitment from Colin Hayes' successor, Andrew Gilfillan, and from our commissioning editor, Alison Sharpe. Alison has steered the project with immense skill and provided us with inspiration, encouragement and good advice. The day-to-day running of the project has been expertly managed by Geraldine Mark, who brought to it her considerable experience as an English language teacher and ELT editor, along with an unerring instinct for how best to present the grammar. By a small-world coincidence, Michael McCarthy was first introduced to the complexities and pleasures of English grammar as a schoolboy by Geraldine's father, Brian Mark, who taught English at Saint Illtyd's College Grammar School, Cardiff, when Michael was a pupil there. Brian Mark, like his daughter, deserves a special thank-you.

CUP also supplied us with corpora and expert computational support from Patrick Gillard, Paul Heacock, Andrew Harley, Ann Fiddes and Dominic Glennon, to all of whom we say thank you. In the final stages of preparing the bulky manuscript for publication, we were privileged to have the editorial expertise, vast experience and eagle-eye of Thérèse Tobin to assist us; Thérèse made invaluable suggestions for clarifying our sometimes unclear statements. Linda Matthews steered the book through its final stages of production; she too deserves our thanks, as do Jane Durkin and Alex Priestley for sales and marketing campaigns. Thanks are also due to Linda Hardcastle for showing such understanding of a long and complex book in the compilation of the index.

A huge amount of background research went into the grammar, and, in addition to Jean Hudson, who worked as a researcher on the project in its earliest stages, we wish particularly to thank Svenja Adolphs, Julia Harrison and Jane Evison for their work in developing the CANCODE spoken corpus and their insightful investigations of it. Without their support as co-researchers, we would have been overwhelmed by the sheer volume of data.

Among university colleagues both authors have shared over the years, certain figures stand out as having profoundly influenced us. John Sinclair was, and remains, the most important inspiration and mentor for us both; his scholarship is unmatched in its originality, breadth and depth. He and other colleagues at the universities of Birmingham and Nottingham have moulded us academically into what we are today; those figures include Margaret Berry, David Brazil, Malcolm Coulthard, Michael Hoey and Walter Nash.

Other British-based colleagues and friends who have supported us and given us ideas and inspiration over the years include Dave Allan, Michael Baynham, Bethan Benwell, Chris Brumfit, Martin Bygate, Lynne Cameron, Joanna Channell, Caroline Coffin, Guy Cook, Sandra Cornbleet, Justine Coupland, David Crystal, Joan Cutting, Zoltán Dörnyei, Amorey Gethin, Sarah Grandage, Peter Grundy, Michael Handford, Martin Hewings, Ann Hewings, Sue Horner, Rebecca Hughes, Howard Jackson, Martha Jones, Almut Koester, Geoffrey Leech, Michael Lewis, Janet Maybin, Tony McEnery, Neil Mercer, Ros Mitchell, Louise Mullany, Felicity O'Dell, David Oakey, Kieran O'Halloran, Antoinette Renouf, John Richmond, Mario Rinvolucri, Paul Roberts, Norbert Schmitt, Mike Scott, Alison Sealey, Paul Simpson, Roger Smith, Peter Stockwell, Michael Swan, Paul Thompson, Ivor Timmis, Brian Tomlinson, Alistair West, Janet White, David Willis, Jane Willis, Alison Wray and Martin Wynne.

From universities and other institutions overseas, inspiration, ideas and friendly support came to us from Jens Allwood, Carolina Amador Moreno, Gabriela Appel, Michael Barlow, Douglas Biber, James Binchy, Anne Burns, Dermot Campbell, Christopher Candlin, Marianne Celce-Murcia, Wallace Chafe, Angela Chambers, Winnie Cheng, Margaret Childs, Brian Clancy, Sylvia de Cock, Susan Conrad, Fiona Farr, Tony Fitzpatrick, Loretta Fung, Sylviane Granger, Carmen Gregori Signes, Michael Halliday, Kieran Harrington, Ruquiya Hasan, Kent Hill, San San Hnin Tun, Paul Hopper, Ken Hyland, Yoshihiko Ikegami, Karen Johnson, Celeste Kinginger, James Lantolf, Diane Larsen-Freeman, Anna Mauranen, Nigel McQuitty, John McRae, Marty Meinardi, Freda Mishan, Bróna Murphy, David Nunan, Aisling O'Boyle, María Palma Fahey, Aneta Pavlenko, Scott Payne, Luke Prodromou, Nikoleta Rapti, Randi Reppen, Antonia Sánchez Macarro, Helen Sandiford, Elana Shohamy, Rita Simpson, Anoma Siriwardena, Diana Slade, Carol Spöttl, Jeff Stranks, Susan Strauss, Merrill Swain, John Swales, Gerry Sweeney, Hongyin Tao, Steven Thorne, Elena Tognini-Bonelli, Geoff Tranter, Amy Tsui, Koen Van Landeghem, Elaine Vaughan, Mary Vaughn, Steve Walsh, Shih-Ping Wang, Martin Warren, Linda Waugh, Fiona Wheeler, Geoff Williams, Brent Wolter and Xuelian Xu.

Others too many to mention have inspired us with conference papers and published work, and to all of them we owe a debt of gratitude. Whatever shortcomings remain in the book, they must rest entirely at our door.

Ronald Carter
Michael McCarthy
Nottingham, 2005

PUBLISHERS' ACKNOWLEDGEMENTS

Development of this publication has made use of the Cambridge International Corpus (CIC). The CIC is a computerised database of contemporary spoken and written English which currently stands at 700 million words. It includes British English, American English and other varieties of English. It also includes the Cambridge Learner Corpus, developed in collaboration with the University of Cambridge ESOL Examinations. Cambridge University Press has built up the CIC to provide evidence about language use that helps to produce better language teaching materials.

The author and publishers are grateful to the following for permission to reproduce copyright material. It has not always been possible to identify the source of material used or to contact the copyright holders and in such cases the publishers would welcome information from the copyright owners.

Advertisement for Satellite trainers, with the kind permission of Reebok International Limited; Unilever UK for, 'I can't believe it's not butter'; Nabisco Foods for, 'Fruitful from Shredded Wheat'; Kraft Foods for, 'Enjoy the smooth, silky taste of Creamery butter'; extracts from the online website of Save the Children Fund, reproduced with the permission of Save the Children; extracts from *The Guardian* and *The Observer* © Guardian Newspapers Limited; for extracts from *Absolute Truths* by Susan Howatch, *The Black Opal* by Victoria Holt, *The Conviction of Guilt* by Lew Matthews, *Codebreaker* by Alastair MacNeill, *The Devil's Door* by Alastair MacNeill, *Dreams of Innocence* by Lisa Appignanesi, *Family Blessings* by Lavyrle Spencer, *Final Resort* by Ian St. James, *For the Love of a Stranger* by Erin Pizzey, *The Glasgow Girls* by Francis Paige, *The Open Door* by Alan Sillitoe, *Rushing to Paradise* by J.G.Ballard, *Testimonies* by Patrick O'Brian and *Walking Back to Happiness* by Helen Shapiro, © HarperCollins Publishers; for extracts from *Desperadoes* by Joseph O'Connor, reproduced by permission of HarperCollins Publishers and Blake Friedmann Literary Agency © Joseph O'Connor, 1994; for extracts from *Lost Children* by Maggie Gee by permission of HarperCollins Publishers and Curtis Brown Group, © Maggie Gee; for extracts from *Yellow Bird* by Trudi Pacter, by permission of HarperCollins and the author; for extracts from *An Indecent Act* by Maria Barrett, *The Ambassador* by Edwina Currie, *Dead & Gone* by Dorothy Simpson, *Siena Summer* by Teresa Crane, *Solomon Grundy* by Dan Gooch, *The Scholar* by Courttia Newland and *What Treasure did Next* by Gina Davidson, © Little, Brown and Company; for extracts from *Two Gentlemen Sharing* by William Corlett by permission of Little, Brown and William Corlett c/o Caroline Sheldon Literary Agency Limited, © William Corlett, 1997; for extracts from *The Keepers* by Pauline Kirk, by permission of Little, Brown and Company and David Grossman Literary Agency on behalf of the author; for extracts from *Another Kind of Cinderella* by Angela Huth, © Angela Huth 1995, reproduced by permission of Little, Brown and Company, Felicity Bryan Agency and the author; for extracts from *Every Man for Himself* by Beryl Bainbridge, by permission of Little, Brown and Company and Johnson and Alcock on behalf of the author; for extracts from *Like* by Ali Smith, by permission of Ali Smith, Xandia Hardie and Little, Brown and Company; extracts from *The Waiting Game* by Bernice Rubens are reproduced by permission of Little, Brown and Company and PFD (www.pfd.co.uk) on behalf of The Estate of Bernice Rubens; for extracts from *Transgressions* by Sarah Dunant, by permission of Little, Brown and Company and Gillon Aitken on behalf of the author; for extracts from *The Angry Mountain* by Hammond Innes, *Arcadia* by Jim Crace, *Carn* by Patrick McCabe, and *Ever After* by Graham Swift, © Macmillan; for extracts from *Cast the First Stone* by Jane Adams, by permission of Macmillan and the author; for extracts from *A Green Bag Affair* by Paul Geddes, *Harvey Angell* by Diana Hendry, *Flight from the Dark, Lone Wolf 1* by John Denver © The Random House Group Ltd; for extracts from *The Tenancy* by Eva Figes by permission of The Random House Group Ltd and Rogers, Coleridge & White Ltd on behalf of the author; for texts from *Act of Valour* by Emma Drummond, *Charlotte Street* by Juliette Mead, *Death Before Dishonour* by Barnaby Williams, *Fault Lines* by Natasha Cooper, *The Keeper* by Eileen MacDonald, *Miles & Flora* by Hilary Bailey, *Mr MacGregor* by Alan Titchmarsh, *Sentimental Journey* by Juliette Mead and *Sour Grapes* by Natasha Cooper, © Simon & Schuster.

Excerpts from the following works are also included:
Emma, Mansfield Park and *Northanger Abbey*, by Jane Austen; *The Tenant of Wildfell Hall*, by Anne Brontë; *A Tale of Two Cities, Dombey and Son* and *Great Expectations*, by Charles Dickens; *The Mill on the Floss*, by George Eliot; *The Mayor of Casterbridge, Far from the Madding Crowd* and *Tess of the D'Urbervilles*, by Thomas Hardy; *Lady Chatterley's Lover*, by D H Lawrence; *Anna Karenina*, by Leo Tolstoy; *Lord Arthur Savile's Crime*, by Oscar Wilde; *To the Lighthouse, The Waves* and *Mrs Dalloway*, by Virginia Woolf.

The following are reproduced with permission of Cambridge University Press: extracts from *Behavioural and Cognitive Psychotherapy* (2002); *Cambridge Advanced Learners' Dictionary*; *Cambridge Encyclopaedia*, Crystal; *Contemporary European History*, 2001, 10 (3); *Environmental Conservation*, (2001); *Environment and Development Economics* (2002); *International Review of Social History*, 46 (2001); *Issues in Applied Linguistics*, McCarthy; *Journal of American Studies*, 2001 35 (1): *Journal of Fluid Mechanics*, 2002; *Journal of Nutrition*, 1993; *Journal of Social Policy* (2002); *Journal of Zoology* (2002); *Materials Development in Language Teaching*, Tomlinson; *More Grammar Games*, Rinvolucri and Davis; *New Cambridge English Course*, Swan and Walter; *New Horizons/Science*; *Key stage 3 Science*, 1995; *Review of International Studies* (2001), 27:265–272 Cambridge University Press Copyright © 2001 British International Studies Association; *Revolutions*, Todd; *The Historical Journal* (2001); *The Politics of the Picturesque*, Copley; *Vocabulary*, Schmitt and McCarthy.

The following adapted sections are reproduced by permission of Oxford University Press from Practical English Usage by Michael Swan © Michael Swan 1980-1995: section on Roman numbers (p. 384); section on notes (p.355); section on *a* and *one* (pp. 385-6); section on singular forms with plural meanings (pp. 386-7); section on areas (p. 388).

Thanks go to the British National Corpus for extracts from the following works: *A Song Twice Over* by Brenda Jagger, Imprint: Fontana Press, 1994; *Billion Dollar Brain* by Len Deighton, Imprint: Arrow Books; *Chymical Wedding* by Lindsay Clarke, Imprint: Jonathan Cape; *The Child Bride* by Philippa Wait, Imprint: Robert Hale Ltd; *Daughters of the Moon* by Susan Sallis, Imprint: Corgi Books; *Frankenstein* by Patrick Nobes, Imprint: OUP, 1994; *Green and Pleasant Land* by Howard Newby, Imprint: Wildwood House; *House of Cards* by Michael Dobbs, Imprint: HarperCollins, 1994; *Jane's Journey* by Jean Bow, Imprint: Hodder & Stoughton Ltd, 1994; *Murder Makes an Entrée* by Amy Myers, Imprint: Headline Book Publishing plc, 1994; *Nice Work* by David Lodge, Imprint: Secker & Warburg, 1994; *Roads that Move* by Walter Perrie, Imprint: Mainstream Publishing Co. Ltd; *Sons of Heaven* by Terence Strong, Imprint: Hodder & Stoughton Ltd.

Contents

Note: the numbers are section numbers, not page numbers.

There are more detailed contents pages at the start of each chapter.

Introduction to the *Cambridge Grammar of English*

Introduction to the *Cambridge Grammar of English*

WHAT IS GRAMMAR? 1

Grammar is concerned with how sentences and utterances are formed. In a typical English sentence, we can see the two most basic principles of grammar, the arrangement of items (syntax) and the structure of items (morphology):

I gave my sister a sweater for her birthday.

Arrangement of items (syntax) 1a

The meaning of this sentence is obviously created by words such as *gave*, *sister*, *sweater* and *birthday*. But there are other words (*I*, *my*, *a*, *for*, *her*) which contribute to the meaning, and, additionally, aspects of the individual words and the way they are arranged which enable us to interpret what the sentence means. For example, we know it is *I* who gave the sweater, not *my sister*, because *I* comes before the verb (*gave*). In English, subjects (the doers of actions) come before verbs in statements. We also know the relationship between the indirect object, *my sister*, and the direct object, *a sweater*, (that *the sweater* was given and *my sister* was the recipient) because indirect objects come before direct objects. We also expect *my* to come before *sister*, not after. These aspects of the arrangement of things in sentences is referred to as syntax. Syntax is one of the two basic principles of grammar.

Structure of items (morphology) 1b

The example sentence also illustrates the other basic principle of grammar. *I* and *my* are two different forms, one with a subject meaning, the other with a possessive meaning, even though they both refer to the same person. *Gave* refers to past time, in contrast to *give(s)*, which refers to present time. *Sweater* is singular; if there were more than one sweater, the form would be *sweaters*. These small items of meaning, such as *I*, *my*, the past form *gave*, a plural *-s* ending, are called grammatical morphemes, and come under the heading of morphology. Morphology is concerned with the structure of words and phrases. It is the second basic principle of grammar.

Acceptable and unacceptable forms 1c

Grammar is concerned with acceptable and unacceptable forms and the distinctions of meaning these forms create. The fact that *sweater* means 'knitted outer garment worn on the upper part of the body for warmth' and that *sister* means 'female sibling' are matters of vocabulary (lexis), but the distinction between present and past, one and more than one, subject and object, possession and non-possession, etc., are matters of grammar. In every language, some forms are acceptable and others are not. So, in English, we can create arrangements of our example sentence which are not acceptable, either syntactically or morphologically:

I my sister gave a sweater for birthday her.

Gave I my sister a sweaters for his birthday.

I gives my sisters sweater a for her birthday.

In this grammar book, we indicate unacceptable forms with a line through the text:

~~I my sister gave a sweater for birthday her.~~

Vocabulary (lexis) 1d

Although some aspects of our example sentence are concerned with lexis, lexis and grammar are not totally independent. A 'sweater' is the kind of thing in the world that English treats as countable (we may have one, two or more of them). However, if I gave my sister 'information', the fact that information is an abstract entity, which English considers to be uncountable, affects the grammar, and the sentence would have to be *I gave my sister some information*. 'I gave my sister an information' would be an unacceptable form.

Phrases 1e

Our initial example sentence may also be seen as composed of units or building blocks of different sizes, not just individual words and their endings. For example, the sentence could be divided up thus:

I | gave | my sister | a sweater | for her birthday.

We have now divided the sentence into its constituent phrases (items which have individual functions in the sentence). It is the phrase *a sweater* which acts as the object, not just the word *sweater*, and the whole phrase *for her birthday* indicates the reason or circumstances of the giving.

Clauses 1f

We could extend the example sentence:

I gave my sister a sweater for her birthday **and** *she bought me a CD for mine.*

We can now see two larger building blocks (in green) in the sentence, connected by *and*. These are clauses (separate units containing their own verbs: *gave/bought*). Grammar is concerned with how the constituent units of sentences (morphemes, words, phrases and clauses) are put together to form sentences.

→ 539 **Glossary** for any unfamiliar terms

Classes of word, phrase and clause 1g

Words are not all of the same type. Some, such as *sweater* and *sister*, are nouns (words referring to entities: persons, things, animals, abstract concepts); some, such as *gave* and *bought*, are verbs (words referring to actions, events or states); and so on. These words belong to different classes.

Equally, the phrases belong to different classes: *for her birthday* and *for mine* are prepositional phrases (phrases introduced by prepositions).

Clauses too belong to classes: some are declarative (they have the subject first and typically make statements), some are interrogative (they have a verb such as *do*, *be* or *have* first, and typically ask questions). Grammar is concerned with how units and classes relate to one another.

Functions 1h

The noun phrases *my sister*, *a sweater* are types of object in our example sentence in 1f, and *for my birthday* and *for mine* are operating as phrases indicating the circumstances. They are referred to as adjuncts. The terms subject, verb, object, adjunct refer to the functions the different phrase-types carry out in the clause. Grammar describes what the acceptable functions are.

Sounds (phonology) 1i

How sentences are spoken is also relevant. The sentence *I do like your car*, on the face of it, seems to break the rule that *do* is not used in statements. However, if the sentence is spoken with appropriate stress, then it becomes acceptable. This is the emphatic *do*, which may be used in statements:

I do like your car.

Phonology (the sound systems of a language) is therefore also connected in important ways with grammar and lexis, and influences the interpretation of sentences.

Choices 1j

Throughout the construction of a sentence, the speaker/writer makes choices. Choices involve things such as number (singular or plural), tense (present or past), definiteness (***a*** *sweater* versus ***the*** *sweater*), etc. Every choice carries a different meaning, and grammar is concerned with the implications of such choices.

WHAT IS THE *CAMBRIDGE GRAMMAR OF ENGLISH*? 2

Usage and acceptability 2a

This book is a grammar of standard British English. Standard British English is a variety of English defined by its grammar, lexis and phonology. There are, of course, other standard varieties of English, for example, standard North American English or standard Indian English or standard Australian English, which may differ quite considerably in terms of pronunciation, but only minimally as far as grammar is concerned. ⇢ **Appendix 530–538** for particular differences in North American English grammar.

However, issues of acceptability are never far from the surface when there is reference to what is standard in grammar or in language use in general. In this book, the following main categories of British English are adopted:

- acceptable in standard written and spoken English (most forms are in this category)
- acceptable in standard written and spoken English but not approved in more prescriptive grammar books and often avoided by many writers of formal English; for example: split infinitives, stranded prepositions, choices between *who* and *whom*
- unacceptable in standard written English but acceptable in standard spoken English (⇢ for example **96** and **97** on **headers and tails**)
- unacceptable in standard written and spoken English but acceptable in many regional varieties of English (⇢ for example **119b** on the use of ***ain't***); such forms are not included in the main description in this book, and are simply referred to occasionally
- unacceptable in all varieties of English (for example a structure such as *he did must speak*); such forms are excluded from this book.*

Where possible in this book, we always give an indication if a particular grammatical usage is likely to be considered non-standard, but we also indicate in which contexts such usage may nonetheless pass unnoticed.

Grammar rules: deterministic and probabilistic 2b

The general lay person's perspective is that grammar is about rules of speaking and writing, but not all 'rules' given by grammarians are of the same kind.

Some rules are deterministic, that is, they are rules which always apply. For example, the definite article always comes before the noun (we say *the cup*, not *cup the*), or indicative third person singular present tense lexical verbs always end in *-s* (we say *she works*, not *she work*).

Other rules are probabilistic, that is to say, they state what is most likely or least likely to apply in particular circumstances. For example, in the overwhelming majority of cases, a relative pronoun (e.g. *who*, *which*, *that*) must be used to refer to the subject of a relative clause:

We met a woman ***who*** *had lived in Berlin during the 1980s.*

However, in informal spoken styles, the relative pronoun may often be omitted, especially after a *there* construction:

There was a shop in the village sold home-made ice cream.
(or: There was a shop in the village which/that sold home-made ice cream.)

* Our thanks to Susan Hunston for suggesting this list of categories.

It is not a rule that the relative pronoun **must** be omitted; it **can** be omitted. The rules concerning its use are therefore probabilistic (it is most probable in most cases that the relative pronoun will be used). In this book, many of the rules given are probabilistic, since they are based on observations of what is most likely and least likely in different contexts in real spoken and written data.

Descriptive versus prescriptive approach 2c

A descriptive approach to grammar is based on observations of usage; it states how people use the grammar of a language. A prescriptive approach to grammar is based on the idea that some forms are more 'correct' or more associated with 'good usage' than others. Prescriptive rules are often social rules that are believed to mark out a speaker or writer as educated or as belonging to a particular social class. Examples of prescriptive rules are:

> DO **NOT** END A SENTENCE WITH A PREPOSITION.
> (e.g. Do not say *This is something you should not be involved* ***in***; say *This is something* ***in which*** *you should not be involved*)
>
> DO **NOT** SPLIT AN INFINITIVE.
> (e.g. Do not say *I expect* ***to*** *shortly* ***welcome*** *him here*; say *I expect* ***to welcome*** *him here shortly*)

Examples are given throughout the book of contexts of use in which prescriptive rules do or do not apply, where this is useful to language learners. The book also contains a number of specially written panels that highlight common prescriptive rules, discuss attitudes to the rules and examine how they do or do not apply in different contexts of use (→ for example 337).

The main approach taken in this book is descriptive. The emphasis throughout the book is on describing the ways in which speakers and writers of English use the language to communicate with one another, as evidenced in large numbers of spoken and written texts from all over the British English community. The approach taken is, we believe, compatible with a pedagogical grammar which is written primarily for advanced learners of English. It is therefore important that learners are aware of the social importance which attaches to certain prescriptive rules while at the same time being aware of the way in which English is used by real speakers and writers of the language. Issues relevant to a learner's grammar are explored further at several places below.

Grammar as structure and grammar as choice 2d

The book regularly draws attention to the implications of different grammatical choices and gives the user opportunities to observe and learn about grammatical choices in relation to particular contexts in which the language is used.

The *Cambridge Grammar of English (CGE)* makes a distinction between grammar as structure and grammar as choice. Grammar as structure means: What rules does one need to know in order to construct a sentence or clause appropriately? An example of a structural rule would be that the determiner *none* must be followed by *of* (*none of my friends*, as opposed to *none my friends*).

On the other hand, grammar frequently involves ellipsis, which is the absence of words which can be understood from the surrounding text or from the situation. For example the ellipsis of the subject noun or pronoun in expressions such as *Looking forward to seeing you*, *Don't know* and *Think so* is largely the speaker's/writer's interpersonal choice. Interpersonal choices are choices which are sensitive to the relationship between the speaker/writer and the listener/reader. In such a case as this, grammar as choice means: When is it normal to use ellipsis? Are some forms of ellipsis more likely to be used in spoken than in written modes? What kinds of relationship does it project between speakers and listeners? Are the forms linked to greater or lesser degrees of intimacy and informality?

Another example of grammar as choice would be the use of the past simple and the past progressive tense in reported speech. For example, the most frequent form of speech report is the past simple, as in:

*She **said** the central heating needed to be repaired.*

But the past progressive form can also be used. This is especially common in spoken rather than in written English as speakers can choose to express reports as 'pieces of news' rather than as representations of people's words:

*She **was saying** that she's going to quit her job.*

Both forms of *say* are acceptable but the progressive form is less frequent. It is, however, a choice which speakers or writers can make in particular contexts. In this book, both grammar as structure and grammar as choice are treated, and the grammar of choice is as important as the grammar of structure.

Grammar and lexis 2e

Grammar does not exist separately from other levels of language. There is a close link between grammar and lexis and in this book attention is given to the meaning, structure and formation of individual words. There are also many places in the book where grammatical choices entail particular choices of vocabulary, or vice versa.

The book reflects recent computer-assisted research, which shows the patterned relationship between vocabulary and grammar. For example, the pattern of about twenty verbs in English is verb + *by* + *-ing*, where the verb is followed by the preposition *by* and an *-ing* clause. Most verbs of this kind fall into two main groups, one group meaning 'start' or 'finish', the other group meaning 'respond to' or 'compensate for' something. For example:

*They **started off** by collecting money for children's charities.*

*She **concluded** by singing three songs in Italian.*

*They **responded to** the news by cutting off all communication with the outside world.*

*He **allowed for** the bend by braking sharply.*

→ **539 Glossary** for any unfamiliar terms

Experienced users of English recognise such patterns intuitively but it is often only when computer analysis demonstrates the patterns across many examples of use that they are fully acknowledged. Description of such patterns is becoming a more established feature of many modern grammar books. *CGE* is no exception and lists of words which behave in similar ways to one another are frequently given.

Grammar and discourse 2f

Another important level of language organisation that has received detailed investigation in recent years is the level of discourse. Discourse refers to the patterns of language used beyond the level of the sentence or beyond the individual speaking turn. There has been much description of spoken discourse patterns (e.g. how people open and close conversations; how they organise their speaking turns) and also attention to the ways in which sentences combine to form coherent texts in writing. This book pays attention to such patterns and describes the cohesion of sentences – that is, the ways in which grammatical links across sentences or speakers' turns create coherent texts (→ **214**). Two chapters in this grammar (**123–139** and **140–154**) are devoted to grammar and discourse and to the way in which larger units of meaning are created.

In *CGE* it is not our aim to take a text and then extract atomised, grammatical points from it. Rather, texts are used to illustrate how grammatical meanings are created in actual use. The place, distribution and sequencing of the grammatical feature in its text and context are as important as its actual occurrence. This book is based on insights from the fields of text and discourse analysis, rather than just traditional sentence grammars. The emphasis in *CGE* is, wherever appropriate, on the relationship between choice of form and contextual factors.

In parts the book represents a first step towards a context-based or discourse grammar of English. For example, where it is appropriate, extracts from different written sources are clearly indicated and spoken exchanges are marked and explained with reference to particular contexts and speaker roles. Examples are drawn here from section 126.

[public notice]
*Vehicles parked **here** will be towed away.*

[notice in a train compartment]
***These** seats are reserved for disabled customers.*

[at a travel agent's; the customer has just received his tickets]
Customer: *Right well **this** is all right now is it?*
Agent: ***That**'s the ticket yes.*
(what is *this* for the customer is *that* for the agent)

Grammar and variation: the importance of context 2g

Language variation takes many different forms. Language can vary in levels of formality; it can vary according to the regional or social groups to which speakers belong; it can vary over time; it can vary according to the uses to which it is put.

Certain types of language use are associated with particular forms of activity or registers and are marked by distinctive patterns of use, including distinctive patterns of grammar.

For example, cookery books and instructional manuals use many imperatives; newspaper headlines often deploy highly compressed forms of language; some forms of academic English make particular use of the passive voice; incomplete sentences are commonly used to highlight key information in advertisements and in radio and television news broadcasts. In conversation, too, the choice of one grammatical feature rather than another can depend on the speaker's perception of the relationship they have with other speakers, the formality of the situation or their assessment of the context in which they are communicating.

An important factor that affects the context of communication is whether the medium is spoken or written. Several parts of this book describe differences and distinctions between spoken and written grammar and indicate the different degrees of formality that affect choices of grammar. Wherever necessary to avoid ambiguity, information about the context in which examples typically function, whether predominantly spoken or written, is given. In *CGE* we are assisted in this practice by access to a corpus (··➝ **3a**), which is very carefully annotated with reference to contexts of use.

Grammar and the spoken language 2h

Most books on the grammar of English have had a bias towards the written language. For many centuries dictionaries and grammars of the English language have taken the written language as a benchmark for what is proper and standard in the language, incorporating written, often literary, examples to illustrate the best usage.

Accordingly, the spoken language has been downgraded and has come to be regarded as relatively inferior to written manifestations. Both in the teaching and learning of first, second and foreign languages, and in educational institutions and society in general, oral skills are normally less highly valued, with linguistic expertise being equated almost exclusively with a capacity to read and write.

Until recently, the forms and structures typically found in spoken communication have not been highlighted. It is only recently that advances in audio-recording and associated technology have enabled sufficient quantities of spoken language to be used for analysis. *CGE* draws for its examples of spoken English on the CANCODE corpus (··➝ **3a**). The CANCODE corpus is a collection of everyday informal spoken texts which provides very useful evidence of significant structures, especially as they are found in spontaneous, unplanned, conversational usage. Although the corpus has not been systematically coded for phonetic features and features of intonation, this book has an accompanying CD-ROM in which key sentences, conversational exchanges and patterns of use can be listened to.

A bias towards written grammar means that in some cases appropriate terms for describing particular features of spoken grammar are not available within existing grammatical frameworks. In some cases new ways of describing language (metalanguage) have to be introduced. An example is the use of the terms 'headers' and 'tails' (→ 96 and 97). Thus, structures such as:

header
Her friend, Jill, the one we met in Portsmouth, ***she*** *said they'd moved house.*

tail
He *always makes a lot of noise and fuss, Charlie.*

are unlikely to be found in written contexts but are standard spoken forms. These have, in the past, often been described using metaphors such as left- and right-dislocation, based on the way words are arranged on a page in western writing. We consider these inappropriate to describe spoken grammar, which exists in time, not space.

Another example of differences between spoken and written use involves voice (the choice of active or passive). Voice is more subtle and varied in the grammar of everyday conversation than is indicated in grammar books that focus only on written examples. There is, naturally, a focus on the core *be*-passive in contrast to the active voice, but when we look at a large amount of conversational data, we see that the *get*-passive form is much more frequent in spoken data than in comparable amounts of written data. At the same time it adds a further layer of choice, reflecting speakers' perceptions of good or bad fortune, or of the degree of involvement of the subject. For example:

I'm afraid his car window ***got broken****.*
(an unfortunate outcome)

She ***got herself invited*** *to the official opening.*
(*she* is seen as partly instrumental in being invited)

Detailed attention needs to be paid to such complex phenomena, which might otherwise be underplayed in a book based only on written examples. Where it is appropriate to do so, in *CGE* there is a thorough examination of spoken examples side by side with balanced written examples so that relevant differences can be revealed.

Some people argue that learners of English should not be presented with details of how native speakers speak. The position taken in this book is that such an approach would disadvantage learners. This book presents information about spoken grammar because it is important for learners to observe and to understand how and why speakers speak as they do. To describe these features does not mean that learners of English have to speak like native speakers. *CGE* presents the data so that teachers and learners can make their own informed choices.

GRAMMAR AND CORPUS DATA 3

What is a corpus? 3a

The word corpus has been used several times already in this introduction. A corpus is a collection of texts, usually stored in computer-readable form. Many of the examples in this book are taken from a multi-million-word corpus of spoken and written English called the Cambridge International Corpus (CIC). The corpus is international in that it draws on different national varieties of English (e.g. Irish, American). This corpus has been put together over many years and is composed of real texts taken from everyday written and spoken English. At the time of writing, the corpus contained over 700 million words of English. The CIC corpus contains a wide variety of different texts with examples drawn from contexts as varied as: newspapers, popular journalism, advertising, letters, literary texts, debates and discussions, service encounters, university tutorials, formal speeches, friends talking in restaurants, families talking at home.

One important feature of CIC is the special corpus of spoken English – the CANCODE corpus. CANCODE stands for Cambridge and Nottingham Corpus of Discourse in English, a unique collection of five million words of naturally-occurring, mainly British (with some Irish), spoken English, recorded in everyday situations. The CANCODE corpus has been collected throughout the past ten years in a project involving Cambridge University Press and the School of English Studies at the University of Nottingham, UK. In *CGE* dialogues and spoken examples are laid out as they actually occur in the transcripts of the CANCODE recordings, with occasional very minor editing of items which might otherwise distract from the grammar point being illustrated.

The CANCODE corpus is a finely-grained corpus. The CANCODE research team have not simply amassed examples of people speaking; they have tried to obtain examples from a range of sociolinguistic contexts and genres of talk. There is considerable advantage in being able to demonstrate statistical evidence over many millions of words and broad general contexts.

Using the corpus 3b

Grammar, like vocabulary, varies markedly according to context, allowing speakers considerable choice in the expression of interpersonal meanings (that is, meanings realised in relation to who one is speaking to rather than just what one is saying). A carefully constructed and balanced corpus can help to differentiate between different choices relative to how much knowledge speakers assume, what kind of relationship they have or want to have, whether they are at a dinner party, in a classroom, doing a physical task, in a service transaction in a shop, or telling a story (for example, our corpus tells us that ellipsis is not common in narratives, where the aim is often to create rather than to assume a shared world). By balancing these spoken genres against written ones, our corpus can also show that particular forms of ellipsis are widespread in certain types of journalism, in magazine articles, public signs and notices, personal notes and letters and in certain kinds of literary text. In descriptions of use, the most typical and frequent uses of such forms are described in relation to their different functions and in relation to the particular contexts in which they are most frequently deployed. (→ **3h** below)

CGE is a grammar book that is informed by the corpus. The word 'informed' is used advisedly because we are conscious that it is no simple matter to import real data into a reference book in the belief that authentic language is always the right language for the purposes of learning the language. In places, this means that corpus examples which contain cultural references of the kind that are so common in everyday language use are either not selected or, while ensuring that the key grammatical patterns are preserved, are slightly modified so that they do not cause undue difficulties of interpretation. It is our strong view that language corpora, such as the Cambridge International Corpus, can afford considerable benefits for language teaching but the pedagogic process should be informed by the corpus, not driven or controlled by it.

Information on frequency 3c

The corpus was analysed in a variety of ways in the preparation of this book. One way was to compile frequency lists. A frequency list simply ranks words, phrases and grammatical phenomena (e.g. how many words end in *-ness* or *-ity*, or how many verb phrases consist of *have* + a verb ending in *-en*) in a list. In this way, we are able to see not only which items are most and least frequent, but also how they are distributed across speech and writing and across different registers (e.g. newspapers, academic lectures, conversations at home). For example, the list of the twenty most frequent word-forms in the CIC for spoken and written texts (based on five-million-word samples of each) are different.

The twenty most frequent word-forms in spoken and written texts

	spoken		written
1	*the*	1	*the*
2	*I*	2	*to*
3	*and*	3	*and*
4	*you*	4	*of*
5	*it*	5	*a*
6	*to*	6	*in*
7	*a*	7	*was*
8	*yeah*	8	*it*
9	*that*	9	*I*
10	*of*	10	*he*
11	*in*	11	*that*
12	*was*	12	*she*
13	*it's*	13	*for*
14	*know*	14	*on*
15	*is*	15	*her*
16	*mm*	16	*you*
17	*er*	17	*is*
18	*but*	18	*with*
19	*so*	19	*his*
20	*they*	20	*had*

In the spoken list, *I* and *you* rise to the top, indicating the high interactivity of face-to-face conversation. *Know* is at number 14, indicative of the high frequency of the discourse marker *you know* (→ **106b**), and *mm* and *er* reflect the frequency with which listeners vocalise their acknowledgement of what the speaker is saying, or whereby speakers fill silences while planning their speech in real time or while hesitating. *It's* and *yeah* reflect the informality of much of the talk in the CANCODE spoken corpus.

Information on concordance 3d

Another way the corpus was analysed was in terms of concordance. Concordances help researchers see how words are actually used in context. Words or phrases which researchers are interested in are displayed in a vertical arrangement on the computer screen along with their surrounding co-text: we see what came just before the word and what came just after. For example, these sample lines from a concordance for the adverb *yet* in the spoken corpus show us that a negative environment is very common, but not in questions (negative items and question marks in bold), and that *as yet* is a recurrent pattern. The A–Z entry for *yet* in this book, and much of our grammatical description, is based on this type of observation.

Sample lines from a concordance for *yet*

<$2> Yeah. We have**n't** got any answer **yet**. We'd like it trimming. <$E> laughs 71094002.dcx

the wedding. <$2> I have**n't** got any **yet**. Em <$O69> Janet looked lovely <\$O6 90127004.dcx

but we have**n't** made er any arrangements **yet** it's sort of er a bit too early yet 80339001.inx

? <$1> Sorry? <$2> Has FX arrived **yet?** <$1> Who is this? <$2> MX's f 90449020.dcx

be in. <$2> They have**n't** arrived **as yet**. <$1> <$=> It is a whole <\$=> it 70752001.dnx

yet? <$1> **No not** a price breaker **as yet**. Just their own winter programme. 70764003.dnx

ame in. <$E> laughs <\$E> Erm but er **as yet** it's not available in every store. 90089007.knx

ll over the place. Em we have**n't** got **as yet** a timetable to show you as to what's 90003001.dnx

haven't come have they? <$2> **Not as yet**. No. Normally about two weeks before 70765004.dnx

. Well I said I do**n't** know the story **as yet** <$2> Mm. <$1> <$=> I said But 70365004.dcx

. But they're **not** putting anybody up **as yet** because they have an appeal launch r 70502001.dfx

ms. Er that's still **not** p= er set up **as yet** though. Erm we're gonna do something 70499001.dfx

n't managed to mark any of your work **as yet** but I I promise I'll have it back to 71232001.kpx

manda are you ready for your assessment **yet?** <$F> I think so yeah. <$1> I' 71229001.kpx

Anyway you obviously have**n't** gone back **yet** so <$=> erm I won't be er <\$=> you 70515012.imx

t know. <$G?> <$1> Oh he's **not** back **yet**. <$2> No. <$1> Oh right. < 70584004.dcx

eeks ago. And he he has**n't** written back **yet**. So <$E> laughs </$E> <$1> No. Mm 70645001.dcx

G?>. <$4> Have you changed your bank **yet?** <$3> My turn. <$E> sighs <\$E> 71031003.kmx

<$1> Bye. Cheers. <$3> Wo**n't** be **yet** until I've <$O13> lost <\$O13> a lit 90082002.knx

<$2> Have you seen Beauty And The Beast **yet?** <$1> No I was wanting to go. 70056002.dcx

p to see me every year. She has**n't** been **yet**. And she and I like to trip out on a 71094002.dcx

tomorrow <$6> No. No. **Not** for a bit **yet**. <$3> Good. <$6> We we thought 70499004.dfx

The concordance also gives us a code on the right of the screen (in green here) which tells us what type of conversation each line occurs in, and leads us to the corpus database where we can verify who the speakers are, what age, gender, and social profile they have, how many people were involved in the conversation, where it took place, etc. We are therefore able to say something is in common usage as we see it represented across a range of texts and users in the corpus.

Deciding what to include 3e

In deciding on priorities with regard to the description of items and patterns, both quantitative and qualitative approaches are important. On the quantitative side, the corpus evidence can often show striking differences in distribution of items between speaking and writing. For example, the forms *no one* and *nobody* are, on the face of it, synonymous, yet their distribution across five million words each of spoken and written data is very different, with *nobody* greatly preferred in the spoken corpus, as shown below.

Use of *no one* and *nobody* in spoken and written English

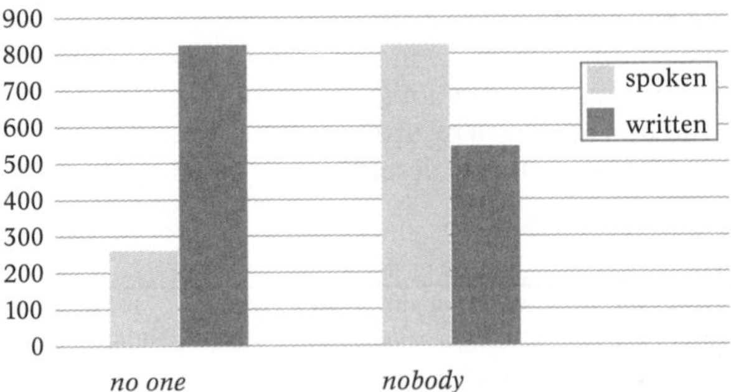

The interpretation of such statistics then depends on a more qualitative interpretation of the data, observing how *nobody* tends to correlate with the more informal end of the spectrum. A similar pattern of usage, in this case more clearly related to formality, can be seen for *who* and *whom*, where *whom* is shown to be relatively rare in conversation, only occurring in more formal contexts.

***Whom* in written and spoken English**

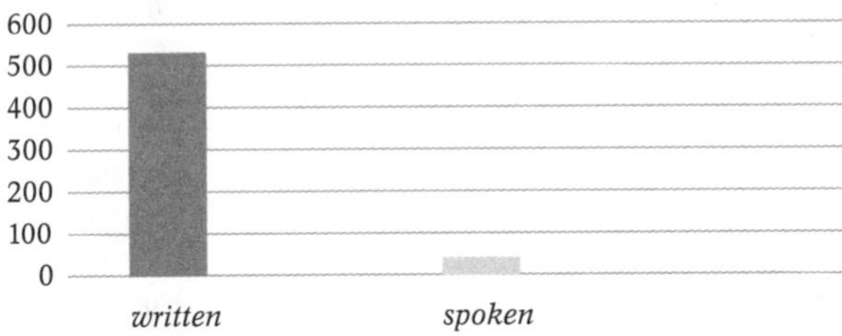

Insights into use 3f

Statistical evidence from the corpus can also give insight into the communicative acts most typically performed by particular items. The next diagram shows the different functions of *what about* and *how about* in the CANCODE corpus. Both forms are used to change the topic in conversation, with *what about* being used to do this more frequently than *how about* (*What about this new airport plan; what do you think of that?*). Another common function for both items is in the turn-taking system, where there is a strong preference for *how about* as a way of selecting the next speaker (*How about you Jean; what do you think?*). When suggestions are being made, both forms seem more or less equally available (*How about a walk before lunch?*) (→ also **421a**).

***What about* and *how about* in conversation**

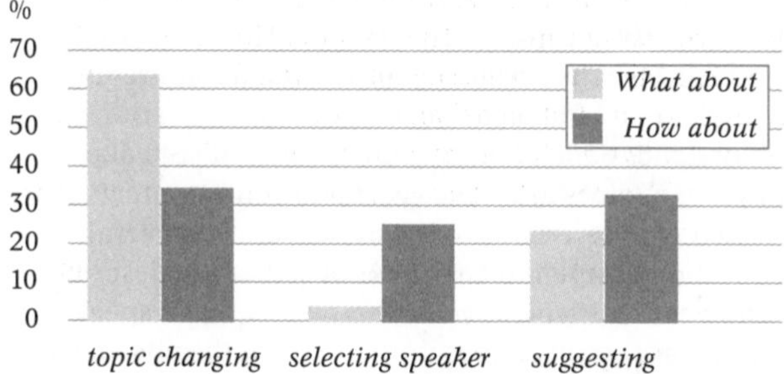

Word clusters 3g

Searching a corpus also continually reveals new insights into language structure and use. For example, research for this book has revealed the importance of word clusters and grammar.

Word clusters are groups of words that often occur together; some consist of just two words, e.g. *you know*, some are longer, e.g. *on the other hand*. Some of the most frequently repeated clusters reveal grammatical regularities. They often merit special consideration outside of the normal structural rules as described in the rest of this book, since they perform important basic functions in everyday usage, such as a turn-taking function in a conversation. These word clusters are sometimes different in spoken and written texts but such clusters are an important overall component in speaking and writing a language fluently since they can operate as the frequent and regular building blocks in the construction of meaning.

Research has highlighted patterns that include a range from two-word to six-word clusters and different patterns exhibit different ranges of meaning. It is possible that further research will demonstrate that lines between the vocabulary and the grammar of a language need to be drawn less sharply. The research is ongoing and new descriptions of the functions of clusters are being formulated. In *CGE* the main findings concerning clusters are presented in **503–505 Appendix: Word clusters and grammar**; however, readers will find a number of observations placed in key places throughout the book (particularly, for example, in chapters on spoken grammar, on the noun phrase, and on prepositions and prepositional phrases). The appendix on word clusters highlights possibilities in description, but corpus research is a constant and ever-developing feature of the study of grammar, and subsequent editions of *CGE* may well contain a separate chapter or chapters devoted to word clusters.

Frequent, common and preferred patterns 3h

Throughout *CGE* particular patterns are said to be frequent or common, either in the language as a whole or in speech rather than in writing or in formal rather than informal contexts of use. Sections 3a–3g above indicate how in this book a corpus is consulted before statements concerning the frequency of grammatical patterns are made.

As we have seen, some patterns are frequent but not acceptable in standard grammar while some patterns are non-standard in written usage but frequent in informal spoken varieties and perfectly acceptable in those varieties. Section 2a above indicates the range of possibilities. We believe information about frequency is important, especially for learners of a language.

A corpus also enables us to indicate which patterns are 'preferred'. Speakers and writers have choices and some choices are more typical in some contexts than in others. Preferences are attested with reference to the corpus and in several places throughout the book the choices open to a speaker or writer are described with an indication of which choices most typically occur. The fact that a speaker may choose the form which is the most typical does not mean that the alternative forms are incorrect or non-standard. The term 'preferred' as used in *CGE* highlights the most frequent choices made by users of the language.

Learner corpus 3i

We also had access during the writing of this book to a large learner corpus consisting of texts produced by learners of English from a wide range of lingua-cultures, coded for error and inappropriate use. This, along with our own language-teaching experience and that of our reference panel, has enabled us to give warnings of common areas of potential error where appropriate. These error warnings are signalled by the ✪ symbol.

HOW *CGE* IS IS ORGANISED 4

CGE is organised differently from other contemporary books on the grammar of English. Our coverage is, we believe, extensive, and major areas of description of the grammar of English are treated. However, as argued in section 2b above, this book is unique in the attention devoted to the spoken language. A high proportion of illustrative examples in *CGE* are drawn from a spoken corpus, a unique A–Z section covers many key words and phrases that have particular prominence in spoken English, and there are several chapters specifically devoted to the structural features of spoken grammar. The organisation of *CGE* reflects this orientation and the first chapters in the book are therefore those most saliently devoted to spoken grammar and to differences and distinctions between spoken and written English grammar. This is not to say that spoken grammar is not treated throughout the book, including the appendices, but it is to underline the belief that spoken and written language need, as far as is practicable, to be accorded equal priority. Previous grammar books have given greater attention to written grammar. *CGE* offers a more balanced approach.

Throughout the book, we make much use of cross references. This is because some of the most common grammatical items in English have many different meanings and uses and their descriptions will consequently be found under different headings in the book. For example, the word *anyway* is used as an adverb, and is also used as a discourse marker in spoken language; the modal verb

Notions and functions

377–407 Modality
408–423 Speech acts
424–433 Questions
434–447 Negation
448–459 Condition
460–471 Comparison

In the six chapters here, core conceptual notions such as negation, condition and comparison are described. The important communicative functions performed by modal verbs and other items are explained in chapters on modality and speech acts.

Information packaging

472–475 Word order and focus
476–487 The passive
488–502 Speech representation

Here the three chapters are concerned with how speakers and writers decide to present information in clauses, by using active and passive voice choices, different word orders and other ways of emphasising things. How speech is represented and reported is also dealt with.

Appendices 4c

The appendices give detailed information on punctuation, spelling, irregular verbs, numbers, measurement, time, nationalities and countries, as well as important differences between British and North American grammatical usage, and an insight into the functions performed by word clusters.

Glossary 4d

The glossary contains brief definitions of all the key grammatical terms used in this book. The glossary also recognises that different grammar books use different terms. The *CGE* glossary refers to terms that are not employed in this book but which are a part of the language used to talk about grammar. Throughout, the aim is to provide an easy navigation between different terminologies and the description of the grammar of English contained in this book.

Index 4e

The comprehensive index is designed to provide access to a wide range of topics and key words covered in CGE.

From word to grammar: an A–Z

From word to grammar: an A–Z

The individual words described here have been selected for special attention because they are:

- very frequent in everyday language
- often polysemous (that is, they have more than one meaning)
- individual in some way in their grammar, possessing characteristics that are worthy of particular note
- known to be difficult for learners of English and often lead to errors.

ABOUT 5

Preposition *about* 5a

The most frequent meaning of *about* as a preposition is 'on the subject of' or 'connected with':

*Er, I'm not too sure **about that**.*

*He became very anxious **about the condition of two of his patients**.*

*We've only just started making enquiries **about him**.*

*I've already told you what I feel **about the appointment**.*

*Why is she always going on **about it**?*

A less frequent use is as a synonym of *round* or *around*:

*The dog was running **about the garden** all day.*

About can be contrasted with *on*, which focuses on more specific and detailed content:

*He gave a lecture **about Karl Marx**.*

*She gave a lecture **on the position of English adverbs in spoken language**.*

Adverb *about* 5b

About is used as an adverb in expressions of time, number and quantity. It is used to express approximation and can be replaced by *around*. It also occurs in the phrase *round about*. It is more common in spoken than in written English:

*I'll see you **about six** then?*

*That was **about six years ago** wasn't it?*

*The suspect was **about 1.7 metres tall**.*

*The main changes took place **round about 1860** at the time of the shift away from agriculture as main source of employment.*

About is rare without a complement. Particular uses are:

*Is John **about**?*
(Is John here/in the neighbourhood/in town?)

*There's a lot of flu **about** at the moment.*

A–Z 18 *Around, round*

103b Approximations

Be about to 5c

Be about to means 'be on the verge of doing something':

*We were just **about to leave**.*

*She looks as if she's **about to burst into song**.*

Common spoken uses of *about* 5d

About is common in spoken English when a speaker is orienting a listener to a topic:

***About that car of yours**, do you still want to sell it?*

***About Fran**, she can call in to see your grandmother, can't she?*

What about is common in questions when the speaker points out something or wishes to orient the listener to a topic:

***What about all the cuts** in education and in housing?*

***What about Andreas**? Isn't he coming with us?*

What about, *how about*, and very informally, *how's about* are commonly used to make suggestions:

***What about moving that bookshelf** into the other room? It would give us a bit more space.*

***How about an ice-cream**?*

***How's about going to Kyoto** for the day?*

421a *What about, what if, how about*

About after nouns 5e

Some common nouns are frequently followed by *about*. These include:

anxiety
argument
assertion
assumption
complaint
concern
debate
discussion
doubt
enquiry
feeling
fuss
idea
information
joke
misgiving
news
point
qualm
question
reservation
scepticism
speculation
statement
story
talk
uncertainty
worry

It is dangerous to make too many ***assumptions about*** *basic cognitive processes.*

She's always making a ***fuss about*** *our bedrooms being untidy.*

Is there any ***news about*** *the people trapped in that avalanche?*

About after verbs 5f

Many common verbs are followed by *about*. They include:

agonise
ask
bother
care
chat
complain
enquire
feel
forget
fret
hear
know
learn
moan
quibble
read
reminisce
speak
speculate
talk
think
wonder
worry
write

They ***agonised*** *for ages* ***about*** *changing their car.*

More and more people are beginning to ***speculate about*** *a change of management.*

About is not used with the verb *discuss*:

We wanted to ***discuss*** *the arrangements for Chinese New Year.*
(~~We wanted to discuss about the arrangements for Chinese New Year.~~)

I wanted to ***discuss*** *ways of improving the essay.*

Note, however, that *about* is used with the noun *discussion*:

Discussions about *the situation took place yesterday.*

About is used after *complain*:

They didn't know what to do when people came to ***complain about*** *the goods they had bought.*
(~~They didn't know what to do when people came to complain the goods they had bought.~~)

About after adjectives 5g

Many common adjectives are followed by *about*. They include:

apprehensive
blasé
cautious
concerned
coy
enthusiastic
excited
fussy
happy
knowledgeable
nervous
optimistic
pessimistic
sceptical
snobbish
sorry
sure
unhappy
upset
uptight
worried

The minister was far too ***blasé about*** *public opinion and in the end the media forced his resignation.*

She's very ***nervous about*** *flying in charter aircraft.*

→ **539 Glossary** for any unfamiliar terms

Ah, I'm really ***sorry about*** *this.*

She is more ***worried*** *than she should be* ***about*** *her exam results.*

ABOVE 6

Preposition *above* 6a

Above means 'higher than'. It has a meaning that is close to the preposition *over*. Its opposites are *below* and *beneath*. In both the following sentences *over* can be substituted for *above*:

There was a faded sign ***above the door.***

Once the plane got ***above the clouds*** *and levelled out, they started to relax.*

Above is preferred when things are at an upper level:

They lived in a small bungalow ***above the village.***
(~~They lived in a small bungalow over the village.~~)

Above can only be used when there is no contact between the people or things referred to. *Over* or *on top of* have a more general meaning and can be used whether or not one person or thing touches or covers another:

He put a light plastic raincoat ***over his jacket.***
(or: on top of his jacket)
(~~He put a light plastic raincoat above his jacket.~~)

Above can be used to refer to a higher part, usually of a building, or to a higher structure or place. It can also be used to refer to an increase in size or scale:

Nairobi is about 2000 metres ***above sea level.***

Their performance was distinctly ***above average.***

Above is also used metaphorically, often meaning 'a long way from' or 'is superior to'. It can also have a sense of being difficult to understand. *Beyond* is also possible in such phrases:

She is ***above suspicion*** *and* ***above reproach.***

I'm afraid that type of mathematics is all rather ***above me.***

Above modifying nouns 6b

Above can be used in writing as a premodifier to refer to something which has already been mentioned in the text. The fixed phrase *the above* means 'the foregoing text'. *Below* cannot be used in this way as a premodifier, and *the below* is not possible:

As we can see from ***the above figures,*** *the profits are likely to be significantly lower this year.*

As we have argued in ***the above,*** *the results are not convincing.*

Both *above* and *below* can postmodify a noun:

*There was noise coming from the **room above**, so I couldn't sleep.*

*The **picture below** is a striking example of new methods of advertising.*

Above is not normally used with numbers. *Over* is normally preferred:

*You can only buy alcoholic drinks here if you are **over 18**.*
(~~You can only buy alcoholic drinks here if you are above 18~~.)

*It'll cost **over a thousand pounds** to repair.*

 25 *Below*; 63 *Over*

ACCORDING TO 7

According to meaning 'as reported' 7a

The most frequent use of *according to* is when reference is made to external evidence to support a statement or an opinion:

***According to the safety experts**, it was all right when they left it.*

*It's the same in every block, **according to Cliff**, the caretaker.*

*This delay, **according to Mr Mckay**, probably violated federal law.*

*It's going to be delayed, **according to what Nick told us**.*

According to is frequently used to refer to statistics, official reports, surveys, opinion polls, studies, research, etc., especially in more formal contexts:

***According to a recent report** by the National Food Alliance, children are being saturated with advertisements for sugar-rich confectionery.*

*And regional government, **according to a poll** taken last month by Gallup, attracts the support of less than one in three of the public.*

Note that *according to* refers to evidence from someone or somewhere else. As such, it usually has a third person referent. It cannot be used to refer to one's own views or statements:

***In my opinion** all those sites should be made green-field sites.*
(~~According to me/according to my opinion, all those sites should be …~~)

According to meaning 'in agreement with' 7b

According to is also used to mean 'in line with', 'in harmony with' or 'depending on'. In this meaning it is most typically not used in front position:

*And is it all going **according to plan** so far?*

If the police acted ***according to the law****, then they should arrest him.*

[talking about placing people on a salary scale]
I'm sure they probably grade people ***according to their experience****.*

Prices vary very slightly ***according to whether*** *you want 'hotel' or 'hostel' service.*

A closely related phrase is *in accordance with*, which is used in formal, written contexts to mean 'in obedience to', or 'strictly following (rules and regulations)':

The Socialist government, elected in 1994, resigned in December, but, ***in accordance with the constitution****, the President had to call on the Socialist party to form another government.*

ACROSS 8

Across is used as a preposition and as an adverb:

It's just not enough time to get ***across London****.*
(preposition)

[giving directions]
A: *You keep going down until you get to the massive traffic-light complex. You know you're at it. It's sort of bright and there's a big main road running* ***across****.*
B: *Right.*
(adverb)

Across is not a verb. The verb form is *cross*:

Every time you ***cross*** *the road, you're worried you're going to get knocked over.*
(~~Every time you across the road, you're worried you're going to get knocked over.~~)

Across can be used to indicate movement or position relative to two sides or extremes of something:

[referring to a newspaper article]
In the paper there's somebody who's going to swim ***across the Atlantic*** *four thousand miles.*

She sat facing me ***across the table****.*

When indicating position relative to another person or thing, with the meaning of 'opposite', 'on the other side of the road to', *across* is used with *from*:

The Town Hall is ***across from the cathedral****.*

Across is often used in contexts of comparisons to indicate a range of something:

The researchers carried out a study ***across 20 countries****.*

Across is also used to refer to the width or diagonal measurement of something. It follows the unit of measurement:

First, a copy; he slipped a minidisk into the port, formatted and labelled it. Barely ***two centimetres across*** *– easy to lose, but easy to hide.*

Across is also used to refer to an area in which things are distributed:

There are other smaller sites, scattered ***across the Caribbean*** *and even in the Mediterranean.*

Across and *over* 8a

Across and *over* are sometimes interchangeable with little difference in meaning:

She walked on ***across the bridge*** *in the bitter wind.*

She put her arm around his waist and led him ***over the bridge****.*

However, when the meaning is 'from side to side' of a surface, *across* is preferred:

Draw a line ***across the middle of the page****.*
(~~Draw a line over the middle of the page.~~)

He glanced at his watch and strode ***across the room****, Julian's dressing-gown flapping around his legs.*
(~~… and strode over the room, …~~)

Across and *through* 8b

When there is a surrounding environment, movement is usually expressed by *through*, not *across*:

It's very pretty in the summer ***walking through the orchards****.*
(~~It's very pretty in the summer walking across the orchards.~~)

 63 ***Over***

ACTUAL, ACTUALLY 9

Actual and *actually* refer to whether something is true or factual. They do not refer to time:

They went into a restaurant … or it was ***actually*** *a café.*
(it was in fact/in reality a café)

I'm not really sure about the ***actual*** *procedure.*
(This means 'the right/correct procedure'; if the meaning had been 'the procedure that is used now', the speaker would have said *I'm not really sure about the* ***present/current*** *procedure*, or *I'm not really sure about the procedure* ***now/nowadays***.)

→ **539 Glossary** for any unfamiliar terms

*She's **actually** working for a computer firm.*
(This means something like 'She is in fact working for a computer firm', or 'Surprisingly, she is working for a computer firm', depending on the context; if we mean 'She is at the present time working for a computer firm', we would say *She's working for a computer firm **at the moment/(right)now.***)

Actual 9a

Actual usually has a meaning similar to 'true', 'real', 'precise', 'right/correct' or 'the thing/person itself/himself/herself':

*I couldn't get an appointment for **that actual day.***
(that precise/exact day)

***My actual involvement** with the project itself was negligible really.*
(my real/true involvement)

[sales assistant (A) talking to a customer in a camera shop]
A: *You don't know which model it is, do you?*
B: *No, I can look it up. Maybe I'll come in with **the actual camera.***
(the camera itself)

A very common expression with *actual* is *in actual fact*, which is an emphatic form of *in fact*:

*But **in actual fact**, a year ago the situation was the same.*

 46 ***In fact***

Actually 9b

Actually can often be used emphatically, especially to refer to something which is in sharp contrast with expectations:

*He **actually admitted** that he enjoyed it.*
(this was unexpected, not normal behaviour for him)

*There **actually is a plant** that produces what is known as 'the curry leaf'.*

*The original connection with Dave was **actually more through jazz** than through folk music.*

Actually often implies a contrast between a desirable and an undesirable situation:

*So, here is a practical seminar that **actually offers solutions** to the challenges women managers face.*
(implied: in contrast to most other seminars)

*Unlike a blender or liquefier, the juicer **actually separates the juice** from the pulp.*

Actually often operates as a discourse marker in spoken language, signalling topic openings, contrasts in topics, specifying within topics, etc.:

[customer (A) at the information desk in a large bookshop enquiring about a technical manual]
A: *Could you tell me where your manuals are kept?* ***Actually*** *I'm looking for a Haynes manual.*
B: *Er what on?*
A: *It's on washing machines.*

[beginning of a one-to-one student tutorial at a university; A is the student]
A: *Where would it be best for me to sit?*
B: *Um, anywhere there's a space.*
[pause]
A: *Well* ***actually*** *there's a couple of things really really quickly to ask you. One is about the draft of my history of English essay.*

When used in questions, *actually* can often focus on 'missing' information which the speaker desires or needs for the purposes of the conversation:

[speakers are already talking about B's father]
A: *What did your dad do* ***actually****?*
B: *Well he was a railway man.*

Actually is often used to hedge statements, making them less direct or less threatening:

I think Sandra would win hands down ***actually****.*

We had an argument ***actually****, a few weeks ago.*

In spoken language *actually* is frequently used in end position, though it may also occur in front and mid positions:

A: *In the afternoon we'll continue with the tour into the training department and on through into the machine division.*

B: *I'd be quite interested in that* ***actually****.*

AFTER, AFTERWARDS 10

Preposition *after* 10a

After is most frequently used with noun phrases referring to time or to timed events:

You get used to that, strangely enough, ***after a while****.*

So I'll do those two classes. I'll start probably ***after the holidays****.*

I was sick and tired of being on my own. I wanted to get home. I mean, ***after nine months*** *I was homesick.*

References to place may also be made with *after*, especially when they are seen as part of a sequence of events in time:

[giving directions to someone]
And ***after the fifth roundabout****, you turn off, and there's another roundabout.*

Adverb *after* 10b

After postmodifying a noun

After may postmodify nouns such as *day*, *morning*, *week*, *month*, *year*, especially in informal speech:

I've got one interview, then, er, a second interview ***the week after****.*
(or, more formal: ... the following week)

A: *And you see yourself as staying round in the London area for the next year or so?*
B: *Oh yeah. Definitely. I mean, for probably* ***the year after*** *as well.*

After premodified by another adverb

After does not normally occur alone as an adjunct. It is almost always premodified by adverbs such as *shortly*, *soon*, *straight*:

[from a text about the young of the shrew, a small mouse-like animal]
Born blind and naked, the young quickly develop a thin coat of hair at around nine days old and their eyes open ***soon after****.*

[a student talking about a difficult period of study]
It's just at this real crossroads at the moment when you're just about to start an essay and then you've got to do something else ***straight after****.*

Occasionally, in informal speech, *after* may occur alone, with the meaning of 'later':

That just reminds me of something. [laughs] *I'll tell you the joke* ***after****.*

Afterwards 10c

Where there is no premodifying adverb (→ **10b** above), *afterwards*, not *after*, is normally used:

Suddenly a black cat ran in front of her. In surprise, she cried out aloud. ***Afterwards****, she felt rather foolish.*
(preferred to: After, she felt rather foolish.)

They laughed together over their tea, but ***afterwards*** *Esther was quiet, analysing what she had been told.*

Afterwards may be premodified by adverbs such as *immediately*, (*not*) *long*, *shortly* and *soon*, and other time expressions involving words such as *days*, *weeks*, *months*, *years*:

She heard a muffled bang, then a car starting ***almost immediately afterwards****.*

When the phone rang again ***shortly afterwards****, he picked up the receiver with regret.*

A few days afterwards*, Italy joined the war, and with immense relief, we gave up the idea of our rescue.*

After + *-ing* clause 10d

When used to link two clauses, *after* followed by a verb in the *-ing* form is many times more frequent in writing than in speech. In informal speech there is a strong preference for a full finite clause:

The police claim he died ***after falling*** *and hitting his head.*

After graduating*, he became a lecturer at the university.*

I was out of work for six months ***after being*** *made redundant.*

After having + *-ed* participle, although it occurs, is rare in both speech and writing. Where it does occur, it often serves to emphasise a contrast between two situations in time:

[part of a speech welcoming a new member of staff in a company]
And ***after having worked*** *very closely with Gerald for so many years, and* ***having had*** *so many people actually believing that he was a member of the company staff, it's very nice finally to be able to welcome him as a real member of staff.* [applause follows]

In most cases, *after* + the *-ing* form of a lexical verb is preferred:

After journeying *more than 11,000 miles, Russell found the man for whom he was searching.*
(preferred to: After having journeyed more than 11,000 miles, Russell found the man for whom he was searching.)

After + finite clause 10e

After may be used with a variety of tense forms and time references to link two clauses:

- Present simple with general present time reference:

  [from an article about John Daly, a well-known American golfer]
  He uses at least a dozen balls per round because they lose their shape ***after*** *he* ***hits*** *them.*

→ 539 **Glossary** for any unfamiliar terms

- Present perfect with general present time reference:

  *All adults, **after** they **have told** off a teenager for not doing his homework, say 'Do I make myself clear?'.*

  [*that* refers to the timing of questionnaires to patients concerning their experience of treatment in the National Health Service in Britain]
  *And I think people would get a better service if that was done, say, a month **after** they'**ve been having** treatment.*

- Present simple with future time reference:

  *Ideally, I'd like to move in straight after that, **after** you **move** out.*
  (~~... after you will move out.~~)

- Present perfect with future time reference:

  *We would love to see you tonight, if it's possible, **after** you'**ve visited** David's mum.*
  (~~... after you will have visited ...~~)

- Past simple:

  A: *And it was only **after** you **married** you discovered all this?*
  B: *Yes.*

- Past perfect:

  *She was glad that she had resisted an impulse to ring Hal again **after** she **had read** his note.*

The perfect aspect versions stress the completion of the event in the *after*-clause and a break in time between the events in the two clauses. The present simple or past simple versions suggest a closer connection between the two clauses, as with *before* (→ 24d).

Other uses of *after* 10f

In informal contexts, *after* is occasionally used as a preposition with the meaning of 'because of' or 'as a consequence of':

[talking about a furniture shop]
***After the experience with the chair**, I don't think I'll buy anything else there.*

*Look at Brian, how healthy he looks **after all that sun**.*

In informal speech, the expression *to be after something* often means 'to want' or 'to look for, to seek':

[customer in a hardware shop]
*I'**m after** a metre of strong chain. Just a metre. It's for a bike you see. You know, just to tie a bike up. I've got a lock and everything.*
(I want/I'm looking for ...)

[customer (A) in a bookshop; *Rough Guides* are a very popular type of travel guide book]
A: *Do you have any of these travel guides, Rough Guide to … wherever?*
B: *Yes, we do. Where in particular **were** you **after**?*
A: *Erm, the south-west of America.*

After all 10g

After all as a conjunction has a concessive meaning, similar to 'besides', or the meaning of 'one should not forget/ignore the fact that …'.

After all may occur in front, mid or end position in the clause. It is normally separated from the rest of the clause by a comma or commas:

*The garage on the main road has been boarded up for some time. It's been boarded up now for nearly seventeen months. It just seems silly. I mean, **after all**, it's unusual to have a petrol station in a fairly quiet residential area.*
(front position)

*But I stuck at it, pretending to get on and take no notice. Because it was, **after all**, none of my business.*
(mid position)

*I don't mind what you buy. It is your money, **after all**.*
(end position)

The other main use of *after all* is as an adverb meaning 'contrary to what was believed or expected'. In this meaning, it occurs almost always in end position, and frequently together with *maybe* or *perhaps*. It is not usually separated by a comma in writing:

*Maybe she's not dating him. I mean, maybe they're just friends **after all**.*
(I thought they were dating. Maybe I was wrong.)

*And then at intervals during the interview, I found him … well, er, creepy really and rather worrying, but then again, at the end, I felt as though I'd done him an injustice and that perhaps he was likeable **after all**.*

*Jeremy looked genuinely pleased to see her and she wondered if they might become friends **after all**.*

AFTER ALL

 10 ***After, afterwards***

AFTERWARDS

 10 ***After, afterwards***

AGAINST 11

Against denoting reactions 11a

Against is used after verbs and nouns denoting (often negative) reactions to situations, beliefs, people, events, etc.

Some common verbs frequently followed by *against* include:

act	*discriminate*	*rebel*
advise	*fight*	*speak out*
argue	*go*	*struggle*
be	*guard*	*testify*
campaign	*have something*	*vote*
decide	*militate*	
demonstrate	*react*	

[talking about speaker B's computer]
A: *One thing you could do is you could actually upgrade this machine.*
B: *I know but I **decided against** it.*

A: *So you think it's fair to **discriminate against** age?*
B: *After a certain age, I think.*

*We will **vote against** it but we will be in the minority.*

Some common nouns frequently followed by *against* include:

accusation	*charge*	*grudge*
action	*complaint*	*law*
aggression	*crusade*	*prejudice*
allegation	*defence*	*protection*
appeal	*demonstration*	*protest*
argument	*discrimination*	*reaction*
battle	*evidence*	*rebellion*
campaign	*fight*	*safeguard*
case	*grievance*	

*She emphasised the need for concerted **action against** poverty and inequality which force children into exploitative work.*

*There is not a scrap of **evidence against** her.*

*There's a **law against** murder but people go out and still murder don't they and rob banks and what have you.*

Against denoting physical contact 11b

Against is frequently used to indicate physical contact between two or more things:

*There was a man leaning **against the wall**.*

[swimming instructor to a learner]
Right, I want to see your arm. That's right. No the other one. Face that way. That one. That's it. Right, I want to see your arm brushing ***against your ear****.*

Against denoting competition 11c

Against occurs frequently with verbs and nouns connected with sport and competing, such as *compete/competition, final, game, match, play, semi-final*:

A: *We used to go there for football. And cricket we used to play on the recreation ground.*
B: *Yes. Mm. And did you have a school team?* ***Play against*** *other schools?*
A: *No we used to* ***play*** *football* ***against*** *other teams but not cricket.*

[*the Clifton Downs* is an area of open land near the city of Bristol in England]
In the holidays sometimes we ***played*** *a hockey match* ***against*** *the Clifton College boys on the Clifton Downs.*

Against, not *with*, is used in sporting contexts with *play* when two teams or individuals compete:

It was three years ago when my volleyball team was selected to ***play against*** *an Italian one.*
(~~It was three years ago when my volleyball team was selected to play with an Italian one.~~)

About, not *against*, is used with *do* to refer to taking action to solve problems:

[speaker is talking about a very noisy party]
They were all out on the street and Jim and Sally couldn't sleep. They had to phone the police. The police couldn't ***do*** *anything* ***about*** *it.*
(~~The police couldn't do anything against it.~~)

Do not confuse *against* and *contrary to*:

Contrary to *what you may read in the guidebooks, very few of the locals actually speak English.*
(~~Against what you may read in the guidebooks, …~~)

ALL 12

Determiner *all* 12a

All is mainly used as a determiner:

All *the tickets are sold out.*

We'll have to get rid of ***all*** *our old furniture.*

→ 539 **Glossary** for any unfamiliar terms

As a determiner, *all* comes before articles, possessives or demonstratives, and before numerals.

	article, possessive or demonstrative	numeral	head noun
all	*the*		*children*
all	*my*		*clothes*
all	*those*		*boxes*
all		*four*	*books*

✪ When *all* refers to an entire class of people or things, *the* is not used:

> ***All dogs** love meat.*
> (every dog in the world)
> (~~All the dogs love meat.~~)

Everybody/everyone is preferred to 'all people'.

> ***Everyone** has to die sooner or later.*
> (~~All people have to die sooner or later.~~)

All of is used before personal, demonstrative and relative pronouns. The object form of the pronoun is used:

> *Thanks to **all of you** for giving up your time to help us.*
>
> *That's very bad news. **All of this** is just too upsetting.*
>
> *They have three sons and two daughters, **all of whom** are married.*
> (~~… all of who are married.~~)

Of is optional before definite noun phrases:

> *I left **all (of) my money** in an account invested in the stock market.*
>
> *Who's going to eat **all (of) this food**?*

Time expressions like *all afternoon, all day, all night* are a special case. They have definite reference but do not require the definite article. However, the definite article is permitted with or without *of*:

> *I spent **all afternoon** at the gym.*
>
> *I spent **all the afternoon** at the gym.*
>
> *I spent **all of the afternoon** at the gym.*

✪ *All*, not *all of*, is used before indefinite plurals and non-count nouns:

> ***All prisoners** of war have rights under international law.*
> (~~All of prisoners of war have rights under international law.~~)
>
> ***All tobacco** is heavily taxed.*
>
> ***All processed food** is fattening.*

All is not used with singular indefinite count nouns; *a whole* is used:

They managed to eat ***a whole chicken.***
(~~They managed to eat all a chicken.~~)

Pronoun *all* 12b

All can be used as an unmodified pronoun, but such usage is formal and infrequent:

***All** are welcome.*

***All** were concerned that something should be done.*
(more typically: Everyone was concerned ...)

***All** is not lost.*

***All** will be revealed in the course of time.*

[newspaper headline]
Minister's ex-secretary tells ***all.***

All is most typically either premodified or postmodified:

In the United Kingdom in 1988, there were nearly 25,000 maintained primary schools, including 586 middle schools deemed primary. ***Almost all*** *were mixed-sex schools.*

It doesn't matter if the car's damaged. ***All that matters*** *is that you're okay.*

I paid him ***all that he wanted.***

When followed by a relative clause, *all* has a similar meaning to 'everything'. *That* may be omitted before a personal pronoun:

They lost ***all that they had earned*** *in the stock market crash.*

I told her to forget ***all that had happened.***

She taught me ***all I know*** *about computers.*

Adverb *all* 12c

All referring to the subject of a clause usually occupies the normal mid position for adverbs (➝ 325):

The members ***all knew*** *what was going on.*

We ***all try*** *our best to be on time.*

This is something that they ***can all do.***

*We****'ve all been waiting*** *for ages.*

We ***could all have made*** *the same mistake.*

They ***are all*** *qualified social workers.*

When *all* refers to a personal pronoun, there is a choice between pronoun + *all* and *all of* + pronoun:

> ***We****'re* ***all*** *thinking the same thing.*
> (or: All of us are thinking the same thing.)

> A: *Are there any cakes left?*
> B: *No, the kids ate* ***them all.***
> (or: No, the kids ate all of them.)

However, in short elliptical responses, the *of* construction must be used:

> A: *Which books do you want to take with you?*
> B: ***All of them*** *if that's okay with you.*
> (~~Them all~~, if that's okay with you.)

All is also used as an adverb to mean 'entirely', 'completely' or 'extremely', especially in spoken English:

> *I've left them* ***all alone*** *in the house.*

> *When I ask you where you've been, you get* ***all upset and agitated.***

> *He took one of the cans from the shelf and the whole shelf* ***all went down.***

> *I got lost and it's* ***all because*** *they gave me the wrong directions.*

> *He got* ***all excited*** *when he heard the news.*

All in fixed expressions 12d

All is particularly common in fixed expressions, especially in spoken English. These are the most common:

All right

All right meaning 'acceptable' or 'okay':

> *Is it* ***all right*** *if she just pops along tomorrow?*
> (also spelled as a single word: alright)

At all

At all as an intensifier in negative and interrogative clauses:

> *No, it isn't exactly modesty. I am not* ***at all*** *certain that I am modest.*

> *Are you* ***at all*** *concerned about interest rates rising?*

When placed at the end of questions, *at all* can also function as a marker of politeness:

> *Do you have any sparkling water* ***at all****?*

And all that

And all that is used as a marker of deliberate vagueness and imprecision:

> *He's into rock music* ***and all that.***

And all

And all (usually pronounced /əˈnɔːl/) can mean 'as well' in informal spoken language:

*They've already had one holiday this year and now they're off to France **and all**.*

Discourse markers

All occurs in a range of fixed expressions which function primarily as spoken discourse markers. In most cases, the markers function to signpost the direction in which a stretch of talk is going or has gone:

***Above all**, the election was won on a sympathy vote.*
(meaning: primarily)

***First of all**, let me thank you for attending this evening.*
(meaning: the first thing I want to say)

***All right**, tell me why you think we should change the schedule?*
(meaning: seeks to establish a new direction in the discourse)

***All the same**, I think there are other points of view.*
(meaning: despite this)

***All in all**, the best team won.*
(meaning: to summarise)

*So you did decide to go to Leeds **after all**, did you?*
(meaning: nevertheless)

A–Z 34 ***Each***; 38 ***Every***

ALLOW

48 ***Let***

ALREADY 13

Already refers to things that have happened or will have happened at a given point in time, and often (but not necessarily) contrary to expectations. It usually occurs in mid or end position; it is particularly frequent in end position in spoken language:

*There are about ten people here **already**.*
(more than we might expect at this time)

*What makes you think he hasn't done it **already**?*

[*The Commons* refers to the elected part of the British Parliament]
*The Commons has **already** agreed that there should be a referendum in which Londoners are asked whether they want a new council and a separately elected mayor.*

'I shall think about it when I get there.'
'By which time, it will be too late to decide where you want to go,' she pointed out.
*'Because you will **already** be there.'*

Front position is uncommon in informal spoken language, but does occur in more formal, written styles:

***Already** younger women without children are more likely than their male counterparts to use the video recorder daily.*

Already is often used with a verb in the past perfect to stress that something was completed before something else happened:

*They **had already made** their plans for various visits before they arrived.*

Do not confuse *already* with *yet*:

*Have you booked a flight **already**?*
(You've done it so soon, have you? It seems very early to book.)

*Have you booked a flight **yet**?*
(We know you have to book one, but I have no idea if you have done it up to this point in time.)

72 *Still*; 81 *Yet*

ALSO, AS WELL (AS), TOO 14

Also 14a

Also is twice as frequent in writing as it is in speech. It may occupy a variety of positions.

Front position

In this position, *also* is used to add a new point or topic to what has been said:

*She felt a little uncertain on her legs. **Also**, it seemed to her that the sounds of traffic were abnormally loud, giving her an odd sensation of vertigo.*

[on the telephone]
*I will give you a ring instead of sending it to you. I can do that. That's no problem. **Also**, how are things down there in Bristol?*

In front position, *also* occurs frequently together with *and*, especially in speech:

*I'll fax through to you the two sheets that have the adverts on, and the address of where you want us to send it. **And also** I'll fax through to you the letter I've received that has the address on.*

Mid position

Also may be used in the normal mid position for adverbs (··> 325). In this position, the meaning of *also* usually refers to the whole clause:

*The boy needs a bath and some food. I don't think he's eaten in a while. He **also needs** clean clothes, which I don't think you'll find at his home.*

*So I've been doing that this week, and I'**ve also been reading**. I've done a lot of reading.*

*She is very approachable and treats everyone equally, but she's not soft. She **is also** very good to staff with domestic problems.*

End position

In end position, *also* normally links two phrases. Items linked by *also* are in green in the examples below:

*Pollution can cause trees and bushes and other things like that to die. And then animals that were in them, like birds and squirrels and things, can die **also**.*

She replaced it [the telephone receiver] *and this time it stayed silent. She went over to the window. The world outside was silent **also**.*

In these end-position examples, *as well* and *too* may be used instead of *also*, especially in speech.

Linking phrases

Also may be used to link various types of phrase:

[in an article about the numbers of people visiting theme parks in Britain]
*But Chessington World of Adventures in Surrey slipped from fourth to fifth as attendances fell 4 per cent to 1.7 million. Thorpe Park, **also** in Surrey, fell by more than 2 per cent, although it still had well over 1.1 million visitors.*

*He had been nervous as he wished them goodbye at the departure lounge, and **also** at the river.*

Too and *as well* cannot normally substitute for this use of *also*.

As well 14b

As well is many times more frequent in speech than in writing, and it is more than twice as frequent in speech as *also*.

✪ *As well* almost always comes at the end of a clause:

*I just ignored it. I think everybody else did **as well**.*
(~~I just ignored it. As well I think everybody else did.~~)

[in a restaurant; A is the customer, B is the waiter]
A: *And can I have special fried rice please.*
B: *Yes.*
A: *Could I have a fried beef in black bean sauce **as well**.*
(~~Could I as well have a fried beef in black bean sauce.~~)

As well as 14c

As well as may join different types of unit to one another.

- Noun phrases:

  My father was an artist ***as well as*** *a priest, which was his profession.*

- Verb phrases:

  I was going to write it myself, so I was going to write ***as well as*** *publish.*

- Clauses:

When *as well as* links a finite clause to another clause, the *as well as* clause has its main verb in the *-ing* form:

> *I am the press officer* ***as well as*** *being the person that has a link in with all of those other communications issues.*
> (~~I am the press officer as well as I am the person that ...~~)
>
> ***As well as*** *working out a post-war settlement, the Paris Peace Conference also gave birth to the League of Nations, which was designed to create a completely new framework of international relations.*
> (~~As well as it worked out a post-war settlement, ...~~)

As well as can be used at the beginning of a sentence. This use is much more frequent in formal writing than in informal speech:

> ***As well as*** *the castle and cathedral, there are other Norman buildings in Lincoln, such as these stone-built houses with round arches.*
>
> ***As well as*** *journalistic skill, being editor teaches you about dealing with stress.*

Front-position *as well as* may occur together with *also* in the second clause:

> ***As well as*** *pointing towards the magnetic north, the compass* ***also*** *points down into the Earth in the northern hemisphere and up out of the Earth in the southern hemisphere.*
>
> ***As well as*** *visiting the centre of the city to buy goods, many people* ***also*** *visit it to enjoy themselves in the theatre or the art gallery, to visit historic buildings, or eat and drink at various restaurants, clubs and cafés.*

Too 14d

Too is much less frequent in speech than either *also* or *as well*. In writing, *too* is only half as frequent as *also*, but many times more frequent than *as well*.

Too is not used at the beginning of a clause. It occurs mostly at the end of the clause, or, in more formal styles, in mid position.

End position

Most occurrences of *too* are in end position. Which part of the clause it refers to depends on context. In the examples below, linked items are in green:

> *Karen's having paté. I'll probably have paté* ***too****.*

> *That was the way she looked at it. And she was dead right,* ***too****.*

> [talking about reading a boring work document]
> *It's as joyful as reading a telephone directory, and as useful* ***too****.*

End-position *too* often occurs in speech after a clause with a fronted complement beginning with *and*:

> *One of her friends was a sort of pioneer at this new school of study. And I decided that was for me. And very interesting it was,* ***too****.*

> [talking about a library book which the speaker has mislaid]
> *It's probably around here then, hiding from me. And a very good book it was,* ***too****.*

Also would not normally be used in these examples. *As well* is possible.

Mid position

In more formal styles, *too* occurs in mid position. In written texts, it is often separated by commas before and after:

> *Her personal life,* ***too,*** *seems happier.*

The meaning, once again, depends on context. This example, out of context, could mean 'her personal life as well as her professional life', or 'her personal life, as well as someone else's personal life'.

Too can occur immediately after the subject, even where auxiliary verbs are present, if it refers directly to the subject:

> *He,* ***too****, was coming to a decision.*
> (he and someone else were coming to a decision)
> (~~He was too coming to a decision.~~)

> *Isabel put her hand to her head and found that her own hat,* ***too****, had gone.*
> (hers and someone else's hat had gone)
> (~~… and found that her own hat had too gone.~~)

However, if *too* links a verb phrase or a whole clause with another, it occurs in the normal mid position, after the first auxiliary verb (→ 325):

> *A formal letter would be sent, and Victor would be grateful if Signor Busi would extend his stay for three more days so that a press conference could be arranged and the timescale for construction plotted. He would,* ***too****, be sending Signor Busi sketches of a small statue which was a birthday gift to Victor from how appropriate! the leading market traders.*
> (he would send a letter, and he would send sketches)

Choosing between *also*, *as well* and *too* 14e

Looking at all three expressions together, in speech *as well* is by far the most frequent, *also* is half as frequent, and *too* is the least frequent. In writing *also* is the most frequent, *too* is much less frequent, and *as well* is the least frequent.

In addition to the cases already mentioned, where one of the three expressions may be preferred to the others (e.g. speech versus writing), there are other cases of differences in the use of *also*, *as well* and *too*.

In imperative clauses, *as well* and *too* are normally preferred to *also*:

> [customer in a post office, buying first-class and second-class stamps]
> *Give me a book of ten first and a book of ten second* ***as well*** *then please.*
> (preferred to: ... a book of ten second also then please.)
>
> *Dave found her the key. 'Have my ring* ***too,'*** *he said, taking it off his finger.*
> (preferred to: 'Have my ring also,' he said ...)

As well and *too* are normally preferred in short responses and elliptical structures:

> A: *I'm looking forward to it. It's going to be good.*
> B: *Yes, I am* ***too.***
> (or: Yes, I am as well.)
> (preferred to: Yes, I am also.)
>
> *And usually, if I can't see who it is when I go to the door, I always ask who it is, and my daughter does* ***as well.***
> (or: ... and my daughter does too.)
> (preferred to: ... and my daughter does also.)

Too is especially common in responses to fixed expressions (e.g. extending good wishes, salutations) and in responses consisting of a single object pronoun:

> A: *All the best. Take care.*
> B: *You* ***too.***
> (preferred to: You as well./You also.)
>
> A: *Right. Have a nice weekend.*
> B: *I shall try. You* ***too.***
> (preferred to: You as well./You also.)
>
> A: *I need to do some serious work.*
> B: *Yeah, me* ***too.***
> (preferred to: Yeah, me also./Yeah, me as well.)

Negative clauses 14f

Where two negative ideas are linked, *either* takes the place of *also*, *as well* and *too*:

> *Bill's not here. I don't think Dave is* ***either,*** *is he?*
> (~~I don't think Dave is also/as well/too.~~)

A: *That's not in paperback yet. It's not been in any book clubs* ***either****, has it?*
B: *No.*
(~~It's not been in any book clubs also/as well/too, has it?~~)

36 *Even*

ALTHOUGH, THOUGH 15

Subordinators *although, though* 15a

Both *although* and *though* can introduce subordinate clauses; *although* is the more formal of the two. *Though* is much more frequent than *although* in spoken and written language taken together.

When used with a subordinate clause **before** a main clause, the meaning is something like 'in spite of the fact that …':

> ***Although*** *a lot of money was thrown into the National Health Service, that money was not being used effectively, which is why they needed more managers.*
>
> ***Though*** *at long last she was by herself once more, she knew this would take some getting used to.*

When used to introduce a clause **following** a main clause, the meaning is something like 'but it is also true that …':

> *We work for what they want, not the other way round,* ***although*** *obviously we advise them.*
>
> *It was really funny actually,* ***though*** *I don't know why.*

In all four examples above, *although* and *though* are interchangeable.

Although, though + reduced clauses 15b

In formal styles, *although* and *though* may be followed by a reduced clause without a verb:

> *Miss D.,* ***although a most tragic case****, had not been dying.*
>
> ***Though a grandfather twice over****, he is tanned, fit and attractive, with keen brown eyes and a lot of hair – except on the top of his bald head.*

Although, though + non-finite clauses 15c

In formal styles, *although* and *though* may introduce a non-finite clause:

> *'The UK,* ***although starting from a higher base than many other countries****, has achieved approximately the same rate of growth as the USSR, and that should worry us,' Sir Denis said.*

*Edith, **though regretting the accident**, was mindful of the irony.*

*The tracks, **though produced a year ago**, are getting top reviews, which, as Mark points out, is vindication of the musical direction they chose to go in.*

Even though 15d

Even is frequently used with *though* (but not with *although*) for emphasis:

*Do you find that you get tired when you're working, **even though** you're a part-timer?*

***Even though** I had nowhere to go, I moved out of the flat.*

A–Z 36c ***Even if, even though*** for a comparison of *even if* and *even though*

Though in non-front clause positions 15e

Though (but not *although* or *even though*) can be used in other positions in the clause apart from at the beginning, with a meaning similar to *however* or *nevertheless*. In spoken language it is particularly common at the end of the clause:

(mid position)
*He knows what's happening. Ken, **though**, doesn't seem to know what's going on.*

(end position)
[speaker is talking about his job]
*It's a bit panicky but I've not got any deadlines like you have, **though**.*

As though 15f

The expression *as though* is very frequent, and has a meaning very close to *as if*:

*You look **as though** you're feeling a bit distracted.*

*You feel **as though** you're battering your head against a brick wall most of the time.*

In both cases, *as if* would be equally acceptable.

ALWAYS 16

Position of *always* 16a

Always usually occurs in the normal mid position for adverbs (→ 325):

*I **always try** and give a taxi driver ten per cent of the fare.*

*He's **always been** very good to me.*

*There **was always** someone in the class that was above everyone else.*

Always is not normally used at the beginning of a declarative or interrogative clause:

*I **always** make sure my doors are locked.*
(~~Always I make sure my doors are locked.~~)

*Do you **always** finish your homework on time?*
(~~Always do you finish your homework on time?~~)

However, *always* often comes first in an imperative clause:

***Always** give way to pedestrians. **Always** be prepared to slow down and stop if necessary.*

***Always** gather herbs for storing on a dry day after the dew has evaporated.*

Some literary styles may occasionally use front position for emphasis:

***Always**, if I asked Mair anything, she would refer the decision to Bronwen.*

***Always**, all the time, men are forcing themselves to do what they do not want to do, and keeping themselves from what they do want to do.*

Always + progressive aspect 16b

Although *always* refers to general states of affairs or to repeated events, and is therefore mostly used with simple tense forms, it also occurs with progressive aspect. Such uses often refer to regular events or states which are problematic or undesired:

*Her group **are always blaming** each other. It's awful, isn't it?*

***I was always lacking** in self-confidence and **lacking** in the confidence to think that I'm acceptable.*

*He'**s always moaning** about money.*

Other uses of *always* 16c

Always is often used with *can* and *could* to refer to options and choices of action which the speaker considers to be freely available:

*Of course, if the worst comes to the worst, I **can always** move in there and rent my house out.*

*We **could always** phone up the ferry people and ask them if they've got any deals going.*

Always frequently occurs as an intensifier with mental verbs such as *think* and *remember*:

A: *They look good down there don't they, those tiles?*
B: *Yeah.*
A: *I **always think** they look lovely.*

*I **always remember** when I was fourteen, fifteen, I wanted to be in the Navy.*

As always 16d

As always is used to refer to a particular event which is seen as typical of all such events:

> ***As always**, she was doing all the talking.*
>
> ***As always**, it's a pleasure to get an email from you.*

For good, for ever and *for always* 16e

References to things which will be permanent are usually made with *for good*, and, more formally, with *for ever* (sometimes written as *forever*), rather than *for always*:

> *If we reject her now, we'll lose her **for good**.*
> (preferred to: If we reject her now, we'll lose her for always.)
>
> *I determined to enjoy every moment that I might carry it **for ever** in my memory.*
> (preferred to: ... that I might carry it for always in my memory.)

For always does occur, but it is rare:

> *'I loved no one before you,' she said. 'I thought we were going to be together **for always**. I took it for granted.'*

Forever and *always* 16f

Forever (usually written as one word; compare *for ever*, **16e** above) has a meaning close to *always* when it is used with progressive aspect to refer to regular and repeated events, but carries an even stronger meaning of undesirability (see **16b** above):

> [*darting about* means 'moving very fast']
> A: *You know, I mean, your day's gone, so you're not relaxing really.*
> B: *No.*
> A: *You'**re forever darting** about here there and everywhere you know. And it's just too much.*

AMONG

 A–Z 26 *Between, among*

ANYWAY 17

Anyway has two main uses: it is used with the meaning 'in spite of other circumstances mentioned', and it is used as a discourse marker to indicate boundaries in the discourse. Because of this second use, it is much more frequent in spoken language than in written.

When used to contrast two sets of circumstances, *anyway* normally occurs in end position:

Some kids will do things and it doesn't matter what they do because the parents won't care ***anyway****.*
(despite what they do)

[customer (B) and server (A) talking about a suit]
A: *Do you want me to wrap it up again for you?*
B: *No it's only got to come out again* ***anyway****.*
A: *Oh, all right then.*
(even if you do wrap it)

As a discourse marker in spoken language, *anyway* occurs in front position, and is used to move to a new phase of a narrative or argument, or to resume a conversation after an interruption or diversion, or to signal a move towards closing the talk:

... she went back to her seat and stood up and sort of started again. ***Anyway****, when I got off the bus the teacher came to me and he said 'Thank you for that'.*
(moving to a new stage in the narrative)

... I'm not that stupid. ***Anyway****, what I was saying was, when I first typed it up, it was like normal spacing and normal character size and I'd done nine pages.*
(resuming the narrative after a diversion or interruption)

But ***anyway*** *we'll continue this discussion when we get into the regulations. I must run cos I have to give a lecture.*
(signalling closure)

Anyway can also have a concessive meaning similar to 'at least', and can be used to limit or restrict a statement or to concede a point. In this meaning it most typically occurs in end position, but may also occur elsewhere in the clause.

I do like where I am, I've noticed there's never really any trouble down here. Well not where I am ***anyway****.*

It was a quiet place, Portland Close. That was the general consensus, ***anyway****.*

Northampton, that's where I live. Well, ***anyway****, that's where I live at the moment.*

APART FROM

A–Z 39 *Except*

AROUND, ROUND 18

Around is used as a preposition and as an adverb. It is alternatively written as *round*. *Round* is more common in spoken English. The primary meaning of *around/round* is that of surrounding or covering all sides of something.

As a preposition

*The plane had to circle **around the town** twice before it could land.*

*They were all sitting **round the fire** and singing songs.*

*The whole organisation was built **around him**.*

*Do you know if there is a florist **round here**?*

*Her whole life revolved **round her mother**.*

*Jeff always seems to know a way **round the problem**.*

As an adverb

*They just sit **around** all day and never seem to do any studying.*

*She's clearly been **around**.*
(been to many places/is experienced)

*He was **around** earlier this morning but he's probably gone home now.*
(in the area where the speaker is)

*Be careful not to leave any purses and wallets lying **around**.*

*That's one of the best cars **around** at the moment.*
(one of the best available/on the market)

With numbers

Around is often used for numerical approximations. It can occur in the structure *around about* or, more frequently, *round about*:

*There were **around 20,000 people** at the concert but we could still see everything on the stage.*

*You have to pay **around £70 a week** for rented accommodation near the university.*

*I'll see you **around four** then.*

*I think it was **round about 1994** when they moved here from Germany.*

Round and round

Round and round is a common fixed expression:

*We just seemed to be going **round and round** in circles and getting nowhere.*

→ also **000 Numerals and vague quantifiers**

AS 19

Preposition *as* 19a

As is used as a preposition, with a meaning of equivalence or comparison:

She was thinking of you, as much **as** *herself.*

His chairmanship may well be criticised **as** *anti-democratic.*

The preposition *as* is often used to talk about the role or function of a person, event or thing. When the noun denotes a specific or definite entity, the determiner is usually optional:

Can you remember **as a child** *whether your parents had any ambitions for you?*

[*Judi Dench* is a well-known actress]
Judi Dench, **as the long-suffering wife**, *was outstanding.*

So, so it comes **as a bit of a shock**.

I used that **as a guideline** *and modified it accordingly.*

As (the) captain, *I have a responsibility to the whole team.*

As + noun can have the meaning of 'in the role of'. It is not the same as *like* + noun, which means 'similar to' or 'in the same way as'. Compare:

1 ***As your tutor***, *I want to give you the best possible advice.*

2 ***Like your tutor***, *I want to give you the best possible advice.*

In **1** the speaker is the listener's tutor. In **2**, the speaker is not the tutor, but wishes to act in a similar way to the tutor.

Comparisons of appearance or behaviour are made with *like*, not *as*:

That dog looks **like** *a wolf.*
(~~That dog looks as a wolf.~~)

Than, not *as*, is used to complete a comparative construction with *more*:

We had more freedom **than** *many kids today.*
(~~We had more freedom as many kids today.~~)

Conjunction *as* 19b

The conjunction *as* can have comparative or temporal and consequential meanings. In its temporal meanings it is a synonym for *when* and *while*; in its consequential meanings it is a synonym for *since* or *because*:

The news from Moscow, **as everyone predicted**, *was excellent.*
(comparative meaning: like)

***As it fell**, it smashed to pieces.*
(temporal meaning: when)

*Drivers are warned to expect massive jams at the weekend **as families return home**.*
(temporal meaning: while)

***As it was getting late**, they decided to book into a hotel.*
(consequential: because)

467a *As ... **as*** for detailed discussion of *as* and *as ... as ...* in comparisons

49 *Like*

ASK (FOR) 20

Ask has the meaning of requesting somebody to do or say something or to tell somebody about something. *Ask for* has the meaning of requesting somebody to give something.

The basic complementation pattern with *ask* is ditransitive (*ask somebody something*) (286), and it is frequently used in reporting structures:

*Can I **ask you a question**?*

*Why don't you **ask that man the way**?*

*Why don't you **ask them how much** it costs?*

*Can I **ask you who** I should go and see?*

*She **asked me if** I needed anything.*

Ask for is used with a direct object or an object + prepositional complement construction:

*She's not the kind of person who **asks for help**.*

*We'll have to **ask** the caretaker **for the keys to the room**.*

Ask can be followed by a direct object, especially in the expressions *ask a question* and *ask the way/ask the time*:

*The audience **asked** a lot of **questions**.*

*I'm not so sure of the roads round here. I think we'd better **ask the way**.*

Ask is often used with a direct object with reference to sums of money, usually for selling and renting things:

[speaker B wishes to rent out a flat and a garage]
A: *How much are you **asking**?*
B: *We're **asking £180 per week** for the flat plus £30 a week for the garage.*

Ask + direct object + *of* occurs in some common expressions:

I need to ***ask a big favour of*** *you.*

I know it's ***asking a lot of*** *Ranji but can't he cover my shift for me tomorrow?*

Both *ask* and *ask for* can be used with object + *to*-infinitive:

I ***asked the whole group to wait*** *in the market square.*
(asked somebody directly)

I ***asked for the car to be repaired*** *on the same day.*
(requested that something should happen)

In very formal contexts, *ask* (with the meaning of 'request') may be followed by a *that*-clause with a verb in the subjunctive mood:

In his will, he ***asked that his ashes be scattered*** *upon the open sea.*

AS WELL (AS)

A–Z 14 *Also, as well (as), too*

AT 21

At commonly refers to time and place. The basic meanings and uses of *at* are best understood by comparing it with *in* and *on*.

At, in, on (time) 21a

A basic distinction between *at* and *in* depends on whether reference is made to a point (*at*), or an extended place or time (*in*):

The Edinburgh train leaves ***at*** *seven thirty* ***in*** *the morning.*
(*seven thirty* is a point in time; *the morning* is an extended period of time)

Some further examples of *at* and *in*, referring to time

things seen as a specific point in time (*at*)	things seen as an extended period of time or as a location within longer periods of time (*in*)
I didn't know if you would have time off ***at half-term****.*	*Here are some references to Russian poetry written* ***in the early 20th century****.*
I'm sorry, Jenn has got someone with her ***at the moment****.*	*He'll be free at about three. Could you wait here* ***in the meantime****?*
I'm wondering when I could come and pick up visiting cards that I ordered from you ***at the beginning*** *of October.*	*Maybe we should aim for a little bit of caution* ***in the beginning****, and try and get it right.*
Okay, we could meet ***at 4 o'clock*** *but why don't we meet* ***at lunchtime*** *instead?*	*Okay, he'll give you a ring* ***in a few days.***
Retirement for all civil servants is ***at 65****.*	*I retire* ***in three years' time****.*

With particular days, or parts of particular days, *on* is used:

We always like to meet for lunch ***on a Friday****.*

They love to have their grandparents with them, especially ***on a birthday****.*

You can't beat a walk ***on a fine spring morning****.*
(compare a more general reference: You can't beat a walk in the morning.)

References to important days are seen in terms of whether they are points on the calendar, parts of the day in general, or as particular days:

calendar points, specific periods, or location within longer periods (*at*, *in*)	particular days (*on*)
The semi-finals are ***in the morning*** *and the finals* ***in the afternoon****.*	*We had croissants* ***on the morning of the wedding****.*
Unemployment fell ***in April*** *in all regions and age groups.*	*At half-past four* ***on the afternoon of 8th April 1912*** *– the weather was mild and hyacinths bloomed in window boxes …*

At, *on*, *in* (place) 21b

At is used to describe a position or location seen as a point:

He was standing ***at the ticket barrier****, holding a bunch of red roses.*

We're going to meet ***at the service station*** *and then go on to Bristol in one car.*

At is used to describe locations at firms, companies, workplaces and educational institutions in a particular place:

[*Boots* is a UK pharmaceutical company]
She works ***at the Boots warehouse*** *in Beeston.*

[*Next* is a UK high-street clothing store]
I think you can buy the same thing cheaper ***at Next****.*

Both our childen are ***at Leeds Metropolitan University****.*

At is used to refer to activities which involve a group of people:

He's ***at a concert*** *until about eleven this evening.*

How many are going to be ***at the lecture****?*

On is used to describe a position along a road or river or by the sea or by a lake:

We can stop off at a café ***on the way****, can't we?*

It would be nice to live ***on the coast****, wouldn't it?*

The nicest hotel is ***on Lake Garda****.*

In is used to talk about locations within a larger area:

Look it up. I think you'll find it on page 32, ***in lines 24 to 28****.*

*She's always sitting **in the back row**.*
(the row is a larger area and she occupies one point in it)

*We're planning to spend a fortnight walking **in the mountains**.*

*He was born and brought up **in South Wales**.*

*Here are some worksheets that the teachers use **in class**.*

At after verbs and nouns — 21c

At is used after a number of verbs in order to underline actions towards somebody or something. It is common after verbs of perception and communication:

*I **shouted at** him but he took no notice.*

*Stop **looking at** me like that!*

*She **frowned at** the suggestion and went rather pale.*

*My comments weren't **aimed at** you.*

At is used after adjectives referring to skills, competencies and reactions:

*She is **bad at** communicating her ideas.*
(~~She is bad in communicating her ideas.~~)

*I'm not very **good at** making decisions.*
(~~I'm not very good in making decisions.~~)

*When he was at school he was **brilliant at** French.*

*He was **indignant at** their unruly behaviour.*

*He is **angry at** being left out of the squad for the European matches.*

BACK — 22

General meanings of *back* — 22a

Back refers to the rear area of something (the opposite of 'the front') and can be used as a noun or as a noun modifier:

*Put the name and address on **the back**.*
(noun: the rear side of the envelope/paper)

*Do you know you've left your **back door** open?*
(noun modifier: the rear door of a house or car)

When referring to the human body, *back* describes the rear surface between the shoulders and the waist:

*It was very uncomfortable for a long time. I had to sleep on my **back**.*

*I've been experiencing **back** pain the last few days.*

→ **539 Glossary** for any unfamiliar terms

One of the commonest meanings of *back* is when something returns to an earlier situation or position, or moves in the opposite direction to how it moved before:

*We went by coach and **came back** by train.*

*Anyway, the bank said, 'Well, Mrs Hogan, **come back** next week and we'll see what we can do for you.' So I **went back** the following week and they reimbursed me for most of it.*

Back does not mean the same as *again*. *Again* implies repetition, *back* simply means returning something to its former position or situation:

[discussing a jumper damaged in the wash; *send it back* means 'send it back to the shop/manufacturer from where it was bought']
A: *I've just noticed. Do you know what's happened to your jumper? Have you seen it?*
B: *What, on there? That always happens to my jumpers.*
A: *Ah, that's dreadful though. Could you not send it **back**?*
(~~… send it again?~~)
B: *Send it **back**?*
(~~Send it again?~~)
A: *Yeah. Brand new, isn't it?*
B: *I've only washed it once.*

*I'm sorry. Could you say that **again**?*
(Could you repeat that?)
(~~I'm sorry. Could you say that back?~~)

Back can also mean 'moving away from something or keeping one's distance from something':

*Why should I stand **back** and watch my kids have to go through this at age sixteen?*

Back + dynamic and stative verbs 22b

Back may be used with dynamic verbs such as *come, drive, go, get, look, take, travel*, as well as stative verbs such as *be* and *lie*:

*I remember a few years ago I was **driving back** from Wimbledon …*

*Mohammed's taken Said to visit a friend and will **be back** later.*

At the back and *in the back* 22c

When *back* refers to a point or position in space, *at* is used. When it refers to an area or enclosed space, *in* is used:

[speaker at a conference]
*Can you hear me **at the back**? I just want to check that the microphone's working.*
(speaker considers the 'back' of the hall as a position or point)

[offer to a passenger in a car]
Would you prefer to sit ***in the back****?*
(*the back* is seen as a part of, or area in, the car)

Back + here, there, home 22d

Back is often used with the adverbs *here*, *there* and *home*:

Meet me ***back here*** *at five o'clock.*

I got ***back home*** *at quarter to eleven, which was okay.*

Back + time expressions 22e

Back can be used with time expressions to emphasise that something happened a long time ago:

And I got involved in quality circles ***back in 1988****.*

Well I used to leave my bike around Truro, I was so naive ***back then****, I just used to leave it unlocked.*

Back can also be used with *a while* instead of *ago* in informal contexts:

A while back *he told me all about a long talk the two of you had when you were walking through the art gallery.*

BECAUSE/COS 23

Because is a subordinating conjunction which introduces clauses of cause and reason:

The government will not act ***because economic factors influence their thinking****.*

Because the snow had set in*, we decided to abandon the excursion to the mountain top.*

Because of is a two-word preposition:

Because of the heat*, we spent most of the time in the pool.*

I'm only here ***because of you****.*

Cos (which can also be spelt *'cause*) is a reduced form of *because*. It can be used in all the examples above. It is widely used in spoken and more informal varieties of English. *Cos* is a way of representing in writing the reduced pronunciation (/kəz/ or /kɔz/) of the word that is common in informal speech across the range of ages, social classes and educational background:

We're not going to the club ***cos*** *it's just too expensive.*

[two teachers speculating about the salary of a colleague]
She's probably on the first allowance ***cos*** *she was probably earning about eighteen thousand.*

In spoken English *cos* often functions more like a coordinating than a subordinating conjunction. In these instances *cos* invariably follows the main clause and functions to add to the information in the main clause:

She doesn't like animals ***cos*** *she says we should keep the house clean. And she does, doesn't she?*

What does he look like? ***Cos*** *I've never actually met him.*
(*cos* here explains why the speaker is asking the question)

BEFORE 24

Preposition *before* 24a

Before is most frequently used with noun phrases referring to timed events:

[speaking to a tennis player]
What kind of thoughts come into your mind ***before a match****?*

[travel agent to customer]
The tickets normally come about ten to fourteen days ***before departure****.*

References to place may also be made with *before*, especially when they are seen as part of a sequence of events in time:

[university literature seminar]
And it's clear I think ***before the end of the first chapter****, probably* ***before the end of the first paragraph****, that actually that is not Jane Austen's point of view nor is it an objective factual point of view.*

Before, by, till/until

If something has to be done *before* a certain point in time, then when that point arrives, the specified action must already be completed:

[tutor to student concerning handing in assigned work]
You'll have to give it to me ***before Tuesday*** *cos I'm going away on Tuesday.*

If something must be done *by* a certain point in time, that point is the last moment at which the specified action can be completed:

I need to be back in Cardiff ***by eight o'clock*** *on the Friday morning.*
(no later than eight o'clock)
(~~I need to be back in Cardiff till eight o'clock on the Friday morning.~~)

If something is done or happens *till/until* a point in time, it starts before that point and continues up to that point:

I'm going to be away ***till August****.*
(my absence will continue up to August)

Compare:

I won't be there ***till three o'clock.***
(I will be there at three o'clock but not before)

I'll be there ***by three o'clock.***
(I may arrive before three o'clock and will be there no later than three o'clock)

Adverb *before* 24b

Postmodifying a noun

Before often postmodifies nouns such as *day, morning, night, week, month, year*:

A: *There was a dreadful tragedy in Australia just yesterday I think.*
B: *Was there?*
A: *Or* ***the day before.*** *Yes.*

A: *Delia had her second day off school ill a week last Wednesday.*
B: *A week last Wednesday. So did she get to the concert?*
A: *Yes. We got to the concert. That was* ***the week before.***
B: *Ah yes. Yeah.*

As adjunct

Before relates earlier events to the moment of speaking or to a point of time in the past:

A: *Does this look different to you?*
B: *Yeah. We haven't been in this building* ***before.***
(up to the moment of speaking)

It was a new team. They hadn't worked together ***before.***
(up to that point in the past)

Before + *-ing* clauses 24c

When used to link two clauses, *before* followed by a verb in the *-ing* form is many times more frequent in writing than in speech. In informal speech there is a strong preference for a full finite clause:

As they talked, Sonia walked past. She spied them and waved, ***before walking*** *on, heading towards Denver.*

Add the lemon juice, and stir. ***Before serving,*** *remove the red chilli.*

Before + finite clauses 24d

Before may be used with a variety of tense forms and time references to link two clauses:

- Present simple (with future meaning):

A: *When you go and vote, what sort of consideration do you give* ***before*** *you actually* ***decide*** *who you're going to vote for?*
B: *Well it's very hard really.*

→ 539 **Glossary** for any unfamiliar terms

- Present perfect:

  A: *The instructions are on there.*
  B: *Okay.*
  A: *And it's quite important to get them well-boiled cos otherwise we'll die of poisoning.*
  B: *Right. What from beans?*
  A: *Yeah. If you eat those* ***before*** *they'****ve*** *even* ***been soaked*** *or anything, it can kill you I believe.*
  B: *Right.*

- Past simple:

  A: *What did she do* ***before*** *she* ***married****?*
  B: *Hm?*
  A: *What sort of work did she do* ***before*** *she* ***married****? Did she ever tell you?*
  B: *I don't think she ever did anything.*

- Past perfect:

  He died in hospital. And ***before*** *he'****d gone*** *into hospital, he kept saying to my mother 'I've got something I've to sort out. I've got to go to the solicitors'.*

  The perfect aspect versions stress the completion of the event in the *before*-clause and a break in time between the events in the two clauses. The present simple or past simple versions suggest a closer connection between the two clauses, as with *after* (→ **24d**).

Premodification of *before* 24e

Before may be premodified by adverbs such as *just, immediately, shortly* and *long*, and by time expressions involving words such as *days, weeks, months, years*:

We arrived ***just before*** *you.*

She was lying in bed sick and I'd known her ***about two years before****.*

Beforehand 24f

Beforehand is often used as an alternative to *before* as an adverb, especially when the reference to timed events is less specific. It is more frequent in informal speech than in writing:

[talking about an overseas teaching scheme and an information booklet about it]
And this is good because it tells you about the history and what the requirements are. And it says also this is to be used as a resource book. So it's good to read that ***beforehand****.*
(before doing anything else in connection with the scheme)

Beforehand may be premodified by adverbs such as *immediately*, *just* and *shortly*, and other time expressions involving words such as *days*, *weeks*, *months*, *years*:

*He'd bought his tickets **months beforehand** and was really looking forward to it.*

*He will get the bill **a week or two beforehand**.*

Other uses of *before* 24g

In more formal contexts, *before* is often used with the meaning of 'in front of':

*Gertie and I had said goodbye to all our old schoolfriends, to the school itself, and the way of life which had come to an end after more than six years. The long end-of-term holiday was **before** us – only it was more than the end of term for us.*

*When the case came up **before** the Crown Prosecution Service, it was returned for lack of evidence.*

*We promise today, **before** the whole country, that free elections will be established as soon as it is safe to do so.*

Before long is a common expression meaning 'after a short time':

[about the breeding of calves for their meat]
*The newly-born calf is put into a tiny wooden crate. **Before long**, it will be unable to stand properly or turn around in its cramped 'home', and will develop deformed joints. Because people like their veal to be very white, the calves are fed solely on an iron-deficient liquid diet.*

*They were lying in a long line near the entrance, their faces covered by their blankets. They were so very quiet it was hard to know whether any one of them was still alive. Many did die **before long** and were replaced by others whose time had come.*

BELOW 25

Preposition *below* 25a

Below is most commonly a preposition and means 'lower than'. It has a meaning which is close to *under*. Its opposite is *above*. In both the following sentences *under* can be substituted for *below*:

*The water was now just **below her waist** and she was beginning to panic a little.*

*Once the plane got **below the thunder** clouds, the turbulence subsided.*

Below is preferred when things are not literally or directly *under* but at a lower level:

*We were 784 metres above sea level and 160 metres **below the actual summit**.*
(~~We were 784 metres above sea level and 160 metres under the actual summit.~~)

Under is preferred to *below* when one thing touches or covers or hides something else. *Underneath* is only used to refer to physical position:

He put a thick winter vest ***under his jacket.***
(*underneath* is possible but not *below*)

[describing a flood]
Some cars parked near the river were almost completely ***under the water.***

Below is also used to refer to lower levels of more abstract notions and to numbers, especially statistics:

The Dead Sea is about 400 metres ***below sea level.***

When they reached the summit, it was already several degrees ***below zero.***

[about the population of Scotland]
By 2025 it will be approaching 4.9 million and by 2040 it could fall ***below 4.6 million.***

The school's examination results were distinctly ***below average.***

Below is not used in references to people's age:

You can only buy a ticket here if you are ***under 18.***
(~~You can only buy a ticket here if you are below 18.~~)

Below is used metaphorically, often meaning that something is beneath or inferior to something else or that something has less power or authority. With this meaning *below* can be substituted by *beneath*:

He won't take on any job which he thinks is ***below him.***

She is in charge of the whole hospital and has three smaller units ***below her.***

Adverb *below* 25b

Below is also used as an adverb, especially with reference to the lower decks of a boat or ship:

[talking about being on a ferry]
It was getting cold on deck so we went ***below.***

Below may postmodify a noun:

The village below *was silent in the midday sun.*

Below is used in writing to refer to something that will be mentioned later in the text:

As we can see from the export data cited and summarised ***below****, the results are very different from what the company was expecting.*

As we will argue ***below****, the history of this decade tells a different story.*

A–Z 6 ***Above***

BENEATH

 25 *Below*

BESIDES

 39 *Except*

BETWEEN, AMONG 26

Between and *among* are prepositions. *Between* focuses typically on two things which are clearly separated. *Among* focuses on things which are not clearly separated because they are part of a group or crowd or mass of objects and entities:

*They built a hotel **between the hills**.*
(probably with one hill on either side)

*It is a lovely hotel set **among the hills**.*
(probably surrounded by hills)

Most commonly, *between* introduces a prepositional phrase in which two singular or plural noun phrases are joined:

*In many cameras, the distance **between the lens and the film** can be altered so that the focus of the picture is sharp.*

*There is a distinction **between what's written and what's spoken**, of course.*

*The managing director was determined to set a distance **between himself and his employees**.*

The complement of *between* can also be a comparison of times or of a numeric value, which is **not** possible with *among*:

*She lived in Japan **between 1994 and 2000**.*
(~~She lived in Japan among 1994 and 2000.~~)

*Three years ago the television companies agreed to pay a royalty of **between 15 per cent and 35 per cent** to musicians and actors on all tapes sold.*

A large number of nouns, and some verbs, are often followed by *between*. The most frequent nouns are: *connection, difference, distinction, link, relationship*. Verbs frequently followed by *between* are: *choose, differentiate, distinguish, divide*. *Among* is not strongly related to preceding nouns or verbs:

*Unfortunately, he could see no **connection between** his behaviour that night and the fact that his friends no longer phoned him.*

*What's the **difference between** writing for children and writing for adults?*

Among creates a sense of being a part of or surrounded by or included in something else. *Among* is typically followed by a plural noun phrase:

I grew up ***among the most majestic pine forests*** *… I took them for granted, never knew how beautiful they were.*

She was far from home, living ***among strangers****, but she was very happy there.*

Do you happen to have my copy of Macbeth ***among your books****?*

I'd put her ***among the top 20% of students in the class****.*

Note also the two phrases *among others* and its variant *among other things*:

One of their hopes, ***among others****, is that more financial information will have to be disclosed, and more people will be made punishable for breaking the rules.*

The review body will discuss this, ***among other things****; but the broad outline of the new system has been approved.*

Amongst is sometimes used as an alternative to *among*. It is more formal and generally less frequent:

Industrial organizations are ***amongst*** *the most fragile in the world.*

Between can sometimes be used to refer to more than two people or things, especially where the people or things are seen as individually separated from one another:

I gave her money for the three children to divide ***between them****.*

There are some big gaps ***between the floorboards*** *in our living room.*

BIT, A BIT (OF) 27

Bit + nouns 27a

Bit often has a deliberately vague and informal meaning:

I've done a few ***bits*** *of shopping.*

The unit is over in the accident and emergency ***bit*** *of the hospital.*

A bit (of)/bits (of) can denote large and small quantities and can refer to both abstract and concrete things. It is an informal alternative to *some*, or *a piece of/pieces of*, or *a part of*, depending on the type of noun it occurs with:

It's ***a*** *nice* ***bit of land*** *you have here.*
(or: piece of land)

Don't they need ***a bit of furniture*** *before they can move in?*
(or: some furniture)

*We went to the auction and got three nice **bits of furniture**.*
(or: three nice pieces of furniture)

*It's okay. You gave me **a bit of your sandwich** and I'll give you **a bit of mine**.*
(or: a part of your sandwich ... a part of mine)

*We only watched **a bit of that documentary**, but it looked interesting.*

*I need **a bit of peace and quiet**.*

*It looks like you've lost **a bit of weight** already.*

A bit of a is used with nouns which have a gradable meaning, and has a meaning similar to 'quite a':

*It's **a bit of a problem**, I'm afraid.*

*Don't you think she's been **a bit of a fool** about all this?*

Adverb *a bit* 27b

A bit commonly functions as an adverb. It is a more informal alternative to *a little*:

*They had got **a bit tired** working at the computer.*

***Wait a bit**, can you. I'll be down in a minute.*

A bit is used to modify comparative adjectives and comparative determiners. It is not normally used to modify comparative adjectives before nouns:

*It was **a bit more** entertaining than the last play we saw.*
(~~It was a bit more entertaining play.~~)

*The beach was **a bit nicer** than we'd been led to believe.*

***A bit less** noise please!*

*She needs to show **a bit more** enthusiasm for her work.*

When used with non-comparative adjectives and determiners, the meaning is often negative and critical:

*It's **a bit extravagant**, isn't it?*

*He's **a bit old** to be driving, I think.*

*She's been trying to tell him what to buy. That's **a bit much**, I think.*
(*a bit much* is an idiom meaning 'unreasonable')

A bit (or *a little bit*) often has a hedging function:

*It still hurts **a bit**.*
(It still hurts, but not much.)

*I was **a little bit** annoyed, to tell you the truth.*
(... slightly annoyed ...)

The phrase *not a bit* is used in responses to deny or repudiate something:

A: *I hope he didn't hurt your feelings?*
B: ***Not a bit.***
(Not at all.)

A good bit, a fair bit, quite a bit 27c

A good bit, *a fair bit* and *quite a bit* are fixed phrases. Unlike most other meanings with *a bit (of)*, these phrases refer, often by means of understatement, to large quantities:

*He left **quite a bit of** money, you know, in his will.*

*She's **a fair bit** older than he is. About 15 years, I think.*

 50 ***Little, a little, few, a few***

BOTH 28

With nouns preceded by determiners, *both* and *both of* occur:

both	*both of*
*We have, in **both those** markets, spent a lot of time and effort on public relations.*	*The problem is **both of those** statements are true, aren't they?*
*This year we've had **both your** nieces here, haven't we?*	*And what changes have you had to make to **both of your** lives in order to accommodate your baby?*

However, determiners are often omitted after *both*:

*I also told **both neighbours** on **both sides** that I was going to be away for that fortnight and could they keep an eye out in the day because there wouldn't be anyone in during the daytime.*

When *both* is part of a subject or object which has a pronoun head, it may be followed by *of* + an object pronoun. Alternatively, *both* may postmodify a subject pronoun or an object pronoun:

	both of + pronoun	pronoun + *both*
subject	***Both of them** were sitting there looking up at it like that.*	***We both** play the violin.*
object	*Do you two want a lift? I can take **both of you.***	*Which do you prefer? Cos I like **them both.***

The *both of* + object pronoun construction is generally preferred after prepositions:

*I think there's different information **on both of them.***
(preferred to: … different information on them both)

*That's going to be helpful for **both of us**, really, isn't it?*
(preferred to: … helpful for us both)

The object pronoun + *both* construction is not used:

1 where a pronoun is the complement:

A: *There's nothing new happening.*
B: *No.*
C: *You know.*
A: *And that's **both of you**?*
(~~And that's you both?~~)
C: *Yes.*

2 in elliptical short answers:

A: *Which one was that? Is that the eldest?*
B: ***Both of them.***
(~~Them both.~~)
A: *They both came over did they?*
B: *Yeah.*

3 where there is a pronoun phrase in apposition:

*Were your mum and dad Irish, **both of them**?*
(~~Were your mum and dad Irish, them both?~~)

In informal speech, *the* may precede *both of* + pronoun:

*Oh, look, I don't know. You decide, **the both of you.***

If *both* refers to the subject of a clause, it may be used in the normal mid position for adverbs (→ 325):

*We **both decided** he was going to be a ballet dancer.*

[addressing two little children]
*Shall I sit in between so you **can both look** at the story together?*

*These **are both** £79.*

Both may be used alone in short questions and answers. *The both* is not used:

A: *Do you want rice, Bob, or noodles?*
B: ***Both.***
(~~The both.~~)

Neither of is usually preferred to *both … not* in negative clauses:

***Neither of them** can walk very far.*
(preferred to: ~~Both of them can't walk very far.~~)

Both ... *and* is used to emphasise the link between parallel constructions, and is stronger than simple coordination with *and*:

Knowing ***both*** *Pat* ***and*** *Fran Powell, I would be careful if I were you.*
(~~Knowing both Pat and knowing Fran Powell, I would ...~~)

Military technology being used for cordless phones will ***both*** *cut out static* ***and*** *prevent eavesdropping.*

BRING, TAKE, FETCH 29

Bring, take 29a

To understand the difference between *bring* and *take*, it is important to observe how the direction of the action relates to the speaker and listener.

Bring typically means movement with something or someone either from the listener's location to the speaker's or vice versa:

[a bottle of water has just been opened; speaker goes towards the kitchen]
I'll ***bring*** *some fresh glasses.*
(she will come back with the glasses to the place where the listener is)
(~~I'll take some fresh glasses.~~)

I had a load of equipment and stuff I couldn't possibly ***bring*** *on a bicycle so I just* ***brought*** *the minibus here.*
(movement to where the speaker is now)

Bring can also mean movement with something or someone from a third-party location to the speaker's or listener's location:

They've been very kind to me over the year and he's just ***brought*** *me a turkey. So I can't grumble.*
(movement with something by a third person to the speaker's location)

[B's sister has just returned from a holiday]
A: *Did she* ***bring*** *you a present?*
B: *Yes, she did.*
(~~Did she take you a present?~~)
(movement with something by a third person to the listener's location)

Take typically means movement with something or someone from the speaker's or listener's location to a third-party location:

A: *What time's your flight? I can* ***take*** *you to the airport.*
B: *Oh, thanks.*
(~~I can bring you to the airport.~~)
(movement to a third-party location; neither the speaker nor the listener are at the airport)

A: *She was sick all Saturday. She was sick Saturday night.*
B: *So it's gone on for quite a long time really, hasn't it?*
A: *Well it has. That's why I **took** her to the doctor's.*
(movement with someone from the speaker's location to a third-party location)

Where both parties involved in the action are third parties, either *take* or *bring* may be used, depending on whether the speaker sees things from the agent's (*take*) or the recipient's (*bring*) viewpoint:

*Every morning she **brings** (or **takes**) dad a cup of tea in bed.*

The most common errors with *bring* and *take* involve a failure to orientate to the direction of the action:

*I **take** my cat to my neighbour's house once a week, to play with my neighbour's cat, to let it have fun with other cats.*
(~~I bring my cat to my neighbour's house once a week~~ …)
(the movement is to a third-party location, not to the speaker's location)

*I always encourage my children to **bring** their friends home and to invite them for birthday parties.*
(~~I always encourage my children to take their friends home~~ …)
(the movement is to the speaker's location, not to a third-party location)

Fetch 29b

Fetch means to go to another place to get something or someone and bring them back:

*Will you go and **fetch** some milk from the fridge, please.*

*I can **fetch** Mick from the station tomorrow if you like.*

A–Z 30 *Come, go*

BY

A–Z 24 *Before*

COME, GO 30

To understand the difference between *come* and *go*, it is important to observe how the direction of the action relates to the speaker and listener.

Come typically means movement either from the listener's location to the speaker's or vice versa:

A: *Are you **coming round** for coffee tomorrow? I'm here on my own.*
B: *Oh are you?*
(movement from listener's to speaker's location)

[speaking on the phone]
I'll ***come to your place*** *at about six and pick you up.*
(movement from speaker's to listener's location)
(~~I'll go to your place at about six and pick you up.~~)

Come can also mean movement from a third-party location to the speaker's or listener's location:

A student ***came to me*** *last night and complained about noise upstairs.*
(movement by a third person to the speaker's location)

A: *I was talking to Gary and Olivia.*
B: *They're* ***coming to see you*** *next weekend I gather.*
A: *That's right. Yes.*
(movement by a third person to the listener's location)

Come is also used with the meaning of accompanying the speaker or listener to a place:

We're going to the cinema Robin. ***Are you coming****?*

[*Super-buy* is a large supermarket]
A: *We were thinking of trying to have a trip to Super-buy at some point.*
B: *I'll* ***come with you****.*

Go typically means movement from the speaker's or listener's location to a third-party location:

A: *Every time I* ***go to Super-buy****, no matter what time I go, I have to queue.*
B: *Mm.*
A: *There's two things that put me off the idea of* ***going to big supermarkets like that****. One is finding somewhere to park and the other is queuing to pay for your goods.*
(movement to a third-party location; neither the speaker nor the listener are at a supermarket)

A: *We drove up into Malaysia.*
B: *And did you* ***go to Kuala Lumpur*** *then?*
A: *No. We* ***went to Melaka****.*
(movement to a third-party location; neither the speaker nor the listener are in Malaysia)

Where both parties involved in the action are third parties, either *go* or *come* may be used, depending on whether the speaker sees things from the agent's (*go*) or the recipient's (*come*) viewpoint:

Much as he had ***come to her*** *when life got too complicated and sad, she now turned to him.*
(seen from the recipient's (her) viewpoint; if *gone* had been used, the movement would be seen from the agent's (his) viewpoint)

Do not use *go on/off* for *get on/off*:

*He put his newspaper down and **got off** the train at the next station.*
(~~He put his newspaper down and went off the train at the next station.~~)

*When you **get on** the plane they offer you a drink.*

When reference is made to a whole trip to and from a place in the present perfect, *been to* is used, not *gone to*:

A: ***Have you been to** Bristol recently?*
B: *No. Not for years.*
(~~Have you gone to Bristol recently?~~)

Present perfect with *go* typically indicates that the subject is still absent:

A: *What about Lou? Did you ring Lou?*
B: *I haven't rung Lou, no. Actually. No, **he's gone to** Edinburgh this weekend so he won't be at home now.*
(Lou is in Edinburgh at the moment of speaking)

Go in, *go into* and *come in*, *come into* mean to enter. *Go to* and *come to* mean to visit or make a trip to a place:

*The idea is that people who **go to foreign countries** should have a lot of respect for other races and different religions.*
(~~The idea is that people who go in foreign countries should have a lot of respect ...~~)

*He had **come to Greece** in the summer on vacation.*
(~~He had come in Greece in the summer on vacation.~~)

 29 ***Bring, take, fetch***

COS

 23 ***Because/cos***

DO 31

Forms of auxiliary verb *do* 31a

Do is used to form the interrogative and negative of lexical verbs (except copular verb *be* and some uses of lexical verb *have*).

person	interrogative	negative declarative	negative interrogative
present tense: all persons except third singular	***Do I*** *know Helen?* *What* ***do you*** *want?* ***Do we*** *really have to do it?* ***Do they*** *sell posters?*	***I don't*** *eat much meat.* ***You don't*** *look old enough.* ***We don't*** *think about it.* ***They don't*** *get back till Tuesday.*	***Don't I*** *know you?* ***Don't you*** *think dad's looking better?* *Why* ***don't we*** *put it to a vote?* ***Don't they*** *look after her?*
present tense: third person singular	***Does anybody*** *want boiled rice?*	***She doesn't*** *eat lunch.*	***Doesn't anybody*** *ask you about that tee-shirt?*
past tense: all persons	***Did I*** *get my change?* ***Did you*** *hear what I said?* *Where* ***did he*** *work?* ***Did we*** *talk about that last time?* ***Did they*** *hire a car?*	***I didn't*** *say that.* ***You didn't*** *try hard enough.* ***Roger didn't*** *have any coffee.* ***We didn't*** *go upstairs.* ***They didn't*** *hear anything.*	***Didn't I*** *sign it?* ***Didn't you*** *tell them the dates?* ***Didn't he*** *turn up?* ***Didn't we*** *have a leaflet?* ***Didn't they*** *come from an academic background as well?*

In more formal styles, or careful speech, or when auxiliary *do* or *not* is stressed, *don't, doesn't* and *didn't* may be spoken and written as *do not, does not* and *did not*:

- Formal styles:

  At an acrimonious meeting, 182 members voted for his adoption, 35 against, four put up their hands as abstentions and 61 ***did not*** *vote.*

  The public affection for the Queen ***does not*** *extend to her family.*

- Careful speech, stressed auxiliary or stressed *not*:

  If I never have to see another doctor's surgery or hospital outpatient clinic, then I would be extremely, extremely happy. I ***do not*** *like being ill.*

Other contracted forms of *do* and *did* 31b

In informal speech, *do you* and *did you* may be contracted to /dju/ and written as *d'you*:

What about roads? ***D'you*** *think less should be spent on the roads?*
(Do you think …)

D'you *get my message?*
(Did you get my message?)

After *where, who, what, why* and *how, did* may be contracted to /d/ in informal speech, and written as *'d*:

*Where'**d** you put the scissors?*
(Where did you put the scissors?)

A: *What'**d** you say?*
(What did you say?)
B: *I said why are you depressed?*

*Why'**d** she ring back?*
(Why did she ring back?)

Emphatic declarative form of *do* 31c

Do, does, did are also used for the emphatic declarative:

*I've got some nice shrubs here which I **do** like.*

*But I think it **does** affect the quality a little bit.*

*He **did** mention that getting the public involved sometimes was a waste of time.*

Do in tags and as a substitute verb 31d

The forms of *do* in the table above (31a) and the infinitive *to do* are used in tags and checks, and in substitute clauses to repeat the idea of the main clause:

*You like lemon chicken, **don't** you, Maureen?*

*She doesn't go short of anything, **does** she?*

A: *It went straight into his eye.*
B: ***Did** it?*
A: *Yeah.*

*I wouldn't intrude in any way on any academic problem because I don't have the necessary qualification to **do** so.*

⇢ also **98 Questions and tags** and **130 Substitution**

Lexical verb *do* 31e

Do as a lexical verb is used to indicate activity of some kind. It collocates strongly with nouns denoting physical and mental activities:

*They think the women are the ones who go out and **do the shopping**.*

*He kept asking me if I'd **do a painting** of him.*

Other everyday nouns of this type include:

cleaning	*dishes*	*research*
course	*homework*	*washing (up)*
decorating	*housework*	*work*
degree	*job*	
diploma	*project*	

A very common pattern is *do* + quantifying expression + activity noun:

*Do you **do a lot of skiing**?*

*I managed to **do a bit of theatre-going and concert-going**.*

*Let's now make the beds and **do some hoovering** if that's all right.*

Other everyday nouns that occur in this construction include:

cooking	*reading*	*swimming*
exercise	*sightseeing*	*walking*
fishing	*singing*	*writing*
gardening	*studying*	

Do and *make* 31f

Do is often used with nouns that can also be used with *make*. *Do* focuses on the activity itself, while *make* focuses on the end product of the activity:

*Do you want me to **make** some potato salad? Cos Mick said he'd **do** a potato salad and another sort of salad and I've just been on the phone to Jane as well, she says she's gonna **do** a rice salad.*

A–Z 51 *Make*

DOWN 32

Down is used as a preposition indicating movement or position:

*They **drove down the hill** too quickly and didn't see the bend.*

*The supermarket**'s down the hill**, then turn right. You can't miss it.*

*Pamela **lives** just **down the road**.*

Down is also used as an adverb:

*They were **waving** a flag up and **down** and looking very anxious.*

*You've **come down** from Portland, have you?*

Down can also be used as an adjective. It is almost exclusively used predicatively and it has a wide range of meanings which are often metaphoric and often negative:

*She's a bit **down**.*
(sad)

*The computer's **down** again.*
(not working)

*Don't be too **down** on them. They haven't done this before.*
(critical)

Down can also be used as a verb:

*He **downed** his opponent in the third round.*
(knocked down, defeated)

DURING 33

During is used to refer to extended events or periods of time. Reference may be to the whole time of the event, or to something that occurred while the event was taking place:

*You're not allowed to smoke **during the flight**.*
(the whole flight)

***During that week** it was the birthday of our son.*
(at a point in the week)

During and *for* are different. *During* is not used with numbers and quantitative time expressions:

*I worked there **for three years**.*
(~~I worked there during three years.~~)

However, *during* is used with *the last* + quantitative time expressions:

*Have you seen him at all **during the last few days**?*

During is not used to introduce clauses:

***While I was sitting there**, the nurses were talking in the corridor.*
(~~During I was sitting there, the nurses were talking in the corridor.~~)

 43 ***For***

EACH 34

Each other 34a

By far the most common construction with *each* is *each other*, which is used to refer to a reciprocal event or state, where the subject and object are both agents and recipients of the same process:

*I mean, you two have known **each other** for a long time, haven't you?*

[talking about the subjects of study at a university]
*The Business Studies and the Computing actually complement **each other** very well.*

A: *We don't mind being with* ***each other*** *in the day.*
B: *Yeah.*
A: *Some couples ... I've got friends who say I'm happily married but I couldn't be locked in a house for five years with my husband.*

Although *each other* most frequently refers to only two people or things, this is not necessarily so, and it may refer to larger groups, especially in informal speech. In this way, it is an alternative to *one another*:

Our next generation in the family, they're all very close to ***each other****, if you know what I mean.*

She said it was all right at the beginning of the year, they all moved in together, but this is the third year they've all lived together, and she said, 'Oh so many arguments'. She said, cos they know ***each other*** *so well now, instead of talking about* ***each other*** *behind their back, they just have full blown arguments to their face.*

Each other's can be used as a possessive determiner:

We like ***each other's*** *company.*

✪ *Each other* cannot be used as the subject of the clause. *Each of us/each of you/each of them*, or *we each/you each/they each* is used:

Each of us *must return to continue the fight in our own towns.*
(~~Each other must return to continue the fight in our own towns.~~)

We each *make our own decisions.*

Each other and *one another* are often used interchangeably, with little difference in meaning:

His last wife was Chinese, and they lived in separate houses, but not far away from ***one another****.*
(or: ... not far away from each other.)

Oh this is Peggy Ann. We've known ***one another*** *now for, what, fifteen years.*

However, while *each other* can be used to emphasise the individuality of the relationship between one person or thing and another, *one another* can be used to focus on people and things as groups:

It is natural for people to be interested in ***one another's*** *affairs in the country, and anything of that nature was sure to be talked about: but this time there was much more talk than usual.*
(people seen as an undefined group)

The high valleys of Graubünden were virtually isolated from ***one another*** *until well into the nineteenth century.*
(all the valleys seen as a group)

Each and *every* 34b

Each refers to individual things in a group or list of two or more entities. It is often similar in meaning to *every*, but *every* refers to a group or list of more than two entities. Compare:

1 ***We each*** *make our own decisions.*
(stresses individual members of a group)

2 ***Everyone*** *makes their own decisions.*
(stresses the group as a totality)

While example **1** could refer to two people or more than two people, example **2** can only refer to more than two people.

Adverbs such as *almost*, *practically* and *nearly* are used with *every*, but not with *each*:

> *You walk down any street and basically* ***almost every*** *building is falling down.*
> (~~... and basically almost each building is falling down.~~)

Each, *each of* and *each one of* 34c

Each is followed by a singular noun:

> *He turned up fairly regularly at the same time* ***each day****.*
> (~~... at the same time each days.~~)

Each of is used before other determiners and before object pronouns:

> *What we did was carry out group discussions in* ***each of the*** *countries within the target market.*
>
> *These are bookmarks. I have one for* ***each of you****.*
>
> *The hotel manager charged* ***each of them*** *£10 for three single rooms, totalling £30.*

Each of with a plural noun as subject is normally followed by a singular verb, though this rule is sometimes ignored in informal speech:

> ***Each of those*** *parallel dimensions* ***is*** *equally possible.*

For greater emphasis, *each one of* may be used with determiners and pronouns. If the phrase with *each one of* is the subject, the verb is singular:

> *Well, there's six doctors now. Six. And* ***each one of them has*** *a computer station.*

Each + pronouns/possessives 34d

Each may be used with plural pronouns and possessives, especially in order to express neutral gender:

> ***Each person*** *should contribute to old-age care insurance, which would be triggered if* ***they*** *became in need of care.*
> (preferred to: ... if he became in need of care.)

539 **Glossary** for any unfamiliar terms

*How can we lay the foundation of children's educational achievements within the confines of the National Curriculum while simultaneously helping **each child** take pride in **their** cultural accomplishments, care for others and care for the world in which **they** live?*

Each referring to a subject 34e

When *each* refers to the subject of the clause, it can occur in the normal mid position for adverbs (→ **325**):

*They **each agreed** to pay £20.*

*We **each have** a responsibility.*

*We **had each been** given a whole loaf of bread.*

 **12 *All*; 28 *Both***

ESPECIALLY 35

Do not confuse *especially* and *specially*. *Especially* means 'particularly' or 'above all'. *Specially* is not normally used in this way:

*The most damaging economic and political effects of the Depression were felt in Japan, and **especially** in Germany.*
(~~... were felt in Japan and specially in Germany.~~)

*The demands of putting all children through the National Curriculum make it more difficult for teachers to cope with disruptive behaviour. This is **especially true** of primary schools.*

Specially is used to indicate the specific intention(s) behind an action:

[referring to the processing of applications for political asylum]
*All asylum claims are considered by **specially trained** caseworkers.*
(the caseworkers are trained intentionally for this job)

*Cows are also **specially bred** to create genetically good milk makers.*

*I did that **specially for you**.*

However, in informal spoken language, *specially* is sometimes used to mean 'particularly' or 'above all':

A: *If somebody is ill do you think, if the treatment isn't going to work, do you think that hospitals should stop treating patients?*
B: *I think **specially in the case of children** they shouldn't stop.*

EVEN 36

General meaning and use of *even* 36a

Even refers to extreme or unexpected things. When it refers to a whole event, it operates as a mid-position adverb (→ 325):

*Some of the members thought I was being very disloyal. They **even accused** me of being in the pay of European dealers, which I had to get them to deny because it was certainly not true.*

*Sadly he can't drive, he can't walk, he **can't even answer** the door.*

[speaker talking about fears for his children]
*There **are even** drugs at school, so I really fear for them and hope that they don't get caught up with it.*

Even can come before the verb in a non-finite clause:

*The potatoes grow without **even looking** after them. We just plant them.*

Even can come before any particular clause element that the speaker/writer wants to focus on:

***Even a ship made with prime materials and the best British engineering** could hardly stand such a battering.*
(focus on subject noun phrase)

*Queen Street today drove me absolutely mad, you know. Because you could hardly walk around there. And it was never like that years ago, **even on a Saturday**.*
(focus on the adjunct)

*One of the targets is for people to take moderate exercise, typically walking and cycling, for around 30 minutes, five times a week. Yet studies suggest that fewer than one in 20 children achieves **even this**.*
(focus on the object noun phrase)

When used to focus on a particular clause element, the negative form of *even* is *not even*:

[speaking of someone born in 1915]
*When Ann was born, the idea of space travel, that men could go to the moon, was considered pure science fantasy. **Not even science fiction**.*

In informal speech *even* may occasionally occur in end position:

*He had loads of injections and then they gave him proper stitches and it was really bad, it was really traumatic for me and my brother **even**.*

Even + comparatives 36b

Even frequently occurs with comparative adjectives and adverbs:

We finish at three but some people have to leave ***even earlier*** *than that.*

By saying ***even*** *earlier*, the speaker is implying that three o'clock is already very early. Compare:

We finish at three but some people have to leave ***earlier*** *than that.*

Here there is no necessary implication that three o'clock is 'early', and the speaker could have said 'some people have to leave before that'.

Other examples with comparatives:

You know you've gone a long way this year. You'll go ***even further*** *next year.*

The alternatives were scratched because they were ***even more*** *time-consuming.*

→ also **460-471 Comparison**

Even if, even though 36c

Even if can have either a hypothetical meaning (i.e. the speaker does not know if something will be the case or not) or a concessive meaning (the speaker concedes that something may well be the case). *Even though* tends to be used only in concessive contexts:

We'll go for lots of walks, ***even if the weather's horrible.***
(hypothetical)

So I know something about the deal ***even if my information is rather out of date.***
(concessive: I accept my information may be out of date)

I kind of have the impression that I really like London now, ***even though I didn't enjoy it at the time.***
(concessive)

In informal speech, where the meaning of *even if* is obvious, *even* is sometimes omitted:

I'll finish that skirt tomorrow ***if it kills me.***
(even if it kills me)

Even and *also* 36d

Even refers to extremes. *Also* simply adds another piece of information, but does not carry the meaning of surprising, unexpected or extreme events. Compare:

[said by a speaker at the closing ceremony of a big international conference]
I've enjoyed the conference very much. I ***also learned a lot*** *from the talks I attended.*

*I've enjoyed the conference very much. I **even learned a lot** from the talks I attended.*
(That surprised me. I thought I knew everything already!)

 14 *Also, as well (as), too*

Even so, even then 36e

Even so has the meaning of 'nevertheless', 'despite this', or 'however'. It occurs mostly in front position in the clause, but may also occur in end position, especially in informal speech:

A: *I mean originally it was going to start on the first of January, and then they realised they simply couldn't do it because Rita was going to be away anyway all of December.*
B: *Right.*
A: *But **even so**, I still think it was quite hurried.*

Even then can also mean 'despite something that was/is/will be already true'. It is most typically used in front position in the clause:

[woman talking about how she went into labour when pregnant]
*So I was admitted to hospital, but **even then** it was another two days before she was actually born.*

EVER 37

Ever is used in interrogative clauses and negative declarative clauses to mean 'at any point in a given period of time':

[talking about childhood]
***Did you ever play** football in the streets?*

***I haven't ever had** anything like that happen to me.*

Ever occurs in affirmative relative clauses in superlative contexts, and often with expressions such as *the first time, the only time*:

*Yet he still admired her **more than** any woman he had **ever** met.*

*It is the **funniest film** I have **ever** seen in my whole life.*

*It was **the first time** I've **ever** seen him get nasty.*

Not ever (and the contracted form *n't ever*) is generally equivalent to *never*. However, in declarative clauses it is far less frequent than the equivalent form with *never*:

*But, given that he is so bright and capable, was he **not ever** enticed to make money legally?*

*I have**n't ever** flown.*

Ever can be used immediately after *if* or separated from it in the clause:

*Here's my address. **If ever** you're in Glasgow you must come and see us.*

*I tell him outrageous things about Kevin which I shouldn't and Kevin would kill me **if** he **ever** heard.*

Ever can premodify the intensifiers *so* and *such* for extra emphasis:

*I'm **ever so** thirsty.*

*My grandma was **ever so** sweet.*

*He's **ever such** a nice guy.*

*Do you know, I heard **ever such** a funny story.*

Ever may premodify *since* used as a time preposition or conjunction to emphasise that something has been true right from the beginning of a specified period of time:

*We've been a bit nervous **ever since we got burgled**.*

Ever since may also be used as an adverb:

*I lost touch with him about ten years ago and I've been trying to get back in touch with him **ever since**.*

Ever is used with comparative *as* … *as* … to indicate a persistent or permanent characteristic of someone or something:

A: *I saw Harold the other day.*
B: *Oh yeah. How is he these days?*
A: *He's **as crazy as ever**.*

Ever may be used as an adverb (most typically occurring before adjectives and noun phrases) meaning 'always', in more formal styles:

*She was a small, handsome woman, modestly dressed and **ever ready** with a smile or a word of encouragement if you were feeling down.*

*'Oh dear, what's up with you guys now?' she asked, **ever the nosy one**.*

Yours ever and *as ever* may be used in leave-takings in letters, emails, etc. *Yours ever* is rather formal; *as ever* is informal:

I will let you know as soon as I have more news.
Yours ever,
Charles (Bowen)

Anyway, I'll talk to you later.
As ever,
Jen

→ **208 *Whatever, whoever, whichever***

EVERY 38

Every refers to the total number of something. It is followed by a singular noun and, if it refers to the subject of the clause, by a singular verb:

> ***Every area*** *of the country* **has** *got a Community Health Council.*
> (~~Every areas … have got …~~)
>
> ***Every day*** *we went somewhere different, didn't we?*
> (~~Every days …~~)

The negative of *every* is normally *not every*:

> *Certain members of this family had a curiously shaped lower lip, which stuck right out; it even became known as the Habsburg lip. But* ***not every*** *member of the family had this.*
> (preferred to: … every member of the family did not have this.)
>
> A: *Do you buy lottery tickets* ***every*** *week?*
> B: ***Not every*** *week.*

Every cannot be used alone, without a noun or without *one*:

> *Unable to find it, she then checked the front door, and* ***every window*** *in the house: as yesterday,* ***all*** *locked.*
> (~~… as yesterday, every locked.~~)
>
> [someone describing how he made sure a paved area in his garden was level]
> *All I did was formed sections. We just put pegs in the ground and a piece of wood, to make sure* ***every one*** *was level.*
> (*every one* = every section)

Every one of is used before pronouns and determiners. *Every one* is written as two words (compare *everyone*; ··➤ **38a**):

> *I agree with* ***every one of them.***
>
> *There were no newcomers.* ***Every one of the refugees*** *was known to her by sight.*

34 *Each*

Pronouns and possessives that refer back to *every* are normally singular, especially in more formal styles, and especially when the referent is non-human:

> ***Every generation*** *and* ***every decade*** *throws up* ***its*** *own particular set of problems.*

In less formal styles, the pronoun or possessive may be plural:

> *In some companies* ***every group*** *has to move every two years to force* ***them*** *to get rid of material which* ***they****'re not using.*
> (instead of: … to force it to get rid of material which it's not using.)

If the subsequent reference applies simultaneously to all members in the group, plural pronouns and possessives are used:

> ***Every woman** walking down the main shopping street paused outside Henry's plate-glass windows. As the jackets caught **their** eyes, **they** assessed them, coveted them and quite a number of window shoppers made a decision to buy.*
> (~~As the jackets caught her eyes, she assessed them~~)

When *every* is used with a numeral expression and a plural noun, it refers to regular intervals of time or numbers:

> *There's one teacher to **every forty-five kids**.*

> *I go to my doctor regularly. I go and see him **every four weeks**.*

Compare the typical use of *every* with a singular noun:

> *I put my money in the bank **every Friday**.*
> (~~every Fridays~~)

Single is often used to emphasise *every*:

> ***Every single** word has been checked to make sure that it reflects modern usage.*

> *We have to log **every single** complaint and pass it on to our district office.*

Every one and *everyone* 38a

Every one, written as two words, is used to refer back to a noun already mentioned:

> *Then taking deep breaths she gathered up the fallen **CDs**, taking great care and attention with **every one**, checking it for dust or damage, reuniting it with its box and putting them all back on the shelf.*
> (*every one* = every CD)

Everyone, written as one word, means 'every person':

> *Say hello to **everyone**.*

Everyday and *every day* 38b

Everyday, written as one word, is an adjective meaning 'routine', 'normal', 'ordinary':

> *We don't discuss **everyday boring things**, you know, we try and discuss the things that are maybe out of the norm a little bit.*

Written as two words, *every day* is an adverb phrase of frequency:

> *And we went **every day** into the zoo.*

Every other 38c

Every other means 'every second one', 'alternate':

> ***Every other Thursday*** *we get together and have a briefing session for half an hour.*

Everybody/everyone, everything, everywhere 38d

Everybody/everyone, everything and *everywhere* are written as one word. They are used with singular verbs:

> ***Everybody gets*** *up and* ***dances*** *and* ***has*** *a good laugh.*
>
> *In the summer* ***everything gets*** *relocated.*
>
> *It was after midnight and* ***everywhere was*** *closed.*

Everybody and *everyone* may be the subject of imperative clauses, in which case the base form of the verb is used:

> *Come on!* ***Everybody sing*** *together!*

Everybody and *everyone* are very close in meaning. However, *everybody* is very much more frequent in spoken language than in written language, and *everyone* is more frequent in written language than in spoken language.

EXCEPT 39

Except as a preposition is used to exclude people or things from a generalisation:

> *Nothing now remains* ***except the factory*** *itself.*
>
> *There was no noise,* ***except the sound of cutlery*** *on plates.*
>
> *Everyone seems to be in on it* ***except me.***
> (*be in on it* = know what's happening)
>
> *I've never seen any policeman on foot* ***except on football match nights*** *and that's when they're leaving the police station and heading towards the football ground.*

Except may be followed by an infinitive without *to* when a general statement or general category is modified to include an exception of some kind:

> *What could you do,* ***except try*** *and put them all behind you?*
> (infinitive without *to*)

An infinitive with *to* is used in other situations, when the meaning is 'except in order to':

> *I never got in touch with that doctor again,* ***except to pay*** *his bill.*
> (~~I never got in touch with that doctor again, except pay his bill.~~)

An infinitive with *to* is normally used when reporting that someone withholds information or action:

He wouldn't tell me what he was up to, ***except to say*** *that it was a secret.*

The other things I could not talk about, ***except to joke*** *a little about him being near with the money.*

An *-ing* form may follow *except* if the clause refers back to a verb normally followed by an *-ing* form:

[*Malahide* is a beach area]
We went into the railroad station then and went to Malahide and had a lovely day out, which I don't remember very much ***except*** *collect****ing*** *a whole lot of shells.*
(I *remember* collect*ing* shells.)

Except for 39a

Except is often followed by *for* + noun phrase:

We went up and down the main street and we couldn't find a proper restaurant ***except for one Italian place****.*

He and his mother were living quite happily over on the other side of the island. There was no involvement from me ***except for an annual phone call*** *to check they were okay.*

When *except* is used without *for*, it normally occurs after generalising words such as *all*, *everything*, *everyone*, *no*, *anybody*, *whole*, etc. (→ the examples in **39** above). If there are no such generalising words, *except for* must be used:

The church was silent and dark, ***except for*** *the rustle of leaves against the door.*
(~~The church was silent and dark, except the rustle of leaves against the door.~~)

The river was deserted, ***except for*** *a couple of small boats.*
(~~The river was deserted, except a couple of small boats.~~)

When there is a generalising word, there is usually a choice of *except* or *except for*:

I met ***all*** *the England football team* ***except (for)*** *David Beckham.*
(generalising word: *all*)

Conjunction *except* 39b

Except (*that*) is often used to introduce clauses, with the meaning of 'but' or 'however'. This is particularly so in informal spoken language:

It was quite a happy time, ***except that I was very lonely****.*

He looks, more or less, just like a normal lad. ***Except he isn't****.*

[*a Tamagochi* is a kind of electronic 'pet']
A: *We'd prefer you to have a hamster than a Tamagochi. And it's not going to cost that much more for a hamster.*
B: ***Except you need to buy food****.*

Except and *apart from* 39c

Apart from does not always mean the same as *except*.

Apart from often means 'in addition to' or 'besides'. In such cases, it cannot substitute for *except*:

There are other people I have to think of ***apart from you.***
(~~There are other people I have to think of except (for) you.~~)

Anybody else want ice cream ***apart from the kids****?*
(in addition to/besides the kids)

On other occasions, the two expressions are interchangeable:

We've got no other holidays planned ***apart from Copenhagen.***
(or: … except for Copenhagen)

EXPECT 40

If someone *expects* something to happen, it means there is a strong probability or belief that it will happen or be true:

A: *I* ***expect you know Paris.***
B: *Mm, a bit, yes.*
(You probably know Paris. It would surprise me if you did not.)

A: *Oh, I hope we do all right.*
B: *I* ***expect you will.*** *You've established quite a formidable reputation now.*
A: *Do you think so?*
(You probably will do all right; I predict you will do all right.)

Expect, *hope* and *wait*

Hope refers to what someone desires/wants/wishes:

[A is making an informal speech at B's birthday party]
A: *I'm very pleased to be here and I wish you many happy returns of the day and I* ***hope you have a happy birthday*** *and a happy time.*
B: *Thank you very much.*
(I want you to have a happy birthday)
(~~I expect you have a happy birthday~~)

[announcement as a plane is coming in to land]
Captain Martinez and his crew ***hope you have had a pleasant flight.***
(~~Captain Martinez and his crew expect you have had a pleasant flight.~~)

Wait for refers to time. If one *waits for* something, one passes time until it arrives:

Come on! Hurry up! I'm ***waiting for you****!*
(~~Come on! Hurry up! I'm expecting you!~~)

I gave him the essay a week ago, and now I'm ***waiting for feedback.***
(I have to just pass the time until he gives me his comments on the essay.)

→ 539 **Glossary** for any unfamiliar terms

Constructions following *expect* 40a

- Same subject for *expect* and verb following: *expect* + *to*-infinitive:

  [referring to returning a pair of trousers to the shop where they were bought]
  *They said, 'When did you buy them?' I said, 'Well it was in the summer, so **I** don't **expect to have** my money back, but, you know, I would like to change them please, cos they're falling apart.'*

  ***The new appointment** is **expected to commence** in early 1996.*

- Different subject for *expect* and verb following: *expect* + object + *to*-infinitive:

  ***I** didn't **expect them to contact** me.*

  *His life was very pure, and **he expected other people to be** as pure as he was.*

- Same or different subject for clause following: *expect* + (*that*-)clause:

  ***I expect it's** from Russia. It's like one of those Russian dolls.*

  ***I expect I'll** get to meet all of them soon.*

  When a (*that*-)clause is used, *I expect* often occurs in end position in informal spoken language:

  > *It would be less trouble for them, **I expect**.*

> *Expect* + (*that*-)clause normally refers to predictions. If *expect* refers to assumptions about how things are or should be, then the infinitive construction is used:
>
> *I do **expect to be respected** by my younger colleagues.*
> (~~*I do expect (that) I'm respected by my younger colleagues.*~~)
>
> *Children **expect to get expensive presents** for their birthdays.*
> (~~*Children expect (that) they get expensive presents for their birthdays.*~~)

- With an object:

  *If I'd written to him, I would have **expected a reply** back in writing.*

  *His wife's **expecting a baby**.*
  (= is pregnant)

  This latter use (referring to pregnancy) can be intransitive in informal contexts:

  *She's **expecting**.*

- With adverbs:

  Back, *here* and *in* often occur after *expect* + direct object:

  *I didn't **expect** you **back** quite so soon.*

  [shopkeeper to customer]
  *I think we've sold out actually. Someone asked us for this the other day. I know we're **expecting** some **in**.*
  (we are expecting to get some in stock soon)

Expect so, expect to 40b

Expect so may be used in short answers instead of repeating a *that*-clause:

A: *Will we have to wait until he changes his swimming routine?*
B: *I* ***expect so****.*

→ 130 Substitution

Expect to, like *hope to*, *like to* and *want to*, is used in short answers instead of repeating an infinitive construction:

A: *Well we've managed to get through it.*
B: *Yes. Good.*
A: *Really, cos we didn't* ***expect to****.*
(~~Really, cos we didn't expect.~~)

A–Z 49 *Like*; 75 *Want*

Expect and progressive form 40c

Progressive forms of *expect* normally occur with a direct object or with the *to*-infinitive construction, not with a *that*-clause:

He seems to be ***expecting some kind of response****.*
(+ direct object)

I let myself in with my key, not ***expecting to find*** *anyone working late on a Tuesday evening.*
(+ *to*-infinitive)

However, a *that*-clause may follow the progressive form occasionally in informal speech:

There was never once that she said, 'Oh, go on without me,' you know. Cos I was fully ***expecting that*** *we would some days leave her behind at the hotel, while we went off on a trip.*

Expect of, expect from 40d

Expect of refers to what someone thinks others ought to do, or how things ought to be:

A: *I thought you meant that was your personal discipline, to work until eight at night.*
B: *Oh yeah. Well it is and it isn't. You need to do it just to keep up with* ***the amount of work that's expected of you****.*
(the amount of work your employer/your teachers think you ought to do)

I don't think you should ***expect too much of it*** *too soon.*

Expect from refers to what someone predicts or thinks is likely about a person or situation:

It was run with the efficiency you'd ***expect from Hilary****.*
(because we know Hilary, one could predict that)

He looked very much as I'd ***expected from his voice*** *over the phone: a little man in his late fifties.*
(... as I had predicted from his voice)

EXPLAIN 41

✪ The complementation pattern for *explain* is object + prepositional phrase, not an indirect and direct object:

	object	prep phrase
Do you think you could ***explain***	***this paragraph***	***to me****?*

(~~Do you think you could explain me this paragraph?~~)

Explain can simply be used with an object noun phrase or a clausal object:

He ***explained the situation****.*

I can't think of any other way to ***explain it****.*

They wrote me a long letter ***explaining why it took eighteen months****.*

In informal speech, *explain* is sometimes followed by *about* + noun phrase when it refers to a general topic or event:

[referring to making a complaint at a hospital]
So when you complained, did you ***explain about the injection****?*

FAIRLY

 66 *Quite*

FALL 42

✪ Do not confuse the past tense forms of *fall* and *feel*.

present	past	-*ed* participle
fall	***fell***	*fallen*
feel	***felt***	*felt*

Their dad had a crash and their car ***fell*** *into the sea.*
(~~Their dad had a crash and their car felt into the sea.~~)

He ***fell*** *in love with one of his classmates.*
(~~He felt in love ...~~)

I completely forgot to phone her back. I ***felt*** *really awful about that.*

Fall and *fall down* are used differently. *Fall* simply implies downward movement. *Fall down* implies falling or collapsing suddenly from one's normal position, often including damage or injury:

House prices ***fell*** *by five per cent last month.*
(~~House prices fell down by five per cent last month.~~)

Now it was winter and the leaves had ***fallen*** *from the trees.*
(~~Now it was winter and the leaves had fallen down from the trees.~~)

[speaker is worrying about not having health insurance]
What if you ***fall down*** *and break a bone? Then you're off work sick and all that and your treatment's at the hospital.*

FELL

 42 *Fall*

FETCH

 29 *Bring, take, fetch*

FEW, FEWER

 50 *Little, a little, few, a few*

FOR 43

For is commonly used to express the recipient of an action or a thing:

Look what Kathy made ***for Heather****.*

I've bought something ***for you****.*

For is used with expressions indicating a period of time:

We went to Ireland ***for a week****.*

Let it dry ***for a few moments****.*

For is used to refer to specific periods of time such as public holidays and seasons:

I usually go there ***for the New Year****.*

We'll be in Scotland ***for the whole summer****.*

Do not confuse *for* and *in* when referring to time:

I'm going on holiday ***for a month****.*
('I'm going on holiday *in* a month' would mean 'I leave one month from now')

 33 *During*; 70 *Since*

For + *-ing* form may refer to the purpose or function of something or how something is used:

> [referring to a conversation with a shop assistant]
> *He said 'What sort of knife do you want?' I said 'Oh just something* ***for camping.****'*

For + *-ing* form may refer to the reason for an event:

> *He got called an idiot* ***for being honest.***

For is not normally used to express one's intention:

> *My wife and I go there to see my mum.*
> (~~My wife and I go there for seeing my mum/for to see my mum.~~)

In very formal styles, *for* followed by a finite clause can be used to indicate the reason for something, and is a synonym of *because*:

> *It was a pity that I could not understand her,* ***for I am sure she would have been most interesting.***

GET

 30 ***Come, go***

GO

 30 ***Come, go***

HARDLY 44

Hardly is a negative adverb; it normally means 'almost not at all'. It is not the adverb form of the adjective *hard*:

> *I could* ***hardly*** *get out of the car.*
> (I almost could not get out at all)

> *The poor woman can* ***hardly*** *walk.*
> (she can almost not walk at all)

The adverb form of *hard* is *hard*:

> *I've been* ***working hard*** *and I've been travelling all the time.*
> (~~I've been working hardly and I've ...~~)

Because *hardly* has a negative meaning, it is used with *any, anyone, anybody, anything* and *ever* in negative clauses, not with *no, none, no one, nobody, nothing* or *never*:

> *There had been* ***hardly any*** *contact between them for years.*
> (~~There had been hardly no contact between them …~~)
>
> ***Hardly anybody*** *turned up today, actually.*
> (~~Hardly nobody turned up today, actually.~~)
>
> *I* ***hardly ever*** *see her. We're not very close.*
> (~~I hardly never see her.~~)

At all may be used with *hardly* for greater emphasis:

> *I* ***hardly*** *smoke* ***at all.***

Another use of *hardly* is to reject or to distance oneself from an idea:

> *He could* ***hardly*** *say no to such a request.*
> (it was virtually impossible to say no)
>
> *Well, you're* ***hardly*** *good friends with Jenny, are you?*
> (it would be wrong/absurd to say that you were good friends)

In more formal styles, *hardly … when* is used in front position with subject-verb inversion to refer to something happening immediately after something else:

> ***Hardly had the tour come to an end when*** *we were off to Japan, which was a very different experience to my first visit.*

HERE, THERE 45

Here typically refers to the speaker's location and sees the position of people and things from the speaker's point of view. It may be used with static and dynamic verbs:

> *We've* ***lived here*** *over 16 years now.*
>
> ***Come here****, Max.*

There typically refers to the listener's location or a third-party location and sees the position of people and things from the listener's or a third-party point of view. It may also be used with static and dynamic verbs:

> [on the phone]
> *Oh, you're in Rome! What are you* ***doing there****?*
> (listener, not speaker, is in Rome)
>
> *If we leave here at six, we should* ***get there*** *by eight or eight-thirty.*
> (at a place where neither listener nor speaker is at present)

Here and *there* correspond in their speaker-listener relationship to *this/these* and *that/those* respectively, and frequently accompany the related demonstrative:

[teacher addressing a computer class]
I think the idea today is that everyone will have a go at ***this*** *machine* ***here****. It's quite simple to use.*

Is ***that*** *coffee* ***there*** *mine?*

Here and *there* also correspond in their speaker-listener relationship to *come/bring* and *go/take* respectively, and frequently accompany the related verb:

They ***came here*** *about 15 years ago.*

She has a cottage on the coast and ***goes there*** *to paint.*

Bring *that tray* ***here****, would you.*

[talking about a restaurant]
She ***took*** *Lars* ***there*** *for a meal when he came to stay.*

 **29 *Bring, take, fetch*; 30 *Come, go***

Here, there in front position 45a

Both *here* and *there* are used in constructions which involve subject-verb inversion. These include everyday routine patterns such as *here is x, here comes x*, and *there is x, there goes x*, and subject-verb inversion in more formal styles where *here* and *there* are used emphatically in front position.

- Everyday usage:

  Hurry up! ***Here comes the bus.***

  Here's my taxi. *I'll have to go now.*

  [speakers approaching a train platform, just as their train is leaving]
  There goes our train*! We've missed it.*

  [handing someone a cup of coffee]
  Here's your coffee.

  [pointing to a book on the table]
  There's that book I was telling you about *if you want to have a look at it.*

- More formal styles:

  She was attracted by this place, and ***here was her opportunity of remaining.***

  The door opened slowly and ***there stood Miss Louise.***

Subject-verb inversion of the types exemplified above do not occur when the subject is a pronoun:

A: *Where's the tin-opener?*
B: *Oh I saw it earlier …* ***here it is.***
A: *Thanks.*
(~~Oh I saw it earlier … here is it.~~)

There goes our train! *We've missed it.*
There it goes! *We've missed it.*
(~~There goes it! We've missed it.~~)

Here's, said when handing or giving something to someone, is often used instead of *here are* with plural noun phrase subjects in informal contexts. Similarly, *there's*, when indicating or pointing to something, is also used with plural noun phrase subjects in informal contexts:

[parents trying to persuade young children to write some placards welcoming their pop music idols to their home town]
Come on, write out the sign that says 'We love you' on it. Come on, go on, ***here's your pens*** *and here's your paper, go and write it out because we've got to go now.*

There you are. ***There's your pills.***

Initial *here* and *there* with a subject + *be* and without subject-verb inversion often occur as emphatic markers, especially in spoken narratives:

[an elderly person who has just developed a skin rash has been told she may be allergic to something]
Well I've never been allergic to a thing in my life. And ***here I am****, seventy-odd, just starting.*

[health worker talking about eating garlic]
I stink of garlic again. It's very embarrassing. This poor patient was really ill and ***there I was****, breathing garlic over her.*

Here and *there* both have more abstract uses. They can refer to parts of the surrounding text. *Here* tends to be used cataphorically (referring forward in the text), while *there* tends to be used anaphorically (referring back in the text):

[writing about the British Government's annual budget; *Kenneth Clarke* was at the time the Minister responsible for the budget]
The Budget was remarkable for missed opportunities rather than new measures. In my opinion, ***here*** *is what Kenneth Clarke should have done. Childcare: At the moment, employers are the only ones to receive tax incentives for this. … Far better would be a system of vouchers for parents who could themselves choose the childcare they prefer and the location.*

[*Tony Adams* and *Stuart Pearce* are footballers]
Tony Adams impressed me, along with Stuart Pearce. And ***there*** *lies the big problem. Both put in good performances, but they are not the long-term future of English international football.*

There is often used to signal the end-point of a conversation in more formal contexts such as meetings and interviews:

[BBC radio interviewer, concluding an interview with Jack Straw, a British Government Minister]
And ***there*** *we must leave it. Mr Straw, Many thanks.*

→ **539 Glossary** for any unfamiliar terms

Here, there after prepositions 45b

Here and *there* both frequently follow prepositions:

[assistant to customer in a café where customers can choose to eat food in the café or take it away]
*Is it **for here** or to take away?*

*There's been a lot of crime **round here**.*
(in this neighbourhood)

*Ugh, it's quite hot **in here**, isn't it?*

A: *Where's the dog's squeaky toy?*
B: *There it is, **under there**.*

[speaker B has just asked where a particular restaurant is]
A: *You know that area where the theatre and the Casino is?*
B: *Yeah. Yeah.*
A: *It's **near there**.*

Here/there you are 45c

Here you are and *there you are* are both used when handing or giving something to someone, often something which has been requested or sought:

A: *Where's the dictionary?*
B: ***Here you are**.*
A: *Ah, thanks.*

[A hands B some money]
A: ***There you are** Jessica.*
B: *Oh, what's that for?*
A: *To help you when you have your holidays.*
B: *Oh thanks, Edward.*

In informal contexts, *here you go/there you go* are used instead of *here you are/there you are* when handing or giving things to people:

A: *Can you pass me the butter?*
B: ***There you go**.*
A: *Thanks.*

People often announce their own or others' arrival with *here* + subject pronoun + *be*:

A: *Hi! **Here we are**! Sorry we're late.*
B: *Hi there!*

There + subject pronoun + *be* is often used to announce the moment of finding or meeting someone or something the speaker has been looking for:

*Ah, **there you are**, Nick! I've been looking for you all morning.*

On the telephone 45d

Here is often used by speakers to identify themselves on the telephone or in voicemail messages:

[voicemail message]
*Hello, **Terry Fitzmaurice here**, calling to speak to Jack at 10.35am Tuesday.*

Hello there 45e

There is often used in informal situations after *hello* and *hi*:

A: ***Hello there**. How's things?*
B: *Hi. Fine. And you?*

HOPE

A–Z 40 *Expect*

IN

A–Z 21 *At*

IN FACT 46

In fact is normally used to say that expectations were not fulfilled and that assumptions may need to be modified or corrected. It is typically used in front position, and occasionally, in more formal contexts, in mid position. In spoken language it may be placed in end position:

A: *Did she pass the exam?*
B: *She did. **In fact, she got** a distinction.*

*Since 1989 the emission of pollutants **has in fact fallen**, but only because the economy has collapsed.*

*That wasn't a very nice thing to say to me, was it? **Quite horrible, in fact**.*

In fact is also used to supply additional information:

*We met Jane for lunch. **In fact**, we spent the whole afternoon with her.*

Related phrases used in similar ways include *in actual fact, as a matter of fact, in point of fact*:

*They lived somewhere near here, **in actual fact**.*
(more emphatic version of *in fact*)

As a matter of fact, more people are going to New Zealand now than ever.

A–Z 9 *Actual, actually*

IN FRONT (OF)

A–Z 62 *Opposite, in front (of)*

JUST 47

Just has a number of meanings.

Just for emphasis

Just has a meaning of 'simply' or 'absolutely'. It is used to create emphasis, and is especially common with reference to negative situations:

*It's **just not right**.*

*Because otherwise Saturday will be **just a nightmare**.*

*It's **just terrible**, isn't it, the way they ignored all the protests.*

*The weather was **just perfect**.*

***Just one of those things**, isn't it?*

***Just be quiet**, will you!*

Just meaning 'exactly'

Another meaning of *just* is 'exactly':

*That's **just what I wanted**.*

*It's **just right** for you.*

A: *Where does it hurt?*
B: [pointing to one side of her wrist] ***Just here**.*

Just meaning 'only'

Another meaning is 'only':

*The eighteenth century reveals a complex overlapping not **just of economic and aesthetic** but also of political **issues**.*

[doctors talking about doing late-night calls to patients]
*... and I can't see that **just one doctor** is sufficient really.*

Just meaning 'recently'

Just can also mean 'a very short time ago, recently':

*I've **just finished** painting the bathroom.*

*They had **just appointed** her to the post of supervisor.*

[to a little child]
*You want more? You **just said** you weren't hungry!*

Just with expressions of time and place

Just frequently occurs before expressions of time and place. It often functions to minimise the time and distance involved:

*Can you wait **just a minute**?*

*It's **just at the end** of the Clifton road.*

*I always called at my mother's **just down the road**.*

Just as a softener

A common function of *just* in spoken English is to downtone or soften utterances:

*Could I **just ask** you something?*

*My dad's ambitions really are … are for us all to be religious and **just sort of to be happy** and erm have enough money and things.*

*I was **just wondering** when you thought we should meet tomorrow?*

*Do you think you … can you **just pop this in the post** on your way home?*

LESS

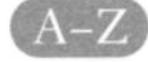 50 *Little, a little, few, a few*

LET 48

Let is followed by an infinitive without *to*:

*I'll **let** you **have** a look at it.*
(~~I'll let you to have a look at it.~~)

*He **let** them **put** some boxes in the basement.*

Let is not normally used in the passive when it means 'allow/permit':

*The families were not **allowed** to see the children.*
(~~The families were not let see the children.~~)

Imperative *let* 48a

Let's is used to form the first person plural imperative, often used for making suggestions:

***Let's** talk about cricket.*

***Don't let's** quarrel about it; it's not worth it.*

Let's is also used frequently in informal speech with a singular meaning referring to the speaker. In this situation, *let's* is more informal and less direct than *let me*:

> ***Let's*** *have a look on the computer for you.*
> (more formal: Let me have a look on the computer for you.)

The full form *let us* occurs in formal contexts:

> ***Let us*** *pray.*
> (used in Christian religious ceremonies to announce the beginning of prayer)

> ***Let us*** *fight together to overthrow the last remnants of the cruellest regime in English history.*

Let is also used for third person imperatives:

> A: *Sylvia is outside. She wants to see you.*
> B: *Oh,* ***let her*** *wait.*

Imperatives with *let* may form their negatives in two ways: *let's/let us + not* and *don't let's*. The first is more common:

> ***Let's not*** *be silly about it.*

> ***Let us not*** *be blind to the true facts.*
> (more formal)

> ***Don't let's*** *fall out.*

Third person imperatives with *let* form their negative with *don't*:

> ***Don't let*** *anyone fool themselves that's the end of it.*

Let meaning 'rent' 48b

Let used alone with a direct object means 'to rent something to someone':

> *They* ***let their house*** *for a thousand pounds a month while they were abroad.*

Let alone 48c

The expression *let alone* is used after a negative statement or with reference to a problematic context, to refer to how unlikely something is by comparing it with something even less likely:

> *I have no idea what I'll be doing in five months,* ***let alone five years.***
> (to predict five years ahead is impossible because even to predict five months ahead is impossible)

LIKE 49

Like means 'similar to'. It often occurs with verbs of sensation such as *look, sound, feel, taste, seem*:

*People **like him** should be put away in prison.*

*She's **like her father**.*

*That **looks like a winner**.*

*It **tastes like pineapple**.*

Like has functions similar to those of an adjective. It is gradable and has attributive uses:

*He's **so like** his father.*

*She is **more like** her sister than her daughter.*

*We are completely **of a like mind** on this issue.*

Like is also used as a conjunction. It is an informal alternative to *as*. In some traditional grammar books and style manuals, using *like* as a conjunction is considered incorrect:

*He involved the staff in everything, **like** a good manager should do.*

Like is used as a noun-suffix meaning 'similar to':

*She looked ill and was wearing a **ghost-like** cream cloak.*

Like in spoken English 49a

One of the most frequent uses of *like* in spoken English is to focus attention, usually by giving or requesting an example:

A: *I fancy going somewhere really hot for holiday this year.*
B: *What, **like** the Equator or the Mediterranean or **like** ...?*

When examples are asked for, a common structure in English conversation is *like what?*:

A: *What did you get up to today?*
B: *Not a lot. There were a few computer things going on.*
A: *Hmm, **like what**?*

Like can be placed in end position in order to qualify a preceding statement. It also indicates that the words chosen may not be appropriate:

*Then she got out of the car all of a sudden **like**, and this bike hit her right in the back.*

*It was a shattering, frightening experience **like**.*

→ 539 Glossary for any unfamiliar terms

Like is very commonly used (particularly among younger speakers) as a marker of reported speech, especially where the report involves a dramatic representation of someone's response or reaction:

So this bloke came up to me and ***I'm like*** *'Go away, I don't want to dance'.*

And ***my mum's like*** *non-stop three or four times 'Come and tell your grandma about your holiday'.*

In some cases *like* acts as a 'filler', enabling the speaker to pause to think what to say next or to rephrase something. Pauses (...) can occur either side of the word:

They think that ... ***like*** *... by now we should be married and if we were married then it's okay* ***like*** *... to get on with your life and do what you want.*

Like is also used in the structure *it + be + like*, a phrase which introduces an example or analogy of some kind:

It's like *if you go to another country you always get muddled up with the currency in the first few days.*

It's like *when I go to the doctor's there's always loads of people in the surgery breathing germs all over you.*

Be like and *look like* are not the same. *Be like* refers to someone's character or personality, *look like* refers to their appearance:

A: *What's your new teacher* ***like****?*
B: *Oh, he's nice. Very patient with us.*

A: *Would you recognise her again? What does she* ***look like****?*
B: *Mm. Short dark hair, quite tall.*

19 *As*

LITTLE, A LITTLE, FEW, A FEW 50

Determiner *(a) little, (a) few* 50a

A little is used with singular non-count nouns. *A few* is used with plural count nouns. They have a meaning similar to 'a small quantity/number of':

Can you give me ***a little help*** *with the garden?*

All tomatoes benefit from ***a little fertiliser****.*

There are still ***a few names*** *left on the list.*

I've met him ***a few times*** *at our music sessions.*

Little (without *a*) is used with singular non-count nouns. *Few* (without *a*) is used with plural count nouns. They both have negative meanings. They suggest 'not as much as may be expected or wished for':

*There was **little chance** of them winning.*

*She has **little** real **enthusiasm** for yoga; she only goes because her friends go.*

***Few supporters** turned up at the meeting.*

Compare:

*He made **a few films** during his career in London.*
(several)

*He made **few films** during his career.*
(not many)

Of is employed after *a little* and *a few* when they come before definite noun phrases:

*Thanks, I'll have **a little of the** soufflé, please.*

*I wish more people had **a little of your** enthusiasm.*

*Only **a few of the** members turned up.*

*I'll have **a few of those** strawberries, please.*

Pronoun *(a) little*, *(a) few* 50b

(A) little and *(a) few* can be used as pronouns. *Little* and *few* (without *a*) only occur in more formal contexts:

A: *D'you want some more soup?*
B: *Give me just **a little**.*

A: *Did everyone turn up?*
B: *Well, **a few** came, but a lot of them didn't.*

***Little** has been written on this topic.*

***Few** would disagree with his election to the chair of the association.*

*She said **little** but it had an impact on everyone there.*

Fewer and *less* 50c

Although, traditionally, *fewer* is the comparative form used with plural count nouns and *less* is used only with singular non-count nouns, increasingly, in informal spoken situations, *less* is used with plural count nouns:

*So would you say you had **less ambitions** then, ten years ago?*
(traditionally correct usage: fewer ambitions)

[complaining about poor conditions in schools in Britain]
*They need good teachers, they need warm classrooms and they need **less children** in the class.*
(traditionally correct usage: fewer children)

→ 539 **Glossary** for any unfamiliar terms

Adverb *(a) little* 50d

A little functions as an adverb of degree, and is a more formal alternative to *a bit*:

[physiotherapist talking to a patient]
Try stretching your left leg ***a little****.*

[garage mechanic talking to a customer]
We've re-tuned the engine ***a little****, so it should be starting okay now.*

A little is not used as an adverb in negative clauses. *A bit* is used instead. The meaning is '(not) at all':

*You have****n't*** *changed* ***a bit****! You still look twenty.*
(~~You haven't changed a little! You still look twenty.~~)

A little premodifies adjectives, determiners and adverbs, including comparative forms, and is a more formal alternative to *(a) bit*:

She's just ***a little agitated*** *about it so please try to persuade her to talk.*

They are both ***a little confused*** *and disoriented.*

Was the plot ***a little thin****?*

'I'm leaving now!', she said ***a little angrily****.*

[talking about a washing-machine]
This model is ***a little less*** *efficient and economical.*

A: *How do you feel today?*
B: *Er,* ***a little better*** *thanks.* (more formal)

A: *How do you feel today?*
B: *Er,* ***a bit better*** *thanks.* (less formal)

I'm still hungry so I'll have ***a little more*** *spaghetti, please.*

If *little* is used as an adverb in front position, subject-verb inversion occurs:

Little did we think *six months ago we'd be going to another funeral in the same family now.*

Not a little as a premodifier can be used as a more formal alternative to 'rather' or 'very':

The management team were ***not a little*** *frustrated by the lack of progress in the negotiations.*

→ **470 Comparison and other word classes** for further discussion of comparative and superlative forms *less, least*

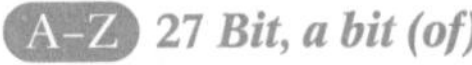
27 Bit, a bit (of)

MAKE 51

A number of constructions follow *make*.

- Object:

  *Look, I **made a mistake**. I'm sorry.*

- Object and adjective complement:

  *Travelling **makes me hungry**.*

- Object and noun complement:

  *When we decided that we'd book the holiday, we came home and about two or three days later we decided that it was time that we got married. We **made it a honeymoon**.*

- Indirect and direct object:

  *She **made me a cup of coffee** in the kitchen.*

- Object + prepositional phrase with *for*:

  *You've got to see your own doctor and he'll **make an appointment for you**.*

- Object + adjective/noun complement + prepositional phrase with *for*:

  *Don't **make it difficult for us**.*
  (adjective complement)

  *So what would **make it a good quality experience for you**?*
  (noun complement)

Make + infinitive without *to* 51a

When *make* means 'force to do' or 'cause to feel' something, it is not followed by *to* in the active voice:

*He **makes** me laugh.*
(~~He makes me to laugh.~~)

*What **made** you choose this job?*
(~~What made you to choose this job?~~)

However, in the passive voice, the *to*-infinitive is used:

*Why should I **be made to feel** guilty for things I didn't do?*

*I **was made to sign** the statement.*

Make and *do* 51b

Make, rather than *do*, emphasises the end product of an action more than the activity itself:

*Shall I just **make a pot of tea** then?*

*I went and worked in a factory **making plastic bags**.*

→ 539 Glossary for any unfamiliar terms

Make, not *do*, collocates strongly with noun objects referring to speech acts connected with communication. These include:

apology	*excuse*	*point*
comment	*generalisation*	*remark*
complaint	*list*	*request*
decision	*note*	*speech*
enquiry	*phone call*	*statement*

> *I* ***make this comment*** *because there may be some students who have experienced the same experience as I have.*
> (~~I do this comment …~~)

> *I rang the switchboard and asked if they could put me through to the person I could* ***make a complaint*** *to.*
> (~~… the person I could do a complaint to.~~)

Other common noun collocations with *make* rather than *do* include *attempt, effort, fuss, improvement, mistake, noise, profit.*

Many nouns can collocate with both *do* and *make*. *Do* tends to emphasise the activity involved, while *make* emphasises the result or end product:

> *I hadn't* ***done a tour*** *for three years, so I was a bit apprehensive, but decided to go.*
> (the writer is probably apprehensive about the work and activity involved)

> *We* ***made a tour*** *of the old printing house. It was quite an experience.*
> (emphasis on the experience that resulted from the tour)

31 ***Do***

Made from, made of, made out of, made with 51c

Made from is often used to describe manufacturing processes:

> *Paper is* ***made from fibres*** *which have some tensile strength.*

> *A traditional-style chef's hat,* ***made from 100% cotton****, completes the look.*

Made of emphasises the inherent material or qualities of something, and has a meaning similar to 'composed of':

> *A large ship floats although it is* ***made of heavy metal****.*

> *Different metals are* ***made of different kinds of atoms****.*

Made out of usually refers to something that has been transformed from one thing into another:

> [speakers are talking about a kind of bag that is made using the stalks of rice plants]
> A: *It's rice.*
> B: ***Made out of rice****?*
> A: *Yeah.*
> B: *How can it be?*
> A: *Well it's* ***out of the rushes****, isn't it? It's* ***made out of the green, the reed****. The plants, isn't it? Twisted.*

According to the Aztecs, the world is ***made out of a goddess who was torn apart by some gods****.*
(she was a goddess, but she was re-made)

Made with is most often used to describe the ingredients of food and drink:

I went away and sat in a nearby café where they served me slices of tortilla ***made with aubergines and garlic****.*

Did you ***make*** *this* ***with fresh mushrooms or dried ones****?*

MEAN 52

Talking about language 52a

Mean is used to talk about understanding language:

What does 'claim' ***mean****?*

A very common error is forgetting that *mean* is used with *do/does* in the interrogative:

What ***does*** *'claim'* ***mean****?*
(~~What means 'claim'?~~)

If we want to refer to someone's intended meaning in saying or writing something, we use *mean by*:

A: *So how well do you think you knew them?*
B: *What do you* ***mean by*** *'knew'?*

Mean when referring to intended meaning is normally only used in simple tense forms, but in informal spoken language it is used occasionally in progressive aspect:

*I'****m*** *not* ***meaning*** *to sound derogatory here.*

The bathroom window may be missing but that's not what I ***was meaning****.*

Discourse marker *I mean* 52b

I mean is a very frequent discourse marker in spoken language, used when a speaker elaborates, expands on or clarifies what they are saying:

See what I'm getting at here? ***I mean****, can you see the principle?*

Portsmouth's bigger than Worcester, ***I mean*** *Portsmouth's a big place.*

Speakers also use it for self-correction:

I know he's Portuguese, ***I mean*** *Brazilian, but he's probably read quite widely in Latin American literature.*

539 **Glossary** for any unfamiliar terms

When *I mean* occurs at the end of a sequence, it usually indicates that the immediately preceding statement is a clarification:

She's very young to be a chef, to be training as a chef, ***I mean.***

Does she smoke? Heavily, ***I mean****?*

I mean can function as a hesitation marker and is often followed by a pause. In such instances *I mean* is often used to soften statements or to correct understandings:

A: *What did you make of the match?*
B: *Well,* ***I mean****, it was a bit too competitive.*

She's a bit upset at the moment. ***I mean****, erm, … she's had a bad time recently so I don't really want to bother her.*

I mean commonly occurs with the phrase *you know* in the very frequent spoken expression (*you*) *know what I mean*, which functions primarily to check comprehension and to indicate that the speaker and hearer share a point of view:

She's very nervous, ***you know what I mean****, she just can't concentrate properly.*

✪ *I mean* is not used to preface a statement of one's opinion:

> ***I think*** *Britain should join the single currency as soon as possible.*
> (~~I mean Britain should join the single currency as soon as possible.~~)

Expressing intentions 52c

When followed by a *to*-infinitive, *mean* is used to express intentions or to refer to intended outcomes:

A: *Where were you? I've been worried sick?*
B: *Sorry Anne, I didn't* ***mean to worry you****. I just lost track of time.*

[about the Russian Space Station, *Mir*]
Mir was only ***meant to last*** *for five years.*

The past progressive and perfect progressive forms are often used for indirectness or politeness when expressing intention, especially with *ask*:

I ***was meaning to ask*** *you, did you learn anything useful from that gunman you caught at the docks this morning?*

*I****'ve been meaning to ask*** *you if you ever found out about Larry.*

Keep is also used with *mean to* in informal spoken language to express long-standing intention:

So it's just rusted now. I ***keep meaning to get*** *it fixed, but that's another expense.*

The passive 52d

The passive, *be meant to*, often has the meaning of 'be supposed to':

*You're forty minutes late. You'**re meant to** phone and let me know what you're doing.*

Expressing necessity 52e

Mean in the active voice is often used with a modal meaning, expressing necessity. In this case verbs which follow are in the *-ing* form:

*The race usually starts at three, so that often **means leaving** the house at two.* (I have to leave at two)

[*Shepperton* is a famous film studio]
*We had to be on the set at Shepperton by seven a.m. That **meant being** in make-up by six.*

Expressing significance 52f

Mean can be used to refer to how important or significant people and things are in our lives. In this sense, the preposition *to* follows:

*Money? What does it **mean to** me? Absolutely nothing.*

*I also know how much your career **meant to** you at that time.*

MIND 53

The verb *mind* is most commonly used in two interrogative forms, *do you mind* and *would you mind*, to ask permission and to make polite requests. Both forms may be followed by *if* or an *-ing* form:

***Do you mind if** I smoke?*

***Would you mind if** I open the window?*

***Do you mind putting** your dog back on a lead?*

***Would you mind checking** that for us, please?*

Mind is also used in the negative declarative form to ask permission and to make polite requests, frequently with a tag:

***You don't mind** if I smoke, **do you**?*

***You wouldn't mind** carrying this? Thanks.*

Would you mind and *do you mind* 53a

Both *would you mind* and *do you mind* are used to make polite requests. *No* as an answer indicates willingness:

A: ***Would you mind** feeding the cats while we're away?*
B: ***No**, no problem.*

A: *Erm, about this press release. I was thinking you would be the better authority to write it than me, actually.* **Do you mind** *putting something on paper?*
B: ***No**, I'll do that.*
A: *That'll be great.*

Would you mind is more frequent in requests in everyday conversation than *do you mind*.

Most occurrences of *do you mind* in conversation are followed by *if I/if we …*, and involve asking for permission:

A: ***Do you mind if I** sit here?*
B: ***No.***

No, not *yes*, is the normal, polite answer to requests with *would you mind/do you mind* (*to mind* means 'to object', therefore the listener answers: '**No**, I do not object to, or have any problem with, your request.'):

A: ***Would you mind** photocopying these for me?*
B: ***No.***
(B: ~~Yes.~~)

Other expressions with *mind* 53b

The expression *if you don't mind* is also used to make statements less direct, or a little more polite, and to protect the feelings or dignity of the listener:

***If you don't mind**, I won't have any coffee this morning.*

***If you don't mind me saying so**, she shouldn't speak to her mother like that.*

I don't mind can be used to sound politely non-commital when responding to suggestions, enquiries about preferences, and offers:

A: *What do you want to do this evening?*
B: ***I don't mind.***

A: *Would you like tea or coffee?*
B: ***I don't mind.***

The expressions *I wouldn't mind* (+ *-ing* clause or a noun phrase) and *I don't mind if I do* indicate a positive preference or desire for something:

***I wouldn't mind having** two weeks' holiday right now.*
(I would really like to have two weeks' holiday right now.)

*I must say **I wouldn't mind a coffee**.*
(I would really like a coffee.)

A: *Want to try some home-made pasta?*
B: *Yes. **I don't mind if I do**.*
(Yes. I'd like to.)

Mind is used to issue warnings:

[public announcement on London Underground as train doors are closing]
***Mind** the doors!*
(Be careful of the doors.)

[warning passengers of a gap between the train and the platform edge]
*Passengers are requested to **mind** the gap when alighting from this train.*

***Mind** you pay the bill each month.*
(Be sure to pay the bill each month.)

Never mind is used, mainly in spoken language, to make someone feel better about something or to tell them not to do something because it is no longer important:

***Never mind**, you can try again next year.*

***Never mind** about the cups, just collect up all the glasses.*

Mind you is used as a discourse marker in informal spoken language, with a meaning of 'however' or 'on the other hand'. When used without *you*, it most typically occurs at the end of the utterance:

*The car is a bit too expensive. **Mind you**, it's got a diesel engine so that's good for economy.*

*He's putting on more weight each week. He did go to the gym this week, **mind**.*

NOW 54

Now is most commonly used as an adverb of time. It can also take on nominal functions such as subject in a clause and as complement of a preposition:

*We should go **now**. We're late.*
(adverb of time)

***Now** is the time to act.*
(subject in a clause)

*I hadn't realised **until now**.*
(complement of a preposition)

*Use this old box **for now**. I'll fetch a new one later.*
(complement of a preposition)

→ **539 Glossary** for any unfamiliar terms

Now also has a general meaning of 'nowadays':

People used to cook three meals a day. ***Now*** *nobody cooks. They just eat out of a microwave.*

Now may be premodified. *Just now*, *right now* and *only now* are common:

A: *When did you see her?*
B: ***Just now*** *in the café.*
(very recently, in the immediate past)

I want you to go to bed ***right now****.*
(straight away, in the immediate future)

In formal contexts, when front-position *now* is preceded by *only*, subject-verb inversion occurs:

Only now do I really understand *what she meant.*
(at this moment and not before)

Now … now is used in more formal literary contexts to describe an altered sequence of actions. In such a structure *now* occurs at the beginning of a clause:

Now *splashing each other noisily,* ***now*** *just serenely floating on the surface, they were all swimming in the lake.*

Now (*that*) can also be used as a conjunction. In spoken and informal uses *that* is often omitted:

Now that *it's stopped raining, we can get on with repairing the wall.*

Now *Ian's left university and is earning some money at last, we can have a proper holiday ourselves.*

Now can be used for emphasis. It frequently occurs at the beginning or end of an imperative clause:

Now *hurry up. We're already half an hour late.*

Don't forget ***now****. It's a very important day for the family.*

The expression *now now* is used to calm somebody down when they are agitated:

Now now*, don't get too upset, it'll all get sorted out, I'm sure.*

Now (or sometimes *now then*) is used as a discourse marker to indicate that a new idea is being introduced, to mark a topic shift or to mark a boundary between stages of a conversation:

Now*, what we want to do today is to cover the workings of the personnel department of the company.*

Right, ***now****, let me see, you haven't visited the church before have you?*

Now then*, which of you wants to go to the Theme Park?*

They lived in Shanghai and had two grown-up sons, George and Matthew. ***Now****, Matthew had worked in the USA and trained as an investment banker, whereas George had left school at 16.*

OF 55

Of is a preposition that introduces a relationship between words, phrases and clauses. It is one of the most frequent words in English. One of its most frequent functions is to introduce prepositional phrases which are complements of nouns. The noun + *of* + noun phrase pattern is very common:

These are ***the important institutions of justice*** *and law enforcement.*

There is unlikely to be ***any loss of electrical power*** *during this time.*

She kept ***a diary of the events of every day****.*

Why do you have such ***a low opinion of British newspapers****?*

The most frequent examples of *of* in informal spoken English are in structures such as *kind of* and *sort of*:

She's ***kind of*** *concentrating on her diet at the moment.*

He's ***kind of*** *interested in starting a new course, isn't he?*

It's a ***sort of*** *apple. They're really quite nice and sweet.*

Of commonly occurs in the pattern noun + *of* + noun phrase to denote groups, parts and quantities:

That's a very good ***cup of tea****.*

A member of staff *will meet you at reception to answer any questions you may have.*

The avalanche started right at ***the top of the mountain****.*

Hasn't he earned ***loads of money*** *from investing in South East Asian banks?*

Of also indicates that something belongs to something or else has particular attributes:

The ***roof of the house*** *was blown off.*

I can't say I like ***the colour of her hair****.*

Of frequently occurs in descriptions to mark identity:

It is ***a novel of considerable wit and intelligence****.*

The thief was identified as ***a girl of thirteen****.*

→ 539 **Glossary** for any unfamiliar terms

The structure determiner + *of* + noun is also frequent in expressions of quantity (→ 191):

__45% of salaries__ exceed £50,000.

__Some of my best friends__ are musicians.

__Twenty of the applicants__ are EU nationals.

Of is optional with *all, both, half*, except before the object pronouns *me, you, it, him, her, us, them*:

__Both (of) the dogs__ have been prize winners at top dog shows.

__All of you__ will be held responsible for the results.
(~~*All you will be held responsible for the results.*~~)

 12 *All*; 28 *Both*

Of occurs after certain adjectives (when used predicatively) and verbs. Among the most common adjectives are *afraid of, aware of, fond of, tired of, full of, capable of*. Among the most common verbs are *think of, talk of, accuse (someone) of, rob (someone) of*:

I was very __aware of__ your objections to the plan.

She had grown __fond of__ her new life in Spain.

What do you __think of__ his new girlfriend?

The police __accused__ him __of__ taking the money without permission.

The structure *be* + *of* + noun phrase occurs in formal contexts:

Her decision __was of no comfort__ to him.

Here is an offer which will __be of interest__ to all amateur golfers.

We are glad to __be of service__ to our customers.

OF COURSE 56

Of course is used to indicate that someone knows something or is assumed to know something or should not be surprised to know something:

__Of course__, you'll have to get up before six o'clock each day.

You should, __of course__, not try to do too much until you've got over the illness.

I didn't stay there long, __of course__.

Of course is used as a polite and positive reply to questions that ask for agreement, even if the answer disagrees, and to requests:

A: *I suppose I was stupid to marry him in the first place?*
B: ***Of course** you weren't.*

A: *Can I borrow the car tonight?*
B: *Yes, **of course**, but I need it back by ten thirty.*

Of course is not used in reply to genuine information questions where the asker could not be expected to know the answer:

A: *Where did you go for your holidays?*
B: *We went touring in southern Spain.*
A: *Nice. Did you get to Granada?*
B: *Yes, **we certainly did**.*
(~~Yes, of course.~~)

A: *Is this the bus for the city centre?*
B: *Yes, **it is**.*
(~~Yes, of course.~~)

Of course is used to show concession in an argument. It is sometimes preceded by *but*. It has a meaning of 'needless to say' or 'it goes without saying':

*I think they'll probably need at least two more staff. **Of course**, they will have to prove first that they are overworked.*

*Nobody understood the arguments he was making about the history of science but **of course** not a single student was brave enough to admit it.*

OH 57

Oh is used as an interjection and as a discourse marker. As an interjection it expresses surprise, disappointment and pain. As a discourse marker, *oh* is used in particular to respond to new information or to indicate that a speaker has just discovered something surprising. The extent of the surprise can sometimes be indicated by a marked tone of voice which is represented in writing by *ohoh* and *oooh*:

A: *Tim's coming tonight as well.*
B: ***Oh**, I didn't realise.*

A: *I know you've got to get a visa for China first.*
B: ***Oh**, I see.*

***Oh**, yeah, that's right. Okay, I'll write to them right away.*

***Oooh** no!!! Please don't say we have to go through that tunnel again.*

Oh often occurs together with other interjections or with discourse markers. It commonly occurs at turn boundaries, mainly to indicate that a speaker is responding to a previous stretch of discourse and is introducing a new phase of talk:

***Oh** well, I suppose we'd better be leaving. It's getting rather late.*

***Oh**, what was I going to ask you? **Oh** yes. Who's in charge of car parking?*

In some cases *oh* combines with expletives to indicate an intense expression of feeling:

***Oh my goodness**. Look at her dog. It's bigger than her.*

***Oh hell**! I've left my credit cards in the shop.*

A–Z 69 ***Right, rightly***; 76 ***Well***

Oh is used to indicate that the speaker is making a direct quotation from the words of another. The interjection *oh* functions to mark that the quotation is beginning:

*So mum came rushing in and she's **oh**, you've really done it now haven't you?*

*I thought to myself **oh**, I'd better start improving or I'm not going to keep the job.*

Oh is also used in wish constructions, usually in more formal contexts:

***Oh** for a nice cup of tea! I'm exhausted.*

***Oh** that they could do something about it!*

OKAY/OK 58

Okay (also spelled *OK*) is an informal word with a range of uses. *Okay* indicates that what is said is accepted or agreed with:

A: *How about a drink?*
B: ***Okay**, I'll join you in ten minutes.*

***Okay**, I was probably wrong to react like that but I was angry.*

Okay frequently functions to indicate a change of topic or to signal that a new stretch of discourse is beginning. When used in this way, *okay* often occurs together with other discourse markers such as *right* and *now*:

***Okay**, let's now move on to the history of colonial expansion in that region in the late eighteenth century.*

***Okay**, right, I think we should try something different.*

*Now, **okay**, you go first.*

Speakers also use *okay* to check that they have been understood. It usually occurs at or near the end of an utterance:

*Now are you all sure you understand why this happened. Yes? **Okay**? Good.*

Okay is used in closing sequences:

***Okay**, so, it was nice talking to you.*

***Okay**, well, I'd better be getting on or I'll be late.*

Okay is also used as an informal adjective (usually predicative) to denote a satisfactory or unproblematic state or situation:

He was ill for quite a time but it looks like he's ***okay*** *again now.*

A: *Are you sure it's no trouble?*
B: *No, that's quite* ***okay****.*

Is it ***okay*** *for us to smoke in here?*

He's an ***okay*** *teacher, isn't he?*
(attributive use: less common)

Okay is used as an adverb in informal speech, meaning 'all right':

She did ***okay*** *in her exams, so she's going to college in the autumn.*

Okay can also be used in informal contexts as a verb, meaning 'officially to approve something':

Has he ***okayed*** *your essay draft?*

I'm phoning to ask if you've been able to ***okay*** *my car insurance?*

ON

 21 *At*

ONCE 59

Adverb *once* 59a

Once is used as an adverb with a meaning of 'on one single occasion':

I only went to London ***once****. Never again.*

Take three tablets ***once*** *a day after meals.*

In formal contexts, *once* can refer to an indefinite time in the past with a meaning of 'at one time':

The swords ***once*** *belonged to a tribe of warriors living in the mountains.*

He knew that future generations would not comprehend the horrors of war that ***once*** *so appalled him.*

Once is not used to talk about an indefinite time in the future. Normally the phrases 'some time' or 'one day' are used:

Why don't you come down ***some time*** *to Devon to see the family?*
(~~Why don't you come down once to Devon to see the family?~~)

Noun *once* 59b

Once can be used as a noun in the expressions *the once* and *this once*, usually with *just*. This structure is more common in informal spoken contexts:

A: *How many times did you go there?*
B: ***Just the once.***

Just this once *I'll let you have the CD player.*

Conjunction *once* 59c

Once is used as a conjunction meaning 'as soon as' or 'when'.

Future or conditional forms occur in the main clause, not in the *once*-clause:

What's he going to do **once** *he finds out he has been left out of the team?*
(as soon as he finds out/when he finds out)
(~~What's he going to do once he will find out …~~)

Once *you've passed your exams, we'll pay for a holiday for you.*

The structure *once that* is not used:

Once I know when she's arriving, I'll let you know.
(~~Once that I know …~~)

Once is used for all times other than the immediate present. In this meaning it is replaced by *now that*:

Now that *I'm lying down, I feel a lot better.*

Once *I'm lying down, I usually feel better.*

Once *I was lying down, I felt a lot better.*

Once *you're lying down, you'll feel a lot better.*

In formal written styles, *once* may occur with clausal ellipsis:

Once *inside the house, the three men were arrested immediately by police officers.*
(Once they were inside the house …)

Once in fixed expressions 59d

Once occurs in many fixed expressions. Most of these are expressions of time. Some common examples are:

at once (immediately, simultaneously)

all at once (suddenly)

once upon a time (used at the beginning of traditional stories)

once in a blue moon (rarely, seldom)

once in a while (not very often)

once or twice (very occasionally)

once and for all (completely, finally)

ONE 60

One can be a numeral, a personal pronoun, and a noun-substitute.

Numeral *one* 60a

As a numeral, *one* can be a determiner or a pronoun:

I just have ***one question*** *to ask you.*
(determiner)

One morning *he just got up and left. We've never seen him since.*
(determiner)

My ***one regret*** *is that I never visited Thailand when I lived in the region.*
(determiner)

I don't need a lot. Just give me ***one*** *for now.*
(pronoun)

One can also be a substitute form for a singular or plural count noun:

A: *How about a coffee?*
B: *OK, I'll just have a small* ***one****.*

Are these the ***ones*** *you ordered?*

A: *Can you pass me the shoes?*
B: *Which* ***ones****?*
A: *The red* ***ones****.*

One is not used to substitute for non-count nouns:

A: *Have you got any sugar?*
B: *Yes.*
A: *Can I borrow* ***some****?*
(~~Can I borrow one?~~)

When *one* substitutes for a noun, it refers back to a previous noun and cannot normally be used to refer forward:

I saw a black car at the traffic lights. But it was a very old ***one****.*
(~~I saw a black one at the traffic lights. But the car was a very old.~~)

→ 60c

Personal pronoun *one* 60b

As a generic personal pronoun, *one* can be used with the meaning of people in general and is common in making generalisations, especially in more formal styles. It has third person singular concord:

***One** never knows, does **one**?*

***One** should not let dogs into the country without proper checks. I think those quarantine laws are quite right.*

*Retirement allows **one** to pursue new interests and hobbies.*

You and *they* are also used in a similar way. However, *one* includes the speaker in the generalisation:

*Does **one** eat durian in Malaysia?*
(includes the speaker, who is there or has an interest in going there)

*Do **they** eat durian in Malaysia?*
(refers to others)

One's functions as a possessive determiner:

***One's** country is important but it is in **one's** family that true loyalty is to be found.*

Oneself is the reflexive pronoun formed from *one* (→ **201** and **202** for **possessive and reflexive pronouns**):

***One** should give **oneself** more credit, shouldn't **one**?*

In traditional formal usage, it is considered inappropriate to mix *one* with other third person singular pronouns:

***One** should always be careful before giving **one's** address to someone.*
(~~One should always be careful before giving his/her address to someone.~~)

Noun substitute *one* 60c

When *one* is used as a noun substitute, it is not used immediately after *some*, *any*, *both* and numbers, unless there is a modifier of the noun:

A: *Are there any yoghurts for breakfast?*
B: *I bought some yesterday.*
(~~I bought some ones yesterday.~~)

A: *Which one do you want?*
B: *I'll take both if that's okay.*
(~~I'll take both ones if that's okay.~~)

A: *How many of those ribbons did you get?*
B: *I bought six **red ones** and three **blue ones**. Is that enough, do you think?*

One is not normally used after noun modifiers:

Do you need lettuce or carrot seeds?
Do you need lettuce seeds or carrot seeds?
Do you need lettuce seeds or carrot?
(~~*Do you need lettuce seeds or carrot ones?*~~)

However, *one* is used with noun modifiers that denote what something comprises or contains:

That's the book I wanted. It's ***the Economic History one****.*

A: *Do you want the cheese roll?*
B: *No, I'll have* ***the salad one*** *please.*

Note also that in informal styles *one* can be premodified by a possessive determiner:

A: *I couldn't use the copier today.*
B: *Neither could I.* ***My one*** *was broken too.*

✪ When *one* refers back to a previous noun and is modified by an adjective, a determiner must be used:

The hotel that we had booked turned out to be ***a*** *luxury* ***one****.*

The French dictionary is totally different from ***the*** *Spanish* ***one****.*
(~~*The French dictionary is totally different from Spanish one.*~~)

A or *one* 60d

A/an is the unmarked indefinite article. *One* may be used as an emphatic alternative to *a/an*:

There was ***a*** *car parked outside her house.*
(unmarked)

There was ***one*** *car in the car park.*
(emphatic: 'only one', where there might typically be more)

ONLY 61

Adverb *only* 61a

Only is primarily an adverb. With numerical expressions it has a meaning of 'no more than' and in temporal expressions it has a meaning of 'not until' and 'no longer ago than'. Another meaning is 'cannot but':

There were ***only six*** *of us at the seminar.*

They are really sorry but they are ***only*** *coming* ***on Sunday****.*

I was talking to them on the phone ***only last night****.*

→ 539 Glossary for any unfamiliar terms

Travellers to this remote village ***can only wonder*** *at its complete peace and serenity.*
(cannot but wonder; cannot do anything other than wonder)

Only can indicate an undesirable outcome:

Don't go and see the film. You'll ***only*** *be disappointed.*

As an adverb, the position of *only* varies, and often intonation or context is required to make clear what is modified by *only*. Its most common position is, however, mid position (⇢ 325). When *only* modifies a subject noun phrase, it has to precede it:

He only rinsed *the cups; he doesn't even know how to wash up properly.*

Such investments ***are only some of the ways*** *in which you can prepare for retirement.*

Only I *saw David leave; the others were too busy to notice.*

Only a small number of banks *stay open after 4 p.m.*

Adjective *only* 61b

Only can be an adjective with a main meaning of 'single':

My ***only complaint*** *was that the service was slow.*

She's the ***only one*** *they are prepared to confide in.*

Did you know he's an ***only child****?*
(he has no brothers and sisters)

Only if 61c

When *only* is used before *if*, either immediately before or in a previous clause, the meaning is 'provided that' or 'not … unless':

Visitors will ***only*** *be admitted* ***if*** *the proper attire is worn.*
(or: Visitors will be admitted **only if** the proper attire is worn.)

If only 61d

If only is used to express a strong wish:

If only *I could get enough money together, I could go and work in Australia for a year.*

Only + *to*-infinitive 61e

Only is used before a *to*-infinitive in order to introduce an action or event which is sudden and a little unexpected. This use is usually formal and literary:

The music shop ordered 50 copies of the CD, ***only to discover*** *that the songs were sung in a foreign language.*

He stopped the car, ***only to start*** *it again violently.*

When the Second World War broke out, he tried to enlist, ***only to be rejected*** *on the grounds of ill-health.*

Only + subject-verb inversion 61f

When *only* modifies an adverbial phrase or clause in front position, subject and verb are inverted. This style is very formal and occurs mainly in writing:

Only *in summer* ***do you see*** *people making such fools of themselves.*

Only *when we got home* ***did we realise*** *we'd left the keys behind.*

Only just 61g

Only commonly modifies *just* in references to very recent events:

We've ***only just*** *got here. When did you arrive?*

Only just can also have a meaning of 'with very little to spare' or 'barely managed':

A: *Is there enough for everyone?*
B: ***Only just.***

There was so much traffic I ***only just*** *managed to make the flight.*

Conjunction *only* 61h

Mainly in informal spoken English, *only* is also used as a conjunction with the meaning of 'but':

I would come, ***only*** *I don't know what to wear.*

Okay, I'll let you bring your golf clubs. ***Only*** *please hurry up.*

It's more or less the same in Cyprus, ***only*** *even hotter in July.*

OPPOSITE, IN FRONT (OF) 62

Do not confuse *opposite* and *in front (of)*.

If two people, A and B, sit *opposite* each other (e.g. at a table in a restaurant), then A and B are facing each other (i.e. they are looking towards each other).

If A sits *in front of* B (e.g. in a cinema or lecture hall), then B is behind A (i.e. looking at the back of A's head):

A: *Where's this pizza place we're going to?*
B: *It's* ***opposite*** *Philips', next to the Lyons coffee shop.*
A: *Oh right.*
(on the other side of the street from Philips')

[talking about a minor road accident]
The car ***in front of*** *me stopped suddenly and I went into the back of it.*
(my car was driving behind the car I hit)

539 **Glossary** for any unfamiliar terms

In front of is often used for things people have in their hands or immediately before them and which are connected with an activity they are engaged in. It is also used to mean 'in the presence of someone':

[doing business over the phone]
A: *Have you got that price list **in front of you**?*
B: *I have. Er, hold on a minute. Yes.*

*Some people spend all evening **in front of the television**.*
(watching television)

[talking about a gift]
*I don't want you to open it **in front of all your family**.*
(in the presence of all your family)

OVER 63

Preposition *over* 63a

As a preposition, *over* typically refers to movement or position at a higher level than something else:

*The planes flew low **over the village**.*

*Didn't the designer recommend hanging the lamps **over the tables**?*

The movement can also be 'across':

*They came **over the road** to say hello to us.*

*I lost my wallet on the train coming **over from Paris**.*

Over and *all over* have a meaning of covering something or being 'throughout' something:

*Why do prisoners always arrive at prisons and police stations with a blanket **over their heads**?*

*Put a cloth **over that food**. There are flies everywhere.*

*Her books were **all over the room**.*

*They have offices **all over the world**.*

Over also occurs with reference to extended periods of time:

***Over the past three months** the situation on both sides has improved considerably.*

*Read it **over the holidays**. You'll enjoy it.*

Over also has a meaning of 'more than' a particular number, or limit:

*They must be **over seventy**. It's great, isn't it, that they still fly to Australia twice a year.*

*That's the second time he's been caught driving **over the speed limit**.*

*He now earns **over £100,000** per year.*

Adverb *over* 63b

Over used as an adverb usually indicates movement above something or someone:

*I didn't hear what she said because a plane **flew over** just at that moment.*

Be over is a very common construction meaning 'finished', 'at an end':

*The interviews should **be over** by about three, so I'll see you then.*

*You're too late. The match **is over**.*

In informal spoken English in particular, *over* has a meaning of 'some distance from the location of the speaker or listener':

***Over in Australia**, they have Christmas dinner on the beach.*

*Why don't you come and sit **over here**?*

*We're going **over to Jack's** for the afternoon.*

*As you come round the corner, you'll see the church **over to the right**.*

Prefix *over* 63c

Over is also frequently used as a prefix referring to an excess of something:

*The government has launched its most stinging criticism yet of **overpaid** directors of public utility companies.*

*He's a good trainer but is known for **overworking** his horses.*

*His approach to the whole topic was **over-elaborate**.*

OWN 64

Own most commonly postmodifies possessive determiners. It emphasises exclusive possession:

*She has **her own** room on the top floor.*

*They have always wanted to have **their own** house in France.*

*It's **the company's own** logo and we think it works well to help sell the product.*

*I suppose we have to learn from **our own** mistakes.*

Own is not used after *a* or *the* and not used alone. The use of *of* + possessive determiner + *own* allows a preceding use of determiners in the noun phrase:

*They have **their own** apartment in the centre of Athens.*
(~~They have an own apartment in the centre of Athens.~~)
(~~They have own apartment in the centre of Athens.~~)

*They have two adopted children and **two children of their own**.*
(~~They have two adopted children and two own children.~~)

*It's nice for them to have **a garden of their own**.*

*He wanted to have **some music of his own** so he bought 20 CDs all at once.*

539 Glossary for any unfamiliar terms

Own can be intensified by *very*:

*He's just bought his **very own** car.*

*It was Laura's **very own** engagement present to them.*

PERSON 65

The noun *person* has two plural forms, *persons* and *people*. *Persons* is used in more formal, legalistic contexts; *people* is the more widely used plural:

*She's just a horrible **person**.*

*There are a lot of nice **people** at our school, aren't there?*
(~~There are a lot of nice persons at our school, aren't there?~~)

*During the 1980s, less than 5 per cent of the US federal budget was spent on programmes that supported families with children, while nearly 24 per cent of federal resources were spent on **persons** over the age of 65.*
(formal)

PRETTY

 66 *Quite*

QUITE 66

Quite + gradable adjectives and adverbs 66a

Quite can be used as an intensifying adverb with gradable adjectives and adverbs, with a meaning similar to 'rather', 'fairly' or 'to a considerable degree':

*But it's going to be **quite interesting** driving home tonight, cos it's the first time I've used it in the dark since I put my headlights back in.*

[showing someone round a house]
*Here's the front room … second reception room … large kitchen … **quite pleasant**, isn't it?*

*Things began to get worse **quite quickly**.*

Quite + non-gradable adjectives and adverbs 66b

Quite can also be used with non-gradable adjectives and adverbs, with the meaning of 'totally/completely':

*It was **quite impossible** to have a conversation with him.*

*I don't know whose coat it is, but it's **quite definitely** not mine.*

Quite + nouns 66c

Quite a/an is used before a noun or before a noun modified by a gradable adjective.

When used before a noun, it is very emphatic, and means 'a considerable' or 'a noteworthy example of':

*It's **quite a drive** from here to north Wales, about five hours.*

*You've got **quite a garden** here, wow.*

When used with a gradable adjective + noun, *quite a* means the same as 'a fairly/a rather':

*You also need to be flexible and have **quite a strong stomach**.*
(or: … a fairly strong stomach)

*I thought he was **quite a nice person**.*
(or: … a rather nice person)

With non-gradable adjectives and adjectives of extreme or intensified meaning followed by nouns, the word order is often *a quite* + adjective + noun:

*She was **a quite superb teacher**.*

*The foundations of the English Channel, its geological framework, formed gradually, but its final shaping was **a quite different** and perhaps even catastrophic **event**.*

Quite the + adjective + noun may also occur in affirmative clauses in very formal styles, with the meaning of 'absolutely'. It is most common with superlatives:

[referring to a TV review in the *Guardian*, a British daily newspaper]
*'"After Dark"', the Guardian once said, was '**quite the best idea** for television since men sat around the camp-fire talking while, in the darkness round them, watching eyes glowed red.'*

Quite + comparatives 66d

Quite is not used alone before a comparative. Normally *a lot* or *a bit* is added:

*He was **quite a lot older** than her, and had children that needed looking after.*
(~~He was quite older than her …~~)

*As I say, I had my babies **quite a bit earlier** than these ladies.*
(~~… I had my babies quite earlier than these ladies.~~)

Quite + verbs 66e

In informal spoken language, the only verbs which commonly occur with *quite* in affirmative clauses are *like*, *enjoy*, *understand* and *agree*. *Quite* occupies the normal positions for mid-position adverbs (→ 325). It can have a range of meanings from 'a bit' to 'totally/completely', depending on context:

*But your dad **quite likes** people to have an opinion so then he can argue with them.*
(likes a great deal)

*I **quite enjoy** working in a team.*
(enjoy a great deal)

*I **quite agree** that the people in public school get a better education because their parents can afford it.*
(agree totally)

In formal written styles, *quite* occurs with a wider range of verbs in affirmative clauses:

[referring to beehives]
*He **has quite forgotten** to replace the roof on the second hive and **quite omitted** to inspect the remaining hives.*
(completely forgotten … completely omitted)

*It was a solemn amusement, and I preferred to fish in remote places: it **quite spoiled** my pleasure if other people were near, to watch, to ask whether I had caught anything.*
(totally spoiled my pleasure)

Not quite 66f

Not quite means 'not completely'. It may be used with adjectives, adverbs, nouns, prepositional phrases and *wh*-clauses:

*Well, if I come I'll just turn up, but, er, as I say, I'm **not quite sure** yet.*
(not 100% sure)

*It's **not quite on the same scale**.*

*I think she looks a bit ill in it. **Not quite her colour**.*

*It's **not quite what I'm looking for**.*

Not quite may also be used with verbs:

*I do**n't quite understand** that.*
(I don't understand that completely.)

Quite a bit, quite a few, quite a lot 66g

Quite a bit and *quite a few* refer to large amounts and quantities, just as *quite a lot* does:

*He'll probably be able to contribute **quite a bit**, I think.*
(he will contribute a lot/a great amount)

*It's a sort of well-established place. It's been there **quite a few** years.*
(it's been there a considerable number of years/many years)

*We talked about it **quite a lot**, you know.*

Short responses with *quite* 66h

Quite may be used in short responses in more formal spoken styles, especially with *yes* and *well*, to express strong agreement:

A: *Of course, I don't know many of them now. I only know those that have had older children, you know, like Maria.*
B: *Yes* ***quite****.*

A: *Probably the 'Sun' is the most popular paper, isn't it, unfortunately.*
B: *Well* ***quite****.*
A: *And this probably says quite a lot about English people, I suppose, in general.*

Quite right is commonly used in short responses to show agreement:

A: *Though there may be some people who are not very at ease with writing and who might prefer to speak to someone.*
B: *Yeah.* ***Quite right****.*

Quite, pretty, fairly and *rather* + gradable adjectives and adverbs 66i

Quite, *pretty*, *fairly* and *rather* can have very similar meanings when premodifying gradable adjectives and adverbs with the meaning of 'to a considerable degree'. The main difference between them is the words they collocate with. There is overlap in collocation (e.g. they all collocate frequently with *good* and *easy*), but there are also noticeable differences.

Pretty tends to collocate more with subjective words describing negative aspects of situations (e.g. *awful, bad, boring, dire, grim, nasty, rough*), and is much more frequent in informal spoken contexts than in formal writing:

[speaking of an emergency on an underground rail system]
A: *And all of a sudden the power went off and we went into pitch blackness.*
B: *Oh. My goodness me.*
A: *And we were a long way down underground.*
B: *Yeah. Yeah. I bet that was* ***pretty awful****.*

Fairly is also much more frequent in informal spoken contexts than in formal writing. It collocates with a wide range of adjectives and adverbs:

Everything should be ***fairly straightforward*** *once you get the hang of it.*

I think it was on TV ***fairly recently****.*

Quite is many times more frequent than *pretty* and *fairly*, in both spoken and written language, and has a wide range of collocates.

Rather tends to collocate with gradable adjectives and adverbs of negative meaning (e.g. *unpleasant, alarming, awkward, disappointing*), especially words relating to lack of colour or excitement/vitality (e.g. *bland, dull, drab, seedy, shabby, soulless, run-down, unexciting*), or words relating to unexpectedness/strangeness/eccentricity (e.g. *odd, unusual, comical*). It is much more frequent in formal written contexts than in informal spoken contexts:

George was dressed in a ***rather dull*** *dinner suit cut in a fashion of twenty years earlier.*

We do look ***rather comical****, don't we?*

A–Z 67 *Rather*

Do not confuse the spelling of *quite* with the adjective *quiet*:

It's ***quite*** *cold today.*
(~~It's quiet cold today.~~)

A common error involves the confusion of *quite* and *very* in negative clauses:

We moved because the hotel was not ***very*** *good.*
(~~We moved because the hotel was not quite good.~~)

RATHER 67

Intensifying function of *rather* 67a

With adjectives and adverbs

Rather can be used to intensify an adjective or adverb. It has a meaning similar to *quite* when *quite* is used with gradable adjectives, but *rather* often occurs in negative contexts, or in contexts indicating an unexpected or surprising degree of something:

I've got a ***rather dominating mother****.*

We passed some ***rather nice old houses*** *on the main road.*

We got it dished out ***rather quickly****, didn't we?*

Rather may also modify a prepositional phrase:

I'm afraid I find myself ***rather out of my depth****.*

With noun phrases

Rather can modify a noun phrase with *a/an*:

I thought it was ***rather a nuisance*** *really.*

The room was ***rather a mess****, the counter still covered with cake pans.*

When *rather* modifies a noun phrase with an adjective and indefinite article, the word order may be *a rather* + adjective, or *rather a* + adjective. *Rather a* is more common in written style:

He looks like the owner of ***a rather posh*** *Greek restaurant.*

This conference takes ***a rather different*** *line to those we have had in the past.*

You wondered suddenly if you hadn't made ***rather a rash*** *decision.*

This puts me in ***rather a rebellious*** *mood.*

The expression *a long time* is not normally interrupted by *rather*:

It was ***rather a long time*** *ago, but never mind.*
(preferred to: ~~It was a rather long time ago, …~~)

With verbs and clauses

Rather as an intensifying adverb can modify a verb or clause. It occupies the normal positions for mid-position adverbs (→ 325):

Dorothy's conversation ***rather led me to believe*** *that she thought it was time Lawrence married.*

[to 'blot your copybook' means to do something that causes someone to be angry with you]
He had ***rather blotted his copybook*** *by charming her mother.*

Rather is often used in this way with verbs such as *enjoy, hope, like, want*:

He ***rather hoped*** *she would throw the whole thing into the garbage and demand to be taken to the Ritz.*

Bill Partridge was definitely coming. Mick MacBride ***rather liked*** *that.*

 **66 *Quite***

Rather + comparisons and *too* 67b

Rather can occur in a variety of constructions related to comparisons. They tend to occur in more formal contexts:

The Minister seemed in ***rather better*** *spirits than his hosts, and apologised for keeping them all up so late.*

He was tall and thin, with a face ***rather like*** *a sad old horse.*

You were ***rather less*** *pleased to see your brother this morning than you were last night.*

It can also be used with *too*:

'You can't go,' he said ***rather too*** *desperately.*

Would rather for expressing preference 67c

Would/'d rather + infinitive without *to* means 'would prefer'. When two alternatives are stated, it is used with *than*:

*She****'d rather struggle on*** *with what money she can raise from the banks.*
(~~She'd rather to struggle on …~~)

*I****'d rather read*** *a book* ***than*** *a professional magazine.*

*I****'d rather stay*** *dirty* ***than*** *wash in that water.*

When it is used with past time reference, *would rather* is followed by infinitive *have* (without *to*) + *-ed* participle:

*The people **would rather have died** than let the old-style conservatives back into power again.*

If the preference is for someone or something else to do something, then a past tense is used in the reported clause, even when the reference is present or future time:

***You'd rather they did**n't say much about it then?*
(You would prefer them not to say much about it then.)

*I'll call Madeleine if **you'd rather she was** present.*
(I'll call Madeleine if you'd prefer her to be present.)

However, in informal speech, an object pronoun plus infinitive without *to* may occur:

***I'd rather them give** it to a younger person.*

***I'd rather it be** your career than my career that is affected.*

When the reference is past time, the past perfect may be used:

***You'd rather he'd waited** a few days, would you, Sergeant?*

Negative

When the subject of the main clause and the reported clause are the same, the negative of *would/'d rather* is *would/'d rather not*:

***I'd rather not** smoke in front of them.*
(~~I wouldn't rather smoke in front of them.~~)

*Doctors have to do a lot of things that people **would rather not** know about.*

Tags

Tags following *would rather* are simply formed with *would*:

*You**'d rather** do something else, **would you**?*

***I'd rather** go now, **I would**.*

Rather modifying a clause 67d

In formal written styles, *rather* as an adverb may link two clauses, where the situation in the second clause is seen as preferable to that in the first:

*Let no self-reproach weigh on you because of me. It is I, who should **rather** reproach myself for having urged my feelings upon you.*

Do not confuse this formal use of *rather* with *better*:

[from a student essay]
*In conclusion, I shall say that it is not a good idea to keep animals, we should **rather** leave them free and observe them in their natural habitats.*
(~~... we should better leave them free and observe them ...~~)

Rather than 67e

Rather than is used to link two parallel words, phrases or clauses where one is considered preferable to the other. It occurs most commonly in mid position between the two compared items, but can be used in front position:

Linda just phoned me wondering whether she should come over ***in the near future rather than in the summer****.*

[customer enquiring about hi-fi in a shop]
I was just wondering whether it would be better to get ***a really expensive portable one rather than a very cheap stack system****.*

The people would be a lot fitter if they didn't have a car because they'd have to ***walk places rather than just get the car*** *to go round the corner shop or something.*

Rather than encouragement*, he would hear* ***words such as 'You will not do anything in life'****.*

Rather than, not just *than* alone, is used when there is no other comparative form present in the sentence:

A doctor may ask, then, whether it is fair to prolong the life of an old person ***rather than*** *to save that of a child.*
(~~A doctor may ask, then, whether it is fair to prolong the life of an old person than to save that of a child.~~)

Or rather 67f

Or rather is often used for self-correction:

Apparently in this situation the decision to stop treatment was taken by the chief authority, ***or rather****, the Health Chief of the Dunbridge Health Authority.*

Rather as a response token 67g

Rather may occur in responses to indicate enthusiastic acceptance or agreement. This usage is more associated with speakers of higher social classes or with older speakers:

[A is explaining to B how university websites often have email addresses listed for staff and students]
A: *So, say you want to contact a professor in Birmingham, you could find out his email address.*
B: *Oh right. That's all right.*
A: *And this is the same for students now, so it'd be good for friends if they want to find you.*
B: *Oh yes* ***rather****. Yeah.*

REALLY 68

Really is an adverb that is commonly used to emphasise or question the factuality or truth of what is said:

Do you ***really*** *have to go now? Can't you at least wait until the evening?*

Do you think he is ***really*** *hungry or is he just pretending?*

He calls himself her personal assistant but he is ***really*** *just the driver.*

Really is often used to intensify gradable adjectives and adverbs:

I made a ***really delicious*** *soufflé. It was easier than I thought.*

I didn't expect to lose but she played a ***really excellent*** *game.*

She looks ***really sweet*** *in that outfit, doesn't she?*

He drove ***really fast*** *all the way and it certainly frightened me.*

Really is used to reduce the force of negative utterances:

I'm not ***really*** *angry, just a bit cross.*

Really is commonly used to soften what has just been said. In this function it can occur at the end of utterances:

A: *What do you think they should do about it?*
B: *Oh, I don't know* ***really****.*

I don't think we can do that sort of thing ***really****.*

Not really is also commonly used to soften a bare *no*-answer.

[in a travel agent's; A is the customer]
A: *Erm I'm looking to get away mid, end of June, thereabouts.*
B: *Right. Anywhere in particular?*
A: *Erm no, no* ***not really****. But I want to be in a hotel.*

Really also has a concessive meaning of 'despite what has just been said':

He's got a terrible temper, but he's a lovely guy ***really****.*

Really is also used as a response token to show interest and surprise. It contrasts with minimal response tokens such as *uhuh* or *mmm* and indicates greater interest in what is being said:

A: *We stayed at a hotel on the south coast.*
B: ***Really****?*
A: *Yes, it's very pretty, isn't it?*
B: *I think we've stayed there.*

A: *Shares have fallen more than 20% over the past decade.*
B: ***Really****?*

Really can also function to invite continuation by a speaker or offer a confirmation that the conversation can continue:

A: *That e-travel company we used last year went bust last week.*
B: *Did they* ***really****?*
A: *'Fraid so.*

A: *I've just … I've been sorting out those tapes. And erm filling in application forms for the Tower of London job.*
B: *Er which?*
A: *The Tower of London. It's a conservation job.*
B: ***Oh really****?*
A: *Yep.*
B: *Wonderful.*

Really is sometimes used as an adjectival modifier in a shortened form, *real*, in very informal spoken language:

Why don't you try? It's ***real*** *easy to work.*

It was ***real*** *good, that sandwich. I think I'll order another one.*

RIGHT, RIGHTLY 69

The two main lexical meanings of *right* are **1** the opposite of 'left'; **2** 'correct' and 'appropriate, fair'. *Right* is used as an adjective and as an adverb. The adverb form *rightly* corresponds only to the meaning of 'correctly' and is normally only used as an adverb showing stance (→ **111**):

Take a ***right turn*** *at the next crossroads.*

He injured his ***right eye*** *in the accident.*

Bear right *at the road junction.*

You are right *and she is wrong.*

I got the number right *this time when I phoned her.*

I rightly assumed *that I was going to be sacked.*

She was scared to death and, ***quite rightly in my opinion****, called the police.*

When used predicatively, *right* only has a meaning of 'correct' or 'fair':

It is entirely ***right*** *to insist on high training standards for the diving instructors.*

A: *Is this the train for Newcastle?*
B: *Yeah, that's* ***right****.*

When modifying prepositional phrases, *right* normally means 'exactly' or 'just':

Give me a couple of minutes. I'll be ***right with you****.*

She arrived ***right after*** *they did, just a few minutes before midnight.*

Right as a modifier also means 'all the way', 'completely':

Cut the grass ***right down****. It'll grow again in a few days.*

We drove ***right up to*** *the very north of Scotland.*

He must be a ***right idiot****. You mean he didn't back all the files up?*

Right also occurs adverbially in certain fixed expressions, where *rightly* might be more normally expected. Here *right* cannot occur before the verb:

It ***serves*** *you* ***right****.*
(you deserve that punishment)

We ***guessed right****. They're closing the shop next week.*

Right is particularly common in spoken English as a discourse marker to indicate that a new action or sequence of thought is about to begin:

Right*, let's try to decide how we should change the traffic light system in the city centre.*

Right*, let's go.*

Right also occurs as a synonym for 'okay', 'we agree':

A: *See you tomorrow, then.*
B: ***Right****.*

A: *I think she's just gone too far this time.*
B: ***Right****. I'll have a word with her about it.*

In the above four examples *all right* can be used as well.

Right can also function to check understanding or to check that someone agrees with what is said. It functions in a manner similar to a tag question and has a meaning similar to 'okay':

It's available as a CD-Rom, ***right****?*

So I knocked at the door and it seemed like no one was in – so I knocked again, ***right****, and it was just so quiet and I got a bit scared, even though I knew it was silly.*

Now, we've covered the origins of the War of Independence, ***right****, and next week we go on to the consequences.*

Right also functions as a backchannel marker. It does not engage with the speaker as directly as markers such as *really*, and can provide a more neutral response to what has been said:

A: *I told them I would resign.*
B: ***Right****.*
A: *But I'm not sure whether I'll go through with it.*
B: *Oh* ***right****.*

ROUND

 18 *Around, round*

SINCE 70

Since has two main meanings, referring to time and referring to reasons.

Since referring to time

I haven't seen Paul ***since Ken and Margaret got married.***
(I haven't seen them from that point in time until now)

She's been doing it ***since the beginning of March.***
(from that point in time until now)

Do not confuse *since* and *for*. *Since* refers to points in time, *for* refers to extended periods of time:

She's been away ***for a couple of days.***
(~~She's been away since a couple of days.~~)

I've been here ***for three weeks.***
(seen as a period of time)

I've been here ***since three weeks ago.***
(seen as a point in the past)

Since referring to reasons

Since is used when the reason for something is presumed to be already known to the listener:

Since *around 30% of the contents of the average dustbin is made up of kitchen waste, it makes sense to encourage more people to compost rather than dump it.*
(or: As we know, around 30% of the contents of the average dustbin is made up of kitchen waste, so …)

Compare *because*, where there is no necessary implication that the reason is already known:

It may be ***because*** *they don't know what the guidelines are.*
(this is a possible reason, we do not know)

Tense-aspect patterns with *since* 70a

Tense-aspect in the main clause

- Present perfect or past perfect:

I've been *awake* ***since*** *half past four this morning.*
(~~I'm awake since half past four this morning.~~)

I hadn't been *to Barcelona* ***since*** *1988 so I was looking forward to it.*

- Present tense or past tense:

  You're looking *better* ***since*** *you got back from the north.*

  Joe's *the one person Martha really* ***cares*** *about* ***since*** *she lost her mother.*

Present simple and past simple are often used instead of present perfect and past perfect with the construction *it* + *be* + time period + *since*:

*It'****s*** *months* ***since*** *I've been out for a coffee anywhere.*
(or: It's been months since I've been out ...)

It ***was*** *years* ***since*** *I'd seen him.*
(or: It had been years since I had seen him.)

Tense-aspect in the *since*-clause

- Past tense; *since* refers to a point in time:

  Can you tell me what's happened ***since*** *we last* ***met****?*
  (from that point in time until now)

- Present perfect; *since* refers to an event leading up to now or still relevant:

  Since I've been *at Durford, which is two years now, Rod's been a tremendous support in putting through some of the changes that we've needed in managing our production systems.*
  (during the two-year period of time)

In informal speech, the present perfect may sometimes be used to refer to completed events in the past:

When I went back, it was when I was still at school. My dad took me back when I was about fifteen. I think I was about fifteen, fourteen, somewhere round there. It's a very long time ***since I've been*** *back.*

Since + *-ing* form 70b

Since referring to time may be followed by the *-ing* form of a verb where the subject is the same in both the main and subordinate clause:

She'd only had a couple of hours' sleep ***since arriving*** *in Oxford the previous day.*

Since having *done that big piece of work, I'm finding it quite difficult to get back into working really.*

This does not occur when *since* refers to reasons:

Since I didn't have *medical insurance, I would have to pay for everything out of my pocket.*
(~~Since not having medical insurance ...~~)

Since, since then 70c

Since referring to time may be used alone as an adverb when the time reference is understood:

And then a bit later on, the next-door neighbour on this side had the son and daughter-in-law over for a meal, and when they got outside, their car was missing and it hasn't been found ***since.***
(understood: since that day)

More specific reference may be made with *since then*:

I mean that's twenty years ago. Traffic has obviously doubled or trebled ***since then.***

When *since* is used in this way, it normally occurs in end or mid position in the clause with present perfect tense:

*She****'s since had*** *a burglar alarm installed.*
(understood: since the time she was burgled)

The consultant who was in charge of your case ***has since retired.***
(understood: since the events we are talking about)

Since then normally occurs in front or end position, but not normally in mid position:

But ***since then****, we've been up and down the country to all these other places.*

It's grown enormously ***since then.***
(~~It's since then grown enormously.~~)

Ever since 70d

Ever since is a more emphatic form of *since* in its references to time (not in its reference to reasons):

Ever since *I was 12, I've thought about being Olympic champion.*

She's been a bit nervous ***ever since*** *we got burgled.*

It may also be used as an adverb phrase:

And people say she was murdered down at the lake. And she's haunted the castle ***ever since.***
(understood: ever since the day she was murdered)

Questions with *since when* 70e

Questions with *since when* do not normally allow separation of *when* and *since*:

Since when *have you spent so much time with your son?* ***Since when*** *have you two been such close friends?*
(~~When have you two been such close friends since?~~)

→ 539 **Glossary** for any unfamiliar terms

Long since 70f

Long since normally means 'a long time ago, a long time before that':

Spontaneous adventures, the essence of her youth, had ***long since*** *ceased.*
(understood: had long ago ceased/had ceased long before that time)

His hair had ***long since*** *thinned, and as he offered his hand, I noticed the blue rivulets of age.*
(His hair had thinned long before that moment …)

Since and *from* 70g

From is sometimes used instead of *since*, especially with reference to distant historical times:

This unhappiness has been going on ***from the earliest historical times****: our whole history is a tale of unhappiness, with war following war, each crueller and bloodier than the last, until in our day we wipe out a hundred thousand with one bomb.*
(or: This unhappiness has been going on since the earliest historical times …)

However, *from* also refers to the starting point of completed periods of time, whereas *since* refers to periods of time continuing up to the point of speaking or writing:

[Margaret Thatcher's period as British Prime Minister was finished when this text was written; *since* would have suggested it was still continuing at the time of writing]
Italy has had the fastest rate of growth of the big four European economies during the past decade – yes, even faster than Margaret Thatcher's Britain if one takes the full period of her office ***from*** *1979.*

A–Z **43 *For***

So 71

Adverb *so* 71a

So is a degree adverb, and typically modifies adjectives and adverbs. It has a meaning of 'to this extent':

I'm sorry I'm ***so late****. The traffic was just a nightmare.*

It doesn't always work out ***so neatly****.*

Why is he ***so grumpy*** *first thing in the morning?*

So also has an intensifying meaning similar to 'very' or 'really':

I spent the morning in Foxton Park and it was ***so nice and peaceful****.*

That's ***so kind*** *of you. Thanks very much.*

You must meet him. He's ***so good-looking****.*

You should have heard her. She sang ***so wonderfully****.*

So + adjective/adverb + *that*-complement clause indicates that something is of such a degree that it produces the outcome described in the *that*-clause:

I felt ***so upset that I just didn't know what to say****.*

It all happened ***so quickly we hardly noticed it****.*

So may also premodify quantifiers such as *much, many, little, few*:

There were ***so many*** *people in the queue I just gave up and went home.*

She just has ***so little*** *sympathy for others.*

So is often used to indicate size or extent in the same way as *this* is used, and is typically reinforced by hand gestures which roughly indicate size:

[indicating the size of a garden plant container, with the hand held palm-downward about half a metre above the ground]
It's about ***so big****.*
(or: It's about this big.)

So is also occasionally used as a manner adverb, with a meaning of 'like this':

Just bend your knees – ***so****.*

In informal spoken language, especially in the usage of younger speakers, *so* may occur as an intensifier before an adjective negated with *not*. In such cases, *so* is heavily stressed. In traditionally correct and more formal usage, an adjective with a negative prefix is the preferred form. *So* can also be used as a more intense and expressive alternative to the adverb phrases *just* or *just like*, and can be followed by any class of item (e.g. verb, noun, prepositional phrase):

[BBC radio travel reporter recounting a tough mountaineering expedition]
And I'm thinking 'I'm ***so not fit*** *for this expedition'.*
(preferred formal usage: I'm so unfit for this expedition.)

I was ***so not ready*** *to take an exam that day.*
(preferred formal usage: I was so unready/unprepared to take an exam that day.)

I'm ***so not*** *going to do that.*
(preferred formal usage: I'm just not going to do that.)

Younger speakers also use *so* as an intensifier with noun phrases, though such usage is considered incorrect by many speakers:

[teenager commenting on a mobile phone]
That phone is ***so*** *last week.*
(it is out of date, not the latest model)

That's ***so*** *Sandra. I knew she wouldn't help us.*
(That's typical of Sandra.)

✪ *So* is not used before an adjective that is used attributively. *Such* must be used instead:

*I took **such nice photos** in the park yesterday.*
(~~I took so nice photos in the park yesterday.~~)

So is not used to modify noun phrases:

*She is **such a quiet girl**.*
(~~She is so a quiet girl.~~)

*It took **such a long time** to get to Scotland.*
(~~It took so long time to get to Scotland.~~)

*And there were **such tall buildings**!*
(~~And there were so tall buildings!~~)

Pro-form or substitute word *so* 71b

So is also used as a pro-form or substitute word. As a pro-form, *so* occurs in reduced clauses with modal and auxiliary verbs and copular verb *be*, to express the meaning 'also' or 'similarly, in the same way'. This use of *so* is followed by inversion of the subject and verb:

Her luck ran out while she was away from home. ***So did his.***

*Ian's a teacher, and **so is his sister**.*

A: *I've got loads of work to do though.*
B: ***So have I.***

A: *Donald can stay at a local hotel.*
B: *Well, **so can I** if it's inconvenient to stay at your place.*

So is used as a clausal substitute after verbs such as *assume*, *be afraid*, *believe*, *hope*, *imagine*, *reckon*, *think*:

A: *Is Thomas coming to the meeting tomorrow?*
B: ***I believe so.***

A: *Will you still be here next time I call?*
B: ***I hope so!***
(note that the opposite of *so* in this type of construction is *not*, e.g. *I hope not.*)

*You're very bright, Zoe. Everybody says **so**.*

So they say, *so everybody says*, *so they tell me*, *so everybody tells me*, *so I'm told*, *so I gather/believe/understand* and similar expressions indicate that the listener has already been informed of something. They are common in responses. With these verbs, *so* often precedes the verb:

A: *It was the American who got the job.*
B: ***Mm, so I understand.***

Subordinator *so* 71c

As a subordinating conjunction, *so* introduces clauses of result, consequence and purpose. Purpose clauses may include an optional *that*:

I had nothing to eat at lunchtime ***so I'm very hungry now.***

Let's talk her into coming for her birthday ***so she won't be alone.***
(or: Let's talk her into coming for her birthday so that she won't be alone.)

So as and *so as not* introduce non-finite *to*-infinitive clauses of purpose, and normally occur in more formal contexts. Often the 'purpose' is to avoid an undesired consequence:

They decided to go ahead with the wedding, ***so as to avoid upsetting everyone.***

He said he was busy, ***so as not to hurt her feelings.***

Discourse marker *so* 71d

In spoken English the most common use of *so* is as a discourse marker. Typically, it functions as a connecting or summarizing marker, usually in front position:

I said – Well have you booked me an ambulance. ***So*** *she says – Oh I'll put you through to the ambulance department. They said that an ambulance had been booked for me but it hadn't.*

[discussing whether to eat a pudding or keep it till the following morning]
A: *I'm not having it cold in the morning. Oh.*
B: *Oh.*
A: ***So*** *what sort of pudding is it?*

A: ***So****, what are we going to do tonight?*
B: *Well, I'd like to stay at home. I've loads to do.*

Right, ***so****, let's get going. Let's say goodbye to everyone.*

With *yes-no* questions it is often an appeal for confirmation: 'am I right in thinking that …?':

[discussing a complaint letter written by speaker A]
A: *It just isn't right.*
B: *Mm.* ***So*** *did you feel that the points that you made in your original letter were all covered in this reply?*
A: *Oh yes. I think they've answered me very well indeed.*

A: *Things have changed then.*
B: *They have certainly changed.*
A: *Okay.* ***So*** *you can't really remember your parents having any sort of ambitions for you or even for themselves?*
B: *No.*

→ **539 Glossary** for any unfamiliar terms

So is not used alone in responses to express surprise. *Really* is typically used in such cases:

A: *She doesn't have a TV set at all. She never has had one.*
B: *Oh, really?*
(~~Ah, so?~~)

The expression *Is that so?* occurs in responses to express surprise:

A: *When I came back she was in the car waiting for me!*
B: *Oh,* ***is that so****?*
A: *Yes!*

STILL 72

Still has three main meanings as an adverb:

1 that something is continuing, often for a longer time than expected
2 that something is true in spite of something else, or in contrast to something else
3 that something is not moving or should not move.

Still for something continuing in time 72a

[*beach huts* are small wooden huts which people own or rent at seaside resorts]
Do they ***still*** *have beach huts down in Weymouth?*

[speakers are talking about a cinema, *The Regal*, which has since closed]
I came here in 1966 and The Regal was ***still*** *going then.*

Still can indicate that the speaker/writer thinks that the continuation of a situation is not desired or is surprising in some way, especially when stressed and in negative constructions:

I still don't *know what we're going to do with those tins.*
(I wish I did know)

They bought an old cooker months ago and ***they still haven't*** *installed it.*

Note the word order in these emphatic negative constructions: *still* comes between the subject and the first auxiliary or modal verb. Compare the normal mid position for adverbs, which is after the first auxiliary or modal verb (→ 325).

The negative of *still* is *no longer, not any longer* or *no more, not any more*:

A: *Are you still working in Birmingham?*
B: *No,* ***not any more/not any longer****.*
(~~No, not still.~~)

Still, yet, already

Still does not mean the same as *yet* or *already*. *Yet* is used mostly in questions and negatives to talk about things which may be expected but which have not happened, or things about which the speaker wonders if they have happened up to that point in time:

A: *Have you looked in that journal you got from Mrs Martin* ***yet****?*
B: *No. I will, honestly.*

Already refers to things that have happened, often to the surprise of the speaker:

A: *Have you* ***already*** *eaten that?*
B: *Sorry, yes, I was really hungry.*
(~~Have you still eaten that?~~)

 13 *Already*

Still for something that is true in spite of other things 72b

[speaker is complaining about the cost of birthday presents for children]
I said we would spend £70 per child, which is ***still*** *a lot of money.*

[talking about an old motorbike]
I offered him £300 but ***he still wouldn't*** *sell it.*

Note the word order with this negative emphatic use of *still* (→ 72a above).

Still indicating lack of movement 72c

We just couldn't ***sit still*** *any longer. We just had to get up and dance.*

Apparently you're supposed to ***stand still*** *and shout and scream as loud as possible.*

Front-position *still* 72d

Front-position *still* often has a meaning similar to *on the other hand* or *nevertheless*:

I worked in the coal mines but I was out of work at 50 because the mines closed. But ***still****, who isn't out of work these days?*

I don't really like weddings. ***Still****, I'll have to go or they'll be offended.*

STUFF

 74 *Thing, stuff*

TAKE

 29 *Bring, take, fetch*

THEN 73

Then is an adverb which refers to a particular time in the past or future:

We used to go to Italy every year by car. But we were very young ***then.***

The new carpet can't be delivered for six weeks so I suppose we'll just have to wait until ***then.***

Then also has a meaning of 'next' or 'after that' and commonly occurs with *and*:

The guides took us all over the city. First to the castle ***and then*** *to the museum* ***and then*** *to the cathedral.*

Tidy your room first. ***Then*** *you can both go out. Okay?*

Then sometimes occurs in the main clause of a conditional sentence when the main clause comes after the *if*-clause, to emphasise the conclusion drawn from that condition:

If you wear that outfit, ***then*** *I'm going to have to wear a jacket.*

If there is a town called Cordoba in Spain, ***then*** *there will probably be cities with the same name all over South America.*

If you feel you should do it, ***then*** *do it.*

In spoken English, *then* often occurs in responses with a meaning of 'in that case':

A: *I can't really afford it but I think I need it.*
B: ***Then*** *why don't you buy it?*

A: *How did she play?*
B: *She was the best in the team.*
A: *So you think she might get a further trial* ***then****?*

Then and *so* can both have a meaning of 'since that is the case' or 'because that is so'. They are both common in responses where they indicate that something logically follows from what has just been said:

A: *It costs much less to run a diesel car.*
B: ***Then*** *I guess we should get a diesel.*
(or: So I guess we should get a diesel.)

However, *then* is not used when the same speaker connects two statements and the second statement follows from the previous one. In such cases *so* is used:

It's going to cost us too much to fly, **so** *we're going by train.*
(~~It's going to cost us too much to fly, then we're going by train.~~)

Then also frequently co-occurs with the discourse markers *well*, *now*, *right* and *okay*:

Well then*, what should we do about it?*

Now then*, I think it's probably time to take a break.*

Okay then*, you go first. You've given many talks like this before and I'm just a bit nervous.*

 71 *So*

THERE

 45 *Here, there*

THING, STUFF 74

Thing 74a

General noun

Thing is a general noun which is widely used to refer to physical objects, abstractions such as ideas and statements, and situations, events, actions, experiences and states:

Can you pass that ***thing*** *over there on the bed?*

What shall I do? I haven't ***a thing*** *to wear.*

Can you put all your ***things*** *in the suitcase?*

Love is a very peculiar ***thing****.*

Let's see how ***things*** *develop.*

These ***things*** *take time.*

A holiday? That's just the ***thing*** *for you.*

They're interested in all ***things*** *Japanese.*

As ***things*** *stand now, the plane won't be taking off for another couple of hours.*

A: *Hi, Pat. How's* ***things****?*
B: *Fine, thanks. How are you?*

Referring back

Thing is commonly used to refer back to something that has already been mentioned. It may also refer back generally to actions:

While I was away, my parents sold all my music CDs and cassettes – these were ***things*** *I'd had since I was a school kid.*

She was really shouting at him, ***a thing*** *I've never seen her do.*

Alternative to *something*, etc.

Thing can be used instead of common pronouns such as *something, anything* and *nothing*. When used as part of a negative expression, *thing* is more definite and emphatic. The pronouns *something, anything* are less open to modification than the noun *thing*:

I can't think of ***one thing*** *we could have done to prevent it.*
(more emphatic than 'I cannot think of anything we could have done' or 'I can think of nothing we could have done')

I could not think of ***a single thing*** *to say.*

In cleft constructions

Thing is particularly commonly used in cleft constructions. It is also common with *to* and *that*-clauses:

The ***thing*** *I want* ***to*** *know is how they managed to miss the bus.*

The ***thing*** *she said* ***to*** *remember was to ask for a discount as soon as we arrive.*

The most obvious ***thing to*** *do is to contact your insurance company.*

In cleft constructions which involve comparison, *thing* is needed:

The most obvious ***thing*** *to do is to keep out of the rain.*
(~~The most obvious to do is to keep out of the rain.~~)

The thing is

The phrase *the thing is* is frequent in spoken English and functions as a discourse marker which focuses attention on what follows and usually signals that there is a problem. The verb form *is* tends to be stressed. *The* is commonly ellipted in informal use:

The thing is *... erm ... we don't have any money left.*

Yeah, but, you know, ***thing is****, she's left it rather late.*

The expression *the thing is* is treated by speakers as a fixed item, and in many cases in informal speech an 'extra' *is* is added as speakers feel a need to have a verb in the clause. When this happens, the first *is* is stressed:

The thing is is *no one wants to take responsibility for paying for it all.*

Vague reference and hedging

Thing enables speakers, in particular, to avoid precise reference and to hedge statements so that they are neither too assertive nor too direct. The word occurs in phrases such as *things like that, kind of thing, sort of thing*, which enable speakers to refer vaguely to categories, on the assumption that the listener will understand what is included in the category:

There isn't time for sending invitations out and ***that kind of thing****, is there?*

A: *So, er, you want the suitcase left upstairs?*
B: *Yeah cos I've got* ***things like plates and stuff*** *to pack yet.*

She's making a lot of cakes and goodies ***and things*** *for Chinese New Year.*

I was a wrestling coach and ***things like that*** *and in New York I used to be a bouncer.*

I'll see you next week then; perhaps we can, like, have lunch, ***sort of thing****.*

Thing is commonly used with a preceding noun modifier to describe phenomena which are either recent, difficult to categorise or best described in deliberately vague terms:

I think ***the whole Euro thing*** *has got completely out of control.*

This new man thing *may have gone too far. More of them than ever are going shopping.*

[reference to public reaction after the death of Princess Diana]
***The whole Diana thing** is very unBritish. It shows they are not cold and unemotional after all.*

Lucky thing, etc.

Thing marks both positive (usually affectionate) and negative attitudes, mainly when accompanied by appropriate adjectives:

*Our dog's getting a bit old now, **poor thing**.*

*You **lucky thing**! I suppose you are on your third holiday this year.*

*We found the book distasteful and don't intend to stock **the thing** on our shelves.*

Thingy, etc.

The words *thingy*, *thingummy*, *thingamabob* and *thingamajig* are also used in similar ways and offer a more colloquial alternative. Such words are normally used with reference to objects in the immediate situation and are not widely used as alternatives to *thing*:

*Can you get me that little metal **thingy** over there on the workbench?*

Stuff 74b

Stuff is also one of the most frequent nouns in spoken English. It functions in very similar ways to *thing*, though it is a non-count noun. It commonly occurs in vague expressions such as *stuff like that*:

*Where can I put my **stuff**?*
(or: Where can I put my things?)

*I can't remember. All that chemistry **stuff** is just too hard to learn.*

*Don't give me all that **stuff**. You've nothing to apologise for.*

*There wasn't much to do really. Just a few shops, a small beach, a few sailing boats and all **that kind of stuff**.*

*He just told us to try hard **and stuff like that**.*

THOUGH

15 *Although, though*

TOO

14 *Also, as well (as), too*

UNDER

25 *Below*

UNTIL

 24 *Before*

WAIT FOR

 40 *Expect*

WANT 75

Want has three basic meanings:

1 *Tell me what you **want** to do.* (wish/desire)
2 *My hair **wants** cutting.* (needs – always with *-ing* form)
3 *You **want** to sign that credit card immediately.* (you should/I advise you to)

2 and **3** are more associated with informal spoken language. Only meaning **1** occurs with *want* in the progressive form.

Want + infinitive 75a

Want is used with an infinitive, including when the subject of the verb in the complement clause is another person or thing; it is not used with a *that*-clause:

***I want him to think** about his future.*
(~~I want that he thinks about his future.~~)

Want always requires complementation, either an object or an infinitive *to*-clause, even in reduced clauses (e.g. short answers):

A: *What shall I do with the knife?*
B: *Leave it there. Gladys **wants it**.*
(~~Leave it there. Gladys wants.~~)

A: *Why aren't you eating?*
B: *Because I don't **want any**.*
(~~Because I don't want.~~)

A: *I've made some cakes, d'you **want one**?*
A: *Yes, please.*
(~~D'you want?~~)

A: *Are you coming with us tonight?*
B: *No thanks, I don't **want to**.*
(understood: … come with you)
(~~No thanks, I don't want.~~)

A: *Well, that's what she said, anyway.*
B: *I don't know why she keeps saying that. It's not as if I **want her to**.*
(~~It's not as if I want her.~~)

Want + *it* 75b

In informal spoken language, even when the object is first mentioned as an indefinite entity, the object of *want* can be *it*, rather than *one/some/any*:

*There's olive oil if you **want it**.*

*I can have a day off when I **want it**.*

*There's a toilet there if you **want it**.*

Want with *wh*-words, *want* with *if* 75c

With *wh*-words, it is often not necessary to use the infinitive marker *to* after *want*:

*Later in life you can do **what** you **want**, go out **when** you **want**, study **when** you **want**.*

*You can come in and pick it up **whenever** you **want**.*

*You can go **wherever** you **want** and still be bored.*

However, in such cases, *to* can be used:

*You can leave **whenever** you **want to**.*

With *if* the infinitive marker *to* is often omitted in affirmative clauses:

*You can come later **if** you **want**.*

However, *to* is normally used with *if* in negative clauses:

*You don't have to do it **if** you don't **want to**.*

Want with progressive verb forms 75d

Although *want* mostly occurs in simple tense forms, in informal spoken language it often occurs with progressive forms. The use of progressive often expresses tentativeness, indirectness or politeness:

*What we**'re** really **wanting** to do is to make sure people have one name they can contact.*

[telephone enquiry to travel agent]
*Oh, hello, my husband and I **are wanting** to go to the Hook of Holland next weekend.*

*I**'m wanting** desperately to do the right thing.*

The progressive is also used to emphasise an ongoing or repeated process:

[tennis player speaking]
*The coach **was wanting** us to win big matches and things like that.*

→ 539 **Glossary** for any unfamiliar terms

*We**'ve been wanting** to get it under way for years, and now I think it'll go in leaps and bounds.*

A: *How do you encourage your own children as regards education?*
B: *It all depends on what they**'re wanting** to do.*

Want + *-ing* form 75e

Want is often used in informal contexts with a verb in the *-ing* form to express a meaning of necessity:

*The grass **wants cutting**.*
(needs to be cut)

*The fridge **wants cleaning** out.*

The meaning of *want* + *-ing* form can also correspond to a pseudo-passive construction:

*I've got some pictures I **want enlarging**.*
(which I want to have enlarged)

Want and speech acts of advice/warning 75f

Want to is used in informal spoken language to advise, recommend or warn (most commonly with a second person subject). It is almost always in present tense, and is often followed by a *be* + *-ing* verb form:

*Put some more water in. **You don't want to make** it too strong.*

[talking about whether young people should look to the future or more to their present needs]
*At that age you need a bit of both. **You want to be looking** ahead and **you want to be improving** your skills as well.*

WELL 76

Well is an adverb and a discourse marker.

Adverb *well* 76a

As an adverb, *well* has the meaning of 'satisfactorily':

*I slept really **well** last night.*

*She talks **well** for a two-year-old, doesn't she?*

Discourse marker *well* 76b

A main function of *well* as a discourse marker is to indicate that the speaker is thinking about things:

A: *What do you think of the department's plan?*
B: ***Well**, let's see, it's certainly better than the last one, I'll say that.*

A: *Why did she say that?*
B: ***Well**, I don't know, I mean, maybe she wants to move house.*

Well normally occurs at the beginning of a turn. But it can occur in the middle of an utterance if a speaker is revising what is said or is searching for an alternative expression:

*I never said I was happy, **well**, all right then, I might have said I was not unhappy.*

Well also indicates that the speaker is saying something which contrasts with what has just been said or which does not follow the expectation of what was said:

A: *You always go out to your evening class on a Tuesday.*
B: ***Well**, tonight I'm too tired and I'm staying in.*

A: *D'you live in Cambridge?*
B: ***Well**, near Cambridge.*
(B cannot answer the *yes-no* question with a *yes* or a *no*; *well* shifts the predicted direction)

Well can also signal that something surprising is about to be announced:

*You know I said I went to Jill's last night, **well**, you'll never guess who I saw there.*

Well can sometimes signal the opening or closing of a topic or speech event:

***Well**, let's get started, shall we?*

***Well**, that's all for now. We'll see you again at the same time next week.*

Well commonly clusters with other discourse markers, adverbs and adverbial phrases:

***Well, actually**, I don't think she has agreed.*

***Well, as a matter of fact**, I've bought a flat in the village.*

Well is also used, often in a cluster with other words, to mark attitudes and feelings, usually in response to a situation:

***Well, well, well**, I never knew that.*
(surprise)

***Well really**, that's awful behaviour.*
(anger)

***Oh well**, there's not much we can do about it.*
(resignation)

A good dictionary will give further information about the range of attitudes that are conveyed by *well*.

539 Glossary for any unfamiliar terms

WHATEVER 77

Whatever is a determiner, a pronoun and an adverb.

Determiner *whatever* 77a

As a determiner, *whatever* commonly appears in a noun phrase with a clausal complement:

***Whatever money I have** has to go on food.*

***Whatever choice you make** will be the right one.*

*They had to rely on **whatever food they were given by the villagers**.*

Pronoun *whatever* 77b

As a pronoun and head of a noun phrase, *whatever* can occur in interrogatives:

***Whatever** does she see in him?*

***Whatever** is he doing with that car?*

Whatever meaning 'regardless of' 77c

Whatever also occurs in subordinate clauses and has a meaning of 'no matter what', 'regardless of', 'it makes no difference':

***Whatever** you decide to do in the future, you can rely on our support.*

*Okay, let's go, **whatever** the weather.*

***Whatever** new clothes she bought, she always ended up taking them back.*

Adverb *whatever* 77d

Whatever can also function as an adverb in negative and interrogative clauses with a meaning of 'at all'. It can be substituted by the form *whatsoever*, which adds further emphasis, especially in negative phrases:

*He has **no respect whatever** from the people he works with.*

*Are there **any objections whatever** to his proposal?*

*They have **no interest whatsoever** in football.*

Whatever for vagueness 77e

Whatever is used, especially in spoken English, to indicate a deliberately vague or non-committal reference, especially when the exact name or meaning of something or someone is not known. It can be used to continue a list:

*So you log on and just click the songs and artists you need using that search tool **or whatever**.*

Now to prepare the soup we need shallots, tomatoes, chillies, red peppers and vegetable stock and then all those herbs ***and whatever.***

Whatever for lack of interest 77f

Whatever can indicate agreement but it can also create a negative tone and indicate either lack of interest or that agreement is a token or unwilling agreement. In such examples the form is often ellipted:

A: *I thought we'd go to southern Italy this year. I think that those southern parts are a lot less crowded.*
B: *Yeah,* ***whatever you think.*** *That's fine.*
(whatever it is you think)

A: *So, shall I invite them round?*
B: *Sure.* ***Whatever.***
(whatever you like)

WHILE 78

While is a subordinating conjunction and a noun.

Conjunction *while* 78a

As a conjunction, *while* corresponds in meaning to the preposition *during*:

While *you're at the swimming pool, I think I'm going to pop into town.*

I made three phone calls ***while*** *they were at lunch.*

Some members of the audience fell asleep ***while*** *he was talking to them.*
(Some members of the audience fell asleep during his talk.)

Within a sentence, *while* is used to refer to a simultaneous time relationship between two actions or states:

Geoff phoned ***while*** *you were walking the dog.*

While *I watched the match, Jill watched a film on the other TV.*

Was the package delivered ***while*** *I was working out at the gym?*

While can be used in clauses where the subject and the verb *to be* are ellipted:

While *holidaying in Malaysia, they received the news that their daughter had secretly married.*
(While they were holidaying in Malaysia …)

While *on the subject, why don't we write a joint letter of complaint to the hotel?*
(While we are on the subject …)

Do not depress the button ***while*** *dialling.*
(… while you are dialling …)

539 **Glossary** for any unfamiliar terms

While can also be used to contrast two ideas or statements; a clause with *while* is put first and is then followed by a contrast. In this meaning, no time relationship is expressed:

> ***While*** *it is clearly a good idea to involve them, I don't think they should be included in everything.*
>
> ***While*** *the university regrets the incident, it cannot be held responsible for cars parked in its car parks.*

Whilst

Whilst is a more formal alternative to *while* and is normally only found in writing:

> ***Whilst*** *the company accepts the apology, it is still to decide whether to take matters further.*

✪ *As* and *while* are sometimes confused. *As* not *while* is used to describe two situations which change in parallel:

> ***As*** *they get more experience, their tactics will become more sophisticated.*
> (~~While they get more experience, their tactics will become more sophisticated.~~)

A–Z 19 *As*

Noun *while* 78b

As a noun, *while* frequently occurs in a number of fixed phrases. Most of the phrases have a temporal meaning:

> *It'll take quite* ***a while*** *before they're finished.*
> (a period of time)
>
> *The captain will be there* ***in a while*** *to help out.*
> (in a short time)
>
> *And* ***all the while*** *they continued the protest and even began to shout as the councillors went into the building.*
> (during this time)
>
> *We'll definitely make it* ***worth your while****.*
> (worth your time)

Other uses of the noun *while* include: *a good/long/short/little while, some while ago, after a while.*

WITH 79

With is a preposition which has a basic spatial meaning of 'in the same place as' or 'being alongside':

> *Coffee* ***with cream*** *£1.50.*
>
> ***With the tip****, the bill came to over £100.*

*We are **with you** all the way in this. You are quite right to insist that she stops smoking.*
(*with* is metaphorical here, meaning 'we agree')

*I'm sorry, I'm not **with you**.*
(*with* is also metaphorical here, meaning 'I don't understand you')

In many uses, *with* indicates particular personal attributes:

*That girl **with the red hair** looks like a fashion model.*

With can also be used to show an instrument. This meaning can be extended to include a reference to 'means' and 'manner':

*They opened the package **with a knife**.*

*They reacted **with great excitement**.*

*Handle **with care**.*

With can also mean 'because of having' or 'as a result of having'. These meanings are especially common in spoken English:

***With all this work**, I'd better stay in tonight.*

***With John away**, we've got a spare bed after all.*

*We found it difficult to sleep in the hotel **with all those kids on motorbikes** down in the plaza.*

In reports (e.g. sports reports, weather reports) *with* can have a meaning of 'as well' or 'and additionally'. It is followed by a verb in the *-ing* form:

*Roma completed a much deserved victory **with** di Canio **scoring** again in time added on for injury.*

*The weather for the south of England is likely to remain unsettled **with** showers **crossing** most regions in the late evening.*

When indicating reasons and outcomes, *with* or *what with* is often linked to giving reasons and explanations about adverse or problematic circumstances. *With* commonly occurs in subordinate clauses with an *-ing* form of the verb. The verb can sometimes be omitted:

A: *Do you still listen to Scottish music?*
B: *Since this pair have arrived, very very little, cos you just don't have the time, and **with** the new house and **with** the garden.*

***With** friends like this, who needs enemies?*

***With** there **being** no buses, we had to get a taxi, which cost us a fortune.*

***What with** it **being** student night as well, there were no tickets left to get in to the club.*

***With** half the staff (**being**) at the conference, several classes had to be taught together.*

***With** (**having**) all this work, I'd better stay in tonight.*

→ 539 **Glossary** for any unfamiliar terms

As a preposition, *with* commonly occurs with words which express emotions:

She was green ***with*** *envy.*

The group leader became very angry ***with*** *their drunken behaviour.*

Down ***with*** *socialism!*

Come on, into the bath ***with*** *you!*

WORTH, WORTHWHILE 80

Worth 80a

Worth is used with anticipatory *it* + a verb in the *-ing* form (not a *to*-infinitive) to state whether the speaker thinks something is a good idea:

If you get a good reliable car, ***it's worth keeping*** *it, isn't it, because if you get a bad car, it keeps costing you money.*
(here the first *it* is the anticipatory *it*; the second *it* is the object of *keep*, i.e. the car)
(~~it's worth to keep it~~)

A person or thing may also be the grammatical subject of a clause with *be worth* + *-ing* form:

He *might not be* ***worth marrying*** *if he works for the railways. They don't earn much.*

It's an interesting book. ***It's worth reading.***
(here *it* refers back to the book)

It (be) worth it can be used to refer to clauses or sentences:

I'm not going to argue about semantics. ***It's*** *just* ***not worth it.***

I went without all the luxuries to stay with the children. But ***it was worth it.***

I think ***it was worth it****, giving up what I was doing.*

Worthwhile 80b

The adjective *worthwhile* is commonly used with anticipatory *it* + *-ing* form:

It *might be* ***worthwhile taking*** *the car, you know.*

It (be) worthwhile is used in a similar way to *it (be) worth it* (→ **80a** above), to refer to clauses or sentences:

A: *It's not that far away from London. And there are lots of villages where you can rent workshops, and out in the countryside.*
B: *Mm. I bet that's expensive round here, though. I imagine it could be very expensive. I don't know whether* ***it would be worthwhile.***

Worthwhile is occasionally written as two words (*worth while*) when it is used predicatively, and, especially in informal spoken language, *while* may be preceded by a possessive determiner:

It might be ***worth their while*** *to just buy a mobile phone, to be honest.*

YET 81

Time adverb *yet* 81a

Yet as a time adverb is used most frequently in negative clauses and in interrogative clauses, especially in informal spoken language. Its other uses account for only a small number of occurrences.

Interrogative clauses

Yet as a time adverb means 'from an indefinite moment in the past up to the moment of speaking', and it includes the notion that events were expected to have happened or are expected to happen at some point in the future, or that their occurrence was or is desirable in the view of the speaker:

*Have you heard from your husband **yet**?*
(I/you were expecting this to happen or considered it desirable)

A: *Have you phoned up your sister **yet**?*
B: *No I haven't.*

Negative questions with *yet* can express an even stronger expectation or desire that something should happen or should have happened:

*Is he home **yet**?*
(affirmative question: expectation that he will be home at some point)

*Has**n't** Richard arrived **yet**?*
(negative question: even stronger expectation at the moment of speaking that he should have arrived)

*Samantha, have**n't** you finished **yet**?*
(speaker feels Samantha should have finished by now)

Negative clauses

Statements with *yet* express an expectation on the part of the speaker that events should or will take place at some point in the future. Most statements with *yet* are negative, especially in informal spoken language:

[speaker B, Deirdre, is asked what she wants to study at university]
A: *What about you, Deirdre? What are you going to do?*
B: *Erm, I'm going to go for Arts as well, but I don't know.*
A: *Yeah. But you do**n't** have to make a decision **yet**.*
B: *Yeah.*
A: *I mean, you could spend the first two months going to every single lecture till you made up your mind, you know.*

A: *What time is it?*
B: *It's **not** even four o'clock **yet**.*
A: *Oh, that's fair enough.*
B: *It's quarter to four.*

→ 539 **Glossary** for any unfamiliar terms

Affirmative clauses

Affirmative statements with *yet* are closer in meaning to *still* (see below), and *yet* most typically occurs in end position. It expresses the persistence or continuation of a situation, even when one might have expected it not to persist or continue:

[ships and boats are often referred to as *she* rather than *it*]
Toby said: 'She should be called the Old Lady of the Seas. Do you know, she is thirty-five years old? Most would have been thinking of retiring. But there is life in the old lady ***yet****. She is the finest ship I ever sailed in …'*
(or: there is still life in the old lady/there is life in the old lady still)

[speaker B has returned from a holiday]
A: *Did you take enough money in the end?*
B: *Oh yes. I brought a lot back. Because I didn't pay for my trip to Grenada. I have that to pay for* ***yet****.*
(or: 'I still have that to pay for'; one might reasonably have expected the trip to Grenada to have already been paid for, like the rest of the speaker's holiday)

With superlatives

Yet as a time adverb often follows superlatives:

His latest film is his ***best yet****.*
(His latest film is the best one he has made up to now.)

[about an artist named Keith Ball]
But back to his work as an artist: this summer Ball got his ***biggest*** *break* ***yet*** *when he was awarded $15,000 from the Pollock Krasner Foundation in New York.*

Future plans are on a much bigger scale, with vast segments of the sea recreated in some of the ***largest*** *aquaria* ***yet*** *to be seen in Britain.*

Have yet to, be yet to

The modal expression *have to*, and less frequently the modal *be to*, occur in more formal styles with *yet* in the fixed sequences *have yet to* and *be yet to* to refer to events which are considered necessary or due to happen but which have not happened so far:

[review of a new computer program]
Pricing ***has yet to*** *be finalised but it will sell in the US for $49.95, so a £49.95 price tag is more than likely.*

For reasons Neil ***had yet to*** *understand, Caroline seemed pleased that Dr Barbara had become more authoritarian.*

Compulsory seat-belts ***have yet to*** *have any noticeable effect on road accident statistics in Britain, despite many exaggerated press reports. Experts agree that it is far too soon to tell how many lives the belt law has saved.*

Of all the seasons, spring is perhaps the finest for walking as the crowds ***are yet to*** *arrive and the cliff-top flora is at its most vivid.*

The international community ***is yet to*** *declare what measures it intends to implement to help to resolve this crisis. There is now a real concern that any escalation in the conflict could lead to a major refugee crisis in an already overloaded region.*

As yet

As yet only occurs in negative statements (not in questions):

> [A is the store assistant; *Delta* and *Switch* are types of debit card]
> A: *We will be taking Delta and Switch in every store by the end of the year.*
> B: *Oh right.*
> A: ***As yet** it's not available in every store.*

Concessive conjunct *yet* 81b

Yet is used with a concessive function, with a meaning close to 'but', 'nevertheless', to indicate that the action, state or event in the previous clause should be seen or evaluated in the light of the *yet*-clause. It often occurs after *and*:

> *Connie felt dim with terror, **yet** she stood quite still, touching the flowers.*

> *All this sounds a very old story now! **And yet** it is not such a long time ago.*

This meaning of *yet* is more frequent in written language.

Intensifier *yet* 81c

Yet often occurs as an intensifier, with a meaning similar to 'even', especially with *more*, *another* and *again*:

> *Nature is already taking a hammering from intensive farming and the introduction of genetically modified crops may push **yet more** species over the edge.*

> *The cook arrived with **yet another** plate of cake.*

> A: *I mean, the big supermarkets stayed open till twelve o'clock at night.*
> B: *So small businesses lost out **yet again** because of the supermarkets.*
> A: *Mm.*

Yet, still, already 81d

Still with affirmatives refers to the continuation of an action, state or event:

> A: *I haven't any great desire to go abroad actually, you know.*
> B: *Yes, there's **still** a lot of places in this country I'd like to see.*

> A: *We've **still** got a pot of rice pudding in our fridge from Andrew's last visit.*
> B: *Have you?*
> A: *So we'll have to eat it.*
> B: *Don't you like it?*
> A: *Yeah I do, I just don't think of eating it.*

Yet or *already* cannot replace *still* in such contexts.

→ also **81a**

With negatives, *still* indicates that the speaker considers the continued absence or non-occurrence of something to be undesirable:

> *I* ***still*** *haven't found Marie's phone number. I know I wrote it down.*
> ('I haven't found it yet' would simply mean that it is missing up to the moment of speaking; 'I still haven't found ...' emphasises the continued inability to find the phone number)

Note also the difference in position between *yet* and *still* in negative clauses. *Yet* normally occurs after the lexical verb:

> *I haven't* ***finished yet****.*

More formally, *yet* occurs after the first auxiliary verb or modal verb and after *not*:

> *The contractors* ***had not yet*** *finished work on the road.*
> (written: more formal)

Still normally occurs before the first auxiliary or modal verb:

> *You know, it's dark now and she* ***still hasn't*** *arrived.*

More formally, *still* occurs after the first auxiliary verb and before *not*:

> *An agreement* ***has still not*** *been reached.*
> (more formal)

Informally, *still* occurs before copular verb *be*; more formally, *still* occurs after copular *be* and before *not*:

> *The man* ***still wasn't*** *satisfied.*
> (informal)
>
> *She* ***was still not*** *certain that she believed him.*
> (more formal)

A–Z 72 *Still*

Already refers to an action, state or event which has occurred or may have occurred before the moment of speaking. *Already* may sometimes suggest surprise on the part of the speaker or that something is unexpected:

> *Is it seven o'clock* ***already****?*
> (the speaker did not expect it to be so late; compare 'Is it seven o'clock yet?', which would be more neutral, with the expectation that seven o'clock may be not far off)

A–Z 13 *Already*

Introduction to grammar and spoken English

Introduction to grammar and spoken English

SPOKEN LANGUAGE 82

Until recently, items and structures most typically found in spoken communication have not been fully described. Most grammars of English have had a bias towards the written language. It is only recently that advances in audio-recording and associated technology have made it possible for sufficient quantities of spoken language to be used for analysis.

This chapter focuses on spoken English in its own right. Most chapters of this grammar book include mention of differences between spoken and written grammar and aspects of context that affect choices of grammar. Those chapters give more detailed examples of items and structures described in this chapter.

It is difficult fully to represent spoken grammar in a written book. Although the corpus used as the source of examples in this book provides useful evidence of spoken usage, the corpus has not been systematically coded for phonetic and prosodic features. Variations in stress, intonation contour, voice quality and other aspects such as loudness and tempo, rhythm and length of pauses are not indicated. And the citations from the corpus are presented in written form so that there always remains an underlying bias towards writing in the transcription itself.

This bias towards written language also means that appropriate terms for describing special features of spoken grammar are not always available in existing grammatical frameworks. In some cases new terminology has to be introduced. An example is the use of the terms *headers* and *tails* in 96–97.

The chapters on spoken English in this book are constructed on the basis of four main features of spoken language:

1 Spoken language happens in real time and is typically unplanned.
2 Spoken language is most typically face to face.
3 Spoken language foregrounds choices which reflect the immediate social and interpersonal situation.
4 Spoken language and written language are not sharply divided but exist on a continuum.

The four features overlap. For example, the very fact that spoken language typically occurs face to face means that it is usually unplanned. It should also be acknowledged that written language involves social and interpersonal choices, for example in the writing of personal letters or emails, or in constructing persuasive arguments.

EVERYDAY INFORMAL CONVERSATIONS 83

The following extract from an informal, casual conversation illustrates several of the important features of informal spoken grammar. The features are used regularly by speakers of British English across different regions and contexts of use and by speakers of different ages, genders, social classes and occupations. Potentially problematic areas for a traditional, written-based grammar book are highlighted in bold.

[Four speakers are sitting at the dinner table talking about a car accident that happened to the father of one of the speakers. At the end of this sequence they switch to another topic. *I'll just take* ***that*** *off* and *Have you got hold of* ***it***? are references to a large pan which is on the dinner table.]

The = sign indicates an utterance which is cut short
The + sign indicates an interrupted turn which continues at the next + sign

A: *I'll just take that off.* ***Take that off.***
B: ***All looks great.***
C: [laughs]
B: *Mm.*
C: *Mm.*
B: *I think your dad was amazed wasn't he at the damage.*
A: *Mm.*
B: *It's not so much the parts. It's the labour charges for=*
D: ***Oh that. For a car.***
B: *Have you got hold of* ***it****?*
A: *Yeah.*
B: ***It was a bit erm=***
A: *Mm.*
C: *Mm.*
B: ***A bit.***
A: *That's right.*
B: ***I mean*** *they said they'd have to take his car in for two days. And he said all it is is straightening a panel.* ***And they're like,*** *'Oh no. It's all new panel. You can't do this'.*
C: ***Any erm problem.***
B: ***As soon as they hear insurance claim.*** *Oh. Let's get it right.*
C: *Yeah. Yeah.* ***Anything to do with+***
A: ***Wow.***
C: ***+coach work is er+***
A: ***Right.***
C: ***+fatal isn't it.***
A: ***Now.***

The following features can be observed:

1 Sentences in the written sense (i.e. units beginning with capital letters, consisting of at least one main clause and ending in a full stop) are difficult to identify in spoken language. What seems more important is the production of adequate communicative units and the taking of turns rather than the transition from one sentence to another.
2 Speech is marked by small units of communication often consisting of just single words or phrases, rather than complete sentences, and these units may be separated by pauses, intakes of breath, falls and rises in pitch, and so on (e.g. *Oh that. // Right. // Any problem.*).

→ 539 **Glossary** for any unfamiliar terms

3 The minimal unit of communication is the tone unit, which consists of at least one intonation contour which ends in a rising or falling tone. If a unit does not have one such intonation contour, it is heard as incomplete. A tone unit typically coincides with a clause, hence the clause may be considered the basic unit of grammar in spoken language, but tone units can also be phrases or single words:

Complete tone units: stressed syllables in bold capitals

*I'm **LOO**king for a **PEN**cil.*

***AREn't** you **REA**dy?*

*I **KNOW**! it's **CRA**zy!*
(two tone units: two falling tones)

***DID** she?*

***ANY**way.*

***ME**?*

Incomplete tone units: stressed syllables in capitals

I'm LOOking for a …
(incomplete because no rising or falling tone is present, only a level tone)

DID she …

4 Speakers' turns, unlike written sentences, are not neat and tidy. The speakers regularly interrupt each other, or speak at the same time, intervene in another's contribution or overlap in their speaking turns. And any transcript of a real conversation is much less tidy than the layout of a dialogue in a drama script or in a course book for learning a language.

5 Listeners are not just passive recipients. There are back-channel items (e.g. *Mm*, *Yeah*), by which listeners give feedback, and other (normally supportive) responses (e.g. *Right*).

6 There are abandoned or incomplete structures (e.g. *It was a bit erm … A bit.*). 'Incomplete' structures rarely cause any problem of understanding, and can be collaboratively completed by others. For example, the utterance *For a car* shows one speaker completing the utterance of another.

7 References to people and things in the immediate situation may be incomprehensible to an outsider reading the transcript. The speakers say *Take **that off*** and *Have you got hold of **it**?*. Without being present at the time of speaking or without a considerable amount of previous text, it is not clear at all to an outsider what *that* and *it* refer to, or *off* where it is supposed to be removed.

8 'Subordinate' clauses are present but they are not always obviously connected to any particular main clause (e.g. the clause *As soon as they hear insurance claim*).

9 There are structures which are difficult to label (is the second *Take that off* an ellipted form of *I'll just take that off*? Is it an imperative? What is the status of *And they're like*? *Like* appears to function here to mark a direct speech report (i.e. *And they said …*). (For this use of ***like***, → **49** and **501e**.)

10 Ellipsis is common (e.g. [it] *All looks great.*). Ellipsis occurs when words usually considered 'obligatory' (e.g. a subject for a verb in a declarative clause) are not needed because they can be understood from the immediate context or from the knowledge which is shared between speakers. For speakers and listeners, there are no words 'missing', and what we call ellipsis is simply an economical and sufficient form of communication which is different from the typical grammar of written English, where greater elaboration and specification is usually necessary because the written text is usually being read at a different time and place from when it was created.

11 Some 'words' have an uncertain status as regards grammar. (e.g. *Wow. Now.*) For example, *wow* has an exclamative function, showing the speaker's reaction to something that has been said or that has happened, and seems to stand on its own. *Right* and *now* at the end of the extract seem to be organisational or structural (rather than referring to time), functioning to close down one topic or phase of the conversation and to move on to another phase. This use of *right* and *now* is a discourse-marking use. Such frequent words often connect one phase of the discourse with another and are outside of 'grammar' when grammar refers to the structure of phrases, clauses and sentences. → **113 Interjections** and **106 Discourse markers**

12 Despite these special characteristics of spoken transcripts, it is important to remember that the majority of grammatical items and structures are equally at home in speech and writing. In this chapter the emphasis will be on those structures which are most frequently found in the everyday informal conversations in the spoken corpus used in the creation of this book and which differ most markedly from the grammar of the texts in the written corpus.

THE NOTION OF STANDARD SPOKEN GRAMMAR 84

The term 'standard grammar' is most typically associated with written language, and is usually considered to be characteristic of the recurrent usage of adult, educated native speakers of a language. Standard grammar ideally reveals no particular regional bias. Thus 'Standard British English' grammar consists of items and forms that are found in the written usage of adult educated native speakers from Wales, Scotland and England and those Northern Irish users who consider themselves part of the British English speech community.

The typical sources of evidence for standard usage are literary texts, quality journalism, academic and professional writing, etc. Standard grammar is given the status of the official record of educated usage by being written down in grammar books and taught in schools and universities.

Spoken transcripts often have frequent occurrences of items and structures considered incorrect according to the norms of standard written English. However, many such forms are frequently and routinely used by adult, educated native speakers. Examples of such structures are split infinitives (e.g. *We decided **to** immediately **sell** it*), double negation (e.g. *He **won't** be late **I don't** think*, as compared to *I **don't** think he **will** be late*), singular nouns after plural measurement expressions (e.g. *He's about six **foot** tall*), the use of contracted forms such as *gonna* (*going to*), *wanna* (*want to*), and so on.

Standard spoken English grammar will therefore be different from standard written English grammar in many respects if we consider 'standard' to be a description of the recurrent spoken usage of adult native speakers. What may be considered 'non-standard' in writing may well be 'standard' in speech.

Speech and writing are not independent. Although some forms of spoken grammar do not appear in writing (unless in written dialogues), there is considerable overlap and there is an increasing range of forms appearing in informal written texts which previously were only considered acceptable in speech. In **120** the presence of typically spoken grammatical forms in such contexts as emails and internet chat-room exchanges is discussed.

Grammatical acceptability 85

In this book the following criteria* are adopted for grammatical acceptability in British English to determine whether or not an item or structure is included.'Widespread' here means across speakers of both genders and across a wide range of ages and social and regional backgrounds.

- Included: in widespread use in both the written and spoken corpus (most forms are in this category).
- Included: in widespread use in both the written and spoken corpus but not approved in more prescriptive grammar books and often avoided by many writers of formal English, for example, split infinitives, stranded prepositions (e.g. *That's the woman I gave it* ***to***, compared with *That's the woman* ***to*** *whom I gave it*).
- Included: rare or not occurring in the written corpus but widespread and normal in the spoken corpus (⇢ for example, **96 Headers** and **97 Tails**), and vice versa.
- Not included: regionally or socially marked in the written and/or spoken corpus but widespread and normal within major regional/social varieties of British English (⇢ for example, the use of *ain't*, **119b**).
- Not included: non-occurring and unacceptable in all varieties of British English (for example a structure such as *he did must speak*).

SPOKEN GRAMMAR AND REAL-TIME COMMUNICATION 86

Unplanned speech 86a

Spoken language is normally unplanned. There are occasions when what is said is memorised or read aloud from a script, but speech mainly takes place in real time. It is 'online' communication, it is spontaneous and there is normally very little time for advance planning.

Because thinking time is limited, pauses, repetitions and rephrasings are common. The flow of a communication may also be affected by interruptions or by overlaps with other speakers or by external factors in the speech situation (e.g. a phone ringing may take someone temporarily away).

In writing there are usually opportunities to plan and hierarchically structure the text. The writer can usually rephrase or edit what is written. In speech, utterances are linked together as if in a chain. One piece of information follows after another and speakers have few opportunities for starting again.

* Our thanks to Susan Hunston for suggesting this list of categories.

Simple phrasal structures 86b

Structures which are often quite complex in writing (e.g. heavily modified noun phrases, embedded clauses) are often simplified in real-time informal speech. Some examples are discussed here and in **94 Situational ellipsis**.

Pronouns

The 'online' nature of spoken communication means that pronouns are often preferred to nouns. Pronouns are only rarely modified and are therefore easier to construct and allow speed of communication. They also indicate the shared context of the speakers and reflect the face-to-face nature of the communication, where references are often to persons and things in the immediate situation.

Pronouns referring to things in the shared context are in bold in this extract:

[four people are assembling a child's portable bed, for which they have instructions]
A: ***It** should fit there cos **it**'s not that big I don't think.*
B: ***It**'s warm in here, shall I turn **that** down?*
A: *We've got the instructions anyway.*
C: *I thought you'd organised **it** ... just put **it** by the window or something.*
D: *D'you want me to take **that**?*
B: *Ooh ... then there's bedding for about ten people here* [laughs].

Full noun phrases

The use of multiple modifiers before a head noun in a noun phrase rarely happens in everyday informal speech. Speakers are alert to the constraints which listeners are under in processing information. In informal conversation there is an overwhelming preference for a very simple structure of determiner (+ one adjective) + noun such as:

*Yeah it's **a big house**, **six bedrooms**.*
(compare the possible alternative: It's a big, six-bedroom house.)

*It's **a large house**, lovely, just right.*

However, in writing, it is not difficult to find more complex adjectival structures:

*Living in **a big, dirty, communal house** eating rubbish ...*

*The **cosy, lace-curtained** house ...*

Simple noun phrases are not a *rule* of spoken grammar, but it is a very strong tendency. Any speaker may use a structurally complex noun phrase in spoken communication (for example in a public speech or presentation), but in casual conversation they will probably be heard as rather formal. Similarly, a writer may wish to create a more informal, interactive and dialogic style and may make such choices for different expressive purposes.

Phrasal chaining

The constraints of thinking-time mean that speaker turns typically contain phrasal chunks of information built up in stages, often by means of sequences of adjective phrases or of simple noun phrases. This accounts for the basic characteristic of spoken grammar as being more like the strung-together coaches of a train or links of a chain rather than a carefully constructed hierarchy of embedded structures, one inside the other:

> *For that time of year you need a polo-shirt or something,* ***light, cool,*** *you know* ***short sleeves, cotton.***
> (compare: a light, cool, short-sleeved, cotton shirt)
>
> *I mean Andy is very* ***talented*** *...* ***good teacher, good diplomat, nice bloke.***
> (compare: Andy is a nice, talented, good, diplomatic person and teacher.)

→ **167–175 The noun phrase**, **197–212 Pronouns** and **140–154 Grammar and academic English** for a wider range of examples of premodification and postmodification with reference to nouns and pronouns in both spoken and written contexts

→ also **236–241 Adjectives and adjective phrases**

CLAUSE COMBINATION 87

Real-time communication 87a

One of the most notable features of clause combination in informal spoken English is the way in which clauses are strung together in a sequence with one clause unit added to another in a non-hierarchical way.

The needs of real-time communication do not allow the speaker time to construct over-elaborate patterns of main and subordinate clauses. Much more common are sequences of clauses linked by coordinating conjunctions (*and*, *but*, *or*) or by simple subordinating conjunctions such as *because* (frequently contracted to *cos*) and *so*, which often function more like coordinating rather than subordinating conjunctions:

> [the speaker is talking about her friend, Melanie, who was looking for a part-time job]
> *Well, no, Melanie's actually still a student* ***and*** *she still has ten hours of lectures a week,* ***so*** *she works in McDonald's in her spare time* ***cos*** *she needs the money* ***and*** *she works in McDonald's in Hatfield ...*
>
> [the speaker is describing a motor accident in which she was involved]
> *I was driving along talking to Sue* ***and*** *we'd, like, stopped at some traffic lights* ***and*** *then – bang – there was this almighty crash* ***and*** *we got pushed forward all of a sudden.*
>
> [speakers are talking about discrepancies in a colleague's wages]
> A: *I bet they've paid her for Sunday not paid her for the Bank Holiday, Friday and Monday.* ***Cos*** *that would make your nine hours wouldn't it.*
> B: *Yeah.* ***Cos*** *she's got the Saturday down the same as I did* ***cos*** *we all did the Saturday.*

 **23 *Because/cos***

Subordinate clauses 87b

Informal spoken English includes subordinate clauses that occupy complete speaker turns. Such clauses often occur in conversation when one speaker takes over and maintains another speaker's topic or when another speaker provides a further comment. They often occur after a pause, or after brief feedback from a listener and often function to evaluate what has been said (such clauses are in bold in the examples below):

A: *So I turned round and chased after him.*
B: ***Just as I would have done.***

[talking about what is covered in an insurance policy]
A: *Oh I – I don't remember.*
B: *I just got liability.*
A: *Just liability.*
B: ***Which is good enough.*** *At least it's insured.*
(comment after feedback from the listener)

A: *Well actually one person has applied.*
B: *Mm.*
A: ***Which is great.***

A: *They charge nearly a hundred pounds a week. But that's the average there, you know.*
B: *Mm.*
A: ***Though it's all relative I suppose.***

For further examples ⇢ **123–139 Grammar across turns and sentences**

Clausal blends 87c

Sometimes clausal 'blends' occur. A blend is a syntactic structure which is completed in a different way from the way it began. The blend is, however, usually communicatively complete, effective and easily understood:

In fact, that's why last year they rented a nice house, in er Spain, was it, is that it was near the airport.
(more likely in writing or careful speech: The reason they rented a nice house in Spain last year was that it was near the airport.)

They've nearly finished all the building work, hasn't it?
(more likely in writing or careful speech: They've nearly finished all the building work, haven't they? Or: All the building work has been finished, hasn't it?)

POSITION OF ITEMS 88

The nature of spontaneous speech means that items often appear in positions that are dictated by communicative needs and by people's thoughts as they unfold. Compared with written English, in much casual conversation in English, positioning is generally more flexible.

Adjuncts may occur after tags, and adjuncts which do not normally occur in end position in written text regularly occur in end position in informal speech:

*Spanish is more widely used isn't it **outside of Europe**?*
(compare: Spanish is more widely used outside of Europe, isn't it?)

*I was worried I was going to lose it and I did **almost**.*
(compare: I was worried I was going to lose it and I almost did.)

*You know which one I mean **probably**.*
(compare: You probably know which one I mean.)

*Are my keys in the door **still**?*
(compare: Are my keys still in the door?)

PAUSING, REPEATING AND RECASTING 89

Pausing 89a

Pauses can be unfilled or filled. An unfilled pause is simply a silence, normally only a silence of a second or two. Longer silences are rare in casual conversations and may be heard as problematic by participants. Unfilled pauses tend to occur when a shift in topic or a change in direction is about to occur. They often coincide with syntactic boundaries such as clause units:

Pauses of longer than one second are indicated by dots [...]
A: *I spoke to her last night and ... well, she's not going to take the job.*
B: *How is he taking the divorce thing?*
A: *Okay, I suppose ... Are you planning on shopping this afternoon?*

A filled pause is marked by a vocalisation such as *er* or *erm* (also written as *uh* and *um*) or a lexical form such as *like, well, you know*. A filled pause can mark a shift in topic, especially when accompanied by discourse markers such as *right* or *well* or *okay* (which commonly initiate a new stretch of discourse). They may also often indicate that speakers have not finished what they want to say and wish to continue:

*I suppose, **er**, she'll, she'll take over next week then?*

[A is on the telephone, then finishes that conversation (*Bye bye.*) and speaks to B (*Sorry about that.*)]
A: *Thanks ever so much. Bye bye. Sorry about that.*
B: *That's okay. **Er, right**, where were we?*

Filled pauses frequently precede important lexical choices underlining that the speaker takes time to select the appropriate expression:

*I, **erm**, I'm not sure what we should do here, are you?*

*It was the, **er**, the director, wasn't it?*

*I was on my way there and, **erm**, got lost, I'm afraid.*

*I think she was a bit **er** upset.*

Repeating and recasting 89b

Under the pressure of real time, speakers may repeat words or phrases or recast what they are saying. This is perfectly normal in spontaneous speech, and is not to be taken as a sign of sloppy or lazy performance:

The = sign indicates an utterance which is cut short
The + sign indicates an interrupted turn which continues at the next + sign
[speaker is an insurance salesperson explaining different kinds of cover]
A: *With third party fire and theft in fact if you'd had that cover+*
B: *Mm.*
A: *+in the event of an accident **erm you you wouldn't have to pay anything. But erm you'd ha= I mean you'd have You wouldn't have to pay anything towards the claim but you'd have to sort your own damage to your car out.***
B: *Right.*
A: *Whereas we'd pay for **the third party, like, the other others involved.***
B: *I see right yeah.*
(despite hesitations and recasting, the message is clearly comprehensible to the listener)

Repeats are one way in which speakers may buy more time for thought. Repetition often occurs at the beginning of an utterance or clause:

***I, I'm, I'm** not sure **he'll he'll** be able to arrange that at such short notice.*

*I can't tell you, I'm afraid. **It, it** ... would cause too much emotional damage.*

Recasting is another feature of real-time communication. Sometimes speakers say things too quickly and need to backtrack, in the process reformulating words and phrases; sometimes they need to qualify what was said previously:

*That's such a limited attitude, **well, okay, I know it's cautious and sensible and not just limited** but I think we've got to take more risks.*
(rephrasing and modifying the word *limited*)

[OHP = overhead projector]
*Before we start ... **before we go into that level of detail**, I'm going to write it on the OHP.*
(rephrasing the subordinate clause)

→ **539 Glossary** for any unfamiliar terms

Sometimes speakers search for the right phrasings and do not find them. The desired word may be supplied by another speaker. Sometimes speakers choose not to find the right phrasings, or utterances are left incomplete, with an implicit understanding formed between the speakers:

A: *I really like the Greek salad, it's the cheese,* ***the the***
B: ***Feta***
A: ***The Feta, that's it****. It's strong but I really really like it.*

[The = sign indicates an utterance which is cut short]
A: *There was* ***sort of like*** *a concrete* ***er er sea er wa= what's it called****?*
B: *Defence.*
A: ***Sea defe=*** *thank you. Sea defence.*

A: *Have you got hold of it?*
B: *Yeah.*
A: *It was* ***a bit erm=***
B: *Mm.*
C: *Mm.*
A: ***A bit=***
B: *That's right.*

ORGANISING THE DISCOURSE 90

Spoken language often looks chaotic and unorganised, as many of the examples above might suggest. However, speakers do need to organise their discourse. They need to preface what they are going to say, and to reflect back upon what they have said. They also need to mark the openings and closings of topics and of whole conversations.

Specific words and structures are often used to mark boundaries in conversation between one topic, one stage or phase of the conversation, or one bit of business and the next: for example, items such as *anyway*, *right*, *okay*, *you see*, *I mean*, *mind you*, *well*, *so*, *now*. These items are called discourse markers. Discourse markers help with the planning and organisation of speech. Structurally, discourse markers function outside the boundaries of the clause. Brief examples are given here; for more detailed treatment, ⇢ **108**.

It is their function as organisers of larger stretches of spoken language that qualifies words or phrases or other structures for classification as discourse markers. For example, *anyway* may be used as an adjunct within the clause, but can also function as a discourse marker indicating some sort of shift in the direction of the conversation:

I shouldn't be jealous but I am ***anyway****.*
(adjunct modifying the second main clause)

A: *Sorry. You know what I mean. Sounds like you're gonna post it or something.*
B: *No.*
A: *Oh dear.* ***Anyway****, I'll have to go cos I've got to ring Bob.*
B: *Right.*
(discourse marker, signalling a desire to close the conversation)

Similarly, *right* can be an adjective or adverb, but as a discourse marker it often signals that a speaker is ready to move on to the next phase of business:

***Right**, we'd better try to phone and see what they have to report.*

For further discussion of discourse organisation, ··➤ **123–139 Grammar across turns and sentences** and **242–249 Adverbs and adverb phrases**

A–Z 17 ***Anyway***; 52 ***Mean***; 54 ***Now***; 57 ***Oh***; 58 ***Okay/OK***; 68 ***Really***; 69 ***Right, rightly***; 71 ***So***; 76 ***Well***

SPOKEN GRAMMAR AND INTERPERSONAL COMMUNICATION 91

Spoken language is most commonly an interactive, face-to-face process. Meanings are often created by referring to shared knowledge or by an understanding based on context or because what is referred to is physically and visually present before the speakers. Many items and structures in spoken grammar, therefore, reflect the interpersonal dimension rather than the content of the message. They are outlined here and dealt with in detail in the chapters and sections referred to.

Deictic expressions such as *in here*, *over there*, *that one*, *this here*, *right now*, *then* are common (··➤ 93). Situational ellipsis (e.g. someone asking someone: *Finished?*) is common because points of reference are often obvious to participants (··➤ 94). Speakers also perform regular checks that understanding is shared and they work hard to provide orientation for listeners and engage them by means of headers (··➤ 96), tails (··➤ 97) and tags (··➤ 98). Discourse markers (··➤ 108) also play a vital part in maintaining a listener's involvement.

In informal, face-to-face conversations speakers are often careful not to sound too assertive or direct; normally they do not wish to seem impolite to their listeners. They are also careful not to sound over-precise, which might be taken to be threatening or pedantic. Consequently, polite forms and indirect language, purposefully vague language and approximations (··➤ 103) are much in evidence and in ways which would be unusual in most written contexts.

From utterance to discourse

From utterance to discourse

INTRODUCTION 92

Sections 82–91 outlined some key features of spoken language, especially the way face-to-face conversations are tied to the participants and the immediate situation in which they are speaking in real time.

In this chapter, 92–103, we consider how grammatical features in spoken utterances reflect the creation of discourse rather than just the internal construction of phrases, clauses and sentences. We use the term 'utterance' to refer to complete communicative units, which may consist of single words, phrases, clauses and clause combinations spoken in context, in contrast to the term 'sentence', which we reserve for units consisting of at least one main clause and any accompanying subordinate clauses, and marked by punctuation (capital letters and full stops) in writing.

This chapter considers how speakers orient themselves to the situation of speaking, centred on the notion of deixis. Deixis concerns the way speakers refer to people and things in terms of time and space, all in relation to the moment and situation of speaking. For example, the basic meanings of *I* and *you* in English are 'person speaking' and 'person addressed', respectively, and who the words refer to will change every time the speaker changes. Similarly, an object which is *this cup* for a speaker may be referred to as *that cup* by a listener who is separated from the speaker in space or time:

A: *What's* ***this*** *box* ***here****?*
B: *I don't know. Trash.*

[at a travel agent's; the customer (A) has just received his tickets]
A: *Right well* ***this*** *is all right now is it?*
B: ***That****'s the ticket yes.*
(what is *this* for the customer is *that* for the agent)

→ 93

This chapter also considers how speakers encode assumptions about what can be understood from the situation without being said, and what cannot, as reflected in the phenomenon of situational ellipsis. Ellipsis, or absence of references to entities which are obvious to all participants, is common in informal speech:

A: *Finished yet?*
B: *Not yet.*
(obvious to the listener that the speaker means '*Have you* finished yet?')

→ 94

This chapter also examines how listeners respond to messages and show their 'listenership', for example by the use of response tokens, i.e. single words and phrases that represent much more personally and affectively engaged alternatives to bare *yes* and *no*:

> [talking about food preparation]
> A: *Actually these things should be marinated the night before.*
> B: ***Exactly**. **Oh absolutely**. Actually er yeah. Even the vegetables, Karen.*

The chapter then describes how speakers package the information in their messages with the listener firmly in mind (e.g. by the use of headers, informative items that precede the conventional clause structure and make the clause easier to process):

> (header) ↓
>
> ***My father**, **he**'s been in hospital three times already.*

→ 96

In addition, the chapter considers how speakers create interactive exchanges by the use of questions and tags (short structures typically found at the end of clauses, such as *You like mushrooms, **don't you**?*) (→ 98).

Another important feature of spoken discourse is the purposive use of vague language (such as *sort of*, *whatever*) to project particular kinds of relationships between speakers (→ 103).

The way speakers organise their utterances into coherent discourse and monitor it in relation to its reception by listeners is covered in the next chapter, in the section on discourse markers (→ 108).

DEIXIS: VIEWPOINT AND TIME AND PLACE REFERENCES 93

General 93a

Deixis refers to the way speakers orient themselves and their listeners in terms of person, time and space in relation to the immediate situation of speaking. Deictic features occur in both written and spoken language. For example, a written notice might say *Vehicles must not be parked **here***, where *here* most likely refers to the immediate environment of the notice itself. However, deictic items are more common in spoken English as the relationship between the discourse and the situation is typically more immediate.

References to the immediate situation are achieved mainly by means of determiners such as *this*, *these*, *that*, *those*, adverbs such as *here*, *now*, *there*, *then*, *ago* and personal pronouns such as *I*, *we*, *him*, *us*. Deictic words are especially common in situations where joint actions are undertaken and where people and things referred to can be seen by the participants. The following examples contain deictic items (in bold) which orient the listener interpersonally (who is referred to), temporally (when) and spatially (where). Note how the meaning of *we* can differ between being inclusive and exclusive:

[message left on an answerphone]
I'm phoning up about ***this*** *trying to set up a meeting and various other things* ***I*** *believe. Erm there's a centre staff meeting at two on Friday twenty fourth. And* ***I*** *was thinking perhaps* ***we*** *could meet in the morning beforehand if* ***you****'re going to be free* ***that*** *day. Anyway er give* ***me*** *a ring.* ***I'm*** ***around tomorrow****. Though* ***tomorrow afternoon*** ***I'm*** *not* ***about*** *because* ***I've*** *got an appointment at the hospital. So* ***I*** *don't know how long* ***I'll*** *be* ***there****. But* ***I'm*** ***here tomorrow morning*** *Friday so ring.*

We in this case includes the speaker and the listener. Note also how references such as *around* and *about* could mean the speaker's home or place of work, depending on where the speaker is or on what the common understanding of *around* and *about* are between the speaker and listener:

[in a restaurant]
Waiter: *Right ladies.*
Customer A: *Shall* ***we*** *order some starters?*
Customer B: *Yeah.*
Customer C: *Yeah.*
Customer A: *Er, sesame prawn toast.*
Waiter: *Yeah.*
(*we* in this case includes A, B and C, but excludes the waiter)

A: *What are you doing at Christmas?*
B: ***We****'re having my brother and a friend for lunch on Christmas Day.*
A: *Right. Mm.*
B: *But otherwise* ***we****'re not doing a great deal.*
A: *Okay. And New Year's Eve or New Year's Day?*
B: *No* ***we*** *don't really bother.*
A: *Right.*
(*we* excludes the listener)

I'd *like to pop in to* ***that*** *little shop* ***over there*** *before* ***we*** *leave.*
(*we* in this case may or may not include the listener(s), depending on context)

This, that, these, those 93b

Referring to physical closeness and distance

This and *these* are used to refer to things which are close in space and time:

I like ***this*** *hotel, don't you?*

I'm sorry, he's not here. He's away ***this*** *week.*

In ***this*** *lecture we shall be looking in particular at Shakespeare's History Plays.*

Have you finished with ***these*** *newspapers?*

That and *those* refer to objects and people that speakers may not easily identify from the immediate situation or that are more distant in space and time:

Could I see ***that*** *video on the shelf up there?*

We should move ***those*** *chairs into the corner of the room.*

Do you remember ***that*** *Sunday in Jeddah? It was the busiest day of the week.*

On the telephone

Especially in telephone calls and in answerphone messages *this* is used as a demonstrative pronoun to identify the speaker and *that* is used to ask the identity of other speakers:

*Hello, **this** is David Locastro speaking. I'm calling at 12.30 your time on November 9th to leave a message for Virginia Cortes.*

*Is **that** Nicola? Hi, **this** is Carol Jordan here.*

Referring to psychological closeness and distance

This can be used to underline or highlight that the speaker thinks something is important or newsworthy and will probably be familiar to the listener, instead of using unmarked *the*:

*One of the strategies is **this** new attack on long-term unemployment.*

This focuses or highlights new topics, making them more immediate and significant:

*A quarter of people in the group resigned, didn't they, and **this** has led to other people protesting too. But what can we do?*

That can distance the speaker from aspects of the topic:

*You can't say women shouldn't be allowed to drive trucks because they can't work the long hours. **That**'s just sexist.*

This and *that* sometimes express contrasts in emotional distance (sometimes called emotional deixis) and can signal different attitudes. *This* normally conveys a more positive and involved attitude whereas *that* suggests a more detached and possibly critical attitude:

*Now tell me what you think of **this** new girlfriend he's got?*
(compare the more disapproving: Now tell me what you think of that new girlfriend he's got?)

Similarly, *that* sometimes carries a feeling of dismissal or rejection of something as problematic:

[speakers are discussing new parking restrictions which have been introduced and a proposal to change the existing voucher system for parking]

A: *They've just brought all **that** parking in. There's nothing much you can do about it.*

B: *Yeah. Abolition of the car-parking voucher scheme. How can he do **that**? He can't do **that**. It's not in his power to do **that**.*

C: *What's he saying?*

B: *He says he's gonna abolish the parking scheme. Which is obviously stupid. You know the voucher scheme.*

C: *Mm.*

B: *Which, obviously everyone wants to get rid of **that** stupid voucher scheme.*

In narratives

In narratives, anecdotes, jokes and similar forms, *this* can be used instead of the indefinite article *a/an* to create a sense of immediacy when introducing important people and things in the story:

> ***This*** *girl Susanna knew in New York, she went to live with* ***this*** *guy called Ché.*

That can be used in narratives instead of the definite article *the* to refer to things that are well known to listeners:

> *Then we drove round* ***that*** *big roundabout and over* ***that*** *bridge, you know the one just as you come into Norwich.*

→ 196f, 196g

SITUATIONAL ELLIPSIS 94

Situational and other kinds of ellipsis 94a

Ellipsis can be either situational, textual or structural. Situational ellipsis means not explicitly referring to people and things which are in the immediate situation, such as the participants themselves:

> A: *Don't know what's gone wrong here.*
> B: *Oh. Need any help?*
> (situational; understood: **I** don't know ... **Do you** need ...)

> *He applied and got the job.*
> (textual; understood from previous clause: ... and **he** got the job.)

> *The car he was driving was stolen.*
> (structural; optional use of *that*: The car **that** he was driving ...)

Although ellipsis is often defined as the absence of elements normally required by the grammar (e.g. a subject before a tensed verb form), in reality nothing is 'missing' from elliptical messages; they contain enough for the purposes of communication. It makes more sense to say that writing and formal speech typically need to elaborate more for the sake of readers/listeners and so 'add' items that might otherwise be unnecessary in everyday informal speech.

Situational ellipsis may involve understood references to a range of expressions relating to people and things:

> ***Didn't know*** *that film was on tonight.*
> (understood: **I** didn't know ...)

> ***Sounds*** *good to me.*
> (understood: **It/that/something obvious in the situation** sounds ...)

> ***Lots of things*** *to tell you about the trip to Barcelona.*
> (understood: **There are/I've got/we've got** lots of things ...)

> [at a dry-cleaner's; speaker B is leaving a pair of trousers for cleaning]
> A: ***Wednesday*** *at four be okay?*
> B: *Er, yeah, that's fine ...* ***Just check*** *the pockets a minute.*
> (understood: **Will/would** Wednesday at four be ... **I'll/let me** just check ...)

Initial elements 94b

In spoken language, the most common kind of situational ellipsis involves initial elements in phrases and clauses, especially at the beginning of a speaker's turn. A normally expected determiner may be absent from a noun phrase, or the initial preposition from a prepositional phrase, or an initial auxiliary verb and its subject may be unnecessary where the meaning is obvious to all participants. This is particularly common in informal conversation:

A: *Where's that cheese we bought?*
B: ***Fridge** I think.*
(understood: **In the** fridge I think.)

A: ***Seen** that photo? The photo of mum when she was young?*
B: *Yes.*
(understood: **Have you** seen that photo?)

Interrogatives with no auxiliary or subject 94c

Auxiliary verbs and second person subject pronouns are often considered unnecessary in interrogative clauses:

Started yet?
(understood: **Have you** started yet?)

Hi Jim. Playing tonight?
(understood: **Are you** playing tonight?)

Hi, Colin, been working?
(understood: ... **have you** been working?)

Got any money?
(understood: **Have you** got any money?)

Interrogatives: subject pronoun and no auxiliary verb 94d

In interrogatives, an initial auxiliary is often unnecessary, even when the subject is present:

***You been** eating the biscuits again?*
(understood: **Have** you been eating ...?)

***The dog bothering** you? Shall I throw him out?*
(understood: **Is** the dog bothering you?)

A: ***Anybody want** soup?*
B: *No thank you.*
(understood: **Does** anybody want soup?)

✪ This type of ellipsis does not normally occur with *I*:

Am I interfering?
(~~I interfering?~~)

Copular verb *be* 94e

In interrogatives, initial copular verb *be* is often not needed before *you* (and less frequently *we* or *they*):

A: ***You*** *all right for coffee, mum?*
B: *Yes, I'm all right, thanks.*
(understood: **Are** you all right ...?)

You *sure you don't want a lift?*
(understood: **Are** you sure ...?)

You *the person who wanted a ticket?*

We *the people you were looking for?*

They *your friends or are they just people you work with?*

In interrogatives, initial *be* and the subject may both be unnecessary before adjectival complements:

[waiter to customers]
Ready *to order?*

[host to child during a meal]
Too spicy *for you?*

Declaratives: no subject pronoun 94f

Initial *I*

Initial *I* is often unnecessary in declaratives in informal speech, both with auxiliary and modal verb structures and with lexical verbs (especially mental process verbs such as *think, reckon, guess, hope, like, love, wonder, suppose*):

A: *What's the matter?*
B: ***Can't*** *find my glasses.*
(understood: **I** can't find my glasses.)

Like *your new car.*
(understood: **I** like your new car.)

A: *Chocolate?*
B: *No.* ***Don't want*** *any more, thanks.*

[guest (A) and host (B) at dinner table; *afters* is an informal word for dessert]
A: *That was lovely.*
B: ***Hope*** *you've got a little bit of room left for afters.*

[talking about a house infested with mice]
A: *They used to wake us up in the night didn't they, scurrying up the walls.*
B: *Yeah.* ***Wonder*** *how they got up walls.*

This also occurs frequently in short replies such as: *don't know, can't remember, think so, hope so*:

A: *Can you make those changes to the list?*
B: *Yeah.* ***Think so****, yeah.*

→ 539 Glossary for any unfamiliar terms

Both *I* and the auxiliary verb may be absent from initial position in declaratives:

> [end of conversation]
> *Okay then. Talk to you later.*
> (understood: **I'll** talk to you later.)
>
> *Love to meet her.*
> (understood: **I'd** love to meet her.)

Pronouns cannot be omitted in all cases. Note that the examples above are all informal, and involve mostly auxiliary and modal verbs, and verbs such as *think, hope, wonder*. In most other cases, a subject pronoun must be used:

> *Did you meet Robbie? He was there at the same time as you.*
> (~~Did you meet Robbie? Was there at the same time as you.~~)
>
> A: *Will your mother be here too?*
> B: *Yeah, she's coming.*
> (~~Yeah, is coming~~)

We and other subject pronouns

We and second and third person subject pronouns are less likely to be absent, but may be if the referent is obvious (but → *it* in **94g**):

> A: *How's Fiona?*
> B: *Oh she's fine.* ***Works*** *too hard, that's her only problem.*
>
> *I've never had a holiday like it in my life.* ***Never spoke*** *to me. He never spoke to me all the time we were there.*
> (understood: **He** never spoke to me.)
>
> A: *My brother and his son built the patio for us.*
> B: *Really?*
> A: *Yeah.* ***Came*** *here a couple of summers ago and did it.*

Question tags

Subject pronouns are most typically absent in declarative questions when accompanied by a question tag:

> [*brothers* here refers to a religious order of teachers]
> A: *And did you ever, did you ever know any of the brothers down at the school when Bernard went there?*
> B: *No, I didn't.*
> A: ***Never met*** *any of them,* ***did you****?*
> B: *No, no.*
>
> A: ***Got*** *lost, did they?*
> B: *Yes, they did and it was not for the first time.*
>
> ***Need*** *a ticket,* ***do we****?*
>
> ***Fooled*** *you then,* ***didn't I****?*

Not all cases of this kind are genuine ellipsis. The following may be seen simply as a variation on typical word order:

*Get **the hang of it**, did you?*
(Not: ~~You get the hang of it, did you?~~)
(understood: **Did you get** the hang of it?)

***Looking** much better, he was.*

It and demonstratives 94g

Subject pronoun *it* and demonstrative pronouns are often not needed:

A: *Oh is this a new one?*
B: ***Looks** like it, yeah.*
(understood: **It** looks like it, yeah.)

A: *It says Duscellier.*
B: ***Doesn't** make any sense.*
(understood: **It/that** doesn't make any sense.)

[students talking about a party]
*Like that one we went to in Birchfield Road. **Turned out** to be something Dave had something to do with.*

Initial *it* is frequently unnecessary in short replies such as *could be*, *might be*, *should be*, *probably is*, *usually is*, *must have been*, *could have been*, *might have been*, *should have been*:

A: *It was white chicken in something.*
B: *Chilli, was it?*
A: ***Could** be.*

A: *He was stuck for eleven hours at Heathrow airport.*
B: ***Must have been** awful.*

Initial *it* plus auxiliary verb are often omitted in references to weather and temperature:

***Raining** again.*
(understood: **It's** raining again.)

***Looking** brighter at last.*

***Been** cold lately.*

Initial *it* and copular verb *be* may both be unnecessary when the referent is obvious:

A: *What do you think of it?*
B: ***Excellent**.*
(understood: **It is** excellent.)

A: *I just thought it might help others.*
B: *Yes yes.*
A: ***No good** for me now. It's too late.*

→ 539 **Glossary** for any unfamiliar terms

The same applies to initial pronoun subject *that* in conventional responses such as *that's true, that's correct, that's good*:

A: *I'm sure Tony doesn't get much sleep.*
B: ***True.***

A: *So, how are you doing?*
B: *I'm all right.*
A: ***Good.***

Existential *there* 94h

Initial existential *there* (and its accompanying verb *be*) may be considered unnecessary:

Must have been *half a million people.*
(understood: **There** must have been half a million people.)

Nobody *at home, by the look of it.*

[talking about the activities of mysterious neighbours]
Yeah, they do seem to be dragging stuff about. It's really weird. ***Seems*** *to be more stuff come out than gone in.*

Verb ellipsis in directives 94i

Occasionally the verb may be understood in a directive:

[teacher to pupils]
Hands up.
(understood: **Put your** hands up.)

Everyone ***into*** *the garden. We want to take a photo.*
(understood: Everyone **come/go** into the garden.)

[airport public announcement]
Mr Ken Wilson ***to*** *airport information please.*
(understood: **Will** Mr Ken Wilson **go** to airport information please.)

Determiners 94j

Articles considered obligatory in formal speech and especially in writing may be unnecessary in informal speech when the referent is obvious:

[customer in a café]
Black coffee*, please.*
(understood: **A** black coffee, please.)

A: *Where do you want this?*
B: ***Bottom shelf****, please.*
(understood: (**On**) **the** bottom shelf, please.)

[doing a job; addressing the person helping]
Right, ***hammer*** *please.*
(understood: Right, **the** hammer please.)

[BBC radio news anchorman]
Time *is twenty to nine.*
(understood: **The** time is twenty to nine.)

Other determiners may also be similarly unnecessary:

A: *Hi Brian.*
B: *Hi.*
A: *How's it going.* ***Flat*** *ready yet?*
(understood: (**Is**) **your** flat ready yet?)

A: *Ooh, what's the matter?*
B: *Mm.* ***Neck****'s aching. I don't know what I've done. Must have twisted it.*
(understood: **My** neck's aching.)

[talking about a dog]
Look at him. ***Tail****'s wagging. He's happy.*
(understood: **His** tail's wagging.)

Conditional *if* 94k

Conditional *if*, where considered obligatory in formal speech and especially in formal writing, may occasionally be absent from initial position:

They turn up *at any point, just let me know.*
(understood: **If** they turn up ...)

[host at table]
You want *anything else, just help yourself.*

Fixed expressions 94l

Many everyday fixed expressions are prone to ellipsis of initial elements, since these can be assumed to be known by all participants:

[said just as rain starts to fall]
Good thing *I remembered the umbrella.*
(understood: **It is a/It was a** good thing ...)

Oh, ***good job*** *I've left a little hole, then.*
(understood: **It's a** good job ...)

Other common expressions that occur with initial ellipsis include:

(There's) no point in ...

(It's) not worth ...

(It would be) best if you ...

(I'll) see you later/tomorrow/soon ...

(I'll) be seeing you ...

(You) never know, ...

Prepositions 94m

Prepositional meaning is often obvious in context and prepositions may not be necessary:

A: *Where does she live?*
B: *Don't know.* ***The south*** *I think.*
(understood: **In** the south ...)

A: *Where is the post office actually?*
B: ***Top*** *of Churchill Street, on your right.*
(understood: **At the** top ...)

Absence of prepositions is particularly common in informal styles, in expressions which refer to place and especially to time, including expressions of duration and frequency:

I've got to make a number of trips this May, ***Dubai, Hong Kong, Berlin*** *just for starters.*
(understood: ... **to** Dubai, **to** Hong Kong, **to** Berlin ...)

She's been like that ***two or three days*** *a week.*
(understood: She's been like that **for** two or three days a week.)

Why don't you both pop round ***Saturday evening****?*
(understood: Why don't you both pop round **on** Saturday evening?)

In informal speech prepositions often do not occur in expressions of measurement and in precise expressions of time:

He's ***the same level*** *as you.*
(understood: He is **at** the same level as you.)

A: ***What time*** *are we meeting?*
B: ***Ten o'clock.*** *Is that okay?*
(understood: **At** what time ..., **At** ten o'clock ...)

Stranded prepositions (→ 257) may sometimes be unnecessary with expressions of place and time:

They have ***no place to go.***
(understood: They have no place to go **to**.)

You've got less than an hour ***to finish*** *the job.*
(or, more formal: ... less than an hour **in which** to finish the job.)

RESPONSE TOKENS 95

General 95a

Some adjectives and adverbs are many times more common in spoken language than in written language because of their frequent use as response tokens. These include *absolutely, certainly, definitely, fine, good, great, indeed, really*. In spoken grammar, the term 'response token' better describes their function of referring to a whole preceding utterance rather than their word-class identity as adjectives or adverbs:

A: *We've decided to go to Greece this year, probably in early June.*
B: ***Really.*** *That sounds nice.*

A: *That's a fair comment, isn't it?*
B: ***Absolutely.***

A: *It's more for the kids, isn't it?*
B: *You think so?*
A: *Yeah* ***definitely.***

A: *I reckon she won't last long in that job.*
B: ***Possibly.***

A: *She's obviously going to tear it up and throw it in the bin.*
B: ***Precisely.***

A: *Well, you wear a little black dress to clubs or to a party.*
B: *Yeah* ***exactly.***

Some response tokens are strongly associated with particular contexts. *Fine* most typically occurs in making arrangements and reaching decisions. *Certainly* most typically occurs in reply to a request for a service or favour (compare *definitely* in the example above, which, although close in meaning to *certainly*, strengthens the force of a response and would be inappropriate in the restaurant context below):

A: *Okay. I'll see you a bit later then.*
B: ***Fine.***
A: *In the morning, whenever.*

[to a waiter]
A: *Can I have the bill please?*
B: *Yes,* ***certainly.***
(B: ~~Yes, definitely.~~)

Adjectives such as *excellent, fine, great, good, lovely, right, perfect* offer positive feedback to the speaker and often mark the boundaries of topics where speakers express their satisfaction with phases of business such as making arrangements, agreeing on courses of action, and marking the satisfactory exchange of information, goods and services:

[at a travel agent's; A is the assistant]
A: *There you go. There's your ticket. And your accommodation there. Insurance, and just some general information.*
B: ***Excellent. Right.***

[dealer (A) and customer (B) in a car spare-parts depot]
A: *I'll get one of the lads in to come and do it for you.*
B: ***Lovely.***

Response tokens also frequently occur at the beginning of longer responses, typically as a preface to a comment on the preceding utterance:

[colleagues at work]
A: *You can make it, you can meet me later if you want.*
B: ***Fine****. Whatever. I've got nothing new.*

Premodification 95b

Many response tokens may be premodified by intensifying adverbs which add further emphasis:

[woman talking about giving birth]
A: *Dick was very excited cos at one point they asked for hot towels.*
B: *Oh.*
A: *Just like the movies. So he skipped off down the corridor to get the hot towels.*
B: *Oh* ***jolly good****.*

[discussing tenancy problems in rented accommodation]
A: *Isn't there something in your tenancy agreement about it? You have a written agreement don't you?*
B: ***Most definitely****.*

Negation 95c

Absolutely, *certainly* and *definitely* may be negated as response tokens by adding *not*:

[speaker A is considering buying a CD player for the first time]
A: *... but then I'd have to go out and buy lots of CDs wouldn't I?*
B: *Well yes. I suppose you would.*
A: *There's no point in having a thing if you can't play them. Haven't got any.*
B: ***Absolutely not. Absolutely not****.*

[discussing the difficulty of studying in the evenings after working all day in a day job]
A: *Seven o'clock in the evening after a day at work is not really quite what you need, is it?*
B: *No.*
A: *Hm.*
B: ***Definitely not****.*
A: *No.*

Pairs and clusters 95d

Response tokens often occur in pairs. This is particularly evident when a topic is being closed down or at a boundary in the talk when another topic is introduced. The pair function both to signal a boundary and to add satisfaction or agreement or simply to express friendly social support. Occasionally, triple response tokens occur:

[waiter (A) and customer (B) in a restaurant]
A: *If you need some more just order some more. All right?*
B: ***Right. Fine.***
A: *Okay. Thank you.*
B: *Thank you.*
A: *You're welcome.*

[couple asking permission to look at a disused railway line]
A: *It went through, it goes through. Straight, straight on.*
B: ***Right. Wonderful. Great.*** *Can we look round then?*
A: *Yes certainly.*
B: *Thank you.*

Response tokens may also cluster in consecutive series across speakers, providing multiple signals that a conversation is about to be terminated while at the same time consolidating interpersonal relationships. Often they occur together with other markers of closure such as thanks, checks, confirmations and greetings. Clustering is especially frequent in telephone conversations, where there are often pre-closing and closing routines:

The = sign indicates an utterance which is cut short
[telephone call concerning a printing order]
A: *Do you think it needs editing?*
B: *Erm I shouldn't think so.*
A: ***Good. Brilliant. Okay, well*** *I'll be round to pick it up.*
B: ***Okay.***
A: *Pick it up today.*
B: ***Okay*** *Jack.*
A: *Have you got the compliment slips?*
B: *Yes.*
A: *On all er=*
B: *They they look very good.*
A: ***Great.*** *Yes.*
B: ***Fabulous.***
A: ***All right.*** [laughs]
B: ***Okay.*** *Thanks for that.*
A: ***Okay*** *Len.*
B: ***Cheers.***
A: ***Bye.***
(*all right* and *okay* may be seen as pre-closing; *cheers* and *bye* close the call)

[giving street directions]
A: *You'll come to a stop sign, take a right and just follow it all the way out.*
B: *Oh.* ***Perfect.***
C: ***Great.***
B: ***That's excellent. Thank you very much.***
C: ***Thank you so much. Thanks.***

539 **Glossary** for any unfamiliar terms

Other types of phrase and short clause also function as response tokens. Common ones include:

Is that so?	*Not at all*	*Of course*
By all means	*True enough*	*What a pity!*
Fair enough		

⇢ also **242–249 Adverbs and adverb phrases**

 **56 *Of course*; 58 *Okay/OK*; 69 *Right, rightly***

HEADERS 96

Headers and clause structure 96a

The dominant word order in English in both speech and writing is the declarative S-V-X where S is the subject of the clause, V is the verb and X is any other item that may be present, e.g. an object (O) or an adjunct (A). The theme (what the speaker wants to talk about or the point of departure of the message) is usually the subject of the clause (⇢ 472).

Fronting may be used to emphasise what the speaker considers to be especially significant. The word or phrase which is fronted and which comes first in the clause is highlighted or 'thematised' by the word order. Adjuncts are frequently fronted for emphasis in both spoken and written language (⇢ 473), and objects and complements can also be fronted. This is particularly common in spoken language:

I like David but ***Pat*** *I find rather odd.*
(fronting of the object *Pat*)

I think we tried to see too much. ***Naples*** *I remember but all those other towns along the coast are a bit of a blur.*
(fronting of the object *Naples*)

[trying to find a library book that is on *short loan*, i.e. must be returned after only a very short period]
A: *There's another short-loan book round here somewhere that I have to get in and I don't know where it is. Yes. That one and there's another one. Not one on the floor down there is there?*
B: *No.*
A: *It's probably around here then. Aha. Hiding from me. And a* ***very good book*** *it was too.*
(fronting of subject complement)

These fronted elements still remain within the clause structure:
[C = subject complement]

C	S	V	A
a very good book	*it*	*was*	*too*

(non-fronted: it was a very good book too)

However, in spoken English a particular type of structure is common where an item within the clause structure is placed before the clause and repeated (usually as a pronoun) in the clause itself. When such an item occurs before the clause, the structure is called a header:

← header → ← clause →
S V C

The teacher with glasses, he *seems very nice.*
(non-fronted: The teacher with glasses seems very nice.)

Types of header 96b

A header most typically consists of a noun phrase followed by one or more pronouns which refer back to the noun phrase. In some grammar books this feature is called left-dislocation. In this book the term 'header' is preferred, because the word 'dislocation' suggests that a very common spoken structure is odd or in some sense 'in the wrong place'. Also, there is no left or right in spoken English. These are metaphors of the space on a typically western, written page. Spoken language exists in time, not space:

That leather coat, it *looks really nice on you.*

The white house on the corner*, is* ***that*** *where she lives?*

[talking about a baby called *Jamie*]
Jamie*, normally, you put* ***him*** *in his cot and* ***he****'s asleep right away.*

Paul*, in this job that* ***he****'s got now, when* ***he*** *goes into the office,* ***he****'s never quite sure where* ***he****'s going to be sent.*

Headers may be complex, with semantically connected noun phrases (NP1, NP2, etc.) strung together in apposition or simply adjacently, leading to the noun phrase which is the subject of the following clause:

NP1 NP2 NP3
Madge, one of the secretaries at work, her daughter *got married last week.*

My friend, Janet, her sister *has just emigrated to Brazil.*

[a *Ford Escort* is a model of car]
His cousin in London, her boyfriend, his parents *bought him a Ford Escort.*

Such strings of noun phrases help to provide orientation for the listener, who can then more easily identify the main topic. They often lead the listener from given or known information to new topical information. Headers of this kind do not normally occur in written English, and though they may look strange when transcribed and written on the page, they are normal, frequent, and pass without comment by participants.

Headers may also be non-finite clauses:

Going round museums and art galleries, it*'s what my mum and dad like doing.*

Walking into that room, it *brought back a load of memories.*

→ 539 **Glossary** for any unfamiliar terms

Headers may also occur in interrogative clauses:

***Your sister**, is **she** coming too?*

***That new motorway they were building**, is **it** open yet?*

Headers can occur with a (normally stressed) *there* subject pro-form:

*Now **Rio de Janeiro**, **there**'s a fabulous city.*

Headers and clause elements 96c

Headers commonly refer to the subject, object, object complement or prepositional complement in a following clause:

***Owen**, **he**'s my favourite nephew.*

***Joe**, I've never seen **him** at a single football match this season.*

[talking about a local character's nickname]
***'The Great Maurice'**, they used to always call him **that**, didn't they?*

***Anita**, you should at least feel sorry for **her**.*

The preposition is not included in the header:

*They booked the hotel for Pamela but, **Dave**, they left it to **him** to find a room for himself.*
(~~They booked the hotel for Pamela but, to Dave, they left it to him to find a room for himself.~~)

Headers often function like titles or headlines in narratives or in jokes:

***The time we were living in Hong Kong**, I suppose we were a lot wealthier then …*
[story continues]

The = sign indicates an utterance which is cut short
A: *Well, **the time I nearly crashed the car**, I was driving late one night=*
B: *You'd forgotten to turn your lights on=*
A: *Yes, and I just didn't see the car in front.*

TAILS 97

Tails and clause structure 97a

Tails are similar to headers in that items are placed outside the s-v-x clause structure (→ above, 96), but they occur after the clause. Tails are typically noun phrases. They clarify or make explicit something in the main clause. Most commonly, a tail consists of a full noun phrase which clarifies or repeats the referent of a pronoun in the clause that comes before it. Like headers, tails feature only very rarely in written English but are a standard feature of informal spoken grammar:

←—— clause ——→ ←—— tail ——→
***He**'s amazingly clever, **that dog of theirs**.*

Tails are sometimes referred to as 'right-dislocated' structures, but in this book we do not use that term for the same reason that we do not use the term 'left dislocated'.

Types of tail 97b

Tails are most typically noun phrases, but may also be prepositional phrases or clauses:

> ***They****'re incredibly nice,* ***our neighbours****.*
>
> *I put it* ***there****,* ***on the fridge****.*
>
> *I find it very frustrating* ***that****,* ***not being able to remember people's names****.*
>
> *I find* ***it*** *annoying that* ***they didn't tell us****.*

More complex noun phrases can also form tails:

> ***It*** *never occurred to me,* ***the danger I was in****.*
> (preferred in writing: The danger I was in never occurred to me.)
>
> ***That*** *was our only chance of a holiday,* ***that weekend in Rome seeing Rita****.*
> (preferred in writing: That weekend in Rome seeing Rita was our only chance of a holiday.)

Tails may also occur in interrogative clauses:

> *Are* ***they*** *both at university,* ***your brother's kids****?*

Tails often occur with statement tags. Sometimes the tail noun phrase may be accompanied by an auxiliary verb or copular verb *be* in the same form and polarity as in the main clause:

> ***It's*** *an exciting place, Hong Kong is.*
> (or: It's an exciting place, Hong Kong.)
>
> ***They're*** *from all over the world, those photos are.*
>
> [two friends in a restaurant]
> A: *What are you going to have?*
> B: *I can't decide.*
> A: ***I'm*** *going to have a burger with chilli sauce, I am.* (statement tag)
> B: *Mm yeah,* ***it's*** *a speciality here, the chilli sauce is.* (tail)
>
> ***She hasn't*** *been here before, Judith hasn't.*
>
> ***It's not*** *very good, that cake isn't.*

Tails also frequently occur with tag questions and can be placed either before or after the tag:

> ***They*** *do take up a lot of time, I suppose, kids,* ***don't they****?*
>
> *Cos* ***they*** *tend to go cold,* ***don't they****, pasta?*
>
> ***It****'s not easy to eat,* ***is it****, spaghetti?*

→ 539 **Glossary** for any unfamiliar terms

Where the tail consists of a pronoun alone, the object pronoun, not the subject pronoun, is used:

> ***I'm** hungry, me. I don't know about you.*
> *(~~I'm hungry, I.~~)*

> ***He**'s crazy, him.*

When demonstratives are used in the tail, they must agree in number with the preceding pronoun:

> ***It**'s a speciality of the region, that.*

> ***They**'re lovely potatoes, these.*

Tails and clause elements 97c

Tails most typically refer back to subjects in the preceding clause. They can also refer to objects or complements or adjuncts:

> *She's never had **one** before, a mosquito bite.*

> *I reckon we'd been **there** before as children, don't you, to Lowestoft?*

Tails are listener-sensitive. The tail clarifies what may not have been understood by the listener. The tail can also reinforce and add emphasis to an already explicit referent:

> A: *Did **Max** help you?*
> B: *Yes, he moved all my books.*
> A: *He said he'd try and help out.*
> B: *Yeah, **he** was very helpful, Max.*

> ***They**'re an odd couple, those two.*

> ***They** look good down there, don't they, those tiles?*

> ***That**'s what I like most, people with real team spirit.*

Tails frequently occur in statements in which the speaker is evaluating a person or thing or situation:

> ***She**'s a great tennis player Hiroko is, isn't she?*

> A: ***It**'s not nice juice, that isn't.*
> B: *I'll still try some.*
> A: *Where's your glass?*

QUESTIONS AND TAGS 98

General 98a

The formation of questions is treated in 424–433. Here in section 98 the question forms examined are more likely to occur in informal speech than in formal speech or writing and therefore more properly belong to the grammar of spoken English. In particular, question tags feature frequently in spoken English and serve to engage the listener and invite convergence with the speaker.

Question tags and intonation 98b

The forms and functions of question tags are described in 431.

Rising and falling intonation may combine with question tags to produce a variety of meaning types. Bold type indicates where the tone might typically occur.

Falling tones (↘)

type	polarity	falling tone ↘	falling tone ↘	expected answer
1	affirm. + neg.	*You've worked* ***hard,***	***haven't*** *you?*	*Yes.*
2	neg. + affirm.	*He didn't* ***get*** *it,*	***did*** *he?*	*No.*
3	neg.* + affirm.	*Nobody* ***knows,***	***do*** *they?*	*No.*

* In this case, the negative element is contained in the subject *nobody* (similarly: 'Nothing happened, did it?' 'We hardly see her, do we?').

Type 1 contains an affirmative statement by the speaker in the main clause, and an expectation of a *yes*-answer as confirmation in the tag.

Types 2 and 3 contain a negative statement by the speaker in the main clause, and an expectation of a *no*-answer as confirmation in the tag.

Falling tone plus rising tone (↘ ↗)

type	polarity	falling tone ↘	rising tone ↗	expected answer
4	affirm. + neg.	*You've worked* ***hard,***	***haven't*** *you?*	Neutral (*yes* or *no*)
5	neg. + affirm.	*He didn't* ***get*** *it,*	***did*** *he?*	Neutral (*yes* or *no*)
6	neg.* + affirm.	*Nobody* ***knows,***	***do*** *they?*	Neutral (*yes* or *no*)
7	affirm. + affirm.	*Kate* ***has*** *gone,*	***has*** *she?*	*Yes.*

* Clausal negation with *nobody*.

Type 4 contains an affirmative statement by the speaker in the main clause, and a more neutral expectation (i.e. of a *yes*- or a *no*-answer) in the tag.

Types 5 and 6 contain a negative statement by the speaker in the main clause, and a more neutral expectation (i.e. of a *yes*- or a *no*-answer) in the tag.

Type 7 contains an affirmative statement by the speaker in the main clause, and a more affirmative expectation (i.e. of a *yes*-answer) in the tag.

Tag patterns in requests 98c

Interrogatives that function as requests often have the pattern of negative clause + affirmative tag, with the fall and rise intonation pattern. Requests expressed with tag questions are usually quite informal. Bold type indicates where the tone might typically occur.

Interrogatives as requests

polarity	falling tone ↘	rising tone ↗
neg. + affirm.	*You couldn't carry* ***this*** *for me,*	***could*** *you?*
neg. + affirm.	*You haven't got any chocolate* ***bis****cuits,*	***have*** *you?*

Position of question tags 98d

Question tags typically come at the end of the clause, but in informal spoken language, they can interrupt the clause:

> ***That's*** *odd, isn't it, from a tutor?*
>
> ***It was*** *perhaps your team, was it, that was round there?*

In reporting structures, the question tag may occur before the reported clause, especially if the reported clause is felt to be unusually long:

> [commenting on the recipes of a famous cookery-book writer]
> ***You*** *always* ***know****, don't you, that what you make will be suitable, and light, and that it will taste all right too.*

Anticipatory *it* clauses may also be interrupted by a question tag:

> ***It's*** *true, isn't it, what they said about him?*

Fixed tags in informal speech 98e

Some tags in informal spoken language do not vary in form. They include items such as *(all) right, okay, yeah, eh, don't you think?*. They are normally used to check that something has been understood or to confirm that an action is agreed:

> *So we're meeting at 7 outside the pizza place,* ***okay****?*
>
> *Let's stop talking in circles,* ***right****?*
>
> *Don't tell anyone about this,* ***yeah****?*
>
> *Oh well, what on earth can we do about it,* ***eh****?*

✪ *No* is not normally used in this way:

> *He's a really nice person, isn't he?*
> (~~He's a really nice person, no?~~)

A-Z 69 ***Right, rightly***

ECHO QUESTIONS 99

Echo questions are very common in spoken language. They typically have declarative word order and include a *wh-* word:

A: *Big day tomorrow. Got to go to the Phoenix.*
B: *Got to go to* ***where****?*
A: *Got to go to this very formal meeting of all these academic people.*

also 432

One common type of echo question involves requests to clarify noun phrases or parts of them which may not have been heard correctly. They are formed with a determiner and *what*:

[talking of problems with European bureaucracy]
A: *What was it? The European Commission?*
B: *Mm. Translation service.*
A: ***The what****, sorry?*
B: *Translation service. And they were just so badly organized. It was just unbelievable.*

A: *That looks like a dinosaur.*
B: *Like* ***a what****?*
A: *A dinosaur.*

A: *But apparently the president of the guild, he's a really nice bloke Alex says, cos, you know, she does all the party stuff.*
B: *Does* ***the what stuff****?*
A: *She does all the politics of the department stuff.*
B: *Politics.*

FOLLOW-UP QUESTIONS 100

A variety of common follow-up question-types occur in speech.

Reduced questions with *wh-* words

Reduced questions with *wh-* words and stranded prepositions (257) are particularly frequent:

A: *Margaret wants to talk to you.*
B: *Oh,* ***what about****?*
(or, more formal: About what?)

A: *You're not staying in tonight, you're going out for dinner.*
B: *Oh.* ***Where to****?*
A: *I'm not telling you, a surprise.*

The follow-up question may consist of a *wh-* word alone or a *wh-* word + a substitute word:

A: *Is he warden of the whole thing?*
B: ***Who****?*
A: *Doctor Thornton.*
B: *I don't know.*

[in a restaurant; A is the customer, B is the waiter]
A: *I'll have that one.*
B: ***Which one****?*
A: *The king prawn in lemon sauce.*

Tag questions

The follow-up question may function as a signal of engagement and attention by the listener. Such questions are typically tag questions. Their function is often very similar to that of supportive responses such as *uhum?*, *yeah?* and *really?* (95):

A: *I went to school with her.*
B: ***Did you****?*
A: *Mm.*

A: *And on mama's tree she's got some raspberries and tomatoes.*
B: ***Does she****? That's great.*

The follow-up tag question may consist of a doubling of this type of structure for emphasis, most typically with a negative clause followed by an affirmative tag, but occasionally with two affirmatives. This usually expresses a strong reaction. A typical intonation pattern is shown:

[talking of firms taking over other firms]
A: *And they've taken over Walker's too.*
B: *Oh* ***they haven't, have they****?*

A: *He thinks you're coming to pick him up.*
B: *Oh* ***he does, does he****?*
A: *Yeah, that's what he said.*

Follow-up tag questions in informal spoken language often simply function to keep the conversation going by inviting further responses from the listener. A typical intonation pattern is shown:

[talking about how quickly a popular type of cake gets eaten by family members]
A: *Have you noticed it always disappears?*
B: ***Yeah, it does, doesn't it****?*
A: *I've got two now,* ***yes****, it* ***does always disappear, doesn't it****?*
B: ***Yeah****.*

Formulaic questions

A number of follow-up questions are formulaic and serve as ways of expanding the discourse or requesting further specification. These include *How come? So what? What for?* and *Like what?*:

[*the shuttle* here is a train which carries cars constantly back and forth between Britain and France]
A: *The shuttle would be out of the question, you see.*
B: ***How come***?
A: *Well, the shuttle is where you take your car on.*
(*How come* = Why?)

A: *I finished loads of odds and ends.*
B: *Did you?* ***Like what***?
A: *Like, my programs. Finished that off.*
(*Like what* = What, for example?)

TWO-STEP QUESTIONS AND RESPONSES 101

Questions in spoken English can involve a two-step process. One question may act as a preface for another question. In such cases, the listener may feel that the first question is too direct or too general and so the speaker shows sensitivity to the listener's reaction by anticipating a response:

What does stalking consist of? *I mean, what was she doing exactly?*

Yes-no questions are only rarely self-contained. While they may function to elicit specific information, such questions are normally asked as a preface to further questions. For example, the question *Are you going to the match tonight?* anticipates an answer which may then be followed by a further more personal or specific question:

A: ***Are you going to the match tonight***?
B: *Yeah, I am.*
A: ***Do you mind if I tag along***?
B: *Sure. We're leaving around seven.*

A: ***Are you in this Sunday afternoon***?
B: *I expect so. I think we might be going out later.*
A: ***Okay, do you mind if I pop round to pick up the drill***?
B: *Of course not.*

Another form of two-step question is the pre-question:

A: ***I wondered if I might ask something***?
B: *Sure.*
A: *Would you be able to write a reference for me?*

Can you tell me something? *What time is the rubbish collection on Mondays?*

Another type of two-step question involves projected answers in a two-step process:

Where are you going? ***Into town***?

What time did you say they were coming back? ***Seven***?

PREFACE QUESTION: *(DO YOU) KNOW WHAT?* 102

The formulaic question *(Do you) know what?* is used as a preface to what the speaker considers newsworthy or important information:

A: ***Do you know what****?*
B: *What?*
A: *Roger's mum's bought Rachel a jumper. Isn't that sweet?*
B: *Yeah.*

VAGUE EXPRESSIONS AND APPROXIMATIONS 103

Vague language 103a

Being vague is an important feature of interpersonal meaning and is especially common in everyday conversation. It involves the use of words and phrases such as *thing, stuff, or so, like, or something, or anything, and so on, or whatever, kind of, sort of.*

Vague language softens expressions so that they do not appear too direct or unduly authoritative and assertive. It also is a strong indication of an assumed shared knowledge and can mark in-group membership: the referents of vague expressions can be assumed to be known by the listener.

There are times where it is necessary to give accurate and precise information; in many informal contexts, however, speakers prefer to convey information which is softened in some way. Such vagueness is often wrongly taken as a sign of careless thinking or sloppy expression. Vagueness is motivated and purposeful and is often a mark of the sensitivity and skill of a speaker:

Between then and ***like*** *nineteen eighty four I just spent the whole time, I mean for that whole* ***sort of*** *twelve year period* ***or whatever****, erm I was just working with just lots and lots and lots of different people.*

I was down in er a place called erm, down in the Urals as well, erm Katherineburg. It's ***kind of*** *directly east of Moscow.*

There are occasions where vague language is necessary and where its absence would make the message too blunt. In the following example it would be pointless to list every available drink and the vague usage simply keeps options open. Both speakers know from their shared cultural knowledge just what is included in *or something* and what is excluded:

[speaker B has suggested taking a visitor to a local coffee shop]
A: *She doesn't like coffee.*
B: *Well, she can have an orange juice* ***or something****.*

Purposefully vague language occurs in writing and in speech. For example, academic writing contains vague expressions which enable writers to hedge the claims for their theories and research findings.

The vague expressions *and things*, *and stuff* and *and that* are particularly flexible and can be used to refer to a wide variety of phrases and whole clauses. These expressions are extremely frequent in informal spoken language. In the following examples, all relevant vague expressions are in bold:

The + sign indicates an interrupted turn which continues at the next + sign
[describing a craft shop]
A: *It's more like a* ***sort of*** *gallery. Just* ***sort of*** *arty. Well no it's* ***sort of*** *arty* ***things****. It's got jewellery and+*
B: *Oh right.*
A: *+erm loads of really nice greetings cards.* ***Sort of*** *hand-made greetings cards* ***and things****.*

A: *And erm again I say that there isn't anywhere for children to play and if they do the way the cars come round sometimes+*
B: *Mm.*
A: *+they can easily be knocked over* ***and things****.*
B: *Mm.*
A: *They run from the grass over onto the back onto the pavement and it's very easy for children to get knocked over like that.*

I really don't know about their environment management systems ***and stuff****.*

They've got a form. They give you a form. You have to fill it in ***and stuff****, cos if you don't you won't get an interview.*

All university is about is opportunity, isn't it. You know it's just having had the time and the money and without the commitment or responsibilities like a family and a house ***and that****.*

[*to have a lump in one's throat* means to feel very sad and ready to cry]
A: *I had a big lump in my throat and I couldn't understand it. I mean there was no reason for me to cry* ***or anything****. Nothing really horrible happening. I guess I must be really tired though cos* ***like****+*
B: *Oh yeah you've been working quite hard* ***and that****.*
A: *+I've been working hard and I've been travelling all the time* ***and all that sort of thing****.*
B: *Yeah.*
A: *So I just couldn't cope with it.*

A–Z 74 ***Thing, stuff***

Approximations 103b

There is a wide range of expressions used with numbers and quantities which enable speakers to give approximations rather than being absolutely precise and perhaps being heard as pedantic. Approximations are used for the same interpersonal reasons as the vague expressions in **103a**.

Adverbs and prepositions

Adverbs and prepositions are most commonly used to express approximation:

I'll see you ***around*** *six.*

*There were **roughly** twenty people turned up.*

*I had the goldfish for **about** three years.*

*That laser printer can do **round about** six pages a minute.*

***Up to** three hundred new cars had been delivered before the fault was discovered.*

The basic meaning of most of the common expressions is 'approximately', although the word *approximately* itself is more commonly used in writing and only normally occurs in formal speech. Prepositional phrases indicating approximation are also more common in formal speech and in writing:

*The plane will settle at its cruising altitude of **approximately** 11,000 metres.* (spoken, formal)

*Losses which were **in the region of** thirty thousand pounds daily were reported by three of the airlines.*
(spoken, formal)

... odd; ... or so

Number + *odd* is used when the figure quoted may be slightly higher than the actual number. A hyphen is used when the expression is written:

*We've got sixty-**odd** people coming later in the day.*

*They'll charge thirty-**odd** pounds.*

Number + head noun + *or so/or thereabouts/or something* are also used in such situations. *Or thereabouts* is more formal than *or so*, and *or something* is the most informal:

*They'd been playing maybe, what, five minutes **or so**.*

*OK, we'll pay the higher deposit. What was it again? It was three hundred and eighty pounds **or thereabouts**, wasn't it?*

*It weighed about twenty kilos **or something**.*

Odd is not used in this way:

*They'll only take twenty minutes **or so**, won't they.*
(~~They'll only take twenty minutes odd, won't they?~~)

... or; ... -ish

Or between numerals also indicates that it would not normally be appropriate to specify more precisely:

*It'll cost you five **or** six pounds to park but it'll save you a long walk into the town.*

The suffix *-ish* is also used, especially in informal speech:

*So, er, we're meeting seven**-ish** or maybe a bit later.*

*I think he's fifty**-ish** but he looks a lot younger actually.*

Exaggeration

Deliberately exaggerated reference to numbers and quantities is another form of approximation:

> A: *How much would it cost to re-lay the lawns?*
> B: *It'll cost* ***thousands****. I don't think we should even think about it yet.*

> *I've told him* ***hundreds*** *of times to put the alarm clock on but he just doesn't listen.*

> *She's very well qualified. She's got* ***loads and loads*** *of letters after her name and qualifications and things.*

Similar expressions include:

ages	*heaps*	*oceans*
crowds	*lots*	*tons*
dozens	*masses*	*zillions*

Clusters

Vague markers and approximations sometimes cluster together:

> *The room will take* ***up to*** *two hundred* ***or so*** *people, won't it,* ***or something like that****?*

More or less is common as a vague expression in spoken language, but it is hardly ever used before numerical expressions. It is generally used to refer vaguely to completion of an action or event, or to hedge (i.e. be less assertive about) a description of something. It may be used before or after the phrase it refers to. It often means something like 'virtually', 'practically', 'just about':

> *I think she's sort of* ***more or less*** *finished with it.*

> *They're* ***more or less*** *the same.*

> *They've got everything,* ***more or less****.*

> *They'll charge thirty-****odd*** *pounds.*
> (~~They'll charge more or less thirty pounds.~~)

A–Z 18 ***Around, round***; 49 ***Like***; 71 ***So***; 74 ***Thing, stuff***; 77 ***Whatever***

From discourse to social contexts

From discourse to social contexts

INTRODUCTION 104

Spoken interaction may range from being intimate and informal to being formal and distant. Often the distance between speakers is dictated by social factors such as interpersonal relationship, the setting or the respective power and social status of the participants.

There is a variety of grammatical options open to speakers to mark intimacy or distance. These range from different formulaic greetings and farewells to the ways in which people address or name one another, or the way they use clause types or tense and aspect choices to show degrees of politeness. Writers typically cannot see who they are speaking to and often have to 'project' an ideal reader for their purposes (e.g. typical educated reader of novels, or typical teenage magazine reader).

The more dynamic and face-to-face nature of spoken communication also means that speakers have to choose the best ways to organise and sequence their messages for the benefit of their listeners and in collaboration with them. This involves 'marking' the discourse, signalling for the listener what is happening using the discourse-marking resources of the language.

Speakers also express stances, attitudes and feelings towards their messages and reactions to what others say, all in real-time face-to-face interaction, with listeners' sensitivities in mind. Spoken grammar therefore also has important affective features.

Speakers choose how to address others. For example, when do speakers use *sir* or *madam*? When do they address people directly by name?

This chapter looks at some of these central social, contextual and affective functions of grammar and spoken English. Sections 105–113 are concerned with the general class of pragmatic markers (items which mark speakers' personal meanings, their organisational choices, attitudes and feelings). These include: discourse markers and how speakers use them to structure and organise the discourse and to monitor the state of the unfolding talk (→ 106–110); stance markers, which express speakers' attitudes and positions (→ 111); hedges, which enable speakers to make their utterances less assertive (→ 112); and common interjections, which encode speakers' affective reactions (→ 113). The chapter then considers taboo language (→ 114), and greetings and farewells (→ 115), and examines vocatives and other aspects of personal address (→ 117–118). Lastly, the chapter returns to a focus on the differences between speech and writing and the notion of standards, concluding with a look at how the grammars of speech and writing are becoming blended in new forms of electronic communication (→ 119–122).

PRAGMATIC MARKERS 105

Pragmatic markers are a class of items which operate outside the structural limits of the clause and which encode speakers' intentions and interpersonal meanings. Pragmatic markers include discourse markers, which indicate the speaker's intentions with regard to organising, structuring and monitoring the discourse (→ 106), stance markers, which indicate the speaker's stance or attitude vis-à-vis the message (→ 111), hedges, which enable speakers to be less assertive in formulating their message (→ 112), and interjections, items which indicate affective responses and reactions to the discourse (→ 113).

DISCOURSE MARKERS 106

General characteristics 106a

Discourse markers are words and phrases which function to link segments of the discourse to one another in ways which reflect choices of monitoring, organisation and management exercised by the speaker. The most common discourse markers in everyday informal spoken language are single words such as *anyway*, *cos*, *fine*, *good*, *great*, *like*, *now*, *oh*, *okay*, *right*, *so*, *well*, and phrasal and clausal items such as *you know*, *I mean*, *as I say*, *for a start*, *mind you* (for a more complete list, → 107–110 below).

Phrases as discourse markers

Discourse markers are outside of the clause structure. They serve to indicate various kinds of relationship between utterances, and simultaneously indicate social relations regarding power and formality. In the following examples, the first group show highlighted items used within the clause; the second group show the same items used as discourse markers:

- In-clause use; non-discourse-marking:

  I didn't really need it but I bought it ***anyway****.*
  (*anyway* functions as a concessive adjunct meaning 'despite [not needing it]')

  You know *what we need? Another helper.*
  (*You know* functions as reporting verb with the clause *what we need* as its object)

  I bought extra food ***so*** *we'd have enough in case more people turned up.*
  (*so* functions as a subordinator introducing an adverbial clause of purpose)

- Discourse-marker use:

  [speaker is describing the different types of house in his neighbourhood]
  You've got high rises, you've got terrace houses, ***you know****, bungalows on the edge and everything.*
  (*you know* monitors the state of shared knowledge and projects an assumption that the listener shares the speaker's perspective on typical kinds of house)

[speaker A has been telling a story about a long, difficult drive from England to Wales; the speakers digress for a while to talk about whether you have to pay to cross the suspension bridge which links England and Wales]
A: *But you only pay one way.*
B: *Oh do you?*
A: *Yeah you only pay going into Wales. You don't pay coming out.*
B: *Oh. Right.*
A: *But er yeah, **anyway**, we drove in the rain and the dark for eight hours.*
(*anyway* functions to signal a return to the main narrative after a digression)

[speaker A is a financial adviser who is advising B and C on borrowing money to buy a house; a *first-time buyer* is a person who has never owned a house before]
A: *You've probably got some burning questions to ask me. 'How much can we borrow and how much is it gonna cost?' Am I right?*
B: *Yes.*
A: *Okay, **so**, if you just tell me a little bit about yourselves. Are you first-time buyers?*
B: *Yeah. We're first-time buyers.*
(*so* marks a transition between the opening part of the discussion and the main business)

Use of discourse markers

In social terms, discourse markers enable the speaker to exercise control in the discourse and they are power-related (e.g. in classrooms, it is usually only the teacher who can exercise such control with utterances such as ***Right**, let's do an exercise*). In this example of a university lecturer teaching, it would be odd and socially inappropriate for any student to use discourse markers in the way the lecturer does. The lecturer's role is to sequence the material coherently and carefully monitor its reception:

[university science lecture]
*We can then have toxic effects. **Right**. These again can be direct. They can be subtle. But they cause lots and lots of injuries. **Right**. Here's an example of one. There's a section of normal liver. **Right**. The thing to notice is that all cells, all the cells look roughly the same. **Right**. So we've got at the top we've got portal triad. At the bottom we've got central vein. **Right**.*

Forms 106b

Discourse markers are a lexical rather than a grammatical category, but their classification in terms of the conventional major word classes (noun, verb, adjective, adverb) is problematic since they stand outside of phrase and clause structures, and they are best considered as a class in their own right.

Phrases as discourse markers

A variety of types of word and phrase commonly function as discourse markers. Most typically, certain words otherwise classed as adverbs and adjectives frequently function as markers (*anyway*, *good*, *well*, *right*) and some (e.g. *right*, *well*) function more frequently as markers than as adjectives or adverbs. Other items can also function as discourse markers, for example phrases (*at the end of the day*, *in other words*), clauses (*you see*, *you know*, *to put it another way*, *look*, *listen*, *there you go*) and miscellaneous other items (*okay*, *cos*, *no*, *now then*, *so*, *yes/yeah*). Many of these are exemplified below.

Clauses as discourse markers

Whole clauses can function as discourse markers. For example, the clause *as I was saying* typically relates one statement to a preceding statement and can be used either to mark backward reference to an earlier stage in the discourse or to resume after an interruption. Similarly, the clause *talking about X* typically marks the linking of a current or earlier topic to a new one introduced by the speaker:

The = sign indicates an utterance which is cut short
[A has been talking about the internet; B interrupts to give back A's change after purchasing drinks with A's money]
A: *Not bad hey. We could do that.*
B: *There's your change.*
A: *Oh cheers. Yeah, the scar=* ***as I was saying****, er,* ***talking about*** *the internet, the scariest thing I've seen on the internet* [laughs] *is Ted's page.*
B: *Oh I've not seen it.*

I mean, *you know* and *you see* can sometimes be used within clauses as subject – verb (s – v) structures, or outside of the clause structure, as discourse markers. When these expressions are inserted parenthetically within a sentence, then their function as discourse markers is clearer:

- Non discourse marking:

S – V	O (clause as object)
I mean	*what I say.*
You know	*that I want to speak about it to him privately first.*
You see	*loads of people at clubs that haven't got good figures wearing short skirts.*

- Discourse marking:

[*5.1* is the name of a version of a computer programme]
A: *She hasn't got 5.1 on her machine but her partner can load it if we can lend her the disks.* ***I mean****, am I at liberty to let these disks go outside the company?*
B: *Erm.*
A: *I don't know how many they're licensed for either?*
B: *Eight.*
(*I mean* as discourse marker, marking the statement following as a rewording or clarification or expansion of the previous one)

The + sign indicates an interrupted turn which continues at the next + sign
[complaining about restaurant prices]
A: *But when you say have a coffee or something or a soft drink it just mounts up actually.*
B: *Mm. Yes. And you see prices going up er say to four ninety nine+*
A: *Mm.*
B: *+or five ninety nine.*
A: *Yeah. Yeah. Yeah.*
B: ***You know** and people don't sort of perceive that er it's really expensive. But when you think about it, **you know**, just the basic dish, four ninety nine or five ninety nine. Five or six pounds.*
A: *Yeah.*
B: *Plus, **you know**, the little bits and pieces.*
A: *Yeah. Yeah.*
(*you know* as discourse marker, marking statements as assumed shared knowledge or uncontroversial or logically linked)

A: *Do you not normally come here for your Delenia products?*
B: *Oh well it varies.*
A: *Right.*
B: *I don't have a set place. **You see** I move around quite a lot with work so I just go wherever I can pop into.*
(*You see* as discourse marker, linking a statement with its explanation)

Grammatical forms of discourse markers

Different grammatical forms can fulfil the same marking function. For example, the following forms can all be used to prepare the listener for a new topic or for a shift in the current focus of the topic:

***Incidentally**, Rita's going to come round tonight.*
(adverb)

***By the way**, Rita's going to come round tonight.*
(prepositional phrase)

***While I think of it**, Rita's going to come round tonight.*
(finite clause)

***Speaking of which**, Rita's going to come round tonight.*
(non-finite clause)

***Listen**, Rita's going to come round tonight.*
(imperative clause)

***Hey**, Rita's going to come round tonight.*
(interjection)

Spoken features of discourse markers

Prosodic information can sometimes help to indicate differences between discourse markers and other parts of speech or clausal functions. For example, if the word or phrase occupies its own tone unit, and if there is a brief silent pause or breath pause after the expression (e.g. *You know* [pause] *she didn't like it*), this usually indicates that the function is that of a discourse marker (→ also **106c**).

Typical functions 106c

Discourse markers not only organise the discourse but can indicate degrees of formality and people's feelings towards the interaction. A selection of discourse markers is indicated in bold in the extracts below and their typical functions are commented on in the tables that follow them.

Informal interactions

The = sign indicates an utterance which is cut short

[end of a sales transaction in a shop; A is the assistant, B is a customer]

A: ***Right*** *that comes to er seventy three eighty six. Thank you.* ***Right*** *I just need you to sign there.*

B: *Thank you.*

A: ***Well*** *the weather's turned up today anyway.*

B: *Mm, it's nice isn't it.*

A: *It's breezy though.*

B: [laughs] *Dick said it's been going on forever. He said it's been raining for about=*

A: *It's been raining, we had a snow blast, we had a snowstorm last weekend there.*

B: *Mm.*

A: *Amazing stuff.*

B: ***Great****. Thanks.*

A: ***Good****. I'll give you a receipt for that.* ***There you go****.*

B: ***Great****. Thanks. Thank you.*

Functions of discourse markers

marker	comment
right (×2)	mark the boundaries between stages of the discourse (between the handing over of money and the signing of the sales invoice)
well	marks a topic shift (to the topic of the weather)
great (×2) and *good*	mark both the conclusion of the transaction and (simultaneously) both parties' mutual satisfaction and informal sociability
there you go	marks the completion of the handing over of goods and receipt in an informal, friendly way

Formal interactions

Such informal markers as occur in the shop transaction may not be appropriate in other social contexts (e.g. transacting a last will and testament with a lawyer, receiving a parking fine from a traffic warden), even though the same organisational functions may be performed.

Discourse markers often indicate power relationships in the ways they are used to structure and control the discourse. In the following extract from a conversation between a university professor and a PhD student, the professor uses discourse markers which indicate his authority in the conversation and his ability to control it (marked in bold). The student does not have the same access to conversational control in this situation. Also, neither of the two speakers uses markers such as *great* or *there you go*, which might project too informal a relationship in this context:

The = sign indicates an utterance which is cut short
The + sign indicates an interrupted turn which continues at the next + sign
[A is a university professor, B is a PhD student]
A: *I told you officially if you're registered for a PhD all along+*
B: *Yeah.*
A: *+then we don't need to worry. I just need to confirm that progress is satisfactory.*
B: *I see. My worry is, is the feeling, my worry is, is whether you like what I'm doing or not. That's my feeling.*
A: ***Ah well*** *if I didn't like it, I would have told you.*
B: *I see.*
A: *Mm. I'm very happy. I wasn't happy a year ago+*
B: *I know.*
A: *+but now I'm happy.*
B: ***So*** *I'm going to apply for another year in=*
A: *Yes.*
B: ***So*** *this is only till the end of June+*
A: ***Good.***
B: *+**so** I hope+*
A: ***Good.***
B: *+you know that by June we can=*
A: ***Well*** *by June I should be able to say that everything is in place. The hypotheses are formulated. Evidence is produced. You know, forty thousand words have been written, which nearly they have.*
B: *Uhuh.*
A: *Erm literature review completed. Er and some analysis completed. And so on. And that the remaining year will be spent putting the finishing and final touches to the thesis because you'll have to submit it in about April next year so that we can examine you in June next year and you can have time to do any corrections that are deemed before going home in August. Or September. Er. That's the way to see it isn't it.* ***Yeah.***
B: *Yeah. Mm.*
A: ***Okay.*** *Er, I must go off to a meeting.*

Functions of discourse markers

marker	comment
ah well	marks a shift to a 'dispreferred' or divergent next utterance: the professor diverges from the student's line of argument
so (×3)	mark conclusions reached by the student
good (×2)	mark the professor's satisfaction with the direction of the discussion
well	marks the professor interrupting or pre-empting the student's conclusion in order to present his own conclusion
yeah	marks the professor's assumption that the student will concur with his view of the situation
okay	marks the professor's desire (and power) to end the conversation

COMMON SPOKEN DISCOURSE MARKERS 107

The most frequent discourse markers in spoken English are the single-word items *anyway*, *cos*, *fine*, *good*, *great*, *like*, *now*, *oh*, *okay*, *right*, *so*, *well*.

Some discourse markers (e.g. *oh*, *mind you*, *right*, *you know*) are restricted to spoken English or to written reports of speech or written texts imitating a spoken style. Others, such as *well*, may occasionally occur in informal writing but are otherwise exclusive to spoken English.

Discourse markers occur in writing, and some types of marker for organising written texts are very rare in everyday speech (e.g. *the end*, *section 3*, *introduction*, *in sum*, *thirdly*). In this chapter we focus only on those markers which are common in speech.

DISCOURSE MARKERS: ORGANISING THE DISCOURSE 108

Opening up and closing down 108a

Openings

Openings and closings are opportunities for speakers to manage the discourse in terms of launching and concluding topics, opening, concluding or temporarily closing a whole conversation, re-opening previously closed or interrupted conversations. Some of the most common and frequent markers function to facilitate openings and closings of these kinds, for example, *so*, *(all) right*, *right then*, *now*, *good*, *well*, *okay*, *anyway*, *fine*:

[opening an academic discussion]
Right*, I suppose we should begin by considering the tricky question of the Norman invasion.*

[two friends in a café; small talk about different types of coffee]
A: *Have you ever tried the different coffees?*
B: *No.*
A: *No. I haven't either.*
B: *Flavoured coffees?*
A: *Yeah. Er well even the ones that they have here.*
B: *You know I wouldn't know the difference I don't think.*
A: *I don't know if I would either. No. I thought you know the way you just you know you ask for coffee and they just give you something.*
B: *Yeah. No. I've never tried them.*
[Pause]
A: ***So*** *how's Laura getting on?*
B: *I think she's just looking forward to coming home.*
(pause, then *So* marking the opening of the speaker's main topic: Laura)

In more formal speech, *now* can occur to mark the opening of a phase of talk or of a new topic, or to mark a rhetorical shift of some sort from one important aspect of a topic to another almost like paragraph changes in written texts:

[beginning of a university lecture in medicine]
***Now**, can you all hear? Er if it is too loud do let me know. Erm two weeks ago I had a patient who had difficulty swallowing. I operated on her six years ago because she had a nasty cancer of the stomach. We'd done quite a big operation and she's done remarkably well. But now she came back unable to swallow. **Now**, we did lots of tests on her and it's pretty obvious she'd got a cancer back again. Very near where the previous one was. Right in the middle there* [points to diagram]. ***Now**, what do you do? She's quite elderly. Er her life was becoming a misery.*

Closings

Pre-closings and closings can also be facilitated by the use of discourse markers. These typically involve *(all) right*, *so*, *anyway*, *okay*, *well* and, particularly at the pre-closings of service encounters, *fine*, *lovely*, *good*, *great*:

[on the telephone]
***So**, I thought I'd better just ring and check.* [other speaker speaks] *I see. **Right**. **Anyway**, I'd better go, cos I'm actually ringing from the medical room.*
(signals of pre-closing)

[conclusion of a discussion concerning a printing job]
A: *And then we actually want overheads, not just colour copies.*
B: *Yeah.*
A: *Six sets.*
B: *Six sets of each.*
A: ***Fine**.*
B: ***Fine**.*
A: ***Right**. I'll see you tomorrow.*
B: ***Okay**.*
A: ***Okay**. **Lovely**.*
B: *Yeah.*
A: *Thanks Jim.*
B: *Bye.*
A: *Bye.*

The = sign indicates an utterance which is cut short
A: *Haven't I missed something? A car went out of control or something? Wendy went i= I don't know. My daughter went into the Post Office and they were all discussing it. A car had gone out of control I think. **Oh well**.*
B: *Er **anyway** I'd better get back.*
A: ***Anyway** see you later.*
B: *Bye.*
A: *Bye.*
B: *Ta ta.*

539 **Glossary** for any unfamiliar terms

The + sign indicates an interrupted turn which continues at the next + sign
A: ***Well** I'd better go and finish this lunch+*
B: ***Okay then.***
A: *+cos we're rather hungry.*
B: *Yeah.*
A: *And Paul is waiting by the door.*
B: *Oh I see. **Right.***
A: ***Okay.***
B: ***Okay then.** See you later.*
A: *Bye bye.*
B: *Cheers. Bye.*

Sequencing 108b

Relationships of sequence can be signalled by discourse markers. Such markers indicate explicitly the order in which things occur or how different segments of a discourse are being organised. They also mark how one thing leads to or leads back to another. Among the words and phrases which mainly signal such relationships in spoken language are:

and
and then
finally
first (of all)
firstly (more formal than *first*)
for a start
going back to
in general
in the end
in the first place
last of all
lastly
next
on top of that
second
secondly (more formal than *second*)
so
there again
third(ly)
to sum up
what's more

[enquiring about flights at a travel agent's]
A: *Erm I was wondering if you could give me some information about flights to Spain please.*
B: *Whereabouts in Spain?*
A: *Erm well **first of all** do you know if er Bilbao is the closest airport to San Sebastian?*
B: *I think it is actually, off the top of my head, cos er, there's not many that we do up in the north at all. I know you can get a flight there from Luton.*
A: *Right.*
B: *Right.*
A: *All right. Erm er er er I'd like to go to … from London to Bilbao on Sunday the third of May.*
B: *Yeah.*
(*first of all* marks that the question must be dealt with before the customer can state the desired booking)

[talking about problems connected with giving money to charities]
You know you give them money and you're trying to be nice and kind but it doesn't work out like that. Because ***for a start*** *half the money that goes over there, there's some eaten up in administration costs. That's not charity is it. That's paying people to supposedly help others.*
(*for a start* suggests this is the first and probably most important of a number of points)

[university lecturer discussing forces that can operate negatively on the human body; he has just been discussing pressure, in connection with deep-sea diving]
I've only seen it once when somebody came up like that and er your lungs are actually dropping out of your mouth. So it's quite a serious diving injury. ***Next*** *we have radiant energy. Right. You're all familiar with sunburn which is an example of radiant energy. Right.*

[tutor commenting on a student's essay; several points have already been made]
Finally*, the argument needs supporting with more evidence concerning the tactics adopted by the Spanish invaders.*

Speakers often use the letters of the alphabet, A and B (and occasionally extending to C, but not beyond), to sequence points or arguments:

[recounting a negative experience of making a complaint at a clinic]
A: *Yes I mean really they wanted me out of the way so they could get on* ***A*** *with the clinic that was really going on which was a totally different clinic.*
B: *I see.*
A: *And* ***B*** *get me out of the way before anybody else arrived and complained as well.*

The marker *going back to X* enables speakers to jump back to a topic that was talked about earlier. It is often preceded by *but*:

The = sign indicates an utterance which is cut short
The + sign indicates an interrupted turn which continues at the next + sign
[speakers were talking about the writer, Faulkner; now they are discussing the writer, Chandler, author of *The Big Sleep*]
A: *The Big Sleep was 1946.*
B: *Yeah. I think he worked on that.*
A: *I think it was yeah.*
B: *And it= Basically it also distracted from work he was doing on his novels. He didn't have time. There was a big sort of hiatus between forty two and forty eight where he did no+*
A: *Yeah.*
B: *+he did completely no work on his novels. So.*
A: *Right.*
B: *Yeah.*
A: ***But*** *erm* ***going back to*** *Faulkner I I mean I'm I don't know much about him. When did he actually die or where? Or=*
B: *Sixty two. Erm he went to a sanatorium.*

→ also **123–139 Grammar across turns and sentences** for more detailed treatment of such items with particular reference to written text

Topics: marking boundaries and linking segments 108c

One of the main functions of discourse markers in spoken language is to mark topic boundaries, indicating the beginning or end of a topic or a transition from one topic or bit of business to another:

[answerphone message]
Hiya. It's Nora. Erm I think you probably rang me earlier this evening. Erm if you haven't gone to bed, you can ring me back. ***Okay*** *bye bye.*
(marking the boundary between the message and the goodbye)

A: *And how's Ricky, your boyfriend?*
B: *He's fine. Yeah.*
A: *That's good.* ***So*** *what are you doing at the weekend? Anything?*
B: *Er Ricky's, he's working.*
(marking the boundary between asking about the boyfriend and introducing the new topic: the weekend)

Another main purpose of discourse markers is to signal coherent links between one part of a topic and the next part. Discourse markers help speakers to negotiate their way through talk, checking whether they share a common view of the topic and of the nature of the unfolding discourse with their listener:

The = sign indicates an utterance which is cut short
The + sign indicates an interrupted turn which continues at the next + sign
[speaker A resumes a phone call after an interruption by another caller]
A: *Hi. Sorry about that mad woman on the line.* [laughs] *Erm what's erm=* ***Oh yeah*** *er do you have a contact number for Amanda Short+*
B: *Yeah.*
A: *+erm* ***cos*** *I'm trying to firm up delivery dates and I think everyone's on schedule for a first of April delivery, which is brilliant.*
B: *Yeah.*
A: ***And*** *erm she's the only one that I haven't heard from so+*
B: ***Right.***
(*oh yeah* marks a link between the interrupted topic and its resumption; *cos* marks the reason/justification/explanation for asking the question, rather than acting as a causal subordinator; *and* marks the continuation of the explanation; *right* marks the listener's satisfactory reception of the message)

 17 ***Anyway***; 58 ***Okay/OK***; 69 ***Right, rightly***; 71 ***So***

Topics: focusing attention, diverting, shifting, resuming 108d

Focusing attention

Attention or focus can be directed to a topic or to a phase of the talk by a number of discourse markers. Common examples are *now*, *hey*, *ah*, *oh* and imperative verb forms (*look*, *listen*, *just think*, *remember*). The main function is to focus the attention of the listener on what the speaker feels is important:

Hey*, I wanted to ask you something. What was it?*

Listen*, we've been talking about this for ages. We need a decision.*

[discussing earrings which speaker B wants speaker A to wear at B's wedding]
A: *No. I don't like them.*
B: *You're going to wear them.*
A: *No I'm not.*
B: *Yes you are.*
A: *Sam please.*
B: ***Look** it's our wedding.*
A: ***Look.*** [sighs] *Please will you just humour me? I've had a terrible day.*
B: *Oh. And I haven't?*
A: *Do you know what time I had to get up this morning? Six o'clock.*

Diverting

Oh often indicates that the speaker is about to create an unexpected diversion in the conversation:

The + sign indicates an interrupted turn which continues at the next + sign
A: *So you get the prestige of working for the University of Bristol with living in the country in a nice big open environment which is+*
B: *Yeah.*
A: *+more appealing when you're a bit older isn't it?*
B: *Suppose so.*
A: *That's my theory anyway.*
B: *Never really thought about it like that.* ***Oh*** *I forgot. Your washing's up there. Sorry just noticed it.*
A: *Oh you've not even put it out or anything.*
B: *Sorry, I forgot about it.*

The = sign indicates an utterance which is cut short
A: *Anyway he's not that much younger. I mean he's older than Mark and Mike. But erm he's erm=*
B: ***Oh*** *what's Mark's other name?*
A: *Hubbard.*
B: *Hubbard.*

 **57 *Oh***

Shifting

Well most typically signals a shift in the projected or expected direction of the discourse, or a response which might not have been anticipated by the speaker:

A: *Did you enjoy the film?*
B: ***Well,*** *we enjoyed the first half but after that I'm not sure.*
(*yes-no* question, but B feels the question cannot be answered by just *yes* or *no*)

A: *What do we do about the traffic?*
B: ***Well,*** *how about leaving earlier so we miss the worst of it?*
(against the anticipation that the question represented a serious problem)

Resuming

So and *anyway*, often accompanied by expressions such as *where was I?*, *where were we?*, *what was I saying?* or *oh yes/yeah*, can be used to resume an interrupted or diverted topic:

The = sign indicates an utterance which is cut short

[in the middle of telling a story]

A: *She says 'Oh darling do wear something nice.' You know. 'Mark Darcy will be here.' And she turns up and she's wearing something hideous and they've told him that she's very bookie. That she's a secretary to a publisher or something like that.*

B: *Bookie?*

A: *Bookie.*

B: *What's that?*

A: *Likes books.*

B: *Oh right. Oh.*

A: ***Anyway** erm. Where was I?*

B: *Mm. You were erm=*

A: ***Oh yeah**. She goes to this Christmas party and he's been told to talk to her about books because she's a secretary or something.*

(resuming the story after a diversion to explain the unusual use of the word *bookie*)

[interrupted anecdote]

A: *Is that your writing?*

B: *No. Don't know why that's there. Cos I put that on. But I lent it to this= Do you know that girl I hate, can't remember her name, whatever.* ***So** what was I saying?*

A: *That annoying one, Joan.*

B: *Yeah.* ***So** he went to this thing and presented all these proposals that he'd got.*

(resuming the main topic after trying to remember someone's name)

MONITORING THE DISCOURSE 109

Reformulations 109a

Some discourse markers enable speakers to monitor and manage the ongoing discourse by commenting explicitly on the process of talking itself.

Discourse markers can signal reformulations or alternative expressions, indicating that the speaker has not selected the most appropriate way of expressing things and is adding to or refining what they say with a more apt word or phrase. Among such markers are:

as I was saying	*if you like*	*in other words*
as it were	*in a manner of speaking*	*not to say*
I mean		*or rather*

so to speak	*that's to say*	*to put it bluntly/ mildly*
strictly speaking	*to put it another way*	*well*

Jim was exhausted and dehydrated. ***To put it another way****, he was completely knackered.*

He's been too easy-going, ***not to say*** *careless and stupid, walking across that mountain at nightfall and on his own too.*

The hotel simply hasn't done its job properly. ***In other words****, we're very unhappy and we'd like a refund.*

The cottage is in a small town, ***well****, a small industrial town, if you like.*

Monitoring shared knowledge 109b

Two of the most common discourse markers are *you know* and *(you) see*. Both these markers signal that speakers are sensitive to the needs of their listeners and are monitoring the state of shared knowledge in the conversation.

(You) see projects the assumption that the listener may not have the same state of knowledge as the speaker:

You see*, since I've damaged my back in that fall, I find it difficult to climb the stairs without help.*
(speaker cannot assume the listener knows this)

You do it like this. Cut the branches right back, ***see****, then cut them into smaller pieces.*

You know projects the assumption that knowledge is shared or that assertions are uncontroversial, and reinforces common points of reference, or checks that the listener is following what is being said:

If you got the earliest train in the morning and then, ***you know****, like, got the last train back at night, it might be cheaper that way.*

DISCOURSE MARKING IN RESPONSES 110

Discourse markers are an important resource for listeners to indicate their involvement with what is being said and to manage their own responses.

(All) right can be used to indicate positive responses and to signal agreement to a proposed action:

A: *I think we should go to the garden centre first.*
B: ***Right****, that's fine by me.*

Response tokens such as *(all) right, I see, good, great, fine* and *okay* show that the listener is receiving the message and is at the same time channelling back support

→ **539 Glossary** for any unfamiliar terms

for what the speaker is saying. The response token can simultaneously signal boundaries in the discourse and send back signals of sociability. Such markers are a sign of active and cooperative listening:

A: *So first of all, we have to meet Kulvinder cos she's got the car.*
B: *I see.*
A: *Then we'll pick up Sue.*
B: ***Right.***
A: *So we'll come round to your place around seven.*
B: ***Okay, I see, right**, thanks a lot.*

↠ also **95, Response tokens**

A–Z **69 *Right, rightly***

STANCE MARKERS 111

A number of common expressions mark the speaker's stance or attitude towards the message. Among the expressions which most frequently signal stances, attitudes and points of view towards segments of discourse are:

actually
admittedly
amazingly
basically
certainly
clearly
confidentially
doubtless
essentially
frankly
to be frank
fortunately
honestly
to be honest
hopefully
ideally
if you ask me
I'm afraid
I must admit
I must say
I think
in fact
indeed
literally
naturally
no doubt
obviously
of course
predictably
putting (or *to put*) *it mildly/bluntly*
(quite) rightly
really
sadly
seriously
(I'm) sorry
strictly speaking
surprisingly
thankfully
to tell you the truth
understandably
undoubtedly
unfortunately

*The team are doing badly and, **quite frankly**, I think he should be replaced by someone who knows what he's doing.*

*I'll have to call you back, **I'm afraid**. Okay?*

[explaining to someone how to use dial-up internet on a home computer]

A: *So now* ***obviously*** *when you're on the internet, if someone tries to phone you, they'll just get an engaged tone.*

B: *Right.*

A: *Okay. But if you wanna use the telephone you just log off. Pick up the telephone and dial. And that's it.*

B: *Okay. So* ***basically*** *if I'm on the internet for an hour or something, people can't phone in for an hour.*

A: *Yeah.*

B: *Okay.*

A: *That's just something you get used to.*

The = sign indicates an utterance which is cut short

[at a travel agent's; A is the assistant]

A: *Is it okay to send the information to your mother? I mean it's not a surprise holiday or anything?*

B: *Oh, well* ***to be honest actually*** *she doesn't know that I'm making these arrangements.*

A: *Oh lovely.*

B : *So it would* ***actually*** *be better if it was=*

A: *So if you could give me your postcode.*

B: *Oh, it's the same* ***actually****.*

A: *It is?*

B: *Yeah.*

 9 ***Actual, actually***; 46 ***In fact***; 52 ***Mean***; 68 ***Really***

HEDGES 112

Speakers are often careful not to sound too blunt and assertive, and a variety of markers exist to hedge (i.e. to express degrees of assertiveness). A range of expressions are used in everyday spoken language to downtone the assertiveness of a segment of discourse. These include:

apparently	*kind of*	*probably*
arguably	*like*	*roughly*
by any chance	*maybe*	*sort of*
I think	*perhaps*	*surely*
just (about)	*presumably*	

A: *I just turned round to her and said 'Let me use your phone.' It wasn't aggressive. I wasn't violent.*

B: *Well* ***apparently*** *you snatched the phone off the lady.*

A: *No I didn't.*

[talking about spring flowers in speaker A's garden]
A: *Angela planted them. There's crocuses around the base of the trees but they're* ***just about*** *gone* ***I think.***
B: *Oh right. Yeah. Cos it's been very mild hasn't it.*
A: *It's been very mild.*
B: *Yeah.*
A: *We had snowdrops but the frost* ***kind of*** *killed them* ***I think.***

A: *It's warm in here isn't it.*
B: *It is warm in here now. Yeah.*
A: *Turn the radiator down a little bit* ***perhaps.***
B: *Yeah.*

I mean ***roughly*** *it's going to cost about another thousand pounds.*

⇢ also **103a Vague language**

47 *Just*; 49 *Like*

INTERJECTIONS 113

The term interjection normally refers to exclamative utterances consisting of single words that do not easily fit into the major word classes (noun, verb, adjective, adverb) such as: *bother, crikey, damn, god, goodness (me), gosh, (good) heavens, hooray, jeez, ooh, oh no, oops, ouch, ow, ugh, tut-tut, whoops, wow, yippee, yuk.*

All these items express positive or negative emotional reactions to what is being or has just been said or to something in the situation. Interjections are especially common in spoken language and rare in writing except in written representations of speech:

A: *You know Hilary? She got married last week.*
B: ***Gosh!*** *That's quick. How long has she known him?*
(expresses surprise; *Crikey/wow* are alternatives here)

Ouch, *that hurt.*
(expresses a reaction to pain)

Oops, *I shouldn't have said that, should I?*
(expresses a reaction to having unintentionally done something inappropriate)

A: *The bus has already gone.*
B: ***Damn.*** *Now I'm going to have to walk home.*
(expresses irritation at bad luck or inconvenience)

Ugh, *I can't eat any more of this.*
(expresses a negative reaction to unpleasant sensations)

They're here at last. ***Yippee!***
(expresses excitement)

A: *Come and look at the sunset.*
B: [goes to the window] ***Wow**, yeah, fantastic.*
(expresses strong surprise or a reaction of awe and wonder)

***Tut-tut**. That's the second time this week you've forgotten my coffee.*
(expresses disapproval, often in a mock-humorous way)

Other items include:

phew (expresses relief)

hooray (indicates delight at a particular outcome)

aargh (indicates general displeasure or unhappiness)

urgh (expresses a strong negative reaction of displeasure)

poo (reaction to an unpleasant smell)

yuk (reaction to something unpleasant, e.g. a taste)

ooo (reaction of pleasure or delight)

SWEARING AND TABOO EXPRESSIONS 114

General 114a

Swearing and the general use of taboo words is increasingly heard in spoken English both in private and in public settings (including radio, TV and films). Although there are some forms of swearing that are less offensive than others, most features of swearing involve taboo words. Learners of English should exercise great care concerning such usages.

The use of taboo words and phrases projects either a close, intimate relationship with the person or group to whom they are addressed (so that one feels free to use taboo words) or else a threatening and hostile relationship. In such contexts it is difficult for learners of a language to know the precise strength of such expressions.

Most taboo words and phrases in English exist under two main headings of religion and parts of the body and bodily processes, especially those associated with either sexual activity or with using the toilet. The most common taboo expressions in this category involve the words *fuck* (to have sexual intercourse – the word is used as a noun and verb forms) and *shit* (bodily excrement – the word is used as a noun and a verb).

A good dictionary will cover the main meanings of these and similar words; this section pays particular attention to grammatical patterns. A rough guide is also given here concerning the relative strength of swearing expressions. A very strong expression, which is likely to be shocking or threatening in most non-intimate situations, is given five stars (*****); a less strong expression, likely to cause little or no offence, is given only one star (*).

In general, swearing which involves 'religious' taboo expressions is likely to be weaker than swearing that involves 'parts of the body' taboo expressions, although people with strong religious views may be offended by both. Learners are advised against using such expressions, although, especially in informal contexts and in films and on TV, etc., it is likely that such uses of language will be heard.

Swearing often takes the form of interjections (→ 113). This can involve single words or short phrases or clauses that are used to express a variety of strong feelings, in particular, annoyance, frustration and anger:

__Damn__! That's the third time this week the car has broken down. (*)

__Christ__! Why didn't you tell me? I could have stopped them!! (**)

__Shit__! I shouldn't have used that kind of nail. I've broken the lock. (****)

Oh __fuck it__! I can't find the address. (*****)

__Christ almighty__! They've actually won their first match. (**)

Well, __I'll be buggered__! How did you manage to find that? (****)

__Fuck me__! That's not what she told me. How can that possibly be true? (*****)

Wh-exclamatives with taboo words are also sometimes used:

__What the hell__ are you doing letting that dog out without a lead on! (*)

__What the fuck__ have I done with my glasses! (*****)

[said in response to the phone ringing very late in the evening]
__Who the fuck__ is that! (*****)

Taboo naming expressions 114b

Taboo naming expressions are commonly used to insult another person. Sometimes the insult is serious and sometimes it can be playful and affectionate. Only the immediate context of the use of the expression will indicate which meaning is intended. Insulting by swearing is particularly common with vocatives (→ 116):

__Lucky bastard__! How did you manage to get the day off? (***)

Come here, you daft __prick__. (***)

Ruth, __you bitch__! Why did you tell her? Can't you keep a secret? (***)

Taboo naming words such as *arsehole, bastard, bugger, bitch, cow, get/git, prick, tit, twat/twot*, are preceded by *you* when addressed directly at the listener, while *the* is most commonly used to refer to third parties:

I hope it's your hormones, __you stupid cow__. (***)

I always give him money, and then when I ask him, he never gives it, __the bastard__. (***)

I mean when he doesn't sort of trust his own kids sort of thing. Do you know what I mean? I mean he might be disappointed in me sometimes but I still love __the old bugger__. And there's no two ways about that really, is there. He's always dad. (***)

You and *the* are sometimes ellipted, since the referent is usually obvious:

> *Get up, **lazy cow**! (***)*
> (Get up, (you) lazy cow.)

> *I lent the key to Dave. **Daft bastard** lost it. (***)*
> ((The) daft bastard lost it.)

Taboo intensifiers 114c

Taboo expressions are frequently used as intensifying adverbs or adjectives. The words *bloody* and *fucking* are especially common in this function. When these are used as adverbs, post-intensifier *well* is often used for further emphasis:

> *Where's the **bloody** key? (*)*

> *That's **fucking** marvellous, that is, isn't it? It's **fucking-well** snowing again. (*****)*

Unlike *shit*, *fuck* and *bugger*, *bloody* is not used on its own as an interjection. *Bloody hell!* is the usual interjection form:

> *Oh **fuck**! I forgot to post that letter. (*****)*
> (or: Oh shit/bugger! But not: ~~Oh bloody!~~)

> A: *Do you know how much they're going to cost? Hundred thousand pound.*
> B: ***Bloody hell!** Crazy isn't it? (**)*

GREETINGS AND FAREWELLS 115

Greetings usually involve an exchange of the same or very similar words and expressions. Different expressions mark different levels of formality. In general, the briefer the structure, the more informal the greeting or farewell is:

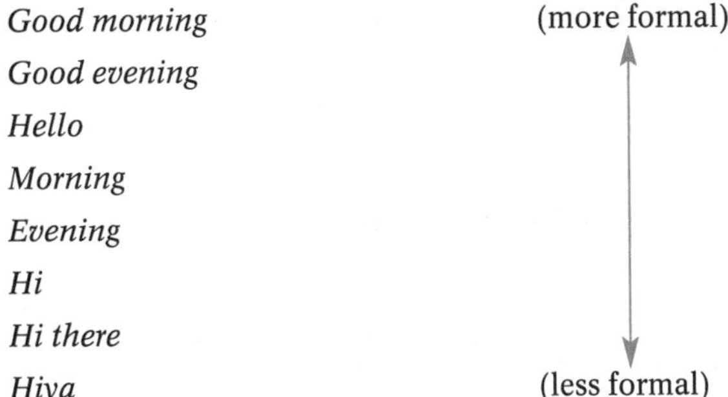

Note that *good evening* but not *goodnight* may be used as a greeting. *Goodnight* is used either when leaving someone in the late evening or night, or just before going to bed or to sleep for the night:

> [B has just arrived at A's house]
> A: *Hello Terry.*
> B: ***Good evening.***
> (not: ~~Goodnight.~~)

539 **Glossary** for any unfamiliar terms

When leaving people, the same conventions regarding formality apply as when meeting and greeting people:

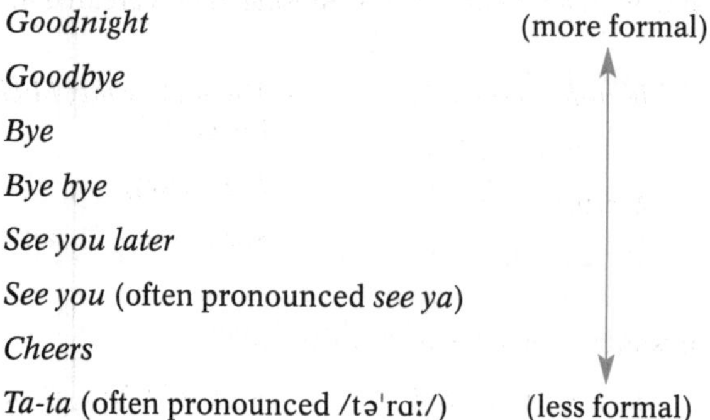

VOCATIVES 116

Unlike many other languages, English does not have ways of addressing people formally or informally by means of different pronouns or other grammatical devices. In English, the relative formality of terms of address is managed by means of vocatives, i.e. the use of the addressee's name (*Jane*, *Mr Lambert*) or a term of kinship (*mum*, *grandad*) or endearment (*darling*, *love*).

Vocatives occur frequently in spoken English. They occur in written English but in more restricted contexts such as salutations in letters (*Dear X*) or in direct-speech reports. In spoken English they are more closely connected with social intimacy and distance in interpersonal relationships and with the marking of discourse boundaries (they occur frequently at topic boundaries, → 118e).

English also does not have any standard polite way of addressing strangers. For example, in British English it is very difficult to know how to attract the attention of a stranger in the street who may have dropped something. *Sir! Madam!* are not commonly used in this situation, and *hello*, *sorry* or *excuse me* are most likely to be used to attract attention.

TYPES OF VOCATIVE 117

Names and titles 117a

Vocatives include various forms of people's names and titles:

People's names and titles

form	example
full first name	***Laura**, have you got a minute?*
abbreviated first name	*Can you give me a hand, **Pete**.* (Peter)
nickname	*Hi, **Red**. How are you?* (to a red-haired man)
title plus family name	***Mr Roberts**, could I have a word with you?*
title alone	*Thank you, **doctor**.*

Abbreviating first names

First names can be familiarised by abbreviating the name (often to a single syllable) or by ending the name with an *-ie* or *-y* form. Among names created in this way are:

Anthony (Tony)
Antonia (Toni)
Devinder (Dev)
James (Jamie)
Jennifer (Jenny, Jen)
Judith (Jude, Judy)
Matthew (Matt, Matty)
Michael (Mike, Mick, Mickey)
Rajiv (Raj)
Susan (Sue, Susie)

The following abbreviated or 'short' forms are less transparent:

Catherine (Kate, Katie, Kit, Kitty)
Deborah (Debbie, Debs)
Dorothy (Dolly, Dot)
Edward (Ted, Teddie)
Elizabeth (Betty, Liz)
Geraldine (Gel)
Julie (Jules)
Richard (Dick, Rick, Ricky)
Robert (Bob, Bobby)
Terence (Terry, Tel)

Degrees of formality

Using full, unabbreviated first names is more formal than using abbreviated forms. Using full family names and family names with titles is more formal still, indicating a greater social distance between speakers:

*Now, **Jennifer**, you've passed the test. So well done … but we'd like you to do just one part again.*

*May I introduce you? **Professor Jackson**, this is Martine, our new secretary.*

***Doctor Jones**, there's a telephone call for you on line 3.*

Family-name-only vocative is rarely used among adults in British English, except in strict institutional contexts, and generally only by a senior person addressing a junior person (e.g. teacher to school student, army officer to subordinate, employer to servant).

The use of the academic titles *doctor* or *professor* as vocatives is not normal without the family name of the individual:

***Professor** Smith, could I give you my essay?*
(~~Professor, could I give you my essay?~~)

Doctor can be used as a vocative without the family name only to a medical doctor:

*Do you think it's serious, **doctor**?*

Some other titles of rank and profession can be used alone:

[radio interviewer interviewing a military general]
*Now **general**, you have considerable experience of guerrilla warfare.*

[addressing a Roman Catholic priest]
***Father**, can I buy a ticket for the charity dinner?*

Terms of kinship and endearment 117b

Family terms include *mother* (usually formal), *mum*, *mam*, *mummy* (to refer to a mother), *father* (usually formal), *dad*, *daddy*, *pappa* (to refer to a father), *pops*, *granpa*, *granpy*, *gramps* (to refer to a grandfather), *gran*, *granma*, *nana*, *nan* (to refer to a grandmother), *bruv* (a brother), *sis* (a sister), *cuz* (a cousin). Such vocatives indicate degrees of intimacy and closeness between speakers:

*I'll tell you what, **mum**, you're going to be a bit cross about it.*

*You can lend me five pounds, can't you **sis**?*

Terms of endearment include: *darling*, *dear*, *poppet* (usually to a little child), *love*, *luvvie*, *sweetheart*. They may combine with names:

*Can you put the coffee on, **sweetheart**?*

***Mike**, **love**, could you take this out to the back yard for me. Ta.*

General plural vocatives 117c

General plural vocatives (e.g. *folks*, *everyone/everybody*, *children*, *boys*, *lads*, *girls*, *guys*, *ladies*, *gentlemen*) are used to address groups:

*What are you planning to do tonight, **folks**?*

***Children**, could you all pay attention please.*

[announcement at a conference lecture]
***Everybody**, could you all hand in your evaluations as you leave, please.*

Impersonal vocatives 117d

Someone/somebody can be used as an impersonal vocative to summon any one of a known group of people:

*Answer the door, **someone**! I'm in the bathroom.*

Honorifics 117e

Honorifics such as *sir* or *madam* are respectful and deferential. They most commonly occur in service encounters. *Sir* and *miss* are generally used to address male and female school teachers (but not teachers in higher education):

[in a shop]
*What can I get you, **madam**?*

[in a school classroom, to the teacher]
***Sir**, he won't let me finish the experiment.*

Sir and *madam* are rare as vocatives in British English outside of service situations. Male strangers may be addressed as *mate*, but this does project a high degree of informality and should be used with care:

*Excuse me, **mate**, do you know where Parton Street is?*

There is no equivalent accepted term for addressing a female stranger, though *love* (often written as *luv*) is sometimes used in this way. However, many women object to this use of *love* or *(my) dear* as patronising or sexist.

Calling people by the name of their occupation is less common and depends on the social status of the occupation. Some which do occur include *doctor* (medical), *driver*, *nurse*, *minister*, *officer*, *waiter*:

[passenger to bus driver]
*Can you let me off here please, **driver**.*

[radio interview with a government minister]
*Now, **minister**, how would you explain this to the electorate?*

*Excuse me, **waiter**, sorry, could we have some more water, please?*

DISCOURSE FUNCTIONS OF VOCATIVES 118

Summons 118a

Vocatives are used to call or summon a person:

***Sue**! Your cup of tea is poured.*

Turn management 118b

Vocatives function in the management of speaker turns, although this is not an especially common function in face-to-face spoken discourse. They are used to identify an addressee, to nominate a next speaker or to soften an interruption:

A: *I should have some change.*
B: *I owe you too don't I, **Jodie**.*
C: *Yes you do.*

The = sign indicates an utterance which is cut short
The + sign indicates an interrupted turn which continues at the next + sign
[speakers are looking at a document about the rules of credit unions]
A: *Whereas the the bank er the credit union made provision with disclosure may be able to enter into contracts with= In other words if the bank want to see the= to find out where money+*
B: *Hang on **Geoff**. I've not got a seventy six two now.*
C: *Yeah.*
B: *Is that what you're up against?*
A: *Yeah. It says that any member= any person can erm any er er member+*
B: *Any member or any persons having an interest in the funds.*

Vocatives occur frequently in radio phone-ins and similar non-face-to-face contexts. The vocative is used for managing the talk – that is bringing callers in, controlling their talk and dismissing them when their contribution is deemed to be sufficient:

A: *Welcome back to the programme. **Alistair**, thanks for your call. Enjoyed talking to you. Now it's Jack on line 2. Hi, **Jack**? Good afternoon to you. Hello there.*
B: *Hello.*
A: *Hi how are you?*

Ritual and sociable contexts 118c

Vocatives often occur ritualistically, for example, to identify participants when food is being served, even though it may be obvious from gaze and body orientation who is being addressed. In such contexts vocatives can occur alone as a single turn:

[a hostess is offering and serving food at a dinner table]
A: *Bits of everything here. **Richard**?*
B: *No thank you.*
A: *No? **Pauline**?*
C: *Fine thank you.*
A: ***Kevin**?*
D: *No. I'm full.*

Vocatives also often occur in contexts where the purpose is purely sociable and where no real information is exchanged (phatic contexts), e.g. greetings, *how-are-you*'s, remarks about the weather:

The = sign indicates an utterance which is cut short
The + sign indicates an interrupted turn which continues at the next + sign
[two colleagues, A and B, are talking informally about vocational courses they may be allowed to go on and C enters in the middle of the conversation; *hiya* and *hey* are very informal alternatives to *hello*]
A: *I mean it's obviously been passed okay by Pat Cromwell and ultimately that's the person who's making the decisions+*
B: *Mm.*
A: *+as to who goes on it as far as I'm concerned. And=*
C: *Hiya **Lynn**.*
B: *Hey **Pat**.*
A: *Hiya **Pat**. Erm.*
B: *So that's=*
A: *that's the+*
B: *Yeah.*
A: *+decision out of my hands.*

Softening and lessening threats to dignity 118d

Vocatives are commonly used to mitigate a threat to the listener's dignity or to soften an utterance. A vocative is not normally threatening and indicates solidarity and membership of a group:

[group of female young friends discussing eating and weight problems]
A: *You're not fat **Jane**.*
B: *I will be if I'm not careful.*

Vocatives can soften utterances which may possibly threaten, challenge or offend another speaker. In these functions the vocative typically occurs at or near the front of an utterance or in a mid position:

A: *So she's gonna try and go into school. But she's got an arrangement that she'll come for er er if she can't manage next week.*
B: *But **Sally**, she's old to be teaching.*

*I'm sorry to have to tell you, **Daria**, that you haven't been successful.*

Vocatives are also used to make requests more indirect and to lessen the imposition:

A: *Will you put on the fish, **Nancy**, so that it'll heat, the fish now.*
B: *Oh yeah.*

Topic management 118e

Vocatives also function similarly to some discourse markers (··❯ 106). They mark the way in which a topic is managed between speakers in so far as they occur at boundaries where topics are launched, expanded, shifted, changed or closed. As part of the management of a topic, speakers may name another conversational participant in order to validate or confirm an assertion:

The + sign indicates an interrupted turn which continues at the next + sign
[the speakers are discussing A's deceased mother; a *Geordie* accent is the accent associated with the area of Newcastle in north-east England]
A: *And she said when she came down here to Bristol she er she had a Geordie accent and all the kids used to+*
B: *Well she would have.*
A: *+make fun of her.*
B: *She would have.*
A: *Yeah.*
B: *Of course.*
A: *Where were you born then, **Mary**?*
B: *In Bristol.*
A: *You're a Bristol girl.*
B: *Yeah.*
(Mary is already the addressee; the vocative coincides with a topic shift)

A: *It was the right place, was it?*
B: *Yes. The right place. Yeah. Yeah.*
C: *They were horrible.*
D: *Do you know the people,* ***dad****?*
C: *Yeah.*

In the above examples the vocatives do not simply identify the addressees. A shift of conversational topic or an encouragement to continue and expand a topic is indicated. In both the above extracts the vocative occupies end position. In the following extract it occurs close to the topical information that needs to be confirmed. In this example A calls on his wife, B, to confirm certain information:

[speakers are discussing a well-known family of traditional Irish musicians]
A: *Er we we were in er Cork weren't we,* ***Barbara****, and we heard his brother. Which brother was it we heard?*
B: *Er, Sean, I think.*

Joking, banter 118f

The vocative frequently co-occurs with light-hearted joking talk and supports the friendship and intimacy normal on such occasions:

[three female students share a house; one has a new kitchen whisk]
A: *Seen my new whisk?*
B: *Oo.*
C: *Oo.*
A: *Nice, isn't it?*
B: *Is that to make your omelettes with?*
C: *Very domesticated,* ***Tracy****.*

The = sign indicates an utterance which is cut short
A: *Are you not studying today or whatever?*
B: *I don't know.*
C: *No. I mean we study yeah. We study ghost stories.*
D: *Yeah.* [laughs] *We study how to frighten ourselves.*
A: *Social hi= social history is it?*
D: *I'll tell you something,* ***mum****. Social scary. Social scary.*
B: *Social mystery. Not social history. Social mystery.*

In such instances vocatives are commonly in end position.

Positions of the vocative 118g

Several positions are available for the vocative. It may occupy the whole speaker turn. It may occur at the beginning of a speaker's turn (front position) or in the course of the turn (mid position), or at the end (end position). End position is by far the most frequent. Mid-position vocatives are not so frequent and are normally preceded by some sort of discourse marker prefacing the main utterance:

> *Tell me, **Margaret**. Er, you more or less got where you are today more or less off your own bat.*
>
> [*North West Tonight* is the name of a TV news programme; *Old Trafford* is a sports ground]
> *Just, just on that, **Lilian**. It may have occurred to you already, but North West Tonight are doing some filming at Old Trafford.*

STANDARD AND NON-STANDARD SPOKEN GRAMMAR 119

General 119a

In **84** the notion of standard spoken grammar was described in relation to standard written English. In this section some features of non-standard spoken grammar are described. Learners of British English are likely to hear these forms.

In **85** five main categories or levels of acceptability for spoken and written forms of grammar were outlined. For purposes of discussion in this section, each category has a number to mark the different levels. 'Widespread' here means across users of both genders and across a wide range of ages and social and regional backgrounds.

1. In widespread use in both spoken and written language (most forms are in this category).
2. In widespread use in both written and spoken language but not approved in more prescriptive grammar books and often avoided by many writers of formal English, for example, split infinitives, stranded prepositions (e.g. *That's the woman I gave it **to***, compared with *That's the woman **to** whom I gave it*).
3. Rare or not occurring in writing but widespread and normal in spoken language (··➤ for example, **96 Headers** and **97 Tails**), and vice versa.
4. Regionally or socially marked in writing and/or spoken language but widespread and normal within major regional/social varieties of British English (··➤ for example, the use of *ain't*, **119b**).
5. Non-occurring and unacceptable in all varieties of British English (for example a structure such as *he did must speak*).

It is important, however, to note that what is acceptable may vary from one context or from one personal relationship to another.

Common forms of spoken grammar 119b

Accusative personal pronoun as subject

*I don't know how but **me** and my sister got lost in the market.* (level 3)
(the level 1 form would be: my sister and I got lost ...)

Zero plural for nouns of measurement

*That's twelve **foot** long. You need something a lot shorter.* (level 3)
(level 1 form: twelve feet long ...)

What as a relative pronoun

*That's the house **what** she rented.* (level 4)
(level 1 form: the house that/which ...)

Them as demonstrative determiner and pronoun

*Did you get **them** photos we sent round?* (level 4)
(level 1 form: get those photos ...)

A: *What are the right plants then?*
B: ***Them** over there, the peonies.* (level 4)
(level 1 form: those over there ...)

Ain't as a negative contraction

*I know something. That **ain't** the answer.* (level 4)
(level 1 form: that isn't ...)

→ also **120** for *innit*, which may be regarded as a variant of *ain't it*

Double and multiple negation

*She has**n't** got **no** sense at all, she has**n't**.* (level 4)

*I have**n't** got **nothing** to say to **no one**.* (level 4)

→ also **438a Double negatives and usage**

Patterns with past and *-ed* participle verb forms

These range from past forms used as *-ed* participle forms, *-ed* participle forms used as past forms and base forms used as past tenses:

*She's been so worried she's **hid** in her room.* (level 4)

*Yeah, it's good, innit, I **seen** it there yesterday.* (level 4)

*She's already **give** it to me, thanks.* (level 4)

Subject/verb concord

This is a very common area of variation in spoken grammar. Patterns occur involving singular noun + plural verb, plural noun + singular verb and structures involving existential *there*, in particular, in which a singular verb is followed by a plural complement. This last structure is very common in spoken English and is becoming established as a standard form:

*It **were** too heavy to move. You need a winch of some sort.* (level 4)

*We **was** frightened like. That's why we didn't call her.* (level 4)

***There's** three other people still to come.* (level 2)

REPRESENTING SPEECH IN WRITING 120

In writing, the expressive character of spoken language is represented by reproducing the sound of core words and phrases as accurately as possible. There is a wide variety of possible variants but the most common transcriptions are:

I don't wanna do it. (want to)

Havva nice day. (have a)

That's great innit? (isn't it?)

I dunno and she dunno. (don't/doesn't know)

I'm gonna have an iced coffee. (going to)

Dad, you just gotta look at this. (got to)

I hafta go now. (have to)

SPEECH INTO WRITING: THE SPOKEN-WRITTEN CONTINUUM 121

Informal writing 121a

It would be a mistake to assume that the forms of grammar common in spoken English are exclusive to speech. Though rare in written English, situational ellipsis, in particular, appears appropriately in written contexts and is especially common in signs and notices as well as faxes, email and internet communications. The relative immediacy of email communication means that informality is the preferred style and ellipsis marks both informality and a relative symmetry of relationship in the exchange:

[inter-company fax]
*Could you email Kyle Barber and ask him for a quote for a laptop? **Said** we'd let Tatchell have one for himself as part of the deal. Compaq or Toshiba. At least 40gb hard disk and 528Mb RAM. **Good deal**, tell David. **Worth** the laptop. **More** in the pipeline.*

In the structure *Good deal, tell David*, the ellipsis and word order (more typically in writing: *Tell David (that) it is a good deal*) are grammatical features which are much more common in speech than in writing but which are becoming standardised in many written communications.

Email messages and personal letters may often display ellipsis of initial elements, especially the pronoun *I*, indicating their status as something midway between written and informal spoken messages:

[email message]
*Hi, Anne. **Just got back** from a terrific conference in Stockholm.*
(understood: I've just got back ...)

[personal letter closing]
*Well, **must go** and bake some bread now. **Will write** again soon. Love, Jane.*
(understood: **I** must go and bake .../**I** will write again soon.)

→ 539 **Glossary** for any unfamiliar terms

Formality in letter closings can be lessened by using ellipsis.

Ellipsis in letter closings

neutral/more formal	less formal (ellipted)
I look forward to hearing from you	*Look forward to hearing from you*
I hope to hear from you soon	*Hope to hear from you soon*
With regards from	*Regards*
With best wishes	*Best wishes* or *Best*
Yours sincerely	*Sincerely*

Postcards and other short written messages 121b

Postcard greetings texts conventionally use a great deal of ellipsis of the verb *be* and of initial elements:

> *Ireland as green as everyone said it was. Having a great time. Weather up and down, but beats work any day. Love, Nigel and Louise.*
> (understood: Ireland **is** as green as everyone said it was. **We're** having a great time. **The** weather **is** up and down, but **it/this** beats work any day.)

Clauses and sentences in informal writing 121c

Headers and tails, along with tags, so common in speech, also occur increasingly in informal writing:

> *He's a man who loves to play tricks on people* ***is TV presenter Noel Edmonds****.*
> (a more 'written' version of this sentence would be: 'TV presenter Noel Edmonds is a man who loves to play tricks on people'. The tail not only adds emphasis to the statement but it also imparts an informal character to the writing.)

The following examples, taken from an advertisement for the Chrysler Jeep Cherokee vehicle, indicate the spread into written text of irregularly punctuated clause fragments more commonly associated with spoken grammar (→ **87b**):

> *In these parts, you'll need a car that'll keep you on the road as well as take you off it.* ***Which is why the locals drive a Jeep Cherokee*** *... Instead of the usual soggy 4×4 handling, the Cherokee is taut and responsive. Not only does this make it safer to drive, it also makes it more exciting to drive.* ***As does the 4 litre engine under the bonnet****.*

Journalists also achieve impact and get on a 'conversational' wavelength with their readers by using common spoken discourse markers and purposefully vague language as well as response tokens such as *definitely*, *certainly*, *exactly*, which in the following examples serve as 'replies' in projected conversational exchanges:

> [magazine article]
> ***So*** *there I was sitting in Mick Jagger's kitchen while he went about making us both afternoon tea.* ***Well****, you can imagine how long it took to get him to talk about the band's latest album.* ***Exactly****. You've got it. Over two minutes.*

[magazine article]
He was talking about sport, Wimbledon, the World Cup, US Open Golf ***and that sort of stuff****.*

Advertisements and slogans 121d

Advertising copy writers in their advertising slogans often imitate the kinds of situational ellipsis found in conversation. By these means they attempt to achieve impact and a casual, almost chatty informality in the promotion of their products:

[magazine advertisement]
Thinking about cosmetic surgery?
(understood: **Are you** thinking about cosmetic surgery?)

[magazine slogan]
Coming soon ... the one you've been waiting for!
(understood: **It's** coming soon.)

NEW MODES: INTERNET DISCOURSE 122

Informal emails are most typically exchanged between participants who know each other. Chat-room messages may involve 'conversations' which are built up over a period of time; or they may involve participants who behave as if they are in a virtual space or 'room', often with an assumed name or identity.

Emails and instant messages are often informal and can be written online with only a few seconds between one response and another. Similarly, chat rooms involve almost immediate speaking turns. They are written but they have the character of spoken language. They are a new and distinct mode of written-spoken English.

The following transcript is an example of how spoken and written forms overlap. It is from an internet chat in which two people with the log-in pseudonyms of Cato and Regent talk with each other (the use of dots ... indicates that the dialogue has been edited for reasons of overall length):

Cato: *hi buddy!!! ;-)*
Regent: *hiya, wassup?*
Cato: *I been working SOOOO HARD!*
Regent: *did you know that your warning level is 0%* [see below]*
Cato: *well when I was on with Julia she gave me a 20% warning*
Regent: *what does it mean?*
Cato: *if someone misbehaves you can send them a warning ...*
Regent: *ok how do you do it*
Cato: *click on the warn button ...* [15 second pause]
Cato: *have you died or something?*
Regent: *all right hold your horses stop rushing me*
Cato: *sorry ;-)*
Regent: *SLOW DOWN*
Cato: *ok, slow*
Regent: *slooooooooow dn*

Cato: *sssssllllllooooooowwwwww* ...
Regent: *bye everyone, bye bye*
Cato: *tarra luv!*
Regent: *good init?*
Cato: *yeh hehehe*
Regent: *;-)*
Cato: *hooorah!*
Regent: *amazing*
Regent: *silly tune aint it*
Cato: *you can go now you passed the smiley test*
Regent: *bye*
Cato: *byyyyyeeeee.*

The exchange is marked by attempts to represent speech in writing. Examples are: *wassup* (what's up?), *tarra luv* (goodbye love), *init, aint it* (isn't it?).

Although the medium used is written and responses are typed on a keyboard, a number of features of the chat-room language are very close to spoken English:

- A 'smiley' ☺ is created using the punctuation marks ;-) to imitate a human smile.
- Laughter is represented (*hehehe*).
- Spelling is creatively manipulated in order to reproduce particular sounds and familiar intonation patterns (e.g. *sssssllllllooooooowwwwww*).
- Non-verbal reactions and farewells (e.g. *SOOOO* and *byyyyyeeeee*) and punctuation, in particular, are used to act as a channel for the expression of feelings.
- Capitalisation and exclamation marks are exploited to underline what both participants see as an interaction in which emotional reactions and responses are given.

It is likely that such new modes will continue to create new forms of spoken English in writing.

* [In this particular chat room the software technology allows the creation of a 'buddy' list which participants can store electronically; it also sends a 'clanging' message every time a new chatter (chat-room term for a person who chats) enters the chat room; and a 'warn' button is available by which participants can send each other warnings if they use offensive language such as swearing. Excessive use of offensive language can mean that the offender is automatically removed from the chat room.]

Grammar across turns and sentences

Grammar across turns and sentences

INTRODUCTION 123

This chapter (123–139) looks at grammar beyond the level of the sentence. In particular, it examines how grammatical links across sentence boundaries in writing and across speaker-turn boundaries in spoken language create textual cohesion. Cohesion is the sense of semantic unity possessed by texts as opposed to random sequences of sentences. Cohesion is created by cohesive links between sentences.

The following extract is from a written text – an encyclopedia – about the process of mining. Examples of cohesive links between sentences are marked in bold:

> ***Mining***
> *The* ***extraction*** *of useful* ***mineral substances*** *from the earth, either near the surface or at some depth.* ***It was*** *practis****ed*** *in prehistoric times, widely us****ed*** *in classical times, and be****came*** *highly developed after the introduction of mechanical power. In surface, strip, and open-cast* ***mining, the soil*** *is stripped away, and* ***the ore, coal, clay, or mineral*** *is* ***dug*** *directly. At* ***greater depths the deposits*** *are approached by horizontal* ***tunnels dug*** *from vertical* ***shafts (drifts)****. Variants of* ***these digging methods*** *are adopted for different geological situations.* ***Other methods*** *of* ***mining*** *may be devised for particular* ***substances****.*

Marked in bold are examples of lexical items which repeat or restate earlier content (*mining* ➛ *mineral*; *substances* ➛ *substances*; *dug* ➛ *dug*), or which are semantically linked in some way (*mining* ➛ *extraction* ➛ *tunnels* ➛ *shafts*; *the earth* ➛ *the soil*). Also marked are grammatical words which refer the reader to entities in the text (*mining* ➛ ***it***; ***these*** *digging methods* ➛ ***other*** *methods*) and examples of grammatical repetition (e.g. past tenses). This chapter describes such grammatical links which enable a string of sentences in sequence to be read as a semantically cohesive text.

COHESION AND COHERENCE 124

Cohesion refers to the grammatical and lexical means by which written sentences and speakers' utterances are joined together to make texts. A text may be written or spoken, and spoken texts are typically constructed by more than one person.

A text is cohesive if, as a whole, the sentences and spoken utterances are semantically linked and consistent. A random set of unconnected sentences or spoken utterances just thrown together will probably not be cohesive; readers and listeners will not be able to see links between each sentence/utterance.

The coherence of a text depends on more than its lexical or grammatical properties. A text is coherent if its semantic and pragmatic meanings make sense in its real-world context to readers/listeners. Coherence depends on the reader/listener being able to interpret the message in relation to its context.

Coherence depends partly on the way that a writer or speaker assumes knowledge of the world and of the context on the part of readers or listeners, and partly on what sorts of clues and signals the writer/speaker puts into the text. Such clues and signals include the linguistic items which provide cohesive links between sentences, as exemplified in **123**, above.

Cohesion is largely a grammatical property of texts, but lexis can also play a part in linking sentences (⇢ the text extract in **123** above). For example:

I went to the dentist. I was nervous. I don't like injections.

Among these sentences there is grammatical cohesion which results from the parallel sequence of personal pronouns and past tenses, but the text coheres because of our knowledge that dentists administer pain-killing injections before dental treatment and that these can be painful and make some patients nervous. Thus the lexical items *dentist*, *nervous* and *injections* are linked coherently through semantic associations made by the reader.

Likewise, punctuation and the layout of the text can indicate how it should cohere. ⇢ **506 Appendix: Punctuation**

In this chapter the emphasis is on the grammar of texts and the part played by grammar in achieving textual coherence.

REFERENCE 125

Speakers and writers can make reference to people, places, things and ideas in a variety of different ways, as in these examples:

1 A: *Abigail didn't go?*
B: *No,* ***she*** *was at* ***her*** *mum and dad's.*

2 [these sentences are the opening sentences of a chapter in a novel]
They *pressed round him in ragged fashion to take their money. Andy, Dave, Phil, Stephen, Bob.*

3 [speakers are looking at photographs]
A: ***That****'s a lovely one of you,* ***that*** *is.*
B: *Yes. I like* ***that one****.*

In **1**, *she* and *her* refer to a person already identified in the text (*Abigail*).

In **2**, *they* refers to people who are identified later in the text (the names in the second sentence).

In **3**, *that* and *that one* refer out from the text to things in the situation itself (the photos that the speakers are holding).

The references in **1** and **2** are endophoric (they operate within the text). The references in **3** are exophoric (they operate between the text and the external world).

Endophoric references are of two types: anaphoric (those which refer back to something earlier in the text) and cataphoric (those which refer forward to something later in the text).

Different kinds of reference

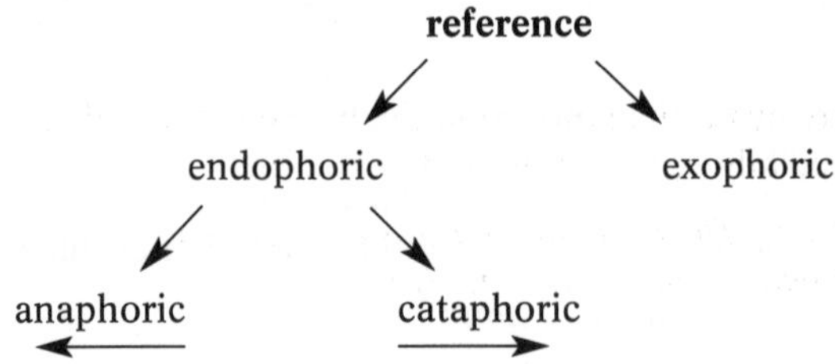

REFERRING EXPRESSIONS 126

Endophoric (anaphoric and cataphoric) and exophoric references are made using referring expressions. The people and things they refer to are called referents.

There are a number of types of referring expression. Among the most common are:

pronouns (for example, *he, she, it, mine, yours, this, that, these, those, some, none*)

determiners (for example, *the, this, that, these, those*)

adverbs (for example, *here, there, then*).

In the following examples the referring items are in bold, and the referents are in green:

*The children looked tired. **They**'d been travelling all day.*
(anaphoric reference)

*A smartly-dressed lady entered the shop. **This** lady had spent over one hundred pounds the day before.*
(anaphoric reference)

*They arrived at the resort. **Here** at last was a place they could relax.*
(anaphoric reference)

[blurb on the back cover of a paperback novel]
*For a split second, **she** saw her own death, a gunmetal face fixed on the sky, all around the faces and voices of Carn as **she** had known it. Josie Keenan had come home to the town of Carn, the only home **she** knew.*
(cataphoric and anaphoric reference)

[public notice]
*Vehicles parked **here** will be towed away.*
(exophoric reference)

[notice in a train compartment]
***These** seats are reserved for disabled customers.*
(exophoric reference)

[on a sign, accompanied by a direction arrow]
*More antiques **this** way.*
(exophoric reference)

ENDOPHORIC REFERENCE 127

Anaphoric reference

Anaphoric references are by far the more common type of endophoric reference, and are created most typically by pronouns and determiners:

> *New talks are under way. The outcome of **these discussions** may well determine future US attitudes towards trade with the EEC.*

There is lexical cohesion in this example between the two synonymous words *talks* and *discussions*, but the cohesion of these two sentences also depends on the anaphoric reference of the determiner *these*, which makes *talks* and *discussions* co-referential (i.e. they refer to the same thing, they have the same referent).

Cataphoric reference

Cataphoric references are considerably less common, especially in informal spoken language:

> [radio phone-in programme host]
> ***This** is the number to call if you want to give us your opinion: 0207600600.*

> *Now **here** is a recipe which you are certain to find tempting. It's one my mum used for making pecan pie.* [recipe then follows]

In fiction and journalism, cataphoric reference to a person or thing by means of a pronoun often creates a sense of suspense and involvement:

> ***He** was arrested late last night. James Gregg knew little about the circumstances of his arrest because at the time he was unconscious.*

Fixed expressions

A number of other fixed expressions allow anaphoric and cataphoric reference. Words and expressions such as *the former, foregoing, previous* create anaphoric reference, while words and expressions such as *below, as follows* and *the following* create cataphoric reference:

> *All of **the foregoing** needs of course to be put in its social and political context.*

> *On **the previous** page you will find details of our new offer as well.*

> *See **below** for more detailed instructions.*

> *I regret to inform you that your application is invalid for **the following** reasons.*

Longer reference

Words such as *this, which* and *such* can also be used to refer endophorically to segments of the text longer than just a noun phrase. That is, they may refer to preceding or following words and phrases, a previous or upcoming whole sentence or, sometimes, a whole stretch of text:

> *He is very experienced. **This is why** we should invite him.*

> *It's the best low-fat spread. **Which is why** you should keep loads in your fridge.*

→ **539 Glossary** for any unfamiliar terms

Nobody has a bad word to say about her. ***Such*** *is her popularity.*

Well, ***this*** *is what the timetable says: buses every other hour but no service on Sundays.*

It, this and *that* referring to segments of text 128

The impersonal pronoun *it* and the demonstrative pronouns *this* and *that* are used in different ways to refer to segments of text or to ideas in the text.

It

It is used to continue reference to an entity which has already been established as a topic in the text:

The girl was so ecstatic afterwards, she had such a wonderful smile on her face. ***It*** *was a sight I shall never forget.*
(*It* refers neutrally to the girl's ecstatic behaviour and smile)

It cannot be used to refer back to a title/heading or sub-title/sub-heading of a text. In such cases *this* is used or the full noun phrase is repeated:

[*veggies* means vegetarians]
Quorn or Mycoprotein
This *is a relatively new foodstuff which is sold as a meat substitute with a chicken-like texture.* ***It's*** *rich in protein and contains no animal fat and many veggies eat* ***it****.*
(note how *it* is used to refer back once 'quorn' is established as a topic, but *it* cannot be used in the first sentence to refer back to *quorn* in the title.)

Or:

Quorn or Mycoprotein
Quorn *is a relatively new foodstuff* …

But not:

Quorn or Mycoprotein
~~*It*~~ *is a relatively new foodstuff* …

It is not used when the referring pronoun is stressed:

She's proved herself as a writer, Mel. ***That*** *you can't deny.*
(stressed fronted pronoun object; *this* could have been used, but not *it*)

This, that

This is used to signal that an entity is a new or important topic in a text, or to refer to entities which the writer wishes to highlight or closely identify with:

If there is something that you particularly like that is fortified with vitamins you could try writing to the manufacturer and asking where they've come from. ***This*** *not only helps you, it also lets the manufacturer know that people do care about what they're eating.*

That highlights entities less emphatically than *this*, and is often used to refer to facts, assertions, etc. which are of temporary interest but which are not major topics in the text. There is often a sense that the writer wishes to indicate a distance from the proposition or entity referred to:

Then, feeling rather foolish, he turned and hurried away down the drive. ***That*** *was a hopeless beginning, he thought, as he returned to the house.*

That is also frequently used to refer to events and entities remote in time and space, or to ideas and propositions associated with another person or another participant in the discourse:

When I left that place, I realized there was something I could do about it – I could make sure I didn't eat those pigs or those hens or any animals. I also decided there and then to work to end this exploitation. ***That*** *was a few years ago but my feelings haven't changed one bit.*

After a while Norrie suggested his brother, Alan Paramor, the music publisher, should help look after me. ***That*** *seemed fine to us.*

TEXTUAL ELLIPSIS (*YES I DID.*) 129

Textual ellipsis refers to items which are normally treated as required by the grammar to complete the meaning but which are not present because they can be recovered by a listener or reader from the preceding or following text.

Verbs, especially the verb *be* (as copular or auxiliary verb), modal verbs, and *do* and *have* as auxiliary verbs, are regular triggers for ellipsis of complements and linked lexical verbs:

A: *I think you're right to find out more before you decide.*
B: *I know I* ***am****.*
(understood: I know I am right to find out …)

A: *Can you hear that noise?*
B: *Yes, I think I* ***can****. What is it?*
(understood: I think I can hear that noise.)

A: *Did you ring Jeff?*
B: *No I* ***didn't****. Sorry, I forgot.*

She used to heap food onto his plate so as he'd get fat. But he never ***did****.*

An auxiliary or modal verb, or copular verb *be*, often make repetition of a lexical verb unnecessary when contrasting subjects (in green in the examples) are present:

But I still don't see how you ***can help me****, or how anybody* ***can****.*

He ***was a football fan****. I* ***was*** *as well.*

Sometimes a contrast in tense/modality/polarity can prompt ellipsis:

The idea of sending her into a mental home is dreadful and we know that it ***would*** *do her no good. There is only one thing that* ***will****. That is the only chance for her, if she could be with you.*
(understood: There is only one thing that will do her good.)

I feel that if you ***can*** *help somebody you* ***should****.*

→ **94 Situational ellipsis** for further examples and discussion of ellipsis

SUBSTITUTION 130

General 130a

When substitution occurs, a substitute form is used instead of repeating a word, phrase or clause which occurs elsewhere in the text. In the following extracts, substitute forms are marked in bold:

Mrs Smith had been able to tell her what no one else could have **done**.
(*done* = told her)

A: *Matthew, have you counted the plates?*
B: *There are twenty two.*
A: *Twenty two.*
C: *Oh my.*
A: *Oh there's still some underneath there. Can you get those out.*
B: *Twenty two yeah. I did check.*
A: *There should be a few little* **ones** *around.*
D: *They're big* **ones***, aren't they?*
C: *There's some big* **ones** *over there, Pauline.*
(*ones* in each case is understood as substituting for 'plates'.)

A: *I'll see you in the morning before I go home.*
B: *Well, I hope* **so**.
(understood: Well, I hope you'll see me/we'll see each other.)

Substitution may be anaphoric (referring back) or cataphoric (referring forward) in the text. Cataphoric substitution is considerably less frequent than anaphoric, and is usually only found across clause boundaries rather than sentence boundaries:

- Anaphoric:

  A modem is the equivalent of a phone for your PC. You'll need **one** *if you want to use email or connect to the net.*

- Cataphoric:

  If you're ever looking for **one***, there's a screwdriver in that drawer.*

A–Z 60 *One*

Substitute forms 130b

There are several different types of substitute form. They include indefinite quantifying pronouns, substitute *do*, substitute *so*, and expressions such as *the same*, *thus*.

Indefinite quantifying pronouns

(a) little	*any*	*either*
another	*both*	*enough*
all	*each*	*few*

half	*neither*	*several*
less	*none*	*some*
many	*one(s)*	
much	*other(s)*	

*In wealthier countries, people tend to eat more foods like sweets, chocolate, cakes, crisps and snacks – all foods that are high in fat or sugar, or often **both**.*

A: *D'you know a lot of people there?*
B: *Mm, not **many**.*

A: *Do you like the yellow roses?*
B: *I prefer the red **ones**, actually.*

The substitute verb *do*

Do may substitute for a verb and any elements of complementation accompanying it:

*Many of the renewable sources of energy are 'clean' sources. They do not cause pollution, as coal, gas, oil and nuclear energy **do**.*
(*do* substitutes for 'cause pollution')

A: *Who picked her up at the airport, you?*
B: *No, Diane **did**.*

(··› 133 below)

Substitute *so*

So may substitute for a *that*-clause complement, especially when it is the complement of a reporting verb:

A: *It's difficult to manage, isn't it?*
B: *Yes, very much **so**.*

A: *D'you think they'll be interested?*
B: *I would say **so**, yes.*
(*so* substitutes for '(that) they'll be interested')

(··› 134 below)

Complement phrases: *the same, likewise, similarly, thus*

The same, *likewise*, *similarly* and *thus* typically substitute for predicative complement phrases and clauses:

A: *Nice to meet you anyway.*
B: ***Likewise**.*

*It's just really depressing you know. For me it is anyway. No, not only for me really, it is for the rest of the staff as well because everyone feels **the same**.*

ELLIPSIS VERSUS SUBSTITUTION 131

Often it is difficult to distinguish between ellipsis and substitution, since forms such as *some*, *any*, *much* can perform both functions (compare *ones* and *none*, which are clearly substitute forms):

A: *Do you seek any guidance from me?*
B: *I ask **none**, sir. But I have thought it possible that you might have it in your power, if you should deem it right, to give me **some**.*
(*none* is clearly a substitute for 'no guidance from you'; *some* could be seen as a substitute for 'guidance' or as ellipsis of 'some guidance')

SUBSTITUTION FOR NOUNS 132

One, some, ones 132a

One and *some/ones* are the most common items used to substitute for count nouns.

One can be used alone as a substitute or with premodification and/or postmodification:

*I want **a** decent **notebook** anyway. Where can I get **one**?*
(understood: Where can I get a decent notebook?)

*Most **diseases** have been around for a very long time, but not all of them. There is **a new one called Lyme disease**. Lyme disease has been studied only since 1975.*

*'Well, I shall get **a manager** somewhere, no doubt,' said Henchard, with strong feeling in his tones. 'But it will be long before I see **one that would suit me so well**!'*

Ones cannot be used alone in this way. Where there is no premodification or postmodification, *some* or *any* are used as a plural substitute:

A: *Do you want some stamps?*
B: *Well I haven't got **any**. Have you got **some**?*
A: *I've got some. I don't know if I've got enough for all those letters.*
(~~Well, I haven't got ones. Have you got ones?~~)

Ones is always premodified and/or postmodified:

[a punt is a flat-bottomed boat]
A: *Apparently they cost about £8,000, those punts.*
B: *They're incredibly expensive.*
A: *Mm.*
B: *You can get them cheaper. **Fibreglass ones** are cheaper than wood.*

[A comments on B's socks]
A: *They look like your dad's.*
B: *No they're not actually. They're mine but they're boys' school socks really. Cos I just wanted **some grey ones that were long enough to come out of the top of my boots**.*

For non-count nouns, *some*, not *one/ones*, is used as a substitute:

> *We need a bit more furniture in here. We'll have to get* ***some*** *when the sales are on.*
> (~~We'll have to get one(s) when the sales are on.~~)
>
> A: *What's it like, that tea, then?*
> B: *Mm, nice.*
> A: *Can I try* ***some****?*

That, those 132b

That and *those* are used as substitutes in formal contexts instead of *the one/the ones* for non-count nouns where the substitute noun phrase is taking the place of a definite noun phrase:

> [from a text about computer storage media]
> *The most commonly used removable drive technology is derived from* ***that*** *found in conventional hard disks, which not only gives you high capacities but also provides fast performance.*
> (… is derived from 'the technology' found in …)
>
> *There are several different kinds of sign language. The most widely used are* ***those*** *which have developed naturally in a deaf community, such as the American, British, French, and Swedish Sign Languages.*
> (or, less formal: The most widely used are the ones which have developed naturally …)
>
> *The results were compared with* ***those*** *obtained from the best research laboratories.*

In more formal styles, and especially in academic style, *that of/those of* is used instead of *the one of/the ones of* or *the … one/the … ones*, and is preferred to the possessive *X's one/X's ones*. This usage is frequent within and across clauses. It is much less frequent across sentences:

> *He founded a school modelled on* ***that of*** *Confucius.*
> (~~He founded a school modelled on the one of Confucius.~~)
> (preferred to: He founded a school modelled on Confucius's one.)
>
> *Comic books are generally collaborations between a writer and an artist. In a process similar to* ***that of*** *making movies, writers' scripts are implemented and interpreted by artists.*
>
> *The chief sea-connecting canals are* ***those of*** *Suez and Panama.*
> (~~The chief sea-connecting canals are the Suez and Panama ones.~~)

That can only substitute for a thing, and not normally for a person or animal. *Those* may substitute for persons, animals or things:

> *I overheard them talking. They're looking for the girl.* ***The one*** *who was in all the papers.*
> (~~I overheard them talking. They're looking for the girl. That who was in all the papers.~~)

→ 539 **Glossary** for any unfamiliar terms

Today most of the Greenlanders live near the coast, particularly in the south west. Here, snow lies only in the winter and people can graze sheep, cows and reindeer and grow crops. ***Those who*** *live further north earn their money mainly from fishing.*

None, enough 132c

Indefinite quantifying pronouns (207) are also used to substitute for noun phrases:

The survivors then spoke up, backing the corporal's claim that they were left in a copse facing overwhelming machine-gun fire while their leaders went off supposedly to make contact with each other. ***None*** *had heard an order to retreat, so they stayed until all their comrades had been killed and the options were die or run.*

Spencer's getting a huge lot of money. The others don't get ***that much****.*
(informal; more formal: The others don't get so much.)

A: *Do we have bread?*
B: *Yes, but not* ***enough*** *for breakfast.*

They had found each other's company delightful, stimulating. Yet ***each*** *was wary of using* ***the other****; and, paradoxically, that had turned them into comrades, co-conspirators, almost.*

SUBSTITUTE VERB *DO* 133

Do, do so, do it, do the same are used to substitute for a verb and whatever complementation accompanies it:

[reminiscing about olden days]
A: *We had a milkman that had a horse and cart.*
B: *Yes. We* ***did*** *too yes.*
(understood: We had a milkman that had a horse and cart too.)

[assistant at a cosmetics counter in a store, explaining the qualities of a face cream to a customer]
A: *That will definitely offer you some protection. And even in the coldest weather it's almost like putting a cushion across the face to repel the harsh winds and things and stop your skin drying out as well.*
B: *Right. Okay. I'll have a think about it.*
A: ***Yes do.***
B: *Thank you very much.*

A: *Can I borrow these scissors?*
B: *Yes, of course,* ***do so****.*
(more formal; understood: Yes, of course, borrow the scissors.)

I asked him if he had ever lost his temper with the press. He replied that he had never ***done it*** *in public but always made sure that the journalist concerned knew how he felt.*

A: *I employed a lawyer. Would you try to defend yourself or not?*
B: *I would* ***do the same*** *as you.*

⇢ also **129 Textual ellipsis** for uses of *do*

Substitution of a lexical verb and its complement also occurs with a modal or an auxiliary verb + *do*:

A: *You could resign.*
B: *Yes,* ***I could do****, I suppose.*

A: *Have you rung Jo?*
B: *Yes,* ***I have done*** *but she wasn't in.*

Do so occurs in tensed and non-tensed forms (⇢ 215). *Do so* is generally used in more formal contexts:

If you are intending to do a reasonable amount of cycling, it is advisable to bring your own bike as the ones available for hire are of an inferior quality. If you ***do so****, bring a good lock as bike theft is a problem here.*
(tensed)

One of the main problems has been clearing away the many unexploded bombs left from the war. Many villagers have been killed ***doing so****.*
(non-tensed)

[*neural networks* are a type of information network in a computer]
Neural networks, on the other hand, don't look for absolutes, but for patterns in data. ***Having done so****, they can then try and establish relationships between those patterns.*
(non-tensed)

Do so, *do it* and *do that* are often interchangeable, but there are occasions where one form is preferred over the others. *Do so* is generally the most formal of the three.

Do so is often preferred for making general reference to a series of actions or events:

[talking about a famous horse race in the streets of Siena, Italy]
For the best view you need to have found a position on the inner rail by 2pm (ideally at the start and finish line), and to keep it for the next six hours. If you haven't ***done so****, there's really no rush, as you'll be able to see a certain amount from anywhere within the throng.*

Do it is often preferred for making a more direct or precise reference to an action or event:

A: *I can't eat any kind of buttery stuff on pasta. It makes me feel sick.*
B: *Really.*
A: *I* ***did it*** *once and I woke up in the middle of the night and was sick.*

Do that is often preferred in contrastive situations:

A: *I also think that if someone knows that they are terminally ill … at the moment they've not got that right to ask the doctor to switch the machine off.*
B: *Euthanasia.*
A: *I think they ought to be able to* ***do that*** *rather than suffer.*

SO AS A SUBSTITUTE FORM 134

So substituting for an adjective

So can substitute for an adjective predicative phrase:

It was the house that had been empty, years ago. It had remained ***so*** *for a long time.*

I am angry. I have been ***so****, many years.*

Cataphoric reference to an adjective complement is also possible with *so*, but it is very infrequent and rather formal:

He was, and remains ***so****, very conscious of his responsibilities.*

More so, less so

More so and *less so* operate as comparative substitutes:

The prospect of a summer here, in the drowsy warmth of the south, had always been a pleasant one. Now it was ***more so****.*

Some dangers, like industrial spying or sabotage, are obvious. Others ***less so****.*

So substituting for *that*-clause

So is also used as a *that*-clause substitute:

And I know she's fond of Nicky. She told me ***so****.*
(understood: She told me that she is fond of Nicky.)

A: *Does the hotel have room service?*
B: *I believe* ***so****.*

The negative of *so* when substituting for a *that*-clause is *not*:

A: *Are they all arriving at the same time?*
B: *I hope* ***not****.*

A: *Did she say when she'd be back?*
B: *No, I'm afraid* ***not****.*

This type of substitution with *so* and *not* is common after the following verbs, especially in conversational responses:

appear	*be afraid*	*expect**
assume	*believe*	*guess*

hope
*imagine**
presume
*reckon**
seem
suppose
*think**

Those verbs with an asterisk (*) often occur with *so* but are less likely to be used followed by *not*:

A: *Is Jake coming too?*
B: *I* ***don't*** *think* ***so****.*
('I think not' is also possible, but infrequent and very formal)

A: *I wonder if she went with them?*
B: *I* ***wouldn't*** *imagine* ***so****.*

But note that *hope* is always used with substitute *not*, rather than negative declarative:

A: *You've spelt her surname wrong, haven't you?*
B: *Oh, I hope* ***not****.*
(~~Oh, I don't hope so.~~)

So with reporting verbs

Substitute *so* sometimes occurs in initial position in short responses with reporting verbs (e.g. *say, tell, hear, read*):

[talking of problems of obtaining home insurance]
A: *There's so many places that won't insure you now unless you've got locks on your doors and windows.*
B: ***So*** *I heard.*

A: *Alex Pruitt has been the subject of an internal investigation at Langley.*
B: ***So*** *Ruiz told me.*

So in exclamations

In exclamative responses, substitute *so* can precede the subject and verb *be* or a modal or auxiliary verb:

A: *The water-butt's completely empty.*
B: *Oh yes,* ***so*** *it is!*

A: *Oh, you've got oil stains on your trousers.*
B: *Oh,* ***so*** *I have!*

So meaning *as well*

Initial *so* often occurs, with a meaning similar to *as well* or additive *too*. This is particularly common in short responses and with pronoun subjects. Subject-verb inversion follows:

A: *I love those red tulips.*
B: ***So*** *do I.*
(or: I do too.)

→ 539 **Glossary** for any unfamiliar terms

A: *Well, we're ready.*
B: ***So** are we. Let's go.*

*Well, I've packed my case, and **so** should you, I think. We haven't got that much time.*

The negative is formed with initial *neither* or *nor*, or with *not* … *either*. In the case of negatives beginning with *neither* or *nor*, subject-verb inversion follows:

*Frank didn't go and **neither** did we in the end.*

A: *Oh, I haven't got any small change at all.*
B: ***Nor** have I.*

A: *I haven't got a fork.*
B: *Oh, Anne has**n't** **either**. I'll get some.*

 71 ***So*** for further examples

COHESION AND COMPARATIVE FORMS 135

Comparative forms across clauses and sentences can signal cohesion:

*Jim can play pool better than me. He's had **more** practice.*
(understood: … more practice than I have)

*Continuing south, you'll feel like an insignificant speck at the feet of the city's tallest structures. For a **better** view of them and their surroundings, take the short monorail ride to Harbor Island.*

460–471 Comparison

COHESION AND LINKING ADJUNCTS (*IN ADDITION, HOWEVER*) 136

General 136a

Linking adjuncts explicitly indicate the semantic relationship between two clauses or sentences or paragraphs (335):

[description of the city of Cardenas in Cuba; *bite its lip and bide its time* means 'be patient and wait (to get regeneration funds)']
*Many of its buildings, particularly the fortifications overlooking the harbour, are in need of renovation, but, with Havana and Trinidad eating up most of the regeneration budget, it seems that Cardenas will have to bite its lip and bide its time. It is, **nonetheless**, a charming little city and worth a look.*

*His face and hands were black with dirt. **In spite of this**, Catherine was very glad to see him and rushed up to kiss him.*

[from a book about how second-language learners acquire vocabulary]
Second-language learners usually have to learn at a rate faster than the 'natural' rate of first-language acquisition. ***In addition****, early stages of second-language acquisition involve a relatively small number of high-frequency words, for which there is a greater pay-off instructionally.* ***However****, second-language learners may also have a greater need to use context.*

Linking adjuncts can co-occur with coordinating conjunctions (in green in the examples below), in which case they follow the conjunction:

So I would like you to read the documents in order to improve or at least confirm your own knowledge and understanding of the network set up here. But ***secondly****, it's important not only that you can answer students' questions but you can tell them where the information is available to them.*

Something happened to you and ***as a result*** *your arm was broken.*

Linking adjuncts are a large class which includes single-word and phrasal items. The most common ones are listed in **136b–136j** (classified according to the semantic relations which they signal). Most of these linking adjuncts are more frequent in formal styles and in writing, but some (marked with *) are more frequent in informal spoken contexts.

Additive (*also, likewise*) 136b

Additive linking adjuncts indicate that the second text segment adds to, gives further or more specific information on, reinforces or expands in some way the information in the first. These include:

Single-word

again	*correspondingly*	*likewise*
also	*equally*	*moreover*
besides	*furthermore*	*too*

And I should have told you about things here. I often thought about it, then I thought no, it's too complicated. I didn't want to involve you. ***Besides****, you don't tell me much these days. It's not like it used to be.*

Phrasal/clausal

above all	*in particular*	*to crown it all**
*as well**	*on top of it all**	*what's more*/what is more*
in addition	*to cap it all**	

(*particularly frequent in informal spoken contexts)

539 **Glossary** for any unfamiliar terms

[about a network of young people in Scotland who call themselves *Article 12*, and who speak out on issues affecting children and young people's lives]
The name Article 12 comes from Article 12 of the UN Convention on the Rights of the Child, which says that young people have the right to express their views on any matter affecting them. ***Above all****, young people want politicians to listen to their opinions and to use their experience to build a better future.*

Resultative (*so, therefore*) 136c

Resultative linking adjuncts indicate that the second text segment expresses a result or outcome of the events or states described in the first. These include:

Single-word

accordingly	*so*	*therefore*
consequently	*then*	*thus*
hence		

After a few years riding the crest of an economic wave, New Zealand has recently seen a downturn in the economy and a resulting dive in the value of the New Zealand dollar. ***Consequently****, most things will seem fairly cheap by European and North American standards.*

Phrasal/clausal

as a consequence	*as a result*	*of course*

My friend Jessica always wanted to be called Jessie but she introduced herself as Jessica. ***As a result*** *everybody called her that.*

Contrastive (*rather, on the contrary*) 136d

Contrastive linking adjuncts indicate a contrast between the information in the first text segment and that in the second. These include:

Single-word

alternatively	*otherwise*	*rather*
instead		

We'll have to invite him. ***Otherwise****, he'll be offended.*

Phrasal/clausal

in/by comparison	*more accurately/more precisely*	*on the other hand*
in/by contrast	*on the contrary*	*then again**

(* particularly frequent in informal spoken contexts)

Few countries have satisfactory legislation on pesticides or the trained manpower to enforce it. ***In contrast****, extensive use of pesticides in Europe, North America and Japan is backed by government legislation or voluntary schemes that provide farmers with detailed advice.*

*We've got computer facilities in the student union. And we've hopefully got some people from the Computer Centre who might be able to help a bit. But **then again** if you're interested in computers it's very easy to learn quickly by yourself.*

Time (*eventually, then*) 136e

Time linking adjuncts indicate a relationship of sequence in time between the information in the first text segment and that in the second. These include:

Single-word

afterwards	*meanwhile*	*subsequently*
eventually	*originally*	*then*
*meantime**		

(*particularly frequent in informal spoken contexts)

*When thousands of seals began dying in European waters during 1988, pollution was first blamed for the tragedy. Tests **subsequently** showed the actual cause was a virus.*

Phrasal/clausal

after that	*in the meantime*

*Her printer is useless, it takes like 45 minutes to print anything out. **In the meantime** I've lent her mine.*

Concessive (*anyway, though*) 136f

Concessive linking adjuncts indicate that the speaker or writer is prepared to accept part of an argument or proposition (that part expressed in the second text segment) which typically in some way contrasts with what has already been stated. These include:

Single-word

admittedly	*however*	*still*
*anyhow**	*nevertheless*	*though*
anyway	*nonetheless*	*yet*
besides	*only**	

(*particularly frequent in informal spoken contexts)

[talking about the risks of a serious industrial accident at a nearby factory]
*I mean they can't just close their eyes and say 'Oh no, it doesn't exist'. That's my opinion, **anyhow**.*

*They sat in Mrs Constantine's overcrowded parlour, where each small table bore its burden of photographs and ornaments and the walls were crowded with pictures. **Nevertheless**, it was cosy and comfortable with a fire burning cheerfully.*

Phrasal/clausal

after all	*for all that*	*mind you**
all the same	*in any case*	*of course*
at any rate	*in any event*	*on the other hand*
at the same time	*in spite of that*	*that said*

(*particularly frequent in informal spoken contexts)

Don't get too excited! This could come to nothing. ***On the other hand****, it might work.*

Inference (*then, in that case*) 136g

Inference linking adjuncts indicate that the speaker/writer infers or concludes something in the second text segment, based on the evidence of the first text segment. These include:

Single-word

otherwise	*then**

(*particularly frequent in informal spoken contexts)

[at a travel agent's; A is the assistant]
A: [showing a brochure] *Perhaps I could give you this actually. There's some suggestions for destinations.*
B: *Oh right.*
A: *And so to go out via Taipei. Out to Tokyo. And then back via Bangkok. And Delhi as well by the looks of it.*
B: *Yes. Oh right. Can I take this brochure* ***then****?*
A: *Oh, certainly yes.*

Phrasal

in that case

If we try to imagine what's the worst possible accident we can imagine, right, it would be if all of this store of gas got released, you know, for whatever reason, if everything went wrong and the whole lot got out. Now ***in that case*** *we'd end up with a much bigger cloud of gas that would travel further before it got completely blown away, right, and couldn't affect anybody.*

Summative (*overall, in short*) 136h

Summative linking adjuncts indicate that the second text segment represents a summary or summing-up of the first. These include:

Single-word

altogether	*so*	*therefore*
overall	*then*	*thus*

[speakers talking about how they spent their holiday]

A: *And I mean that was second-hand the bike that I bought for Jenny because I couldn't see the point in spending for a brand new one when she's going to have outgrown it, you know, in a little while anyway. And she doesn't go out that much anyway.*

B: ***So overall** you'd say you had a fairly happy holiday this year?*

A: *Oh yeah. Yeah.*

C: *Yeah we enjoyed it. Yeah.*

Phrasal/clausal

all in all

in conclusion

in short

in sum

in summary

to conclude

to sum up

to summarise

[beginning of final paragraph in a book review]

***In sum**, this is a good book to have in your reference library – providing you have other sources of information on which to draw.*

Listing (*firstly, lastly*) 136i

Listing linking adjuncts indicate that the text segments in which they occur form part of a list of segments. These include:

Single-word

a, b, c, etc.

finally

first(ly)/second(ly)/ third(ly), etc.

lastly

next

one, two, three, etc.

then

There are two problems with assuming that our figure applies to the whole Chinese population.

***First**, we 'measured' lefthandedness by looking at which hand each student wrote with. This is only a restricted definition of lefthandedness.*

***Secondly**, the student population may not be representative of the population as a whole. But we do not believe that any bias in the sample would account for the difference between Gooch's figure of 18 per cent and ours of 3 per cent.*

Phrasal/clausal

first of all

*for a start**

for one thing … for another thing

in the first place/in the second place

last of all

on the one hand … on the other hand

to begin with/to start with

(*particularly frequent in informal spoken contexts)

A: *But do you think these hopes and ambitions for the children now are very different from the ones your parents would have had for you?*

B: *Yeah. Definitely.*

A: *In what way?*

B: *Well, I don't think they'd have been worried so much about us going out and getting a job, **for a start**.*

539 Glossary for any unfamiliar terms

Meta-textual (*namely, so to speak*) 136j

Meta-textual linking adjuncts indicate that the text segment they introduce either explains, paraphrases, exemplifies or relates topically to the previous segment or represents a temporary digression from the previous segment or a shift in topic. These include:

Single-word

incidentally	*namely*	*well**
indeed	*now*	

(*particularly frequent in informal spoken contexts)

A: *We never do much at Arthur and Clarissa's in the mornings, as you know.*
B: *How is he,* ***incidentally****?*
A: *Oh Arthur is better than he was two years ago.*

Phrasal/clausal

*by the way**	*in other words*	*that is*
for example	*or rather*	*that is to say*
for instance	*so to speak*	*to put it another way*

(*particularly frequent in informal spoken contexts)

A: *I'm wallpapering this week and doing all the little jobs, you know, that need doing.*
B: *Oh I know. I know.*
A: *Isn't it boring.*
B: *Yeah. Oh, how did you get on* ***by the way*** *at the doctor's? Er you went on Friday.*
A: *Oh I'll tell you about it over the weekend.*

[review of the technical features of a digital camera]
You can even automatically place images in prespecified positions in documents. ***In other words****, it is the shape of digital cameras to come.*

54 *Now*; 76 *Well*

Coordinating conjunctions (*and, but, or*) and sentence boundaries 137

In writing, the coordinating conjunctions *and*, *but* and *or* are traditionally viewed as being inappropriate as the first item in a sentence. However, they frequently occur as sentence beginners in both speech and writing, though less so in very formal and academic writing styles. In this way they provide important cohesive links between sentences, and should not be thought of as 'bad style':

> *A universal cry of horror and fury arose: Vengeance! The bodies of the victims were loaded on a cart lit with torches. The cortege moved back amidst curses at a funeral pace.* ***And*** *in a few hours Paris was covered with barricades.*

> *Glass could be impregnated with inorganic pesticides, then ploughed into the land.* ***Or*** *pellets impregnated with trace elements could improve the diets of cattle; in impoverished pastures similar pellets would protect cattle from parasites.*

PARALLELISM AND REPETITION 138

Often sentences and utterances may be seen to be cohesively linked because of parallel grammatical features. Such features are common in literary and other creative styles (e.g. music lyrics):

> [text from a novel; parallel tense/aspect choices are in bold]
> *From being afraid of nothing he **had become** wary of everything, yet he was exalted on realising that all his actions so far **had been rooted** in an alien timidity. He **hadn't been born** that way. Circumstances **had made** him so. The jungle **he had been brought up** in **had instilled** nothing but fear, **which had shaped** all his decisions. The Malayan forest **had been** congenial.*

In the following extracts, lexical repetition combines with parallel structures and repeated grammatical items (comparatives, reporting verbs, modal verbs, *-ing* forms and *-s* forms):

> *They were Zoe's age. Old**er**. Not much old**er**. Smart**er**, hard**er** than Alma's daughter but how would I know? **she thought**, despairing, **she might** have chang**ed**, **she must be** chang**ing** ... **She might** be in **love**. **She might love** a stranger. Alma tried to reconstruct her train of thought. It was something to do with **love**, **she thought**. **Loving the** picture. **Loving the** painter. **Love** somehow let**s** you into **the** picture. Allow**s** you to enter. **Love** allow**s**.*

> [a group of young female students are chatting on a Sunday evening in their shared accommodation]
> A: *I like **Sunday** nights for some reason, I don't know why.*
> B: [laughs] *Cos you **come home**.*
> C: *I **come home**.*
> B: *You **come home** to us.*
> A: *And we don't go out.*
> B: ***Yeah yeah**.*
> C: ***Sunday**'s a really nice day, I think.*
> B: ***It** certainly **is**.*
> C: ***It's a really nice** relaxing **day**.*
> B: *It's an earring, **it's an earring**.*
> C: *Oh lovely, **oh**, **lovely**.*
> B: ***It**'s fallen apart a bit but ...*
> C: ***It**'s quite a nice one actually, I like that.*

COHESION AND COHERENCE IN PARAGRAPHS 139

Paragraphs consist of an indeterminate number of sentences, but often a particular sentence may stand out as being more important than the others and provide important clues as to textual coherence. For example, the first sentence of a paragraph often indicates what the whole paragraph will be about, and is sometimes called the topic sentence. Equally, the final sentence in a paragraph may represent the logical conclusion or a summary of all the previous sentences.

→ 539 **Glossary** for any unfamiliar terms

In the following extract, the first sentence in the paragraph flags what the whole paragraph will be about (forming a friendship with one's dictionary) and sets the syntactic framework (the initial modal adjuncts in bold) for the subsequent sentences:

> [new paragraph in the introduction text to a learners' dictionary of English]
> ***Maybe** people see their dictionary as a friend. **Perhaps** a bond is created in all the hours that a learner spends together with a dictionary. **Perhaps** some of the character of the book rubs off on the reader.*

Wh-cleft structures and similar foregrounding structures (→ **475d**, **475**) may signal that the sentence in which they occur is a key sentence in the paragraph:

> [*UFO* = unidentified flying object]
> *Of course many pitfalls may lie in wait at this point of the research. But it is possible, with caution, to isolate categories of UFO with general characteristics. An example of one category of UFO, which some researchers have pinpointed, is of objects with an ovoid shape from 1 to 3 metres in diameter, which rotate on a vertical axis, close to the ground, and which appear to emit a wide range of electromagnetic radiation. Perhaps **what is most important is** that the nature of such identifiable UFO categories, and the conditions under which they might be observed, are predictable, after careful analysis of the data. Scientific searches, with appropriate instrumentation, are now able to prove once and for all that these UFOs do exist, and can provide information about their nature. To distinguish such phenomena from more dubious data, we propose that they should be renamed 'UAPs', for unidentified atmospheric phenomena, as this seems to be an appropriate and adequate description.*
>
> ***What is lacking at this stage is** for some imaginative research laboratory or university department to contact serious UFO researchers and design an experimental study for these UAPs. In the US, Harley Rutledge, head of the physics department at Southcast Missouri State University, has conducted a pilot study, with some encouraging results.*

Cohesive ties may operate across paragraph boundaries as well as sentence boundaries, especially determiners, comparative expressions and linking adjuncts:

> [from a book discussing different types of language-teaching material]
> *With international materials it is obvious that the needs of individual students and teachers, as well as the expectations of particular schools in particular countries, can never be fully met by the materials themselves.*
>
> ***Indeed, most users** seem to accept that what they choose will in many ways be a compromise and that they will have to adapt the materials to their situation.*

[from a book of tasks and activities for second-language learners]
Competitive activities that pit pairs against pairs and threes against threes are excellent for fostering collaboration and mutual help within each team. In this heightened atmosphere a lot of learning takes place without the students noticing they are 'studying'.

In many of ***these activities*** *the students' language task is to look at a set of sentences and decide which are correct and which are wrong. We believe that this testing of their own criteria is central to students building up a strong internal monitor to help them speak and write correctly.*

Pronoun ties alone may often be felt to be too weak across paragraph boundaries, and a definite determiner + noun may be preferable, as in the example above, where *these* used alone, without repeating *activities* in the second paragraph, may not have provided a strong and clear enough link. Equally, to have said 'their language task' instead of *the students' language task* in the second paragraph may not have been felt to be a strong enough tie.

Grammar and academic English

Grammar and academic English

INTRODUCTION 140

Academic writing and speaking take place in a variety of contexts. Student essays, assignments, presentations, dissertations and theses, lectures, tutorials, conference papers, books and articles by professional academics, all have different formal conventions, but all have a great deal in common in terms of grammar.

Academic writers and speakers mainly communicate with other academics and therefore can refer to things in complex and condensed ways, taking for granted that their readers and listeners share the grammatical conventions and contextual frames of reference to interpret them.

In general, academic language, especially writing, has quite complex structures and is more formal and impersonal in style than everyday language. The structuring and signposting of academic texts is important, and in spoken academic language, such as lectures and demonstrations, the spoken words are often accompanied by handouts, projected images, the whiteboard, etc., all of which have an effect on the grammar used (e.g. deictic words referring to diagrams and visuals: *here*, *above*, *see Table Two*, *in this chart*, etc.).

Much of the grammar of academic English is shared with that of English as a whole, and there are no special structures which are unique to academic English and never found elsewhere. On the whole, the grammar of academic English is closer (in both its spoken and written forms) to the grammar of general written English than to the grammar of general spoken English.

Where grammatical structures and items have been indicated as associated with written language in this book, then by and large such features are appropriate to academic English, with the exception of places where we have mentioned specialist registers such as journalism, advertising and specific literary conventions.

This chapter (140–154) focuses on items and structures which are common in academic language and which characterise it. We distinguish where appropriate between written and spoken academic styles. The chapter examines how information is packaged (typically in rather dense noun phrases), how tense, aspect, voice and modality are used to structure and signpost texts and to create an appropriate relationship with the listener/reader, how pronouns create such relationships, how sentences are typically linked, and how specific conventions are used (e.g. citing, abbreviations).

INTEGRATING INFORMATION IN THE NOUN PHRASE 141

The noun phrase is an important structure in academic English. Academic style, especially in writing, packs a great deal of information quite densely into noun phrases.

Noun phrases in academic writing tend to be more complex than in everyday, non-academic speech (→ 141e) or informal writing, especially in terms of modification and the embedding of elements, all of which serve to integrate different types of information in the noun-phrase structure.

Premodifying: classifying and evaluating 141a

Adjectives of classification (i.e. those which refer to the type or category of something, e.g. *chemical, Asian, metallic, conical, prehistoric*) and noun phrase premodifiers (→ 170a) are frequent, especially in scientific and technical writing. Unlike in informal conversational language, several premodifiers often occur, combining both adjectives and noun phrase modifiers.

In the examples, noun phrases are in green, premodifiers are in bold type:

[fluid mechanics text]
*The effect of **bottom** scattering on **swell** propagation is illustrated with **numerical model** computations for the **North Carolina continental** shelf using **high-resolution** bathymetry and an **efficient semi-implicit** scheme to evaluate the **bottom scattering source** term and integrate the **energy balance** equation.*

[about C.P. Scott, Editor of the *Manchester Guardian* newspaper]
*At the same time, Scott rejected the **prevailing contemporary** notion that the press should merely 'represent' the readers' interests.*

*Thornes & Shao (1991b) tested the sensitivity of individual meteorological parameters in a **road weather information** system by using a range of input values.*

Evaluative adjectives (those which give subjective judgements, such as *interesting, ground-breaking, misguided, excellent*, etc.) are more frequent in humanities subjects, where opinion and personal stance are often foregrounded. Such adjectives are normally gradable and may be premodified by adverbs of degree:

(noun phrases in green, premodifiers in bold type)

*The literature of Latina writers, like other ethnic literatures, examines in **very commanding** and **provocative** ways the construction of identity in the American context.*

*In the **familiar** territory of women's work, oral histories of societies at war have opened up a **far more fragmented** past experience than the narrative of social progress might suggest.*

Premodifying: coordination and hyphenation 141b

Premodifiers are often coordinated in academic styles, thus avoiding repetition of the noun head:

(noun phrases in green, coordinated premodifiers in bold type)

*For both **normal and oblique** incidence, the **stochastic and deterministic** theories are equivalent in the limit of long propagation distances.*
(compare with the uncoordinated alternative: For normal incidence and oblique incidence, …)

... and that sole parents and disability support pensioners should be required to demonstrate some form of ***social or economic*** *participation in return for receiving income support.*

Hyphenated compound adjectives are frequent, and these also contribute to the integration and condensation of information. They often reflect the condensation of a noun and its complement phrase:

(noun phrases in green, hyphenated premodifiers in bold type)

Spiral galaxies have a ***disc-like*** *appearance, with distinct,* ***spiral-shaped*** *arms on which most of the stars reside.*
(compare the noun-complement alternative: Spiral galaxies have an appearance similar to a disc, with distinct arms in the shape of a spiral on which most of the stars reside.)

These unusual outcomes have a number of ***policy-relevant*** *implications for sustainable development.*
(compare: ... a number of implications (which are) relevant to policy for sustainable development.)

Premodification of adjectives 141c

Adjectives are frequently premodified by adverbs in academic style:

[*SMS* = 'safe minimum standard' for the conservation of endangered species]
Arguments for the SMS are typically invoked in settings involving considerable uncertainty and ***potentially irreversible*** *losses.*

[describing an experiment to test people's anxiety levels, involving them making a speech while looking at a computer monitor screen where an 'audience' is displayed; the subjects have to imagine the audience is real]
High and low ***socially anxious*** *individuals were asked to make a speech to a monitor displaying six people whom they believed to be watching them live.*

Post-head elements: defining and specifying 141d

Postmodified and complemented noun phrases are extremely frequent in academic English because of the frequent need for definition and specification. All the types of postmodification and complementation described in **The noun phrase** are used; → 171–172.

Prepositional phrases are very frequent, and may consist of several occurring together:

(noun phrases in green, prepositions beginning post-head elements in bold type)

From their differing positions ***within*** *the family, men and women separately weighed the potential benefits and risks* ***of*** *migration.*

*The Bragg scattering **of** random, non-stationary surface gravity waves **by** random topography **on** a gently sloping bottom is investigated.*

Embedded prepositional phrases are common. This is another important aspect of integrating the maximum amount of information in the noun phrase:

(noun phrases in green, prepositions beginning embedded phrases in bold type in the examples)

[a *vole* is a small, mouse-like creature]
*In a field study **on** the behavioural response **of** grey-sided voles Clethrionomys rufocanus **to** predator odour, ear tattoos were used for individual marking of the voles in the field.*

a field **study**

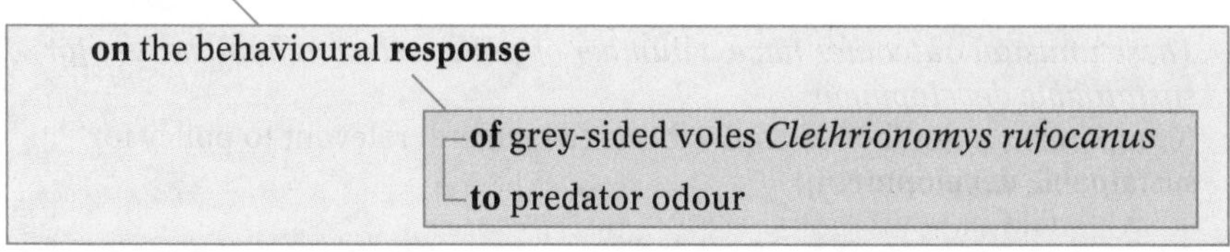

*This article demonstrates the connection **between** journalism, patriotism, and the culture **of** public discussion **in** late Victorian Britain.*

the **connection**

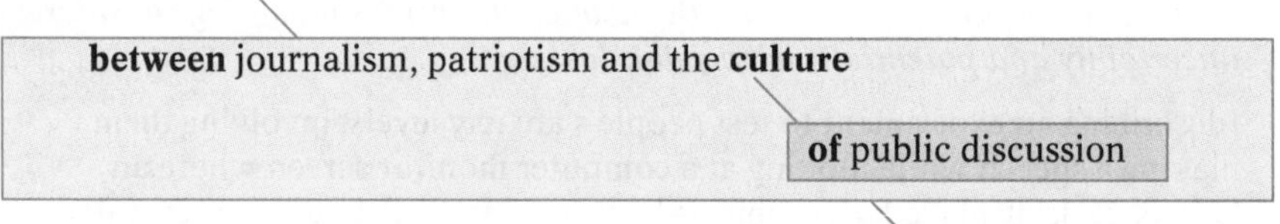

in late Victorian Britain

Postmodification by non-finite clauses is frequent in academic style:

(noun phrases in green, postmodifying clauses in bold type)

*The Latina writers **interviewed** consider their work to have a legitimate place in the canon of North American literature.*
(compare the finite alternative: The Latina writers who were interviewed …)

[from an article on nutrition, involving giving restricted amounts of food to laboratory rats]
*In previous studies the precise measurement of spontaneous activity was not possible in experiments **involving the laboratory rat** and, therefore, the energy **expended in relation to activity** and its role in adaptation to feed restriction could not be assessed.*

Noun phrases in spoken academic styles 141e

Spoken academic styles vary from being rather formal (e.g. large, formal lectures) to quite informal (e.g. small-group tutorials where teacher and students have built up a relaxed, friendly relationship). Noun phrases more typical of written styles, with much premodification and postmodification, occur in formal lectures, etc.

(noun phrases in green, premodificaton and postmodificaton in bold type)

[lecture on English literature]
But despite the apparent diversity of opinion, Anti-Pamelists were united on what they saw as three serious problems. All of which pertained to ***the earlier apparently subversive*** *part* ***of the novel****.*

[endocrinology lecture]
So you ought to be able to work out what seventy per cent of sixteen point eight millimoles per minute is in terms of ***the proximal tubular sodium*** *reabsorption* ***per minute****.*

In more informal lecturing styles and in informal tutorials and classes, typical spoken noun phrases are common, where information is added incrementally rather than integrated into a single noun phrase:

(noun phrases in green, noun heads in bold type)

[informal literature seminar]
It is a fascinating ***question****. It's a* ***question*** *of the kind that I don't think we pursue enough. And it's* ***one*** *that I'm still wrestling with.*
(compare an integrated alternative: It is a fascinating and under-researched question which is the subject of continuing investigation.)

→ also **142 Nominalisation** and **175 Formation of nouns (nominalisation)**

NOMINALISATION 142

Noun phrases are often used in academic style as an alternative to longer, clausal constructions, thus enabling the writer/speaker to integrate a considerable amount of information into the noun-phrase subject slot or object slot in the clause. This process, using a noun phrase to express a meaning more typically associated with an item from another word class, is called nominalisation.

Nominalisations include nouns which express verb-type meanings and adjective-type meanings. They are more frequent in written academic styles than in spoken:

[*IR* = the academic discipline International Relations]
The result was an IR canon, of the 'Plato to Nato' variety, which was substantially anachronistic. ***Its dismantling*** *over the last twenty years has much to do with efforts in the area of conceptual history. Despite this, and the* ***keenness*** *of post-positivist IR theorists to display an historical* ***consciousness****, IR and history maintain an uneasy* ***association****.*
(compare: *It was dismantled* over the last twenty years, and this has much to do with efforts in the area of conceptual history. Despite this, and the fact that post-positivist IR theorists *are keen* to display the fact that they *are* historically *conscious*, IR and history continue *to be associated* uneasily with one another.)

[*marking* and *recapture* refer here to capturing and marking animals for scientific research]
*The time lag between **marking** and first **recapture** was higher than the lag between second and third **recapture**, which indicates a trauma caused by the marking procedure.*
(compare: The time lag between *when we marked the animals* and *when we first recaptured them* was higher than the lag between *when we recaptured them for the second and third time* ...)

TEXTUAL SIGNALS 143

Textual signalling refers to how certain types of word signal the structure or organisation of the text. Textual signals guide the reader around the text and point to how the writer/speaker wants the text to be interpreted.

Signalling with *it*, *this* and *that* 143a

Reference to textual segments is an important aspect of academic style. The impersonal pronoun *it* and the demonstrative pronouns *this* and *that* are used in different ways to organise references to text segments and are frequently not interchangeable:

*For example, interacting with native speakers is obviously a Social Strategy, but if **it** is part of an overall language learning plan, **it** could also be a Metacognitive Strategy.*

*Low-luminance flickering patterns are perceived to modulate at relatively high rates. **This** occurs even though peak sensitivity is shifted to relatively low temporal frequencies.*
(the whole of sentence one is the topic of sentence two)
(~~It~~ occurs even though peak sensitivity is shifted to relatively low temporal frequencies.)

[anatomy lecture]
*And then that's what's called acoustic shadowing, you see, nothing getting through the back, there's a black shadow behind it. **This** is because this is a densely calcified gallstone sitting in his gall bladder.*
(*This* refers to 'acoustic shadowing ... nothing getting through the back, there's a black shadow behind it' and makes those clauses the new topic for discussion)

[genetics lecture]
*As I say, you'll learn more about the genetic codes which relate GAG to glutamate and GUG to thyamine in one of the other lectures in the course. **That** is another way of expressing the flow of information from DNA to proteins. Right.*

→ **128** for a full account of these uses of *it*, *this* and *that*

TEXTUAL SIGNALS: THE VERB PHRASE 144

General 144a

The verb phrase is important in academic discourse as the place where a number of textual signals of various kinds occur. These include using tense-aspect choices to mark the status of a quotation or citation vis-à-vis the writer's/speaker's current position (➝ 144b–144d below), or the use of modal verbs for hedging propositions (altering their level of assertiveness; ➝ 146 below) as a way of forestalling a challenge to or rejection of a claim.

Academic language has characteristic uses of tense and aspect which relate to important academic textual functions. These include:

Signposting

Tense-aspect choices refer the reader/listener backwards and forwards in the text. For example: *In this chapter we **have looked** at the process of compound formation.*

Structuring

Particular tense-aspect choices tend to be associated with particular parts of academic texts. Abstracts, summaries, concluding sections of academic books, papers and presentations, etc. usually have typical tense-aspect patterns associated with them (e.g. present simple in abstracts, ➝ 144b).

Reporting/narrating

Tense-aspect choices have become institutionalised for reporting and narrating experiments and studies, and for stating findings and conclusions, etc. (e.g. past simple narrating experimental procedures, ➝ 144c).

Citation

Tense-aspect choices have become institutionalised for citing and quoting one's own work and the work of others in different ways (➝ 144d).

The present simple 144b

Abstracts/summaries

The present simple form often appears in abstracts and summaries of academic works such as articles, chapters, dissertations, theses, essays:

> *This article **looks** at the effect of transoceanic migration on rural Sicilian families. The author **focuses** on the conflicts, stresses and transformations experienced by members of transnational families.*

Reporting findings

The present simple form is often used to report the outcome, results or findings of a piece of research (➝ 144c to compare the use of the past simple to narrate details of experiments):

> *This paper discusses some asymptotic uniform linearity results of randomly weighted empirical processes based on long-range dependent random variables. These results **are** subsequently **used** to linearize nonlinear regression quantiles in a nonlinear regression model with long-range dependent errors, where the design variables can be either random or nonrandom. These, in turn, **yield** the limiting behavior of the nonlinear regression quantiles. As a corollary, we*

__obtain__ the limiting behavior of the least absolute deviation estimator and the trimmed mean estimator of the parameters of the nonlinear regression model.

Reporting significant aspects of people's work

The present simple form is often used to report major tenets or central aspects of the work of other academics, especially where such work is considered important or relevant to the present context:

As Wittgenstein __suggests__, there is no such thing as a private language.

[lecture on text linguistics]
Halliday __argues__ that there are three basic transitivity choices. Okay. And he __calls__ them process options.

However, where the citation reports experiments and specific studies, the past simple is preferred.

Unlike previous work, our study personally __followed__ subjects rather than relying on record linkage methods to obtain information on death. In addition, we __examined__ mortality differences for men and women at several points from the beginning of the illness and over its course.

Creating synopses of fictional plots in works of literature

The present simple is used to summarise the plot/events in e.g. novels and plays:

Four men once close to Jack Dodds, a London butcher, __meet__ to carry out his peculiar last wish: to have his ashes scattered into the sea. For reasons best known to herself, Jack's widow, Amy, __declines__ to join them.

The past simple 144c

Referring to the procedures used in individual studies

The past simple form is common when academics refer to the procedures used in their own and others' individual experiments and studies:

[reporting one's own experiment/study]
In two studies, 65 three-year-olds, 57 five-year-olds, and 74 adults __viewed__ video clips of animals or inanimate objects being transported by a person. For each clip, the child __was__ asked whether the animal or object was moving.

[reporting experiments/studies by others]
Bogren et al (2000) statistically __modelled__ the magnitude of such temperature deficits with respect to solar elevation.

The present perfect 144d

Citing

Citing with the present perfect simple is similar to the use of the present simple form (→ 144b), and can sometimes occur as an alternative to the present simple, but the present perfect is especially used to emphasise current relevance or continuing debate:

Berg and Hudson (ch. 6; Hudson 1989) __have emphasised__ that modern factories need not have been large, yet the factories nonetheless were closely divided in their labour.

Schneirla (1966) ***has used*** *the concept of 'experience' to mean all kinds of stimulative effects from the environment.*

Recapitulating

The present perfect simple is used to summarise or recapitulate points or arguments in the discourse up to a particular moment, especially in concluding sections:

What is more, the qualitative analyses in this chapter ***have illustrated*** *crucial aspects of the lexical characteristics of everyday spoken language, and although we* ***have argued*** *against over-generalisation from one-off analyses, it is true that one does not need much data to see the same features constantly recurring.*

[literary stylistics seminar]
But of course we ***have talked*** *about the shape of the poem and that's where I want to go next. So if you have a look on the next sheet. We***'ve talked** *about lexis. We***'ve talked** *about morphology so far, and what we're looking at now is graphology. That is the actual shape on the page.*

Ongoing processes

The present perfect progressive is not typically used in concluding sections of academic texts, but may be used to refer to an ongoing process in the discourse up to a given point:

[discussing the way the playwright, Samuel Beckett, uses the space of the theatre stage]
*This pure space, which has only extension but no location, is quite different from the theatrical spaces I'***ve been discussing** *so far.*

[embryology lecture]
*And probably the surgical procedures that we***'ve been talking** *about while thinking of ways of correcting before birth can have a major effect.*

In general, progressive verb forms are not frequent in academic citations and in the structuring of academic texts (→ 144e), since academic texts are usually concerned with things that have permanent and long-lasting relevance, rather than temporary or unfolding relevance.

Modal expressions 144e

Will/shall/'ll

An academic writer/speaker may use *will/shall/'ll* to refer forward in a written text or in an academic presentation (e.g. a lecture), to outline or point to things which are to be found later in the text.

Both simple and progressive forms are used. Progressive aspect is especially used when the writer/speaker refers to events which will be repeated or be constant over longer stretches of text.

Shall, especially, indicates an undertaking by the writer/speaker to do the action referred to:

Radiant energy plays a vital role in astrophysical scenarios, and often appears as an equal partner to matter in determining the nature of physical processes which govern different structures. So we ***shall*** *next* ***consider*** *different types of radiant energy which exist in nature and how they interact with matter.*

It seems to me that this second case, in which coordination gives way to subordination, often holds in the works of Pascal that I ***shall be discussing****.*

[discussing the body displays and vocal displays made by animals]
In the different subsections of this section, I ***will discuss*** *different possible mechanisms underlying aspects of display development and their interrelationship.*

[immunology lecture]
*Let's now just concentrate on the B cells for a few minutes. And then we****'ll*** *come back to the T cells.*

As is true with all verb contractions, the contracted form *'ll* is not normally used in written academic style (→ 144f).

Be going to

Be going to is often used for forward reference in spoken academic style but is generally not used for this purpose in written academic style:

[law lecture]
But do you think that there is a point where the position of consumers has to be looked at very differently from businesses? [pause] *We****'re going to*** *talk about this more next week because we****'re going to*** *be talking about the Unfair Term.*

Verb phrases: contractions 144f

Contracted verb forms are generally avoided in academic writing:

It is *doubtful that such a project ever existed.*
(~~It's doubtful that ...~~)

[discussing the influence of the philosopher Schopenhauer on the novelist D.H. Lawrence]
I am *not saying that Lawrence* ***did not*** *read the other essays or even 'The World as Will and Idea';* ***I am*** *saying that* ***there is*** *no evidence that he did, and* ***we cannot*** *assume any but the briefest familiarity with Schopenhauer's system.*
(~~I'm~~ not saying that Lawrence ~~didn't~~ read the other essays or even 'The World as Will and Idea'; ~~I'm~~ saying that ~~there's~~ no evidence that he did, and ~~we can't~~ assume any but the briefest familiarity with Schopenhauer's system.)

Spoken academic presentations, however, often use contracted forms:

[university tutorial group; lecturer speaking about the writer, Jane Austen]
*Maxims usually express a commonsense point of view and Jane Austen****'s*** *full of that commonsense.*

[immunology lecture]
*And you can see that this is very similar to the picture we****'ve*** *looked at previously but we****'ve*** *added on two more molecules. So here****'s*** *our surface of the T cell.*

ACTIVE AND PASSIVE VOICE IN ACADEMIC DISCOURSE 145

Passive voice is common in academic discourse since it is often felt necessary to shift the focus from human agency to the actions, processes and events being described. In academic writing in particular, foregrounding the writer/researcher in such processes is often felt to be inappropriate (··› also 148):

> *A total of 14 case studies **were recorded**. The data **were analysed** using principles of conversation analysis and thematic analysis set within a hermeneutic interpretative framework. In order to illuminate presentations of autonomy in practice, focus-group discussions with nurses and older people **were used** as part of the interpretative process. **I discuss** the factors that prevented the operationalisation of an individualised rights-based concept of autonomy for older people.*

Note how the research process is described in the passive voice (*were recorded, were analysed, were used*), while the author changes to active voice (*I discuss*) when signposting the section dealing with personal stance and evaluation of the research.

Passive voice (along with the present tense, ··› 144b) is particularly prevalent in abstracts to academic papers and articles:

> *The urban hierarchy of an English region in the period 1300–1540 **is defined**, using both documentary and archaeological evidence. The part of the East Midlands studied – Leicestershire, Northamptonshire and Rutland – contained twenty towns. 'Benchmarks' for placing towns in the hierarchy **are explored**, including population, topography, social structure, occupational diversity, marketing and migratory networks, administration, and civic and material culture. The conclusion **emphasizes** the common urban characteristics of all of the towns studied, the compatibility of written and unwritten evidence, and the stability of the urban system.*

Note here that active voice (*emphasizes*) occurs with the impersonal subject *the conclusion* (compare the alternative constructions which would foreground the researcher: *I conclude/I emphasize in the conclusion*).

However, personal subjects and active voice verbs do occur frequently in academic discourse, particularly where a researcher is laying claim to a different or new approach to something, or contrasting their approach with that of others:

> *The acquisition of the English past tense inflection is the paradigm example of rule learning in the child language literature and has become something of a test case for theories of language development. This is unfortunate, as the idiosyncratic properties of the English system of marking tense make it a rather unrepresentative example of morphological development. In this paper, **I contrast** this familiar inflection with a much more complex morphological subsystem, the Polish genitive.*

Personal subjects and active voice are also common where speakers/writers provide textual signposting:

> *Throughout the literature, these pedagogical themes emerge: build a large sight vocabulary, integrate new words with the old, provide a number of encounters with words, promote a deep level of processing, facilitate imaging and concreteness, use a variety of techniques, and encourage independent learner strategies.* ***I will now discuss*** *each item in turn.*
> (compare: Each item will now be discussed in turn.)

✪ *I think* is less commonly used in academic writing than in everyday language, and expressions such as *in my view/opinion, I would argue/suggest, it is reasonable to suppose/conclude/suggest/*etc. are preferred when the writer is giving a personal opinion:

> *For example, the counting system, with its decade structure, certainly helps us to make complicated arithmetical calculations, but the experience of doing so also transforms our understanding of quantity, according to Vygotsky. It is a simple, testable and provocative idea whose time,* ***in my view****, has still to come.*
>
> ***I would argue that*** *different models are appropriate at different times.*
> (~~I think (that) different models are appropriate at different times.~~)

Get-passives are very rare in academic writing, but are more frequent in spoken academic style:

> [lecture about the alimentary system]
> *So particularly in middle-aged people who take Amatrozol, they're at a great risk of food poisoning because the bugs which the acid kills off don't* ***get killed*** *and they make it down through the gastrointestinal tract and give them a nasty case of food poisoning.*
> ('...are not killed' would be expected in written academic style)

Get-passives and *be*-passives may occur side by side in spoken academic style:

> [microbiology lecture]
> *Many viruses* ***get taken*** *up by cells of the immune system of one sort or another. And they* ***get transported*** *to the lymph nodes and swollen lymph nodes is a common feature of many virus infections. And what's happening is that as the virus* ***is taken*** *to the lymph nodes, there is an intense immune response within the lymph nodes so the lymph node swells in an attempt to try and eliminate the virus infection.*

HEDGING AND BOOSTING 146

Academic texts are most frequently characterised by a desire to avoid making claims and statements that are too direct and assertive, since academic discourse is often about theories, conclusions drawn from evidence, exchanging viewpoints, and so on, rather than hard, indisputable facts. Therefore, hedging (making a proposition less assertive) is very important in academic styles. Less often, it is sometimes also necessary to assert a claim or viewpoint quite directly and more confidently, a process we shall refer to as boosting.

Hedging and boosting are principally realised through modal expressions and through the use of simple tense forms. We also examine the role of adverbs and other constructions in asserting (boosting) and hedging.

Modality and tense-aspect 146a

Will is used to make confident predictions or to assert known or accepted facts:

Represented as a value between zero and one, X ***will*** *approach unity in perfectly flat and open terrain, whereas locations with obstructions such as buildings and trees* ***will*** *cause X to become proportionally less (Oke, 1992).*

[pathology lecture]
*Right. Red blood cells leaving the capillaries and then entering the tissues. They'****ll*** *break down there and haemoglobin* ***will*** *be released and the tissue* ***will*** *turn black and eventually* ***will*** *go.*

Must is used to make confident predictions or conclusions:

Such changes ***must*** *be due to changes in motivational organization of social behaviour.*

Must is also used in boosted directives to the reader/listener to pay attention to particular points:

We ***must*** *remember, however, that migrants may not need information about more than one destination.*
(compare the weaker: We should remember, however, ...)

It is useful to try to apply these general stages when considering any piece of worked stone. As always, they are meant to help us understand the processes and as such are merely an intellectual framework. Therefore one ***must not*** *apply them too rigidly.*

The unmodified simple forms of verb tenses are used to make non-hedged assertions:

Attachment, then, ***results*** *in close and prolonged proximity of bacterial digestive enzymes with the substrate.*
(compare the hedged: Attachment, then, may/can/could/might/should result in close and prolonged proximity of bacterial digestive enzymes with the substrate.)

→ 539 Glossary for any unfamiliar terms

*Adams **believed** that the Washington government must, for material as well as moral reasons, fight an aggressive war for American commerce.*
(compare: Adams may have believed/Adams probably believed ...)

Hedging: modality 146b

Can, could, might and *may*

Broadly speaking, *can, could, might* and *may* are used in academic style in the same way as they are used in general English, but one or two usages which are more frequent in academic style are worth noting. Academic English often needs to state possibilities rather than facts, and academics frequently hypothesise and draw tentative conclusions.

Can is often used to make fairly confident but not absolute assertions, in contrast with *could, might* or *may* (see below):

*These new insights into the multiple meanings of family **can** help us understand the experience of transnational migration.*
(asserting a claim of what is normal, i.e. almost equivalent to 'these new insights ... help us understand ...', but framed as 'usually/normally' rather than 'always')

Could and *might* are used for more tentative assertions:

*One **could** say that our concept of selfhood is radically contaminated by the mind-set of 'this is mine', 'I am this'.*

[consultant (A) tutoring a student doctor]
A: *Right. Very good. What do you think **might** have happened since he left hospital that caused this ulcer to break down yet again?*
B: *He **could** have either occluded his graft.*
A: *Yes.*
B: *Or the area **could** have become infected.*
A: *Okay. Now is there any clinical evidence that he **might** have occluded his graft?*

[on the behaviour of young birds]
*Thus, one **might** conclude that the predisposition to respond to pattern or flicker only affects the further development of a preference in that it **might** help to guide the young bird towards objects having these characteristics.*

A particular use of *may*, which is very common in academic texts, is to describe things which are likely to occur or which normally do occur. In this usage it is a formal equivalent of *can*:

*Parallel vertical pipes, several centimetres long and 1–2 mm thick, are common in much of the unit, but especially in the middle part, where there **may** be several in each cm horizontal section.*

[on mental health and mental retardation]
*The anger experience **may** culminate in a variety of behavioural reactions, including aggression or withdrawal.*

May is also widely used in a more general way in academic texts to make a proposition more tentative. *May* is less tentative than *could* or *might*:

*This change **may** also have been in progress in other counties.*

[*CFS* = chronic fatigue syndrome]
*Overall, one **may** conclude that the present study has shown that patients with CFS have psychomotor impairments, problems maintaining attention, and are visually sensitive.*

Would

Would is frequently used to hedge assertions which someone might challenge and to make argumentative claims less direct when used with speech-act verbs such as *advocate, argue, assume, claim, propose, suggest*:

*Given this, we **would argue** that the Iowa sample has provided a unique opportunity to examine a number of important questions regarding schizophrenia, including the issue of mortality.*

*Theoretically, one **would assume** that this increased bacterial mass would synthesize more enzymes.*

[lecture on the teaching of language and literature]
*And students think that by reading a text, getting the information from it, they have understood it. They are, I **would suggest**, full of the understanding of one level: the referential meaning.*

Would is also frequently used with *appear* and *seem*:

*It **would seem** that in this domain, as in so many others, the north was more favoured than the south.*
(compare the more assertive: It seems that in this domain …)

Should and *ought to*

Should allows the writer/speaker to describe desired or ideal situations. It is less strong than *must*:

*However, to assess different advantages and disadvantages in other circumstances, the chosen method **should** be examined critically before use.*
(compare the stronger: … the chosen method must be examined …)

Ought to is occasionally used in this way in academic style, but is much less frequent than *should*:

*Our use of the term 'stable' **ought to** be defined here.*

Should is used to hedge conclusions and predictions, but it expresses confidence in the probability that a situation will occur in a particular way:

*The overall agreement of the results **should** allow us to accept them with some confidence.*
(compare the more direct: … the results allow us to accept …)

→ 539 **Glossary** for any unfamiliar terms

[English literature lecture]
Okay. You ***should*** *be able to see the connections already and hopefully you can see what Anderson is saying in this extract.*

Hedging: other expressions 146c

Hedging in academic texts is often carried out by the use of a range of adverbial and prepositional constructions (plus some other types of expression). Their full effect can often best be observed by removing them from the example sentences quoted here.

Common hedging expressions include adverbs such as:

apparently	*generally*	*roughly*
arguably	*likely*	*seemingly*
broadly	*normally*	*surely*
evidently	*partially*	*typically*
frequently	*probably*	*usually*

It was, ***arguably****, the strongest leadership the department had ever had and it used its resources well.*

They are both from ***roughly*** *the same period in the middle of the sixteenth century.*

Yet, ***seemingly*** *for Bakhtin, though material forces no doubt exist, what determines that we know about them at all are intersubjective human relations.*

Common prepositional phrases and other expressions used as hedges include:

as a (general) rule	*in a way*	*in some respects/in many respects*
broadly speaking	*in most cases/in the majority of cases*	*more or less*
generally speaking	*in principle*	*roughly speaking*
in a sense	*in some senses*	

Survey researchers have ***as a rule*** *understandably preferred to make use of established diagnostic categories, rather than have to develop their own new ones and then try to persuade clinicians to accept these.*

[critique of a collection of political essays]
Thus the essays were, ***in a sense****, out of date when they appeared, yet the cultural tradition which they articulate and to which they contribute remains a part of the German scene to this day.*

This summary ***more or less*** *encapsulates the thesis advanced by Glynn in his new and wide-ranging history of arms races and arms control.*

Hedging and impersonal constructions 146d

Propositions may be hedged by the use of impersonal *it*-constructions with passive voice which enable the writer/speaker to avoid the more direct commitment to a proposition which a first person *I/we* + active voice may create:

> ***It is suggested*** *that the analytic procedures illustrated in this paper be applied to more widely-used oral testing instruments in order to evaluate their utility in eliciting conversational interaction.*
> (compare the more direct and personal: I suggest that ...)

Such impersonal *it*-constructions may also be used simply to hedge a proposition by attributing it to other, unnamed experts:

> ***It is claimed, or tacitly assumed,*** *in narrative studies that temporality should be explored in narrative texts where it functions as a dominant principle of organization.*

A range of impersonal *it*-expressions are common in academic texts to attribute propositions to unnamed people. These include:

it is (widely) accepted	*it is believed*	*it is/has been said*
it is generally agreed	*it is/has been claimed*	*it is/has been suggested*

> ***It is generally agreed*** *that one of the most influential reports published during the war was the Beveridge Report, published in 1942, which mapped out the future welfare state.*
>
> *Literature,* ***it is claimed,*** *seeks to recapture and reconstruct tradition.*

The use of a raised subject as an alternative to anticipatory *it*, similarly, enables the writer/speaker to make a less direct commitment to a proposition. Common passive expressions of this type include:

be believed to	*be found to*	*be shown to*
be claimed to	*be said to*	*be thought to*
be considered to	*be seen to*	

> *The value placed on children* ***is believed to have changed*** *from pre-industrial societies to the present time.*
>
> *Operating practices* ***are said to have been*** *a major obstacle to improvement.*

Boosting 146e

Boosting in academic texts, to make a claim more assertively, is often carried out by the use of a range of adverbial and prepositional constructions (plus some other types of expression).

→ 539 **Glossary** for any unfamiliar terms

Common boosting expressions include adverbs such as:

categorically	*indisputably*	*plainly*
certainly	*inevitably*	*undeniably*
clearly	*irrefutably*	*undoubtedly*
definitely	*observably*	*unquestionably*
emphatically	*obviously*	

This is ***clearly*** *a very restrictive hypothesis, which requires verification, and Lightfoot suggests that language change represents a useful testing ground.*

While most people were ***indisputably*** *poor, the economy had a considerable surplus above basic subsistence needs, although much of that surplus was concentrated in the hands of those in the top 10 per cent or so of the income distribution.*

Yet utilities and transport ***unquestionably*** *provide a service rather than a commodity.*

Other expressions used in boosting include:

for sure/for certain	*there is/was no doubt that*
*it is/was clear/obvious/ indisputable/*etc. *that*	*without doubt*

It was clear that *the Danes would remain neutral, although they offered to approach Catherine II in order to sound her out on a possible settlement.*

In the early nineteenth century this was ***without doubt*** *true of much of the Nord region and the Normandy textile area.*

PERSONALISING AND DE-PERSONALISING: PRONOUNS 147

I versus *we* 147a

The personal pronoun *I* is used in academic discourse for self-reference, particularly when referring to one's own stance (one's position or viewpoint) or conclusions, or when contrasting one's own approach with that of others. It commonly occurs with verbs expressing stance, particularly in humanities disciplines, and particularly in spoken academic style. Such verbs include:

accept	*assume*	*suggest*
advocate	*believe*	*suppose*
agree	*consider*	*suspect*
argue	*propose*	*think*

__I consider__ it unlikely that instruction accounts for anywhere near as much vocabulary growth as does incidental acquisition from context during reading.

[pathology lecture]
Right. We've got production of toxins. An endotoxin or an extra toxin. Right. __I assume__ you know the difference between the two. So we won't go into it.

I can occasionally be used with a generic meaning, particularly in the discipline of philosophy:

To guarantee the truth of my belief that you are in pain, __I__ need only determine whether the relevant physical, criterial conditions are satisfied. But if __I__ believe that being in pain involves something distinguishable from the satisfaction of such public conditions, __I__ am in serious philosophical trouble. Could it be that what __I__ assume to be other people are people in appearance only?
(*I* here refers to any person who thinks/acts in the way described)

We is typically used to refer to more than one author of an academic paper or article. Nowadays it is becoming less frequent for single authors to refer to themselves in the first person plural:

[paper by two authors]
In this paper __we__ report our experience with ear-tattooing in order to compare it with other methods used for marking small mammals.

The other characteristic use of *we* is to refer to the speaker/writer and listener/reader together, creating a sense of an academic community shared by all participants in the discourse:

[virology lecture]
__We__ know the molecular biology of this virus in very great detail. __We__ know the sequence of the genome from end to end. Now __we__ know the proteins encoded by that genome.

Single authors may sometimes use *we* as an inclusive strategy to carry the reader along with them in the unfolding argument or presentation of facts, even though it is the single author who has presented the arguments or facts:

In describing the process of gravitational instability __we__ have oversimplified matters a little.

We also occurs in textual signposting, where the writer/speaker is orienting the reader in some way, or pointing to links within the text to other parts of the text:

It is true, as __we__ have seen elsewhere in this book, that individual changes may aid or impair communication to a limited extent.

→ **539 Glossary** for any unfamiliar terms

You and *one* 147b

You and *one* can both be used to refer to people in general, and to the academic community of writer(s)/speaker and readers/listeners. *You* is less formal than *one*.

You in these generic uses is frequent in both written and spoken academic style, although it is considerably less frequent than *we* in written academic texts:

We could argue, however, that the probability of an uptake event is not fixed, but varies in a predictable way. It is possible, for example, that the more words ***you*** *already know, the easier it is to acquire the meaning of new words that* ***you*** *encounter.*

[from a text about the architecture of cathedrals]
If ***you*** *consider, for example, the plan of the Cistercian monasteries, where the church was designed to receive abbot, monks, lay brothers and the congregation, it was the position allocated to each of these elements within the edifice which led to its being partitioned.*

[virology lecture]
We'll see in some detail in a bit, viruses are quite unique in the way that they carry their genetic material and the most important feature is that viruses will only carry RNA or DNA. ***You*** *never find both in the same virus particle.*

One is also used with generic reference to people in general or to the academic community of a particular discipline, but it is considerably less frequent than *we* or *you*, especially in spoken academic style:

On biological grounds ***one*** *might suspect that the changes induced by early life experience are in an evolutionary context adaptive.*

[lecturer in History of English tutorial session]
I mean this theory that showed through analogy, now I think it's absolutely right, but I suppose ***one*** *has to say 'probably' because of course no one exactly knows how this happened.*

Mixing of *one* and *you* occurs in the same discourse, especially in spoken contexts:

[immunology lecture]
One *has to actually have the T cells there to isolate the T cells and show that they are reacting against a specific antigen. And are therefore said to be the main mediators of cell mediated immunity.* ***You*** *actually need the T cells themselves to demonstrate that they are responding to the antigen and having an immune effect.*

OTHER IMPERSONAL CONSTRUCTIONS 148

It-constructions 148a

Anticipatory *it* is frequently used in passive-voice clauses with or without an explicit agent to create an impersonal structure. This enables writers/speakers to distance themselves from assertions (→ also **146d Hedging and impersonal constructions**):

***It** has generally been accepted **by scientists** that models with fewer parameters and which make predictions are better models.*
(compare the more direct: scientists generally accept …)

***It** is argued that in the latter two cases, the default-like character of one of the affixes is attributable to the properties of the relevant inflectional subsystems, not to the predispositions that children bring to the language-learning task.*
(compare: I argue that …)

See also the next example below in **148b Existential *there***.

Existential *there* 148b

Existential *there* constructions are also regularly used instead of personal ones (note also impersonal *it* in this example):

[*marking* and *recapture* refer here to capturing and marking animals for scientific research]
*The time lag between marking and first recapture was higher than the lag between second and third recapture, which indicates a trauma caused by the marking procedure. However, **there was** no evidence of any weight loss as reported for other marking methods, and most of the tattooed animals did not show any behaviour indicating irritation after being marked. **It is concluded** that ear-tattooing, as an alternative to other methods of marking small mammals, is useful even in the field.*
(compare the more personal: However, I/we found no evidence …)

[endocrinology lecture]
*So as the fluid fluxes through this segment of the nephron its osmotic concentration goes from two ninety up to twelve hundred milliultinals per kilo and then back down to one eighty milliultinals per kilo. Now **there are** certain things to note as a consequence of that.*
(compare: We/you should note certain things as a …)

There + *exist* is also found in formal academic styles:

*This is similar to cognitive knowledge, in which **there exist** universally valid concepts to which each individual object could belong.*

Third person self-reference 148c

Academic writers often refer to themselves as 'the author', 'the (present) researcher', and often refer to their own work impersonally. This is especially the case in abstracts and other types of summary:

[article abstract, written by the article's author]
***This article** looks at the effect of transoceanic migration on rural Sicilian families. **The author** focuses on the conflicts, stresses, and transformations experienced by members of transnational families. … **This essay** highlights the deeply gendered nature of transnational migration, and the role of the family in altering ideas of husband, wife, mother and father.*

→ **539 Glossary** for any unfamiliar terms

IMPERATIVES AND RHETORICAL QUESTIONS 149

Imperatives

Imperatives occur in academic contexts most typically when the reader/listener is invited to consider or pay particular attention to something.

Some verbs in the imperative are particularly common in written texts. These include *consider, note, notice, observe, recall, remember, see*:

*For example, **consider** the way people often construe behaviour problems in boys who do and who do not have mental retardation.*

[text linguistics lecture]
*But the grammatical subject is also the agent, that is if the subject is doing something to the object. Okay. **Remember**, the grammatical subject is not always the agent.*

Let us, and in spoken contexts *let's*, are also common in academic discourse to direct a collective focus of attention on the part of writer(s)/speaker and readers/listeners:

*First, **let us perform** a comparative examination of two examples.*

[lecture on the alimentary system]
*So **let's look** now at their targets and in particular the dietary carbohydrates.*

First person *let me* is also common when the speaker/writer is signalling some upcoming aspect of the text. It is similar in function to *I shall/I will* (➔ above, **144e**):

[referring to the William Shakespeare play, *Romeo and Juliet*]
*With all this context in mind, **let me** return to the final scene of 'Romeo and Juliet' and to my questions (1) and (3): what would an audience in the mid 1590s actually have seen; and, equally important, so what?*

Rhetorical questions

Rhetorical questions and questions which the questioner immediately answers are frequent in academic contexts, since writers and speakers often wish to anticipate questions readers and listeners may be posing in their minds, or else wish to raise those same questions in the mind of the reader/listener prior to answering them:

*If the northwest-European-origin slaveowners had operated as if the slaves resembled life-cycle servants, **what might we expect to observe**?*

***Why is it that quasar activity declined in the universe both at high redshifts and at low redshifts**? If the conventional picture of quasars is correct, then …*

SENTENCE PATTERNS 150

In general, academic writing displays quite complex sentence patterns, including frequent use of all the types of subordination which occur in general English usage (➔ **310–317**).

Non-finite subordinate clauses are particularly common:

Surprisingly, the pioneers of modern urban healthcare supported a 'return to nature' by mobilizing anti-urban and pro-rural discourse. ***Comparing*** *Nottingham and Saint-Etienne, this article addresses the politics that produced this paradox.*

To explore *further the perceptual component, we measured perceived temporal frequency in human subjects with unilateral optic neuritis for whom optic nerve transmission is known to be relatively slow and generally similar to the normal physiological state under low luminance.*

Ellipted subordinate clauses are also frequent:

Specifically, ***when asked*** *in the post-use interviews how using the computer-tutor influenced their behaviour, students most commonly mentioned an increase in their level of effort.*

This approach could admit the possibility of conflict between an individual's use of freedom and the attainment of happiness ***while denying*** *that happiness could be attained without freedom.*

Clauses with *as* ... **151**

As-clauses referring to the works of other academics are an alternative to a reporting + reported clause structure:

By contrast, ***as*** *Gombrich* ***has remarked****, little value was placed on clarity in Renaissance iconography.*
(or: By contrast, Gombrich *has remarked that* little value was placed on clarity in Renaissance iconography.)
(By contrast, ~~as Gombrich has remarked that~~ little value was placed on clarity in Renaissance iconography.)

As-clauses often occur in the passive in academic style to exemplify or compare or to cite something/someone. In such cases, an *it*-subject is not used:

Hume's contention can be avoided by the use of inverse probability, ***as was seen*** *in Chapter 7, and although the justification of induction has always been a notorious problem, yet empirically, as Ramsey argued (Sahlin, 1990), induction is convincing because it is successful.*
(Hume's contention can be avoided by the use of inverse probability, ~~as it was~~ seen in Chapter 7, ...)

The same is true when subject-verb inversion occurs after *as*:

When total study time was limited but local study time was free, ***as was the case*** *in Experiment 2, the experimental subjects allocated more study time to items in the non-mobilized category, whereas the control subjects allocated an equal amount of time to items in both categories.*
(When total study time was limited but local study time was free, ~~as it was the case in Experiment 2,~~ ...)

539 **Glossary** for any unfamiliar terms

LINKING ADJUNCTS 152

The use of linking adjuncts (→ 136) is important in academic language, especially in writing, to give coherence to the text and to organise it.

Academic English uses many linking adjuncts which are not frequent in everyday conversational English. The following occur frequently in academic contexts but only very infrequently in day-to-day conversational language:

- Additive: adding further ideas (→ 136b):

additionally	*in addition*	*similarly*
equally	*likewise*	
furthermore	*moreover*	

The national income grew roughly 2.5 times between 1945 and 1990 and earnings in real terms grew, if anything, even more rapidly. Household income gained ***additionally*** *from the higher proportion of women in paid jobs.*

- Resultative: expressing causes, reasons, results, consequences (→ 136c):

accordingly	*hence*	*in view of this/that*
as a consequence	*in consequence*	*therefore*
as a result	*in (the) light of this/that*	*thus*
consequently		

The behaviour of dark matter is governed entirely by gravitational forces, and ***hence*** *is easy to incorporate theoretically – both in calculations and in computer simulations.*

- Contrastive: contrasting, opposing (→ 136d):

by/in contrast	*nevertheless*	*on the one hand … on the other hand*
conversely	*nonetheless*	
however	*on the contrary*	

Histories of literacy and print culture had also cultivated an interest in visual media. These studies ***nonetheless*** *generally focused on print rather than writing.*

- Organisational: organising and structuring the text, listing:

finally	*in conclusion*	*in summary*
firstly, secondly, thirdly	*in its/in their turn*	*lastly*
in brief	*in short*	*respectively*
	in sum	*subsequently*

This reviewer might wish to question particular judgements here and there, but ***in sum*** *this is a fascinating and thought-provoking book.*

Note also that a number of non-finite clausal constructions are used in academic texts to signal summaries (*to sum up*, *summing up*, *to conclude*, *to summarise*).

→ also **123–139 Grammar across turns and sentences** and **335 Linking**

Problems with linking adjuncts 153

Certain linking adjuncts typical of academic style are often misused.

On the contrary, by contrast, on the other hand

On the contrary, *by contrast* and *on the other hand* are different. *On the contrary* rejects a previous statement in favour of an opposite one:

> *Such complex impressions on the part of teachers by no means arise from ignorance or prejudice:* ***on the contrary****, they are the result of powerful, historically informed, shared perspectives on musical reality.*

By contrast and *on the other hand* hold two statements up for consideration and comparison/contrast, but do not reject the first one:

> *Criminality in pre-industrialized Europe is thus characterized more by violence against persons than by property crimes such as theft. Modern society,* ***by contrast****, is thought to experience more theft than violence.*

> *Athenian public buildings and spaces were magnificent. Private houses,* ***on the other hand****, seem to have been small, and minimally furnished.*
> (both statements are true, but are presented for contrast with each other)

First(ly) and *at first*

First or (more formally) *firstly*, not *at first*, is used to label the first item or point in a list:

> *In this paper we* ***firstly*** *review the empirical studies carried out by Annett. We* ***then*** *discuss the ways in which genotypes are identified within the Annett studies, we show that this is inefficient, and then describe a more powerful and sensitive method that we use in our own empirical study.*

At first is used to contrast two different situations in time:

> *Employment had* ***at first*** *been only too full, and the economy was overloaded.* ***But by the end of the period*** *the very idea of full employment seemed illusory and even Keynes' view that 5 per cent was a reasonable level to aim for would have seemed highly optimistic.*

Last(ly) and *at last*

Last(ly), not *at last*, is used to label the final item or point in a list:

> *As a rule the multiple-function centres were the first to acquire the innovation; they were* ***followed by*** *the prefectoral towns,* ***then*** *by industrial towns, and* ***lastly*** *by those not dominated by any single activity.*
> (…, ~~then by industrial towns, and at last by those not dominated by any single activity.~~)

At last is used to indicate that something happens, but later or after a longer period of time than was hoped or expected:

> *By 1937 activity was 70 per cent higher than five years earlier. Much more than a recovery from the depression, or even a result of substituting home production for imports, the upsurge has been interpreted as being the structural change that the 1920s failed to achieve (Richardson 1967). New industries were* ***at last*** *replacing the old staples.*

OTHER ASPECTS OF ACADEMIC STYLE 154

The grammar of titles and sub-titles 154a

Titles of academic works often use the *-ing* form of the verb in a non-finite clause to indicate research activity directed towards a stated goal or some ongoing process. Examples of titles of books and papers:

[book title]
*Negotiat**ing** Service: Studies in the Discourse of Bookshop Encounters*

[title of a paper in a musical education journal]
*Rais**ing** standards in performance*

[title of a paper in a behavioural sciences journal]
*Vary**ing** the scale of financial incentives under real and hypothetical conditions*

The preposition *towards* is often used in academic titles to indicate tentative proposals or initial explorations in new theory. Examples of book titles:

*EC Regionalism at the Turn of the Millennium: **towards** a new paradigm?*

***Towards** more Effective Supplementary and Mother-tongue Schools: guidelines*

***Towards** a Reference Architecture for Natural Language Generation Systems*

Punctuation 154b

Academic writing has developed punctuation conventions which are normally observed when writing essays, papers, articles and books.

Quotations

For punctuating quotations, a variety of conventions exists, often depending on individual publishers or journal styles, or the rules of individual institutions. Some typical examples are given here.

No punctuation of the quoted words if indented
Longer quotations from people's works often occupy their own paragraph and are usually indented further than the current paragraph indentation. In this case, no quotation marks are used.

Single or double quote marks within the body of the text
Although considerable variation exists, there is a tendency to prefer single quotation marks, particularly when citing single words or short phrases. If double quote marks are used, they are more likely to enclose longer quotations. Single quotes may also be used to draw attention to a particular nuance of a word or an unusual use of it, or to question a term or concept:

Communication in the ELT classroom is a highly complex, complicated and elusive phenomenon: 'a problematic medium' (Cazden, 1986: 423).

Pomerantz reports (1986: 227) that formulations "assert the strongest case in anticipation of non-sympathetic hearing" and hence are frequently used in complaining.

Use of the colon to introduce quotations
The colon is often used to introduce quotations where they do not form a continuous sentence with the author's own text (see also the example beginning 'Communication in the ELT classroom ...' above):

As Young reminded his audience: In the beginning of the war we advertising men had very little standing.

Where the quotation forms a continuous sentence with the author's own text, no punctuation other than quote marks is necessary:

Robert Crassweller, Trujillo's biographer, notes that America's unfamiliarity with the Dominican Republic is "a fact that must be included among the curiosities of the region".

Bibliographic citations

There are different ways of punctuating bibliographical citations. Most typically, a citation appears within round brackets in the text:

Thornes & Shao ***(1991b)*** *tested the sensitivity of individual meteorological parameters in a road weather information system by using ...*

Where the whole citation is already within parenthesis, commas typically separate authors' names and dates, and the semi-colon is used to separate different citations:

*The dominance of X as a controlling parameter for RST has also been found in many other studies (e.g. Barring et al.***,** *1985***;** *Elliasson***,** *1996***;** *Upmanis***,** *1999). The impact of X will be most noticeable during times of high atmospheric stability, when potential radiation losses are at their greatest.*

Where specific page numbers are given in a citation, the colon is normally used:

*'Situation' and 'sequence' are two concepts which Winter, working with written sentences, sees as fundamental in the interpretation of sequences of clauses in text (Winter, 1982***:** *2).*

Titles and sub-titles

A title and sub-title are often separated by a colon. This usually indicates that the sub-title is an explanation or paraphrase of the title:

[title of an article in an academic book]
*Focus on the language learner***:** *motivation, styles and strategies*

[title of a chapter sub-section in an academic book]
*Dark matter***:** *weight without light*

→ **539 Glossary** for any unfamiliar terms

Bibliographies and lists of references 154c

Conventions exist for the ways in which bibliographies and lists of references are laid out in academic books, papers and essays. These sometimes depend on individual publishers or conventions adopted by colleges and universities, but some are widely used internationally, for example the APA (American Psychological Association) system, which lays out bibliographical references in the following ways (note the use of commas, full stops, colons, italics and brackets). The examples given here are APA style; other systems (e.g. Harvard, MLA) may be quite different.

Books

author	date	title of book	place of publication	publisher
Biber, D.	(1995).	*Dimensions of Register Variation.*	Cambridge:	Cambridge University Press.

(APA)

Biber, D. (1995) *Dimensions of Register Variation*, Cambridge University Press, Cambridge.
(Harvard)

Biber, D. Dimensions of Register Variation. Cambridge: CUP, 1995.
(MLA)

Papers in academic journals

author	date	title of article	journal	volume and issue	pages
Sinclair, J.	(1996).	The search for units of meaning.	*Textus,*	9(1),	75–106.

Articles/chapters in books

author	date	title of article/chapter	name(s) of book editor(s)
Bakhtin, M. M.	(1986).	The problem of speech genres.	In T. W. McGee & C. Emerson & M. Holquist

	title of book	page numbers of the article	place of publication	publisher
(Eds.),	*Speech Genres and Other Late Essays*	(pp. 60–102).	Austin:	University of Texas Press.

Abbreviations used

The following abbreviations often appear in textual and bibliographical references:

& = and

cf. = compare

edn. = edition

ed(s). = editor(s)

et al. = and other authors

ibid. = the same place in a work already referred to

ms. = manuscript

no. = issue number

op. cit. = the work already referred to

p. = page pp. = pages

Trans. = translator/translated by/translation

vol. = volume

Introduction to word classes and phrase classes

Introduction to word classes and phrase classes

INTRODUCTION 155

This chapter (155–166) explores the types and functions of words and how they form phrases. The chapter introduces terminology and definitions and lays a basis for more detailed treatment in a number of subsequent chapters. The main word classes dealt with in this chapter are: noun, verb, adjective, adverb, preposition and conjunction. Word classes are traditionally called parts of speech.

A further word class, determiner, is dealt with in **176–196 Nouns and determiners**. There are also minor word classes such as interjections (*ouch*, *oi*, *oh*, *ah*). However, these minor types operate outside of the clause and sentence structure.

➔ **113 Interjections**

Word classes can be either open or closed. Open classes admit new words, whereas closed classes are a more limited set and only rarely admit new words. For example, nouns are an open class and new nouns are created all the time; pronouns, however, are a closed class and it is not easy to create new pronouns. Thus, the growth of the internet has resulted in many new nouns such as *blog* (from 'web-log'), *smiley*, *spam*, *hypertext*, but the new written pronoun *s/he* has failed to become universally established.

Many languages use word endings to distinguish between nouns and verbs and other word classes. In English different word classes can be formed by the process of derivation using suffixes. For example, the suffix *-ment*, when added to the verb *amaze*, changes the word class to the noun *amazement*. However, although English uses such word endings, they are not a reliable guide to word class; for example, *augment* is a verb, and *comment* can be a verb or a noun, depending on context.

Word endings can also be inflections, which indicate categories such as tense, person and number. The inflection *-ed* can change a verb from present to past tense (*walk/walk**ed***), and the inflection *-s* can indicate third person singular concord with a subject. But inflections do not change the word class. *Walk* and *walked* are both verbs.

➔ **258–268 Word structure and word formation**

A word may have more than one grammatical form. For example, *sing* belongs to the word class of verb and yet has several different forms such as: *sings*, *singing*, *sung*, *sang*. We refer to the word *sang* as the past form of the word *sing*. It is common for a single form to have different grammatical functions. For example, in the case of the verb *cut* the present and past form of the verb are the same. There is, however, only one underlying form in each case: *sing* and *cut*.

Items within a particular class may consist of more than one word. For example, the phrasal verb *take off* (as in *take off your coat/take your coat off*) consists of two words but operates syntactically and semantically as a unified item.

Underlying forms are called lexemes. For example, the word *water* has a similar meaning when used as a noun (*I drank the water*) and when used as a verb (*I must water the plants*) but it is a different lexeme in each case. A lexeme can only belong to one word class. So *I **watered** the plants* involves the same lexeme as *I must **water** the plants*, but a different lexeme from *I drank the **water***. Forms such as *water*, *waters*, *watering* and *watered* are grammatically distinct forms of the same lexeme, the verb *water*.

Sometimes differences in pronunciation distinguish words with identical forms. For example, *refuse* (/rɪˈfjuːz/ verb, meaning to decline) and *refuse* (/ˈrefjuːz/ noun, meaning household rubbish) or *row* (/rəʊ/ noun, meaning a line of seats) and *row* (/raʊ/ verb, meaning to quarrel).

Words can be converted from one class to another and new words are often formed in this way. For example, the noun *fax* has been converted into a verb *to fax*. The adjective *hopeful* has been converted into a noun and is used in contexts such as *There were three hopefuls being interviewed for the job*.

Words combine to form phrases. Each word class has a corresponding phrase class. This book has chapters dealing with noun phrases, verb phrases, adjective phrases, adverb phrases and prepositional phrases. Because of the complexity of determiner phrases, a special chapter is devoted to them.

Sections 156–166 contain basic definitions of six major word classes: nouns, verbs, adjectives, adverbs, prepositions and conjunctions.

NOUNS 156

Nouns: forms 156a

Nouns are the largest class of words. They denote classes and categories of things in the world, including people, animals, inanimate things, places, events, qualities and states. For example, *accident*, *cat*, *club*, *competition*, *conscience*, *garage*, *soldier*, *pride*, *James*, *Paris* are nouns.

Suffixes

Nouns are not usually identifiable by their form. However, common derivational suffixes which may enable words to be recognised as nouns include:

suffix	nouns	suffix	nouns
-age	*wastage, postage, mileage*	*-ist*	*artist, realist, pessimist*
-al	*approval, withdrawal*	*-ity*	*practicality, identity*
-ant	*deodorant, disinfectant, itinerant*	*-ment*	*amazement, containment*
-dom	*kingdom, wisdom*	*-ness*	*fitness, toughness*
-ee	*referee, tutee*	*-ship*	*ownership, studentship*
-er, -or	*trainer, runner, actor, vendor*	*-tion, -sion*	*addition, caption, extension*
-hood	*childhood, girlhood*	*-tude*	*altitude, multitude*
-ing	*building, fencing*	*-y*	*entry, discovery*
-ism	*socialism, idealism*		

The suffixes can be added to verbs and adjectives to form nouns:

verb	noun
amaze	*amazement*
contest	*contestant*
refer	*referee*
survive	*survivor*
write	*writer*

adjective	noun
bright	*brightness*
happy	*happiness*
loyal	*loyalist*
rapid	*rapidity*

Conversion

Conversion can also occur from verbs to nouns. Examples include:

*a **desire** to do something*

*a **lack** of something*

*a **cheat***

*a long **walk***

*a **pay rise***

Occasionally, adjectives may be converted to nouns:

*He's a **regular** at our local pub.*

*The clubs are mostly full of young **singles**.*

Prefixes and compounds

New nouns can be formed by other means, for example by prefixes (e.g. *non-event*, *pre-meeting*) and by compounding (e.g. *mousepad*, *website*).

→ **258–268 Word structure and word formation** for further details

Singular and plural

Most nouns have a singular and plural form which can be distinguished by different inflectional endings. The most common plural form is *-(e)s*. For example, *cat–cats*, *wish–wishes*. Some nouns have irregular plurals, mainly because they reflect older English forms or are derived from foreign words. Examples of these are: *ox–oxen*, *alumnus–alumni*.

Gender

The gender of nouns is significant in some languages. Nouns in English do not in themselves have masculine or feminine gender. They do, however, sometimes refer to male or female people or animals, or consist of a pair where one is used as the neutral term covering both sexes and the other is more marked. For example, *host–hostess*, *father–mother*, *widower–widow*, *dog–bitch* (where *dog* is the neutral term).

Nouns: types 156b

Nouns differ in their types of meaning, for example common nouns (e.g. *table*, *boy* and most nouns) versus proper names (e.g. *Joanna*, *New York*), or concrete nouns (*cup*, *bus*) versus abstract nouns (*love*, *beauty*).

The major grammatical distinction in English nouns is between count nouns and non-count nouns. English treats some things as units which can be counted and some things as indivisible wholes. Count nouns refer to people and things which can be counted. Non-count nouns refer to things which are treated as indivisible wholes which cannot be broken down in order to be counted:

count nouns	non-count nouns
a dog – dogs	*butter, oil, advice, furniture, belongings, trousers*
church – churches	

For some nouns the singular and plural forms are the same (e.g. *sheep*, *series*, *deer*).

Nouns: syntactic characteristics 156c

Nouns can be recognised by the following syntactic characteristics:

- They may be preceded by determiners:

  ***the** young boy*

  ***my two** cats*

- They may be modified by adjectives:

  *a **large** pizza*

  *those **lovely** flowers*

- They may be premodified by other nouns:

  *a **university** degree*

  *a **computer** programmer*

When a noun is head of a subject noun phrase, it agrees in person and number with the tensed verb of the clause:

*My throat **is** sore.*
(agreement between singular noun and the present tense of *be*)

*Their apologies **were** accepted.*
(agreement between plural noun and the past tense of *be*)

NOUN PHRASES 157

Noun phrases: form 157a

Nouns act as the main words, or heads, of noun phrases. A noun phrase usually consists of a head along with modifiers or a complement. Modifiers occur before the head (premodifiers) and after the head (postmodifiers).

Premodifiers include determiners (words such as *a*, *an*, *the*, *this*, *all*, *any*, *some*), adjectives (*blue*, *cautious*, *economic*, *old*) and other nouns (*government*, *school*).

539 Glossary for any unfamiliar terms

Postmodifiers include prepositional phrases (*the cafeteria **in the building**, an insurance policy **with profits***), relative clauses (*the student **who needed to speak to you**, the report **that was published in 1997***) and adverb phrases (*the room **upstairs**, the lecture **yesterday***).

Complements occur after the head and function to complete the meaning of the noun (*the body **of a young woman**, the suggestion **that we should refuse to pay***). Postmodifiers give extra information and are not necessary for the meaning to be completed. Complements complete the meaning of the noun.

In the following examples, the whole of the noun phrase is green and the head is in bold:

*The **problem** cannot be solved.*

*All the **offices** in the building are closed.*

*He is an old **man** who lives near us.*

***Divorce** was inevitable.*

The head of a noun phrase can also be a pronoun instead of a noun:

***She** was very unhappy in her new job.*

***Someone** was looking for you earlier.*

Noun phrases: functions 157b

Noun phrases can act as the subject (S), object (O) or complement (C) of a clause (noun phrase in green, head in bold):

S O
*Her **brother** mended our **car**.*

C
*You're a good **friend**.*

Noun phrases can be the complements of prepositions:

*I did it **for** the **children**.*

Less often, noun phrases may occur as clause adjuncts (modifying the clause in some way, most typically in terms of time):

*I saw him the following **day**.*

→ **167–175 The noun phrase; 176–196 Nouns and determiners; 197–212 Pronouns**

VERBS 158

Verbs: forms 158a

Verbs are the second largest class of words. Typically, verbs denote actions, events, processes and states. For example, *sing, consult, eat, argue, break, sleep, encounter.*

Suffixes

Some verbs are recognised from their endings, but most verbs are not identifiable from their form. Suffixes which can denote verbs include:

suffix	verbs	suffix	verbs
-ate	*hyphenate, chlorinate*	*-ify*	*beautify, identify*
-en	*widen, sadden*	*-ize, -ise*	*realize, industrialise*
-iate	*differentiate, appreciate*		

Conversion

Verbs may be formed by conversion from other word classes. Examples include:

- verbs related to nouns:

  *to **corner** a thief*

  *to **hand** something to someone*

  *to **position** a table*

- verbs related to adjectives:

  *to **calm** someone*

  *to **empty** one's glass*

  *to **humble** oneself*

Verbs which have the same form as other word classes are recognised as verbs by their syntactic functioning in context:

*What **sort** of camera have you got?*
(noun)

*Can you **sort** the potatoes into large ones and small ones?*
(verb)

*It's a **narrow**, twisty road.*
(adjective)

*That would **narrow** our options considerably.*
(verb)

*Did you go **up** the tower?*
(preposition)

*They're going to **up** the wages of all the part-timers.*
(verb)

⇢ **539 Glossary** for any unfamiliar terms

Prefixes

Prefixes are also used with verbs to create new verbs. The most common prefixes used with verbs are: *un-*, *out-*, *over-*, *under-*:

verbs	new verbs with prefixes	verbs	new verbs with prefixes
pack, lock	*unpack, unlock*	*eat, charge*	*overeat, overcharge*
live, do	*outlive, outdo*	*estimate*	*underestimate*

Regular and irregular

Verbs are either regular or irregular. The regular form simply adds inflections to the base form without internal change. Verb inflections indicate number agreement and whether the form shows tense (present or past) or not:

base form	*cough*
present form	*cough*
-s form	*cough**s***
-ing form	*cough**ing***
past form	*cough**ed***
-ed participle	*cough**ed***

Only the verb *be* has separate inflectional forms for all of the different categories of form:

base form	*be*
present form	*am, are*
-s form	*is*
-ing form	*being*
past form	*was, were*
-ed participle	*been*

Irregular verbs have a variety of types of ending and internal change applied to the base form. There are approximately two hundred and fifty irregular verbs in English. Almost all irregular verbs are irregular only in terms of their past form and *-ed* form. For example:

base form	*speak*
present form	*speak*
-s form	*speak**s***
-ing form	*speak**ing***
past form	*sp**oke***
-ed participle	*sp**oken***

→ 529 Appendix: Irregular verbs

Multi-word verbs

Multi-word verbs are verbs which consist of more than one word. The most common type of multi-word verb comprises a verb followed by one or more particles (usually prepositions or adverbs or both) which combine with the verb to form a single syntactic and semantic unit. In all respects multi-word verbs behave in the same way as single-word verbs and are lexical verbs in their own right. Examples of multi-word verbs are: *give in, look after, look up to, put up with, catch up on*.

⇢ **235 Multi-word verbs**

Verbs: types 158b

There are three main grammatical classes of verb: lexical, auxiliary and modal.

Lexical verbs are the biggest class and include most verbs. Lexical verbs denote types of action, state or event (e.g. *walk, shine, think, drive, feel, shout, buy, fall*). They are an open class, and new verbs are frequently created.

Auxiliary verbs are a closed class consisting of *be, do* and *have*. Auxiliary verbs add information to the lexical verb, indicating clause type (e.g. interrogative, negative), aspect (progressive and/or perfect) and passive voice. *Be, do* and *have* can also be used as lexical verbs.

Modal verbs are a closed class consisting of core modal verbs (*can, could, shall, should, will, would, must, might, may*), semi-modal verbs (*dare, need, ought to, used to*) and modal expressions (*be able to, have (got) to*). Modal verbs add information to the lexical verb, mainly concerning degrees of certainty and necessity. Modal verbs do not inflect for tense, person or number, and only display historical remnants of tense contrasts, such as *can–could, will–would*.

Verbs: characteristics 158c

A typical verb can be recognised because it follows the subject noun phrase, agrees with the subject noun phrase in person and number and can indicate tense (except for the modal verbs, ⇢ **158b**). For example, *dream* and *walk* can be either nouns or verbs but can be identified by their respective syntactic properties:

*That was **a very frightening dream**.*
(noun)

*The character **dreamed** that she was in outer space.*
(verb in past tense)

***The space walk** was the most exciting event.*
(noun)

*She **walks** too quickly for me.*
(verb in present tense, agreement in person and number with subject)

⇢ also **260 Word formation; 529 Appendix: Irregular verbs** for full list of irregular verbs; **213–216 The verb phrase 1** for further details concerning verb structure and morphology, and word order for verbs and verb phrases

VERB PHRASES 159

Verb phrases: forms 159a

Verbs act as the heads of verb phrases. The head is the first verb in the verb phrase, and it determines the form of what may follow.

A verb phrase may consist of a lexical verb only but may also include auxiliary verbs or modal verbs. In the following examples verbs are in bold:

*I **asked** you.*
(main verb only: lexical verb *ask*)

*I **could**.*
(main verb only: modal verb *could*)

*I **have asked** you.*
(auxiliary verb *have* + main verb)

*I **must ask** you.*
(modal verb *must* + main verb)

Modal verbs and auxiliary verbs precede lexical verbs. A modal verb (**modal**) and auxiliary verbs (**aux**) can occur together. The modal verb comes first. More than one modal is not permitted but there may be several auxiliary verbs:

modal aux
A: *We **should have bought** it there and then.*

modal aux
B: *Yes, we **should have**.*

modal aux aux
*They **must have been talking** about it for ages.*

modal aux aux aux
*It **might have been being used** at the time.*

Where there are combinations of modal verbs and auxiliary verbs, the order of these is modal verb ➛ perfect *have* ➛ progressive *be* ➛ passive *be* ➛ lexical verb:

	modal	perfect	progressive	passive	lexical verb	
It	***might***	***have***	***been***	***being***	***used***	*at the time.*

Each element requires a particular kind of complementation to follow it:

a The modal verb must be followed by the bare infinitive (without *to*).
b The perfect *have* must be followed by the *-ed* participle.
c The progressive *be* must be followed by the *-ing* form.
d The passive *be* must be followed by the *-ed* participle.

➛ **217–226 The verb phrase 2**

Auxiliary *do* is required to form negatives, interrogatives and emphatic forms when the lexical verb is not preceded by any other auxiliaries:

*She **doesn't** smoke.*
(negative)

***Did** you buy a newspaper?*
(interrogative)

*I **do** like your skirt.*
(emphatic)

The verb phrase (in bold below) begins the predicate part of the clause (in green below). This is the part which elaborates what the subject is, does or experiences:

subject **predicate**
*Josh | **might need** to leave early.*

Verb phrases: tensed and non-tensed forms 159b

Verb phrases are either tensed or non-tensed. Tensed verb phrases show contrasts in tense. They also show contrasts in number and person:

*She **works** hard now but she **worked** even harder during the whole year.*
(contrast in tense: *works/worked*)

***He's** too old but **we're** not.*
(contrast in number and person: singular/plural; 3rd person/1st person)

Non-tensed forms of the verb are:

- the base form (e.g. *work*) used as the imperative form (*Come on! **Work!***) or as the subjunctive (*They insisted she **work** the same hours as everyone else.*) (→ 229)
- the infinitive with *to* (e.g. *she tried **to work***)
- the *-ing* form (*she's **working***)
- the *-ed* participle (*she has **worked***)

The time references of non-tensed verb phrases are understood in terms of the time references of main-clause verbs:

***Exercising** every day, he still **did** not lose weight.*
(past reference understood from *did*)

***Attracted** by low prices, tourists **flock** to the islands every year.*
(present reference understood from *flock*)

***To be** there for eight o'clock we'**ll** have to leave at about six.*
(future reference understood from modal *'ll*)

Verb phrases: aspect 159c

Verb phrases can also indicate aspect. The two aspects are progressive and perfect. Aspect adds information about the speaker's perspective on time.

Progressive

The progressive aspect is formed with auxiliary *be* form and the *-ing* form of a lexical verb. It adds information to the verb concerning the speaker's perception of events as unfolding in time, without reference to starting or finishing points:

*We**'re leaving** now.*

***I was walking** into town yesterday, and I saw Sue outside the cinema.*

Progressive aspect may occur in verb phrases involving modal verbs:

*We **could be waiting** for ages.*

*I **might be working** next Saturday.*

Progressive aspect does not combine with non-tensed verbs in the *-ing* form:

***Sitting** there like that, you remind me of my father.*
(~~Being sitting there like that, you remind me of my father.~~)

Progressive aspect may combine with a *to*-infinitive verb phrase:

***To be buying** shares, you need to know the stockmarket really well.*

Perfect

The perfect aspect is formed with auxiliary *have* and the *-ed* form of a lexical verb. It gives information about the duration of events and the relationship of events to one another in time:

*I**'ve made** a lot of friends since I moved here.*

*We**'d forgotten** all about it.*

The perfect aspect may occur in verb phrases which include modal verbs:

*He **could have rung** me.*

The perfect aspect may occur with non-tensed verbs in the *to*-infinitive and the *-ing* form:

***To have read** my emails, she'd have needed to know the password.*

***Having bought** it, we ought to use it.*

Perfect and progressive combined

Perfect aspect and progressive aspect may combine in the verb phrase:

*I**'ve been looking** for you.*

*She should **have been studying**, not watching TV.*

Verb phrases: voice 159d

Verb phrases also indicate voice. The passive voice is usually formed with auxiliary *be* and the *-ed* participle of a lexical verb (→ **479 on the passive with *get***). Voice gives information about the roles of different participants in an event (e.g. who the agent was, who the recipient was):

*I **was stung** by a wasp.*

***Was** she **promoted**?*

Passive voice may occur in verb phrases involving modal verbs:

*He could **be charged** with murder.*

Passive voice may occur in non-tensed verb phrases involving the *-ing* form and the infinitive:

***Being left** here waiting like this, I'm inclined to walk out and say 'forget it'.*

***To be accepted** completely, you have to live here a long time.*

Passive voice may combine in the verb phrase with progressive and perfect aspect:

*Our car **was being repaired** at the time.*

***I've been asked** that question many times.*

Verb phrases: mood 159e

The verb phrase also expresses contrasts of mood. Mood refers to the factual or non-factual status of events. Non-factual here means events which do not happen or are only desired. The moods of English are indicative, imperative and subjunctive.

The indicative is a factual mood. It is by far the most frequent mood, and involves all the choices of person, tense, number, aspect, modality and voice discussed above:

***I'll give** you a call in the week.*

*We **were talking** about this the other day.*

The imperative mood is a non-factual mood and is used to issue directives. It involves the base form of the verb:

***Sign** here, please.*

*Just **leave** it on the table.*

The subjunctive mood is a non-factual mood and is very rare in English. It refers to wishes, desires, etc. It is used after a very limited number of verbs (e.g. *suggest, insist, recommend, demand*), occasionally after conditional subordinators (e.g. *if, lest, on condition that, whether*) and occasionally after expressions of necessity (e.g. *it is important/imperative/essential that*).

The subjunctive occurs only in very formal styles. It involves the base form of the verb, with no inflections:

They insisted that she ***consult*** *a psychiatrist and, fortunately, Laura had the strength to insist that it* ***be*** *a woman.*

The subjunctive form of the verb *be* may occur as the base form *be* or as hypothetical *were* (for all persons). The *were* subjunctive is especially used after *if*, *as if*, *though* and *as though*:

[from a hotel workers' manual, describing how to deal with customer complaints in the restaurant]
The kitchen and restaurant staff must be contacted immediately and the cause for complaint dealt with. The guests must be persuaded to return to the restaurant, where it is imperative they ***be*** *served with a more than satisfactory meal and* ***be*** *completely pacified.*

I can remember it as if it ***were*** *yesterday.*
(or, non-subjunctive: I can remember it as if it was yesterday.)

→ **217–226 The verb phrase 2** on tense and aspect; **377–407 Modality** on modal verbs and related forms

ADJECTIVES 160

Adjectives: forms 160a

Adjectives describe properties, qualities or states attributed to a noun or a pronoun.

Adjectives cannot necessarily be identified by their form. However, some suffixes are associated with adjective formation, and many adjectives can be seen to be derived from nouns and verbs:

suffix	adjectives related to nouns	suffix	adjectives related to nouns
-al	*accidental, professional*	*-less*	*hopeless, harmless*
-ful	*beautiful, useful*	*-ly*	*brotherly, friendly*
-ic	*heroic, optimistic*	*-ous*	*virtuous, courteous*
-ish	*foolish, boyish*	*-y*	*sandy, watery*

suffix	adjectives related to verbs	suffix	adjectives related to verbs
-able	*drinkable, understandable*	*-ive*	*attractive, explosive*

Adjectives may also be derived from other adjectives, through the use of suffixes or, more commonly, prefixes:

*green**ish***

*short**ish***

***im**possible*

***dis**respectful*

***ir**responsible*

***un**fortunate*

A group of adjectives with the prefix *a*- are derived from verbs:

afloat

asleep

awash

ablaze

awake

Adjectives: gradability 160b

Adjectives are either gradable or non-gradable. Gradable adjectives can be seen as existing along a scale. For example, it is possible to say that something is *a bit* ***dangerous*** or *extremely* ***dangerous***. *Dangerous* is a gradable adjective. Most adjectives are gradable. Gradable adjectives tend to have an antonym (opposite), for example, *hot–cold*, *high–low*, *strong–weak*.

Non-gradable adjectives cannot be modified on a scale. A person is either *married* or not, *female* or not, *dead* or not, and one cannot be *very married* or *rather female*. Non-gradable adjectives classify and categorise things.

An inflectional property of gradable adjectives is that they can occur in a comparative or superlative form. Some common everyday adjectives add -*er* or -*est* to form the comparative and superlative:

larger, largest

sillier, silliest

fast, fastest

Other adjectives require *more* and *most* (or *less* and *least*) to convey the same gradable contrasts:

the more difficult task, the least difficult task

the most interesting person

the more expensive of the two

A few gradable adjectives change form completely (e.g. *good, better, best*; *bad, worse, worst*).

ADJECTIVE PHRASES 161

Adjective phrases: forms 161a

An adjective phrase can consist of a single adjective or an adjective which is modified or complemented.

Adjectives are typically modified by adverb phrases (in bold):

*That's **really** interesting.*

*He's a **very** tall man.*

*That's not good **enough**.*

*It's **too** expensive.*

*They were only **very slightly** injured.*

Occasionally, modification may be by a noun phrase (in bold):

*She's only **seven years** old.*

*His farm is **300 acres** bigger than his brother's.*

Adjectives can be followed by complements, most commonly in the form of a prepositional phrase (in bold), or also by a *that*-clause (in bold). Different adjectives require different complementation patterns:

*Lucy is proud **of you**.*

*Lucy is good **with children**.*

*Lucy is keen **on golf**.*

*Lucy is safe **from criticism from her family**.*

*Lucy is clever **at avoiding work**.*

*Lucy is sure **that she saw someone**.*

Adjective phrases: attributive and predicative 161b

Two main syntactic functions of adjective phrases are attributive and predicative.

An adjective phrase is attributive when it modifies a noun or pronoun:

*the **tall**, **grey** building*

*an **interesting** idea*

***poor** you!*

*a court **martial***

An adjective phrase is predicative when it occurs in the part of the sentence which says what the subject is, does or experiences (the predicate):

*The teacher was **ill**.*

*That's **very good**.*

*It made me **really nervous**.*

Most adjectives can be used in either way, but some adjectives have only an attributive or only a predicative function (→ 240).

ADVERBS 162

Adverbs are a class of words which perform a wide range of functions. Adverbs are especially important for indicating the time, manner, place, degree and frequency of an event, action or process.

Adjectives and adverbs are frequently based on the same word. Most adverbs have the form of their related adjective plus *-ly* ending:

*She's a **beautiful** girl.*
(adjective)

*She sings **beautifully**.*
(adverb)

*They were **careful** not to wake the baby.*
(adjective)

*They walked **carefully** across the narrow bridge.*
(adverb)

Other suffixes which denote adverbs are *-ward(s)* and *-wise*:

-ward(s)	-wise
homeward(s)	*clockwise*
northward(s)	*lengthwise*
onward(s)	*edgewise*
outward(s)	

A number of adverbs have the same form as adjectives (e.g. *hard, outside, right, straight, late, well*). A number of adverbs (e.g. *just, quite, so, soon, too, very*) are not related to adjectives at all.

Some adverbs may inflect for comparative and superlative forms:

soon – sooner – soonest

hard – harder – hardest

little – less – least

far – farther/further – farthest/furthest

ADVERB PHRASES 163

Adverb phrases: forms 163a

An adverb acting as the head of an adverb phrase may be modified by another adverb (in bold) and/or followed by a complement (in bold):

It all happened **rather** suddenly.

Funnily **enough** *I didn't notice it.*

Most surprisingly **for her**, *she decided to emigrate to Australia.*

Complement patterns of some adverbs may be the same as the complement patterns of their related adjectives:

It was **unfortunate** for us *that we got there too late.*
(adjective)

Unfortunately for me, *they'd closed early that day.*
(adverb)

Adverb phrases occur as the complement of *be*, typically indicating location:

Is *the dog* **upstairs**?

Your glasses are **there**, *on the table.*

Adverb phrases frequently occur as modifiers of verbs:

She works **really slowly**.

I swim **regularly**.

Adverb phrases frequently modify adjectives and other adverbs:

It was **extremely** cold *out there.*

They did the test **very** competently.

Adverb phrases can also modify noun phrases (including pronouns) and prepositional phrases:

That was **quite** a match.
(adverb + noun phrase)

Didn't he manage to speak with **nearly** everyone there?
(adverb + pronoun)

We followed the path **right** to the end.
(adverb + prepositional phrase)

Adverb phrases may also modify determiners, especially quantifiers:

Almost all *of those books are useless.*

There's **very** little *chance of that happening.*

Hardly any *of his colleagues believes him.*

Adverb phrases: functions 163b

As well as giving information on the time, place, manner and degree of an action, event or process, adverb phrases can also have a commenting function, indicating the attitude and point of view of the speaker or writer towards a whole sentence or utterance. In such cases they are referred to as sentence adverbs:

__Actually__, it's nearly midnight.

__Officially__, I can't tell you the results but I'll find a way.

Adverb phrases can often indicate a relationship between two clauses or sentences (e.g. one of cause and effect, one of concession, one of temporal sequence). In such cases they are called linking adverbs:

Although in principle agriculture ought to be a net producer of energy, converting the sun's energy into the calorific value of food, modern agriculture is actually a net consumer. We are __consequently__ eating up our energy resources.

Philip got the sack and __then__ we heard Liam was sacked too.

Adverb phrases can occupy a range of positions at the front, in the middle and at the end of a clause.

→ **242–249 Adverbs and adverb phrases**

PREPOSITIONS 164

Prepositions are a closed word class. New prepositions cannot easily be formed.

Prepositions express a relation in time between two events or a relation in space between two (or more) things or people. They can also express a variety of other, abstract relations:

They left __after__ six o'clock.

__During__ the film she fell asleep.

They decided to meet __in__ a park.

He dealt __with__ the problem.

The most common prepositions are: *about, after, as, at, by, during, for, from, in, of, off, on, to* and *with*. Most prepositions consist of a single word but some prepositions may be considered as consisting of more than a single word (e.g. *in front of, outside of, out of, next to*).

Some of these words may also be used as adverbs (e.g. *about, round/around, by, off, out, over*):

We were just touring __around__, stopping off here and there.

She's not here. She's __out__.

Prepositions are almost always followed by a prepositional complement. Usually, the complement is a noun phrase but it can also be a whole clause:

The doctor gave her a lot of information ***about*** *the tablets*.
(noun phrase)

I'll take her ***to*** *where they last met*.
(clause)

A particularly common prepositional complement is the nominal *-ing* form of a verb. Prepositions may not be followed by other forms of a verb:

He was jailed ***for murdering*** *his close friend and flatmate.*
(~~He was jailed for murder/murdered his close friend ...~~)

By talking *to all the witnesses, the police eventually managed to reduce the number of suspects.*

An adjective or an adverb may sometimes act as complement to a preposition:

in *short*

by *far*

until *now*

at *first*

before *long*

Prepositions may be modified by a small set of adverbs (e.g. *right, straight*):

We went right ***down*** *the coast.*

Will you go straight ***to*** *your sister's house or stop on the way?*

Some verbs require prepositional complements, and are termed prepositional verbs. The verb determines what preposition must follow. Different verbs require different prepositions. Examples are *confide in, cope with, depend on, look after*. (→ **235f Prepositional verbs**):

You should learn to ***confide in*** *your friends.*

They will have to ***look after*** *their father.*

PREPOSITIONAL PHRASES 165

Prepositions act as the head of a prepositional phrase. A prepositional phrase is formed when a preposition combines with a complement. Prepositional phrases can function as a postmodifier or complement of a noun, as an adjunct in the clause and as a complement of a verb or adjective:

We saw a girl ***with*** *a small dog*.
(noun phrase postmodifier: *a girl with a small dog* = a girl who had a small dog; additional information about the girl, but not necessary to complete the meaning of 'girl')

We saw the outline ***of*** *a man against the window.*
(noun phrase complement: *outline* needs a complement to complete its meaning – an outline must be an outline of something)

He writes well ***on*** *the whole.*
(adjunct, modifying the clause)

I'll deal ***with*** *that.*
(complement of a verb)

I must admit I felt very sorry ***for*** *her.*
(complement of an adjective)

250–257 Prepositions and prepositional phrases

CONJUNCTIONS 166

Conjunctions express a variety of logical relations between phrases, clauses and sentences. Conjunctions can be divided into coordinating conjunctions and subordinating conjunctions.

Coordinating

A coordinating conjunction is used to link elements of equal grammatical status. A coordinating conjunction can link elements of any size, from morphemes (e.g. prefixes) to sentences. The main coordinating conjunctions are *and*, *or*, *but*:

He collects pre- ***and*** *post-war cameras.*
(linking prefixes)

There are two ***or*** *three houses nearby.*
(linking words)

The wind was really cold ***and*** *absolutely biting.*
(linking phrases)

You can join now ***or*** *you may prefer to wait* ***and*** *discuss things with your partner.*
(linking clauses)

If she had been in London she would have walked out and taken a taxi home. ***But*** *she was on Richard's territory now and she couldn't do that.*
(linking sentences)

Correlative conjunctions consist of two items, each of which is attached to an element to be coordinated. The most common correlatives are *either … or …*, *neither … nor …*, *both … and …*:

The class can meet | ***either*** *on Friday at 9 |* ***or*** *on Thursday afternoon at 4.30 |.*

| ***Neither*** *I |* ***nor*** *my family | feel that an interview is appropriate at this time.*

She | ***neither*** *eats meat |* ***nor*** *drinks coffee |. What a dreary existence.*

Subordinating

Subordinating conjunctions only relate clauses to one another. They make the clause they introduce a subordinate clause (one which is dependent on a main clause). Common subordinating conjunctions are: *after, although, as, before, if, since, that, until, when, whereas, while*. Some subordinating conjunctions consist of more than one word: *as long as, as soon as, except that, in order to, in order that, provided that*:

> *They had to cancel their holiday in Brazil* ***because*** *Anne's mother was seriously ill.*
>
> ***As*** *you have not explained your action, the school will be making a formal report on your behaviour.*
>
> ***In order to*** *reach the village, walkers need to be prepared for a steep climb.*

Some subordinating conjunctions may be modified by adverbs:

> *Just* ***when*** *I arrived, I got a phone call.*
>
> *Ever* ***since*** *I heard about it, I've been afraid to go out after dark.*

→ **304–318 Clause combination**

The noun phrase

The noun phrase

INTRODUCTION 167

Structure 167a

Noun phrases consist minimally of a noun or pronoun, which acts as the head of the noun phrase. The head may be accompanied by dependent elements before or after it. The following are examples of noun phrases; heads are in green, words in black are dependent elements:

music

summer

we

him

a dog

the old man

that table in the corner

a nice day at the beach

the sofa we bought in the sale

➔ also **176–196 Nouns and determiners**; **197–212 Pronouns**

Function 167b

Noun phrases are referring expressions and are used to refer to particular instances or general classes of people and things.

Noun phrases typically function in the clause as subjects, objects, complements and occasionally as adjuncts:

Functions of noun phrases in the clause (noun phrases in green; heads in bold)

subject	verb	object	complement	adjunct
*My **father***	*used to play*	*the **piano***		
She	*was*		*a fairly average **swimmer***	
*The **children***	*loved*	***him***		
*His **body***	*was found*			*the next **day***

Noun phrases frequently occur as the complements of prepositions:

*We usually go **to** our local gym **at** the weekends*

Noun phrases also occur in the noun phrase +'s possessive determiner construction:

*the average meat-eater**'s diet***

*the biotechnology department**'s long-awaited new building***

→ **176–196 Nouns and determiners**

Other less frequent functions of noun phrases include:

*The train was an hour **late** leaving Milan.*
(premodifier of adjective)

*Two days **before** we left, we still hadn't heard from her.*
(premodifier of conjunction)

*We agreed that two meetings **ago**.*
(premodifier of adverb)

*He lives three houses **along our street**.*
(premodifier of prepositional phrase)

*She watches children**'s TV** in the afternoon.*
(the 'descriptive' use of the *'s* construction)

→ **197–212 Pronouns, 236–241 Adjectives and adjective phrases, 242–249 Adverbs and adverb phrases** for premodification and postmodification of pronouns and the role of adjectives and adverbs in postmodifying structures

HEADS 168

The head of a noun phrase may be a noun or a pronoun:

*My **father** worked there three years ago.*
(noun as head of noun phrase)

***He** was a friend of Jean's.*
(pronoun as head of noun phrase)

Simple heads 168a

A simple head consists of one noun. The following noun phrases have simple heads:

*my **sister***
*the larger **size***
*a new **home** for the children*
*a government **report***
*this year's **budget***

Compound heads 168b

Structure of compound nouns

Compound nouns consist of a noun head with another item (most typically a noun, but it may also be an adjective or verb) placed before it in a very close syntactic and semantic relationship. The initial item most typically identifies a type of the class of entities denoted by the final noun. For example, a *video shop* is a type of shop; *orange juice* is a type of juice:

video shop	*window box*	*blackboard*
orange juice	*sports centre*	*grindstone*
petrol station	*greyhound*	

The elements in compounds are closely bound to each other syntactically and cannot normally be interrupted by other elements (e.g. *a motorway **petrol station***, not a ***petrol** motorway **station***). Compounds are therefore best considered as single heads in the noun phrase. Their typical stress pattern is with stress on the first item (***petrol** station*, ***black**board*, ***grind**stone*).

Compound nouns and noun modifiers

The borderline between compound nouns and noun phrases acting as premodifiers of noun heads is not always clear. However, the preferred stress pattern for compounds, with stress on the first item, is usually an indication that the nouns are considered as an 'institutionalised' unit (stressed items in bold):

***car** park*	***bus** stop*	***safety** helmet*

The noun modifier construction has the stress on the noun head:

*a fur **coat***	*that government **report***
*several volunteer **helpers***	*bathroom **door***

Meaning of compound nouns

The compound noun structure is extremely varied in the types of meaning relations it can indicate. It can be used to indicate what someone does (*language teacher*), what something is for (*waste-paper basket, grindstone*), what the qualities of something are (*whiteboard*), how something works (*immersion heater*), when something happens (*night frost*), where something is (*doormat*), what something is made of (*woodpile*), and so on.

Proper names

Compound nouns are common in proper names and titles. Most typically, these have the stress on the final noun:

*Narita **Airport***	*Head**teacher***
*New York City **Hall***	*Ronald **Bickerton***
*The London **Underground***	*Mary **Prosser***
*Prime **Minister***	

Writing compound nouns

Familiar compound nouns (usually those involving short, monosyllabic nouns) are normally written as one word:

postman	*bathroom*	*lampshade*

There is some inconsistency, however. Some compounds are written with a hyphen:

pen-friend	*tee-shirt*	*belly-dancing*

In the case of some pairs, hyphens, separate words and words joined together are all equally possible:

post-box	*post box*	*postbox*

Normally, if a compound is perceived as a single word, it tends to be written as a whole word without a space or a hyphen. Hyphenation is less common in American than in British English.

··› **265 Compounds** for further information on noun compounds

··› **507–511 Appendix: English spelling** for spelling and use of hyphens and apostrophes involving noun compounds and other types of compound

Other categories of compound noun

Nouns combine less frequently with other units including adverbs, prepositions and other parts of speech to form compound nouns. The most common categories of compound are nouns which are joined by *of*, *at* or *in*, compound nouns formed from phrasal verbs, and compound nouns which are linked by *and* or are otherwise hyphenated.

- Examples of compound nouns joined by *of*, *at* or *in*:

right-of-way	*stay-at-home*	*brother-in-law*
commander-in-chief		

- Examples of compound nouns formed from phrasal verbs:

runner-up	*passer-by*	*take-over*
stand-by	*lay-by*	

- Noun + *and* + noun compounds are often called binomial phrases. The nouns in such pairs may be singular or plural in form, and are usually fixed in their order. Frequently occurring examples are:

aims and objectives	*research and development*
ladies and gentlemen	*size and shape*
health and safety	*policy and resources*
presence and absence	*theory and practice*
strengths and weaknesses	*trial and error*

Plurals

Some countable compound nouns do not form plurals in entirely regular ways. The most common plural form is made by adding *-s*. So the plurals of *lay-by* and *take-over* are *lay-bys* and *take-overs*.

In certain noun + adverb/prepositional phrase combinations, the plural *-s* is usually added to the noun. So the plural of *mother-in-law* is *mothers-in-law*, *commander-in-chief* has the plural *commanders-in-chief*, and *passer-by* has the plural *passers-by*. However, occasionally, plurals of some of these compounds may be attached to the final item of the compound, especially in informal speech:

*I've got two brother-in-law**s**.*

Pronoun heads 168c

A pronoun may act as the head of a noun phrase. The pronoun may be a personal, possessive or demonstrative pronoun:

***She** hates **me**.*

***It** happens all the time.*

*I'll take **that**.*

*Is **this yours**?*

DEPENDENT ELEMENTS 169

Determiners, modifiers and complements 169a

A noun acting as the head of a noun phrase is often accompanied by one or more dependent elements, before and/or after the head. Pronoun heads are only rarely accompanied by other elements.

Noun heads may have three types of dependent element: determiners, modifiers and complements.

Determiners

Determiners indicate the type of reference made by the noun phrase (e.g. definite, indefinite, possessive) (→ **176–196 Nouns and determiners**). Examples of determiners:

***The** tall woman*
(definite reference)

***My** old school*
(possessive reference)

***That** person*
(demonstrative reference)

Modifiers

Modifiers indicate qualities and attributes of the noun head (e.g. subjective qualities, physical attributes such as size, colour, material, location in space and time, restricted reference to a particular entity). Examples of modifiers:

*those **big** boxes **in the garage***

*a **little red** lever **which controls the temperature***

Complements

Complements complete the meaning of the noun head. For example, nouns such as *fact, claim, suggestion, idea, thought, statement* are always 'about something' and the complement completes the necessary information. Examples of complements (in green):

*the **fact** that he was no longer a little boy*

*an American expert's **claim** that the monsters were wiped out after a massive meteorite created devastating climatic changes 65 million years ago*

*the **body** of a young man*

Pre- and post-head dependent elements 169b

Two types of dependent element may come before the head in the noun phrase (i.e. they act as pre-head elements): determiners and premodifiers.

Two types of dependent element may come after the head in the noun phrase (i.e. they act as post-head elements): postmodifiers and complements.

Complements versus postmodifiers 169c

Complements and postmodifiers are different in their function. Postmodifiers specify which person or thing or type of person or thing is being referred to. The major postmodifier is the relative clause. All the other postmodifiers can be paraphrased by a relative clause. For example, 'the house nearby' can be paraphrased as 'the house which is nearby'; 'the girl in jeans' can be paraphrased as 'the girl who is wearing jeans'.

Complements complete the meaning of the noun phrase. In the noun phrase *the **claim** that they have nuclear weapons*, the underlined words complete the meaning of *claim* (a claim must be 'about something'). Complement prepositional phrases cannot be paraphrased with relative clauses:

***a rise** in interest rates*
(~~a rise which is in interest rates~~)

*the **mother** of three little children*
(~~the mother who is of three little children~~)

More than one complement can occur together:

*The **gift** | of the estate | to the National Trust | meant more people could visit it.*

*The **statement** | by the driver of the vehicle | that he did not see the lorry | was rejected by the Court.*

539 **Glossary** for any unfamiliar terms

More than one postmodifier can occur together:

*The **girl** | in jeans | in the corner | with that tall American student* |.

Complements and postmodifiers can occur together. The complement comes first because it is so closely associated semantically with the head:

complement postmodifier

Students | of astronomy | at Cambridge | all get very high grades.
(~~Students at Cambridge of astronomy all get very high grades.~~)

Order of pre- and post-head elements 169d

The table below shows the order of the pre- and post-head elements in the noun phrase. Because they indicate the type of reference for the whole noun phrase, determiners come before premodifiers. Because complements complete the meaning of the head and are therefore closely associated with the head, they precede postmodifiers.

Order of elements in the noun phrase

pre-head		head	post-head	
determiners	premodifiers		complements	postmodifiers
		silence		
those		***books***		
	cheap | red	***shoes***		
its	*smooth | wood*	***surface***		
my own	*personal*	***space***		
some	*baked*	***potatoes***		
many	*big*	***towns***		*nearby*
the	*first*	***chapter***		*of the book*
all	*university*	***students***		
the		***killer***	*of seventeen-year-old Maria Nixon*	
a		***mother***	*of two children under five*	
the		***car***		*(that) he was driving*
some	*recent*	***films***		*which have been on general release and which have made millions of dollars*
a		***letter***		*saying when it will happen*
a	*long-awaited | government*	***report***		*published last week*
a		***drawer***		*full of pens and pencils*
his	*recent*	***claim***	*that he was innocent,*	*which was broadcast on state radio and TV*

176–196 Nouns and determiners; 236–241 Adjectives and adjective phrases

MODIFIERS 170

Types of premodifier and postmodifier 170a

The main types of premodifier are:

- adjective phrases:

  a ***different*** *bus; a* ***very important*** *meeting; a* ***stabbing*** *pain; a* ***hastily written*** *request*

- noun phrases:

  a ***stone*** *wall;* ***media*** *hype; a* ***first-year undergraduate*** *seminar*

The main types of postmodifier are:

- full relative clauses:

  the newspaper ***I have always bought****; the fighting* ***which accompanies every international football match between the two countries***

- *-ing* relative clauses:

  that short fat man ***walking through the shop***

- *-ed* relative clauses:

  the six Cuban nationals ***held in custody by rebel soldiers***

- *to*-infinitive relative clauses:

  We had a long journey ***to make before nightfall.***

- prepositional phrases:

  Those piles ***on the floor*** *are exam papers* ***from last year.***

- adjective phrases which include a complement of the adjective:

  a jacket ***similar to yours****; parents* ***eager to support their children's efforts***

Noun phrases can involve several of the above elements. The table shows examples of noun phrases which include premodification and postmodification occurring together:

Noun phrases with premodification and postmodification

determiner	premodification	head	postmodification
the	*small | stone*	*cottage*	*which he bought three years ago*
an	*ancient | market*	*town*	*in the heart of the country*
a	*new | staff*	*structure*	*for the company*
some	*very sudden*	*changes*	*caused by an area of low pressure*
many	*brave*	*soldiers*	*willing to volunteer*

→ 236–241 Adjectives and adjective phrases

Premodification involving noun phrases 170b

Even though premodifying noun phrases may have plural reference, they are singular in form:

the ***postgraduate*** *regulations*
(i.e. the regulations for postgraduates)
(~~the postgraduates regulations~~)

✪ This is particularly notable with expressions of measurement:

a ***three-day*** *journey*
(~~a three-days journey~~)

a ***300-seat*** *auditorium*
(~~a 300-seats auditorium~~)

Several noun premodifiers often occur together. This occurs frequently where it is important to compress as much information as possible in a limited space:

cottage-style kitchen *window*

two-button cotton summer *jacket*
(product description)

Italian pesto chicken *pasta*
(menu or description of a food dish)

Such structures also occur in everyday usage when speakers need to convey detailed information economically:

That ***first floor flat front door*** *key needs replacing.*

I've got ***twenty year-three geography*** *essays to mark.*

Sometimes this kind of information packing can cause ambiguities, though alternative interpretations are usually resolved in context:

a ***French Canadian literature*** *professor*

This phrase could be interpreted as 'a professor of Canadian literature who is French' or 'a professor of literature who is a French Canadian' or 'a professor of French Canadian literature'.

→ also **174 The noun phrase in speech and writing**

Noun modifier versus prepositional phrase 170c

In general, noun modifier and compound structures are preferred to noun + prepositional structures when referring to familiar, everyday entities:

a world map
(a familiar object)

a map of the Nile Delta
(a less common combination; preferred to 'a Nile Delta map')

road signs
(familiar and everyday sights)

signs of frustration
(occurring in more specific circumstances – preferred to 'frustration signs')

In the case of phrases which refer to units, parts and collections of things, normally referred to as partitive expressions (*a piece of paper*, *a bunch of roses*, *four slices of ham*), noun + preposition + noun forms are preferred. Thus *four slices of ham* is preferred to *four ham slices*.

55 *Of*

→ also **179 Partitive expressions**

POSTMODIFIERS 171

Clauses as postmodifiers 171a

Finite relative clauses

Clauses acting as postmodifiers are relative clauses. Finite relative clauses are introduced by the pronouns *who*, *whom*, *whose*, *which*, *that* or a 'zero' relative pronoun:

*That's the **group** to whom they should consider making an incentive payment.*

*The police haven't even interviewed those **people** whose house was burgled.*

*I've left some **books** which you'll need in the main office.*

*That **car** that she wanted has been sold.*

*Did you make the **call** he asked you to make?*
('zero' relative pronoun)

→ **204 Relative pronouns**

Postmodifying relative clauses are of two types: defining and non-defining. A defining relative clause identifies the noun which it postmodifies and distinguishes it from other nouns. In the following sentence, *who lives abroad* tells us that there is more than one sister and identifies the one who lives abroad as the one who is ill:

*His sister **who lives abroad** got taken seriously ill.*

Non-defining relative clauses provide further information about the preceding noun but do not identify it. In the following sentence, the relative clause simply adds extra information about the sister, rather than defining her:

*His sister, **who lives abroad**, got taken seriously ill.*

The different punctuation reflects these differences in meaning.

Defining and non-defining relative clauses are also termed restrictive and non-restrictive clauses.

→ 317 Relative clauses

Non-finite relative clauses

Postmodifying relative clauses may also be non-finite. The common types of non-finite relative clause are (in green):

- *-ing* clauses:

  *It's got **a walled garden** consisting of a stone arch and two sections for vegetables.*

  ***The guy** running the event looks pretty well-off, doesn't he?*

- *-ed* clauses:

  ***The effort** required to lift these weights is considerable.*

  ***The protests** caused by the lack of tickets were the responsibility of the organisers.*

- *to*-infinitive clauses:

  *He certainly is **an actor** to watch out for.*

  ***Pictures** to be seen in the gallery include a fine eighteenth-century watercolour.*

Non-finite relative clauses can be defining or non-defining:

*I'm looking for **a house** to buy.*
(defining)

***A large sum of money**, donated by Petsmart foods, has also been invested in improved kennel facilities.*
(non-defining)

Prepositional phrases as postmodifiers 171b

Prepositional phrases are an extremely common type of postmodifier. They function in a manner similar to defining relative clauses:

***Cars** with disc brakes on all four wheels have been proved to be safer.*
(Cars which have disc brakes on all four wheels ...)

The five main proposals *in the plan were considered at yesterday's meeting.*
(The five main proposals which are in the plan ...)

*He has lots of friends but that was **a friend** of long standing.*
(... but that was a friend who was of long standing)

COMPLEMENTS 172

Clauses as complements 172a

Types of noun that take complement clauses

The majority of the nouns that take complement clauses are nouns which are derived from verbs (e.g. *suggestion* is derived from *suggest*) or nouns which are semantically related to verbs (e.g. the nouns *author* and *writer* are related to the verb *write*).

That-clauses

Clauses acting as complements are often *that*-clauses. On the surface these may resemble postmodifying defining relative clauses with *that*. However, the difference can be demonstrated:

The suggestion ***that they put forward*** *was accepted.*

The suggestion ***that he should resign*** *was accepted.*

In the first sentence, which involves a postmodifying relative clause, the *suggestion* is defined and identified, and *that* can be substituted by *which* or it can be omitted (i.e. the clause can have a zero relative pronoun). In the second sentence, *that* cannot be omitted (i.e. the clause cannot have a zero relative pronoun), *which* cannot substitute for *that*, and the whole clause completes the meaning of the 'suggestion'.

Noun complement clauses with *that* are very common in formal written contexts, especially academic writing and journalism:

The fact *that he was calm did not influence the jury.*

Why has ***the impression*** *that he is about to give large sums of money to the cause grown up so quickly among his supporters?*

The belief *that prejudice is largely an ethnic issue has dominated the political agenda.*

Other types of clause

Less common types of noun complement clause include:

- *to*-infinitive clause:

  The decision *to go ahead was not a popular one.*

- defining *wh*-interrogative clause:

  That's part of ***the reason*** *why we bought it.*

- *as to* + *wh*-clause (mainly with *whether*):

  There were a number of ***reservations*** *as to whether they should be allowed to participate.*

The *as to* structure is particularly common in writing in more formal contexts.

Prepositional phrases as complements 172b

The most frequent prepositions used in prepositional complement structures are *to*, *of*, *in*, *for* and *with*:

*Has she forgotten about **her right** to compensation?*

*Just don't lose **your belief** in his talent, will you.*

***The relationship** with neighbouring countries has markedly improved in recent years.*

A noun may take more than one prepositional phrase complement:

*Let there be **government** | of the people | by the people | for the people |.*

*The **statement** | by the driver | to the police | about the incident | was crucial.*

→ 250–257 Prepositions and prepositional phrases

NOUN PHRASES OCCURRING TOGETHER (IN APPOSITION) 173

Noun phrases which refer to the same entity can occur together in a clause. The feature is called 'apposition'. The nouns can follow each other in sequence (often separated by commas in writing).

Apposition states the relationship between the nouns, or indicates the relationship with a name, or expresses the first noun phrase as an attribute of the second noun phrase. The second (appositive) noun phrase has the same grammatical status as the preceding noun phrase and the phrases can normally be reversed without altering the meaning:

| The Queen |, | the head of the Commonwealth |, will be accompanied to the conference by the Prime Minister and the Foreign Secretary.

| The head of the Commonwealth |, | the Queen |, will be accompanied to the conference by the Prime Minister and the Foreign Secretary.

Other examples of apposition are:

I'm going to see | my tutor |, | Dr Johnson |, about a change of course.

I saw | the clerk in charge |, | a very dubious-looking individual |.

| Seamus Deane's novel | Reading in the Dark | has been nominated for the Booker Prize.

In written English, apposition is more likely to occur at the beginning of a clause, as in several of the above examples. In spoken English, apposition regularly occurs at the end of a clause but its position within a clause is generally a little more flexible:

When you went in through the apartment door the first thing you saw was | the harbour | – | Sydney Harbour |.

She got me to do | the job | for her, | her fence |.
(the job = repair her fence)

Equivalent information in written discourse is normally given by means of premodifiers:

They've bought | *a new jeep* |, | *a new 2.6 litre turbo-diesel* |.
(preferred in written style: They've bought a new 2.6 litre turbo-diesel jeep.)

In journalistic styles, a characteristic order of common nouns preceding proper nouns often occurs:

| *Former Prime Minister and scourge of Europe* |, | *Margaret Thatcher* | *spoke out today.*

··➣ **96 Headers** and **97 Tails** for apposition-related structures

THE NOUN PHRASE IN SPEECH AND WRITING 174

There are differences in spoken and written uses of modifiers and complements.

Speech

In spoken English, especially in informal contexts, the clauses are sometimes strung together in a sequence. In narratives, in particular, information is built up more gradually and in smaller units. In the following examples post-head elements are in bold and the head is in green:

[spoken]
*There's just so many things **that we've got to tell them about and that they've got to just sit down and listen to and that they'd better do something about**.*

[spoken narrative]
*While we were on one of those Breton holidays she swam so far out that she met the only other person **who could swim, who turned out to be an Austrian** and that was only the beginning **of our link with Austria**.*

Writing

In some registers of written English, especially those where space is restricted, complex premodifiers are more common than simple ones and in certain written varieties pre- and post-head elements are likely to occur together. In many of the following examples, a lot of information is compressed into the noun phrase, often because space has to be saved (e.g. in the case of newspaper headlines). In the following examples, pre- and post-head elements are in bold and the head is in green:

[advertisement]
***Lightweight training** shoes **with dual density midsole**.*

[menu]
***Lightly battered** prawns **with a spicy Thai red curry sauce**.*

[personal contact advertisement – newspaper]
***Attractive, fun-loving** male **of independent means** seeks **mid-thirties** partner with a view to marriage.*

[small advertisement offering things for sale, etc. – magazine]
Delightful lakeside country house *hotel* ***with own frontage, jetty and yacht for hire.***

[personal contact advertisement – newspaper]
Slightly balding but fit and active *divorcee* ***with two young children, nine and seven,*** *seeks* ***sport-loving, energetic*** *companion.*

→ 236–241 Adjectives and adjective phrases

→ also 82–91 Introduction to grammar and spoken English

 55 *Of*

Post-head elements enable the user to define and specify things more precisely. In written styles, post-head elements help to create a characteristic descriptive style of the kind found, for example, in guide books and in promotional information about services and products. In the following examples post-head elements are in bold and the head is in green:

[text on a cereal packet; the cereal is called *Fruitful*]

Fruitful from Shredded Wheat
Full of Fruit

Enjoy succulent sultanas ***combined with plump raisins dried in the Californian sun and blended with hazelnut pieces.*** *Crunchy slices* ***of golden banana, mixed with juicy pieces of papaya and tender toasted coconut.*** *Discover the tempting taste* ***that's bursting with delicious fruits and crunchy wholewheat goodness.***

[estate agent's particulars]
Imaginatively restored Georgian terraced house ***with fitted kitchen leading to a spacious patio and a large vegetable garden.***

In technical and scientific English, heavy use of post-head elements involving clauses and prepositional phrases serves to elaborate and package a lot of information within the noun phrase:

[an advertisement which in this case sells the product it advertises by means of a more technical register]
The armchair design allows infinite combinations ***of seat tilt, leg support and back rest angle, providing every facility from fireside chair to full-length single bed.***

Formation of nouns (nominalisation) 175

Nouns can be formed from other parts of speech, most commonly verbs. For example, the verb *fly* can be converted into the nouns *flying* and *flight*. The adjectives *bright* and *long* form the nouns *brightness* and *length*. The process is called nominalisation. The nominalised form is used more in written and formal contexts:

*We **fly** at seven o'clock this evening.*
*Our **flight** is at seven o'clock this evening.*

*Mr Hamson **donated** £2000.*
*Mr Hamson made a **donation** of £2000.*

*I was dazzled by the extremely **bright** lights.*
*I was dazzled by the extreme **brightness** of the lights.*

*They **partied** all night and we decided to **complain** to the hotel.*
*We decided to make a **complaint** to the hotel about their all-night **parties**.*

In each example here, the second sentence contains one or more nominalised forms. This results in a more formal expression of the equivalent meaning in a different word class.

Sometimes the noun is derived from another part of speech to which it is related. Sometimes the noun is formed metaphorically rather than derived (morphologically) from another part of speech:

*They were able to **get to** the computer once a week.*
***Access** to the computer was once a week.*

*Mobile phones are **getting much better** technically.*
*There have been many technical **advances** with mobile phones.*

Nominalised forms can sometimes be used without reference to an agent and in certain contexts this can mean the cause or agent can be concealed or made less important:

*The **closure** of the factory caused 200 workers to lose their jobs.*
(compare: Meteorcorp closed the factory and 200 workers lost their jobs.)

*The **dismissal** of the union leaders was immediate.*
(compare: The director of the company dismissed the union leaders immediately.)

Another type of nominalised structure, common in everyday usage, is the delexical verb phrase + noun phrase structure. Delexical verbs include *go*, *get*, *make*, *do*, *take* (→ 475a). Delexical structures often offer an informal equivalent to a full lexical verb phrase:

*They **got a divorce** in 1998.*
(compare the more formal: They divorced in 1998.)

*He hasn't **done any painting** since he retired.*
(compare: He has not painted since he retired.)

→ **142 Nominalisation** in **Grammar and academic English**

Nouns and determiners

Nouns and determiners

INTRODUCTION 176

This chapter is divided into two main parts. The first part (177–186) pays particular attention to the features of nouns, and the second part (187–196) describes the features of determiners.

Nouns

Nouns can be divided into two major grammatical types, count nouns and non-count nouns. Their grammar differs principally in terms of whether they can express contrasts of number.

Count nouns are the largest group of nouns. They denote entities which are treated as units. They refer to objects, people, abstract entities, etc. which are seen as easily counted (e.g. *leaves*, *cups*, *footballers*, *cousins*, *results*, *ideas*). Count nouns are also known as countable nouns.

Non-count nouns denote things treated as non-divisible. They refer to entities which do not have clear boundaries (e.g. *cheese*, *music*, *sand*, *water*, *love*, *advice*, *air*, *progress*, *homework*, *ice*, *coffee*). They show no contrast in number between singular and plural. Non-count nouns are also known as uncountable nouns.

Some things that English treats as non-divisible are easy to perceive that way (e.g. *sand* or *water*) but English also treats as non-count things such as *luggage*, *money*, *furniture*, which are composed of elements which can be counted (e.g. someone's 'luggage' may consist of two cases and a bag; 'money' may consist of six coins and two notes) but which are treated as single indivisible entities.

Count and non-count are not mutually exclusive terms. Many nouns have both count and non-count uses.

There are also other grammatical and semantic types of noun (proper names, plural-only nouns and collective nouns) referred to in this chapter.

Determiners

Determiners indicate the type of reference a noun phrase has; for example whether the determiner is definite or indefinite (*the*, *a*), possessive (*my*, *her*, etc.), demonstrative (*this*, *those*, etc.). Determiners can also indicate number or quantity (*some*, *many*, *twenty*, etc.).

Determiners come first in the noun phrase, before other elements such as adjectives and noun modifiers. They include words like: *a*, *each*, *his*, *my*, *several*, *some*, *the*, *those*, *which*, and numerals such as *one*, *two*, *first*:

*This is **a** message for Helen Crawford.*

*I'm just about to eat **my** pizza.*

*I'm **his** best friend.*

*There have been **three** recent government reports which have looked into the matter.*

The rules for the use of determiners depend on the grammatical type of the head noun of the noun phrase. For example, *a/an* cannot be used with singular or plural non-count nouns such as *furniture, information, outskirts* or *belongings* (→ **178b and 178d**).

COUNT NOUNS 177

Count nouns and determiners 177a

Count nouns denote people and things which are treated as units. They refer to objects, people, abstract entities, etc. which are perceived as easily counted. Count nouns have both a singular and a plural form. The indefinite article *a/an* can be used with count nouns in the singular. Numerals can also be used in front of count nouns:

*I'd prefer **a cat** to **a dog**. **Cats** are interesting.*

***Three cars** were involved in the accident.*

Singular count nouns cannot stand without a determiner:

*Would you pass **the teapot** please?*
(~~Would you pass teapot please?~~)

*Have you ever worked in **a hotel**?*

***This book** is interesting.*

Plural count nouns are used with determiners when a specific meaning is indicated, but without determiners when a general meaning is indicated:

***These hotels** offer you every comfort.*
(specific)

***Your books** have arrived.*
(specific)

***Rats** terrify me.*
(general: all members of that class)

***Hotels** in the area of the Conference Centre are usually booked well in advance.*
(general: the number of hotels in the area or which hotels in the area is not specified)

Count nouns: same singular and plural forms 177b

A limited number of count nouns have an identical singular and plural form:

*We encountered **a series** of problems on the way.*

*The BBC are planning **two** new drama **series** for the autumn.*

Other examples of identical singular and plural forms include:

aircraft	*gasworks*	*species*
*chassis**	*précis**	*rendezvous**
corps (/kɔː/)*	*series*	

* Although the written forms are identical, singular is usually pronounced without the /s/ at the end, plural is pronounced with the /s/ at the end.

Agreement with singular and plural verbs and/or with singular and plural determiners indicates whether the noun is being used with singular or plural meaning:

> ***The aircraft is*** *the same one we flew out to Greece in.*
> ***These aircraft were*** *used in the Second World War and* ***are*** *too old to fly now.*

> ***It's a*** *new* ***series****. They took the previous series off because* ***it was****n't suitable viewing for children.*

> *There* ***are three*** *different* ***series*** *of the computer. We think* ***they were*** *all made in South Korea.*

Many count nouns which refer to animals or birds also have an identical singular and plural form. When an individual creature is referred to, singular determiners and verbs are used, but when referring to several animals in a group or in large numbers, plural determiners and verbs are used:

> *He saw* ***a grouse*** *moving very slowly across the field.*
> ***Grouse are*** *always shot at this time of year.*

> ***A deer*** *attacked a motorist late last night.*
> *There* ***are many*** *lovely* ***deer*** *in the royal park.*

> ***This salmon is*** *not very fresh.*
> ***These salmon return*** *to the same stream every year.*

Other examples are: *bison*, *reindeer*, *sheep*, *fish* (*cod*, *halibut*, *herring*, *mackerel*, *trout* and other fish names).

In the case of many tree- and plant-name count nouns, the singular and plural forms may both be used to express more than one example of the class:

> ***Several beech*** *lined the long path leading to the palace.*

> [*rookeried* means 'containing rooks' nests']
> *When he rode back over the hill to Burlford and took in the timeless cluster of rooftops and church tower, the rookeried* ***beeches*** *behind the Rectory, how did it seem?*

> [text about the spread of different types of tree across Europe in prehistoric times]
> *In time, a broadleaved band of* ***hazel****,* ***wych-elm****,* ***oak*** *and* ***alder*** *grew across southern Britain and mainland Europe, displacing the original forests of* ***birch*** *and* ***pine*** *as winters became less severe and summers lasted longer.*

→ **539 Glossary** for any unfamiliar terms

*Bog-like conditions prevail with **mosses, ferns** and **heathers** attracting fox moths and heather beetles. In damper ground orchids also thrive, sending up spectacular stalks of flowers. Trees too may take root, the stands of **grey willow** and **alder** providing still more shelter.*

*The women sported thistles in their hats or **heather** in their lapels.*

Sort of, type of, kind of, class of + count noun 177c

With expressions such as *sort of, kind of, type of, class of, category of*, singular count nouns normally occur without *a/an*:

*What **type of shop** do you think people use instead of the corner shops?*

[*the Firth of Forth* is a wide river channel in Scotland]
*A famous example of this **kind of bridge** is the road bridge across the Firth of Forth.*

However, in informal spoken contexts, *a/an* may be used:

*What **kind of a dad** are you?*

*What **sort of a bird** was it that you saw?*

*It went away, then it came back. It was that **kind of a flu**.*

When the plural forms *sorts of, kinds of, types of, classes of, categories of* are used, either a singular or plural noun may follow:

[advertisement for a security firm]
*All **types of locks** and security **devices** fitted, and estimates given.*

*There are two **types of microphone**: condenser microphones (otherwise known as electret) which require a battery, and dynamic microphones which do not.*

*What **kinds of ambitions** did you have when you were younger?*

*The banks give different interest for different **classes of deposits**.*

*Various **categories of vehicle** are exempt from the need to obtain an operating licence.*

NON-COUNT NOUNS 178

General 178a

Non-count nouns show no contrast in number between singular and plural. They refer to things treated as indivisible entities, not as separate units. They typically refer to things such as materials and liquids, states of mind, conditions, topics, processes and substances.

There are two types of non-count nouns: singular and plural.

Singular non-count nouns 178b

Singular non-count nouns are not used with the indefinite article *a/an* or in the plural:

I can hear ***music****.*
(~~I can hear a music.~~)

The ***furniture*** *was very old.*
(~~The furnitures were very old.~~)

They got good ***advice*** *from the student counsellor.*
(~~They got a good advice from the student counsellor.~~)
(~~They got good advices from the student counsellor.~~)

Some common examples of singular non-count nouns are:

advice
baggage
bread
cement
cheese
electricity
fun
furniture
happiness
help
information
knowledge
luck
luggage
paint
patience
progress
rain
sand
snow
soap
truth
water
weather
violence

Singular non-count nouns may have concrete meanings (*cheese, furniture, luggage, sand*) or more abstract meanings (*advice, knowledge, patience, progress*).

When concrete nouns are singular non-count, it is usually because they are seen as an undifferentiated mass. The names of many common items of food and drink are treated as singular non-count nouns, as are the names of materials. The nouns in the lists below that are liquids, gases and solids consist of collections of small particles that are not usually divided and so are seen as a whole:

- Food and drink:

bread
cake
cheese
coffee
curry
fruit
jam
juice
milk
oil
pasta
rice
salad
salt
spaghetti
spinach
sugar
tea
water
yoghurt

539 **Glossary** for any unfamiliar terms

- Liquids, gases and solids:

adhesive
air
cement
cloth
concrete
cotton
deodorant
dye
fabric
fog
fuel
fur
gravel
lotion
medicine
metal
ointment
paint
petrol
plastic
sand
smoke
soap
soil
toothpaste
wool

Other languages divide masses and entities differently from English. For example, in some languages *hair*, *spaghetti*, *spinach* and *money* are treated as plural units rather than a singular mass.

The following examples of singular non-count nouns are count nouns in many other languages:

*accommodation**
advice
applause
assistance
baggage
camping
cash
chaos
clothing
cutlery
equipment
evidence
furniture
hair
harm
health
homework
housework
housing
information
knowledge
leisure
luck
luggage
money
music
news
progress
publicity
*research**
rubbish
safety
shopping
spaghetti
spinach
traffic
transport
travel
underwear
violence
weather
work

* may occur as count nouns in non-British varieties of English

*Where have you left your **luggage**?*
(~~Where have you left your luggages?~~)

*There **is** not **much information** about the college.*
(~~There are not many informations about the college.~~)

How ***is*** *your* ***knowledge*** *of the British jail system?*
(~~How are your knowledges of the British jail system?~~)

Your ***hair looks*** *nice.*
(~~Your hairs look nice.~~)

Non-count nouns ending in *-s* 178c

Some non-count nouns end in *-s* but are grammatically singular. They include names of some school/university subjects, physical activities, diseases, and games:

Non-count nouns which end in *-s*

school/university subjects	physical activities	diseases	games
civics	*athletics*	*shingles*	*bowls*
classics	*aerobics*	*measles*	*billiards*
economics	*callisthenics*	*mumps*	*darts*
ergonomics	*gymnastics*		*dominoes*
ethics			*draughts*
linguistics			*skittles*
maths/mathematics			
mechanics			
physics			
politics			
pragmatics			

Another very common word that is singular but ends in *-s* is *news*

Aerobics is *really popular these days, particularly with older people.*

Shingles lays *you low for anything up to six months, doesn't it?*

Bowls is *played by many younger people these days.*

This news is *not so good.*
(~~These news are not so good.~~)

Exceptionally, plural verbs may occur with such nouns when the noun phrase has a more specific reference:

David's ***politics keep*** *getting him into trouble.*
(political views)

They've been running the country for two years now but their ***economics are*** *all wrong.*
(economic beliefs/policies)

539 **Glossary** for any unfamiliar terms

Plural non-count nouns 178d

The following commonly occurring non-count nouns are always grammatically plural:

belongings	*outskirts*	*riches*
congratulations	*particulars*	*savings* (money)
dregs	*pictures* (cinema)	*stairs*
earnings	*premises* (buildings)	*surroundings*
goods	*proceedings*	*thanks*
likes	*proceeds*	
mains	*remains*	

*I understand **congratulations are** due on the new job, by the way.*

*The **outskirts** of the city **are** rather drab and uninteresting.*

*The **proceeds** of the concert **are** all going to charity.*

Some nouns with plural forms have different meanings. For example:

pictures = cinema (now becoming outdated)
pictures = plural of picture

premises = a building or buildings
premises = plural of premise (meaning 'ideas or theory on which an argument is based')

Some plural non-count nouns refer to things perceived as having two parts, e.g. *trousers* have two legs ('bipartite' items):

A: *Where **are** my **jeans**?*
B: ***They're** in the wash.*

Bipartite nouns include garments with two legs worn around the waist (e.g. *jeans*), instruments worn over both eyes or both ears related to sight and hearing (e.g. *headphones*) and tools consisting of two similar parts on a pivot (e.g. *scissors*):

Bipartite nouns

instruments	garments	tools
binoculars	*briefs*	*pincers*
glasses	*jeans*	*pliers*
goggles	*jodhpurs*	*scissors*
headphones	*knickers*	*shears*
spectacles	*overalls*	*tongs*
	pants	*tweezers*
	pyjamas	
	shorts	
	trousers	
	underpants	

This group of nouns is productive in that new nouns (including the names of manufacturers) which fit into these categories generally take on the same syntactic features. Recent examples include:

combats, chinos, Levis (types of trousers)

boxers (underwear shorts)

shades, Ray-bans (types of sunglasses)

In order to refer to more than one example of this type of noun, the partitive expression *a pair of/pairs of* is commonly used:

He needs a new ***pair of glasses****, I think.*
(or: He needs new glasses, I think.)

We bought a small ***pair of binoculars****.*
(or: We bought some small binoculars.)

I'm going to take about ***four pairs of trousers****.*
(~~I'm going to take about four trousers.~~)

In some cases it is difficult to tell whether a singular or plural reference is made:

I didn't buy much but I did buy ***some trousers****.*
(one pair or several could be indicated)

PARTITIVE EXPRESSIONS (*A BIT OF, A PAIR OF*) 179

Sometimes it is necessary to be able to count the things denoted by singular and plural non-count nouns, and especially to count concrete things. Partitive expressions allow this. Examples of partitive expressions are: *bit of*, *item of*, *pair of*, *piece of*. Of these, the most neutral and widely used expressions involve *bit*, *piece* and *item*:

I gave her two ***bits of advice****.*

Some ***items of furniture*** *were destroyed.*

Would you like this ***piece of cheese****?*

Partitive expressions collocate strongly with particular non-count nouns:

a ***loaf of*** *bread*
two ***slices of*** *bread/cake/cheese/chicken breast*
a ***bar of*** *chocolate/soap*
a ***bit of*** *fun*
a ***piece of*** *furniture*
a ***stroke of*** *luck*
a ***spell of*** *bad weather*

→ 539 **Glossary** for any unfamiliar terms

Examples of informal everyday partitive expressions commonly occurring with non-count nouns, both concrete and abstract, are:

bit of	*mass of*	*sliver of*
chunk of	*sheet of*	*spell of*
dash of	*pile of*	*spot of*
drop of	*portion of*	*touch of*
lump of	*slice of*	*trace of*

*There are two **piles of** dirty **washing** over there. Whose are they?*

*He always adds a **nice touch of humour** to the commentary.*

*They say we might just get a **spot of rain** in the late afternoon.*

*We had a **spell of** very mild **weather** in January.*

*Shall I get six **slices of cheese**, or is that not enough?*

Partitive expressions commonly refer to the shape, size, movement or the amount of something:

*There's a whole **stream of people** queuing outside the post office.*

*He gave us a **torrent of abuse**.*

*At the end of the evening several **jets of** coloured **water** and light were sent flying up into the sky.*

*One massive final **gust of wind** blew the tree over on its side.*

Some partitive expressions with *-ful* refer to containers or spaces which commonly hold the item referred to. These include *bowlful of, cupful of, fistful of, handful of, mouthful of, spoonful of*:

*He gave me a **fistful of cash**. I don't know how much it was all together.*

*I always add a **spoonful of salt** to the pasta water.*

The plural of such expressions is usually formed by adding *-s* after *-ful*:

*Just put three **teaspoonfuls** of olive oil and one of vinegar and you have a perfect salad dressing.*

Partitive expressions are often used metaphorically to describe more abstract quantities:

*They had a **slice of luck** when the coach went off the road but didn't hit anything.*

*One had to add a **dash of realism** and a great big **dollop of gratitude** to a situation like this.*

*Only a **handful of people** turned up at the concert. It was very disappointing.*

55 Of

NON-COUNT NOUNS USED COUNTABLY 180

Masses and units

A number of singular non-count nouns can refer both to masses and to units. These nouns can be used with the indefinite article or in the plural when they refer to a particular unit or to units of something, or to different types and qualities of something.

Nouns in this class include those referring to food and drink and other materials and substances. The class also includes some abstract nouns such as *difficulty, experience, failure, injustice, success*. They are often referred to as 'dual class' nouns, because of their ability to operate in two different ways:

*Do you drink **tea**?*
(general, non-count use)

*Three **teas** and **a coffee** please.*
(particular instance(s): a cup/cups of tea/coffee)

*'Dazzle' is **an** excellent **washing powder**.*
(a particular type or quality)

*Do you want some **cake**?*
(general, non-count use; a piece of a big cake)

*Do you want **a cake** with your coffee?*
(an individual item)

*These **cakes** are delicious.*
(a number of individual items)

[describing puffins, a type of sea-bird]
*Since they find **difficulty** in taking off from flat ground, they tend to colonise the steeper slopes first.*

***An** additional **difficulty**, as some see it, is that the country now has multi-party democracy.*
(one individual problem or difficulty)

*I don't foresee any **difficulties**.*
(any set of problems or difficulties)

***Experience** must count for something in such situations.*
(a person's accumulated life experience or work experience)

*It was **a** great **experience**.*
(an individual event as lived through by someone)

*She's had some very odd **experiences**, I must say.*
(odd events have happened to her)

→ 539 **Glossary** for any unfamiliar terms

Mental states

Some of these dual-class nouns referring to mental states can be used with *a/an* but cannot be used in the plural. These include *anger, bitterness, courage, determination, hatred, knowledge, patience, pride, resistance*. When used with *a/an*, such nouns must be modified or used with a complement:

Count/non-count nouns with and without *a/an*

used without a/an	used with *a/an*
... and many members of the middle class still harboured ***deep anger over the economic losses that they had suffered during the 'great inflation'****.*	[literary critic describing a book] *There is wit and candour as well as sorrow, and* **a good, controlled anger***, which never displays itself in censure or rancour.*
The offer from the IRA, to which Blair** has responded with* ***courage and determination****, was on the table last October.* [* Irish Republican Army] [**Tony Blair, British Prime Minister at the time]	*She had locks on her doors and, above all,* ***a determination to be a burden to no one****.*
They had ***extensive knowledge of 'best buy' food and food shops within their areas.***	*And she acquired* ***an in-depth knowledge of the hotel business****.*
It was conversation that proved the downfall of our relationship; that and ***wounded pride****.*	*Senna* not only has a much-improved car but* ***a wounded pride*** *to fire him today.* [* famous motor-racing driver]

Different meanings

A small number of singular non-count nouns are also used as count nouns but with a change in meaning:

I've got loads of ***work*** *I could be doing.*
(non-count: tasks, jobs, things to do)

The announced aim is to display modern ***works*** *of art to a vast new audience.*
(count: creative products by artists, e.g. books, paintings, music)

This will involve extensive engineering ***works*** *on public roads.*
(count: large-scale engineering activities, e.g. *road-works* [building and repairing roads])

Strangely, she disliked ***travel****. She said she had always wanted to be 'home alone'.*
(non-count: the activity or process of moving over longer distances from one place to another)

It has been my privilege to travel, to see a lot of country, and in those ***travels*** *I have learned of several ways to become intimate with the land, ways I try to practise.*
(count: often refers to major expeditions and journeys of exploration, for example, the famous English novel *Gulliver's Travels*)

COUNT NOUNS USED AS NON-COUNT NOUNS 181

Count nouns can be used as if they were non-countable. This often applies to countable food items such as *potatoes*, *onions*, *eggs*, and to any other count nouns which can be seen as a whole:

*Do you use **egg** when you make your own pasta?*

*After the storm, there were bits of **tree** all over the garden.*

Sometimes there is a shift in meaning when a count noun is used non-countably:

*When we lived in the US, wild **turkeys** used to come into our garden.*

*Do you always have **turkey** for lunch?*
(reference to the meat rather than to the bird)

NOUN PHRASE AGREEMENT 182

Noun + verb agreement 182a

Collective nouns, such as *committee, government, team*, can be followed by either a singular or a plural verb form. When the singular verb form and/or singular pronouns are used, the group is treated as a unit; when the plural verb form and/or plural pronouns are used, the noun treats a group as a number of individuals:

***The government has** said **it** will take action.*
(treated as a unit)

***The government have** said **they** will take action.*
(treated as composed of different individuals/departments)

***The team is** in good spirits.*
(treated as a unit)

***The team are** in good spirits.*
(treated as composed of individual team members)

Plural concord is more common than singular in informal contexts. Further examples of collective nouns which behave similarly are:

audience	*company*	*group*
board	*congregation*	*jury*
committee	*crew*	*public*
community	*enemy*	*staff*

Other nouns with variable or otherwise noteworthy agreement patterns include *bulk, couple, majority, minority, number, pair, percentage, proportion, rest, remainder*:

*While some patients in the special hospitals are dangerous, **the majority are** not.*
(typical usage: treated as composed of separate individuals; plural agreement)

→ 539 **Glossary** for any unfamiliar terms

Over 100,000 supporters waited to see the game but ***the majority was*** *outside watching on a large screen.*
(less typical usage: treated as a unified body; more formal)

[from a film review]
The rest *of the cast* ***are*** *okay as well but no one really stands out, and the special effects are merely okay, too.*
(treated as composed of separate individuals)

The rest *of the European Union now* ***seems*** *ready to reluctantly bow to British pressure that justice and home affairs remain primarily a matter for intergovernmental cooperation.*
(treated as a unified body)

There ***were a number*** *of strange facts that were difficult to explain, and the judge decided that she was the murderer.*
(almost always plural agreement even though singular in form)

A couple of *boys* ***were*** *standing at the corner.*
(almost always plural agreement even though singular in form)

Agreement with quantifying expressions 182b

The quantifying expressions *a good deal of*, *a great deal of*, *plenty of* and constructions with *quantity of* and *amount of* are restricted to use with certain types of noun.

A good deal of, a great deal of

These are normally restricted to singular non-count nouns:

Recent comment has been disfigured by ***a good deal of misinformation****.*

He had lost ***a great deal of weight*** *and it made him look taller than ever.*

However, in informal speech, *a good/great deal of* may be used with plural count nouns:

[talking about how men might behave badly when out in all-male company but differently when at home]
I'm quite convinced that ***a good deal of those men*** *would go home to their wives and family and be very loving to their, to their wives and family, be respectful of their neighbours.*

[talking about a tennis club]
There are a couple of adults there that like to play but really there weren't really ***a great deal of players*** *other than the juniors to play with.*

Amount of

In general, constructions with *amount of* are restricted to use with non-count nouns:

We still have ***a huge amount of work*** *to do.*

However, in more informal spoken and written contexts, *amount of* may occur with plural count nouns:

For the cost, the machine seems very good value, especially with ***the amount of accessories*** *supplied.*

Plenty of and *quantity of*

Constructions with *plenty of* and *quantity of* may be used with either non-count nouns or plural count nouns:

No need to rush, we've got ***plenty of time***.

There are ***plenty of reasons*** *for not doing it.*

[describing materials for use with aquarium plants]
A mixture of coarse sand and clay with ***a small quantity of charcoal*** *or charcoal incorporated in granulated clay is suitable.*

He had ***a huge quantity of*** *newspaper* ***cuttings*** *he'd collected over the years.*

A sizeable quantity of drugs*, including heroin, had been found and seized also, along with a veritable arsenal of guns and ammunition.*

Gender and animate/inanimate reference 183

English nouns are not, as they are in some languages, masculine, feminine or neuter. Only pronouns and possessive determiners are marked grammatically for gender (e.g. *he, she, it, his, hers*). However, English does distinguish living (animate) from non-living (inanimate) things. For example, *he, she* and *who* are used to refer to animate nouns; *it* and *which* are used to refer to inanimate nouns:

She*'s a famous* ***actress****. Isn't* ***she*** *the one* ***who*** *was in 'Four Weddings'?*

Here's ***the bag****. Don't forget* ***it****'s the bag* ***which*** *has already been stolen twice this week.*

Animate nouns can refer either to people (personal) or animals (non-personal). Personal animate nouns can be used to refer to both males and females. There are different forms for a small number of personal animate nouns:

actor	*actress*
host	*hostess*
policeman	*policewoman*
steward	*stewardess*
waiter	*waitress*

Some female forms of nouns are no longer used (e.g. *poetess, murderess*), and in some cases the (formerly) male noun is now used to refer to both sexes (e.g. *actor, host*). Usually, gender-neutral nouns are preferred (e.g. *police officer, firefighter, flight attendant*).

Sometimes male and female terms are used as premodifiers to distinguish the gender-reference of the head noun. Examples are: *male model, male nurse, female plumber, boy soprano, women novelists*. These terms are all socially sensitive and should be used carefully.

In some contexts, the word *person* is preferred to *man* or *woman*:

She was elected ***chairperson*** *of the committee.*

He was the best ***spokesperson*** *we've had in a long time.*

Most non-personal animate nouns refer to animals. Animals which have a special place in human society can be referred to by the pronouns *he*, *she* and *who*, especially in spoken language. A degree of subjectivity in labelling the gender of an animal is usually present:

*There's a black dog in the street. **He** looks lost.*

*Is **she** a big eater, your **cat**?*

Some animals are given separate male and female words. These words are mainly used in specific contexts, for example by breeders or vets, or other experts and people working in the field. Common examples are listed below, with the common general name for the animal given alongside.

male	female	common name
lion	*lioness*	*lion*
fox	*vixen*	*fox*
dog	*bitch*	*dog*
tiger	*tigress*	*tiger*
bull	*cow*	*cow*
drake	*duck*	*duck*

When used with human reference, the pronoun *it* normally only applies to babies or to small children and is used both for general reference and for occasions when the gender may not be known:

*Every child misses **its** mother.*

*That baby upstairs. **It**'s always crying.*

[said to a mother about a forthcoming birth]
*Are you going to have **it** at home or in hospital?*

PROPER NAMES 184

Proper names are nouns which give names to people and things. For example, *Mary*, *Jakarta* or *March* are proper names. These nouns are typically used without determiners and do not vary in number. They are written with a capital letter.

Proper names may consist of more than one word: *The Straits Times* (name of an Asian newspaper), *Princess Diana*, *The Hague*, *Kai Tak Airport*, *The Lord of the Rings*, *Mount Kilimanjaro*, *the Nile*, *Shannon International Airport*. When proper names consist of more than one word, the words work together as a single unit.

In some contexts proper names can be treated as count nouns:

*I'm meeting **the Grays** at nine this evening.*
(*Gray* is a family name, and therefore a proper name; *the Grays* refers to the family as a whole, or to specific members of the Gray family)

*There were **three Sues** in my class at school.*
(three single instances of the same name – three girls called Sue)

*Do you have **my Jane Austen**?*
(my copy of a novel by Jane Austen)

*He has **Picassos** in his gallery.*
(paintings by Picasso)

*You don't need to be **an Einstein** to work that out.*
(Einstein was a scientist)

*I remember **the New Year's Eves** we spent together.*

[looking at a baby and commenting on its facial features]
*She's **a real O'Donnell**, isn't she?*

Some proper names are singular non-count nouns, e.g. *Marmite* (a food product), *Dulux* (a brand of paint):

*Would you like some **Marmite** on your toast?*

Some proper names are plural non-count nouns, e.g. *Levis*® (a brand of jeans), *Ray-Bans* (a brand of sunglasses):

*Those **Ray-Bans** were on sale at the duty free at the airport.*

In most cases the proper name is capitalised but some common everyday product names are not capitalised (e.g. *brie, cheddar, sellotape*).

Proper names and agreement
Proper names also involve agreement choices. When specific organisations, institutions and countries are mentioned, plural and singular verb forms tend to be used interchangeably, depending on whether the entity is treated as a single unit or as composed of individuals:

***The CIA is** only acting in the public interest.*
***The CIA are** only acting in the public interest.*

***Vietnam is** refusing to re-join the economic summit.*
***Vietnam are** refusing to re-join the economic summit.*

***The BBC has** a new World Service channel.*
***The BBC have** a new World Service channel.*

Names of geographical features **185**

The English names of rivers have the definite article before them. Note that the article is normally written in lower case:

the Colorado River	*the Amazon*	*the River Thames*
the Yangtse	*the Danube*	*the Ganges*

The names of lakes and of individual mountains do not have the definite article before them. *Lake* or *Mount* often comes before the specific name:

Lake Ontario	*Mount Fuji*	*Popocatepetl*
Lake Geneva	*(Mount) Everest*	*Snowdon*

Exceptions: *the Matterhorn, the Eiger*

→ **539 Glossary** for any unfamiliar terms

The names of ranges of mountains have the definite article before them:

the Alps | *the Himalayas* | *the Andes*

The names of deserts, oceans, seas, groups of islands and major areas and regions have the definite article before them:

the Sahara (Desert) | *the Mediterranean (Sea)* | *the Bahamas*
the Pacific (Ocean) | *the Florida Keys* | *the Steppes*

Some names of buildings, monuments and cathedrals can take a definite article; some do not:

the Houses of Parliament | *the Bundestag* | *Stonehenge*
the White House | *the Taj Mahal* | *Westminster Abbey*

Some names of streets and roads can take a definite article; some do not:

Princes Street | *Piccadilly* | *the Great North Road*
Oxford Street | *Abbey Road* | *the M5, the A34*

Names of regions, countries, nationalities and languages 186

Reference to regions, countries, nationalities and languages is made in English by proper names, adjectives, singular and plural nouns.

Proper names indicate the names of regions and countries:

Asia | *Brazil* | *China*
Africa | *Germany* | *Norway*

Adjectives are used to indicate nationalities or regional identities (bold); some also refer to the languages spoken in the country (in green):

Peru : ***Peruvian*** | *America* : ***American*** | *China* : ***Chinese***
Asia : ***Asian*** | *France* : ***French*** | *Spain* : ***Spanish***

Some nationality adjectives can be used as nouns to refer to the nationality of a person:

a Norwegian | *an Iraqi* | *a Belgian*
a Brazilian | *an Egyptian* | *a Canadian*

(~~an Irish, a Dutch, a French~~)

Plural nouns based on the adjective form are used to refer to the population of a country as a whole:

the Norwegians | *the Algerians* | *the Greeks*
the Malaysians | *the Israelis* | *the Venezuelans*

Nationality adjectives ending in *-ese*, *-(i)sh* or *-ch* do not inflect in this way:

the Chinese | *the Spanish* | *the French*
the Japanese | *the Welsh* | *the Dutch*

(~~the Chineses, the Spanishes~~)

→ **528 Appendix: Nationalities, countries and regions** for a full list

DETERMINERS: INTRODUCTION 187

Determiners indicate the type of reference made by the noun phrase (e.g. definite, indefinite, possessive); they also indicate number or quantity (e.g. *six*, *much*, *some*). Determiners come in front position in noun phrases, before adjectives and noun modifiers. They include words such as *a*, *all*, *each*, *five*, *many*, *my*, *no*, *some*, *the*, *those*, *which*:

*This is **a** complete mess.*

*Where are **my** glasses?*

***Each** time I've tried to sell **the** house I've had **no** buyers.*

*I'm **his** best friend.*

*I've had **several** blood tests.*

All the determiners in English are dealt with in this book. They are:

a/an
all
another
any (strong form)
any (weak form)
both
each
either, neither
enough
every
(a) few, fewer, fewest
half
(a) little, less, least
many, more, most
much, more, most
my, your, his, Jim's, etc.
no
one (numeral) *two, three*, etc.
some (strong form)
some (weak form)
such (anaphoric)
several
the
this, that, these, those
what (interrogative)
what (quantitative)
what, such (exclamative)
which
whose
zero determiner (i.e. no determiner)

Determiners may occasionally be premodified or postmodified:

*Almost **all** libraries have got quite a lot of information on those sorts of things.*

*Many **more** professional couples are opting for larger families.*

***All** but one of the 16 stockmarkets continued to recover this week.*

More than one determiner may occur in the noun phrase:

*I do **all the** housework, I look after **my two** children at the same time, and I'm studying.*

A: *We've had lots of visitors as well haven't we?*
B: *Yeah.*
A: *This year we've had **both your** nieces, haven't we?*

Where more than one determiner can be used together, there is a fixed order in which they occur. The table illustrates the sequence:

The order of determiners

quantifier	article or demonstrative or possessive	numeral	head
all	*my*	*five*	*cousins*
all		*three*	*pages*
both	*your*		*nieces*
half	*a*		*litre*
	my	*first*	*exam*
	those	*two*	*girls*

All, *both* and *half* can come before articles and demonstratives and possessives, but quantifiers such as *any*, *few*, *many*, *more*, *some*, etc. and numerals cannot. Where these quantifiers and numerals do occur first, *of* must be used (→ 191):

*Can I borrow **more of those** disks?*

*I've achieved **some of my** ambitions.*
(~~I've achieved some my ambitions.~~)

***Two of his** children are getting married around the same time.*

DETERMINERS: CHARACTERISTICS OF USE 188

Determiners have particular ways of occurring in noun phrases. In 189–192, four principal ways in which determiners can occur are described:

1 which determiners can occur with which types of head noun (189)
2 whether the determiner can also be used as a pronoun (190)
3 whether the determiner can occur as a pronoun followed by *of* + definite noun phrase (e.g. *some of her friends*, but **not** *this of my food*) (191)
4 whether the determiner can occur with *of* and a possessive determiner (e.g. *a cousin of mine arrived*, but **not** *all best friends of hers were there*) (192)

DETERMINERS AND TYPES OF HEAD NOUN 189

No restrictions 189a

Some determiners may be used with any type of head noun, whether singular or plural, count or non-count.

The determiners which have no restrictions on use with head nouns are:

any (strong form)	*some* (strong form)	*which*
my, your, his, noun phrase + *'s*, etc.	*the*	*whose*
	what (interrogative)	
no		

The following are examples with *any*, *no*, the strong form of *some*, and *whose:*

- Singular count:

  *So that's **no problem**, is it?*

  *He was driving along up there somewhere, to **some village** or other, and all of a sudden this double-decker bus came down the lane.*

  ***Whose idea** was this?*

- Plural count:

  *They've got **no beds** for the children.*

  *It wasn't as bad as **some places**, because it's quite a big shop, and we didn't queue at all.*

  *I can't remember **whose names** were on it.*

- Singular non-count:

  *Unfortunately, the flight's available but **no accommodation**.*

  ***Some chocolate** makes me sneeze, but I haven't worked out why.*

  ***Whose land** are we on?*

- Plural non-count:

  *Why doesn't he have **any scissors**?*

  *He answered the door with **no trousers** on.*

Restricted to singular count or non-count noun 189b

This and *that* are singular and are used with singular nouns. The noun may be count or non-count:

*She arrived home **this morning**.*
(count)

*What's **that book**, Nigel?*
(count)

*It'll take us ages in **this weather**.*
(non-count)

Restricted to singular count noun 189c

Some determiners may only be used with a singular count noun. These are:

a/an	*each*	*every*
another	*either, neither*	*one* (numeral)

*Can I have **a stamp** for this, please?*

***Each task** should take a couple of minutes to do.*

→ **539 Glossary** for any unfamiliar terms

It was in the south part of Dublin and I used to go by tram ***every day*** *all across Dublin. I got to know the city so well.*
(~~I used to go by tram every days …~~)

Quietly Esther checked that ***neither child*** *was watching, then locked the kitchen door.*

Restricted to singular non-count noun 189d

Much and *(a) little, less, least* may only be used with a singular non-count noun:

It's not ***much pay****. There isn't* ***much work*** *for him these days.*

Those animals exported abroad for slaughter are subject to similar mistreatment, as well as long, arduous journeys over hundreds of miles with ***little food*** *or* ***water****.*

Restricted to plural count noun 189e

Both, many, (a) few, the numerals *two, three, four,* etc. and *several* are restricted to use with plural count nouns:

I've been my own boss for ***many years****.*

Brighton is ***a few hours*** *away by train.*

Few books *are, in a strict sense, necessary.*

Restricted to plural count or plural non-count noun 189f

These and *those* are used with plural count or plural non-count nouns:

These trousers *don't fit me any more.*

Those beans *are cooked.*

Restricted to non-count or plural count noun 189g

Some determiners may only be used with a non-count (singular or plural) noun or with a plural count noun. These are:

all	*some* (weak form)	*what, such* (exclamative)
any (weak form)	*such* (anaphoric)	
enough	*what* (quantitative) + relative clause	zero determiner (i.e. no determiner)

We weren't given ***enough information****.*
(singular non-count)

Rising costs of living and mounting unemployment in the aftermath of war fuelled discontent with the colonial state. ***Such discontent*** *could be exploited by nationalist politicians.*
(singular non-count)

What money they made *went entirely to local charities.*
(singular non-count)

[public announcement to passengers about to leave a train]
Please make sure to take ***all*** *personal* ***belongings*** *with you.*
(plural non-count)

All kids *learn through play.*
(plural count)

Well, first of all, have we got ***enough envelopes****?*
(plural count)

But I looked at my father and he laughed like mad and said, 'Oh, she means offer of marriage.' And my mother said, 'Don't put ***such ideas*** *in the child's head.'*
(plural count)

DETERMINERS AND PRONOUNS 190

Determiners used as pronouns 190a

Some determiners may also be used as pronouns (i.e. as the head of their own noun phrase):

Have you finished with ***those videos****?*
(determiner)

A: *D'you want these sunglasses?*
B: *Yes, I'll need* ***those****.*
(pronoun)

Would you like ***some teriyaki chicken****?*
(determiner)

[offering cake to someone]
Would you like ***some****?*
(pronoun)

The next train took us a stage further until it just stopped. We got out and waited for hours at the railway station for ***another****.*
(pronoun, i.e. another train)

The sight of him was a gift of greater value than ***any*** *she'd ever received in her life.*
(pronoun, i.e. than any gift)

He's not my first teacher. I've had ***several****.*
(pronoun, i.e. several teachers)

539 **Glossary** for any unfamiliar terms

Determiners which may also be used as pronouns in this way are:

another	*enough*	*some* (weak form)
any (strong form)	*(a) little, less, least*	*these, those*
any (weak form)	*many, more, most*	*this, that*
both	*much, more, most*	*two, three*
each	*one* (numeral)	*which*
(a) few, fewer, fewest	*several*	*whose*
either, neither	*some* (strong form)	

Determiners replaced by pronouns 190b

The and *a/an* do not occur as pronouns, but their meanings may be expressed pronominally in different forms.

He, she, it and *them* are used as anaphoric pronouns in place of a noun phrase beginning with *the*:

*Have you met **the new boss**? **He**'s very nice.*

*I am thrilled to win **the race** this year, because of all the great horses in **it**.*

*Add **the potatoes** and roll **them** around in the spices.*

One is used as a pronoun in place of a noun phrase beginning with *a/an*:

*He has lost **a son**. I have found **one**.*

Possessive determiners and pronouns 190c

The possessive determiners have the following forms as pronouns (→ **201a**):

possessive determiner	possessive pronoun
my	*mine*
your (singular)	*yours*
his	*his*
her	*hers*
its	(no form)
one's	(no form)
our	*ours*
your (plural)	*yours*
their	*theirs*

***My dad** would beat **yours** in a fight.*

*I've lived **my life**. She's just starting **hers**.*

*You see, they go to **their church** first and we go to **ours**, and then we meet, you know, afterwards.*

If possessive determiners are postmodified with *own*, they retain their form when used pronominally:

> *I always forget birthdays. I have enough trouble remembering* ***my own***.
> (~~I have enough trouble remembering mine own.~~)

Singular *all* + noun may be substituted by *it all* or *all of it*. Plural *all* + noun may be replaced by *we/you/they/us/them all* or *all of us/you/them*:

> *We've got so much stuff, there's no way we're going to eat* ***it all*** *(or* ***all of it****).*
> (~~... there's no way we're going to eat all.~~)

> [to a taxi driver]
> *There are four people. Can you take* ***us all*** *(or* ***all of us****)?*

> *They've all been together from secondary school. Well some of them from primary school. And there's a really strong bond between* ***them all****. And* ***they all*** *care about one another.*

It/you/us/them all cannot be used in a reduced clause when there is no verb:

> A: *Has he eaten the cauliflower?*
> B: *Not* ***all of it****.*
> (~~Not it all.~~)

> A: *Whose are* ***all*** *the books?*
> B: *Harold's.*
> A: ***All of them****?*
> B: *Mm.* ***All of them****.*
> A: *Wow!*
> (~~Them all? Mm. Them all.~~)

When a subject pronoun + *all* is used, *all* occupies the mid position for adverbs (→ 325):

> ***We****'ll* ***all*** *meet again tomorrow.*
> (preferred to: We all will meet again tomorrow.)

→ also **201 Possessive pronouns**

OF + DEFINITE NOUN PHRASE 191

Some combinations of determiners are not permitted (e.g. *some/any* followed by *my/the/this*). However, some pronoun forms of determiners may combine with *of* + definite noun phrase (or definite pronoun) to produce partitive meanings (i.e. expressing a partial quantity or number out of a totality):

> **determiner *of* definite noun phrase**
> *Do you want | some | of | that stuff?*

 **55 *Of***

Determiners which operate in this way are:

- *a/an* (in the form of *one of*)
- *all*
- *another*
- *any* (strong form)
- *any* (weak form)
- *both*
- *each*
- *either, neither*
- *enough*
- *every* (in the form of *every one of*)
- *(a) few, fewer, fewest*
- *(a) little, less, least*
- *many, more, most*
- *much, more, most*
- *no* (pronoun form *none*)
- *several*
- *some* (strong form)
- *some* (weak form)
- *one* (numeral), *two, three,* etc.
- *the* (in the form *those of*)
- *which*

*It was yet **another of those** things that you couldn't describe, but you'd know it when you saw it.*

*He's not going to go back on **any of his decisions**.*

*I don't think we have **enough of that**.*

***Every one of my friends** turned up.*
(~~*Every of my friends turned up.*~~)

***Neither of the men** had said a word.*

*At one time, almost all the drugs in use were extracted directly from plants. **Some of the plants** in your garden may contain essential medical drugs.*

*I'd also like to say thanks to **those of my colleagues** who can't be here tonight.*
(~~*I'd also like to say thanks to the of my colleagues who can't be here tonight.*~~)

***Two of the boys** had nine children between them.*

***Which of those policies** would seem the best?*

OF + POSSESSIVE PRONOUN AFTER THE HEAD NOUN 192

Some determiners may combine with *of* + possessive pronoun used after the head noun:

	determiner	head noun	*of*	possessive pronoun
I run a company with	*a*	*friend*	*of*	*mine.*

Note that the pronoun is in the possessive form, not the object form:

I run a company with a friend of mine.
(~~*I run a company with a friend of me.*~~)

Determiners which may be used in this way are those listed in **191** and in addition *the*, zero determiner, noun phrase + *'s* (the so-called possessive *'s* construction), *this/that/these/those*, *what* and *such*:

*She was moving out and she gave the keys to **some friends of hers**.*

*If **every word of yours** is in there, the person has infringed your copyright.*

A friend of my sister's *took that photo.*

*Besides, you want **any child of yours** to live a long and healthy life.*

That house of theirs *must have cost a fortune to build.*

What money of hers *that was left went to her children.*

*I was just thinking of **old friends of mine** who I grew up with.*
(zero determiner)

POSSESSIVE 'S 193

The possessive *'s* construction is used to describe the possession or attribution of particular things, features, qualities or characteristics. It operates syntactically like the possessive determiners *my, your, his,* etc., and is best considered as a determiner:

*cow**'s** milk*

*goat**'s** cheese*

*men**'s** jackets*

*the school**'s** development plan*

*Jean**'s** bicycle*

*Vietnam**'s** economy*

*America**'s** foreign policy*

The possessive *'s* construction occurs with more complex noun phrases as well as with simple ones:

The Prince of Albania's *daughter*

The director of the company's *statement*

Dr Smith's *patients*

The use of possessive *'s* is sometimes arbitrary. For example, *lamb's liver* is said but not *lamb liver*. On the other hand, *chicken breast* (not *chicken's breast*) is said.

The possessive *'s* is common in general measurements of time:

*today**'s** news*

*yesterday**'s** political party*

*three weeks**'** holiday*

*twenty minutes**'** delay*

The possessive *'s* rather than the noun + noun construction is also used when the reference is more precise and specific:

I always spend ages reading the Sunday paper.
(general reference)

*The recipe you want was in last Sunday**'s** paper.*
(specific, unique reference)

→ **506 Appendix: Punctuation**

NUMERALS 194

Numerals can be either cardinal (e.g. *two, sixteen*) or ordinal (e.g. *first, third*).

Cardinals

Cardinal numbers are used as determiners, but they are also used as head nouns and pronouns. As heads, cardinals are inflected like nouns:

*Only **fifteen** people attended the meeting.*
(determiner)

***Two** cats are always better than **one** cat.*
(determiner)

***Twenty** of our group were German.*
(determiner with *of* + definite noun phrase)

*Troubles always come in **threes**.*
(head noun)

A: *How many screws do you need?*
B: *I just need **two**.*
(pronoun)

When *dozen, hundred, thousand, million* and *billion* are premodified, no final *-s* is used. When they are not modified, plural *-s* + *of* occurs:

five hundred pounds
(~~five hundreds pounds~~)
hundreds of pounds

several thousand people
thousands of people

a few million years
millions of years

Ordinals

Ordinal numbers refer to entities in a series or sequence. They are used as determiners and are normally preceded by other determiners such as the definite article or a possessive determiner:

*It was **the tenth** and final album in a long career.*

*We celebrated **his first** birthday in Hong Kong.*

Ordinals can also be used as the heads of noun phrases:

*I like all of them but **the fourth** was the best.*

*It was calculated in **hundredths** and **thousandths**.*

Ordinals can also be used as adverbs:

*Merry came **third** in the race.*

***First**, we need to clear the chairs away.*

AGREEMENT PROBLEMS WITH DETERMINERS 195

Some determiner phrases present choices of agreement. This principally concerns the use of *none of*, *either of*, *neither of*, *any of*, *half*, and numeral expressions between *one* and *two* (e.g. *one and a half*). There are also cases where singular determiners are used with plural numerals.

None of

In traditional views of grammar and in more formal styles, *none of* + plural count noun has singular concord with a verb. In such usage, *none of* is seen as a negated form of *one*:

> *The other assistants in the shoe shop seemed to manage on their wages. Of course,* ***none of them was*** *supporting a child, and the male assistant got sixty per cent more than the women.*

In everyday spoken and written informal usage, *none of* + plural count noun typically has plural concord with a verb. The plural head noun is treated as the notional subject of the verb:

> ***None of our children play*** *any musical instruments.*

Either of, *neither of* are also used in two ways. Singular concord is more traditional and formal, treating *either/neither* as referring to one of two individual entities. Plural concord sees *either/neither* as implying a pair of entities, therefore greater than one:

> [from a book about sleeping and dreaming]
> *Dreams of being chased, or of flying, are also more frequent than one might expect, given that* ***neither of these events happens*** *very frequently in real life.*
>
> ***Do either of you*** *play golf?*

Any of

Variable concord occurs with *any of*. Singular concord treats *any* as referring to an individual entity. Plural concord can imply either an individual or several individual entities:

> *What right* ***does any of us*** *have to play God?*
>
> ***Do any of you*** *want a ticket for the club dinner?*
> (could be one or more than one individual implied)

One

Variability of agreement occurs with expressions involving *one*. The phrase *more than one* is normally followed by a singular head noun and has singular verb concord:

> *But what we have seen so far is that for every job lost,* ***more than one job has been created.***
> (~~... more than one jobs have been created.~~)

However, in more informal spoken styles, plural head nouns and plural verb concord may occur:

[informal discussion at a meeting]
A: *But there* ***are more than one approaches****. There are many different conflicting approaches.*
B: *Yeah. But we're just reduced to using only one.*

✪ The expression *one and a half* is followed by a plural head noun:

That bottle holds about ***one and a half litres****.*
(~~… one and a half litre.~~)

However, when *a/one* + head noun + *and a half* is used, the head is singular:

That bottle holds about ***a litre and a half****.*

Numerals

✪ *Another*, not *other*, is used with numerals:

I paid him fifty pounds, now we owe him ***another fifty pounds****.*
(~~… now we owe him other fifty pounds.~~)

In informal styles, singular determiners can occur with plural numerals when they are modified:

Let me give you back ***that ten pounds I owe you****.*

That same three milk bottles *were still standing on his doorstep after a week.*

Expressions such as *a good* (meaning 'at least that number') and *a full* (meaning 'a completed number') may be used with plural numerals:

It's ***a good ten miles*** *or more from here.*

She's ***a full three years*** *younger than the next child up.*

A–Z 38 *Every*

IMPORTANT DISTINCTIONS IN THE USE OF DETERMINERS 196

The and zero article 196a

When general reference is made to all members of a class of count nouns or all examples or manifestations of a non-count noun, *the* is not used:

I don't think the internet will ever completely replace ***books****.*
(refers to all books)
(~~I don't think the internet will ever completely replace the books.~~)

Salt *is bad for you.*
(all salt is bad for you)
(~~The salt is bad for you.~~)

Life *has its moments of frustration for all of us.*
(~~The life has its moments of frustration for all of us.~~)

A postmodified noun does not necessarily require *the*; the presence or absence of *the* still depends on whether the reference is general or to a defined sub-class:

Furniture of that quality *is too good for a student flat.*
(all and any furniture of that quality)

[speakers are gluing together a piece of wooden furniture]
A: *Does this stuff really work, this glue?*
B: *Yeah. That's what I've used on* ***the furniture I've made****, you know, the TV table and stuff.*
(specifically refers to only the items of furniture the speaker has made)

The is most commonly used to refer to things which are part of the speakers' shared world. It is a way of saying 'You know which x I am referring to':

If you're going to paint ***the wall****, we'll have to move* ***the furniture****.*
(speaker and listener know which wall and which furniture they are talking about)

A: *How are* ***the children****?*
B: *Fine thanks. Yes, they're doing fine.*
(speaker A does not need to say 'your children' if it is obvious to both speakers whose children are being referred to)

A: *Are you going into* ***the university*** *today?*
B: *I may do. Why?*
A: *Could you drop some books off at* ***the library*** *for me?*
(the university and the library are understood as the ones known to both speakers; it is unlikely B would reply 'Which university? Which library?')

Some and *any*: strong versus weak forms 196b

Some and *any* each have strong forms, which are stressed, and weak unstressed forms. The weak form of some is pronounced /səm/.

The weak forms indicate an indefinite quantity of something:

Would you like ***some cheese****?*

Are there ***any messages*** *on the answerphone?*

The strong forms have different meanings. The strong form of *some* most typically means 'a certain' or 'a particular' when used with singular count nouns:

Some child *was crying behind me throughout the whole flight and I never slept.*

Strong form *some* contrasts with *others*, *all* or *enough* when used with plural count nouns and with non-count nouns:

[talking of student grants]
Some students *get substantial amounts and others get nothing.*

[talking of dried beans that need to be soaked before use]
A: *But dry ones you have to soak them overnight and then get rid of that water and stuff.*
B: *Right. And lentils as well?*
A: ***Some of them**. Not all.*

*We've got **some bread** but not enough for three people.*

Strong form *any* is used most typically with singular count nouns and with non-count nouns to mean 'it does not matter which':

*If you have the warranty, **any authorised dealer** can get it repaired for you.*

***Any fruit juice** will make you sick if you drink enough of it.*

Some, any and zero determiner 196c

Although *some* and *any* indicate an indefinite quantity, they are not used for large or unlimited indefinite quantities. The zero determiner indicates an indefinite quantity without reference to size when used with non-count nouns and with plural count nouns:

*There are **some extra blankets** in the wardrobe if you need them.*
(an indefinite but limited number)

[government spokesman after a major earthquake]
*We need **help** from the international community. We need **tents** and **medicines** and **blankets**.*
(~~We need some help from the international community. We need some tents, some medicines and some blankets.~~)

*Are there **any frogs** in that pond?*
(indefinite but probably limited expectation of quantity)

*Do you have **red ants** in your garden?*
(no expectation about quantity)

Weak form *some* and *any* and clause types 196d

The use of the weak forms of *some* and *any* depends on whether the clause is declarative or interrogative, and whether it is affirmative or negative:

*There's **some** milk in the fridge.*
(~~There's any milk in the fridge.~~)

*There isn't **any** milk in the fridge.*
(~~There isn't some milk in the fridge.~~)

*Is there **any** milk in the fridge?*

*Is there **some** milk in the fridge?*

*Isn't there **any** milk in the fridge?*

*Isn't there **some** milk in the fridge?*

Affirmative and negative clauses

In declarative clauses, *some* occurs with affirmatives but does not occur with negatives. *Any* occurs with negatives but does not usually occur with affirmatives:

*I've got **some** nice French cheese for us.*
(~~I've got any nice French cheese for us.~~)

A: *I'd like **some** apple juice please.*
B: *You'd like **some** apple juice.*
A: *Yes.*
B: *Right.*
(~~I'd like any apple juice please.~~)

*I do**n't** have **any** questions.*
(~~I don't have some questions.~~)

[talking about a recently typed document]
*There are**n't** **any** glaring errors. I mean Jamie's read through it and he has**n't** seen **any**.*
(~~There aren't some glaring errors. I mean Jamie's read through it and he hasn't seen some.~~)

Any can occur in affirmative declarative clauses with an implied conditional meaning and in subordinate conditional clauses:

[radio weather forecast]
***Any** rain will clear by midday.*
(if there is any rain, it will clear by midday)

*If anyone has **any** questions during the day, ask Sam.*

Interrogative clauses

With interrogatives, *some* and *any* are both used to ask questions. *Some* suggests the speaker thinks the answer will fit neatly with the question; *any* is more open-ended and does not necessarily project an answer which the speaker expects:

[hostess to dinner guest at the beginning of the meal]
A: *Would you like **some** soup?*
B: *Mm, please.*
(at this point in the meal, the expectation is that the guest will want soup)

[hostess to dinner guest towards the end of the main course]
A: *Do you want **any** more salad or anything?*
B: *No I'm full thanks Jill.*
(it is less obvious whether the guest will want more or not; the question is more open-ended.)

[in a post office; A is the postal agent, B is a customer]
A: *You want it first class. Let's just weigh it for you then. First class is fifty seven.*
B: *Is there **some** kind of recorded delivery I could send it by?*
A: *Yes, it's another fifty five.*
(the customer's expectation is that there is a recorded delivery system; compare 'Is there any kind of recorded delivery I could send it by?', which would suggest the customer is far less certain whether such a possibility exists)

→ **539 Glossary** for any unfamiliar terms

Because of the difference between a suggestion of agreement with the question and a more open-ended question, *some* is more common than *any* in situations where polite or friendly offers are made, especially offers of food, even though the response may be negative:

A: *Do you want* ***some*** *pudding now Chris?*
B: *No. I'll have it in a minute thank you.*

Negative interrogative clauses

Negative interrogatives with *some* and *any* are used to check the speaker's understanding of a situation.

Negative interrogatives with *some* typically indicate that speakers wish to confirm their positive expectations or assumptions about the situation:

Wasn't there ***some*** *trouble in the village last night?*
(speaker has reason to think there was, and seeks confirmation)

[speaker is sharing out a bar of chocolate]
Don't you want ***some****, Lee?*
(I would expect you to want some, please confirm)

Negative interrogatives with *any* typically indicate that speakers wish to confirm their negative expectations or assumptions about the situation:

[at the dinner table]
A: *Do you want some water? Don't you want* ***any*** *juice?*
B: *No.*
A: *No?*
B: *Mm.*
(I sense you do *not* want juice, please confirm)

also **435c Negative interrogatives and speech acts**

No and *not a/not any* 196e

Affirmative verb + *no* is often used as a more emphatic form of negated verb + *any*:

I ***can't*** *see* ***any*** *reason at all for his behaviour.*
I ***can*** *see* ***no*** *reason at all for his behaviour.*

*These two things are****n't*** *in* ***any*** *way connected.*
These two things ***are*** *in* ***no*** *way connected.*

When *no* + noun is used as the subject of a main clause, *not any* is not normally an alternative:

No vegetables *taste as good as ones straight from the garden.*

This, that, these, those 196f

This, *that*, *these* and *those* are the only determiners which express contrasts of number. *This* and *that* are used with singular nouns; *these* and *those* are used with plural nouns:

*I saw the three students in my office **this morning**.*

*How are we going to afford **that type** of accommodation?*

***Those** young **kids** will cause trouble unless something is done soon.*

Conveying physical distance

The most common function of *this* and *these* is to point to things and people which are close to the speaker/writer in time and space. In general, *this* and *these* can be said to be speaker-oriented, as with *here* (→ A–Z 45 *Here, there*):

*I like **this hotel**, don't you?*

*Will he be coming **this Wednesday**?*

*In **this lecture** we shall be looking in particular at Shakespeare's History Plays.*

*Have you finished with **these newspapers**?*

*You'll need **these coins** for the parking ticket.*

The most common use of *that* and *those* is to refer to objects and people which may not be easily identified from the situation. *That* and *those* are used to refer to things which are more distant in time and space, even though it may be possible to see such things. In general, *that* and *those* can be said to be listener-oriented or oriented towards a third person, place or entity (→ A–Z 45 *Here, there* to compare *there*):

*What's **that** red **mark** on your face?*

*The book had two endings. I prefer the second but **that ending** is a bit too sentimental for me.*

*Could I see **those videos** on the shelf up there?*

*We should move **those chairs** into the corner of the room.*

In more formal styles, pronoun *that* and *those* may be complemented or postmodified:

***Those of you who have registered for the course** will be able to obtain booklists from the departmental office tomorrow morning.*
(complemented)

[quote from the writer George Bernard Shaw]
***Those who can**, do; **those who can't**, teach.*
(postmodified)

Conveying attitude

This/these and *that/those* may also express contrasts in emotional distance and can signal different attitudes. *This/these* can convey a more positive and involved attitude whereas *that/those* suggest a more detached and possibly critical attitude:

*I love **these** new phones that you can take pictures with.*
(can be said even if the speaker is nowhere near one of the phones referred to)

*I'm not going to wear this brown sweater any more. I hate **that** colour.*

*When are you going to finish **that** thesis of yours?*

*I hate **those** big four-wheel-drive cars.*

Use in narratives

This and *these* are used in narratives, anecdotes, jokes and similar contexts to create a sense of immediacy and to encourage a listener or reader to become involved. In these contexts, *this/these* may be seen as highly dramatised alternatives to *a/an* and zero article/*some*:

*Listen, there was **this** Irishman and he met **this** Englishman who was wearing a kilt, right, ...*
(compare: ... there was an Irishman and he met an Englishman ...)

That also has an involving function in narratives; as an alternative to *the*, it refers the listener to something familiar or known to them:

*And we lost our way at **that** big roundabout just outside Norwich.*
(You know the roundabout. Compare: ... the big roundabout just outside Norwich ...)

This for highlighting

In stories and reports, *this* is also used in order to underline or highlight that something is important:

*One of the central planks of the government's programme is **this** new attack on long-term unemployment.*

This and *that* for identification

This and *that* are used to identify oneself or to ask the identity of other speakers, especially in telephone calls and in answerphone messages:

*Hello, **this** is Mike calling to leave a message for David.*

*Is **that** Jenny Chapman? Hello, **this** is Sarah Bennett here.*

This and *that* and discourse segments 196g

This and *that* are used to refer back to things which have already been spoken or written about and to refer forward to things which are yet to be said or written. When used in this way, both determiners signal that something significant has been said or is about to be said. *This* and *that* both refer back but *this* is more frequently used to refer forwards and *that* is generally more emphatic:

*'Woodbrook' by David Thompson: **this** is a novel for anyone interested in Ireland and Ireland's history.*

*The whole area needs to be made a traffic-free zone. **That**'s the problem.*

***This** is the main problem. Organic foods are always going to be more expensive.*

*What do you think of **this**? We leave at 8 this evening rather than tomorrow morning.*

It can also refer back or forward to a specific noun or segment of discourse. But it is not normally used to refer in a general way and is not particularly emphatic:

A: *I seem to get so many of these sales phone calls. Do you get them?*
B: *No.*
A: ***It**'s usually double glazing firms.*
(*it* = the phone calls)

→ also **128 *It*, *this* and *that* referring to segments of text; 143a Signalling with *it*, *this* and *that***

Much, *many* and *a lot/lots* 196h

Although *a lot of/lots of* are not determiners (they are best seen as partitive noun phrases in their own right), they are used in situations where *much* and *many* would be inappropriate.

As with weak forms *some* and *any*, *much* and *many* are used differently with different clause types.

Declaratives

Affirmative declarative clauses prefer *a lot /lots*. *Lots of* is more informal than *a lot of*. *A lot of* and *lots of* can both be used with plural count nouns and with singular non-count nouns:

***A lot of/lots of** students get into debt.*
(preferred in informal contexts to: Many students get into debt.)

*I've got **a lot of/lots of** work to get through today.*
(preferred to: I've got much work to get through today.)

[tutor in informal university seminar]
*Compounding is one of the main forms of word formation in the Germanic languages. That is you just take **lots of** words and stick them together. Erm, Joyce has an example in just before this passage actually. He has a word which he totally invents. Contransmagnificandubantangiality. And all he's done is stick **lots of** words together. You get the idea?*
(*many* would sound far too formal here)

Much and *many* do occur in affirmative declarative clauses, but only in more formal styles:

> *There will be* ***much*** *competition among all those involved to hand out sweeping verdicts on history. The British will be credited (particularly by the British) with having done a splendid and disinterested job.*
>
> *However, Lincoln itself is an area of urban land-use. This means there are* ***many*** *buildings tightly packed together and a large population of over 80,000 people.*

Much is more restricted than *many* in affirmative declarative clauses. For example, it is more restricted to abstract nouns such as *competition*, *controversy*, *effort*, *discussion*. *Much* as a determiner and pronoun also occurs mostly in subject position:

> ***Much*** *has been written on this topic.*
> (~~They have written much on this topic.~~)
>
> ***Much*** *time has already been devoted to this question.*

Much and *many* are used in negative declarative clauses:

> *I have****n't*** *got* ***much*** *room in my flat, well it's just an open-plan flat. So there's literally one room and a bathroom. And it's got a kitchen but it's all open plan. There's* ***not much*** *space.*
>
> *The children do play out on the Green. There are* ***not many*** *places that they can go. And I don't like not having a front window so I can't see them out there.*

Many a + singular noun is used as an emphatic form with a similar meaning to *many* + plural noun, especially with time expressions:

> *Oh, I've said* ***many a time*** *I'm going to go on a diet.*
>
> *It's one of the most dangerous jobs in the world and the firefighters have been grossly underpaid for* ***many a decade****.*

Interrogatives

Much and *many* are used in interrogatives. There is no necessary implication that a large quantity or number are involved:

> A: *Is there* ***much*** *work to do in the garden?*
> B: *Yes, there's* ***a lot*** *to do.*
> (~~Yes, there's much to do.~~)
>
> A: *Were there* ***many*** *people at the pool?*
> B: *Mm, there were* ***a lot of*** *kids there.*
> (~~Mm, there were many kids there.~~)

A lot of and *lots of* are also used in interrogatives, but with more of an expectation that the quantity or number may be large:

> *Were they making* ***a lot of*** *noise? Is that what kept you awake?*
>
> *Have* ***lots of*** *people been congratulating you on your promotion?*

Negative interrogatives are more complex. Negative interrogatives with *much/many* typically seek to confirm the absence of a large quantity of something:

> ***Aren't** there **many** students taking that course?*
> (It seems there are a small number of students; please confirm.)

> A: *Did you **not** get **much** information from them?*
> B: *No.*

Negative interrogatives with *a lot/lots* typically seek to confirm the presence of a large quantity of something:

> ***Aren't there lots** of students taking that course?*
> (It seems there are a large number of students; please confirm.)

Note that, although *much* and *many* are restricted in the syntactic environments in which they occur, *a lot/lots* are far less restricted.

A–Z 27 ***Bit, a bit (of)***; 50 ***Little, a little, few, a few***

Pronouns

Pronouns

INTRODUCTION 197

Pronouns are a closed class of words. Pronouns may substitute for or stand for the references to entities which full noun phrases make:

Your boxes of photos have been delivered. ***They****'re in the kitchen.*
(used instead of repeating the noun phrase in green, to refer to the same thing)

Could ***you*** *carry* ***this*** *for* ***me****?*
(used to refer to people or things in the immediate situation: *you*, the listener; *me*, the speaker; *this*, an object in the immediate environment)

Is there ***something*** *wrong?*
(reference to a general notion, potentially realised by several noun phrases)

They*'ve got speed cameras everywhere these days so* ***you****'ve got to be careful.*
(vague, general reference to groups of people or to everyone)

The interpretation of the meaning of individual pronouns depends heavily on the context in which they occur.

Like nouns, pronouns can act as the heads of noun phrases and function as subject, object or complement of the clause, or as the complement of a preposition:

I *miss* ***you****.*
(pronoun as subject and object)

[identifying someone in a photograph]
That*'s* ***him****, there, standing behind* ***you****.*
(pronouns as subject, complement and complement of preposition)

There are several different classes of pronoun: personal pronouns, possessive pronouns, reflexive pronouns, reciprocal pronouns, relative pronouns, interrogative pronouns, demonstrative pronouns, indefinite pronouns. Each is treated in a separate section in this chapter.

Although pronouns have noun-like characteristics, they are only rarely modified. Exceptions to this rule normally involve postmodification:

I'm talking to ***him*** *over there.*

You *in the corner. Come here please.*

Premodified examples usually involve adjectives:

Have you got a cold again? Poor ***you****.*

Oh, silly ***me****! I went to the post office and still forgot to post that letter.*

PERSONAL PRONOUNS 198

General 198a

Personal pronouns have subject and object forms:

Personal pronouns: subject and object forms

subject	object
I	*me*
you (singular/plural)	*you* (singular/plural)
he, she, it, one	*him, her, it, one*
we	*us*
they	*them*

The subject forms of personal pronouns most typically act as the subject of a clause:

__I__ met a cousin of mine.

__We__'re late again.

→ 198e for 'anticipatory' *it*

The object forms of personal pronouns most typically act as the object (direct and indirect) or complement in a clause or as the complement of a preposition:

I invited __them__.
(direct object)

Give __him__ the map.
(indirect object)

That's __her__. She's wearing the black beret.
(complement in a clause)

I left it to __them__.
(complement of a preposition)

Personal pronouns indicate person, number and gender. *You* is used for singular and plural reference. Only *he*, *him*, *she*, *her* express gender contrasts:

Personal pronouns: person, number and gender

subject	object	person	number	gender
I	*me*	first	singular	
you	*you*	second	singular or plural	
he	*him*	third	singular	masculine
she	*her*	third	singular	feminine
it	*it*	third	singular	
one	*one*	always generic	always generic	
we	*us*	first	plural	
they	*them*	third	plural	

Personal pronouns are most typically used for backward (anaphoric) reference:

*The manager phoned me back. **He** was extremely apologetic.*

Occasionally a personal pronoun may be used to refer forward (cataphorically). Such uses are common in openings to written stories:

***She** was walking along a tree-lined suburban road, unaware of what was about to befall her. Gillian Dawson had never been very aware of the people around her.*

→ **123–139 Grammar across turns and sentences** for further examples

→ also **198d *He/him, she/her, they/them***

I/me 198b

I and *me* refer to the speaker/writer:

[on the phone]
*Hi Ken. It's **me**, Bob. Can **I** speak to Hilary?*
(speaker)

*In this paper, **I** challenge the dominant understanding of autonomy as 'individualism'.*
(writer)

→ **147a *I* versus *we*** for the special academic generic use of *I*

You 198c

You does not distinguish between singular and plural reference, but, in context, the reference is usually clear:

*D'**you** want some more tea, Paul?*
(singular reference)

[host to group of dinner guests]
*Would **you** come to the table now please.*
(plural reference)

You refers most frequently to the immediate addressee(s). But it can also refer more generally to any potential listener(s) or reader(s). This is especially so in advertising texts and public notices. *You* can also have generic reference (to people in general, including the speaker/writer):

*Would **you** all follow me please?*
(listeners)

[slogan of the British National Lottery]
*It could be **you**.*
(any individual addressee could be a winner)

*They do these throw-away cameras. They're about £8. **You** can get a panoramic one and **you** can get a sort of party one with a flash. And **you** can get an underwater one.*
(generic reference)

He/him, she/her, they/them 198d

In general, *he/him* and *she/her* are only used to refer to humans or animals. In traditional formal usage, *he/him* may occur with reference to both sexes. Increasingly, however, gender-neutral pronoun forms are preferred, such as (subject forms) *he/she, he or she, they*, or (in writing) *(s)he*, or *s/he*; (object forms) *him/her, him or her, them*:

A judgment by an Australian court which curtailed the powers of Senate committees prodded the Senate into reform. Now anyone who believes ***he*** *has been injured by a senator's words can ask to have a response written into the Senate's records.*
(traditional formal usage)

Any student who thinks ***(s)he*** *has been unfairly treated can appeal.*
(preferred neutral usage)

The use of *they/them* is particularly common when the reference involves words such as *person, someone, anyone*. It is also used in this book for gender-neutral reference:

How can you expect a person to remember what ***they*** *were doing five years ago?*
(preferred neutral usage in more informal contexts)

[from the section on *will* in this book, 387]
A rarer use of will is in declarative clauses which command someone to do something or insist that ***they*** *do something.*

→ also **198h *They/them***

It 198e

It is used to refer to things as well as to anything which is not obviously either a *he* or *she*:

The aerial on your car is broken off. Look at ***it****.*

Ships, planes, vehicles and other machines (e.g. steam engines) and countries are sometimes referred to by people within the relevant field with a feminine pronoun. However, such usage is considered inappropriate by many people:

She *is the finest yacht I have ever sailed.*

How long have you been flying ***her****?*

In very formal styles, countries may be referred to with *she/her*. Again, such usage is considered inappropriate by many people:

In 1783, France regained Senegal, wihch ***she*** *had lost at the conclusion of the Seven Years War.*

More commonly, *it* is used for countries and machines:

Like most European countries, France imports more food than ***it*** *exports.*

It *has proved in tests to be a quieter plane than the DC-10.*

It is also used as an empty pronoun in anticipatory structures and in references to the weather and the time, as well as more general references to situations:

> ***It**'s nice that you were able to come.*
> (anticipatory; preferred to: That you were able to come is nice.)
>
> ***It**'s raining again.*
>
> ***It**'s getting late.*
>
> *We're going to have to pay all over again. **It**'s crazy.*

➔ **211 Anticipatory *it***

One 198f

One is rare in modern usage, especially in speech, and is confined to formal styles. It may refer to people in general including the speaker/writer, or, more rarely, as an oblique reference to the speaker/writer but excluding the listener/reader:

> [description of the facilities offered by a hotel]
> *Table tennis is on offer, and **one** can also hire bicycles.*
>
> *I don't know whether there are any aspects of the countryside that I don't like, you know. Occasionally there are horrible smells. Well, **one** doesn't like that. But on the whole I like it.*
> (oblique reference to the speaker)

60 *One*

We/us 198g

We/us may be used to refer to different groups of people.

- The speaker/writer(s) and the listener(s)/reader(s):

  A: *Shall **we** have lunch outside?*
  B: *Mm, yes, great idea.*

- The speaker/writer(s) and a third party or parties but excluding the listener/reader:

  A: ***We**'re having some friends around on Saturday, would you like to join **us**?*
  B: *Oh, thanks. Yes. What time?*

- People in general (generic *we*):

  *I'm sounding like a Communist now but **we** should all have the same housing. **We**'re all equal. You know it's sad that there are these divisions.*

We is sometimes used with singular reference, especially by people in authority, for example by teachers to children or by medical staff when addressing patients:

> *How are **we** today, Mr Maclean? Still got chest pains?*
> (meaning: How are you today, Mr Maclean?)

➔ also **147a *I* versus *we* in Grammar and academic English**

They/them 198h

They is used to refer to a specific group of people, animals or things, or, generically, with vague reference to wider groups of people, bodies, institutions, authorities, etc. which exclude the speaker:

*Tell your brother and sister **they**'re always welcome to come and stay. We'd love to see **them**.*
(specific group of people)

[*the M25* is a motorway around London]
***They**'re going to widen the M25.*
(generic reference to a body or authority – here the Highways Agency)

→ **285f Verbs normally only followed by *-ing*** for use of object/subject pronouns and *-ing* forms

PERSONAL PRONOUNS AND NOTIONS OF CORRECTNESS 199

Users of English (even highly educated users) regularly disagree about what is correct or acceptable and incorrect or unacceptable with reference to certain uses of personal pronouns. Choices often depend on whether the context is formal or informal or written or spoken. In very formal usage, subject forms of personal pronouns are used as the complement of *be* or when subject pronouns are joined with *and* or *or* (coordinated):

A: *Who's calling?*
B: *It is **I**.*
(not often used)

*It is **he** who is causing all the trouble.*
(not often used)

***I** and all the family wish you well for the future.*
(formal)

Especially in informal spoken contexts, object pronouns are widely used in similar positions:

[on the phone]
A: *Who's calling?*
B: *It's **me**.*
(almost universally used)

*It's **him** that owns that red car.*
(almost universally used)

***Me** and my wife always go shopping on a Saturday.*
(or: *My wife and **me** always go shopping on a Saturday.*)
(usually only found in speech)

Some pronoun forms may be used in a hypercorrect way. Hypercorrect forms occur when a speaker chooses a highly formal option and uses it universally, without reference to context. The phrase *you and I* can occur as an object and even after prepositions such as *between* and *for*, which normally demand an object pronoun:

She ***wants you and I*** *to be there with her.*
(hypercorrect form)

Between you and I*, he keeps making mistakes while driving.*
(hypercorrect form)

Between you and me*, he keeps making mistakes while driving.*
(preferred, following the rule of preposition *between* + object pronoun)

I've taken notes ***for Mike and I****.*
(hypercorrect form)

I've taken notes ***for Mike and me****.*
(preferred form: object form after a preposition)

In the case of short answers, object pronouns are used in informal contexts. In more formal contexts, subject pronouns are used along with a verb:

A: *I play the piano.*
B: ***Me*** *too.*
(informal)

A: *I swim regularly.*
B: *Yes,* ***I swim*** *regularly too.*
(more formal)

→ also **200 Personal pronouns and spoken English**

Occasionally, in very formal styles, subject personal pronouns may occur as complements in anticipatory *it* structures. However, object forms are more common in everyday usage:

It was ***she*** *who wanted fame, not me.*

It was ***me*** *who left those boxes there. Sorry.*
(typical everyday usage)

When the pronoun is both the object of a previous verb (or the complement of a preposition) and the subject of a following verb, then the object form of the pronoun is used:

Do you want Jess or ***me*** *to phone her?*
(~~Do you want Jess or I to phone her?~~)

It's for ***her*** *to choose.*
(~~It's for she to choose.~~)

Personal pronouns and spoken English 200

In informal spoken English, particular patterns of personal pronoun usage can be observed.

- The structure *me and you* is heard in informal speech, but it is traditionally not considered polite for speakers to put themselves first:

  ***Me and you** should have a talk.*
  (preferred: You and me/You and I should have a talk.)

- *Us* is sometimes used very informally to mean *me*. It is commonly used when making requests, perhaps to soften the force of the request:

  *Can you lend **us** five pounds?*
  (normally: Can you lend me …)

  *Give **us** a kiss.*

  *Could you do **us** a favour? Could you give Joe a message?*

- After *as, like, than, but*, and *except*, subject forms are used in more formal contexts. They are normally followed by auxiliary, modal or lexical verbs:

  *She does the same job **as he does**.*
  (more formal)

  *She can swim better **than he can**.*

  *We certainly work as hard **as she works**.*

- The object forms of pronouns are used in informal contexts:

  *She lives in the same house **as him**.*

  *He keeps his bedroom almost as untidy **as me**.*

  *She can swim better **than him**.*

POSSESSIVE PRONOUNS 201

General 201a

There are two classes of possessive pronoun: possessive determiners and possessive pronouns.

possessive determiner	possessive pronoun
my	*mine*
your (singular)	*yours*
his, her, its	*his, hers, its**
our	*ours*
your (plural)	*yours*
their	*theirs*
one's	*one's**

* only when complemented by (*very*) *own* (→ **201c** below)

Possessive determiners and independent possessive pronouns may be postmodified by *(very) own*:

*It's **his own** fault.*

*Now that you've got **your very own** flat, how does it feel?*

Possessive determiners 201b

Possessive determiners are also called possessive adjectives in some grammar books.

Possessive determiners occur before a head noun and before any modifiers in the noun phrase:

*Here's **their ticket**.*

***Her final exam results** were better than expected.*

[proverb]
*Don't count **your chickens** before they are hatched.*

When a possessive determiner and a possessive *'s* form modify the same head noun, the possessive determiner normally comes second:

*The best man at **Jane's and my wedding** couldn't stop telling jokes.*

(preferred to: The best man at my and Jane's wedding ...)

Possessive pronouns 201c

Possessive pronouns can stand alone as the head of a noun phrase:

*Is this coat **yours**?*

*I can't believe that the house is **ours** at last.*

Its and *one's* only occur as possessive pronouns when complemented by *(very) own*:

*Have you given the rabbit **its dinner** yet?*
(possessive determiner)

*Is this cage the rabbit's? It is **the rabbit's**, surely?*
(~~It is its, surely?~~)

*A cat will use every garden except **its own** as a toilet.*

*It was a new sense of freedom, of a life of **one's own**.*

 **64 *Own***

→ also **192 *Of* + possessive pronoun after the head noun**

→ also **190c Possessive determiners and pronouns** for possessive determiners postmodified by *own* used pronominally

REFLEXIVE PRONOUNS 202

Reflexive pronouns typically refer back to subject forms of personal pronouns. They always end in *-self* or *-selves*.

Reflexive pronouns
myself
yourself
himself, herself, itself
oneself
ourselves
yourselves
themselves

Reflexive pronouns for same subject and object

Reflexive pronouns are commonly used to refer to actions where the subject and object are the same person:

> ***He*** *hurt* ***himself*** *quite badly in the fall.*
> ('He hurt him quite badly' would mean subject *he* and object *him* were two different people)
>
> ***I'm*** *going to get* ***myself*** *a drink? Anyone else want one?*
>
> *When are* ***you*** *going to stop pushing* ***yourself*** *so hard?*

A reflexive pronoun is used to differentiate reference to a subject from reference to somebody else:

> *She looks very pleased with* ***herself.***
> (reference to being pleased 'with her' would indicate reference to somebody else)
>
> ***Children*** *always hurt* ***themselves*** *when they play that game.*
>
> ***Children*** *always hurt* ***each other*** *when they play that game.*
> (one child hurts another child)

Reflexive pronouns for emphasis

Reflexive pronouns cannot occur as the subject of a clause. They may only be used in subject position as emphatic complements of subject personal pronouns:

> ***He himself*** *told me he was intending to retire.*
> (~~Himself told me he was intending to retire.~~)

Reflexive pronouns may also function to emphasise a subject or object consisting of a full noun phrase. In such cases, stress is normally on the reflexive pronoun:

> ***The Head of Department herself*** *knows that the staff are unhappy.*
>
> ***The head of the company*** *wrote to us* ***himself*** *to explain why they had been so slow in sending us the toys.*
>
> *Have* ***the children*** *paid for it* ***themselves****?*

In spoken English, the reflexive pronoun is sometimes used as a header or as a tail:

***Myself*, *I* think it's crazy.**

***He**'d prefer wine, **himself**.*

→ **96 Headers** and **97 Tails**

Reflexive pronouns for politeness

Reflexive pronouns are sometimes used instead of personal pronouns, especially to mark politeness:

*Most people were late, including **us**.*
(more informal)

*Most of the audience arrived late, including **ourselves**.*
(more formal/polite)

After *as for*, *like*, *but for*, *except for*, reflexive pronouns are particularly common, although personal pronouns are also possible in each case. The reflexive use here indicates greater politeness and deference:

*These holidays are designed for people like **yourself**, young, fancy-free and unattached.*
(or: These holidays are designed for people like you, …)

[shop assistant addressing a customer who is considering a garment]
*Is it for **yourself**?*

*As for **myself**, I haven't decided yet.*

Reflexive pronouns meaning *alone*

Reflexive pronouns, with or without the preposition *by*, are also used to mean 'alone, from one's own resources, without help':

*Did she draw that **herself**?*

*I think it would be better if you did it **yourself**.*

*He did it all **by himself**.*

*I can help until 4, then they'll have to manage **by themselves**.*

→ also **283c Reflexive construction**

Reflexive pronouns in other languages

In languages other than English, verbs referring to basic everyday actions often take reflexive pronouns. Such verbs are reflexive in English only if there is a reason to emphasise the action:

He got up, washed, shaved, dressed and had breakfast.
('washed himself, shaved himself, dressed himself' would mean that this is surprising because he is usually unable to do these things on his own)

*She's seven now. She's old enough to wash **herself**.*
(she doesn't need any help)

Other common verbs often used reflexively in other languages but which are not reflexive in English include *concentrate, feel, lie down, sit (down), hurry, open*:

*You must really **concentrate** if you want to learn how to play it.*
(~~You must really concentrate yourself if you want to learn how to play it.~~)

*Does she **feel** sick?*
(~~Does she feel herself sick?~~)

RECIPROCAL PRONOUNS 203

Reciprocal pronouns are used to indicate mutual relationships.

Reciprocal pronouns

reciprocal	reciprocal possessive
each other	*each other's*
one another	*one another's*

*They are always criticising **each other**.*

A: *They both look like **one another**, don't they?*
B: *So they should, they're sisters.*

Both pronouns may be used with the *'s* possessive determiner construction:

*My neighbour and I are always borrowing **one another's/each other's** bikes.*

These pronouns may be compared with reflexive pronouns:

*We entertained **ourselves** when it rained.*
(either the whole group is entertained or each member of the group entertains himself or herself)

*We entertained **each other** when it rained.*
(each member entertains the other members)

 A–Z 34 ***Each***

RELATIVE PRONOUNS 204

Relative pronouns link noun phrases to a relative clause.

Relative pronouns

who	*which*
whom	*that*
whose	

The relative pronoun *who* has an object form *whom* and a possessive form *whose*. In general *who* and *whom* are only used personally (to refer to people). *Who* is commonly used in both object and subject functions. *Whom* is used as object or as the complement of a preposition in more formal contexts:

*That's the guy **who** sold us the tickets.*

*The minister, **who** the media had criticised, eventually resigned his post.*

*After years of drifting apart, he and Helen, **whom** he first met at art college, and **with whom** he has three children, were divorced.*

Whose is not restricted to people. Animals and things can also be referred to:

*Koalas, **whose** nocturnal habits are well known, are unique to Australia.*

*Those are the cars **whose** windows got broken.*

Which is used non-personally (to refer to animals and to things); it is not used personally:

*Why don't you just go to a city **which** is by the sea? What about Barcelona?*

That is more informal than *who* or *which* and refers to people, animals and things:

*That's the guy **that** sold us the tickets.*
(more formal: ... the guy who sold us the tickets)

*Can you suggest a book **that**'s for lighter reading?*
(more formal: ... a book which is for lighter reading)

That is only used in this way in defining relative clauses, not in non-defining relative clauses.

Omitting a relative pronoun in defining relative clauses is more common in informal than in formal contexts:

Here's the book you were looking for.
(or: Here's the book that/which you ...)

The company we invested all that money in has been taken over.
(or: The company that/which we ...)

Which can refer to a whole clause or sentence. This usage is frequent in evaluative statements. *What*, *that* and *how* are not used in this way:

*The whole office entered the fun-run marathon, **which** is pretty good for people who sit down all day.*

*They've won their last three matches, **which** I find a bit surprising actually.*

→ **317a Types of relative clause** for sentential relative clauses

Personal pronouns are not used to repeat or extend relative pronouns:

*He's the runner **who** won the 5000 metres.*
(~~He's the runner who he won the 5000 metres.~~)

*Here's the pen **that** you lent me.*
(~~Here's the pen that you lent me it.~~)

INTERROGATIVE PRONOUNS 205

Interrogative pronouns are used to ask questions.

Interrogative pronouns	
who	*which*
whom	*what*
whose	

Who and *whom* are used alone as noun-phrase heads. *Whose, which* and *what* may be used with a noun head or may themselves act as noun-phrase heads:

> ***Who****'s next?*
>
> *And* ***whom*** *does Margaret meet?*
>
> ***Whose*** *are these socks?*
>
> ***Which*** *colour do you like best?*
> (interrogative pronoun used here as determiner)
>
> ***What*** *number did you write down?*

Who can be used in both subject and object forms. *Whom* is used in object forms and following prepositions in more formal contexts:

> ***Who*** *is your favourite footballer?*
>
> ***Who*** *did the prime minister promote to the cabinet?*
> (or more formal: Whom did the prime minister promote to the cabinet?)
>
> ***Who*** *do you have most confidence* ***in****?*
> (informal)
> (or more formal: In whom do you have most confidence?)

Which can be either personal or non-personal:

> ***Which*** *is your brother's girlfriend, the one with the black jeans?*
>
> ***Which*** *of the juices do you prefer? Orange or pineapple and mango?*

What is only used non-personally:

> *She is just about the most persistent person I've met.* ***What*** *does she want?*

What* versus *which

What is used when specific information is requested from a general or open-ended possible range. *Which* is used when specific information is requested from a restricted range of possibilities:

> A: *I've got your address.* ***What****'s your phone number?*
> B: *Oh it's 267358.*
> (~~Which is your phone number?~~)
> (an open-ended range of possible information)

[looking at a pile of coats]
A: ***Which** is your coat?*
B: *That black one.*

However, where the number of options is shared knowledge among speakers and listeners, *what* + noun is often used in informal contexts. Here, *what* is an interrogative pronoun used as a determiner:

[talking about a shop]
***What side** of the street is it on, left or right?*
(or: Which side of the street is it on?)

A: *Did you see that documentary about the SARS virus last night?*
B: *No, **what channel** was it on?*
(or: Which channel was it on?)

→ also **427 *Wh*-questions**

→ **292d *Wh*-interrogatives**

DEMONSTRATIVE PRONOUNS 206

Demonstrative pronouns are used to point to things. The demonstrative pronouns are *this*, *that*, *these* and *those*. *This* and *that* have singular reference; *these* and *those* have plural reference.

Demonstrative pronouns express contrasts between what is 'near' and what is 'distant', whether in space, time or emotional distance, in terms of the speaker and listener. *This* and *these* are speaker-oriented; *that* and *those* are listener-oriented:

***This** is what we want, a big house with a big garden.*

[shop assistant referring to two sets of earrings, one of which she is holding (*these*) and another set which a customer is holding (*those*)]
*Why don't you take **these**? **Those** look far too large.*

→ **190 Determiners and pronouns**

INDEFINITE PRONOUNS 207

Indefinite pronouns refer to things in a general and open way. They indicate either quantity or the absence of quantity.

There are two main types of indefinite pronoun. The first type consists of compounds which have a second part: *-one*, *-body*, *-thing* linked to *any*, *some*, *no* and *every*.

Indefinite pronouns *-one*, *-body*, *-thing*

someone	*somebody*	*something*
anyone	*anybody*	*anything*
no one	*nobody*	*nothing*
everyone	*everybody*	*everything*

→ **207a *-one*, *-body*, *-thing***

The second type is a much larger group of determiners which can be used as pronouns and which can be followed by an *of* construction:

a few	*few*	*most*
a little	*fewer*	*much*
all	*fewest*	*neither*
another	*least*	*none*
any	*less*	*numerals* (cardinal and ordinal)
both	*little*	*one*
each	*many*	*several*
either	*more*	*some*

⇢ also **190 Determiners and pronouns**, for further examples of these words used as pronouns

__All__ are waiting outside the bus station.

__Many__ apply to join but __few__ are chosen.

You want tickets for the concert. Right, well, __most__ of them have gone already, I'm afraid.

__Neither__ of them has the right qualifications.

Cardinal and ordinal numbers can be used as indefinite pronouns:

I was woken at __six__ every morning by those birds.

The mortar bomb hit the main hospital building, leaving __twenty two__ seriously injured.

Jane, __the third__ of our children, is the brightest.

⇢ also **194 Numerals**

12 *All*; 28 *Both*; 34 *Each*

12 *All* for further distinctions between *all* and *all of*

-one, -body, -thing 207a

There are no significant differences in meaning between indefinite pronouns ending in *-one* and those ending in *-body*. However, *somebody*, *anybody*, *nobody* are used more frequently in informal contexts.

When used as subjects, these indefinite pronouns take a singular, not a plural verb. *Somebody* and *someone* normally only refer to one person:

__Does anyone__ want a lift?
(~~Do anyone want a lift?~~)

***Is nobody** interested?*

***Someone has** left a message for you.*

However, when pronouns are used to refer to these words, plural forms are commonly used:

*If **anybody** knocks at the door, tell **them** I'm out.*

*You'll have to tell **them** I'm busy if **anyone** calls.*

***Nobody** resigned, did **they**?*

***Someone** has lost **their** ticket.*

Although indefinite pronouns are most commonly used for vague and general reference, *somebody/someone* and *anybody/anyone* can have both general and specific reference:

*Will **somebody** be there to meet you at the airport?*
(specific)

***Somebody** isn't telling the truth.*
(general)

*I didn't see **anybody**.*
(specific)

***Anyone** can learn to play the guitar, if they work at it.*
(general)

The pronouns *someone/somebody, something* and *anyone/anybody, anything* are distinguished in similar ways to the determiners *some* and *any* (→ 196d). For example, *someone/somebody* is more assertive and is used in questions in which the speaker thinks that the answer will follow neatly from the question. The pronouns *anyone/anybody* are more open-ended and when used in questions do not anticipate a particular answer:

*Has your mum bought you **something** for the journey?*

*Do you want to buy **anything**?*

*Hasn't **anyone** called a taxi?*

Something and *anything* can be used to ask negative questions. They contrast in meaning:

*Didn't she contribute **something** to the appeal?*
(suggests that she probably did)

*Didn't she contribute **anything** to the appeal?*
(indicates greater uncertainty)

The indefinite pronouns *no one* (which is also written *no-one*) and *nobody* are more definite than *not anyone* or *not anybody*. *Anyone* and *anybody* are used in conjunction with uses of *nothing*:

*I heard that **no one** said a good word about the trip.*

*I did**n't** hear **anybody** say a good word about the trip.*

*Nothing **anybody** says is accurate.*
(~~Nothing somebody says is accurate.~~)

→ 196b–196d for fuller discussion of *some* and *any*

A–Z 38 *Every* for discussion of the determiner *every*, which is included mainly for purposes of contrast with *each*, but which also contains examples of the use of the indefinite pronouns *everything* and *everyone*.

WHATEVER, WHOEVER, WHICHEVER 208

Whatever, *whoever* and *whichever* can be used as pronouns, especially in speech:

*Take **whatever** you want.*

*If I talk to an Irish person or **whoever**, my accent changes.*

A: *Which one shall I get for you?*
B: ***Whichever**. I don't mind.*

In formal use (and often in proverbial expressions) a subject personal pronoun + *who* may be used instead of *whoever*. More commonly, *whoever* or *the person who* are used:

***He who** hesitates is lost.*

*Will **whoever** borrowed my dictionary please return it to my office?*
(or: Will the person who borrowed my dictionary please return it to my office?)

→ 317c *Who* and *whom*

SUBSTITUTE *ONE* 209

Substitute *one* has a plural form *ones*:

*Which **one** would you like?*

*Which **ones** are you taking with you?*

→ 123–139 Grammar across turns and sentences

EMPTY *IT* AND EXISTENTIAL *THERE* 210

The so-called empty *it* and existential *there* do not refer to any object or entity. They are used as dummy subject forms (since a subject is required in non-imperative clauses) and refer generally to situations:

***It**'s very hot today, isn't it.*
(empty *it* used for weather, time and general references to situations)

***It** looks as if the shop's closed early.*

***It** seems as though we might have misjudged her.*

***It**'s time to call a halt to all the arguing.*

***It**'s no use complaining.*

***There** were a lot of people in the town centre.*

***There**'s something I want to talk to you about.*

ANTICIPATORY *IT* 211

If an infinitive or a *that*-clause is the subject of a sentence, *it* is often used as a preparatory or anticipatory subject:

It's been nice to meet you.
('To meet you has been nice' is unusual and, at the least, very formal indeed)

It's silly to let such things upset you.
(preferred to: To let such things upset you is silly.)

***It** was a great shame that they arrived late and missed the start of the play.*
(preferred to the more formal: That they arrived late and missed the start of the play was a great shame.)

It can also be used as a preparatory or anticipatory subject when the subject of the clause is an *-ing* form:

***It**'s no trouble meet**ing** them at the station.*

It can also be used as a preparatory object:

*I consider **it** a compliment getting such a positive response from him.*
(preferred to: I consider getting such a positive response from him a compliment.)

*He made **it** very difficult to like him and his sister.*

It is also used in cleft constructions:

***It** was Sunita who reported them to the police.*
(Sunita, not Jane)

→ **475c Cleft sentences**

→ **128a *It, this* and *that* referring to segments of text**

ARCHAIC FORMS 212

Some older forms of second person singular pronouns such as *thou, thee, thy, thyself, thine* are only found in religious texts, in poetry and in some dialects of English. In contemporary English the equivalents are:

thou : *you* (subject)

thee : *you* (object)

thy : *your*

thyself : *yourself*

thine : *yours*

Verb phrase 1: structure of verb phrases

Verb phrase 1: structure of verb phrases

SIMPLE VERB PHRASES 213

Affirmative

A simple verb phrase has just one verb, which is a lexical verb indicating an action, event or state. The lexical verb shows tense (present or past) and clause type (declarative, imperative or subjunctive:

*She **lives** opposite me.*
(declarative present, affirmative)

*They **took** it home with them.*
(declarative past, affirmative)

***Take** a seat.*
(imperative, affirmative)

*I insist that she **come** along.*
(subjunctive, affirmative)

Interrogative and negative

Simple verb phrases are not used to form interrogatives or negatives. Interrogatives and negatives are complex verb phrases (→ 214), in which auxiliary *do* must be used:

***Do** you **know** Shirley's number?*
(interrogative)
(~~*Know you Shirley's number?*~~)

*Going up to university just **does not appeal** to me.*
(negative declarative)
(~~Going up to university just not appeals to me.~~)

***Don't tell** Brian.*
(negative imperative)
(~~Tell not Brian.~~)

Be and *have* used as lexical verbs are exceptions, forming negatives and interrogatives using simple verb phrases:

***Are** you ready?*
(lexical verb *be*: interrogative)

***Has** she **not** a right to be jealous?*
(lexical verb *have*: interrogative and negative)

COMPLEX VERB PHRASES 214

Elements of complex verb phrases 214a

A complex verb phrase may include one or a combination of the following structures:

- Auxiliary or modal verb + lexical verb:

  *I **do like** pizza.*
  (emphatic auxiliary *do*)

  *I **can't take** any more.*
  (modal *can*)

  Only one modal verb may occur in a verb phrase:

  *He'**ll be able** to get a lift.*
  (~~He will can get a lift.~~)

→ **378 Modal forms** for a full list of modal verbs

- Perfect aspect (auxiliary *have* + *-ed* participle of lexical verb):

  *We'**ve talked** about that.*

- Progressive aspect (auxiliary *be* + *-ing* participle of lexical verb):

  *Tears **were rolling** down my face.*

- Passive voice (auxiliary *be* + *-ed* participle of lexical verb):

  *A Laurel and Hardy film **was banned**.*

Ordering of elements in complex verb phrases 214b

The table shows (from left to right) how the different elements that may occur in complex verb phrases are ordered. The elements are labelled 1 to 5.

The maximum number of different elements is five, but to find all five in one verb phrase is extremely rare.

Ordering of elements in complex verb phrases

			1	2	3	4	5
examples	**A**	*it*	*might*				*rain*
	B	*she*		*has*			*arrived*
	C	*they*			*were*		*working*
	D	*Jamie*		*had*	*been*		*looking*
	E	*it*	*might*	*have*		*been*	*used*
	F	*we*	*may*	*have*	*been*	*being*	*followed*
type of verb			**modal verb**	**perfect auxiliary *have***	**progressive auxiliary *be***	**passive auxiliary *be***	**lexical verb**
ordering principles			must be followed by base form	must be followed by *-ed* participle	must be followed by *-ing* participle	must be followed by *-ed* participle	
meaning			verb phrase has modal meaning	verb phrase has perfect aspect	verb phrase has progressive aspect	verb phrase is passive voice	

The ordering principles in the table mean that if, for example, there is just a modal verb + the lexical verb, the base form of the lexical verb must be used (example **A** in the table). If the modal is followed by auxiliary *have* and a lexical verb, then the next auxiliary or the lexical verb must be in the *-ed* participle form (example **E**).

Example A consists of (**1**) modal verb (*might*) + (**5**) base form.

Example B consists of (**2**) auxiliary verb (*has*) + (**5**) *-ed* participle.

Example C consists of (**3**) auxiliary verb (*were*) + (**5**) *-ing* participle.

Example D consists of (**2**) and (**3**) two auxiliary verbs (*had* + *been*) + (**5**) *-ing* participle.

Example E consists of (**1**) modal verb (*might*) + (**2**) and (**4**) two auxiliary verbs (*have* + *been*) + (**5**) *-ed* participle.

Example F consists of (**1**) modal verb (*may*) + (**2**) and (**3**) and (**4**) three auxiliary verbs (*have* + *been* + *being*) + (**5**) *-ed* participle.

Here are further examples of ordered combinations of the elements. The numbers refer to the table opposite:

combination	example
modal + progressive	*I **might be seeing** Bob.* 1 3 5
modal + perfect	*They **should have finished** a long time ago.* 1 2 5
modal + passive	*If I **may be allowed** to say so, …* 1 4 5
perfect + progressive	*Two men **had been plotting** to rob the train.* 2 3 5
progressive + passive	***We're being fooled.*** 3 4 5
perfect + passive	***I've been asked** to write this report.* 2 4 5
modal + perfect + progressive	*She **must have been talking** to Anthea.* 1 2 3 5
modal + perfect + passive	*But, I mean, I **could have been killed**.* 1 2 4 5
modal + progressive + passive	*The nucleic acid **may be being reproduced** in the nucleus …* 1 3 4 5
perfect + progressive + passive	***It's been being repaired** for the last two years.* 2 3 4 5

539 **Glossary** for any unfamiliar terms

Indication of person and number 214c

The first element of the verb phrase indicates person (first, second or third) and number (singular or plural). However, modal verbs do not show person or number.

Verb phrases indicating person and number

example	person and number	example subject pronouns
work	first person singular or plural	*I, we*
	second person singular or plural	*you*
	third person plural	*they*
works	third person singular	*he, she, it, one*
have worked	first person singular or plural	*I, we*
	second person singular or plural	*you*
	third person plural	*they*
has worked	third person singular	*he, she, it, one*
was working	first person singular	*I*
	third person singular	*he, she, it, one*
were working	first person plural	*we*
	second person singular or plural	*you*
	third person plural	*they*
will work	no person or number indicated	any subject pronoun

Indication of tense 214d

The first element of the verb phrase indicates tense (present or past). Modal verbs do not show tense.

Verb phrases indicating tense

example	tense
look	present
has *spoken*	present
lifted	past
were *laughing*	past
might *break*	no tense

→ **380b Modal verbs and tenses** for historical tense contrasts between *can/could, shall/should, will/would* and *may/might.*

TENSED AND NON-TENSED VERB PHRASES 215

General 215a

Tensed verb forms indicate whether a verb is present or past tense. The *-s* form and the past form of the verb are tensed forms.

The *-ing* participle and the *-ed* participle are non-tensed forms.

The base form may be tensed or non-tensed. When it has a subject, it is tensed (and is called the present form); when it is used as the infinitive form (with or without *to*), it is non-tensed.

Verb phrases which begin with a tensed verb form are tensed verb phrases. They must have a subject, except when they are in the imperative. Verb phrases with modal verbs are treated as tensed (→ 215b, below). Verb phrases which begin with a non-tensed verb form are non-tensed verb phrases. Examples are given in the table.

Examples of tensed and non-tensed verb phrases

	examples	comments
tensed	***I hate*** *carrots.*	first person singular, present tense
	She was *very nice.*	third person singular, past tense
	We spoke *a few months ago.*	first person plural, past tense
	They may get *here by six o'clock.*	modal verb phrase
non-tensed	***Pointing*** *at my forehead, he asked if I had been fighting.*	*-ing* participle; no person, tense or number indicated
	Accompanied *by Professor Saito, she strode round the island.*	*-ed* participle form; no person, tense or number indicated
	To get *there, you take the lift to the third floor.*	base form used as infinitive with *to*; no person, tense or number indicated

Non-tensed verb phrases 215b

Although non-tensed verb phrases do not indicate tense, person or number and usually do not have a subject, their person, tense, etc. are normally understood in relation to items in the main clause:

Waking *up in the middle of the night,* ***he*** *will jot down thoughts on a complicated case.*
(assumed to mean: when he wakes up in the middle of the night)

Introduced *last year by the Ministry of Health,* ***the ban*** *forbade doctors to perform the operation.*
(assumed to mean: the ban was introduced last year)

Core modal verbs do not occur in non-tensed verb phrases. However, the modal expressions *be able to* and *have to* may occur in non-tensed verb phrases:

Being able to *run fast is what you miss as you get older.*

It's not nice ***having to*** *get up at five o'clock in the morning.*

Non-tensed verb forms 215c

-ing participle

-ing participle non-tensed verb phrases may be simple phrases:

Please listen carefully to all the options before ***making*** *your choice.*

Buying *from Save the Children's gift catalogue is easy.*

Complex *-ing* participle verb phrases may occur with perfect aspect or with passive voice or a combination of both. They are more frequent in writing and in formal styles than in informal speech:

> ***Having finished*** *her breakfast, she pushed her plate noisily across the table and the waitress appeared.*
> (perfect aspect)

> *He was released from prison in 1958, after* ***being pardoned*** *by West Germany's president, Theodor Heuss.*
> (passive voice)

> ***Having been asked*** *a few times before to do it and said no, I can't say no this time.*
> (perfect aspect and passive voice)

Progressive aspect does not occur in non-tensed *-ing* participle verb phrases:

> ***Living*** *on my own, I don't cook very often.*
> (~~Being living on my own, I don't cook very often.~~)

-ed participle

-ed participles may occur as simple (non-tensed) phrases:

> *Danzig (Gdansk) became a 'free city',* ***linked*** *by a customs union to the new Polish state, which also gained Upper Silesia, a major industrial area.*

In complex phrases, they combine with the *-ing* participle and *to*-infinitive forms of *be* and *have* to create passive voice and perfect aspect, or a combination of both:

> ***Being consulted*** *on the matter would have been nice too.*
> (passive)

> ***To be forced*** *to leave, be rejected by his own people, must have been a double blow.*
> (passive)

> ***Having written*** *so many letters and not got an answer, I'm not sure it's worth writing another one.*
> (perfect)

> ***To have worked*** *so hard and then to have that done to them overnight!*
> (perfect)

> ***Having been fired*** *only the day before for not doing any work, I was eager to appear busy.*
> (perfect and passive)

> *It was petty of me, I know,* ***to have been irritated*** *by such a fellow, but I was.*
> (perfect and passive)

To-infinitive

To-infinitives may occur as simple non-tensed phrases:

> ***To cope*** *with the extra traffic caused by the university, a new £7-million road bridge will be built over the River Witham.*

They may also be used with *be* and the *-ed* participle as passive voice phrases:

> ***To be deprived*** *of even one hour of sleep was another step towards total exhaustion and collapse.*

They also occur with *have* and the *-ed* participle to indicate perfect aspect:

> ***To have got*** *the 8 o'clock flight would have meant getting up at 4.30.*

They also occur with the *-ing* participle to indicate progressive aspect:

> *How cruel* ***to be having*** *it now, when it was too late.*

Combinations of these structures may also be found:

> *Well I've heard they're supposed* ***to be being pulled down.***
> (progressive and passive)
>
> *And you felt that she ought* ***to have been informed*** *about that?*
> (perfect and passive)
>
> *Whales and other marine animals are thought* ***to have been being killed*** *as a result of the military tests.*
> (perfect, progressive and passive)

CATENATIVE VERB PHRASES (*SEEM TO, MANAGE TO*) 216

Meaning

A catenative verb phrase is one which includes a verb such as *appear to, come to, fail to, get to, happen to, manage to, seem to* and *tend to* with a lexical verb. These verbs have meanings similar to some of the modal verbs or meanings similar to those indicated by aspect choices. However, unlike modal and auxiliary verbs, they behave like lexical verbs in that they construct their complex forms with auxiliary *do*, *be* and *have*.

The catenative verbs express modal meanings, indicating whether something is probable or certain, and aspectual meanings, indicating whether something is achieved or completed:

> *'You* ***appear to be*** *a man of many parts,' she said.*
> (could also be expressed with a modal adverb such as: You are probably a man of many parts.)
>
> *Do you* ***happen to know*** *Suzie's number?*
>
> *He* ***didn't manage to get*** *Anna on the telephone.*
> (He wasn't able to/couldn't get Anna on the telephone.)
>
> *We* ***seem to have been*** *this way before.*
>
> *We don't* ***tend to go*** *to London very often.*

→ 539 Glossary for any unfamiliar terms

The quasi-modal meanings of catenative verbs may be illustrated by the fact that they can be removed without any major change to the meaning:

Do you ***happen to know*** *Suzie's number?*
(or: Do you know Suzie's number?)

Do you ***happen to have*** *a spare pen?*
(or: Do you have a spare pen?)

We don't ***tend to go*** *to London very often.*
(or: We don't go to London very often.)

In the case of *fail to*, a simple negative may be substituted:

The package ***failed to arrive*** *on time.*
(The package did not arrive on time.)

However, non-catenative lexical verbs cannot be removed in this way without major changes to meaning:

I often ***long to change*** *my job.*
(compare: I often change my job.)

→ **285a** where non-catenative lexical verbs which are followed by the *to*-infinitive are dealt with

Passive

Catenative verbs do not occur in the passive. Voice is indicated in the verbs following the catenative verb:

Large sums ***appear to have been removed*** *from the fund without adequate explanation.*
(~~Large sums have been appeared to remove from the fund …~~)

England's market-led success in the last century, for example, ***failed to be matched*** *in equally market-oriented Ireland.*
(~~England's market-led success in the last century, for example, was failed to match …~~)

Progressive aspect

Progressive aspect may sometimes be indicated on the catenative verb itself, and sometimes on the lexical verb which follows it. The table below shows which verbs allow one or both of the options. In cases where both options are possible, the more frequent is marked with (+).

Examples of progressive aspect in catenative verb phrases

	indicated on catenative verb	indicated on lexical verb
appear to	no	*The mood **appears to be changing** slightly.*
fail to	*Leeds University professor Robin Alexander said the latest methods **were failing to teach** children properly.*	no
get to	***I'm getting to know** Damien better.*	no
happen to	no	*I hope you don't mind. I **happened to be passing** and I used to live here once.*
manage to	*I think it's remarkable that we**'re managing to keep** in touch.* (+)	*Some students even **manage to be** '**working** on a play' for their entire three years at university without anyone ever actually seeing so much as a page.*
seem to	*The university **were** hanging on and **seeming to think** the changes would not happen.*	*You **seem to be losing** weight rapidly.* (+)
*tend to**	*Outside London, where jobs are scarce, they **are tending to accept** lower pay rather than fewer staff.*	*It's a bit infuriating cos you **tend to be paying** the Post Office a lot of extra money, or British Telecom.*

* Occurrences of *tend to* with progressive aspect are infrequent in either combination.

Perfect aspect

Perfect aspect may also be indicated on the catenative verb itself or on the lexical verb. The table below shows which verbs allow one or both of the options. In cases where both options are possible, the more frequent is marked with (+).

Examples of perfect aspect in catenative verb phrases

	indicated on catenative verb	indicated on lexical verb
appear to	*The furore surrounding Mr Harvey **had appeared to threaten** East 17's commercial future.*	*He **appeared to have forgotten** I was there.* (+)
fail to	*Sam's team **had failed to get** through the first round and faced a humiliating defeat at the hands of the African team.* (+)	*Add the kind of guilt most people will feel about **failing to have provided** enough protection, or being responsible for an accident, and you have a very dangerous cocktail of traumas to adjust to.*
get to	*By then I **had got to know** David quite well.*	no
happen to	*... Julia, who **had happened to pop** in unexpectedly at precisely the wrong moment, looking for a packet of cigarettes ...*	*But she **happens to have gone** off for the weekend with friends.* (+)
manage to	*They **had managed to have** a quick coffee together on the last day of term.*	no
seem to	*Robert **hadn't seemed to need** him of late, and it had annoyed him.*	*It **seems to have worked**.* (+)
tend to	*It's something we **have tended to try** and focus on.* (+)	*If we're lucky enough to own our own homes, we **tend to have borrowed** either our first mortgage or sometimes a second against it.*

→ 539 **Glossary** for any unfamiliar terms

Verb phrase 2: tense and aspect

Verb phrase 2: tense and aspect

INTRODUCTION 217

English verb phrases give information of different kinds. Verb phrases indicate: tense, which gives information about time, e.g. *I speak* (present tense) versus *I spoke* (past tense); aspect, which gives information about the speaker's perspective on time, e.g. *I spoke* (simple aspect) versus *I was speaking* (progressive aspect); voice, whether active (e.g. *She destroyed it*) or passive (e.g. *It was destroyed*), which gives information about agents and recipients of verb processes. This chapter deals with contrasts between the different tenses (present and past), and the different aspects (progressive and perfect). Voice is dealt with in **476–487 The passive**.

Progressive (also known as continuous) aspect is formed with auxiliary verb *be* + the *-ing* participle of a lexical verb. Perfect aspect is formed with auxiliary verb *have* + the *-ed* participle form of a lexical verb.

Although English does not have a future tense, the term 'future' is often used to refer to modal and aspect combinations, such as 'future perfect' (e.g. ***I will have studied*** *for three hours by the time I finish.*) or 'future progressive' (*She* ***will be arriving*** *tomorrow.*).

Tense and aspect are combined in the verb phrase. The tense is shown on the first verb in the verb phrase (unless it is a modal). All subsequent verbs have non-tensed forms (*-ing* participle, *-ed* participle, or infinitive). A verb phrase may include both aspects, progressive and perfect.

Examples of aspect in present and past tense

aspect	present tense	past tense
progressive	*Why* ***is*** *he smil**ing** like that?*	*Why* ***was*** *he smil**ing** like that?*
perfect	*They* ***have*** *chang**ed** the time.* (*have* is present)	*They* ***had*** *chang**ed** the time.* (*had* is past)
perfect and progressive combined	*He* ***has*** ***been*** *do**ing** some research.*	*He* ***had*** *been do**ing** some research.*

The perfect auxiliary *have* comes before the progressive auxiliary *be* when the two are combined:

perfect progressive
He | ***has*** | ***been*** *work**ing*** | *on Mrs Green's case for almost six years.*
(~~He is having worked on Mrs Green's case~~ ...)

→ **214b Ordering of elements in complex verb phrases**

TENSE 218

English verbs can show two tenses, present and past. Examples are given in the table overleaf.

Examples of present and past tenses

verb form	tense
I ***work*** *here.*	present
She ***is*** *working in London.*	present
They ***have*** *left.*	present
We ***worked*** *all day.*	past
I ***was*** *working in the garden.*	past
It ***had*** *worked well.*	past

The marking of tense on irregular verbs often involves internal sound changes (e.g. *sit–sat, speak–spoke*).

→ 529 Appendix: Irregular verbs

Present tenses are mostly concerned with talking about present time, and past tenses are mostly concerned with talking about past time.

The present tense forms are also used to talk about other kinds of time, especially the future. Present tense forms can also refer to the past. This is particularly true of narratives, where past events may be recounted partly or wholly in the present tense (for example, jokes are often told entirely in present tense). This is sometimes referred to as the 'historic present'. Examples of present tense forms with future and past reference are given in the table below.

Examples of present tense forms referring to future and past time

example	tense	time referred to
They ***are*** *com**ing** to see you next weekend, I gather.*	present	future time (→ 362)
Her daughter ***finishes*** *school tomorrow evening.*	present	future time (→ 369)
And his mum ***says****, 'Homework never killed anybody,' and then he said, 'No, and I'm not going to be the first.'*	present	the past (frequently used for dramatising speech reporting in spoken stories, → 360e)
*Emma, this friend of mine, brought out these photographs of the family through the years and he**'s** look**ing** at them, and he said 'Oh!'*	present	the past (frequently used for dramatising important events in spoken stories, → 360a)

The past tense forms are also used to refer to present time, especially for reasons of politeness or indirectness. This is because the past tense distances an event from the present, and distancing an event can make it more indirect. Examples are given in the table below.

Examples of past tense forms referring to present time

example	tense	time referred to
A: *I wonder**ed** if you* ***felt*** *it would make a difference if more people wrote or telephoned or said what they thought.* B: *Well yes.*	past	present time
[customer on the telephone to a travel agent] *We* ***were*** *wondering about going to Amsterdam. We* ***were*** *wanting to stay in tents or in a caravan or in a bed and breakfast to see what the different prices* ***were****.*	past	present time

As can be seen in the table above, past tense may combine with progressive aspect (*we were wondering/we were wanting*) to further emphasise politeness, indirectness or tentativeness.

→ 408

THE PRESENT SIMPLE 219

The present simple is formed using the present tense form of a lexical verb (the same as the base form) for all persons except third person singular. Third person singular is formed by adding *-s* or *-es* to the base form.

The present simple: formation

1st and 2nd person singular/plural, 3rd person plural	3rd person singular	3rd person inflection
I/you/we/they/the children ***talk*** *a lot.*	*He/she/it/one/the child* ***talks*** *a lot.*	in most verbs *-s* is added to base form
I/you/we/they/the children ***worry*** *about it.*	*He/she/it/the child* ***worries*** *about it.*	verbs ending in consonant + *y*: *y* changes to *i*, and *-es* is added to base form
I/you/we/they/the children ***miss*** *her.*	*He/she/it/the child* ***misses*** *her.*	verbs ending in *s, z, ch, sh* or *x*: *-es* is added to base form

For a small number of verbs ending in a single *-s*, variations are possible in which the *-s* is doubled:

> To *focus*: *He/she/it* ***focuses*** *(or* ***focusses****) on the problem of unemployment.*
> To *bus*: *The primary school* ***buses*** *(or* ***busses****) children in from miles around.* (brings them in a bus)
> To *bias*: *The question* ***biases*** *(or* ***biasses****) people against voting 'yes'.*

There are also some other special cases of spelling and/or pronunciation:

be
I ***am***
you/we/they ***are***
he/she/it ***is***

do
I/you/we/they do
he/she/it ***does*** (/dʌz/)

say
I/you/we/they say
He/she/it ***says*** (/sez/)

have
I/you/we/they have
he/she/it ***has***

go
I/you/we/they go
he/she/it ***goes***

The declarative and interrogative forms of the present simple are shown in the table overleaf.

The present simple: declarative and interrogative forms

declarative		interrogative	
affirmative	negative	affirmative	negative
I/you/we/they ***work.***	*I/you/we/they* ***don't work.*** (informal) *I/you/we/they* ***do not work.*** (more formal)	***Do*** *I/you/we/they* ***work****?*	***Don't*** *I/you/we/they* ***work****?* (informal) ***Do*** *I/you/we/they* ***not work****?* (more formal)
He/she/it/one ***works.***	*He/she/it/one* ***doesn't work.*** (informal) *He/she/it one* ***does not work.*** (more formal)	***Does*** *he/she/it/one* ***work****?*	***Doesn't*** *he/she/it/one* ***work****?* (informal) ***Does*** *he/she/it/one* ***not work****?* (more formal)

THE PAST SIMPLE 220

Regular verbs form the past simple by adding *-ed* to the base form:

*The flight last**ed** ten hours and we land**ed** at 6.30 in the morning.*

*We talk**ed** for hours on the phone.*

Negative and interrogative forms are constructed with auxiliary *did.*

The past simple: affirmative, negative and interrogative forms

affirmative	negative	interrogative
*I miss**ed** it.*	*I **did not/didn't** miss it.*	***Did*** *I miss it?* ***Didn't*** *I miss it? (informal)* ***Did*** *I* ***not*** *miss it? (more formal)*
*He look**ed** well.*	*He **did not/didn't** look well.*	***Did*** *he look well?* ***Didn't*** *he look well? (informal)* ***Did*** *he* ***not*** *look well? (more formal)*

For irregular verbs, the past simple form is the second of the three parts of a verb, which are usually listed as base form – past form – *-ed* participle.

Irregular verbs

base form	past form	*-ed* participle
see	***saw***	*seen*
take	***took***	*taken*
put	***put***	*put*

*I **saw** her earlier.*

*She **took** it home yesterday.*

529 Appendix: Irregular verbs for a list of irregular verbs

Negative and interrogative past simple forms of irregular verbs are formed in the same way as with regular verbs, using auxiliary *did* + the base form:

*I didn't **eat** my lunch.*
(~~I didn't ate my lunch.~~)

*What did he **sing** for you?*
(~~What did he sang for you?~~)

508e Rule 5: Spelling of verb forms and *-ed* forms

TYPES OF TIME REFERENCE 221

The types of time that the verb forms may refer to are quite complex. For example, the present tense forms may refer to a variety of different types of time. A wide range of references is made possible by combining the present tense with progressive aspect (*be* + *-ing*) and/or perfect aspect (*have* + *-ed* participle). The same applies to past time references. Examples are given in the table below.

Examples of tenses for a variety of time references

example	type of time reference
*This soup **tastes** nice.*	the actual moment of speaking ('present time')
*Come on! **I'm waiting** for you.*	the actual moment of speaking ('present time')
*I **work** in a big office.*	time around the moment of speaking ('present time')
*He **is getting** old.*	time around the moment of speaking ('present time')
*Water **freezes** at zero degrees Celsius.*	general time, always true (in this book included in 'present time')
*We **leave** for Italy next week.*	the future, based on a present arrangement or fact (in this book dealt with under 'future time')
*He **is leaving** London tomorrow.*	the future, based on a present fact or already made decision (in this book dealt with under 'future time')
*I said 'You all right, Bill?' He **says**, 'Give me a cigarette.'*	the past, reporting what was said (in this book, dealt with under 'past time')
*She **has aged** a lot. She doesn't look well.*	time beginning in the past and continuing till now (in this book dealt with under 'past time')
***I've been working** hard.*	time beginning in the past and continuing till now (in this book dealt with under 'past time')
*They**'d sold** the house some years before.*	time beginning in the past and continuing till a point in the past (in this book dealt with under 'past time')
***I'd been swimming** so my hair was wet.*	time beginning in the past and continuing till a point in the past (in this book dealt with under 'past time')

- Present time may be seen as the moment of speaking or writing, or the idea of 'time around now', or the more general, permanent time relating to truths and general facts.
- References to present time are made through the simple and progressive forms of the present tense. However, some references to present time may be made using past tense forms (→ 343).
- Past time refers to an earlier time separated from the present. References to past time are usually made with the past tenses (past simple, past progressive, past perfect). However, some past time references may be made using present tense forms (→ 360).
- Future time refers to time after the present, either separated from the present, or seen as starting from the present and continuing forward. References to future time may be made with modal verbs (e.g. *will*, *shall*, *may*) or with the present tense forms (→ 362 and 369).
- References to time beginning in the past and continuing until now are usually made with the present perfect forms, which are dealt with under past time (→ 351–354).
- References to time beginning in an earlier past and continuing until a determined point in the past are usually made with the past perfect forms, which are dealt with under past time (→ 355–357).

ESTABLISHING THE TIME FRAME 222

Explicit time frame

The time frame for the choice of verb tense can be established by the presence of an adjunct or an adverbial clause.

Examples of adjunct or adverbial clause to establish time frame

example	time frame
They're travelling through Italy ***at the moment****.*	present time
She's arriving in Bogota ***next week****.*	future time
Her daughter finishes school ***tomorrow evening****.*	future time
She started ***last Monday****.*	past time
Plymouth has changed ***in the last few years****.*	time leading up to the moment of speaking
His mother had died ***years previously****.*	time before a point in the past
I've known Jill ***since I came here in about 1975****.*	time leading up to the moment of speaking
I really didn't even concentrate on it ***when I was doing it****.*	past time

Implicit time frame

The time frame may be implicit or already established, and simply understood in the context.

Examples of implicit time frame

example	form	implicit time frame
Why ***is*** *he* ***smiling*** *like that?*	present progressive	present time (moment of speaking)
I think you've probably got the wrong number. What number ***did*** *you* ***dial****?*	simple past	past time (you dialled at some point separated from the moment of speaking)
*Ben****'s moving*** *to Manchester so he's selling his house.*	present progressive	future time (he will move at some point soon)
A: ***Have*** *you* ***rung*** *dad?* B: *No, not yet.*	present perfect	time leading up to the moment of speaking, during which you may have rung
I told her ***I'd invited*** *you.*	past perfect	time before a point in the past (before I told her)

ASPECT AND MEANING 223

Aspect refers to the speaker's/writer's perspective on the time of an event.

In English, aspect is concerned mainly with how the speaker perceives the duration of events, and how different events relate to one another in time.

An event may be referred to in different ways, even though the point in time when it occurs may be unchanged. For example, the same event in the past can be referred to by either the past simple or the present perfect, depending on the speaker's perception of the importance or relevance of an event:

A: *They****'ve sold*** *their house there, you know.*
B: *Oh have they. Where have they gone?*
A: *Oh she's a bit fed up really. They* ***sold*** *the house because he wants a job up north.*

The speaker uses perfect aspect (*have sold*) to announce the news of the house sale (a typical use of the present perfect to mark 'newsworthiness') but then uses the past simple (*sold*) when expanding on the details, even though both verbs refer to the same event.

The choice of aspect may also reflect an emphasis on whether an event was long-lasting or just a point in time. It may also reflect whether it is to be seen as temporary or permanent, whether it is/was already in progress when something else happened, whether it is generally or always the case, whether it happens regularly, etc.

English has two aspects: progressive (sometimes called continuous) aspect and perfect aspect.

PROGRESSIVE ASPECT 224

With progressive aspect, the focus is principally on the duration of the event. It may therefore be used to indicate that something is ongoing, unfinished, or that it is extended but temporary. It may indicate that something is/was/will be already in progress when something else happens/happened. In other words, the focus is not on the starting or finishing point of an event, but on the event as seen from its centre. Examples are given in the table below.

Progressive aspect involves the use of auxiliary *be* and the *-ing* form of a lexical verb.

Examples of progressive aspect

	example	form	type of duration
1	[on the telephone] *It's about half past two and* ***I'm approaching*** *Lyon.*	present progressive	an ongoing process at the moment of speaking
2	[*MP* = Member of Parliament] *He* ***has been doing*** *some research for an MP for about a year.*	present perfect progressive	continuing from a year ago till now and possibly into the future
3	*My knees* ***were shaking****.*	past progressive	an ongoing process at the point in the past the speaker is referring to
4	*This* ***had been going*** *on since September.*	past perfect progressive	continuing from September till the moment in the past the speaker is talking about
5	***I'll be working*** *when you get home.*	*will/shall* + progressive (often called future progressive)	will be an ongoing process at the point in the future the speaker is referring to
6	*We****'ll have been living*** *here twelve years soon.*	*will/shall* + perfect progressive (often called future perfect progressive)	will continue from twelve years before till the point in the future referred to ('soon')
7	*It* ***must have been going*** *on for years.*	modal perfect progressive	an ongoing process probably occurring over a period of time leading up to now or up to a point in the past

Some of the sentences in the table above are best understood in contrast with possible meanings of their simple form equivalents.

2 *He has done some research for an MP for about a year.* This sees the action more as a completed event, and could – but not necessarily – mean the action is finished.
3 *My knees shook.* This could mean my knees shook for a defined period of time (e.g. a few seconds) then stopped.
5 *I'll work when you get home.* This could mean 'I'll start work when you get home'.

The infinitive form of the progressive (following verbs such as *hope*, *intend*, *like*, *seem*, *want*, and other structures requiring an infinitive) is formed with *to be* + *-ing* form of the verb:

*He just seemed **to be doing** the same thing we were doing.*

*I don't want **to be walking** round on my own at nights.*

*It's a peculiar essay **to be doing** at university, I would have thought.*

The present progressive 224a

The present progressive is formed with the present tense forms of *be* + *-ing* form of a lexical verb. Examples are given in the table below.

The present progressive: declarative and interrogative forms

declarative		interrogative	
affirmative	**negative**	**affirmative**	**negative**
*I**'m** do**ing** it right.* (informal) *I **am** do**ing** it right.* (more formal)	*I**'m not** do**ing** it right.* (informal) *I **am not** do**ing** it right.* (more formal)	***Am** I do**ing** it right?*	***Aren't** I do**ing** it right?* (informal) ***Am** I **not** do**ing** it right?* (more formal)
*You/we/they**'re** work**ing** on Friday.* (informal) *You/we/they **are** work**ing** on Friday.* (more formal)	*You/we/they**'re not** work**ing** on Friday.* *You/we/they **aren't** work**ing** on Friday.* (informal) *You/we/they **are not** work**ing** on Friday.* (more formal)	***Are** you/we/they work**ing** on Friday?*	***Aren't** you/we/they work**ing** on Friday?* (informal) ***Are** you/we/they **not** work**ing** on Friday?* (more formal)
*He/she/one it**'s** work**ing** today.* (informal) *He/she/it/one **is** work**ing** today.* (more formal)	*He/she/it/one**'s not** work**ing** today.* *He/she/it/one **isn't** work**ing** today.* (informal) *He/she/it/one **is not** work**ing** today.* (more formal)	***Is** he/she/it/one work**ing** today?*	***Isn't** he/she/it/one work**ing** today?* (informal) ***Is** he/she/it/one **not** work**ing** today?* (more formal)

→ 508f Rule 6: Spelling of verb forms: *-ing* forms

The past progressive 224b

The past progressive is formed with *was/were* + *-ing* form of a lexical verb:

*The wind **was** blow**ing** from the north.*

***Were** you expect**ing** someone?*

The table below shows the declarative and interrogative forms of the past progressive.

The past progressive: declarative and interrogative forms

declarative		interrogative	
affirmative	negative	affirmative	negative
I/he/she/it/one ***was*** *runn**ing** late.*	*I/he/she/it/one* ***wasn't*** *runn**ing** late.* (informal) *I/he/she/it/one* ***was not*** *runn**ing** late.* (more formal)	***Was*** *I/he/she/it/one runn**ing** late?*	***Wasn't*** *I/he/she/it runn**ing** late?* (informal) ***Was*** *I/he/she/it/one* ***not*** *runn**ing** late?* (more formal)
You/we/they ***were*** *sleep**ing**.* (informal)	*You/we/they* ***weren't*** *sleep**ing**.* (informal) *You/we/they* ***were not*** *sleep**ing**.* (more formal)	***Are*** *you/we/they sleep**ing**?*	***Aren't*** *you/we/they sleep**ing**?* (informal) ***Are*** *you/we/they* ***not*** *sleep**ing**?* (more formal)

The future progressive 224c

Progressive references to the future are formed with *will/'ll/shall* + *be* + *-ing* form of the lexical verb. The table below shows the declarative and interrogative forms of the future progressive.

The future progressive: declarative and interrogative forms

declarative		interrogative	
affirmative	negative	affirmative	negative
(Subject) ***'ll be*** *wait**ing** at the station.* (informal) *(Subject)* ***will be*** *wait**ing** at the station.* (more formal)	*(Subject)* ***won't be*** *wait**ing** at the station.* (informal) *(Subject)* ***will not be*** *wait**ing** at the station.* (more formal)	***Will*** *(subject)* ***be*** *wait**ing** at the station?*	***Won't*** *(subject)* ***be*** *wait**ing** at the station?* (informal) ***Will*** *(subject)* ***not be*** *wait**ing** at the station?* (more formal) ***Will not*** *(subject)* ***be*** *wait**ing** at the station?* (very formal and now considered archaic)
I/we ***shall be*** *mind**ing** the children.* (more formal)	*I/we* ***shan't be*** *mind**ing** the children.* (informal) *I/we* ***shall not be*** *mind**ing** the children.* (more formal)	***Shall*** *I/we* ***be*** *mind**ing** the children?*	***Shan't*** *I/we* ***be*** *mind**ing** the children?* (informal) ***Shall*** *I/we* ***not be*** *mind**ing** the children?* (more formal) ***Shall not*** *I/we* ***be*** *mind**ing** the children?* (very formal and now considered archaic)

Where there is a choice between *will* and *shall* (i.e. with first person pronouns), the forms with *shall* are more formal than those with *will*.

→ **492d The past progressive** on progressive aspect in indirect reports

PERFECT ASPECT 225

Perfect aspect is concerned with the speaker's perspective on the relationship between one time frame and an event that takes place in another time frame. An event which took place in the past may be seen as relevant to the present moment. Likewise, an event due to take place in the future may be seen as linked to the present moment. The table below gives examples of different time-frame relationships.

Perfect aspect involves the use of auxiliary *have* + *-ed* participle of a lexical verb. The tense may be present or past. Future perfect forms are created using *will/'ll/shall*.

Examples of perfect aspect

example	form	time relationship
*I've **lived** here about 25 years.*	present perfect	the whole period from 25 years ago till now
*The flight is at 7.15. They've **changed** the time.*	present perfect	the time change happened between some unspecified point in the past and now
*I **had finished** just before I went to work.*	past perfect	the time I finished in relation to the time (in the past) when I went to work
*That was about 1936. That was when we came to Stockport. We **had lived** in Manchester before that.*	past perfect	the time we lived in Manchester in relation to 1936
*Yesterday and tomorrow all together I **will have spent** £100 on train fares.*	future perfect	yesterday and the period up to and including tomorrow
*In three years' time, **we'll have lived** here 20 years.*	future perfect	the time between when we started living here and three years in the future from now
*They **may have been** confused.*	modal perfect	a possible event during a time leading up to now or up to a point in the past

The present perfect 225a

The declarative and interrogative forms of the present perfect simple are shown in the table below.

The present perfect: declarative and interrogative forms

declarative		interrogative	
affirmative	**negative**	**affirmative**	**negative**
*I/you/we/they**'ve** work**ed**.* (informal) *I/you/we/they **have** work**ed**.* (more formal)	*I/you/we/they **haven't** work**ed**.* *I/you/we/they**'ve not** work**ed**.* (informal) *I/you/we/they **have not** work**ed**.* (more formal)	***Have** I/you/we/they work**ed**?*	***Haven't** I/you/we/they work**ed**?* (informal) ***Have** I/you/we/they **not** work**ed**?* (more formal)
*He/she/it/one**'s** work**ed**.* (informal) *He/she/it/one **has** work**ed**.* (more formal)	*He/she/it/one **hasn't** work**ed**.* *He/she/it/one**'s not** work**ed**.* (informal) *He/she/it/one **has not** work**ed**.* (more formal)	***Has** he/she/it/one work**ed**?*	***Hasn't** he/she/it/one work**ed**?* (informal) ***Has** he/she/it/one **not** work**ed**?* (more formal)

The past perfect 225b

The past perfect simple forms are the same as the present perfect, but with *had* being used instead of *have* and *has*, and *'d* being used as the contracted form. The table below shows the declarative and interrogative forms of the past perfect simple.

The past perfect: declarative and interrogative forms

declarative		interrogative	
affirmative	**negative**	**affirmative**	**negative**
*I/you/we/they**'d** already **started**.* (informal) *I/you/we/they **had** already **started**.* (more formal)	*I/you/we/they **hadn't** already **started**.* *I/you/we/they**'d not** already **started**.* (informal) *I/you/we/they **had not** already **started**.* (more formal)	***Had** I/you/we/they already **started**?*	***Hadn't** I/you/we/they already **started**?* (informal) ***Had** I/you/we/they **not** already **started**?* (more formal)

continued

declarative		interrogative	
affirmative	**negative**	**affirmative**	**negative**
*He/she/it/one'**d** already **started**.* (informal)	*He/she/it/one **hadn't** already **started**.* *He/she/it/one**'d not** already **started**.* (informal)	***Had** he/she/it/one already **started**?*	***Hadn't** he/she/it/one already **started**?* (informal)
*He/she/it/one **had** already **started**.* (more formal)	*He/she/it **had not** already **started**.* (more formal)		***Had** he/she/it/one **not** already **started**?* (more formal)

Perfect infinitive 225c

The infinitive form of the perfect aspect (following verbs such as *hope*, *intend*, *like*, *seem*, and other structures requiring an infinitive) is formed with *to have* + *-ed* participle:

*I was hoping **to have finished** by now.*

*They don't seem **to have solved** all the other problems.*

*Are you supposed **to have fed** the dog?*

The perfect aspect may also occur in a non-tensed *-ing* form:

***Having arrived** eventually in Salt Lake City at 5.30 a.m. and walked around for a couple of hours, I wandered into a downtown supermarket.*

COMBINING PERFECT AND PROGRESSIVE ASPECT 226

The present and past perfect may both combine with progressive aspect:

***I've been cycling** for years through busy traffic.*

*This **had been going on** since September.*

Types of verb

Types of verb

INTRODUCTION 227

There are three basic types of verb in English: lexical verbs, auxiliary verbs and modal verbs.

Lexical verbs

Lexical verbs can stand alone. Lexical verbs have meanings denoting actions, events and states, and belong to an open class (i.e. new verbs are frequently created):

*They **laughed**.*

*It **rained** all night.*

*We had to **catch** a bus.*

Some lexical verbs such as *appear, be, become, feel, get, look, remain, seem, smell, sound, taste*, which are followed by predicative complements, are called copular verbs:

*He**'s** a teacher.*

*That **smells** good.*

→ 288 Copular complementation

Auxiliary verbs

The auxiliary verbs are *be, do* and *have*. Auxiliary verbs add extra information to the lexical verb.

- Auxiliary *be* is used to indicate progressive aspect (→ 224) and passive voice (→ 478).
- Auxiliary *do* is used in the creation of interrogative, negative and emphatic structures.
- Auxiliary *have* is used to indicate perfect aspect (→ 225).

Auxiliary verbs are usually followed by a lexical verb, but they may occur without a lexical verb in reduced clauses (i.e. clauses with ellipsis). They may also occur in clauses where *do* substitutes for a lexical verb:

A: *Are you hoping to get it finished today?*
B: *Yes, we **are**.*
(ellipsis: Yes, we are hoping to get it finished today.)

A: *Will you ring the electrician?*
B: *I already **have done**.*
(*do* as substitute verb: I already have rung the electrician.)

Be, *do* and *have* can be used as auxiliary verbs or as lexical verbs. In these examples of *be*, *do* and *have* as auxiliary verbs, the lexical verbs are in green:

*He **was** working over there.*

*What **do** they call them?*

***Have** you been home?*

***I've been** asked that question a number of times.*

Examples of *be*, *do* and *have* as lexical verbs:

*That **was** a good meal.*
(also referred to as copular *be*)

*He would need to **do** his exams before he went.*

*Can I **have** a receipt for it?*

Modal verbs

Modal verbs belong to a closed class of verbs whose core members are *can*, *could*, *may*, *might*, *shall*, *should*, *will*, *would* and *must*, along with semi-modals such as *dare*, *need*, *ought to* and *used to*. Modal verbs generally encode meanings connected with degrees of certainty and degrees of necessity:

*We **could** go up and get one.*

A: *I'm sure one day you'll go back to teaching.*
B: *I **might**.*

*We **ought to** do something about that missing roof-tile.*

Modal verbs are usually followed by a lexical verb, but they may occur without a lexical verb in clauses with ellipsis. They may also occur in clauses where *do* substitutes for a lexical verb:

A: *I'll give her a ring.*
B: *Yes, you **must**.*
(ellipsis: Yes, you must give her a ring.)

A: *You know the Philips?*
B: *Well I **should** do.*
(*do* as substitute verb: Well I should know them.)

→ 377–407 Modality

LEXICAL VERBS 228

Regular verbs 228a

Regular verbs, the class to which most lexical verbs belong, have four different forms. These forms realise a variety of functions. The most typical functions are shown in the table below.

Regular verbs: form and function

form	function	example
base form	present tense	*People always* ***look*** *at me.*
	infinitive (with or without *to*)	*I want to* ***look****.* *Let me* ***look****.*
-*s* form	present tense (3rd person singular)	*She* ***looks*** *at everyone.*
-*ing* form	progressive aspect	*What* ***are*** *you* ***looking*** *at?*
	non-tensed in non-finite clause	***Looking*** *ahead, we should book flights for the summer holidays.*
	gerund (nominal form)	***Looking*** *shouldn't offend anyone.*
	-*ing* form adjectives	*They had to work in* ***freezing*** *temperatures.*
-*ed* form	past tense	*We* ***looked*** *for a taxi.*
	-*ed* participle	*I've* ***looked*** *everywhere.*
	non-tensed in non-finite clauses	***Looked*** *at in that way, it seemed less problematic.*
	-*ed* form adjectives	*We had some wonderful Irish* ***smoked*** *salmon.*

The present tense form is the same as the base form for all persons except third person singular, which takes the -*s* form:

I/we/you/they ***look***
(present tense form)

He/she/it/one ***looks***
(-*s* form)

Irregular verbs 228b

Irregular verbs, like regular verbs, have a base form, an -*s* form and an -*ing* form, but they vary in how the functions of the regular verb -*ed* form are realised.

Some irregular verbs have the same form for the base form and for all the functions of the -*ed* form.

All three forms the same

base form	-*ed* form as past tense	-*ed* form as -*ed* participle/adjective/non-tensed
cut	*cut*	*cut*
set	*set*	*set*
shut	*shut*	*shut*

Some irregular verbs have the same form for the base and -*ed* form as -*ed* participle/adjective/non-tensed, but a different form for the -*ed* form as past tense.

Base form and -*ed* participle, etc. the same; past tense different

base form	-*ed* form as past tense	-*ed* form as -*ed* participle/adjective/non-tensed
come	*came*	*come*
become	*became*	*become*
run	*ran*	*run*

Some irregular verbs have three different forms which correspond to the functions of the base and the *-ed* forms of regular verbs.

All three forms different

base form	*-ed* form as past tense	*-ed* form as *-ed* participle/adjective/non-tensed
speak	*spoke*	*spoken*
take	*took*	*taken*
swim	*swam*	*swum*

There are other variations too. ⇢ **529 Appendix: Irregular verbs** for a full list of irregular verbs with their base and *-ed* forms

Be, have, do

Be, *have* and *do* have irregular forms for the present tense:

be	*have*	*do*
I ***am***	*I/we/you/they* ***have***	*I/we/you/they* ***do***
you/we/they ***are***	*he/she/it/one* ***has***	*he/she/it/one* ***does***
he/she/it/one ***is***		

Be also has irregular past tense forms:

I/he/she/it ***was***

we/you/they ***were***

THE BASE FORM 229

The base form functions as the present tense form for all persons and numbers except the third person singular (which uses the *-s* form). (Modal verbs do not show these contrasts of tense, person and number.):

They ***work*** *on exactly the same principle.*

I ***hate*** *carrots.*

The base form functions as the infinitive (with or without *to*):

I hope to ***see*** *you tomorrow.*

I'll let you ***know*** *what's to be done.*

The base form is used for the imperative mood:

Sit *here then.*

The base form also functions as the subjunctive mood (⇢ **159e**) for all persons, including third person singular:

The doctor insisted that he ***go*** *to the hospital for a series of tests.*

THE -*S* FORM 230

The -*s* form is used with third-person-singular subjects (*he/she/it/one* and singular nouns) to indicate the present tense:

*He **lives** at 27 Webber Close.*

*It **depends** on what you want to do.*

*The coffee **smells** good.*

THE -*ING* FORM 231

The -*ing* form is used with auxiliary *be* to form progressive aspect:

*I **was doing** some work for Sally.*

*He**'s looking** well these days.*

The -*ing* form also occurs in non-finite clauses:

***Getting** no reply, she rang the bell again.*

*He stared at me, as if **trying** to make up his mind.*

The -*ing* form functions as the gerund, which is a noun-like (nominal) form which can occur as the head of a noun phrase or as the complement of a preposition:

*When I was a lad, I had to milk cows by hand. Now all **milking** is done by machines.*

*It was a good play, with some very good **acting**.*

*Thank you **for coming**.*

*You can get back to the car park **by going** up to the first floor.*

In its nominal function, the -*ing* form is frequent in noun compounds:

*We need a new **washing machine**.*

*Where are my **walking-boots**?*

The -*ing* form can also act as an adjective:

***Falling** processor prices means this is a good time to buy a new computer.*

THE -*ED* FORM 232

The -*ed* form indicates the past tense:

*I just **phoned** your place.*

*It **looked** a bit big.*

→ **539 Glossary** for any unfamiliar terms

The *-ed* form functions as the *-ed* participle, which is used with auxiliary *have* and *be* to form perfect aspect and passive voice:

*I've **broken** my glasses.*
(perfect aspect)

*I wasn't **offended** by what she said.*
(passive voice)

The *-ed* form also occurs in non-finite clauses:

***Encouraged** by our progress, we decided to go on.*

*Whenever **asked**, show all your documents.*

The *-ed* form is often used as an adjective:

*D'you want **fried** rice or plain?*

AUXILIARY VERBS 233

General 233a

Be

Auxiliary *be* is used with the *-ing* form of a lexical verb to indicate progressive aspect and with the *-ed* form of a lexical verb to indicate passive voice:

*She **was** work**ing** in Glasgow.*
(progressive aspect)

*She **was** rush**ed** to hospital last week.*
(passive voice)

Do

Auxiliary *do* is used with the base form of a lexical verb in negative, interrogative and emphatic structures, and as a substitute for a lexical verb or clause predicate:

*I **do not** trust people who change so abruptly.*
(negative)

***Did** you see Sarah at school?*
(interrogative)

*I'm a good complainer. I **do** complain a lot.*
(emphatic)

A: *I cried.*
B: *Yes I **did** too.*
(substitute)

Have

Auxiliary *have* is used with the *-ed* participle to indicate perfect aspect:

*We **have looked** down there.*

*They **had** already **eaten** when we got there.*

Negative forms and auxiliary verbs 233b

Not is placed after the auxiliary verb to form the negative:

*Pupils **were not** turning up.*
(~~Pupils not were turning up.~~)

*I **have not** left the house.*

The contracted form of the negative (*n't*) is very frequent in spoken language and is also used in informal writing. In writing it is attached to the auxiliary verb, without a space:

*It **hasn't** got any particular sort of name.*

*You **weren't** here yesterday.*

*The locals **don't** mix that well with the students.*

When the contracted forms of *be* (*'m*, *'re* and *'s*) and the contracted forms of *have* (*'ve*, *'s* and *'d*) are used, *n't* is not used:

***I'm not** doing that one.*
(~~I'mn't doing that one.~~)

*We**'ve not** abandoned you.*
(or: We haven't abandoned you.)

Interrogative forms and auxiliary verbs 233c

Interrogative structures involving auxiliary verbs consist of auxiliary + subject + lexical verb:

***Are** the children **looking** forward to it?*

***Has** she **finished** her room now?*

*What **did** your mother **do**?*
(~~What did do your mother?~~)

Auxiliary verbs also occur in corresponding question tags:

*Annabel **has** lost a lot of weight actually, **has**n't she?*

*You **know** what it's like, **do**n't you?*

Contracted forms of auxiliary verbs 233d

Auxiliary verbs have contracted forms which are widely used in spoken language and in informal writing. The contracted forms are written with an apostrophe (') and without a space. The contracted forms are:

be	*do*	*have*
I'm	***d'**you (do)*	*I/we/they**'ve** (have)*
*We/you/they**'re** (are)*		*He/she/it/one**'s** (has)*
*He/she/it/one**'s** (is)*		*I/we/you/he/she/it/one/they**'d** (had)*

→ **539 Glossary** for any unfamiliar terms

*I think **they're** starting it again.*
(they are)

***She's** paying for everything.*
(she is)

*Apparently **it's** what **he's** wanted to do all his life.*
(it is/he has)

Do you frequently contracts to *d'you*. In very informal spoken language, *did you* may also contract to *d'you*:

***D'you** normally have to book?*
(do you)

***D'you** hear what's happened to Ted?*
(did you)

The interpretation of *'s* depends on what follows it. It represents *is* in the present progressive if it is followed by the *-ing* form (*she's eating* = *she is eating*), or if it is followed by an adjective or a noun (*she's lovely* = *she is lovely*; *she's a girl* = *she is a girl*). If it is followed by an *-ed* participle, it can represent *is* in the *be* passive (*she's forgiven* = *she is forgiven*) or *has* in the present perfect (*she's started* = *she has started*). It represents *has* if it is followed by *got* (*she's got* = *she has got*):

*She**'s** turn**ing** into a friend.*
(She is turning ...)

*It**'s** publish**ed** by Cambridge University Press.*
(passive: It is published by ...)

*He**'s** **left**. He left Sunday.*
(He has left.)

The contraction *'d* represents *had* if it is followed by the *-ed* participle (*I'd left* = *I had left*) or by *better* (*I'd better* = *I had better*). It represents *would* if it is followed by the base form (*I'd like* = *I would like*; *I'd have done it* = *I would have done it*), or if it is followed by *rather* or *sooner* (*I'd rather not go* = *I would rather not go*):

*I**'d** phon**ed** and he wasn't there.*
(*-ed* participle: I had phoned ...)

*I**'d** **agree** with Jim with what he's said there.*
(base form: I would agree with Jim ...)

Ellipsis and substitution with auxiliary verbs 233e

Auxiliary verbs occur in clauses with ellipsis and in substitute clauses. The contracted forms are not used:

A: *Are you looking forward to the New Year?*
B: *Oh yes. Yes, I **am**.*
(~~B: Oh yes. Yes, I'm.~~)

He wondered why he'd been put where he ***had****.*
(ellipsis: ... where he had been put.)

I saw her across a crowded room and thought she was really beautiful and that I must speak to her, so I ***did****.*
(ellipsis: ... so I did speak to her.)

He couldn't go so I ***did*** *instead.*
(substitution: ... so I went instead.)

MODAL VERBS 234

General 234a

The core modal verbs are *can, could, may, might, shall, should, will, would* and *must*. Core modal verbs are used with the base form of a lexical verb, without *to*:

Could I speak *to Maureen please?*
(~~Could I to speak to Maureen please?~~)

Core modal verbs are not preceded by the auxiliary verbs:

Can you help *me, please?*
(~~Do you can help me, please?~~)

You mustn't *put it near a naked flame.*
(~~You don't must put it near a naked flame.~~)

Modal verbs may be followed by auxiliary *be* and *have* indicating aspect and voice:

We **could be** *wait***ing** *here for hours. Let's go home.*
(progressive aspect)

I ***might have*** *got killed.*
(perfect aspect)

These gates **will be** *lock***ed** *at 8pm.*
(passive voice)

There are also semi-modal verbs such as *dare, need, ought to* and *used to* (→ 395).

Negative forms of modal verbs 234b

Not is placed after the modal verb to form the negative:

She **could not** *shut her eyes to the daylight.*

I **would not** *wish to disagree.*

The contracted negative *n't* is used in spoken language and in informal writing with *can*, *could*, *should*, *would*, *might* and *must*, and with the semi-modals *ought*, *need* and *dare*:

*I **couldn't** believe it.*

*He **shouldn't** have been irritated by them.*

*I'm told I **mustn't** eat too quickly.*

*She **needn't** worry if she can't get back to me.*

The contracted negative forms of *shall* and *will* are *shan't* and *won't*:

*I **shan't** ask you again.*

*My white shirt probably **won't** fit me.*

Negative forms, uncontracted and contracted, for the core modal verbs

verb	uncontracted negative	contracted negative
can	*cannot; can not*	*can't*
could	*could not*	*couldn't*
may	*may not*	*mayn't* (very rare)
might	*might not*	*mightn't*
must	*must not*	*mustn't*
will	*will not*	*'ll not; won't*
shall	*shall not*	*'ll not; shan't*
would	*would not*	*'d not; wouldn't*
should	*should not*	*shouldn't*

Interrogative forms of modal verbs 234c

Interrogative structures involving modal verbs consist of modal verb + subject + lexical verb:

***Will** you **be** at home Saturday morning?*

***Can** my friend **come** too?*

Auxiliary *do* is not used:

***Can you** tell me where the market is please?*
(~~Do you can tell me where the market is please?~~)

Modal verbs also occur in corresponding tags:

*They **will** make it on time, **won't** they?*

*He **mustn't** shout like that, **must** he?*

*He **could** win, he **could**.*

Contracted forms of modal verbs 234d

Will and *would* have contracted forms which are especially common in spoken language and informal writing. *Will* and *shall* are frequently shortened to *'ll* in declarative clauses:

*We**'ll** see what happens.*
(We will/shall see …)

→ 365 on 'independent' *'ll*

→ **377–407 Modality**

Ellipsis and substitution with modal verbs 234e

Modal verbs occur in clauses with ellipsis. The contracted forms are not used in ellipted clauses and clauses with substitute *do*:

A: *We could get a video couldn't we?*
B: *Yeah, we **could**.*

A: *So will you look after that for us?*
B: *I **will**.*
(~~I'll.~~)

A: *But it might be worth just giving that number a ring.*
B: *Yeah, I **will do**.*
(~~Yeah, I'll do.~~)

MULTI-WORD VERBS 235

General 235a

A lexical verb may combine with a particle to form a multi-word verb which behaves as a single unit of meaning. The particle may be an adverb or a preposition. In the following examples, verbs and their accompanying particles are in bold:

*This **calls for** a celebration.*
(*calls for* = demands/requires)

*They've been **turned down** once already.*
(*turned down* = refused)

*Did mum and dad **get away** all right?*
(*get away* = leave/depart)

*I think I'm going to **drop off** soon.*
(*drop off* = fall asleep)

Some multi-word verbs have two particles:

*He never **looks down on** her for what she's doing.*
(looks down on = disrespects, considers less worthy)

*I don't see why I should have to **put up with** that.*
(*put up with* = accept, tolerate)

The particle is linked closely to the lexical verb, and cannot be separated and fronted in the way it can in other structures:

***Off** she **ran**.*
(verb *run* plus adverb *off*; non-fronted version: She ran off.)

*Mum and dad **got away** all right.*
(~~Away got mum and dad all right.~~)
(multi-word verb *get away* = leave, depart)

***For** Jill I **bought** a necklace.*
(verb *buy* plus prepositional phrase *for Jill*; non-fronted version: I bought a necklace for Jill.)

*This **calls for** a celebration.*
(~~For a celebration this calls.~~)
(multi-word verb *call for* plus object *a celebration*; *calls for* = demands)

The most frequent verbs and the particles they combine with to form multi-word verbs

verb	example particles	verb	example particles
come	*into, off, out, up*	***make***	*for, out, up*
get	*at, away, on*	***pick***	*on, out, up*
give	*in, off, up*	***pull***	*over, through, up*
go	*into, off, on*	***put***	*across, forward, out*
hold	*against, on, to*	***run***	*into, over, up*
keep	*on, up, to*	***set***	*off, out, up*
knock	*about, down, over*	***take***	*back, off, to*
let	*off, out, up*	***turn***	*over, round, up*
look	*after, into, over*	***work***	*on, out, up*

Multi-word verbs fall into three main classes, which are described in subsequent sections:

- phrasal verbs (**235c, d, e**)
- prepositional verbs (**235f**)
- phrasal-prepositional verbs (**235g**)

Particles 235b

The most common particles which combine with lexical verbs to form multi-word verbs are shown in the table below, along with a selection of verbs (and verbs + particles) they combine with.

The most common particles and the verbs they combine with to form multi-word verbs

particle	example verbs (+particles)	particle	example verbs (+particles)
about	*go, hang, knock, mess*	***off***	*come, go, get, take*
ahead	*forge, go, keep, move*	***on***	*come, get, go, put*
around	*come, get, go, knock*	***out***	*break, come, go, put*
at	*come, get, look, play*	***over***	*come, get, go, turn*
away	*get, put, run, take*	***round***	*come, drop, go, hang*
back	*come, get, go, take*	***through***	*come, get, go, run*
down	*break, come, go, put*	***to***	*come, get on, go back, keep*
for	*care, go, look, stand*	***together***	*get, go, pull, put*
in	*come, get, go, take*	***up***	*come, open, pick, take*
into	*break, get, go, run*	***with***	*deal, do away, go, put up*

Other particles include *about, across, after, against, along, apart, aside, astray, away, by, for, forward(s), from, onto, under, upon*:

*She also **came across** as being stupid as well.*
(*came across* = appeared)

*The fridge has **fallen apart**.*
(*fallen apart* = broken into pieces)

*A day didn't **pass by** when I didn't know what was **going on**.*

Multi-word verbs are written as separate words, not as a single word or with hyphens:

*I think I'm going to **drop off** soon.*
(Not: I think I'm going to dropoff soon.)
(Not: I think I'm going drop-off soon.)

Phrasal verbs 235c

Phrasal verbs consist of a lexical verb and a particle. Phrasal verbs may be intransitive or transitive (⇢ 282). In the case of transitive phrasal verbs, the position of the object (in green in the examples below) may vary:

*You're not going to **sort out** your problems in a month.*
(*sort out* = solve)

[to a small child reaching for a drink at table]
*Careful, darling, don't **knock** that **over**!*
(*knock it over* = make it fall)

A number of phrasal verbs are intransitive, i.e. they do not require an object:

*The radio alarm **went off** at the same time as usual.*
(*went off* = rang)

*I waited till the noise of the train **died away** then walked home.*
(*died away* = became inaudible)

Many verbs may be used both transitively and intransitively. There may be a difference in meaning between the transitive use and the intransitive use:

*Oh, better **get back** to reality now I suppose!*
(intransitive: return)

*He wouldn't be able to stand losing Sonnie now. He had to **get** her **back**.*
(transitive: regain her/re-possess her)

*I've got to **set off** at five o'clock.*
(intransitive: begin a journey)

*As soon as he moves, he's going to **set** the alarm **off**.*
(transitive: cause it to ring)

Transitive phrasal verbs 235d

Many phrasal verbs can be used with a direct object. The most frequent include:

blow up
break down
bring up
carry on
check out
close down
drink up
drop off
eat up
fill up
find out
finish off
give away
give up
hand in/out
hold up
leave out
look up
make up
phone up
put off
put on
ring up
rub out
save up
shut down
sort out
take back
take over
take up
tell off
throw away
try on
turn down
wake up
work out
write down

In most cases, the particle may come before or after the direct object (in green in the examples below) if the object is not a personal pronoun:

*In Kent, burglars **blew up** a fireworks factory after trying to break in using oxyacetylene cutting equipment.*
(or: ....burglars blew a fireworks factory up ...)
(*blew up* = made it explode)

*We decided to **put** the meeting **off** for a couple of weeks.*
(or: We decided to put off the meeting for a couple of weeks.)
(*put off* = postpone)

*As usual it will be left to me to **sort** everything **out**.*
(*sort out* = organise)

*But don't **throw away** that fur coat yet.*
(*throw away* = dispose of)

When the direct object is a personal pronoun, the pronoun always comes before the particle:

A: *I've got a nice home.*
B: *Yes.*
A: *But I've got to almost **give** it **away**.*
(~~But I've got to almost give away it.~~)
(*give it away* = take no money for it)

A: ***Leave** me **out**.*
B: *What do you mean 'leave you out'?*
A: *I don't want to go.*
(~~Leave out me.~~)
(*leave out* = don't include)

*They couldn't **wake** her **up**.*
(~~They couldn't wake up her.~~)

If a pronoun object is coordinated with a full noun phrase or another pronoun, the objects may occur before or after the particle:

*The noise **woke** me and my wife **up**.*
(or: The noise woke up me and my wife.)

*He didn't **phone** her or me **up**.*
(or: He didn't phone up her or me.)

[*the OED* = the *Oxford Dictionary of English*]
*I'll have to **look up** that word and its derivation in the OED.*
(or: I'll have to look that word and its derivation up in the OED.

Longer objects tend to come after the particle:

*Yesterday we were just **finishing off** looking at the structure and the land use of city and town.*
(~~Yesterday we were just finishing looking at the structure and the land use of city and town off.~~)

Intransitive phrasal verbs 235e

Intransitive phrasal verbs consist of a verb and a particle without an object.
Frequent phrasal verbs which are used intransitively include:

break down	*go off*	*run away*
carry on	*hang on*	*set off*
drop off	*join in*	*wake up*
eat out	*move in/out*	
get back	*ring off*	

539 **Glossary** for any unfamiliar terms

It was a disastrous day, because the coach ***broke down****.*
(*broke down* = stopped working)

He buys all his own food and he very rarely ***eats out****.*
(*eats out* = eats at a restaurant)

Hang on*. Let me write all this down.*
(*hang on* = wait)

A: *We have to* ***set off*** *at the crack of dawn.*
B: *That's gonna be fun!*
(*set off* = leave, start the journey)

Prepositional verbs 235f

Prepositional verbs consist of a verb and a preposition which are closely syntactically linked with each other. As with other multi-word verbs, fronting of the prepositional complement is not normally possible:

I don't ***approve of*** *his views on war and military things.*
(~~Of his views on war and military things I don't approve.~~)

Prepositional verbs follow different rules from phrasal verbs. The direct object (in green in the examples below) must follow the preposition, even if it is a pronoun:

I couldn't sell my car. I just couldn't ***do without*** *it.*
(~~... I just couldn't do it without.~~)
(*couldn't do without* = need/have to have)

Frequent prepositional verbs include:

approve of	*cope with*	*get over*
break into	*deal with*	*go into*
call on	*depend on*	*lead to*
care for	*do without*	*listen to*
check into	*get into*	*look after*
come across	*get on*	*look at*
come upon	*get off*	*look for*

Common prepositions and some verbs which combine with them to form prepositional verbs

preposition	verbs	preposition	verbs
across	*come, cut, run, stumble*	*of*	*become, consist, despair, hear*
after	*ask, inquire, look, take*	*off*	*feed, get, give, go*
at	*get, glance, laugh, look*	*on*	*bet, depend, lean*
for	*ask, care, go, live*	*to*	*amount, belong, keep, object*
into	*break, bump, delve, launch*	*with*	*agree, break, deal, go*

*Because loads of people **break into** cars, does that make it right?*
(~~*Because loads of people break cars into, does that make it right?*~~)
(*break into* = enter by using force)

*You said you'd already **come across** that sort of stuff in the library.*
(*come across* = found)

*He says it's the pills that's doing it. 'But I can't **do without** them,' he says.*
(*can't do without* = must have)

*I managed to **look after** everybody for a day and a half.*
(*look after* = take care of)

Some prepositional verbs allow an adverb or discourse marker to be used between the verb and the preposition:

*It **depends** entirely **on** what's going on at the time.*

*I **agree**, I think, **with** most of his reasons.*

Verbs in this category include:

agree with	*check into*	*keep to*
apologise for	*consist of*	*laugh at*
approve of	*cope with*	*lead to*
ask for	*deal with*	*lean on*
belong to	*depend on*	*live for*
bet on	*disagree with*	*look at*
break with	*glance at*	*look for*
care for	*go with*	*object to*

Some prepositional verbs take a direct object after the verb as well as an object of the preposition. These include:

associate … with	*deprive … of*	*remind … of*
bombard … with	*protect … from*	*rob … of*
confine … to	*provide … with*	*thank … for*

*You don't **bombard** them **with** new stuff.*

*Local white rulers enforced racial segregation by 'Jim Crow laws' to **deprive** black people **of** civil rights.*

*Just **remind** me **of** your surname again.*

··➝ 539 **Glossary** for any unfamiliar terms

Phrasal-prepositional verbs 235g

Phrasal-prepositional verbs consist of an adverb particle and a preposition. Common phrasal-prepositional verbs include:

catch up on	*get along with*	*look out for*
catch up with	*get on with*	*look up to*
come up against	*listen out for*	*put up with*
do away with	*look forward to*	*watch out for*
face up to	*look down on*	
get away with	*look in on*	

These verbs normally occur in informal contexts:

*I'll **catch up with** you in a minute.*
(*catch up with* = reach, join)

*Let her **get on with** it.*
(*get on with* = continue doing)

*I'm **looking forward to** the weekend.*
(*looking forward to* = anticipating with pleasure)

*You have to **watch out for** the things coming along behind that you can't see.*

A small number of such verbs also take a direct object after the verb as well as an object of the preposition. These include:

fix ... up with	*let ... in on*	*put ... up to*
fob ... off with	*put ... down to*	*take ... out on*

*She's going to try and **fix** me **up with** a bit of part-time work.*
(*fix me up with* = arrange for me)

*Do you **put** that **down to** luck or judgement?*
(*put down to* = think the cause or reason is)

*He was just **taking** his frustration **out on** me, shouting at me and stuff.*
(*taking ... out on me* = causing me to suffer)

Adjectives and adjective phrases

Adjectives and adjective phrases

ADJECTIVES 236

Introduction 236a

Adjectives are the third major open word class in English. They describe the features of persons or things denoted by nouns or pronouns (··› 237 below):

*It's a **nice** room.*

*The service was **awful**.*

*Her father is **German**.*

*She's **beautiful**.*

Adjectives cannot be automatically identified by their form, although certain suffixes typically occur with adjectives (··› 236b below). Many common, everyday adjectives have no form which identifies them as such (e.g. *good*, *nice*, *old*, *wet*). Adjectives are identified most typically by their functions in a sentence.

Suffixes and prefixes 236b

Some suffixes occur typically or exclusively with adjectives.

Suffixes that occur with adjectives

suffix	examples
-able,-ible	*acceptable, usable, inedible*
-al,-ial	*normal, comical, radial*
-ed	*timbered, aged*
-ful	*masterful, wishful*
-ic	*frantic, heroic*
-ical	*hysterical, political*
-ish	*amateurish, childish*
-ive, -ative	*active, attractive, talkative*
-less	*endless, priceless*
-eous, -ious, -ous	*erroneous, anxious, famous*
-y	*angry, busy, windy, wealthy*

As can be seen from the table, adjectives may be derived from nouns (*hero–heroic*, *wind–windy*) or verbs (*accept–acceptable*, *attract–attractive*) by the addition of suffixes.

The prefix *a-* also identifies certain adjectives (e.g. *awake*, *alive*, *ablaze*).

··› also **258–268 Word structure and word formation**

Comparative and superlative inflections 236c

Many one-syllable adjectives, and two-syllable adjectives ending in an unstressed syllable, have inflections to show the comparative and superlative.

Adjectives that inflect

base form	comparative	superlative
fine	*finer*	*finest*
small	*smaller*	*smallest*
young	*younger*	*youngest*
funny	*funnier*	*funniest*
gentle	*gentler*	*gentlest*

However, two-syllable adjectives ending in a stressed syllable and longer adjectives do not inflect. Comparatives and superlatives are formed using *more* and *most* (··➤ 462 and 463).

Adjectives that do not inflect

base form	comparative	superlative
correct	*more correct* ~~*correcter*~~	*most correct* ~~*correctest*~~
memorable	*more memorable* ~~*memorabler*~~	*most memorable* ~~*memorablest*~~

··➤ **460–471 Comparison**

-ing and *-ed* form adjectives 236d

The *-ing* and *-ed* forms of verbs may also function as adjectives:

[cooking instructions on food packet]
*Just add **boiling** water.*

*They only want to travel to **English-speaking** countries.*

*It's not **smoked** salmon, it's **smoked** trout.*

*Even supermarkets now sell **home-made** jams.*

MEANINGS OF ADJECTIVES 237

Types of meaning 237a

Adjectives describe features and qualities of entities (people, animals and things) denoted by nouns or pronouns.

- Some adjectives denote characteristic or inherent properties and qualities which are long-lasting or permanent: *tall, heavy, old, good, rough, true, ugly, red.*
- Some adjectives express transient states and conditions: *hungry, cold, absent, ill, dry, full, lonely.*
- Some adjectives denote relations between entities. These are among the adjectives that require complements (··➤ 238a below): *fond (of), similar (to), aware (of), keen (on/to), far (from).*

- Some adjectives describe entities in terms of their actions: *generous, cruel, talkative, polite, cooperative.*
- Some adjectives classify entities into types: *wooden (spoon), Swedish (film), departmental (meeting), detached (house), organic (vegetables), impressionist (painter), wild (salmon).*

Oppositeness (antonymy) and gradability 237b

Most common adjectives (except the classifying type in **237a** above) are members of a pair of opposites (antonyms). For example:

tall–short; heavy–light; good–bad; dry–wet; dead–alive; absent–present

Many of these are also gradable, i.e. one can differentiate between different degrees of the same property along a scale (→ **238c** and **238d** below):

*He's **quite tall** for his age, isn't he?*

*Your hair's going to be **very wet**.*

ADJECTIVE PHRASES 238

Structure of adjective phrases 238a

Just as nouns and verbs function as the heads of noun phrases and verb phrases, adjectives function as the head of adjective phrases. An adjective phrase consists minimally of an adjective acting as head. The head may be accompanied by modifiers (pre- and post-head) and complements (post-head).

→ **the tables at 169d** and **214b** for comparison with noun phrases and verb phrases

The structure of adjective phrases (adjective phrases are in green; adjective heads are in bold)

example	structure
*She has a **lovely** apartment.*	head only
*It's a rather **unfortunate** name, isn't it?*	premodifier + head
*Shall we see if that's **big** enough?*	head + postmodifier
*She's **advanced** for her age.*	head + postmodifier
*Are you **willing** to volunteer?*	head + complement
*He was very **keen** on sport and nature.*	premodifier + head + complement
*I'm not really **sure** that I can advise you.*	premodifier + head + complement

Some adjective phrases have more complex structures than those in the table. In particular, there are phrases which are split into two parts (discontinuous adjective phrases). These are dealt with in **240d** below.

Premodification and postmodification of adjectives 238b

The most typical premodifiers of adjectives (in green) are adverb phrases expressing degree (bold):

*I was **pretty** upset at the time.*

*That's an **extremely** good camera.*

*I think my jeans are **a bit** damp.*

The major exception is the degree adverb *enough*, which is a postmodifier:

*It's not long **enough**.*
(~~It's not enough long.~~)

Adverbs other than adverbs of degree may also premodify adjectives:

*The house was **unusually** silent that day.*

*It was **wonderfully** peaceful at Gelli.*

*I don't know how **seriously** ill they are.*

Premodification and gradability 238c

Most everyday adjectives are gradable, i.e. they denote qualities, properties, states, conditions, relations, etc. which vary in their degree or extent.

Gradable adjectives can be premodified by degree expressions (usually adverb phrases) which specify different degrees of the feature in question.

Premodification of gradable adjectives

example	comments
*He's **very** tall.* *He's **fairly** tall.*	
*He's **this** tall.*	*This tall* would be typically spoken with a gesture indicating a specific height.
*I didn't realise he was **that** tall.*	*That tall* might refer to a statement made by someone about someone's height or to the moment of seeing someone very tall.
*He is over **two metres** tall.*	*Over two metres* is a noun phrase. Certain adjectives expressing numerically measurable properties may be modified by such noun phrases: *She is **ten years** old; The wood is **two centimetres** thick; You're **ten minutes** late.* A–Z 80 ***Worth, worthwhile***
*He is **so** tall **<u>that he can touch the ceiling</u>**.* *He is **too** tall **<u>to drive</u>**.*	Some degree adverbs (*so, too, as*) need a complement (underlined) to complete their meaning. The complement may be a clause or a phrase; it occurs after the head adjective. The structure is discontinuous (split into two parts, one part pre-head, the other post-head).
*He is **as** tall **as his father**.* *He is tall**er than his sister**.*	The comparative with *as* … *as* and the suffix *-er* have the same function of specifying degree as the various premodifiers. The structure with *as* is discontinuous.
***How** tall is he?* ***How** tall he is!*	Interrogative *how* is used to ask questions or to utter exclamations about degree, but with an important difference in word order.

Non-gradable adjectives cannot normally be premodified in these ways. Non-gradable adjectives include: *automatic*; *dead/alive*; *female/male*; *Irish/Brazilian/Thai*/etc.; *married/unmarried/single*:

This cat is male.
(~~This cat is more male than that one.~~)

This plant is dead.
(~~This plant is rather dead.~~)

Gradable opposites (antonyms) 238d

Open-ended

The most common gradable adjectives occur as pairs of antonyms that denote the upper and lower parts of an open-ended scale:

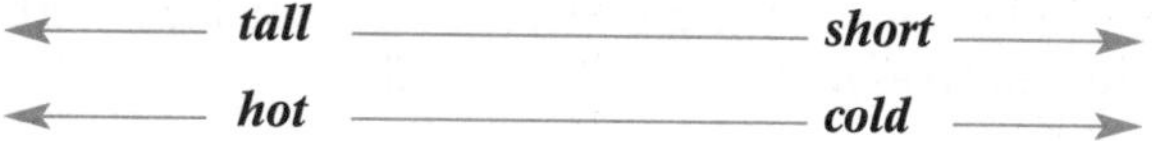

There are no maximum and minimum points on such a scale. Therefore, adjectives of this kind may not be premodified by degree adverbs indicating totality, such as *completely*, *absolutely*, *entirely*, *utterly*, *totally*, *wholly*:

It's going to be an ***extremely small*** *stadium.*
(~~It's going to be a totally small stadium.~~)

I think it's a ***very beautiful*** *statue.*
(~~I think it's a completely beautiful statue.~~)

→ **238e** below for how adjectives may be cross-classified, however

Maximum and minimum

Some other gradable adjectives can denote properties on scales which have a maximum and/or minimum (zero) value:

full ←——————→ ***empty***

possible ←——————→ ***impossible***

Such adjectives can be premodified using degree adverbs like *absolutely*, *completely*, *entirely*, *totally*, *utterly* and other synonyms:

It was ***absolutely full*** *with families with kids.*

He is ***completely blind****, you know.*

So it's ***utterly impossible****, isn't it?*

Other degree adverbs which can premodify gradable adjectives of this second type include *almost*, *barely*, *half*, *scarcely*:

[talking about the colour of water coming out of a tap]
When it comes out it looks ***almost white****, you know.*

I realised I was ***half-naked*** *and fumbled with the buttons of my pyjama jacket.*

Quite

The degree adverb *quite* means 'fairly', 'to some extent' when it premodifies gradable adjectives which occur on open-ended scales, but means 'absolutely' when it premodifies gradable adjectives which occur on a scale which has a maximum and/or minimum (zero) value:

*She's **quite tall** for her age, isn't she?*
(fairly)

*You were **quite right** to refuse to pay.*
(absolutely)

A–Z 66 *Quite*

Cross-classification of gradable and non-gradable adjectives 238e

Although adjectives can generally be classified as gradable or non-gradable, they can be used (often with a shift in meaning or connotation) as if they were members of the other class. For example, if an adjective normally classified as non-gradable is premodified as if it were gradable, it is usually interpreted non-literally:

*They were all being **very Scottish**.*
(probably interpreted as 'behaving in an exaggeratedly or stereotypically Scottish manner')

Similarly, gradable adjectives can be treated as if they were non-gradable and premodified by items associated with non-gradable meanings:

*The weather was **absolutely beautiful**.*
(i.e. it was beautiful to the highest possible degree)

*That suggestion is **totally stupid**.*

Implicit superlatives (*filthy, starving*) 238f

Often, to express an extreme or maximum degree of a property (e.g. *dirty*), an implicit superlative adjective (e.g. *filthy*) is used instead of a more neutral adjective. Such adjectives are often used for special effect or exaggeration, or in intensified responses, and are often premodified by *absolutely*.

Examples of implicit superlatives

more neutral adjective	implicit superlative
*I'm **very hungry**.*	*I'm **starving/ravenous**.*
*I'm **very cold**.*	*I'm **(absolutely) frozen**.*
*His room **is very small**.*	*His room is **tiny/minute**.*
*Their house **is very big**.*	*Their house is **(absolutely) enormous/huge/vast**.*
*We got **very wet**.*	*We got **soaked/drenched**.*
*It was **very hot** in Nevada.*	*It was **(absolutely) boiling/scorching** in Nevada.*
*The kitchen was **very dirty**.*	*The kitchen was **(absolutely) filthy**.*

The use of such implicit superlatives in responses is an important way of showing agreement in conversations:

A: *Oh it's fantastic.*
B: *It sounds* ***absolutely amazing.***

[tasting food]
A: *Is it all right?*
B: *Lovely.*
C: *Yes, it's* ***absolutely delicious.***

Fixed modifiers (*bone dry, as dry as a bone*) 238g

Modifier + adjective collocations (*bone dry*)

There are a large number of idiomatic expressions for indicating maximum degree which consist of fixed modifier + adjective collocations. These are very common in informal spoken language. They include:

bone dry	*pure white*	*stone deaf*
brand new	*rock hard*	*wide awake*
fast asleep/sound asleep	*soaking wet/sopping wet*	
pitch black/pitch dark	*stark naked*	

Her throat was ***bone dry.***

Very soon he was ***fast asleep.***

The flat was ***pitch dark****, with all the blinds shut, blocking out the street-lights and the moon.*

Comparative expressions (*as dry as a bone*)

Similarly, there are a number of idiomatic comparative expressions, which include:

as blind as a bat	*as dry as a bone*	*as white as snow/as white as a sheet*
as deaf as a post	*as heavy as lead*	

You desperately fight to stay on your feet, but you feel weak and dizzy from your ordeal, and your legs are ***as heavy as lead.***

They were clutching each other in shock, and the woman particularly was ***as white as a sheet.***

In informal spoken language, the first *as* is often omitted in these constructions:

She went ***white as a sheet*** *when they told her.*

THE FUNCTIONS OF ADJECTIVE PHRASES 239

General 239a

Noun modifiers and copular complement

Adjective phrases have two main functions within larger structures: they modify nouns (attributive function) and they complement copular verbs (predicative function).

Adjective phrases in the attributive function (bold) modify nouns (in green), normally as premodifiers:

*Only **rich** people can afford a flat in **central** London.*

*Enjoy the **smooth, silky** taste of **Creamery** butter.*

An adjective phrase has a predicative function when it occurs in a clause as the complement (bold) of a copular verb (in green) such as *appear, be, become, feel, get, look, remain, seem, smell, sound, taste*:

*They were always **popular** with the rest of the team.*

*The daily rates for the hotel seem **a bit high**, don't they?*

*That chicken tastes **very odd**.*

Object complements

Adjective phrases (bold) may also occur as object (in green) complements:

*I made him **nervous** before the interview. I suppose he wanted the job too much.*

*We've made the room **tidy** so they can move in when they like.*

Adjectives modifying nouns (attributive function) 239b

An adjective phrase (bold) has an attributive function when it occurs as a modifier in a noun phrase (in green):

*She had a **huge** suitcase.*

*It really is an **incredibly beautiful** place.*

*Students **keen to get the best degree** will pay to go to more expensive colleges.*

Position of adjective

Most typically, an attributive adjective phrase occurs as a premodifier in the noun phrase, coming between any determiners and the head noun:

	determiner	adjective phrase	head
And so you're not sure what	*the*	***really important***	*things are.*

*Elsie's got her **best** hat on.*

If the head of the noun phrase is one of the pronouns *someone, somebody, something, somewhere; no one, nobody, nothing, nowhere; anyone, anybody, anything, anywhere; everyone, everybody, everything, everywhere,* the attributive adjective phrase occurs as a postmodifier:

*There's nothing **good** about being poor.*

*There wasn't really anyone **famous** at Lordsborough [University].*

*There's something **definitely wrong** here.*

Position of adjective and complement

If an attributive adjective has a complement, the whole adjective phrase or just its complement must follow the head noun.

Examples of attributive adjectives with complements

example	type
*Are they a **similar** age?*	adjective with no complement
*Hardin reached under the counter and brought out a badge **similar to the one he was already wearing on his waistcoat**.*	adjective and complement both after the noun head
A: *So how do you see yourselves in twenty years' time?* B: *I would imagine very much in a **similar** position **to my mum and dad now**.*	adjective before the noun head; complement after the noun head

*Helsinki has a character **quite different from the Scandinavian capitals**.*

*You can buy a computer system **good enough for most tasks** for less than £500.*

*It's a **very different** room **from the old one**.*

*I haven't got a **good enough** voice **to sing it**.*

For a number of adjectives, the whole adjective phrase must follow the noun when a complement of the adjective is used. These include *closed, eager, full, happy, keen, open, ready, responsible, (un)willing, worth*:

*Fans **keen to get their hands on the new book** had queued all night.*
(~~Keen fans to get their hands on the new book …~~)

*Events **open to the public** are listed overleaf.*

*By the time we got there, the person **responsible for giving refunds** had gone home.*

*It's a film **worth seeing**.*

Some fixed expressions include postmodifying adjectives, for example *chairperson designate, court martial, President Elect.*

RESTRICTIONS ON THE FUNCTIONS OF ADJECTIVES 240

Adjectives restricted to noun phrases (attributive-only) 240a

Adjectives in the following meaning categories occur only in noun phrases (the attributive function):

- Degree (intensifiers and downtoners), such as: *absolute*, *complete*, *mere*, *perfect*, *proper*, *pure*, *real*, *sheer*, *true*, *utter*, *veritable*:

  *It was **pure** nonsense.*
  (~~The nonsense was pure.~~)

  *This is **sheer** heaven.*

→ 240c

- Temporal ordering, such as: *former*, *latter*, *present*, *future*, *old* (meaning 'of many years' standing', e.g. *an old friend*), *early* (meaning 'of the initial period in the history of something', e.g. *early English literature*), *late* (meaning 'died recently', e.g. *the late Mrs Thompson*):

  *In 1816 he married Charlotte, daughter of the **future** George IV of England, and lived in England after her death in 1817.*

  *The only permanent display is the **late** actor William Holden's collection of Asian and African art.*
  (*late* = recently deceased/dead)

- Restrictive adjectives, such as: *certain*, *chief*, *main*, *major*, *only*, *particular*, *principal*, *sole*, *very*:

  *You know, the **main** reason for being in business at all is profit and that's what you ought to be judging.*

  *He published **major** works on logic and political theory.*

Adjectives restricted to copular complement (predicative-only) 240b

Some adjectives can be used only as a complement to copular verbs (the predicative function), and not attributively. The majority of these are adjectives with the prefix *a-*, and include: *ablaze*, *afloat*, *alive*, *asleep*, *awake*, *awash*:

*The building was **ablaze**, and we were trapped.*
(~~It was an ablaze building, …~~)

*I was **asleep** in bed when she came to tell me.*

Other adjectives that usually occur predicatively are *well* (and *unwell*), and *ill*, referring to states of health:

*His younger brother was **ill**.*

A: *You're looking **well**.*
B: *And you are.*

Very rarely *well* and *ill* may occur attributively with non-specific nouns such as *man, woman, child, patient*, etc., and *health* may occur with *ill*:

*Dad hadn't been a **well** man for years.*

*Whatever feelings a wife may have, she must not add to her **ill** husband's problems.*

*Two **critically ill** patients were admitted by the hospital late last night.*

*He retired because of **ill** health.*

Adjectives with similar meanings can be substituted in the attributive function for some of the predicative-only adjectives. For example, *live* can substitute for *alive*; *lone* can substitute for *alone*; *sick* can substitute for *ill* and *unwell*; *sleeping* can substitute for *asleep*:

*It's better for digestion if the yoghurts are made with **live** cultures.*
(~~alive~~)

*It's very much a book for the **lone** traveller.*
(~~alone~~)

*Her **sick** child keeps stopping her from working.*
(~~ill~~)

[proverb]
*Let **sleeping** dogs lie.*
(~~asleep~~)

Different attributive and predicative meanings 240c

Some of the adjectives used attributively in 240a above have a different meaning when used in the predicative function:

*It's **sheer** chaos.*
(intensifier meaning: attributive only)

*Care is needed on some of the stretches of path because the cliffs are **sheer**.*
(very steep/vertical; may be used attributively or, as here, predicatively)

*... the **late** actor William Holden ...*
(deceased/dead; attributive only)

*The train was **late** again.*
(behind schedule; may be used attributively or, as here, predicatively)

*Of course there's going to be a **certain** amount of risk involved, but you've got to trust me on this.*
(particular but not specified; attributive only)

*I'm not **absolutely certain**, but I think it's very unlikely.*
(sure/definite; normally predicative only)

Complex attributive adjective phrases 240d

When degree modifiers are used in attributive adjective phrases, their position varies. Different degree modifiers require different positions for the adjective phrase in relation to the indefinite article.

Positions of indefinite article and degree modifiers

example	comments
*a/an **very/fairly/moderately/extremely tall** man*	typical position: indefinite article + intensifier + adjective
	quite and *rather* are special cases
	for *quite*:
***quite** a **tall** man*	most frequent position: intensifier + indefinite article + adjective
*a **quite tall** man*	less frequent position: indefinite article + intensifier + adjective
	for *rather*:
*a **rather tall** man*	most frequent position: indefinite article + intensifier + adjective
***rather** a **tall** man*	less frequent position: intensifier + indefinite article + adjective A-Z 66 *Quite*; 67 *Rather*
as/so tall** a man **as him	*as/so* + adjective + indefinite article + noun + complement
*a man **as/so tall as him***	indefinite article + noun + *as/so* + adjective + complement (less frequent in writing but more frequent in informal speech)
*a man **this/that tall***	indefinite article + noun + *this/that* + adjective
***this/that tall** a man*	*this/that* + adjective + indefinite article + noun (less frequent)
***How tall a man** is he?* *I don't know **how tall a man** he is.*	*how* + adjective + indefinite article + noun

*We kept in touch for **quite a long time**.*

*He seemed **a rather childish, impetuous fellow**.*

*But this is not **as big a problem as it might first appear**.*

*He was willing enough, but my sister was good and virtuous, and hated his brother with **a hatred as strong as mine**.*

*It's not **that big a place**.*

ORDER OF ATTRIBUTIVE ADJECTIVE PHRASES 241

Lists of adjectives

When a noun phrase is premodified by more than one adjective, there is a preferred order for the adjectives. For example, colour normally precedes material:

*A **yellow plastic** container was found at the scene of the crime.*
(~~A plastic yellow container was found …~~)

Shape normally precedes material and material normally precedes purpose:

*You need one of those **round**, **wooden**, **bathing** tubs.*

References to place or origin usually come after colour or shape and before material:

*You need one of those **round**, **Swedish**, **wooden**, **bathing** tubs.*
(~~You need one of those bathing, Swedish, wooden, round tubs.~~)

Evaluative adjectives which describe opinions or attitudes often come before more neutrally descriptive ones:

*She's a **remarkable old** woman. She's just got such a **fantastic**, **long** memory.*
(~~She's an old remarkable woman. She's just got such a long fantastic memory.~~)

The most neutral sequence of adjective types may be summarised as:

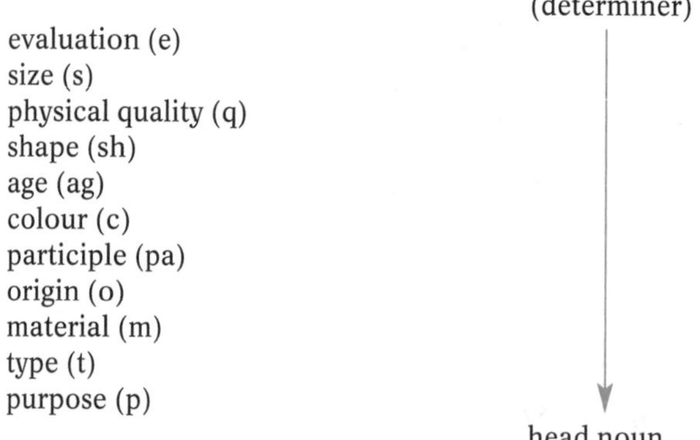

An example including a number of these types would be:

(e) **(s)** **(q)** **(ag)** **(c)** **(o)** **(p)**
*These **wonderful**, **monumental**, **strong**, **old**, **grey**, **Indian**, **log-carrying** elephants of Northern Thailand …*
(an invented example to illustrate the possibilities)

A noun phrase which included all these types would be extremely rare.

Examples of multiple attributive adjectives involving *beautiful*:

(e) (sh)
*You can also sit in the **beautiful semicircular** courthouse and listen to the trial of a farmer accused of fraud.*

It was designed by Bror Marklund and the whole hall unbelievably won the
(e) (o) (p)
*1964 award for the **most beautiful Swedish public** building.*

(e) (pa)
*… the **beautiful walled** city of Avila, birthplace of Saint Teresa; …*

(e) (s) (ag)
*It was a **beautiful little old** church.*

(e) (c) (pa)
*Where was that **just most beautiful black-and-white timbered** house?*

Adjectives joined by *and*

Some lists of adjectives are joined by *and*. When a list of adjectives occurs predicatively, the penultimate and final adjectives are normally joined by *and*:

*It was **wet, wild and windy**. How can anyone forget a night like that?*

And occurs less commonly when the list of adjectives is in an attributive position:

*A **tall, dark, mysterious** stranger entered the room.*

And can occur when two or more adjectives of the same category are used, or when the adjectives refer to different parts of the same thing:

*He drives a **red and black** Ferrari.*

⇢ 539 **Glossary** for any unfamiliar terms

Adverbs and adverb phrases

Adverbs and adverb phrases

INTRODUCTION 242

Adverbs, the fourth major open word class, have strong affinities with adjectives. Many adverbs are derived from adjectives, mostly by adding the suffix *-ly*.
(··› **162 Adverbs** for a full description of the construction of adverbs.)

adjective	adverb
nice	*nicely*
beautiful	*beautifully*
fond	*fondly*
slow	*slowly*

Most adverbs, like most adjectives, are gradable: they can be modified by other (degree) adverbs, including comparative forms, to form adverb phrases which are very similar in their structural characteristics to adjective phrases:

*She sings **really beautifully**.*
(compare: She has a really beautiful voice.)

*He played **more skilfully** this time.*
(compare: He was more skilful this time.)

Adverb phrases most typically function as adjuncts in the clause structure, but may also occur as complements:

*I ate my dinner **very slowly**.*
(adjunct)

*Could you put it **just there** please?*
(complement, required by *put*)

*Your sister's **here**.*
(complement of *be*)

However, adverb phrases differ from adjective phrases in their function. Adjective phrases most typically modify noun phrases (or are used in the predicate of the clause to state a quality of a noun phrase). Adverb phrases typically modify verb phrases, adjectives and other adverbs. Some adverbs modify whole clauses or sentences:

*I think a doctor or a nurse should be a **careful** person, and she isn't.*
(adjective: modifying the noun *person*)

*I was always very **careful** not to offend them.*
(adjective: predicative, describing the subject *I*)

*They walked **carefully** along the edge of the canal.*
(adverb: modifying the verb phrase; answers the question '*How* did they walk?')
(~~They walked careful along the edge of the canal.~~)

Adjectives cannot modify verbs:

She spoke angrily.
(~~She spoke angry.~~)

Here are some examples of how adverbs modify different items:

*Talk **properly**!*
(modifying a verb – *talk*)

*An **extremely** tall man came round the corner.*
(modifying an adjective – *tall*)

*The business in Holland went **remarkably** smoothly.*
(modifying another adverb – *smoothly*)

***Only** someone very stupid would say that.*
(modifying a noun phrase – *someone very stupid*)

*We've got our silver wedding **soon**, so we're planning a few days away.*
(modifying the whole clause)

***Frankly**, when he smiles, it terrifies me.*
(modifying the whole sentence)

Adverbs do not normally have inflected forms, but a few, most of which are identical in form to adjectives, inflect for comparison (e.g. *far*, *fast*, *hard*, *high*, *long*, *low*):

*We haven't got very **far** with that yet.*

*That's probably the area where they've gone **furthest**.*

*But the happy life did not last **long**.*

*You know, she'd be quite happy to stay **longer**.*

465 Comparative and superlative adverbs

ADVERB PHRASES 243

Adverbs function as the head of adverb phrases.

An adverb may function alone as the head of the adverb phrase or it may have dependents of various kinds.

In general, these dependents are similar in type to those found in adjective phrases – partly because most adverbs are related to adjectives and partly because many adverbs, like many adjectives, are gradable.

Examples of simple adverb phrases (head only) and complex adverb phrases (head + dependents) are given in the table below.

Simple and complex adverb phrases (adverb phrases are in green, adverb heads are in bold)

example	dependents
*You **rarely** get a full break.*	head only
***Personally** I'm not fond of ice cream.*	head only
*The six weeks went by very **quickly***	premodifier + head
*Dr Smith wrote back fairly **promptly***	premodifier + head
*It's amazing how **quickly** you get used to it.*	premodifier + head
*But **luckily** enough, neighbours did see them and called the police.*	head + postmodifier
*He plays really **well** for a beginner*	premodifier + head + postmodifier
***Unfortunately** for me, I started to get ill.*	head + complement
*Its body seems to move almost **independently** of the head*	premodifier + head + complement

Occasionally, the structure may be more complex:

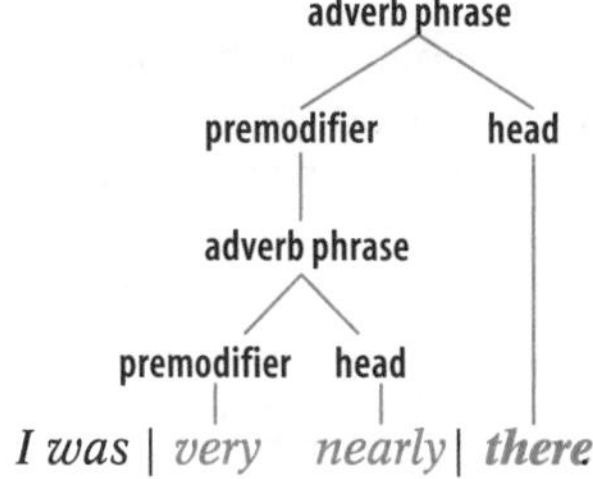

The structure of the adverb phrase may also be discontinuous, i.e. it may consist of a structure which commences before the adverb and is completed after it:

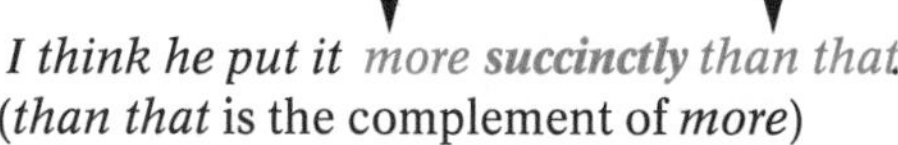

*I think he put it more **succinctly** than that*
(*than that* is the complement of *more*)

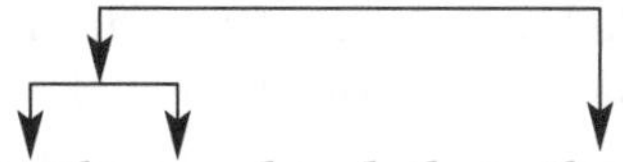

*Nuclear power stations produce electricity much more **cheaply** than other types of power station*

539 **Glossary** for any unfamiliar terms

TYPES OF MEANING 244

There are a number of different types of meaning adverb phrases can have. The important general types are shown in the table below.

Main types of meaning of adverb phrases

type	function	example
manner	refers to how something happens	*Those flowers grow **quickly**, don't they?* *The vicar spoke **very nicely**.*
place	refers to where something happens	*Many **locally** owned bookshops are cutting prices.* *Sign **here** please.*
time	refers to when something happens	*Her father died **recently**.* *He came in **very early**.*
duration	refers to length of time over which something happens	*No, I'm not staying there **permanently**.*
frequency	refers to how often something happens	*I **often** go and see them.*
degree	refers to how much, to what degree something happens	*I was **greatly** relieved when we were finally rid of her.*
focusing	focuses on or specifies an entity	Waiter: *What about you, sir?* Customer: ***Just** ice cream please.*
modal	expresses degrees of truth, possibility, necessity, etc.	*She **most probably** thinks I'm joking.*
evaluative	judges or comments on the event, gives the speaker's opinion	*I **stupidly** forgot to mention the meeting to him.*
viewpoint	expresses the perspective or standpoint from which the speaker sees things	*I **personally** don't think you would hate it, Elaine.*
linking	links and relates clauses and sentences to one another	*She wanted to study but there wasn't any provision. **However**, her younger sisters are now studying.*

→ **326b** and **326c** on the order of adverbs

ADVERBS MODIFYING PHRASES 245

Types of modification 245a

The following types of modification are common. (Adverb phrases are in bold, modified phrases are in green.)

- Adverb phrase modifying verb phrase:

*He's played **extremely well**.*

*She blushed **furiously**.*

- Adverb phrase modifying adjective phrase:

  *It was **perfectly** acceptable.*

  *Her heartbeat was **very slightly** erratic.*

- Adverb phrase modifying adverb phrase:

  *She'd worked **extremely** hard.*

  *It seems to affect different people **completely** differently.*

- Adverb phrase modifying noun phrase:

  *It's a chapel but it's **almost** a cave.*

  *It takes **quite** a dose to reach fatal levels.*

- Adverb phrase modifying prepositional phrase:

  *It's really **right** out in the country.*

  *The situation was **completely** out of control.*

Degree adverbs and focusing adverbs 245b

Degree adverbs and focusing adverbs are the most common type of adverb modifiers of phrases. These include (adverbs in bold, modified phrases in green):

Degree

absolutely	*fairly*	*slightly*
a (little) bit	*highly*	*somewhat*
almost	*a lot*	*terribly*
awfully	*lots*	*too*
completely	*perfectly*	*totally*
doubly	*pretty*	*utterly*
enough	*quite*	*very*
entirely	*rather*	
extremely	*remarkably*	

*I wouldn't mind living **a bit** longer.*

*Oh that will make it **doubly** attractive won't it?*

*The food was **pretty** awful actually.*

***Quite** obviously they don't want to push anything under the carpet.*

*They don't normally have three together so it seemed **rather** strange.*

*He's going to be **terribly** upset.*

*His sister is **totally** different from his brother.*

Focusing

especially	*largely*	*simply*
generally	*only*	
just	*particularly*	

*They'd be upset, **especially** my father, if I didn't try.*

*I just feel **generally** fed up.*

Evaluative adverbs 245c

Evaluative adverbs are also used to modify phrases:

*But something has gone **oddly** wrong in the meantime.*

*The family, two brothers and a sister, lived **curiously** isolated.*

EVALUATIVE, VIEWPOINT AND LINKING (DISJUNCT AND CONJUNCT) ADVERBS 246

Often adverbs are fully integrated in the clause (244 above, the examples of manner, place and time adverbs). However, adverbs may be less integrated in the clause structure and may modify the whole sentence or utterance. Evaluative and viewpoint adverbs often function in this way. Adverbs of this type are referred to as disjunct adverbs:

*What was more, **oddly**, he seemed to have bought enough for two.*
(evaluative)

***Personally**, I think it's a waste of time.*
(viewpoint)

Linking adverbs express a logical relationship (e.g. cause and consequence, sequence in time, contrast) between two clauses or sentences. These may be referred to as conjunct adverbs:

*The overwhelming majority of big-name French chefs are, as they have always been, men. There is one place, **however**, that for 100 years and more has provided an exception – Lyon, close to the Swiss and Italian borders and France's second city.*

*The bad news is that your shares are almost certainly overvalued at present, as is the entire banking sector. The good news is that they are probably worth keeping **anyway**.*

COPULAR VERBS (*BE, SEEM*) AND COMPLEMENTATION 247

Copular verbs such as *be, seem, become, get, grow, look, smell, taste* describe the state of people and things, and are complemented by adjectives, not adverbs:

*Hmm, it **smells** a bit **funny**.*
(~~It smells a bit funnily.~~)

*It **looks interesting**.*

*It **seems odd** that we were not told.*

But some of these verbs can also be used to denote actions, in which case they may be used with adverbs:

*I **looked briefly** through the papers.*
(action of looking)

*She **smelt** it **carefully** before drinking it.*
(action of smelling)

ADVERBS USED AS SHORT RESPONSES 248

Some degree, modal and focusing adverbs occur very frequently in spoken language as single-word responses indicating the respondent's attitude or stance:

A: *That's a fair comment, isn't it?*
B: ***Absolutely.***

A: *It's more for the kids, isn't it?*
B: *You think so?*
A: *Yeah, **definitely**.*

A: *He might have been away at the time.*
B: *Well, **possibly**.*

A: *Didn't you think it was just a joke?*
B: *Yeah, **probably**.*

A: *She's obviously going to tear it up and throw it in the bin.*
B: ***Precisely.***

A: *Well, you wear a little black dress to clubs or to a party.*
B: *Yeah, **exactly**.*

A: *Not easy, mind you, accommodating everything in our bedroom.*
B: *Well, yes, **quite**.*

Not really is also very commonly used in this way to soften a bare *no*-answer:

A: *Have you been in smaller classes before?*
B: ***Not really.***

Note that *certainly* most typically occurs as a single-word reply to a request for a service or favour (compare *definitely* above, which strengthens the force of an utterance):

[to a waiter]
A: *Can I have the bill please?*
B: ***Certainly.***

Intensifying adverbs often occur alone in responses:

A: *It's hot in here.*
B: *Yes, **very**.*

A: *She's a very bright kid.*
B: *She is, yes, **incredibly**.*

→ 95 Response tokens

ADVERBS AND DISCOURSE MARKERS 249

Most discourse markers belong to the general class of adverbs. However, it is their function as organisers of larger stretches of conversation or text which qualify them for classification as discourse markers. The discourse marking functions of adverbs include signalling closure and pre-closure, labelling of text segments, topic changes, asides.

Compare the use of *anyway* as a linking (conjunct) adverb and as a discourse marker:

*I shouldn't be jealous but I am **anyway**.*
(conjunct)

A: *Sorry. You know what I mean. Sounds like you're gonna post it or something.*
B: *No.*
A: *Oh. **Anyway**, I'll have to go cos I've got to ring Bob.*
B: *Right.*
(discourse marker, signalling closure)

→ 108 Discourse markers

Prepositions and prepositional phrases

Prepositions and prepositional phrases

INTRODUCTION 250

Prepositions express a relation in space between two or more entities or a relation in time between two events, or various other abstract relations:

*Don't walk **on** the grass.*

*She fell asleep **during** the film.*

***After** the interview, they phoned the police.*

*She sent me an email **about** the conference.*

Prepositional phrases (in green) consist of a preposition as head (bold), and a complement. The complement is usually a noun phrase, though it may sometimes be an *-ing* clause or, less frequently, a *wh*-clause:

*They decided to meet **in** a park.*

***During** the war they moved **to** Wales.*

*They left just **after** six o'clock.*

*It's a good way **of** losing weight.*

*He passed the exam **by** working every night.*

*She went back **to** where she used to work.*

The complement of a preposition may also be an adverb phrase (usually one of place or time):

*Just come **through** here and I'll show you where the problem is.*

*Many of these treatments were used **until** quite recently.*

Prepositional phrases as complements of a preposition are less common:

*He looked at me **from** behind the tree.*

*I can't see you **until** after lunch.*

Prepositions are not followed by the base form of a verb or by *that*-clauses:

*Where's that thing **for** chopping vegetables?*
(~~Where's that thing for chop vegetables?~~)

They were disappointed that we couldn't come.
(or: They were disappointed by the fact that we couldn't come.)
(~~They were disappointed by that we couldn't come.~~)

We're relying ***on*** *him being there to help us.*
(~~We're relying on that he will be there to help us.~~)

We're looking forward ***to*** *see****ing*** *you soon.*
(preposition *to* + *-ing* form)
(~~We're looking forward to see you soon.~~)

To plus the base form of a verb is called the *to*-infinitive and is not a prepositional phrase:

We're hoping ***to see*** *you soon.*
(*to*-infinitive)

SIMPLE PREPOSITIONS 251

There are over 100 prepositions in English, including complex and marginal prepositions. A list of more than 50 common simple prepositions is given here. Some word pairs have over time become fused as simple prepositions (e.g. *upon*, *into*):

aboard
about
above
across
after
against
along
amid
among
around
as
at
before
behind
below
beneath
beside
besides
between
beyond
but
by
despite
down
during
except
for
from
in
inside
into
like
near
of
off
on
onto
opposite
outside
over
past
round
since
than
through
to
toward
towards
under
underneath
unlike
until
up
upon
via
with
within
without

539 **Glossary** for any unfamiliar terms

COMPLEX PREPOSITIONS 252

Although most prepositions are single words, some pairs and groups of words operate like single prepositions:

__As for__ me, I'd rather have a holiday in January, when it's cold and wet.

The street below was empty __except for__ a girl walking along sobbing quietly and a boy behind her trying to explain.

I'd never say that __in front of__ the children.

There'll be __up to__ 50 people there, I would think.

Pairs and groups of words which function in this way include:

ahead of	*for lack of*	*near to*
apart from	*in addition to*	*on account of*
as for	*in aid of*	*on top of*
as of	*in exchange for*	*out of*
as well as	*in favour of*	*outside of*
because of	*in front of*	*owing to*
but for	*in line with*	*prior to*
by means of	*in place of*	*subsequent to*
by virtue of	*inside of*	*such as*
due to	*in spite of*	*thanks to*
except for	*instead of*	*up to*

PREPOSITIONS AND OTHER WORD CLASSES 253

Prepositions and conjunctions 253a

Some words which are prepositions also function as conjunctions. Among the most common are *after, as, before, since, until*. When followed by a noun phrase, they act as prepositions; when followed by a clause, they act as conjunctions:

__After__ the meeting he rang me to apologise.
(preposition)

__After__ we spoke this afternoon, he rang me to apologise.
(conjunction)

Has morale improved, __since__ his explanation?
(preposition)

Has morale improved __since__ he explained everything to them?
(conjunction)

Prepositions and adverbs 253b

Several words which are prepositions also belong to the word class of adverbs. These are often called prepositional adverbs. Common prepositional adverbs are: *about, across, around, before, beyond, down, in, inside, near, on, opposite, past, through, under, up, within*. Prepositional adverbs normally stand alone:

Too many visitors were left to walk ***in*** *the castle unsupervised.*
(preposition)

We stayed ***in*** *last night.*
(prepositional adverb: *in* = at home)

PREPOSITIONAL MEANINGS: LITERAL AND METAPHORICAL 254

Many common prepositions can indicate a wide range of relations in space and time and other more abstract relations. For example, *at, in* and *on* can express relations in time and space as well as abstract relations:

at *6.30*

in *the garden*

on *New Year's Day*

to feel ***at*** *ease*

the woman dressed ***in*** *white*

a book ***on*** *the history of aircraft*

The more abstract relations indicated by prepositions can often be seen as metaphorical extensions of their literal meanings. This is particularly the case with prepositions which refer to space. Basic spatial prepositions are often extended metaphorically to more abstract meanings:

That map you need is ***behind*** *the filing-cabinet.*
(basic spatial sense)

The whole nation was ***behind*** *the team.*
(gave support)

The socialists are ***behind*** *the communists in the polls.*
(competition as a race)

Who's ***behind*** *his plan?*
(describing agency: Who is responsible for his plan?)

What's the reason ***behind*** *his resignation?*
(describing causes)

Beyond *the gardens, there were open fields.*
(basic spatial sense)

→ **539 Glossary** for any unfamiliar terms

Trigonometry was just ***beyond*** *me.*
(Trigonometry was just too difficult for me.)

You'll need to put a jacket ***over*** *that blouse. It's cold.*

There was a serious dispute ***over*** *performance-related pay.*

Note that, when used metaphorically, the preposition can usually be modified by an adverb of degree:

The team was ***completely with*** *the manager.*
(*was with* = supported)
(metaphorical)

I went on holiday ***with*** *an old friend of mine.*
(~~I went on holiday completely with an old friend of mine.~~)

STRUCTURE OF PREPOSITIONAL PHRASES 255

Premodification 255a

Prepositions may be premodified. This applies mainly to prepositions with a gradable spatial or temporal meaning:

They went deep ***into*** *the forest.*

She doesn't like flying and only started to relax when we were high ***above*** *the clouds.*

It was too foggy to see but the hotel was only a short distance ***in front of*** *them.*

Be careful. The lamp's just ***above*** *your head.*

They arrived just ***before*** *the guests.*

Complementation by a verb 255b

The form of the verb which follows a preposition is the *-ing* form:

Is she responsible ***for handling*** *all the phone calls and for managing the office?*

The new director has devoted herself ***to raising*** *funds.*

Do you think they have any interest ***in selling*** *the house?*

Sometimes the subject of the verb occurs between the preposition and the *-ing* form. If this subject is a pronoun, in everyday informal styles the object form of the pronoun is used:

Within a few hours ***of*** *us* ***putting*** *the ad in the paper, we had over twenty phone calls.*

Because of *them* ***being*** *so reasonable, at least compared with the rest of the group, the airline made them wait to catch the next flight.*

In more formal styles the possessive pronoun form is used:

*Well, this may result **in his receiving** lots of unwanted junk mail.*
(less formal: This may result in him receiving lots of unwanted junk mail.)

also **285f Verbs normally only followed by *-ing***

A number of verbs, such as *arrange, ask, long, wait*, are followed by the preposition *for* + noun/pronoun + *to*-infinitive. In such cases, *for* is not followed by an *-ing* form:

*They've **arranged for** the cases **to be transferred** direct onto the flight.*

*Didn't you **ask for** it **to be delivered** by midday?*

*She's been **longing for** David **to call** her.*

*I've been **waiting for** the bank statement **to clear** it all up.*
(~~I've been waiting for the bank statement clearing it all up.~~)

43 *For*

FUNCTION OF PREPOSITIONAL PHRASES 256

Adjuncts

Prepositional phrases commonly function as adjuncts in the clause:

***During the visit** the inspectors will review the factory very thoroughly.*

Prepositional verbs

Prepositional phrases also commonly function as the complements of verbs. Where a special preposition is required to introduce the complement of the verb, such verbs are called prepositional verbs:

*It **depends on** the weather.*

*Please **listen to** me.*

*She has decided to **confide in** her doctor.*

*I promise to **look at** the results this afternoon.*

235f, 235g

Phrasal-prepositional verbs

Sometimes the preposition is preceded by an adverb particle, and the verb + adverb particle + preposition structure forms a verb with a unitary meaning. These verbs are called phrasal-prepositional verbs:

*I don't know how she'll **put up with** the noise.*

*We're **looking forward to** the match.*

Predicative complements

Prepositional phrases also act as predicative complements, most typically of place:

*I was **at the office** all day.*

*Just put it **on my desk**, please.*

Postmodifiers and complements

Prepositional phrases act as postmodifiers or as complements in noun phrases (in green):

*That guy **in the pub last night** was getting on my nerves.*
(postmodifier)

*It was in the shape **of a triangle**.*
(complement)

They also act as postmodifiers and complements in adjective and adverb phrases (in green):

*She's quite tall **for a five-year-old**, isn't she?*
(postmodifier)

*Both brothers were good **at football**.*
(complement)

*He performed quite well **on the whole**.*
(postmodifier)

*Luckily **for me** there was another train just half an hour later.*
(postmodifier)

Premodifiers

Numerals may be premodified by a prepositional phrase:

*Children of **under** fourteen years of age will not be admitted.*

*It'll cost **just over** two hundred pounds.*

Preposition stranding 257

A preposition is described as stranded when it is separated from its complement:

complement **preposition**
***What** was she referring **to**?*
(preposition stranding)

prep + comp
***To what** was she referring?*
(more formal, without preposition stranding)

In traditional style guides, advice is often given never to end a sentence with a preposition, meaning that prepositions should not be stranded. However, the situation concerning the usage of prepositions is rather more complex than such advice suggests.

Preposition stranding occurs in the following main structures:

*Who did you talk **to**?* (*wh*-interrogatives)

*I need someone to go **with**.* (relative clauses)

*It's the only garage which we have any confidence **in**.* (relative clauses)

*Tell me what they are so afraid **of**.* (indirect *wh*-interrogatives)

*It's being looked **into**.* (passives)

*It's too slippery to walk **on**.* (infinitive complements)

Preposition stranding is common in informal styles. In formal structures, prepositions tend to occur with their complements:

*He is the officer we'd been talking **with**.* (informal)

*He is the officer **with whom** we'd been talking.* (formal)

*Which building was the smoke coming **out of**?* (informal)

***Out of which** building was the smoke coming?* (formal)

When a prepositional phrase is the complement of a verb (*went **to the match*** in the example below), the stranded preposition may occur before or after the prepositional phrase:

*He's the friend I went to the match **with** last Wednesday.*
(or: *He's the friend I went **with** to the match last Wednesday.*)

If the context allows for ellipsis, a reduced *wh*-question may consist simply of a *wh*-word + stranded preposition:

A: *We're **going** on holiday next week.*
B: *Oh, **where to**?*

A: *I've got to buy a birthday card.*
B: *Oh yeah. **Who for**?*

When the meaning is obvious from the text, stranded prepositions of place may occasionally be omitted, especially in informal conversation:

A: *Do you like Tokyo?*
B: *Yes, it's a very safe place to live.*
(understood: Yes, it's a very safe place to live in.)

A: *I'm going out tonight.*
B: *Oh yeah, where?*
(understood: Where to?)

Some prepositions, including frequent prepositions such as *during* and *since*, resist stranding:

***During which of the terms** did it happen, spring or autumn?*
(preferred to: ~~Which of the terms did it happen during?~~)

***Since when** has the train service stopped?*
(~~When has the train service stopped since?~~)

→ also **472–475 Word order and focus; 94 Ellipsis**

5 *About*; 6 *Above*; 7 *According to*; 10 *After, afterwards*; 11 *Against*; 21 *At*; 24 *Before*; 26 *Between, among*; 32 *Down*; 33 *During*; 43 *For*; 55 *Of*; 63 *Over*; 79 *With*

Word structure and word formation

Word structure and word formation

INTRODUCTION 258

Word structure (morphology) 258a

The word is the basic unit which relates the grammar of a language to its vocabulary. Words have internal structure which indicates their grammatical identity (e.g. that the word is plural, or past tense) and their lexical identity (e.g. that the word *unhappiness* is a noun with negative meaning referring to emotions).

Grammar is generally divided into the study of the structure of sentences, which is called syntax, and the study of the internal structure of words, which is called morphology.

Words are composed of morphemes. A morpheme is the smallest unit of meaning. Some words consist of just one morpheme; some consist of several.

In the table below, the words *dog* and *drink* cannot be broken down into smaller meaningful units. They are words which consist of one morpheme.

Examples of words and their morphemes

word	morpheme(s)
dog	*dog*
drink	*drink*
dogs	*dog* + *s*
drank	*drink* + irregular past *a*
drinkable	*drink* + *able*
impenetrable	*im* + *penetr* + *able*
intolerable	*in* + *toler* + *able*
irregular	*ir* + *regular*
midday	*mid* + *day*
homesick	*home* + *sick*
homesickness	*home* + *sick* + *ness*

In the table we may note various kinds of morpheme.

Affixes

Some of the morphemes are attached to the beginning or the end of words. These are affixes. Affixes attached to the beginning of words are prefixes; those attached to the ends of words are suffixes.

Inflectional morphemes

Some of the affixes express grammatical relations (e.g. the *-s* on *dogs* indicates plural; the past form *drank* contrasts with the present *drink*). These are inflectional morphemes.

Derivational morphemes

Some of the affixes express lexical relations by forming new or different words when attached to basic words (e.g. *-able* indicates that something is possible; *mid-* indicates the middle part of something). These are derivational morphemes.

Allomorphs

Some morphemes have a variation in form, even though their meaning is the same (e.g. ***im**-penetrable*, ***in**-edible*, ***ir**-regular*, all meaning 'not'; *-ible* and *-able* both meaning 'can be done'). These variations are known as allomorphs. Allomorphs are also seen in inflections , e.g. noun plurals (*book**s***, *glass**es***) and verb endings (*seem**s***, *watch**es***).

Compounds

Whole words may combine with each other (e.g. *home* and *sick*). Such combinations are called compounds.

Word, stem and base 258b

The form of a word to which prefixes and suffixes attach is called the stem. A simple word of one morpheme consists of a stem only. Words consisting of a stem plus prefixes and/or suffixes are complex words.

Examples of words showing stems and affixes

	word	stem	prefixes/suffixes
1	*snowy*	*snow*	*-y*
2	*untraceable*	*trace*	*un-* *-able*
3	*deduce, reduce, produce*	*-duce*	*de-* *re-* *pro-*
4	*capture, captive*	*capt-*	*-ure* *-ive*
5	*recapture*	*capt-*	*re-* *-ure*

The stem may not necessarily be a whole independent word, as can be seen in the table.

Snow and *trace* are free stems; they can stand alone. The forms *-duce* and *capt-* are bound stems; they can only be used in combination with prefixes or suffixes.

The stem on its own may be restricted to certain combinations. In example **5** in the table the prefix *re-* can only attach to *capture* (we cannot say *recaptive*). In *recapture, capture* is called the base. A base may already include an affix. In the following words, the base is in bold:

***grammar**ian*

***grammatical**ity*

*un**grammatical***

Inflectional morphemes (bold) attach to whole lexemes (in green):

*Grammarian**s** have often disagree**d** on this point.*

*Poetry de-familiarize**s** the everyday.*

*We never send postcard**s**.*

Inflectional morphology of various kinds is central to many of the chapters in this book. This chapter describes the main types of inflection, but deals mainly with lexical morphology, i.e. in the four main word classes, noun, verb, adjective, adverb. Grammatical morphology is dealt with under areas such as tense, aspect, person, voice and number in other chapters.

INFLECTION 259

English does not make much use of word structure to express grammatical meanings and, unlike other languages, the inflection of words is limited. Inflections in English are realised by the suffixes in the table below.

Inflectional suffixes

suffix	examples
noun plurals (e.g. *-s,-es,-en*)	*cars, bush**es**, ox**en***
3rd person singular present tense *-s*	*he work**s**, it rise**s***
past tense *-ed*	*we walk**ed**; I smok**ed***
-ing form as progressive aspect	*she's runn**ing**; we were laugh**ing***
-ed form as *-ed* participle	*they've land**ed**, he was beat**en***
comparative forms *-er, -est*	*he's small**er**, I'm small**est***
negative verb inflection *-n't*	*I ca**n't**; they wo**n't***

Inflection also sometimes occurs through internal vowel or consonant change.

Examples of inflection through vowel or consonant change

*g**oo**se*	*g**ee**se*	plural
*h**a**ng*	*h**u**ng*	past tense
*f**a**r*	*f**u**rther*	comparative
advise	*advice*	verb to noun

Sometimes an inflected form is identical to its non-inflected form (for example, where the singular and plural have the same form). This is called syncretism.

Examples of syncretism

deer	*deer*	plural
set	*set*	past tense, *-ed* participle

Sometimes, an alternative word is used for a particular inflectional meaning, a process known as suppletion.

Examples of suppletion

be	*am, are, is*	present tense
go	*went*	past tense

Inflections do not change the meaning of a word. *Walk* and *walked* have the same lexical meaning; they are forms of the same lexeme. *Responsible* and *irresponsible* have different meanings; they are different lexemes.

539 **Glossary** for any unfamiliar terms

WORD FORMATION 260

Present-day English has four main processes of word formation: prefixation, suffixation, conversion and compounding.

Prefixation

Prefixation involves adding a prefix to a base or stem:

__ante__natal, __ante__room
__de__criminalise, __de__form
__post__-1945, __post__graduate
__pro__-life, __pro__-Europe
__un__tidy, __un__happiness, __un__usual, __un__democratic

Suffixation

Suffixation involves adding a suffix to a base or stem:

age__ism__, terror__ism__
king__dom__, free__dom__
ident__ify__
reason__able__, unprofit__able__
unhappi__ly__, slow__ly__

Conversion

Conversion involves the change of a word from one word class to another. For example, the verbs *to screen* and *to fax* are formed from the nouns *screen* and *fax*. The verb *to narrow* is formed from the adjective *narrow*; the noun *love* from the verb *to love*:

*The film is an absolute **must** for all lovers of Westerns.*
(noun from verb)

*Can we **microwave** it?*
(verb from noun)

*Internet **downloads** can be expensive.*
(noun from verb)

*They decided that they had to **broaden** his appeal.*
(verb from adjective)

Less often, internal vowel change or one form replacing another (suppletion) may indicate a change in word class or sub-class.

Examples of change in word class through vowel change and suppletion

hot	*heat*	adjective ➛ noun
rise	*raise*	intransitive verb ➛ transitive verb (change in sub-class)
deep	*depth*	adjective ➛ noun (plus suffix; similarly, *wide* ➛ *width*)
mouth	*oral*	noun ➛ adjective (suppletion)

Some words can change class by a shift in stress from one syllable to another. Typically, the stress is on the first syllable when the word is a noun and on the second syllable when the word is a verb, e.g. ***re**cord* (noun, with stress on the first syllable) becomes *re**cord*** (verb, with stress on the second syllable).

Compounding

Compounding involves linking together two or more bases to create a new word. Normally, the first item identifies a key feature of the second word. For example, the two bases *head* and *ache* can combine to form the compound word *headache*:

award-winning
helpline
house-proud
input
long-running
postcard

→ 266 Hyphenation

In addition to the main processes, English allows words to be formed by abbreviation (which includes clipping, acronyms and blends) (→ 267a), and back-formation (→ 267b).

PREFIXES 261

The main prefixes used in English

prefix	meaning	examples
a-	(i) in a particular way or condition (ii) without (note different pronunciation)	(i) *awake, asleep* (first syllable pronounced /ə/) (ii) *atypical, amoral* (first syllable pronounced /eɪ/)
anti-	against or opposed to	*antibiotic, anticlimax, anti-nuclear*
ante-	before	*antenatal, antechamber*
auto-	self	*autobiography, autograph*
de-	to reverse, to alter	*decommission, deform, destabilise*
dis-	to reverse, to remove	*disarm, disagree, dismantle, disqualify*
down-	to lower, to reduce	*downsize, downgrade*
dys-	not regular or normal	*dyslexia, dysfunctional*
extra-	beyond	*extramural, extraordinary, extraterrestrial*
half	one of two equal parts	*halfway, half-moon*
hyper-	extreme	*hyperactive, hyperinflation*
hypo-	less than usual, too little	*hypothermia, hypotension*
il-, im-, in-, ir-	not	*illegal, impossible, intolerant, irresponsible*
inter-	between	*interactive, intercontinental, international*
intra-	within	*intra-departmental, intramural*
intro-	directed within	*introvert, introspection*
mega-	very big, important	*megabyte, megastar*
mid-	middle	*midday, mid-September*
mis-	incorrectly, badly	*misinterpret, misunderstand, misinform*
non-	not	*non-smoker, non-stick, non-believer*
over-	too much	*overeat, overindulgent*

continued overleaf

continued

prefix	meaning	examples
out-	go beyond/exceed	*outdo, outshine, outbid*
para-	(i) beyond; (ii) similar or connected to	(i) *paranormal*; (ii) *paramedic, paramilitary*
post-	after	*post-war, postpone*
pre-	before	*pre-1990, predetermined, pre-set*
pro-	in favour of	*pro-Europe, pro-nationalisation*
re-	again	*reapply, refocus*
semi-	half	*semicircle, semiconscious*
sub-	under, below, secondary	*subway, subtitle, subzero, subnormal*
super-	above, beyond, excessive	*superstructure, superhero, supersensitive*
tele-	at a distance	*telecommunication, television, telepathy*
trans-	across	*transatlantic, transmit*
ultra-	extremely	*ultralight, ultrasonic*
un-	(i) remove; (ii) reverse, not	(i) *undress, undo*; (ii) *unhappy, unlucky*
up-	make higher, increase	*upgrade, uplift, upscale*
under-	beneath, less than	*underworld, under-age, underestimate*
vice	deputy	*vice-president, viceroy*

Prefixes which change the class of a word

Prefixes do not typically change the class of a word. One example is the prefix *be-*, which can change a noun into a verb (e.g. *bewitch, besiege*), or an adjective into a verb (e.g. *belittle, becalm*). Similarly, the prefixes *em-* and *en-* can create a verb from a noun or adjective (e.g. *embitter, embolden, encode, endanger, enlarge, enlighten*).

SUFFIXES 262

Prefixes have a semantic role; suffixes also have a semantic role but they additionally change the class of a word. The tables below show the common suffixes by word class (together with an indication of the most common types of class change where appropriate).

Suffixes which form nouns

suffix	examples
-age	(count to non-count noun) *baggage, mileage*
-al	(verb to noun) *arrival, burial, withdrawal*
-ant/-ent	*assistant, coolant, deodorant, student*
-ance/-ence	(verb to noun) *defiance, insistence, pretence*
-arium/-orium	*aquarium, crematorium, sanatorium*
-dom	*boredom, freedom, stardom, wisdom*
-ee	*absentee, devotee, trainee*
-ar/-er/-or	(verb to noun) *registrar, singer, indicator*
-ie/-y	*kiddie, daddy, puppy*
-hood	*childhood, motherhood, knighthood*
-ism	*defeatism, Marxism, pacifism*
-ist	*Buddhist, exhibitionist, impressionist*
-ity/-ty	*deity, rarity, similarity, cruelty, casualty*

continued

suffix	examples
-let/-ette	(diminutives) *hamlet, booklet, kitchenette*
-ment	(verb to noun) *amazement, disappointment*
-ness	(adjective to noun) *friendliness, kindness*
-ary/-ery/-ory	*library, fishery, laboratory*
-(r)y	(verb to noun) *entry, inquiry, bribery*
-ship	*craftsmanship, membership*
-sion/-tion/-xion	*confusion, ammunition, expedition, infection, complexion*
-(at)ion	(verb to noun) *formation, resignation*

Suffixes which form adjectives

suffix	examples
-ble	(verb to adjective) *readable, workable, responsible*
-al	*informal, criminal*
-ed	(noun to adjective) *bearded, long-sighted, short-tailed*
-en	(noun to adjective) *woollen, golden, wooden*
-ese	(noun to adjective) *Japanese, Taiwanese, Vietnamese*
-ful	*grateful, helpful, mindful*
-i	(noun to adjective) *Pakistani, Iraqi, Omani*
-ic(al)	(noun to adjective) *heroic, poetic, historic(al)*
-ish	(noun to adjective) *foolish, Danish, Polish*
-ive	(verb to adjective) *adhesive, offensive, productive*
-ian	(noun to adjective) *Brazilian, Christian, Iranian*
-less	*childless, priceless*
-like	*business-like, rubber-like*
-ly	(noun to adjective) *monthly, yearly, manly*
-ous	*enormous, famous, nervous*
-type	*A-type, Hollywood-type*
-y	*windy, shaky, frosty*

Suffixes which form verbs

suffix	examples
-ate	*dominate, irritate*
-en	(adjective to verb) *harden, lengthen, stiffen*
-ify	*identify, magnify*
-ise/-ize	*caramelise, Americanize*

→ 507–511 **Appendix: English spelling** for *s* and *z* spellings

Suffixes which form adverbs

suffix	examples
-ly	*slowly, aggressively*
-ward(s)	*backwards, homeward(s)*
-wise	*clockwise, edgewise*

Very occasionally, non-suffixed and suffixed forms may be used more or less synonymously (e.g. *disorient/disorientate*; *transport/transportation*).

Change of sub-class

Occasionally a suffix may change a word to a sub-class of the same word class. For example, *gun* and *gunner* are both nouns but one is inanimate, the other animate. Compare also *cook* (person) ➛ *cooker* (thing), *Berlin* (place) ➛ *Berliner* (person), *mathematics* (thing) ➛ *mathematician* (person).

-ish and *-y* in informal contexts 263

The *-ish* suffix is used widely in informal spoken English to soften or hedge numbers and quantities when precise reference is not necessary or is inappropriate:

So we're meeting at eleven, well ***elevenish****.*

I think she's ***thirtyish*** *but she looks a lot younger.*

-ish may occasionally be used on its own in informal conversation. It functions to make something deliberately vague and is not used only to refer to numbers and quantities:

A: *Did you say you'll be here at five?*
B: *Well,* ***-ish****. It depends on the traffic.*

A: *Are you hungry?*
B: ***-ish****. What about you?*

Although *-ish* is most commonly used with numbers, dates, times and quantities, it is a productive suffix and speakers creatively attach it to a wide range of words from different word classes.

Though not as frequent as - *ish*, the *-y* suffix functions in similar ways in informal contexts. It is especially used with colours:

[the speaker is talking about a blouse and is trying to decide what to wear]
But I mean I love the collar and the short turn-up sleeves. You may see them in there in your one pink deep pink and er this beautiful ***bluey*** *turquoise and a* ***beigey*** *colour which I can't wear. If they'd had white I might have tried. Well it still would have stuck out.*

It has a sort of ***woody*** *taste, doesn't it?*

What's that ***plasticky*** *thing sticking out there?*

[the speakers here are deciding about the colour of a pair of cushions]
A: *Well it's a kind of* ***orangey*** *red isn't it.*
B: *Yeah.*
A: *Or is it a* ***reddy*** *orange?*
B: *It's not a* ***reddy*** *orange.*
A: ***Orangey*** *red.*
C: *Or* ***reddish****.*

Note also the changes in spelling which are sometimes necessary with these suffixes (*red* ➛ *reddish* ➛ *reddy; plastic* ➛ *plasticky*)

CONVERSION 264

Conversion involves changing a word from one word class to another but without adding any affix. For example, when the adjective *solid* is turned into the verb *to solidify*, the suffix *-ify* is added. When the adjective *dry* is turned into the verb *to dry* or when the noun *fax* is turned into the verb *to fax*, no affix is added and the process is one of conversion. Most examples involve the conversion of verbs into nouns or nouns into verbs. The main types of conversion are:

- Verbs converted into nouns:

  cure, drink, doubt, laugh, smoke, stop (as in *bus stop*), *walk, work*

- Nouns converted into verbs:

  to bottle, to bully, to elbow, to email, to glue, to group, to head, to ship, to ski, to skin, to tutor

- Adjectives converted into verbs (including comparatives):

  to better, to calm, to clean, to dry, to empty, to faint, to lower, to smooth, to tidy, to wet

- Nouns converted into adjectives:

  ***junk** food, a **rubbish** explanation* (common in spoken English)

Conversion is a process which continues to produce new forms constantly. For example, conversion has most recently produced forms such as *to email, to impact, to text, a download.*

Less commonly, other word classes are involved in conversion:

*That kind of remark only **ups** the stress for everyone.*
(verb from preposition)

*Seeing that play is an absolute **must**.*
(noun from modal verb)

*That's a very big **if**.*
(noun from conjunction)

*You get both **ups** and **downs**.*
(nouns from prepositions)

The conversion of a sub-class of proper noun to common noun is also possible:

*Has anybody seen my **Galsworthy**?*
(copy of a book by Galsworthy)

*He has two **Ferraris**.*
(a car manufactured by Ferrari)

Whole phrases may also be converted, most commonly into adjective compounds:

*I really fancy one of those **four-wheel-drive** cars.*

→ **539 Glossary** for any unfamiliar terms

*Why don't you have a word with that **good-for-nothing** brother of his?*
*It was a **fly-on-the-wall** documentary.*

COMPOUNDS 265

General 265a

Compounds are lexemes formed from more than one base. Compounds are found in all word classes:

nouns: *pop group, car park*
adjectives: *heartbreaking, guilt-ridden, homesick*
verbs: *babysit, dry-clean*
adverbs: *good-naturedly, nevertheless, nowadays*
pronouns: *anyone, everything, nobody*
numerals: *forty-seven, two-thirds*
prepositions: *into, onto*
conjunctions: *although, whenever*

Compounds which have entered the language more recently tend to be nouns, adjectives or verbs (e.g. *answerphone* (n), *hyperactive* (adj), *downsize* (v)).

Compounds have a structure similar to the basic phrase classes such as noun or verb phrases; the final element may be seen as the head, which is modified or complemented:

*day**dream***
(modifier-type: dream during the day)

*guilt-**ridden***
(complement-type: ridden with guilt)

Some compounds involve identical or near identical or rhyming bases. Such compounds are called reduplicative and are often very informal in usage or are used in affectionate talk with and by children. For example, *bow-wow* (dog), *clever-clever, easy-peasy, goody-goody, lovey-dovey, olde-worlde, super-duper, tick-tock* (clock).

Compound nouns 265b

Compound nouns involve a range of different grammatical relationships. The pre-head item is typically a noun, a verb or a word derived from a verb, or an adjective:

noun: ***screw**driver*
verb base form: ***answer**phone*
verb *-ing* form: ***chewing** gum*
adjective: ***happy** hour*

The typical (unmarked) stress pattern is with stress on the first item (e.g. ***screw**driver*, ***happy** hour*), which helps to distinguish noun compounds from noun modifier + head structures, where stress is on the noun head (e.g. *university **degree***, *government **report***).

There is a wide range of possible semantic relationships between the pre-head item and the head. These include:

subject + verb: *headache* (head that aches), *rainfall* (rain that falls)

verb + subject: *warning sign* (sign that warns)

verb + object: *know-all* (a person who thinks they know all), *killjoy* ('kills joy', someone who spoils the enjoyment of others)

object + verb: *carpet-shampoo* (shampoos carpets), *risk-taking* (takes risks), *hair-dryer* (dries hair)

predicative complement + subject: *junk food* (the food is junk), *girlfriend*

prepositional complement: *raincoat* (the coat is for rain), *ashtray*

complement + noun: *chairleg, fingertip* (the tip of the finger)

Compound adjectives 265c

Most compound adjectives end in an adjective (e.g. *air-sick*), or in an *-ing* or *-ed* adjective form (e.g. *heart-breaking, short-sighted, white-washed*). The main relationships between the parts of compound adjectives are as follows:

object + *-ing*/*-ed*: *English-speaking* (speaks English), *confidence-boosting* (boosts confidence), *heart-broken* (the heart is broken by somebody)

verb complement + *-ing*/*-ed*: *far-reaching* (reaches far), *home-made* (made at home)

subject + predicative complement: *top-heavy* (the top is heavy) (A is B)

comparative: *paper-thin* (as thin as paper) (as B as A)

adjective + complement: *fat-free* (free of fat), *user-friendly* (friendly to the user)

adjective + adjective head: *royal-blue, light-green, bitter-sweet*

Note also that some adjective compounds are formed by adding an *-ed* inflection to an existing adjective + noun: *right-angled* (formed from *right-angle*), *left-handed* (formed from *left hand*).

Compound verbs 265d

Compound verbs are far less frequent than compound nouns or adjectives. They may be derived by conversion from another word class, normally an already existing noun compound (e.g. *to daydream, to blackmail, to wait-list*). They may also be derived by a process of back-formation (→ **267b** below) by the removal of a suffix (e.g. *shoplift* from *shoplifting* or *shoplifter*; *babysit* from *babysitting* or *babysitter*). Examples include: *chain-smoke, dry-clean, housekeep, sight-see, spring-clean*.

HYPHENATION 266

The use of hyphens in compounds and complex words involves a number of different rules, and practice is changing, with fewer hyphens present in contemporary usage. For example, compound words may be written as separate words (*post box*), hyphenated (*post-box*) or written as one word (*postbox*). However, in certain forms the rules governing the use of hypens are more regular.

Particular prefixes regularly involve a hyphen (e.g. *ex-minister, post-war, self-interest, quasi-public*).

When a compound premodifies a noun head, a hyphen is normally inserted to indicate which words are compounded (e.g. *a well-known entertainer, twentieth-century Danish architecture*).

Hyphens are normally used in compounds in which the pre-head item is a single capital letter (e.g. *U-turn, X-ray*), and hyphens are sometimes needed to disambiguate different words (e.g. *re-form* = form again, *reform* = change radically).

In numerically modified adjectives, all modifying elements are hyphenated. Note that these forms are only used attributively (e.g. *an eighteen-year-old girl, a twenty-ton truck, a twenty-four-hour flight*).

→ **506 Appendix: Punctuation**

OTHER TYPES OF WORD FORMATION 267

Abbreviation 267a

Abbreviation involves shortening a word. This can be done by means of three main processes: clipping, acronyms and blends.

Clipping

Clipping is a type of abbreviation in which a word is shortened when one or more syllables are omitted or 'clipped'. Proper names for people are commonly clipped:

ad: *advertisement, advert*
decaf: *decaffeinated*
medic: *medical student, doctor*
memo: *memorandum*
lab: *laboratory*
Liz: *Elizabeth*

Acronyms

Acronyms are a type of abbreviation formed when the initial letters of two or more words are combined in a way that produces consonant and vowel sequences found in words. Acronyms are pronounced as words:

*RAM: **R**andom **A**ccess **M**emory*
*NATO: **N**orth **A**tlantic **T**reaty **O**rganisation* /ˈneɪtəʊ/
*Laser: **l**ight **a**mplification (by) **s**timulated **e**mission (of) **r**adiation*

Initials are similar to acronyms but are pronounced as sets of letters, not as words:

*BBC: **B**ritish **B**roadcasting **C**orporation*
*PC: **p**ersonal **c**omputer, or **p**olitically **c**orrect*
*CD: **c**ompact **d**isc*

Blends

Blends are a type of abbreviation in which parts of existing words are combined to form a new word. The process is a notable recent phenomenon:

camcorder: blend of ***cam**era* and *re**corder***
fanzine: blend of ***fan*** and *maga**zine***
heliport: blend of ***heli**copter* and *air**port***
netiquette: blend of *inter**net*** and *et**iquette***
smog: blend of ***sm**oke* and *f**og***

Back-formation 267b

Back-formation is a process of word formation in which what is thought to be a suffix (and occasionally a prefix) is removed. It applies in particular to the process of forming verbs from nouns. The two major sources are nouns and compound nouns ending in *-tion*, or *-ion* and in *-ar*, *-er*, *-or*, *-ing*. But there is also a large miscellaneous group which occasionally includes back-formation from adjectives:

emote: derived from *emotion*
intuit: derived from *intuition*
legislate: derived from *legislation*
televise: derived from *television*

air-condition: derived from *air-conditioner*
commentate: derived from *commentator*
brainwash: derived from *brainwashing*
sightsee: derived from *sightseeing*

enthuse: derived from *enthusiasm*
diagnose: derived from *diagnosis*
legitimise: derived from the adjective *legitimate*

Other types 267c

Occasionally the formation of words may occur by utilising sounds from words with similar associations. For example, words ending in *-ump* such as *dump*, *thump*, *lump* can generate invented words with similar sound patterns and associations of heaviness and hardness (e.g. *whump*, *bubump*, *kerbump*).

Words can be formed from proper names. Examples include: *braille*, *caesarian*, *platonic*, *sadist*, *sandwich* (words formed, respectively, from the names of Louis Braille, Julius Caesar, Plato, the Marquis de Sade and the Earl of Sandwich).

539 **Glossary** for any unfamiliar terms

Sometimes the names of products can be taken over into general use. For example *hoover* and *Mac* are both the names of a company and the general name applied to the object (*Mac* refers to the name of Apple-MacIntosh computers):

I'm just going to ***hoover*** *the lounge before we go out.*

I'm sorry I've got a ***Mac*** *and can't use those files.*

It is very rare for new words to be formed without parts of existing words being in some way involved. An exception to this rule is loan words. These are words that are borrowed from other languages. Relatively recent loan words from the domain of food include: *pizza, salsa, tapas, chapatti*. Loan words are most typically nouns and are not normally subject to any of the processes of word formation, though they may be inflected if they are singular count nouns (*pizzas, chapattis*).

PRODUCTIVITY 268

Not all prefixes and suffixes are equally productive. Some are frequently used to create new words, while others are rarely, if ever, utilised in present-day word formation.

The suffix *-ion* is particularly productive in English and is used to form a large number of high-frequency nouns, e.g. *reunion, confusion, extension, explosion, direction, infection, inflation, intuition, relation, resignation*.

The adjectival suffix *-al* produces a large number of high-frequency adjectives, e.g. *critical, crucial, dental, frontal, typical, vital*.

Prefixes such as *un-* and *de-* and the *-er/-or* suffix are highly productive, with new words constantly being formed.

Rare suffixes such as *-ose* (as in *verbose, jocose*) and *-dom* are rarely used to form new words.

Conversion and compounding are productive in modern English, and new forms occur regularly, especially in technical domains such as computing and in the sciences in general. Almost any noun may potentially combine with any other noun to form new noun compounds.

Acronyms, back-formations and loan words only account for a small amount of the new vocabulary to appear each year in English, but the processes in themselves are productive.

→ **155–166 Introduction to word classes and phrase classes**

→ **507–511 Appendix: English Spelling**

Introduction to sentences and clauses

Introduction to sentences and clauses

THE SENTENCE AND THE CLAUSE 269

The sentence is normally considered to be the largest unit of grammar. Longer stretches of text, such as paragraphs and segments of conversations, are usually regarded as units of discourse. The sentence is principally a unit of written grammar and is normally easily identified by an initial capital letter on the first word and a full stop after the last word. For spoken language, the sentence as a grammatical unit is more problematic (→ 272a below).

Sentences are composed of clauses. The clause is the core unit of grammar. A sentence must include at least one main clause (→ 270 below). A clause consists of two parts: a subject and a predicate. The subject is a noun phrase or its equivalent (e.g. a nominal clause: ***writing novels*** *is not easy*) which indicates the doer or agent of an action, state or event, and the predicate is a verb phrase and any other accompanying elements (e.g. an object or complement):

subject	predicate
We	*baked some potatoes in the fire.*

The subject can be seen as representing a topic (who/what the clause is about – in this case *we*) and the predicate can be seen as representing a comment (what is said about the topic – that we *baked some potatoes in the fire*). The topic and comment together constitute a proposition. Clauses combined together as sentences express various types of relation between propositions.

The clause centres around a verb phrase (in the example above, *baked*), since it is the verb phrase which largely determines what else must or may occur in the clause. A clause most typically consists of a subject (which is a noun phrase), a verb, and other elements which may or may not be necessary, such as an object (which is a noun phrase), a predicative complement (most typically an adjective or noun phrase), or an adjunct (which is typically an adverb phrase or a prepositional phrase):

S	V	O	A
noun phrase	verb phrase	noun phrase	prepositional phrase
I	*'ve got*	*a parcel for you*	*in my car.*

Examples of clauses and non-clauses.

- Clauses (verbs in bold):

  He ***wrote*** *a couple of novels.*
  (one clause: one verb)

  Did *you* ***say*** *tea or coffee?*
  (one clause: auxiliary verb [*did*] and lexical verb [*say*])

*When you **get** there, | **ring** me.*
(two clauses: two lexical verbs with their own accompanying structures)

- Non-clauses:

  the green sofa
  (noun phrase)

  in the garden
  (prepositional phrase)

  Hello
  (greeting formula)

  hopefully
  (adverb)

MAIN AND SUBORDINATE CLAUSES 270

The two main types of clause which can combine to form sentences are main clauses and subordinate clauses. Main clauses are not dependent on any other clause in the sentence, and a sentence must have at least one main clause.

The following are sentences, since they contain at least one main clause.

- Sentences (main clauses in bold):

  I went to speak to them.
  (whole sentence is one main clause)

  I went down to the fish and chip shop** and **I got fish and chips.
  (two main clauses joined by *and*)

  *If I went down there, **I could use the computer and the laser printer.***
  (one subordinate clause [*if*-clause] and one main clause)

The following are not sentences, since they do not contain a main clause. They consist of subordinate clauses, which need to be accompanied by a main clause in order to form a sentence.

- Non-sentences (no main clause):

  before I went

  when I went to Southampton for the day with my friend

  which arrived yesterday

- Further examples of main clauses (in green) with verbs in bold:

  *Oh, she**'s left** some money for you.*

  *Richard **got up** and **walked** over to the window.*

  *I**'ve done** a lot of thinking while you **were** asleep.*

  *As her confidence **grew**, she **started** to get careless.*

The clauses *while you were asleep* and *as her confidence grew* are dependent on other clauses and cannot be sentences on their own. They are therefore not main clauses.

The table below shows examples of sentences with one, two and three clauses. The clauses in the shaded boxes are main clauses; they could form sentences on their own. The clauses in the clear boxes are subordinate clauses; they could not form sentences on their own.

Examples of main and subordinate clauses

	clause	clause	clause
1	*She **took** her duties seriously.*		
2	*That **was** a few years ago*	*but my feelings **have not changed** one bit.*	
3	*When I **left** college,*	*I **couldn't find** any work.*	
4	*He **turned** round,*	*someone **pushed** him*	*and he **fell**.*
5	*As soon as she **opened** the envelope,*	*she **knew** something was wrong,*	*for the first lines of Richard's letter **were** full of apologies and regrets.*
6	*The water **begins** to freeze,and*	*as it **does** so,*	*it **expands**.*

In the table, *but* and *and* are coordinating conjunctions joining clauses of equal status to one another (in this case main clauses). *When*, *as soon as*, *for* and *as* are subordinating conjunctions, indicating a dependent relationship between the clauses they introduce and the main clauses. Coordination (→ 307) and subordination (→ 310) are two principal ways in which clauses are combined to form sentences.

Relative clauses (typically clauses with *who*, *which*, *that* modifying nouns) and nominal clauses are also types of dependent clause. In these cases they are embedded within larger structures:

← subject → verb complement
*The points **that I'm talking about** are similar.*

← subject → verb complement
What we need is more time.

→ **316–317**

SIMPLE, COMPOUND AND COMPLEX SENTENCES **271**

A sentence with one main clause is called a simple sentence:

← main clause →
It snowed last night.

→ also **sentence 1 in the table in 270**

A sentence with two or more main clauses is called a compound sentence:

← main clause → ← main clause →
He should have been here at five** and **he's not here yet.

→ also **sentence 2 in the table in 270**

A sentence with a main clause and one or more subordinate clauses is called a complex sentence. In the example below, || indicates clause boundaries. Subordinate clauses are in green; the main clause is in bold:

> [automatic customer-answering-service at a company]
> *Welcome to [name of company].* || *If you have a touch-tone telephone,* || ***please listen carefully to all the following options*** || *before you make your choice.*

➝ also **sentence 3 in the table in 270**

➝ **506 Appendix: Punctuation** on the punctuation of sentences in writing

SENTENCE AND UTTERANCE 272

The sentence in spoken language 272a

Sentences in spoken language are more problematic than in written language. Speakers take turns to speak, and turns are a basic unit of conversation. A turn ends when the speaker changes.

Many turns in everyday speech consist of long strings of clauses (e.g. when someone is telling a story), unfinished sentences, or just noun phrases, adjective phrases or adverb phrases standing alone. We also find *yes*, *no*, interjections and other miscellaneous word-types standing alone, or sentences 'jointly constructed' by more than one speaker.

A typical transcript of everyday conversation contains many complete and communicatively sufficient units which are not sentences:

> [speaker A is telling speaker B about a computer problem]
> **1** A: *But he's trying to send us an email and I'm having some trouble with the computer you see.*
> **2** B: *Right.*
> **3** A: *You know.*
> **4** B: *Yeah.*
> **5** A: *On my computer when I try to get anything on it.*
> **6** B: *Mm.*
> **7** A: *It's just saying that it's not in the files. I don't know if …*
> **8** B: *Mm.*
> **9** A: *And I'll have to get a disk.*

Speakers often begin new topics or sub-topics with conjunctions such as *but* (turn **1**) and *and* (turn **9**), even after considerable silences.

A turn may consist of just a word or phrase indicating a response or acknowledgement (turns **2** and **4**).

It may not be clear which independent unit a dependent unit is attached to. The prepositional phrase in turn **5** could be treated as attached to turn **1** or turn **7**, or simply as a free-standing and communicatively self-sufficient element.

The 'sentence' is therefore a problematic concept to apply to oral communication.

The utterance 272b

Problems with identifying sentences in informal spoken language mean that it is often useful to distinguish between a sentence and an utterance.

The sentence is a unit of grammar, and must be grammatically complete (i.e. it must have at least one main clause). The utterance is a unit of communication. It must be communicatively and pragmatically complete, but it does not need to be grammatically complete. Communicative means that the utterance communicates a meaningful message, and pragmatic means that it is fully interpretable in its context. Thus a string of words standing alone such as *over to you*, though not a sentence, can be communicative and pragmatically interpretable (e.g. telling someone it's their turn to take over the main speaking role), while a string of words such as *you if on* is unlikely to be either communicatively or pragmatically adequate.

Right and *you know* (turns **2** and **3** in the conversation extract in **272a**), although they are not grammatically sentences, are complete utterances since each one is communicatively and pragmatically complete.

However, in spoken language the general principles for combining clauses can still be seen to operate in broad terms (but ➜ **87b Subordinate clauses**).

SENTENCE TYPES 273

The sentence types take their names from the names of the different types of main clause. The four major types of sentence are:

(x = other elements e.g. objects, complements)

type	structure of the main clause
declaratives	subject + verb + x
interrogatives	auxiliary/modal verb + subject + verb + x
imperatives	verb + x; no overt subject (subject is understood)
exclamatives	introduced by a phrase with *what* or *how* and followed by a subject + verb + x construction

BASIC FEATURES OF CLAUSES 274

Polarity 274a

Polarity, whether the clause is affirmative or negative, is an important feature of clauses. The polarity of the main clause determines the overall polarity of the sentence.

Examples of affirmative and negative polarity

main clause	clause polarity	subordinate clause	clause polarity	sentence polarity
She looked really offended.	affirmative			affirmative
*They **don't** do it during the summer.*	negative			negative
I might want you to do something for me	affirmative	*while I'm away.*	affirmative	affirmative
I'll have it	affirmative	*if you don't want it.*	negative	affirmative
*I'm **not** going*	negative	*if he goes.*	affirmative	negative

Participants, processes and circumstances 274b

Clauses express the relationship between processes (actions, states or events), participants (the people and things who act or are involved in or affected by actions, states and events) and circumstances (e.g. the time, place, manner and surrounding circumstances of an action, state or event).

The process is typically expressed by a verb phrase:

*I'll **post** the letter tonight.*

The participants are most typically expressed by noun phrases:

***I**'ll post **the letter** tonight.*

The circumstances are most typically expressed by adverb phrases or prepositional phrases:

*I'll post the letter **tonight**.*
(adverb phrase)

*Let's go there **after lunch**.*
(prepositional phrase)

Clauses consist of various arrangements of these types of phrase fulfilling the functions of subject, verb, object, predicative complement and adjunct.

Subjects, verbs, objects, complements, adjuncts 274c

A clause centres around a verb phrase and most typically consists of a subject (which is a noun phrase), a verb (which is a verb phrase), and other elements which may or may not be necessary or present. These other elements include an object (which is a noun phrase), a predicative complement (which can be a noun/adverb/prepositional/adjective phrase) or an adjunct (which is typically an adverb phrase or prepositional phrase):

subject	verb	object	adjunct
I	*'ll post*	*the letter*	*tonight.*

subject	verb	complement
I	*feel*	*very tired.*

539 Glossary for any unfamiliar terms

A clause may consist minimally of a verb in the imperative:

Run!
(imperative clause)

Arrangements of subjects, verbs, complements and adjuncts in clauses vary, depending on the pattern of complementation required by the verb (→ 281–289 Verb complementation). The variations in the table below typically occur.

Examples of verb complementation

example (verbs in bold)	pattern
No one | ***laughed.***	subject + verb
She | ***took*** | *a photograph.*	subject + verb + direct object
I | ***'ll give*** | *you* | *a ring.*	subject + verb + indirect object + direct object
He | ***'s working*** | *this afternoon.*	subject + verb + adjunct
We | ***signed*** | *it* | *as a protest.*	subject + verb + object + adjunct
He | ***'ll get*** | *angry.*	subject + verb + subject complement
It | ***made*** | *my clothes* | *dirty.*	subject + verb + object + object complement

→ 275 Basic clause structure

Central and peripheral elements 274d

Central elements

The verb is the most central element in the clause as it tends to determine what else must or may occur in the clause. Next in importance come the subject and object or predicative complement, which express the relationship between participants and the process expressed by the verb.

The central elements subject and verb are the basic obligatory elements of a simple declarative clause. Central elements have a relatively fixed word order in English. The verb, for example, cannot usually be moved:

*You **know** the problem.*
(~~You the problem know.~~)

Objects and predicative complements have slightly more flexibility and occasionally occur in untypical positions for reasons of emphasis:

*Every computer that we looked at was near two thousand pounds. But **this one** I got for twelve hundred, with two hundred pounds' worth of software.*
(object (*this one*) placed before subject (*I*) for emphasis/contrast)

*Well, **rich** they may be, but I'm not sure they're happy.*
(complement (*rich*) placed before subject (*they*) for emphasis/contrast)

Peripheral elements

Adjuncts are normally regarded as peripheral elements in the clause; they are always optional, they are the most mobile elements (they can occupy different positions), and they do not determine what else must occur in the clause.

Adjuncts are even more flexible than objects and predicative complements, and may occur in a variety of positions:

In the morning *we had to pretend nothing happened.*
(adjunct in front position; also possible: We had to pretend nothing happened in the morning.)

We ***sometimes*** *go to Rochester.*
(adjunct between subject and verb; also possible: Sometimes we go to Rochester.)

That young guy seems to deliver the post ***quite often these days****.*
(adjuncts in final position; also possible: Quite often that young guy seems to deliver the post these days./These days that young guy seems to deliver the post quite often.)

Elements outside of the clause structure 274e

Sometimes, especially in informal spoken language, elements occur which are not contained within the clause structure. Items may occasionally occur before or after the clause for emphasis and be repeated in some form within the clause (most typically by a pronoun):

Joe*, I've known* ***him*** *for years.*
(object placed outside the clause, repeated in the clause by pronoun *him*)

It*'s a great city,* ***Dublin****.*
(subject *it* repeated after the clause as a full noun phrase)

→ **96 Headers** and **97 Tails**

Pragmatic markers are also normally considered to be outside of the clause structure. These include discourse markers (words and phrases indicating boundaries in the discourse or words that monitor the state of the discourse in some way), stance markers (words and phrases indicating a stance or attitude to a segment or section of discourse) and interjections:

Well*, what are you going to do with it?*
(discourse marker)

Susie does aerobics, ***you know****.*
(discourse marker)

To be honest*, I don't think I'll go this year.*
(stance marker)

Frankly*, I couldn't care less.*
(stance marker)

Gosh*, that's very cheap.*
(interjection)

→ **105 Pragmatic markers**

Vocatives (addressing someone directly with a name or title) are also considered to be outside of the clause structure:

Would you like another drink, ***Molly****?*

BASIC CLAUSE STRUCTURE 275

In this and the following sections we deal with the basic structure of clauses, focusing on simple declarative main clauses. A simple declarative clause consists of a subject phrase, a verb phrase, any object or predicative complement phrases and optional adjunct phrases.

Examples of simple declarative clauses

subject	verb	object	complement	adjunct
Everyone	*laughed.*			
She	*stole*	*some money.*		
He	*'s*		*my brother-in-law.*	
I	*travelled*			*for a year.*

Subject + verb is the minimal structure for declarative clauses.

CENTRAL CLAUSE FUNCTIONS 276

The following sections (**276–279**) deal principally with the central clause functions of subject, verb (focusing on verb complementation), object and predicative complement. Adjuncts, the other main function in the clause, are optional, mobile elements describing the circumstances of the action or event (··› **280** below) and are peripheral to the structure of the clause.

A separate chapter deals with adjuncts (**319–337**).

Subject 276a

As indicated above (**269**), the clause may be divided into two main parts: the subject and the predicate.

The subject in an active-voice declarative clause is the noun phrase which precedes the verb, and which indicates the 'doer' or agent of an action, or the participant that an event or state happens to or refers to. The subject noun phrase agrees with the verb in person and number. The predicate in a declarative clause is the rest of the clause after the subject, where what the subject is, does or experiences is elaborated.

Examples of clauses showing subject and predicate

subject	predicate
My mother	*was a friend of hers.*
I	*ate too much last night.*
Their dog	*died last week.*
The garden	*looks lovely.*
They	*made him a member of their gang.*

The predicate consists of the verb phrase followed by objects and predicative complements (··→ 278 and 279).

The subject is most typically a noun phrase, though it may sometimes be a *wh*-nominal clause, or, very occasionally, a prepositional phrase. The subject (in green in the examples below) determines the person and number of the verb:

> *My sister **does** singing lessons.*
> (noun phrase: determiner + noun)
>
> *They **have** a matter-of-fact approach to everything.*
> (noun phrase: pronoun)
>
> *Skiing **doesn't** appeal to me.*
> (noun phrase: the gerund *-ing* form of a verb functioning as a noun)
>
> *What we're doing **is** offering a scholarship.*
> (*wh*-nominal clause)
>
> A: *When shall I ring you?*
> B: *After six **would** be best.*
> (prepositional phrase; less common)

The subject comes before the verb in a simple declarative clause, and it is obligatory, except in high-context, informal situations where it may be unnecessary and omitted if it is obvious to the participants:

> A: *Have you been back to the 'Shanghai Palace'?*
> B: *Yeah, I went a few weeks ago. **It**'s a really nice restaurant.*
> (~~Yeah, I went a few weeks ago. Is a really nice restaurant.~~)
>
> A: ***Need** a hammer. Is there one in the garage?*
> B: *Yeah, **think** so.*
> (subjects are obvious to the speakers in the context; more explicit forms: I need a hammer/I think so)

··→ 94 Situational ellipsis

Subject pronouns are nominative in form: *I, you, he, she, it, one, we, they*.

Dummy subjects 276b

Since there must be a subject, 'dummy' subjects sometimes have to be used. Dummy subjects, consisting of *it* or *there*, are subjects considered to have no semantic content but which simply fill the necessary subject slot:

> ***It**'s interesting the way these dresses are so similar.*
> (~~Is interesting the way these dresses are so similar.~~)
>
> ***There** are many ways in which you can use that.*
> (~~Are many ways in which you can use that.~~)

··→ 45f, 45g.

Subject-verb concord 276c

Concord refers to the way words match each other in terms of number, tense, etc. A present tense verb shows concord of number with a third person singular subject by having a final *-s* on the verb:

> ***It takes*** *up a lot of energy.*
> (~~It take up a lot of energy.~~)
>
> ***My dad*** *works there.*

In the present tense, all other persons are followed by the uninflected form of the verb:

> *We love Dublin.*
> (~~We loves Dublin.~~)
>
> *They never **watch** TV.*

In the past tense, all persons are followed by the past tense form of the verb, with no special indication of number. Only the verb *be* has special forms for different persons and number: *am, are, is, was, were.*

The head noun of a subject noun phrase determines number, not other nouns in the noun phrase:

> *The general **quality** of supermarket vegetables **is** very poor.*
> (~~The general quality of supermarket vegetables are very poor.~~)

also **177a Count nouns; 279c**

34 *Each*; 38 *Every*

VERB COMPLEMENTATION 277

General 277a

Complementation is concerned with elements which follow the verb in a declarative clause and which are necessary to complete the meaning of the verb in some way.

Some verbs are complete in themselves and require no complementation (they are used as intransitive verbs), others require single complementation or dual complementation and are used as transitive verbs:

> *She **laughed**.*
> (intransitive: no complement needed; the verb is complete in itself)
>
> *I **spotted** a taxi.*
> (transitive: single complementation needed; the speaker must say what was spotted)
>
> *He **put** it in the rubbish bin.*
> (transitive: dual complementation needed; speaker must say what was put and where it was put)

The different patterns of complementation (⇢ below, the tables in **277c** and **277d**) are dealt with in greater detail in **281–289 Verb complementation**.

No complementation 277b

Some verbs require no complementation. This is known as intransitive use:

*She **died** last week.*

*House prices **have risen**.*

Single complementation 277c

Some verbs are used with single complementation. There are several common types, as shown in the table below.

Examples of single complementation

structure of complementation	example	function of complementation
noun phrase	*I hate **hospitals**.*	object
noun phrase	*I was **the winner**.*	subject complement (gives more information in the predicate
adjective phrase	*She seemed **very nice**.*	about the subject)
prepositional phrase	*It's **near the Boulevard**.*	predicative complements of place/measure/time
noun phrase	*He lives **next door**.*	
noun phrase	*It weighed **about two and a half pounds**.*	
prepositional phrase	*It lasted **for 18 hours**.*	
clause	*I know **you think** I'm crazy.*	object
clause	*I'm **where you should be**.*	subject complement

Dual complementation 277d

Some verbs require dual complementation. There are several common types, as shown in the table below.

Examples of dual complementation (direct objects in green)

structure of complementation	example	function of complementation	type of complementation
noun phrase + noun phrase	*He gave **me** his number.*	two objects, indirect and direct	ditransitive (i.e. two complements)
noun phrase + prepositional phrase	*She sent a letter **to Ivy Bolton**.*	object and prepositional complement	transitive-oblique (i.e. the recipient is referred to 'obliquely' in a prepositional phrase)

continued overleaf

continued

structure of complementation	example	function of complementation	type of complementation
noun phrase + noun phrase	*With more than 50 victories worldwide, golf has made him **a multi-millionaire**.*	direct object and object complement (gives more information about the object)	complex transitive
noun phrase + adjective phrase	*It made me **very ill**.*		
noun phrase + prepositional phrase	*I want to put the picture **over here**.*	direct object and prepositional phrase	locative (locates the object in terms of place or time)
noun phrase + clause	*She told **me** what it was.*	indirect object and direct object	clause (functioning as direct object alongside indirect object)

OBJECT 278

General 278a

Objects are most typically noun phrases. They follow the verb. They may be direct or indirect.

Direct objects indicate the person or thing that undergoes the action denoted by the verb, or the participant directly affected by the action:

*I like **that restaurant**.*

*She kicked **him**.*

*They stole **a van** and then they robbed **a bank**.*

Indirect objects indicate the recipient of a direct object. They are usually people or animals. An indirect object (bold) is always accompanied by a direct object (in green):

*They handed **me** a pile of forms.*

*Her mother sent **her** a cheque for her birthday.*

Direct objects 278b

Direct objects are always noun phrases (or their equivalents, e.g. nominal clauses). The direct object of an active clause can typically become the subject of a passive clause:

*Everybody hated **the teacher**.*
(active: *the teacher* is direct object)

***The teacher** was hated by everybody.*
(passive: *the teacher* is subject)

Examples of direct objects

subject	verb (+ indirect object where required)	direct object
She	*murdered*	***her husband.***
He	*missed*	***this morning's class.***
The police	*came and arrested*	***them.***
He	*loves*	***cycling.***
We	*gave her*	***the tickets.***
I	*understand*	***what you mean.***

Adjuncts (in green) are not normally placed between the verb and the object:

*Mum noticed **a difference** quite quickly.*
(~~Mum noticed quite quickly a difference.~~)

However, in the case of longer phrases or clauses acting as objects, adjuncts may sometimes occur before the object:

*It was a bright room and I noticed immediately **the door which opened on to the balcony.***

→ also **322**

Indirect objects 278c

The indirect object (IO) is the recipient of a direct object (DO), and is most typically an animate being:

IO DO
*She gave | **him** | a large envelope.*

An indirect object always has a direct object accompanying it.

Examples of indirect objects

subject	verb	indirect object	direct object
Diana	*is going to buy*	***Martha***	*a present.*
I'll	*give*	***you***	*a ring.*
Jeremy	*had handed*	***her***	*a card.*

Indirect object or prepositional complement? 278d

With verbs such as *give, buy, send, hand,* when the recipient of the object is expressed as a full noun phrase and the object is an unstressed pronoun, the structure object + prepositional complement is used, not indirect object + direct object:

*I gave **it to Frank.***
(~~I gave Frank it.~~)

*They handed **them to the teacher.***
(~~They handed the teacher them.~~)

→ **277d** on transitive-oblique in the table

COMPLEMENT 279

General 279a

Predicative complements are most typically noun phrases and adjective phrases which follow the verb and give further information about a subject (subject complement) or an object (object complement):

*He's **my brother-in-law**.*
(subject complement: gives information about the subject)

*The students seem **pretty bright**.*
(subject complement)

*They labelled him **a coward**.*
(object complement: gives information about the object)

*It made me **seasick**.*
(object complement)

Complements may also be adverb phrases or prepositional phrases:

*She's **upstairs**.*

*The bus stop is **near the shop**.*

*The lecture is **at three-thirty**.*

Subject complements 279b

A predicative subject complement adds information about the subject:

*He's **a maths teacher**.*
(gives information about the subject, *he*)

The subject complement here is not the same as an object. *He* and the *maths teacher* are the same person. Compare *He married/visited/interviewed a maths teacher*, where *maths teacher* is the object, and a different person from *he*.

Subject complements are most typically noun phrases or adjective phrases.

Examples of subject complements

subject	verb	subject complement	type
We	*became*	***friends.***	noun phrase
He	*died*	***a very rich man.***	noun phrase
She	*'s*	***very lucky.***	adjective phrase
That	*smells*	***good.***	adjective phrase

Verbs which do not take objects are followed by subject complements. These are verbs such as the copular verb *be*, sense verbs such as *feel, look, taste, smell, sound*, verbs of perception such as *seem* and *appear*, change-of-state verbs such as *become, grow, get, go, turn*.

Pronouns

Pronoun subject complements following the copular verb *be* are normally in the object form (*me, you, him, her, it, us, them*):

A: *Who did that?*
B: *It was* ***me****, sorry.*
(~~It was I, sorry.~~)

There's his mother now, that's ***her****.*
(~~..., that's she.~~)

However, in very formal styles, pronoun subject complements with *be* may occur in the subject form, especially in cleft sentences:

It was ***I*** *who told him to go.*
(compare the more informal: It was me who told him to go.)

Number concord with subject complements 279c

In informal spoken language, speakers sometimes have a choice whether to use a singular or plural verb when there is a difference in number between the subject and the complement:

singular subject	plural complement
Another topic of course ***is***	*words that have changed their meaning.*

[talking of a car that is proving difficult to sell]
The only good thing ***are*** *the tyres.*

Normally, and in more formal styles, the subject determines the number of the verb .

Apposition

Adjective and noun phrases separated from the rest of the clause by punctuation or intonation may function in a way very similar to a subject complement:

The crowd *pressed closer,* ***unwilling to miss a thing.***

We'd *just sit there,* ***a couple trying to make it in the world.***

Object complements 279d

An object complement adds information in the predicate about the object:

All that hard work has left me ***exhausted.***
(gives information about the object, *me*)

An object complement is most typically a noun phrase or an adjective phrase. The object complement follows the object.

539 Glossary for any unfamiliar terms

Examples of object complements

subject	verb	object	object complement	type
Ryan	*had (always) called*	*her*	***Katy**.*	noun phrase
He	*makes*	*me*	***happy**.*	adjective phrase
This	*makes*	*the time factor*	***even more pressing**.*	adjective phrase

→ **473b Predicative complements** for marked (untypical) positions of complements

ADJUNCTS 280

All other elements in basic clauses which are not subjects, verbs, objects or complements may be classified as adjuncts. Adjuncts are peripheral, optional elements in the clause, and have a variety of functions. They most typically relate to the circumstances of an action or event, e.g. its time, place, manner, degree, frequency, intensity:

__In the summer__ we __often__ make our own ice cream.

He wrote a letter __every day__.

She was in love with him __in a big way__.

Adjuncts can occupy a variety of positions in the clause, either front position (*In the summer*, above), mid position (*often*, above) or end position (*every day, in a big way*, above).

Adjuncts and complements 280a

Adjuncts modify the verb or the clause but, unlike complements, they do not complete the meaning of the verb and are not required elements:

It rained __in the afternoon__.
(adjunct: indicates the circumstances, i.e. the time when it rained)

I'll put it __in my diary__ now.
(complement: completes the meaning of *put*, which must specify both an object and a location)

→ **169c Complements versus postmodifiers** for the distinction between complements and modifiers

→ **319–337 Adjuncts** for a full account of the different functions and positions of adjuncts

Verb complementation

Verb complementation

INTRODUCTION 281

Verb complementation refers to items which are required to follow verbs of different types in order to complete the meaning of the verb. These items may be noun phrases, adjectives, prepositional phrases or whole clauses, functioning as objects or complements.

COMPLEMENTATION TYPES 282

Intransitive 282a

Some verbs are complete in themselves and do not require any further elements to make their meaning complete; although there may be further elements in the sentence, these are not essential. This is called intransitive complementation. It involves verbs such as:

appear	*drown*	*rise*
arrive	*fall*	*sneeze*
begin	*go*	*snow*
break	*happen*	*stop*
come	*increase*	*swim*
cough	*laugh*	*wait*
decrease	*lie* (tell an untruth)	*work*
die	*matter*	
disappear	*rain*	

*She **died** when she was about twenty-one.*

*The passenger window closed and the car **disappeared** up the driveway.*

*Nothing **happened**.*

*She **laughed** loudly.*

*It **rained**.*

Transitive 282b

Some verbs, when used in the active voice, require further information to complete their meaning and are followed by objects. This is called transitive complementation. In the examples below, the verbs are in bold, the objects are in green. Everyday verbs of this type include:

ask	*forgive*	*offer*
believe	*get*	*produce*
blame	*give*	*put*
bring	*help*	*raise*
buy	*hold*	*receive*
carry	*keep*	*remember*
catch	*know*	*say*
cut	*like*	*see*
describe	*lose*	*suggest*
do	*love*	*take*
enjoy	*make*	*use*
expect	*mean*	*want*
find	*need*	*watch*

I'll have to ***get*** *a new battery for it.*

Raise *your hand if you can hear me.*

Take *what you want.*

Copular verbs 282c

Verbs such as *be, seem, become, feel, remain, smell, taste* are followed by predicative complements, in the form of adjective phrases, noun phrases, adverb phrases or prepositional phrases which give more information about the subject. These verbs are called copular verbs. In the examples, the verbs are in bold, the predicative complements are in green:

It ***seems*** *strange, doesn't it really.*

You ***are*** *the boss.*

The ***cat's*** *in the garden.*

Verbs which may be used transitively or intransitively 282d

Few verbs must always be used intransitively, and many verbs can be used both intransitively or transitively. Sometimes the meaning remains the same whether the verb is used transitively or intransitively, but sometimes there is a change of relationship between the verb and the subject.

→ 539 **Glossary** for any unfamiliar terms

No change in meaning

Some verbs may be used with or without an object with no change in meaning. Such verbs include:

approach	*enter*	*play*
drink	*help*	*win*
drive	*leave*	*write*
eat	*pass*	

Examples of verbs with and without an object – same meaning

with object (in green)	without object
*People make extra money by **driving** taxis.*	*You **drive** along here about two miles.*
*Can I **help** you?*	*How can I **help**?*
*All I need to do is **win** the lottery.*	*You can't **win** all the time.*

Change of subject-verb relationship

Some verbs may be used with or without an object, but the subject-verb relationship is different in each case. Such verbs include:

begin	*drop*	*turn*
change	*increase*	*walk*
close (down)	*open*	*work*
decrease	*slam*	

When these verbs are used with an object, the subject is the agent (doer) of the action. When they are used without an object, the action or event happens to the subject.

Examples of verbs with and without an object – different meanings

with object (in green) subject (underlined) is agent of the action/event	without object the action/event happens to the subject (underlined)
*We **closed** the door and they knocked later.*	*The door **closed**.*
*Sony has **increased** overseas production.*	*Worldwide sales have **increased** by 14%.*
*She **walks** the dog every morning.*	*He **walks** everywhere. I don't think he can drive.*
*How do you **work** this photocopier?*	*The photocopier is not **working**.*

OTHER INTRANSITIVE CONSTRUCTIONS 283

Pure intransitive constructions are those where there is a subject and no requirement of any further elements. However, some intransitive constructions do include information about subject-object relationships, or have parallel transitive constructions with the same meaning.

These constructions include the pseudo-intransitive construction, reciprocal verbs and reflexive verbs.

Pseudo-intransitive construction 283a

Verbs which are normally transitive also sometimes occur intransitively in clauses where the subject is in reality the recipient of the action or event, and where the agent is not mentioned. This type of intransitivity is called pseudo-intransitive. Verbs used in this way include:

clean	*iron*	*read*
close	*keep*	*sell*
cook	*open*	*store*
drink	*pack*	*wash*
drive	*photograph*	
fold	*print*	

These verbs are typically complemented by adverb phrases or prepositional phrases:

*This blouse hasn't **washed** very well.*

[*The Independent* is a newspaper]
*Cusack said, 'One other thing: 'The Independent' are carrying a shortened version of the Choltitz profile of you, Prime Minister. It **reads** very well indeed.'*

*Jack Pritchards' books **sell** by the million.*

Sell also occurs with an object in this type of construction, usually referring to number or quantity:

[referring to a pop music record]
*It eventually **sold** about 500,000 copies so I got a silver disc.*

Reciprocal verbs 283b

Reciprocal verbs such as *divorce, meet, marry* can have the same meaning as their transitively constructed equivalents:

*Frank and Diane **met** in 1979.*
(compare the transitive equivalents: Frank met Diane in 1979./Diane met Frank in 1979.)

*Lily and Tom **married** after a brief courtship.*
(compare: Lily married Tom … Tom married Lily …)

Reflexive construction 283c

A small number of verbs may be used intransitively or with a reflexive pronoun object, though meaning changes occur when the verb is reflexive (→ 202 Reflexive pronouns). These include *brace, dress, undress, wash*:

*Dolly, somewhat excited, had **dressed** and done her hair with care.*

*He dispatched a messenger to the stables to inquire whether the coachman was there; and while the man was gone, **dressed himself** very hurriedly.*

[*brace* here means to tense one's body ready for a negative physical impact]
Sturr ***braced****, as if for a fight.*

[*brace oneself* has a more abstract meaning of being mentally prepared for something negative]
She took a deep breath and ***braced herself****.*

TYPES OF COMPLEMENTATION 284

Complementation primarily concerns transitive and copular constructions, since the intransitive verb construction requires no complementation. There are four general types of complementation:

1 Monotransitive:

verb + direct object

2 Ditransitive:

verb + indirect object and direct object
verb + prepositional phrase (the transitive-oblique construction; → 286e)

3 Complex transitive:

verb + direct object + object complement
verb + direct object + locative complement

4 Copular:

copular verb (e.g. *be, look, seem*) + subject complement

1 Monotransitive complementation

examples (direct object in green)	structures
I ***love*** *fish.*	noun phrase as direct object
He ***thinks*** *[that] I'm right.*	*that*-clause as direct object
We ***understand*** *what you're saying.* *How did you* ***know*** *who to write to?*	*wh*-clause as direct object; *wh*-clause with *to*-infinitive as direct object
They ***decided*** *to buy it.* *We* ***love*** *buying old furniture.*	non-finite clause as direct object (*to*-infinitive or *-ing* clause, depending on verb)

2 Ditransitive complementation

examples (direct object in green, indirect object etc. underlined)	structures
She ***gave*** *me her email address.*	noun phrases as indirect and direct objects
We ***told*** *her [that] she couldn't have them.*	noun phrase as indirect object + *that*-clause as direct object
Oh, don't ***ask*** *me what it is.*	noun phrase as indirect object + *wh*-clause as direct object
I ***offered*** *my condolences to the family.*	noun phrase as direct object + prepositional phrase as oblique complement
Who ***taught*** *you to play the guitar?*	noun phrase as direct object + *to*-infinitive clause

3 Complex transitive complementation

examples (direct object in green, complement underlined)	structures
*It used to **drive** me crazy.*	noun phrase as direct object + adjective phrase as object complement
*She used to **call** her Aunt Susie.*	noun phrase as direct object + noun phrase as object complement
*I certainly **believe** it to be very rare.*	noun phrase as direct object + *to*-infinitive clause as object complement
*I **heard** her scream.*	noun phrase as direct object + infinitive without *to* as object complement
*I **noticed** them doing that.*	noun phrase as direct object + *-ing* clause as object complement
*Let's **get** this stuff washed.*	noun phrase as direct object + *-ed* clause as object complement
*You could **put** the water in a bottle.*	noun phrase as direct object + prepositional phrase as locative complement

4 Copular complementation

examples (complement underlined)	structures
*It **seems** silly.*	adjective phrase as subject complement
She's my cousin.	noun phrase as subject complement
*My husband's office **is** upstairs.*	adverb phrase as subject complement
*It **was** on the floor.*	prepositional phrase as subject complement

The next sections, **285–288**, deal with these types of complementation.

VERB + DIRECT OBJECT (MONOTRANSITIVE COMPLEMENTATION) 285

When a verb requires a direct object, the structure is called monotransitive complementation.

The direct object is typically a noun phrase, but it may also be a clause.

When the direct object is a pronoun, the object form (*me, you, him, her, it, us, them*) is used.

- Noun phrase as direct object:

  *I **took** the last piece of bread.*

  *Do you **remember** her from last year?*

- Clause as direct object:

  *I've **heard** (that) you're retiring.*

  *You always **know** what I'm thinking.*

  *I can't **remember** if it was last month or the month before.*

  *I **remember** staying a couple of nights in the village.*

539 **Glossary** for any unfamiliar terms

Monotransitive complementation and voice: active and passive 285a

Most verbs which can be used with a direct object in the active voice may also be used in the passive.

Examples of monotransitive verbs in active and passive voice

active	passive
*The postman **brought** it and apologised.*	*Our luggage **was brought** to the hotel.*
*Do you want to **keep** the menu?*	*Random access memory is a temporary storage area where information **is kept** while the computer is on.*
*I've just **started** a camera course at university.*	*The fire **was started** deliberately.*

The most common verbs of this type are:

begin	*hear*	*receive*
believe	*help*	*remember*
bring	*hold*	*say*
call	*keep*	*see*
carry	*know*	*start*
close	*like*	*study*
cut	*lose*	*take*
do	*love*	*use*
end	*make*	*visit*
enjoy	*mean*	*want*
expect	*meet*	*wash*
feel	*move*	*watch*
find	*need*	*win*
follow	*pass*	

Fit, *have*, *lack*, *resemble* and *suit* do not allow the passive construction:

*I **had** a weird dream.*
(~~A weird dream was had (by me).~~)

*That **suits** you.*
(~~You're suited by that.~~)

The passive voice gives the speaker/writer the option of omitting reference to the agent of an action. Thus the passive voice alternative of the following newspaper headline presents two options:

PRIME MINISTER ANNOUNCES NEW IMMIGRATION RESTRICTIONS
(active)

NEW IMMIGRATION RESTRICTIONS ANNOUNCED BY PRIME MINISTER
(passive with agent phrase)

NEW IMMIGRATION RESTRICTIONS ANNOUNCED
(passive with agent omitted)

→ also **481 Agent phrases** and **482 Passives without an agent phrase**

That-clause as direct object 285b

A class of verbs with reporting functions connected with speech and thought can occur with *that*-clauses as direct object. The most common verbs are:

accept	*find*	*prove*
admit	*forget*	*realise*
agree	*gather*	*recall*
announce	*guarantee*	*reckon*
argue	*guess*	*recognise*
assume	*hear*	*remark*
believe	*hint*	*remember*
bet	*hold*	*repeat*
check	*hope*	*reply*
claim	*imagine*	*report*
comment	*imply*	*say*
complain	*infer*	*see*
conclude	*insist*	*show*
confess	*know*	*state*
confirm	*learn*	*suggest*
consider	*mean*	*suppose*
decide	*mention*	*suspect*
deny	*notice*	*swear*
discover	*predict*	*think*
doubt	*presume*	*understand*
expect	*pretend*	*warn*
explain	*promise*	*write*
feel	*protest*	

I couldn't ***accept*** *that he was never going to come back.*

Some of the girls ***complained*** *yesterday that we're not cleaning the inside of the fridges.*

*I'd **forgotten** that you'd rung somebody up.*

*Her therapist **held** that it was natural and healthy for human beings to assume that bad things happened only to other people in remote areas.*

*So, every time, I **remark** that he's losing weight.*

*I can **understand** that she must have felt she was under some pressure.*

That is very frequently omitted in such constructions, especially in informal spoken language. Omission of *that* is particularly common after *think*:

*I **think** he's bored with his job.*

Omission of *that* is also common where the subject of the reporting clause and the reported clause are the same:

*The guy now **claims** he didn't do it.*

*I **hope** I've got the right size. It looked a bit big.*

*He **reckons** he's made a mistake.*

There is a tendency to retain *that* in more formal contexts. The retention of *that* is especially evident when the reporting verb is in the passive, and in coordinated reported clauses:

[from a book about volcanoes]
*In chapter three **it was mentioned that** the effect of getting large volumes of water mixed up in a volcanic eruption is to make it more violent.*

*We knew very quickly **that** we could talk to each other about anything **and that** we'd be there for each other.*

Wh-clause as direct object 285c

Many of the verbs which are used with *that*-clauses (→ **285b**) may also be used with *wh*-clauses as direct objects. The most common verbs of this type are:

anticipate	*depend*	*hear*
arrange	*discover*	*imagine*
ascertain	*discuss*	*inquire*
ask	*doubt*	*judge*
care	*enquire*	*know*
check	*establish*	*learn*
choose	*explain*	*mind*
confirm	*find out*	*notice*
consider	*forget*	*observe*
decide	*guess*	*predict*

prove	*say*	*tell*
realise	*see*	*think*
remember	*show*	*wonder*

*Could I possibly **ask** why you're unable to attend?*

*You have to **decide** whether or not you want it.*

*I'll just **find out** who you need to speak to.*

*Nobody can **predict** what's going to happen in life.*

[*tell* here means predict]
*You can never **tell** what he's going to do next.*

Wh-clause with infinitive as direct object 285d

Many of the verbs which can be followed by a *wh*-clause (→ **285c**) can also be followed by a *wh*-clause with *to*-infinitive. The most common verbs are:

arrange	*establish*	*notice*
ask	*explain*	*observe*
check	*find out*	*remember*
choose	*forget*	*say*
consider	*imagine*	*see*
decide	*inquire*	*show*
discover	*judge*	*tell*
discuss	*know*	*think*
enquire	*learn*	*wonder*

*Can you **explain** how to use this machine?*

*I'm just **wondering** what to say to you.*

*The committee reports to the Head of Department, who can then **choose** whether to take action.*

Non-finite clause with or without a new subject 285e

Non-finite *-ing* clauses and *to*-infinitive clauses occur as direct objects. The non-finite clause may occur with or without a new subject.

- Same subject for verb and complement clause:

  *She's **regretted** selling the house.*

  *I'd **hate** to swim in the Thames.*

- Different subject in complement clause:

  *Didn't he **like** you to sit in the room?*

  [*a little sip* means a small amount of a drink]
  *You don't **mind** me having a little sip, do you?*

Note that the new subject is in the object form. (→ also **285f**)

Verbs normally only followed by *-ing* 285f

A number of common, everyday verbs are normally only followed by the *-ing* form as opposed to the infinitive:

*Haven't you **finished** pack**ing** yet?*
(~~Haven't you finished to pack yet?~~)

*They **keep** chang**ing** the timetable and it confuses everybody.*
(~~They keep to change ...~~)

*I **fancy** do**ing** some evening classes.*
(~~I fancy to do some evening classes.~~)

The most common verbs only followed by *-ing* are:

admit
adore
appreciate
avoid
burst out (e.g. *laughing*)
can't help[1]
commence
consider[2]
contemplate
defer
delay
deny
detest
dislike
dread
endure
enjoy
(can) face
fancy
feel like
finish
give up
imagine
involve
keep (on)
lie
loathe
mention
mind
miss
object
postpone
practise
prevent
put off
recall
report
resent
risk
sit
stand (be on one's feet)
can't stand (can't bear)
suggest

[1] *Can't help* may also be followed by *but* plus the base form of the verb: *You couldn't help **but laugh** at it.*

[2] In the meaning of 'think about doing something': *Have you **considered** contact**ing** Mr Stanfield?*

*I really **appreciated** having met them all before.*

*He accepted that he had been abusive but **denied** threatening to kill the barman.*

*I don't really **feel like** going out tonight.*

*Fewer students from poor backgrounds will be **put off** going to university.*

A different subject may occur with some of these verbs. If it is a pronoun, the new subject is in the object form:

*I can just **imagine** him saying that.*

I didn't mind them playing in my garden.

*Do you **miss** him being around?*

In formal styles, the new subject may occur as a possessive form:

*You mean she would **object to** his coming here if she knew?*
(less formal: … object to him coming here …)

Hate, like, love and *prefer* 285g

Hate, like, love and *prefer* can be followed either by *-ing* or by a *to*-infinitive. The difference in meaning is often not great, but *-ing* emphasises the action or event in itself, while the infinitive places the emphasis more on the results of the action or event.

The *-ing* form often implies enjoyment (or lack of it), and the infinitive is often used for expressing preferences:

*I really like my teacher and I like my class. I **like being** in year five.*
(emphasis on the process itself and enjoyment of it)

*I like home-made soup. I **like to make** a panful and then it lasts me a couple of days.*
(emphasis more on result and the habit or preference)

However, when these verbs are used with *would* or *should*, only the infinitive is used, not the *-ing* form:

*I **would** like **to go** to Spain, or somewhere else, such as Italy.*
(~~I would like going to Spain …~~)

In the case of *prefer*, if alternatives are stated, they are linked by the preposition *to*, not infinitive *to*:

*Would you **prefer writing** to **telephoning** if you wanted to put something across?*
(~~Would you prefer writing to telephone if you wanted to put something across?~~)

Verbs with *-ing* or *to*-infinitive clauses and changes of meaning 285h

Some verbs have a different meaning depending on whether they are followed by *-ing* or *to*-infinitive. These include *forget, go on, mean, need, regret, remember, stop, try, want.*

Remember and *forget* with the infinitive refer to necessary actions and whether they are done or not:

*I must **remember to ask** the secretary for his phone number.*

*Oh, what I **forgot to bring** was the candle.*

With *-ing* they refer to memories of the past:

*Do you **remember going** to that place in Manchester?*
(Do you remember when we went to that place …?)

*I'll never **forget landing** at Hong Kong airport for the first time.*
(I'll never forget when we landed …)

Examples of contrasts in meaning between *-ing* and *to*-infinitive

verb	*-ing*	*to*-infinitive
go on	*She **went on sleeping** as the sun crept up.* (she was sleeping, and continued)	*Some people do **go on to have** two, three, or even four face-lifts but this is rare.* (after they have had the first face-lift, they then have a second, etc.)
mean	*Getting the earlier flight **means leaving** here at 6.* (involves/necessitates leaving here at 6)	*I didn't **mean to offend** her.* (intend to offend her)
regret	*You're really **regretting volunteering** now, aren't you?* (you are sorry for what has already happened)	*However, I **regret to say** that I think his judgments on the EC … ought not to be so readily accepted.* (polite form meaning: I am sorry for what I am about to say/do)
stop	***Stop saying** sorry!* (you are saying sorry all the time; do not do it any longer)	*Now and then, one of the players **stopped to light** his pipe.* (stopped playing in order to light his pipe)
try	[about an alarm clock that does not seem to work] ***Try re-setting** it.* (re-set it as an experiment, to see if it works)	*I will **try to remember** not to disturb you.* (I will attempt not to disturb you)

Infinitive clause without a new subject 285i

The most common verbs which may be followed by an infinitive clause without a new subject are:

afford	*attempt*	*continue*
agree	*(can't) bear*	*decide*
aim	*begin*	*demand*
arrange	*choose*	*fail*
ask	*claim*	*forget*

hate *help* *hope* *intend* *learn* *like* *long* *love* *manage* *mean* *need* *neglect* *offer* *plan* *prepare* *pretend* *promise* *propose* *refuse* *remember* *(can't) stand* *start* *try* *want* *wish*

They couldn't ***afford*** *to put the heating on.*

But they are unlikely to forgive the company for ***failing*** *to warn them so many things could go wrong.*

I ***managed*** *to make it sound a lot better than it was.*

Well, Laura, I can't ***promise*** *to be up at four or five in the morning.*

To-infinitive clause with a new subject 285j

Choose, hate, like, love, need, prefer and *want* are the most common verbs which may be followed by a new subject + *to*-infinitive clause. If it is a pronoun, the new subject is in the object form:

She'd ***hate*** *me to remember just that sort of thing.*

They just ***wanted*** *us to be happy.*

-ing clause with a new subject 285k

Hate, like, love, mind and *remember* are the most common verbs which may be followed by a new subject + *-ing* clause. If it is a pronoun, the new subject is in the object form:

I used to ***love*** *him coming to visit us.*

I can ***remember*** *them asking me to carry a bottle of water.*

VERB + INDIRECT OBJECT + DIRECT OBJECT (DITRANSITIVE COMPLEMENTATION) 286

Ditransitive complementation refers to combinations of direct and indirect objects, and direct objects and oblique complements (→ **286e**).

Some verbs are followed by an indirect and a direct object. An indirect object always has a direct object accompanying it.

An indirect object (IO) is the entity affected by (i.e. the recipient or beneficiary of) the direct object (DO). The indirect object comes before the direct object:

S | V | IO | DO

He | gave | me | his number.

Verbs used with indirect + direct object construction 286a

Common verbs which can be used with an indirect object + direct object construction include:

allow	*leave*	*save*
ask	*lend*	*send*
bring	*make*	*serve*
charge	*offer*	*show*
envy	*order*	*spare*
find	*owe*	*teach*
fine	*pay*	*tell*
forgive	*promise*	*throw*
give	*read*	*wish*
grant	*refuse*	
hand	*reserve*	

In these examples, the indirect object is underlined, the direct object is in green:

*He **brought** them some cakes.*

*I **lent** my niece £500.*

*I **offered** him a drink.*

*I **showed** you his photo, remember?*

→ **278** for a full account of direct and indirect objects

Indirect objects and passive voice 286b

Some verbs allow two passive voice alternatives for active clauses with indirect + direct object.

Examples of alternative passive constructions

example	type
IO DO	
*They **gave** the children presents.*	active
***The children** were given presents.*	passive alternative **1** (IO becomes subject)
***Presents** were given to the children.*	passive alternative **2** (DO becomes subject)

Passive alternative 1 (indirect object becomes subject) is the more common.

Verbs which allow alternative passives include:

bring	*grant*	*leave*
give	*hand*	*lend*

offer
owe
pay
promise
read
send
serve
show
teach
tell
throw

***We** were paid lots of money.*
(less frequent: Lots of money was paid [to us].)
(active alternatives: They paid us lots of money./They paid lots of money to us.)

***I** was taught English by her father.*
(possible, but less common or likely, alternative: English was taught to me by her father.)

The verbs in **286e** do not have alternative passives, and only the direct object noun phrase, not the noun phrase which is the complement of the preposition, may become the subject of a passive alternative:

***They** were robbed of all their belongings.*
(possible active clause: Somebody robbed them of all their belongings.)
(~~All their belongings were robbed [of] them.~~)

***She** was charged with murder.*
(possible active clause: They charged her with murder.)
(~~Murder was charged [with] her.~~)

Indirect object + *that*-clause as direct object 286c

Some verbs occur with an indirect object (underlined in the examples) plus a *that*-clause direct object (in green in the examples). For the following verbs the indirect object is obligatory:

assure
convince
inform
notify
persuade
remind
tell

*The bank manager **convinced** them that it was not a good time to start a business.*
(~~The bank manager convinced that it was not a good time to start a business.~~)

Remind her that the committee meeting is on Monday.

With other verbs, the indirect object is optional. A subjunctive verb form (i.e. subject + base form of the verb for all persons) may also occur. These include:

advise
ask
bet
order
promise
show
teach
warn
write

*Kumara left a suicide note **asking** that he **be** buried with his most cherished possessions.*
(subjunctive verb form *be*)

539 **Glossary** for any unfamiliar terms

*This graph **shows** that clocks have got more accurate over the years.*

*They **warned** that this could completely transform the countryside.*

Some verbs allow complementation with a prepositional phrase (underlined in the examples below) plus a *that*-clause direct object (in green in the examples below). These include:

acknowledge	*mention*	*state*
admit	*point out*	*propose*
announce	*prove*	*recommend*
complain	*remark*	*suggest*
confess	*report*	
explain	*say*	

*He did not return to his seat but **announced** to the general assembly that he was very tired.*

*I want an education, **to prove** to society that I am no longer dangerous.*

*I **suggested** to Charlie that he **come** with me but he turned pale at the idea.* (subjunctive verb form *come*)

Indirect object + *wh*-clause as direct object 286d

Advise, ask, inform, remind, show and *tell* may be used with an indirect object (underlined) and a *wh*-clause as direct object (in green):

*I **asked** him why he came.*

*Could you please **advise** me what I should do.*

[lecturer to students at beginning of lecture]
*Just to **remind** you what we covered last time, ...*

Advise, ask, instruct, remind, show, teach, tell and *warn* may be followed by an indirect object (underlined) and a *wh*-clause in the infinitive (in green):

*I'll **ask** Anne what to wear.*

*The pastry chef **showed** him how to create exotic desserts.*

*They should have **told** us what to do if we were dissatisfied.*

Direct object + prepositional phrase 286e

Give to, send to, etc.

Many of the verbs in **286a** can also be used with an object noun phrase and a prepositional phrase with *to*. This construction is sometimes called transitive oblique. The verbs are:

bring	*offer*	*serve*
give	*owe*	*show*
grant	*pay*	*teach*
hand	*promise*	*tell*
leave	*read*	*throw*
lend	*send*	

In these examples, the direct object is in green, the prepositional phrase is underlined:

*George **handed** the bottle to William.*

*She **sent** an email to him.*

*I **taught** English to adults.*

Other verbs may not be used in this way (direct object in green, indirect object underlined):

*I **envied** him his success.*
(~~I envied his success to him.~~)

The choice between using an indirect + direct object structure or an object + prepositional phrase (oblique complement) depends on what the speaker wishes to focus on in the message. As end position in English is generally associated with greater focus, either the direct object (in green) of the verb can be put into focus or the recipient of the direct object (underlined):

*George **handed** William the bottle.*
(end-focus on *the bottle*)

*George **handed** the bottle to William.*
(end-focus on *William*)

However, where two pronouns are involved, the prepositional (oblique) construction is often preferred to an indirect object + direct object:

*She wrote her name and address on the card and **gave** it to me.*
(or: … and gave me it; or, more informal: … and gave it me)

*I think my mother **gave** them to them.*
(preferred to: … gave them them)

Make for, save for

Not all the verbs in **286a** can be used with the oblique construction with a *to*-prepositional phrase. Some verbs are followed by a noun phrase (in green in the examples below) together with a prepositional phrase with *for* (underlined in the examples below). These include:

find	*order*	*save*
make	*reserve*	*spare*

Her mother ***made*** *me a lovely sweater.*

Her mother ***made*** *a lovely sweater for me.*
(~~Her mother made a lovely sweater to me.~~)

I'm going to be late. Can you ***save*** *me a seat?*

Can you save a seat for me?
(~~Can you save a seat to me?~~)

Accuse of, congratulate on, provide with

Other verbs have special prepositions associated with them and are only used in the oblique construction, not with indirect and direct objects. These verbs include:

accuse of	*persuade of*	*serve with*
charge with	*prevent from*	*subject to*
compare with	*protect from*	*suspect of*
congratulate on	*provide with*	*tell about*
convince of	*refer to*	*thank for*
deprive of	*relieve of*	*treat to*
inform of	*remind of*	*warn of*
interest in	*rob of*	
introduce to	*sentence to*	

The police ***charged*** *him with dangerous driving.*

Steven ***introduced*** *him to me.*
(~~Steven introduced me him.~~)

She said she'd ***provide*** *me with a list of all managers.*
(compare: She said she'd give me a list of all managers.)

The steward tried to ***relieve*** *me of my overcoat.*

She ***thanked*** *her colleagues for all the cards and presents.*

I want to ***treat*** *you to a drink.*

Direct object + *to*-infinitive clause 286f

Some verbs may be used with a direct object (in green in the examples below) followed by a *to*-infinitive clause (underlined in the examples below). These verbs include:

advise	*forbid*	*recommend*
ask	*implore*	*remind*
beg	*instruct*	*request*
challenge	*invite*	*teach*
command	*order*	*tell*
direct	*persuade*	*urge*

Did they ever ***advise*** *you to go and see a doctor?*

Sally ***invited*** *her to stay lots of times.*

COMPLEX TRANSITIVE COMPLEMENTATION 287

Complex transitive complementation occurs when a direct object is followed by an object complement or a locative complement (→ **287h**).

Direct object + object complement (adjective) 287a

Many common verbs may be used with a direct object (in green in the examples below) followed by an adjective phrase acting as object complement (underlined in the examples below). These include:

call	*hold*	*send*
consider	*keep*	*think*
declare	*leave*	*turn*
drive	*like*	*want*
find	*make*	
get	*prefer*	

I must ***keep*** *dad's dinner warm.*

The whole of mankind ***makes*** *me angry.*

We ***found*** *the garden slightly disappointing.*

Direct object + object complement (noun) 287b

Some verbs may be followed by a direct object (in green in the examples below) and a noun phrase object complement (underlined in the examples below).

In the sentence *He made her a cake*, *her* is the indirect object and *a cake* is the direct object. In the sentence *He made her a rich woman*, *her* and *a rich woman* refer to the same person; *a rich woman* is the object complement.

Verbs which can be followed by a direct object and a noun phrase object complement include:

appoint	*deem*	*name*
baptize	*elect*	*proclaim*
call	*find*	*pronounce*
christen	*hold*	*rate*
consider	*keep*	*think*
crown	*leave*	*vote*
declare	*make*	

If I never saw them again, I would not ***consider*** *it a loss.*

They ***declared*** *the festival a great success.*

You will, I think, ***find*** *it a comfort in the years ahead.*

You've done these different things and it has ***made*** *you a slightly different person.*

Direct object + *to*-infinitive clause 287c

A number of verbs may be used with a direct object (in green in the examples below) followed by a *to*-infinitive clause acting as the object complement (underlined in the examples below). These verbs include:

allow	*expect*	*permit*
announce	*feel*	*presume*
appoint	*find*	*proclaim*
assume	*force*	*prompt*
believe	*get*	*reckon*
condemn	*help*	*report*
consider	*imagine*	*require*
declare	*inspire*	*suppose*
elect	*intend*	*take*
enable	*know*	*think*
encourage	*lead*	*tip*
entitle	*mean*	*understand*
equip	*oblige*	

Heathcote Williams quite simply loathes the automobile. He ***believes*** *it to be the world's prime source of disease, pollution and war and a destroyer of mind, nature and morality.*

[*Pickfords* is a removal company]
A Pickfords van ploughed its way past me en route from Cadiz to Marbella. I ***imagined*** *it to be transporting a retired English couple's belongings.*

She had never ***intended*** *her work to cause such controversy.*

These constructions can be paralleled in the passive voice, especially with reporting verbs:

He ***is believed*** *to have arrived in Moscow in the last two weeks.*

It has ***been known*** *to happen.*

The polluted waters ***were reported*** *to be moving out to sea.*

Direct object + infinitive clause without *to* 287d

Verbs followed by a direct object (in green in the examples below) and an infinitive clause without *to* (underlined in the examples below) include:

feel	*let*	*see*
have	*make*	*watch*
hear	*notice*	
help	*overhear*	

I ***had*** *him mend that fence for me.*

There's a law firm that will ***help*** *you make a claim against the travel agent if you've had a bad holiday.*

Hilary used to come down here and ***watch*** *me bake cakes.*

Direct object + *-ing* clause 287e

Verbs followed by a direct object (in green in the examples below) and an *-ing* clause (underlined in the examples below) include:

catch	*have*	*overhear*
discover	*hear*	*see*
feel	*leave*	*smell*
find	*notice*	*spot*
get	*observe*	*watch*

→ **539 Glossary** for any unfamiliar terms

*I **found** her <u>bathing the baby, which was lovely</u>.*

*At ten o'clock every Friday they'd **hear** someone <u>walking up the stairs</u>.*

*My next-door neighbour actually said to me that the girl next door to her had **overheard** them <u>talking about breaking into this house on the corner</u>.*

Verbs of perception with *-ing* or infinitive without *to* 287f

Feel, hear, overhear, notice, see and *watch* may be used with *-ing* or the infinitive without *to*. When used with *-ing*, the emphasis is on the action or event in progress; when used with the infinitive without *to*, the emphasis is on the action or event seen as a whole, or as completed:

*Jeff **saw** something **going** on, so he ran out.*
(emphasis is on the event in progress at that moment)
(preferred to: Jeff saw something go on, so he ran out.)

*The girl next door to her had **overheard** them **talking** about breaking into this house on the corner.*
(she heard the conversation in progress, but probably not the whole conversation)

*I've not **heard** him **mention** Glasgow yet.*
(emphasis on the event as a whole, or absence of it)

*In the airport I walked from the coffee bar without paying the bill after I **saw** a mouse **run** unseen by anyone across the bar top.*
(emphasis on the whole, completed event)

Direct object + *-ed* clause 287g

The following verbs may occur with a direct object (in green in the examples below) plus *-ed* (*-ed* participle) clause (underlined in the examples below):

feel (oneself)	*have*	*need*
find	*leave*	*want*
get	*like*	

*I keep meaning to **get** it <u>fixed</u>.*

*He **had** a few things <u>stolen</u>.*

*They **want** him <u>buried there</u>.*

A–Z 51 ***Make***; 75 ***Want***

Direct object + prepositional complement of time or place (locative) 287h

Some verbs, especially verbs of placement and direction, take a direct object (in green in the examples below) and a prepositional phrase locating the object in terms of time or place (locative complement) (underlined in the examples below). Such verbs include:

bring
drive
lay
lead
place
put
send
set
show
stand
take

*Edith **led** her through her own front door.*

*Did you **put** your stuff in our bedroom?*

*He **took** me to a club in Manchester.*

COPULAR COMPLEMENTATION 288

Copular verbs 288a

Copular verbs describe states (e.g. *appear, be, feel, look, seem, smell, sound, taste*) or changing states/results (e.g. *become, get, go, grow, turn out*).

Copular verbs link subjects with subject complements. Subject complements may be adjective phrases, noun phrases, adverb phrases or prepositional phrases.

Adjective phrase complements 288b

Adjective phrase complements (in green) of copular verbs are very common:

- State:

  *They don't **seem** very happy up there, you know.*

  *He **was** too clever for them.*

  *It **looked** a bit big.*

- Change of state/result:

  *Leeds city centre has **become** better.*

  *What makes them **go** pink?*

  *It always **turns out** black.*

- Adjective complements and collocation:

  Some adjective complements collocate strongly with particular verbs, and the verb has a similar function to a copular verb:

  *We **fell** silent as we tried to understand what he was saying.*

  *He just **lay** flat on the bed, without moving.*

  *They won't succeed. Oh no. We'll **stand** firm.*

Other expressions of this kind include *blush red, die young, freeze solid, keep quiet, lie awake, loom large, slam shut.*

→ 539 **Glossary** for any unfamiliar terms

Noun phrase complements 288c

Many verbs which allow an adjective phrase complement also allow a noun phrase complement (in green). These include *appear, be, become, feel, look, remain, seem* and *sound*:

*Samantha's **not** my friend.*

*Well, it **became** a liability.*

*This **looks** a delicious meal.*

*He **seemed** a nice enough lad.*

Some verbs which allow an adjective complement do not normally occur with a noun phrase complement. These include *get, go, grow, smell* and *taste*.

Adverb phrase complements 288d

Be, get, lie, live, remain and *stay* can all be used with adverb phrase complements (in green):

Amy's upstairs, isn't she?

*I'll wait till I **get** home, I think.*

Prepositional phrase complements 288e

Be, get, lie, live, remain, stand and *stay* can all be used with prepositional phrase complements (in green):

*Your glasses **are** on the table. Don't forget them.*

*A memorial to him **stands** in the park which also bears his name.*

OTHER ASPECTS OF COMPLEMENTATION 289

Complementation with *should* and subjunctive mood 289a

A group of verbs with meanings connected with requests and desires can be used with a *that*-clause (in green in the examples below) and the modal verb *should*, or with a subjunctive form. The subjunctive form uses the base form of the verb, and has no third person *-s* in present time reference.

Both forms are associated with formal styles, with the subjunctive form being associated with very formal styles. The verbs include:

agree	*concede*	*insist*
arrange	*demand*	*intend*
ask	*determine*	*prefer*
beg	*ensure*	*propose*

recommend	*require*	*suggest*
request	*stipulate*	

*Robert had **arranged** that the visitors **should** be brought down to his office.*

*Right from the start he would have **insisted** that his son **embark** on a proper profession.*
(subjunctive)

[*the Hollyhocks* is the name of a hotel]
*They **agreed** that they **should** stay at the Hollyhocks, and blushingly **suggested** that they **be** given an adjacent suite of rooms.*
(here *should* follows *agreed*; subjunctive follows *suggested*)

Consider, deem and find 289b

When *consider, deem* or *find* are followed by adjective + *to*-infinitive clause or *that*-clause, the object pronoun *it* must be used after the verb:

*'We **considered it** essential they be separated,' continued Khan, unperturbed.*

*I **find it** very difficult to have my eyes dealt with.*
(~~I find very difficult to have my eyes dealt with.~~)

Complementation and prepositional verbs 289c

Prepositional verbs consist of a verb and a preposition which are closely syntactically and semantically linked with each other (→ **235f**), and as such they are similar to simple lexical verbs. The object (in green) follows the preposition:

*It all **depends on** how much it costs.*
(prepositional verb)

*No-one could **disagree** with that.*
(lexical verb)

→ **235f** for a list of common prepositional verbs

Some prepositional verbs take a direct object (in green) and a complement of the preposition (underlined):

*I **associate** Bristol <u>with many happy memories</u>.*

*The safety goggles are supposed to **protect** you <u>from bits of grit and stones</u>.*

Clause types

Clause types

INTRODUCTION 290

Types of finite clause

In the first part of this chapter (291–294) we consider the different basic types of finite clause. These are declarative, interrogative, imperative and exclamative.

Declarative clauses are typically associated with statements:

She works in publishing.

I've never met his father.

Interrogative clauses are typically associated with questions:

Do you need any help at all?

Has Katie arrived yet?

Imperative clauses are typically associated with directives (commands, orders, etc.):

Get some kitchen paper, will you.

Sign here, please.

Exclamative clauses are associated with exclamations:

What a lovely dress you're wearing!

How ugly it all is!

Main and subordinate clauses

We then consider the characteristics of main clauses and subordinate clauses (295–296). Main clauses are not dependent on any other clauses and can form sentences on their own. Subordinate clauses are dependent on other clauses and can only form sentences by combining with main clauses. Main clauses are in bold:

It hasn't lasted very long.
(one main clause, also one sentence)

I'll see you *when I get back, then.*
(main clause and time adverbial clause)

Will you be at home *if I ring you tonight?*
(main clause and conditional clause)

The guy *who came this morning* ***was very polite.***
(main clause and embedded relative clause)

Push it right down, as far as it'll go.
(main clause and comparative clause)

*Working all day like that **you'll exhaust yourself**.*
(non-finite *-ing* form conditional clause and main clause)

Finite and non-finite clauses

The next sections (297–298) look at finite and non-finite clauses. A finite clause has a verb which indicates tense (i.e. a tensed verb form, → 215). A non-finite clause has a verb with no indication of tense (i.e. a non-tensed verb form, → 215), and depends for the interpretation of its time reference on other clauses in the environment:

*They jointly **earned** £60,000 a year.*
(finite: past tense form)

*Sally just phoned me **wondering** whether she should come over in the near future rather than at New Year.*
(*wondering* is a non-tensed form, but its past time context is interpreted from *phoned*; the clause in green is non-finite)

Tags

The chapter also considers tags (299–303), which are short clauses added on to main clauses either to create questions or to reinforce statements, directives and exclamations:

*You like mushrooms, **don't you**?*

*I'm hungry, **I am**.*

*Pass me that pen, **will you**.*

*What a pretty girl, **isn't she**!*

DECLARATIVE CLAUSES 291

Structure 291a

The word order in declarative clauses is subject (s) – verb (v) – x , where x is any other element present (e.g. object/complement).

Declaratives are most typically used to make statements and assertions:

s v
I | saw | him in the distance.

s v
These days | he | seems | quite happy.

s v
Bob | often | annoys | people.

s v
I | don't put | salt on my food.

Affirmative declaratives 291b

An affirmative declarative clause makes a statement about something that is, as opposed to something that is not.

Examples of affirmative declarative clauses

subject	verb	x
He	*is*	*a good teacher.*
I	*'ve noticed*	*it.*
She	*works*	*in the mornings.*
He	*mentioned*	*that.*

Negative declaratives 291c

Negative declarative clauses negate a proposition. They have the word order subject – auxiliary/modal verb – negative particle – verb – x, where x is any other element present (e.g. object/complement).

Examples of negative declarative clauses

subject	auxiliary/modal verb	negative particle	verb	x
The lights	*were*	*not*	*working.*	
He	*could*	*not*	*afford*	*it.*
He	*did*	*n't (= not)*	*phone*	*me.*
I	*was*	*n't*	*allowed*	*in the room.*

In informal language, especially spoken contexts, the negative particle *not* is contracted to *n't* (though only very rarely with *may* and *used to*, ⇢ **380e** and **400**).

⇢ **437 Negation and mental process verbs** for negation with verbs such as *think, hope, guess, wish*

⇢ also **472–475 Word order and focus**

Declaratives used as questions, requests and directives 291d

Affirmative and negative declarative clauses typically function as statements, but may also occasionally function as questions or requests or directives:

A: ***You want it today***?
B: *Yes, as quickly as possible.*
(question)

A: ***You could put that in the dishwasher for me***.
B: *Okay.*
(directive)

A: *I'm going to have a cake.* ***You haven't got any cakes***?
B: *I have indeed.*
(question)

[fixing an appointment]
A: ***You couldn't make it twelve o'clock.***
B: *Yeah, twelve would be fine.*
(request)

[talking about a child; the expression *to go ballistic* means to lose one's temper in an extreme way]
*He actually had had a temper tantrum for the first time yesterday and his sister took something off him and he went absolutely ballistic and he went '**You don't do that!**' and pushed her.*
(directive)

→ also **430 Declarative questions** and **410a Declarative clauses functioning as questions**

INTERROGATIVE CLAUSES 292

Polar interrogatives: *yes-no, x or y* 292a

Polar interrogative clauses typically function to ask questions to which the answer is *yes* or *no* (*yes-no* questions), or questions with *x or y?* (alternative questions), where the respondent must choose between alternatives.

Normal word order for polar interrogatives is auxiliary/modal verb – subject – verb – x, where x is any other element present (e.g. object/complement).

The auxiliary verb may be *be, do* or *have.*

Examples of polar interrogatives

	auxiliary/modal	subject	verb	x
be	*Were*	*you*	***staying***	*in Cardiff?*
	Are	*you*	***going***	*by boat* **or** *train?*
do	*Do*	*you*	***know***	*the way to the market?*
	Did	*we*	***go***	*twice* **or** *just once?*
have	*Haven't*	*you*	***phoned***	*your sister yet?*
	Have	*you*	***got***	*a pair of scissors* **or** *a sharp knife?*
modal	*Shouldn't*	*we*	***leave***	*it till tomorrow?*
	Could	*we*	***meet***	*for lunch the following Tuesday?*

Wherever there is no auxiliary *be*, auxiliary *have* or modal verb already present, auxiliary *do/does/did* is used.

Where there is more than one auxiliary verb or a modal verb plus auxiliary verb(s), only the first auxiliary or the modal verb precedes the subject.

Examples of polar interrogatives with multiple auxiliary verbs

modal verb/first auxiliary verb	subject	second auxiliary verb	verb	x
Is	*your violin*	*being*	*repaired?*	
Has	*the flat*	*been*	*painted or redecorated*	*recently?*
Could	*it*	*have*	*been*	*like the problem you had before?*
Will	*you*	*be*	*ordering*	*some stuff, then?*

Note that only auxiliary and modal verbs, not lexical verbs, may come before the subject:

	auxiliary verb	subject	lexical verb	
When	***was***	***the book***	***written***,	*do you know?*

(~~When was written the book, do you know?~~)

Sentences with modal verb – subject – verb – x structure also frequently function as requests or as directives:

Could you *give me a call about nine o'clock this evening?*
(request)

Will you *be quiet!*
(directive)

⇢ **412 Modality and directives**

Polar interrogatives with lexical verbs *be* and *have* 292b

Lexical verb *be*

Interrogatives with lexical verb *be* have verb – subject – x word order (verb in bold, subject in green):

Are *they all the same?*

Was *the swimming pool busy?*

Lexical verb *have*

With lexical verb *have*, verb – subject – x word order sounds rather formal. Interrogatives with auxiliary *do* and with *have got* are the preferred forms in informal situations:

*'**Has he** his name on the door?' Mr Laidlaw said suddenly.*
(formal)

Do they have *a lot of toys?*
(informal)

Has she got *any brothers or sisters?*
(informal)

The choice between the inverted form, the *do/does/did* ... *have* form, and *have/has/had* ... *got* form depends on the meaning of *have*. When *have* refers to possession/attribution, all forms are possible:

> ***Has he got*** *his name on the door?*
> (possession/attribution: most informal)
>
> ***Does he have*** *his name on the door?*
> (possession/attribution: informal)
>
> ***Has he*** *his name on the door?*
> (possession/attribution: formal)

Interrogatives in the past tense show a marked preference for the *did* ... *have* form rather than the *had* ... *got* form when referring to possession/attribution:

> ***Did you have*** *a car when you were younger?*
> (more frequent form)
>
> A: ***Had he got*** *a little girl?*
> B: *A little boy.*
> (less frequent form)

When *have* means 'to hold or take part in a habitual event', the *do*-forms are used. The inverted form and the *got*-forms are not used:

> *How often* **do you have** *parties?*
> (refers to regularity of events)
> (~~How often have you got parties?~~)
> (~~How often have you parties?~~)
>
> ***Does Nigel have*** *butter?*
> (Does he normally use/eat butter?)
> (compare: Has Nigel got butter?, which would mean 'Does he possess/has he received butter?')

When *have* is used in the pseudo-passive (→ **480**), the *do/does/did* forms are used, not the inverted form:

> *How often* **do you have** *your car serviced?*
> (~~How often have you your car serviced?~~)

→ **403d *Have to, have got to***

Exclamations with *be*
Clauses with verb – subject – x word order with lexical verb *be* can occasionally function as exclamations:

> *It was a very good school, but* ***was I*** *lamentably ignorant in maths!*

→ **472–475 Word order and focus** and **408–423 Speech acts** for further examples

Negative polar interrogatives 292c

Negative *yes-no* interrogatives are typically used to ask questions which function to check or confirm something which the speaker believes or expects to be the case, or which the speaker considers to be a viable course of action.

The negative is formed with *not*, and is most frequently contracted to *n't*. Sentences with the full form *not* are more formal than those with contracted *n't*:

Wasn't he *here at the party?*

Don't you *want any tea or coffee?*

When the full form is used, *not* comes after the subject:

Could you not *hear me?*
(please confirm, yes or no)

Should we not *photocopy it?*
(I consider this a desirable action)

In very formal, rather archaic literary styles, full form *not* may occur before the subject:

[from *Northanger Abbey* by Jane Austen; speaking about open carriages]
Do not you *think it has an odd appearance, if young ladies are frequently driven about in them by young men, to whom they are not even related?*

Negative interrogatives with modal verbs are also often used to express polite requests or polite commands:

'Please, ***won't you*** *both* ***come*** *through?' Carole said, leading them down the red carpeted foyer and into the dimly lit restaurant.*

Replies to negative interrogatives

Note that a reply which agrees with the proposition in a negative polar interrogative is made with *no*, not *yes*:

A: ***Isn't*** *Margaret here today?*
B: ***No****. She's on holiday.*
(~~Yes. She's on holiday.~~)

A: ***Don't*** *you want any tea or coffee?*
B: ***No****. I've just had breakfast. Thanks anyway.*

However, negative polar interrogatives where the asker is simply checking information believed to be true may be answered with *yes*:

A: ***Isn't*** *she older than her brother?*
B: ***Yes****, she is. There's about three years between them, I think.*
(speaker B confirms what speaker A believes to be true)

Wh-interrogatives 292d

Wh-interrogatives (clauses introduced by *what, when, where, which, who, whose, why, how*) typically function to ask questions which seek information, and cannot be answered simply with *yes* or *no*.

If the *wh*-question-word is the subject or forms part of the subject, then subject – verb – x word order is used, and auxiliary *do* is not used:

S V
Who | *wants* | *more coffee?*
(~~Who does want more coffee?~~)

S V
Whose car | *got stolen?*
(~~Whose car did get stolen?~~)

In all other cases, interrogative word order is used:

O AUX S V
Who | *did* | *you* | *see* | *there?*
(*wh*-word refers to the object)
(~~Who you saw there?~~)

O MODAL S V
What | *can* | *I* | *do* | *to help?*
(*wh*-word refers to the object)
(~~What I can do to help?~~)

A AUX S V
Why | *have* | *they* | *got to* | *sit and wait?*
(*wh*-word refers to the adjunct)
(~~Why they have got to sit and wait?~~)

A AUX S V
When | *are* | *you* | *leaving?*
(*wh*-word refers to the adjunct)
(~~When you are leaving?~~)

C (SUBJ) V S
Whose *shoes* | *are* | *those?*
(*wh*-word refers to the subject complement)
(~~Whose shoes those are?~~)

Wh-interrogatives with lexical verb *have* are formed with auxiliary *do* or the *have got* construction when the *wh*-word refers to an element other than the subject. The formal verb-subject construction is not used:

What do you have *for me? Anything?*
(~~What have you for me?~~)

Why have you got *three email addresses?*
(~~Why have you three email addresses?~~)

Prepositions and particles with *wh*-interrogatives 292e

Wh-words and *wh*-phrases can be the complement of a preposition, in which case the preposition and its complement typically occur together in more formal styles:

> ***To whom*** *did the last item belong?*
> (*wh*-word)

> ***For what purpose*** *could it be used?*
> (*wh*-phrase)

In informal styles, especially in spoken language, the preposition may be stranded (separated from its complement, → 257) and placed at the end of the clause:

> [writing a cheque]
> ***Who*** *do I make it out* ***to****?*

> ***Where*** *do you get them* ***from****?*

In the case of reduced questions, the preposition and its complement normally occur together:

> A: *She was quite upset.*
> B: ***For what*** *reason?*
> (~~What reason for?~~)

> *A marriage of convenience, if ever there was one. But* ***for what*** *motive?*
> (~~But what motive for?~~)

With phrasal verbs, which are combinations of verbs and particles (→ 235c), the particles stay attached to the verb, rather than to the *wh*-word:

> ***What*** *did they* ***get up to****?*
> (What mischief/misbehaviour were they involved in?)
> (~~Up to what did they get?~~)

> ***Which*** *dictionary shall I* ***look*** *it* ***up*** *in?*
> (or, in formal style: In which dictionary shall I look it up?)
> (~~Up in which dictionary shall I look it?~~)

Negative *wh*-interrogatives 292f

In negative *wh*-interrogatives, auxiliary *do* is used in all cases where there is no other auxiliary or modal verb, even when the *wh*-word is subject of its clause:

> ***Who doesn't want*** *tea?*

> ***Which*** *one* ***didn't you use****?*

> ***Why can't I say*** *'Good afternoon, gentlemen and ladies'?*

Indirect interrogatives 292g

Indirect polar interrogatives

When a polar interrogative is reported indirectly, *if* or *whether* is used. *Whether* tends to be more formal.

The reported clause has subject – verb – x word order.

Examples of indirect polar interrogatives

direct interrogative	indirect interrogative
Will you be seeing *them during the week?*	*She asked me* ***if/whether I would be seeing*** *them during the week.*
Did he enjoy *himself?*	*I asked* ***if/whether he had enjoyed*** *himself.*
Does everybody go *or just the ladies?*	*I don't know* ***if/whether everybody went*** *or just the ladies.*
Can I phone *you back?*	*He wondered* ***if/whether he could phone*** *me back.*
Have they been *helpful?*	*She asked* ***if/whether they had been*** *helpful.*

→ **493 Viewpoint: Time and place references** in **Speech representation** for the principles of backshift in tense and deictic changes in indirect interrogatives

When *or not* immediately follows, *whether* is preferred to *if*:

I don't know ***whether or not*** *you'll print this.*
(preferred to: I don't know if or not …)

When *or not* is placed later in the clause, then *if* may be used:

I didn't know ***if*** *I was going to do it* ***or not****.*

In informal speech, interrogative word order may occur as an alternative to an *if/whether* clause:

When I asked her ***was she looking*** *for a job, she said, 'Well, not really'.*
(instead of: if/whether she was looking …)

I wonder ***is that form wrong****.*
(instead of: if/whether that form is wrong.)

Indirect *wh*-interrogatives

When a *wh*-interrogative is reported indirectly, the word order in the reported clause is normally subject – verb – x, not interrogative:

S V
So I asked him ***what*** | ***the arrangements*** | ***were****.*

S V
I phoned up the hospital and asked ***who*** | ***I*** | ***should address*** | *the letter to.*

However, in informal speech, interrogative word order is sometimes used:

AUX S V
She wanted to know ***why*** | ***didn't*** | ***I*** | ***go*** | *too.*
(compare: She wanted to know why I didn't go too.)

Where the subject of the reporting clause and the reported clause are the same, an infinitive construction may be used in the reported clause:

[in a restaurant]
Oh, I don't know ***what to have****. What are you having?*

*How do they decide **who to employ** and who not?*
(*they* decide and *they* employ)

→ also **424–433 Questions** and **408–423 Speech acts**

IMPERATIVE CLAUSES 293

Structure 293a

Imperative clauses typically function to give directives (e.g. commands, orders, instructions).

Imperative clauses do not have an overt subject. They have the word order verb – x. The lexical verb is in its base form (→ **229**):

***Give** me a clue.*

*Just **leave** it there.*

***Tell** me when you've finished.*

***Be** quiet!*

***Don't move**!*

***Let's go** home now.*

Imperatives with subject pronoun

Imperatives may occasionally occur with an emphatic subject pronoun *you*. This may be for contrastive emphasis, or simply to make the imperative stronger:

[speakers are clearing things from the table after a meal]
A: *Shall I take those out?*
B: ***You take** those two out on the tray. And I'll just put this milk away.*

[parent to a child just about to play with a dog]
***Don't you start** teasing him now!*

In very informal spoken contexts, *you* may occur after the verb, especially where speakers are being playful or mildly reproachful:

[mother to young child]
*Come on, **you**!*

An indefinite subject such as *someone/somebody*, *no one/nobody*, *everyone/everybody* may also occur, especially in informal spoken language:

***Somebody get** one more chair, please.*

*Quick! **Everybody hide**!*

Imperative as invitation

The bare imperative may also function to make an offer or an invitation:

***Have** some more coffee.*

*Next time you're in Manchester, **come** and see us.*

The bare imperative is a very direct form in English and should be used with great care in order to avoid the perception of impoliteness. It is **not** generally used to make requests/commands or give instructions (e.g. in service encounters in shops or restaurants) except in cases where people are very familiar with one another, and except where accompanied by *please*.

→ **408–423 Speech acts** for the most common ways of requesting, instructing

[to a waiter]
Could we have the bill please?
(~~Give us the bill.~~)

Just and/or *please* can also soften an imperative:

[customer and market trader]
A: *And some peppers, please.*
B: *Yeah. How many?*
A: ***Just give** me two big ones, **please**.*

Imperatives with *do*

Imperatives with emphatic *do*-auxiliary are perceived as more polite than bare imperatives:

[to guests who have just arrived]
***Do take** your coats off.*

Short imperative answers may consist of emphatic *do* without a lexical verb:

A: *Can I leave this in your office?*
B: *Yes, **do**, by all means.*

Imperatives with *let*

First person plural and third person imperatives are formed with *let*:

A: *Bob's here to see you.*
B: ***Let him** wait. I don't want to see him yet.*

Contracted *let's* is the most frequent form for first person plural imperatives. In very formal contexts, the full form *let us* is used:

***Let's** start, shall we.*

***Let us** remember those who died on this day, twenty-five years ago.*

Emphatic *do* may be used with *let's*:

***Do let's** hurry up or we'll be late again.*

Let's may occur alone in short responses:

A: *Shall we go for a walk?*
B: *Yes, **let's**.*

Negative imperatives 293b

Negative imperatives are constructed with auxiliary *do*. Contracted *don't* is the most common form in spoken language:

Please ***don't tell*** *him until he rings me.*

Don't be *silly.*

In more formal styles the full form *do not* often occurs:

[instructions for keeping a cake fresh for a long time]
Do not store *in a sealed plastic container or in the kitchen, as the humidity will make it sweat and go mouldy.*

Short negative imperative answers or reactions may consist of *don't* without a lexical verb:

A: *Should I tell her, do you think?*
B: *No,* ***don't.*** *It'll only upset her.*

Negative imperatives with subject pronoun

Negative imperatives with emphatic subject pronoun *you* or with an indefinite subject (e.g. *nobody*) may also occur, especially in informal spoken language:

You know we're coming up again next year. ***Don't you worry,*** *Ursula, we'll be up you know.*

I'll tell her. ***Don't you say*** *anything.*

Nobody say *a word, okay.*

Negative imperative of *let's*

The negative of *let's* is most typically *let's not*. Less frequently, *don't let's* may occur:

Let's not *be silly about it.*

Don't let's *confuse the issue.*

In rather formal styles, *let us not* or *do not let us* may occur:

[Trade Union Annual Conference speech]
Let us not *forget that we're not in business to remain in perpetual opposition.*

[Trade Union Annual Conference speech]
Colleagues, ***do not let us*** *shirk from our responsibilities to our fellow workers.*

EXCLAMATIVE CLAUSES 294

Exclamatives consist of phrases with *what* and *how* (or a clause with *how*) followed by a subject – verb – x construction.

They usually express a reaction of surprise or shock or the experience of a strong impression on the part of the speaker.

→ **539 Glossary** for any unfamiliar terms

In writing, they are often punctuated with an exclamation mark (!).

→ **506 Appendix: Punctuation**

What is followed by a noun phrase:

***What a lovely cake** they bought you!*

***What nonsense** you talk!*

How may be followed by an adjective phrase, an adverb phrase or a clause:

***How happy** they both seem!*

***How wonderfully** it worked out!*

***How I wished** I could have been there!*

The exclamative clause may consist of the *wh*-word and a phrase alone, especially in spoken language:

***What** a wonderful thing!*

***How** sad! **How** terribly sad!*

***How** awful!*

Simple exclamatives are not normally constructed with *such* followed by an un-premodified noun:

Wow! What a view!
(~~Wow! Such a view!~~)

However, *such* may occur before a premodified noun:

*What a beautiful house! And **such a wonderful garden**!*

MAIN CLAUSES 295

A main clause is a clause which is not dependent on any other clause in the sentence. A sentence must have at least one main clause.

A main clause must be finite; that is, it must have a verb which is inflected for tense:

A simple diet suits me.
(sentence consisting of one main clause, not dependent on any other clause)

He was very quiet, and he had beautiful manners.
(two independent main clauses joined by *and*)

SUBORDINATE CLAUSES 296

A subordinate clause is dependent on another clause in the sentence. A sentence may not consist of a subordinate clause alone.

A subordinate clause may be finite or non-finite (⇢ 297, 298). Examples of subordinate clauses:

***If people feel good about coming to work**, they will work better.*
(*if*-clause dependent on main clause)

*I laughed at him **when he first asked me**.*
(*when*-clause dependent on main clause)

***To get the morning flight**, we'd have to leave here about eight.*
(non-finite clause dependent on main clause)

***To do it by hand** would be difficult.*
(non-finite clause as subject)

*The people **I work with** are nice.*
(relative clause functioning as postmodifier in the noun phrase)

*It's not really as bad as **most people think**.*
(clause as the complement of a comparative adjective phrase)

Subordinate clauses in conversation 296a

In conversation, subordinate clauses may appear to be used alone, but they are usually dependent on a main clause nearby, spoken either by another speaker or by the same speaker:

A: *You're coming on Friday?*
B: *Yeah. **If I can**.*
(understood: I'm coming on Friday if I can.)

[assembling a piece of flat-pack furniture]
A: *This has got screw holes. Right?*
B: *Right.*
A: ***Which is funny isn't it**. It's not at all obvious what they support.*
(understood: that it has screw holes is funny)

⇢ 87b Subordinate clauses

⇢ 310–317 for a full description of subordinate clauses

FINITE CLAUSES 297

A finite clause contains a verb which is inflected for tense (present or past). Finite clauses typically have a subject, and can be main or subordinate clauses.

Examples of finite clauses

clause	tense
*He **lives** on his own.*	present
***Aren't** you going anywhere in between times?*	present
*I seriously **considered** private health care.*	past
*She always **rings** | when we**'re** out.*	present | present
*We **could** go up and get one.*	modal*

* Some modal verbs have forms which can indicate present and past time reference (e.g. *can/could, shall/should, will/would, may/might*) (→ **380b**). Past forms in such cases are often used to make indirect statements about a present or future situation, or to perform particular speech acts (→ **408–423 Speech acts**):

*I thought I **would** wait and see what happened.*

***Could** you hold this for me, please?*

NON-FINITE CLAUSES 298

Non-finite clauses contain a lexical verb which does not indicate tense. Non-finite clauses can normally only be subordinate, and typically combine with finite ones in sentences.

References to time (and person and number) are normally interpreted from context or from information in the finite clause to which the non-finite clause is related.

Examples of non-finite clauses (non-finite clauses are shaded, verbs are in bold)

type	clause	clause	comments
-ing clause	*The documentary **is** built like fictional drama,*	***following** the parents' anguish and the doctor's anxiety through the months of ups and downs.*	the subject of *following* is *the documentary*, and its time reference is the same as *is* (present time)
-ing clause	*The London Stock Market **welcomed** the news of the deal,*	***marking** the company's shares up 50 pence.*	the subject of *marking* is *the London Stock Market*, and its time reference is the same as *welcomed* (past time)
-ing clause	*At ten o'clock every Friday they**'d hear** someone*	***walking** up the stairs.*	understood past time references: 'someone *was walking* up the stairs'
to-infinitive clause	***To help** the people who travel into the city by car,*	*there **are** multi-storey car parks around the edge of the city centre.*	the subject of *help* is *multi-storey car parks*, and its time reference is the same as *there are* (present time)
-ed clause	***Helped** by her children's schoolteacher,*	*Sue **started** out on the learning process she should have begun 30 years earlier.*	the (passive) subject of *helped* is *Sue*, and its time reference is the same as *started* (past time)
-ed clause	*You **should read** the parts*	***highlighted** in yellow.*	understood present time reference: 'which are/have been highlighted in yellow'

TAGS 299

Tags are a type of clause without a lexical verb but which relate to the verb in the main clause of a sentence.

Tags consist of auxiliary *be, do, have*, lexical verb *be* or a modal verb and a subject (most typically a pronoun). They may have declarative or interrogative word order and may have affirmative or negative polarity.

The four main types of tag are question tags, directive tags, statement tags (also known as copy tags) and exclamation tags:

- Question tags:

  *She's a teacher, **isn't she**?*
  *I haven't shown you this, **have I**?*
  *You've met David, **have you**?*

- Directive tags:

  *Shut the door, **will you**.*
  *Don't stay out too late, **will you**.*

- Statement tags:

  *I'm hungry, **I am**.*
  *She was very kind, **Rita was**.*
  *He's not so tall, **Jim isn't**.*

- Exclamation tags:

  *How strange, **isn't it**!*
  *What a laugh that was, **wasn't it**!*

QUESTION TAGS 300

General 300a

Question tags are used to check or clarify information, or simply to involve the listener in a more interactive way.

Question tags consist of an auxiliary or modal verb or lexical verb *be* + subject pronoun. The subject pronoun repeats the subject of the main clause to which it refers, and agrees in number, person and gender with the subject of the main clause.

Where the main clause contains an auxiliary or modal verb or lexical verb *be*, it is repeated in the tag.

Examples of question tags with repeated auxiliary

	declarative clause	auxiliary/modal verb	subject pronoun
1	***You've** worked hard,*	***haven't***	***you**?*
2	***He didn't** get it,*	***did***	***he**?*
3	***We had** talked about it,*	***hadn't***	***we**?*
4	***I can** do it now,*	***can***	***I**?*
5	***Kate is** Irish,*	***isn't***	***she**?*

→ 539 **Glossary** for any unfamiliar terms

Where there is no auxiliary or modal verb in the main clause, auxiliary *do/does/did* is used in the tag.

Examples of question tags with added auxiliary verb

	declarative clause	auxiliary verb	subject pronoun
6	***He said*** *it's basically the same,*	***did***	***he****?*
7	***Patsy lives*** *in Lincoln,*	***doesn't***	***she****?*
8	[lexical verb *have*] ***They have*** *one every year,*	***do***	***they****?*

Negative tags are normally contracted in informal styles (*doesn't he?, don't they?, weren't we?, isn't it?*, etc.). In more formal styles, uncontracted *not* may occur:

You changed servants at that time, ***did you not****?*

So we're left with three possibilities, ***are we not****?*

Question tag polarity: affirmative or negative 300b

Polarity refers to whether a verb phrase is affirmative or negative. In examples **1**, **2**, **3**, **5** and **7** in the tables in **300a**, there is contrasting polarity between the main clause and the tag:

affirmative / negative
*You |****'ve****| worked hard, |* ***haven't*** *| you?*

negative / affirmative
He | ***didn't*** *| get it, |* ***did*** *| he?*

affirmative / negative
We | ***had*** *| talked about it, |* ***hadn't*** *| we?*

In examples **4**, **6** and **8**, the polarity is affirmative in the main clause and the tag:

affirmative / affirmative
I | ***can*** *| do it now, |* ***can*** *| I?*

The different patterns of polarity combine with intonation patterns to produce a variety of different meanings. ··› 431 for a full account

Main clauses with *am, may, used to, ought to* 300c

Am, may, used to and *ought to* do not follow the normal pattern of obligatory repetition in the question tag. Typical usage is as follows.

Examples of tag questions with *am, may, used to, ought to*

	declarative clause	tag auxiliary/modal	subject
am	***I'm*** *crazy to even think about it,*	***aren't***	*I?*
may	*Jim* ***may*** *be able to help,*	***mightn't***	*he?*
used to	*He* ***used to*** *work with you,*	***did******	*he?*
ought to	*We* ***ought to*** *ring her now,*	***shouldn't*** or (less frequent) ***oughtn't***	*we?*

* The form *used (he)* (or its negative *usedn't*) is now very rare (··› 400).

Main clauses with indefinite pronouns 300d

When the indefinite pronouns *someone/somebody, anyone/anybody, no one/ nobody, everyone/everybody* are used as subjects, the tag pronoun is normally *they*:

> ***Someone** gets your breakfast, **don't they**?*
>
> ***No one** questioned it, **did they**?*
>
> *In small towns in Ireland, **everybody** knows everybody, **don't they**?*

Main clauses with *there is/are* 300e

Tag questions with *there is/are* have *there* as subject:

> ***There's** a lake near the house, **isn't there**?*
>
> ***There were** more younger people in the café, **weren't there**?*
>
> ***There should be** some continuity, **shouldn't there**?*
>
> ***There'd be** more choice, **wouldn't there**?*

Tag patterns in requests 300f

Interrogatives that function as requests often have the pattern of negative clause + affirmative tag, with the fall and rise intonation pattern:

polarity	falling tone ↘	rising tone ↗
neg. + affirm.	*You couldn't carry **this** for me,*	***could** you?*
neg. + affirm.	*You haven't got any **gin**gerbread men*,*	***have** you?*

* A *gingerbread man* is a kind of biscuit.

Question tags with reporting structures 300g

With reporting structures, the question tag usually refers to the reporting clause:

> *I **told** you he would be there, **didn't I**?*
> (~~I told you he would be there, wouldn't he?~~)
>
> *She **mentioned** that Joe was not well, **didn't she**?*

However, with verbs such as *believe, guess, know, reckon, suppose, think*, when used with *I*, the question tag normally refers to the reported clause. This is because expressions such as *I guess, I suppose, I think* are acting more like phrasal discourse markers than main clauses:

> *I think **it's going** to rain, **isn't it**?*
> (~~I think it's going to rain, don't I?~~)
>
> *I suppose **you think** that's clever, **do you**?*

Question tags in non-final position 300h

Although question tags normally occur after the main clause, they may sometimes interrupt the clause, especially in clauses with anticipatory *it*:

*It's odd, **isn't it**, that he should say that?*

*It was perhaps your team, **was it**, that was round there?*

*It's true, **isn't it**, what they said about him?*

In reporting structures, the question tag may occur before the reported clause, especially if the reported clause is felt to be unusually long. The early placement of the tag can also serve to project or acknowledge a shared perspective with the listener:

[commenting on the recipes of a famous cookery book writer]
*You always **know**, **don't you**, that what you make will be suitable, and light, and that it will taste all right too.*

→ **431** on question tags and intonation patterns

DIRECTIVE TAGS 301

Affirmative imperatives may be followed by tags involving *will/would/can/could you*. Such clauses typically function to issue directives:

***Stop** arguing, **will you**.*

***Hold** this rope, **would you**.*

***Be** back by five, please, **could you**.*

Negative imperatives may be followed by *will you*:

***Don't** forget my CD, **will you**.*

Imperative clauses, in more formal styles, sometimes occur with the tag *won't you*. This softens a directive and the utterance may be heard more as a polite request:

***Give** Emma whatever she needs, **won't you**, Hal.*

*'I'd very much like a black coffee,' Amy said. 'Here's the money. **Choose** something for yourself too, **won't you**?'*

First person plural imperatives with *let's* typically have *shall we* as a tag:

***Let's** go home, **shall we**.*

***Let's** not discuss it now, **shall we**.*

STATEMENT TAGS 302

Declarative clauses may be followed by a tag with the same polarity and subject – verb word order. These are called statement tags or copy tags. Such sentences typically make emphatic statements, frequently in evaluative contexts:

affirmative **affirmative**
*She**'s** lovely, **she is**.*

negative **negative**
*It's **not** very good, **that one isn't**.*

*They were pathetic-looking things, **they were**.*

*I'm fed up with it, **I am**.*

The principle of same polarity operates with reduced (ellipted) clauses too:

[speakers are at a nature conservation area]
A: *I don't think we'll see much wildlife today.*
B: ***Not** without binoculars **we won't**.*

[speakers are joking and engaging in word play]
A: *D'you know the definition of a secret?*
B: *No.*
A: *A secret is something only one person knows.*
B: ***Not** where I work **it isn't**.*

→ also **434–447 Negation**

Both *it* and *that* may occur as subjects in tags following main clauses with *it*. Main clauses with *that* normally have *that* as the subject of the tag:

***It**'s about this big, **it is**.*

*Ah, **it** was beautiful, **that was**.*

***That** was the second time, **that was**.*

→ also **97 Tails**

EXCLAMATION TAGS 303

Wh-exclamative clauses may be followed by negative tags with interrogative word order:

***How** strange, **isn't it**!*

***What** a coincidence, **wasn't it**!*

***How** sad we were, **weren't we**!*

Clause combination

Clause combination

INTRODUCTION 304

This chapter (304–318) looks at the ways in which clauses combine with one another to create sentences in written texts and sentence-like structures or clause complexes in spoken texts.

The main ways in which clauses combine to form sentences are by joining clauses of equal syntactic status (coordination) and joining main and subordinate clauses (subordination) (→ 307–317).

This chapter also describes the most common types of subordinate clause, including adverbial clauses, nominal clauses and relative clauses. Comparative clauses (e.g. *We're going to Spain for our holidays, **the same as we always do**.*) are described fully in 471 Comparative clauses.

This chapter also discusses embedded clauses, where a clause becomes a constituent of a phrase (e.g. a postmodifying relative clause in a noun phrase) rather than acting as a constituent of the sentence structure.

In this example, the phrase is in green, the clause is in bold:

*There's one thing **that needs changing***

INDEPENDENT AND DEPENDENT CLAUSES 305

An independent clause is one which does not depend syntactically on another clause. Independent clauses act as main clauses, that is clauses which can form whole sentences on their own.

A dependent clause is one that is syntactically dependent on another clause. Dependent clauses cannot in themselves form whole sentences. Dependent clauses include subordinate clauses (which combine with main clauses to form sentences) and embedded clauses (for example, relative clauses embedded in noun phrases):

main clause **dependent (subordinate) clause**
*I'll do it | **when I've had my lunch**.*

noun phrase **dependent embedded (relative) clause**
*This is | the video | **that I said I'd lend you**.*

Examples of how independent and dependent clauses relate to one another

sentence	
independent (main) clause	**dependent clause(s)**
1 *I was going to take a photograph.*	
2 *Could you just sign that for me please?*	
3 *We would love to see you tonight*	*if it's possible.* (subordinate conditional clause)
4 *That's the thing that annoys me most.*	... *that annoys me most.* (embedded relative clause, acting as postmodifier)
5 *I'll get them to give you a ring.*	... *to give you a ring.* (embedded non-finite clause acting as complement of *get*)
6 *I don't believe what they told us.*	... *what they told us.* (embedded nominal clause, acting as object)

Sentences **1** and **2** in the table are main clauses and complete sentences.

In sentence **3** in the table, the clause *if it's possible* is a dependent clause. It cannot in itself form a whole sentence, and is syntactically dependent on the main clause *we would love to see you tonight.* It is a conditional clause, introduced by the subordinator *if* (➜ **314d**).

In sentence **4** in the table, *That's the thing that annoys me most*, the clause *that annoys me most* is a dependent clause. It cannot in itself be a sentence, and is syntactically a postmodifier of the noun *thing*, and is a relative clause (➜ **317f**).

In sentence **5** in the table, *I'll get them to give you a ring*, the clause *to give you a ring* is a dependent clause. It cannot in itself form a whole sentence, and is syntactically dependent on the main clause. It is a non-finite clause, introduced by the non-tensed infinitive verb form (➜ **317j**).

In sentence **6** in the table, *I don't believe what they told us*, the clause *what they told us* is a dependent clause. It cannot in itself be a sentence, and is syntactically the object of the verb *believe*. It is a nominal clause (it serves a noun-like function) (➜ **316**).

MAIN AND SUBORDINATE CLAUSES 306

The clauses which combine to form sentences are of two kinds: main and subordinate. A main clause can be a sentence on its own. A subordinate clause can only be part of a sentence when it is dependent on the main clause. This can happen either through the use of a subordinator (a word like *as*, *because*, *if*, *since*, *until*, *when*) or by using a non-tensed verb form to create a non-finite subordinate clause. Examples of main (bold) and subordinate (in green) clauses:

I'll see you tomorrow.
(one main clause, one sentence)

I'll call you *when I get home.*
(main clause, and subordinate clause introduced by subordinator *when*)

Looking at it now, ***I don't think it's such a good idea after all.***
(non-finite subordinate clause introduced by non-tensed form *looking*, and main clause)

Examples of subordinate clauses preceding or following a main clause in the sentence

subordinate clause first	main clause	subordinate clause second
	She could do a lot more	***if** she wanted.*
	I'll get back to you	***when** I've had a think about it.*
***Until** he died,*	*nobody knew he was married.*	
***As** I was going upstairs,*	*I tripped on the carpet.*	

In more formal styles, a subordinate clause may interrupt the main clause or interrupt another subordinate clause.

Examples of subordinate clauses interrupting the main clause

	main clause interrupted (formal styles)	
main clause	subordinate clause	main clause (continued)
We should,	***if** we get there early enough,*	*be able to get seats near the front.*
The French in 1993 can,	***if** they wish,*	*vote for the same party in both presidential and assembly elections.*

Example of subordinate clause interrupting another subordinate clause

	subordinate clause interrupted (formal styles)		
main clause	subordinate 1	subordinate 2	subordinate 1 (continued)
She worked there for some time,	***although,***	***as** she herself has told you,*	*she was not happy in her job.*

The choice as to where to position a subordinate clause in relation to a main clause is not a grammatical one as such, but is a question of discourse. In general, subordinate clauses are more marked (i.e. used in an untypical way) when they occur first, and even more marked when they interrupt the main clause.

Placing a clause in a marked position can create emphasis, or may be used to signal a contrast with another clause or sentence. It may also serve to create a coherent link between sentences, or to signal the importance of a piece of information (⇢ **123–139 Grammar across turns and sentences**).

As in the table above, a subordinate clause may be subordinate to (i.e. syntactically dependent on) another subordinate clause, rather than a main clause:

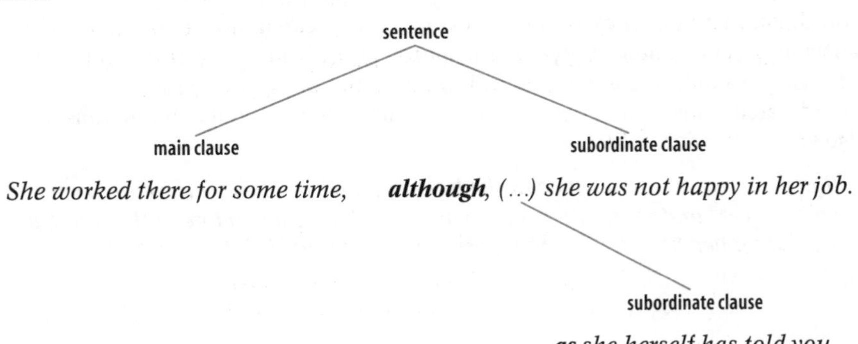

COORDINATED CLAUSES 307

The relationship between two or more clauses in a sentence may be one of coordination, not subordination. Coordinated clauses are clauses which have the same syntactic status.

For example, coordination can take place between main clause + main clause, or subordinate clause + subordinate clause, but not main clause + subordinate clause, and not finite main clause + non-finite clause:

main **main**
finite **finite**
I was there ***and*** *I saw it.*
(~~I was there and if I saw it.~~)
(~~I was there and to see it.~~)

→ **297–298** for the difference between finite and non-finite clauses

Coordination most typically involves the central coordinating conjunctions *and*, *but* and *or*:

Jim brought me here ***and*** *Phil's taking me home.*

[talking about school grades (years) and class teachers]
It will be different *when you're in my year* ***and*** *when you're in Mr Lane's maths group.*

If I have an appointment in the morning ***and*** *if I'm late,* ***what do I do?***

We didn't want to be rude to her *because she's a good customer* ***and*** *because she's such a nice person.*

I've never owned a car before ***but*** *I'm considering buying one.*

I'll phone you later ***or*** *you can give her a ring.*

[employee discussing the problem of freely expressing opinions about her work situation to her employers]
If you complain ***or*** *if you dare to put comments that are not suitable for what they want to hear,* ***then you get a bad reputation.***

Coordination may occur without the explicit link created by a conjunction. This is particularly true in literary style or for special effect in narrative texts. In the following example, clauses are coordinated by the use of commas alone. Coordinated clauses simply placed next to each other without conjunctions are also known as contact clauses:

She made me a cup of coffee in the kitchen, she knew where the cups and spoons were and where the coffee was kept, she sat up on one of the stools and leaned on her elbows on the breakfast bar and said, …

COORDINATORS 308

The most common coordinator is *and*:

main clause 1	coordinator	main clause 2
She's definitely interested	***and***	*she's willing to drive all the way down.*

subordinate clause 1	coordinator	subordinate clause 2
Well, if you don't get a job,	***and***	*if you want to come here for a bit,*

main clause
you're welcome to stay.

The other most common coordinators are *or* and *but*:

She doesn't know if she's right ***or*** *if she's wrong.*

If it's too expensive ***or*** *if it's costing me money, we'll think again.*

I dialled a different number ***but*** *I didn't get a dialling tone.*

Correlative structures are used to coordinate clauses. These are *either … or …*, *neither … nor …*, *not only … but also*:

Either *she could come down here* ***or*** *I could go to Gatwick or Heathrow.*

She was desperate to play down the problem, ***not only*** *to save face,* ***but also*** *to spare you any embarrassment.*

The *neither … nor* construction requires subject-verb inversion in the *nor*-clause:

They [universities] should ***neither*** *remain aloof from what goes on in life,* ***nor should they*** *spend all their time solving industrial problems.*

The same applies to *nor* and *neither* when used singly to link clauses:

Fred Wolf did not come in to join them, ***nor did he*** *appear in the hallway when Edith left.*

I don't know my parents, ***neither did they*** *know theirs.*

MULTIPLE COORDINATION 309

Coordination may involve more than two clauses, especially in informal spoken language. This is called multiple coordination:

It happened in front of the police station. It was the best place to have an accident anyway ***and*** *of course the police officer came* ***and*** *I was a bit shocked* ***and*** *he said 'Get in the passenger seat'* ***and*** *he drove me to the hospital you see.*

[answerphone message]
I'll be driving off down to France ***and*** *I'll try and ring again* ***but*** *remember I'll be in my car most of the day.*

→ **539 Glossary** for any unfamiliar terms

*I'd gone to the bookshop with a friend **and** he went to collect me **and** I was just sitting in the bookshop chatting **and** my husband said, 'That coffee shop over the road,' **and** I thought, 'Oh this is good.' Then you came in **and** Sylvia was having a coffee with us **and** poor James was left running the bookshop **and** nobody had made him a coffee **and** I said 'I know what I'm going to do. Can I buy him a coffee here?'*

Such multiple coordination makes the concept of 'sentence' difficult to apply to spoken language.

SUBORDINATION 310

A subordinate clause is dependent on a main clause or dependent on another subordinate clause, and cannot in itself form a whole sentence.

Subordinate clauses are typically introduced by a class of words known as subordinators (→ **311** and **312** below). Subordinators indicate the semantic relationship between the subordinate clause and the clause it is dependent on.

Subordinate clauses may be finite or non-finite.

→ **297–298** for the difference between finite and non-finite clauses

SIMPLE SUBORDINATORS 311

Simple subordinators are single words (bold in the examples below) which introduce subordinate clauses (in green in the examples below). They include:

after	*in order that*	*whenever*
although	*lest* (formal styles only)	*where*
as	*once*	*whereas*
because	*since*	*wherever*
before	*that*	*which*
for (formal styles only)	*though*	*while*
how	*till*	*whilst*
however	*unless*	*who*
if	*until*	*whoever*
in case	*when*	*whom*
		whose

*The company's director stated that the first six months were good, **although** interrupted by a one-day strike by van drivers.*

*I want to book it **before** we go, really.*

***Once** you get off the escalator, go round and towards the restaurant.*

The Major was concerned at her sudden departure, ***though*** *he knew its cause.*

You can come and pick it up ***whenever*** *you want.*

[person explaining to a doctor how a child came to hurt himself while playing on the bed]
He was okay ***while*** *jumping on the bed, but I didn't know he was going to jump off the bed.*

→ also **204** and **317b Relative pronouns** for *who, whom, which, whose* and *that*

COMPLEX SUBORDINATORS 312

Complex subordinators consist of more than one word and include common expressions ending in *as* and *that* (or optional *that*), plus a small number of other expressions. These include:

as far as	*given (that)*	*in the event that*
as if	*granted (that)*	*providing/provided (that)*
as/so long as	*in case*	*seeing as* (informal styles only)
as soon as	*in order for*	*seeing (that)*
as though	*in order that*	*such that*
assuming (that)	*insofar as*	*supposing (that)*
considering	*insomuch as* (formal styles only)	

So, ***as far as*** *my mother was concerned, I was safe.*

Assuming *he dies first, I get all the money. And* ***assuming*** *I die next, you two just share the money.*

You take it in turns to be on duty ***in case*** *the fire alarm goes off or whatever.*

A: *That'll be fun.*
B: *Oh, Yes. It will won't it,* ***provided*** *it's not too snowy for the planes to get off.*

ELLIPSIS IN SUBORDINATE CLAUSES 313

Subordinators such as *although, if, unless, when, whenever, while* may be followed by ellipsis of subject and copular verb *be*. Such usage is generally associated with more formal styles:

Being part of a group means that you can support each other ***whenever necessary.***
(understood: … you can support each other whenever supporting each other is necessary.)

[in a shop: customer buying nuts; *Brazils* are Brazil nuts]
A: *Can I have a quarter of those please?*
B: *Yes.*
A: *Er, not too heavy on the Brazils* ***if possible****.*
(understood: ... if it/that is possible.)

In reporting structures with common everyday verbs such as *guess*, *hope*, *know*, *say*, *tell*, *think*, omission of *that* is the norm, except in formal styles or very careful speech:

[informal conversation]
I think he's a lovely man.
(less likely: I think that he's a lovely man.)

[written text]
The Mayor hopes visitors will become involved with the village.
(less likely: The Mayor hopes that visitors will become involved with the village.)

He says he's sold his bike, everything he owns, to get money together.
(less likely: He says that he's sold his bike ...)

Backward-referring (anaphoric) ellipsis in subordinate clauses is more common than forward-referring (cataphoric) ellipsis:

You can have that if you ***want to****.*
(anaphoric; understood: You can have that if you want to have that.)

I only go there when I ***have to****.*
(anaphoric; understood: I only go there when I have to go there.)

If you ***can****, do try different methods, techniques to see if you can get more.*
(cataphoric; understood: If you can try different methods, techniques to see if you can get more, do try ...)

If you ***wish****, we can fax it to you.*
(cataphoric; understood: if you wish us to fax it to you, we can ...)

ADVERBIAL CLAUSES 314

Introduction 314a

Adverbial clauses act as modifiers in or of the main clause. They specify circumstances such as manner, time, frequency, place, degree, reason, cause, condition:

Tell me ***after I've eaten my dinner****.*
(time: tell me after dinner)

I feel guilty today ***because I've not paid you that cheque****.*
(reason: I feel guilty today because of the delay)

He says he can't repair the leak ***unless the water is turned off.***
(condition: the water must be turned off or he can't repair the leak)

Adverbial clauses are sometimes divided into two types: adjuncts and disjuncts. Adjuncts are more fully integrated into the clause (compare the general class of adjuncts, **319–337**), while disjuncts are more peripheral, and in writing are often separated from the main clause by a comma:

Your evening class tonight has had to be cancelled ***because the lecturer's ill.***
(adjunct expressing reason)

Somebody could have left it in the corridor, ***because it does happen.***
(disjunct expressing a justification/explanation for what the speaker has just said)

The most common types of adverbial clause are described here. Adverbial clauses of comparison are dealt with in **471 Comparative clauses**

Adverbial clauses: time 314b

Adverbial clauses of time may indicate that events in the main clause occur earlier than, simultaneously with, or later than events in the adverbial clause.

They may be placed before or after the main clause. After the main clause is the more neutral position:

- Main clause event occurs earlier than adverbial event:

  He'd need to do his exams ***before he went.***
  (the exams must happen first, then he can go)

- Simultaneous events:

  I got a sandwich ***while I was out.***
  (I was out and got a sandwich at the same time)

- Main clause event occurs later than adverbial event:

  [computer tutor to pupils]
  Once you've typed that text in, *can you all save the document.*
  (type the text in first, then save the document)

Adverbial clauses: place 314c

Adverbial clauses of place are usually introduced by *where* or *wherever*. After the main clause is the more neutral position:

Everybody knew everybody ***where I grew up.***

He always carried them on him ***wherever he went.***

Adverbial clauses: condition 314d

Conditional adverbial clauses involve the use of *if*, *unless* and a number of other subordinators. These include:

as/so long as	*in case*	*providing/provided (that)*
assuming	*in the event that*	*supposing (that)*
given (that)	*on condition that*	

Conditional adverbial clauses may be placed before or after the main clause. After the main clause is the more neutral position:

*So, **given that Church and politics have so much in common**, is there anything the former can learn from the latter?*

*I only spoke to the police **on condition that I wasn't going to be involved**.*

Conditional clauses can also involve syntactic devices such as inversion with *had*, *should* and *were*. Such clauses may come before or after the main clause:

*I'd have gone there with you **had I known** Philip was going to be there.*

***Should you lose** one of your credit cards, call our emergency helpline.*

→ **448–459 Condition** for a full account of conditional clauses

Adverbial clauses: contrast 314e

Contrastive adverbial clauses are usually introduced by *whereas* or *while/whilst*. After the main clause is the more neutral position:

*Without a car, if you want to go to the seaside then you have to pay for a coach to take you there or a taxi **whereas if you've got your car, you just have to put petrol in it and off you go**.*

*He likes fried rice, **while I prefer boiled**.*

Adverbial clauses: concession 314f

Concessive adverbial clauses contrast expectations between the information in the adverbial clause and the information in the clause it is dependent on. After the main clause is the more neutral position. Concessive clauses are typically introduced by:

(al)though	*no matter wh-*	*while (+ nevertheless)*
even though	*whatever*	*whoever*
if (+ at least/also)	*wherever*	
however	*whether … or*	

*He still plays tennis now and again, **even though he's in his eighties**.*

*Her reputation was growing, and **if her business wasn't going to make her rich, at least** it made her happy.*

***Whatever I do**, I'm compromised.*

Adverbial clauses: reason 314g

Reason clauses are typically introduced by:

as
because
for (formal styles only)
in that
seeing (that)
since
with (informal spoken)

Reason clauses may come before or after the main clause:

__As I trust myself__, I don't need to write a number on it.

Without the columns, the house looked very different, __in that it was the same as any other house in the street__.

He's very intense when it comes to his work. I suppose you have to be, __with doing a PhD__.

Adverbial clauses: purpose 314h

Purpose clauses may be introduced by *in order to/that, so as to, so (that)*. Purpose clauses may also simply be non-finite clauses with the *to*-infinitive. The purpose clause may occur before or after the main clause:

__In order to survive under the water__, fish and other creatures need to get oxygen, just as people do.

All the coordinates are moved around __so as to confuse us__.

Like all boys, he needs stability __so that he can rebel but still know he has security__.

I was ringing up __to enquire whether you've got any news about Alice__.

The negated forms of *in order to* and *so as to* are *in order not to* and *so as not to*:

I'll take my shoes off __so as not to dirty the carpet__.

Adverbial clauses: result 314i

Adverbial clauses of result are mostly introduced by *so*, and *so that* (more formal). Result clauses are placed after the main clause:

Roy's up in Manchester tomorrow, __so he can't come tomorrow__.

She tried to pull away, but he tightened his fingers __so that she could not get free__.

Adverbial clauses: comment 314j

Comment clauses are similar to viewpoint adverbial phrases (→ **246**) in that they express the speaker's or writer's opinion or viewpoint on the events in the main clause. Frequent comment clauses include *as you know, I believe, I daresay, I expect, I presume, I suppose, I (don't) think, so they say/tell me, speaking as …, to be honest.*

Such clauses may occur before or after the main clause, or, in more formal styles, in mid position in the main clause:

To be honest, I haven't really thought about it. (with *To be honest* in bold)

I could ring him, ***I suppose****.*

In any case, my English master, ***as you know****, was Tubby Baxter.*

→ **319-337 Adjuncts** for a full account of adverbial-clause types

EMBEDDED CLAUSES 315

Embedded clauses are dependent clauses which function as constituents of phrases. They are most typically relative clauses, but may also be adverbial clauses, nominal clauses or comparative clauses.

This phenomenon is sometimes called rankshifting since an item associated with a higher rank in the grammar (e.g. clauses are a higher rank than phrases and are constituents of sentences) may occupy a lower rank (e.g. a clause may act as constituent of a phrase).

In the sentence *Two people I know have gone there*, the clause *I know* modifies the noun *people*, and is a constituent of the subject noun phrase (in green in the diagram below):

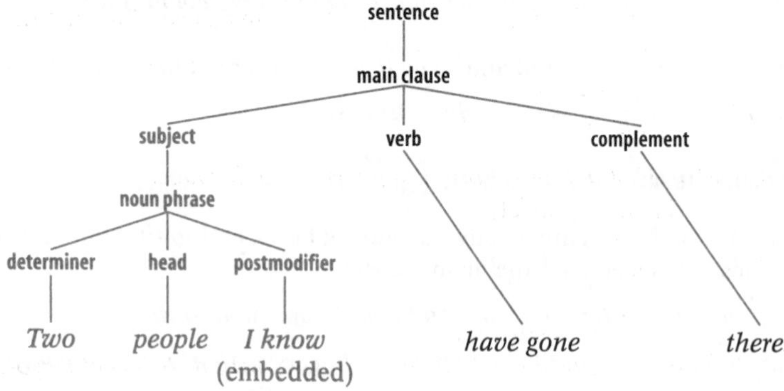

(noun phrase is in green)

Lindum was ***a town*** *| where Roman soldiers* ***could settle*** *with their families | after they* ***had retired*** *from the army.*

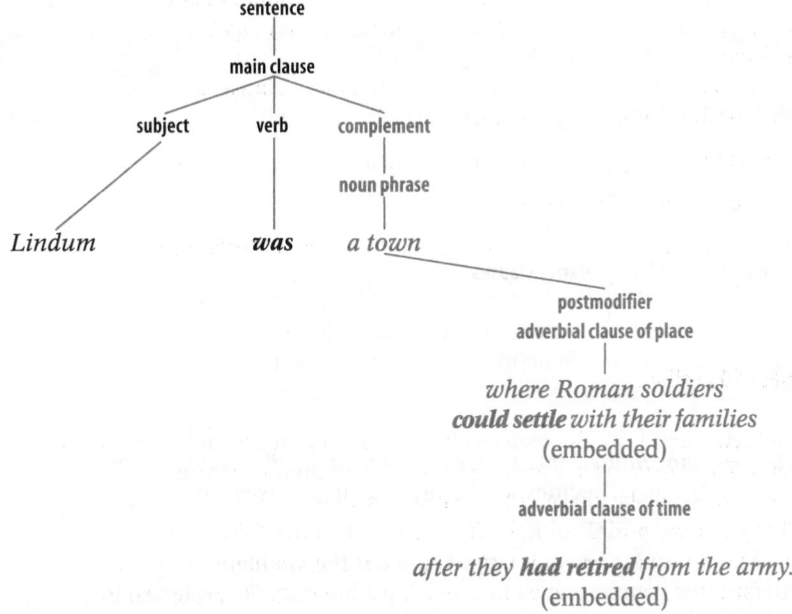

NOMINAL CLAUSES 316

Nominal clauses function in a way similar to noun phrases, in that they may function as subjects or objects/complements in the main clause. Compare the following pairs of examples:

His sincerity *can't be denied.*
(noun phrase as subject)

That one British child in four is born into poverty *is a disgrace.*
(nominal *that*-clause as subject)

I forgot ***his name.***
(noun phrase as object)

I forgot ***to ask how long it would take.***
(nominal infinitive clause *to ask how long it would take* as object of *forgot*, and *how long it would take* as object of *ask*)

The idea was ***a good one.***
(noun phrase as subject complement)

Well the idea was ***that I made tea*** *because Philip was helping us out.*
(nominal clause as subject complement)

Nominal clauses may also be indirect interrogatives:

__What he didn't know__ was the name of the person standing by my side.

They have to decide __who to give the treatment to__.

RELATIVE CLAUSES 317

Types of relative clause 317a

Relative clauses are of two main kinds: embedded clauses which postmodify noun heads, and *which*-clauses referring to a whole sentence or stretch of discourse (sentential relative clauses).

Defining and non-defining relative clauses

Relative clauses (in green in the examples below) may define or describe a preceding noun head (bold in the examples below).

Relative clauses which define the noun are called defining (or, in some grammar books, restrictive):

*The **guy** who shouted must have been on about the seventh floor.*
(defines the guy; specifies which guy is being referred to)

*This is the **problem** which we're having at the moment.*
(defines the problem; specifies which problem is being referred to)

*That **woman** that was here lost all her keys.*
(defines the woman; specifies which woman is being referred to)

Relative clauses which describe the noun are called non-defining (or, in some grammar books, non-restrictive):

*Have you ever heard of **Guy Preston**, who had a hit song with 'Loving Ways'?*
(describes or gives extra information about Guy Preston)

*Erm there's Portugal, there's **Las Palmas**, which is one of the Canary Islands, and there's Rhodes.*
(describes or gives extra information about Las Palmas)

Sentential relative clauses

Sentential relative clauses comment on a whole previous sentence or series of clauses, or a speaker turn, or a longer stretch of discourse. They are introduced by *which*. Their most frequent function in informal spoken language is to express evaluation:

He's always in the office and then he complains about not having any time off and how wonderful he is to the company, which is his own fault.
(comments on the previous clauses)

In conversation, sentential relative clauses may be added by a second speaker:

A: *I should use my qualification but you know I think I'll probably look back if I haven't done something with it and think 'Oh I wonder what, you know, what if I'd ...?'.*
B: *Which is not good*.
A: *Mm.*
(comments on previous clauses/a speaker turn)

[A is a travel agent, B is a customer, discussing flight schedules]
A: *No that's coming back 12 o'clock, coming home midday, but that one, the one going out, it gets in at 7 in the morning.*
B: *Which is fine isn't it?*

Occasionally, the same speaker may add on a sentential relative clause after a response by a listener:

A: *It cost £20.*
B: *Oh right.*
A: *Which I know is quite a lot*.
B: *Mm.*

Sometimes such clauses may be added by more than one speaker:

A: *Any other ideas? Any way you could prop the business up or, you know take ...*
B: *Not at the moment.*
A: *Mm.*
C: *Not without having to go heavily into debt on a mortgage on a re-mortgage or have a personal loan.*
A: *Mm.*
B: *Which is the one thing we don't want to do*.
C: *Which at the moment none of us can afford*.
(two sentential clauses commenting on the notion of 'going heavily into debt')

Relative pronouns 317b

Relative clauses are introduced by relative pronouns. The relative pronouns are *who, whom, which, that* and *whose*. The choice of relative pronoun depends on whether the reference is to:

- a person, animal or thing
- a subject or an object
- a possessive meaning

The choice of relative pronoun also depends on what type of relative clause is involved, whether it is defining or non-defining, or sentential (→ 317a above).

Sometimes the relative pronoun is omitted. This is referred to as zero relative pronoun (→ 317h):

*It's not **a problem I've got**. It's **a problem they've got**.*
(compare: It's not a problem which/that I've got. It's a problem which/that they've got.)

The relative pronouns stand for the subjects, objects or prepositional complements of their clauses, so those clause elements are not repeated in the relative clause:

*He's <u>the man</u> **who** wrote back to me.*
(subject relative pronoun: He's the man. The man wrote back to me.)
(~~He's the man who he wrote back to me.~~)

*This is <u>the problem</u> **which** we're having at the moment.*
(object relative pronoun: This is the problem. We are having the problem.)
(~~This is the problem which we're having it at the moment.~~)

*<u>The woman</u> **who** I gave the form **to** was quite friendly.*
(object of a preposition: I gave the form to the woman.)
(~~The woman who I gave the form to her was quite friendly.~~)

However, occasionally, in very informal speech, an element may be repeated unnecessarily:

[DJ inviting listeners to call in and talk about songs which are very special to them]
*If you have <u>one</u> **that** you're really desperate to tell us about **it**, then give us a ring on 01223 …*
(standard usage: if you have one you're really desperate to tell us about, then give us …)

The + sign indicates an interrupted turn which continues at the next + sign
[customer speaking to a travel agent; *Amtrak* is an American rail company]
A: *So with this Amtrak thing then, basically that's just <u>a voucher</u> **that** I take **it** to the station+*
B: *Right.*
A: *+when I want to start using it.*

Such usage may be explained by saying that sometimes speakers 'change direction' during their utterances so that two standard structures blend. This is a normal, common feature of speaking in real time and should not be seen as deviant or 'wrong'.

What is not used as a relative pronoun in standard usage:

*But Simon Quigley was there, **which** was very nice.*
(~~But Simon Quigley was there, what was very nice.~~)

Who and whom 317c

Who refers to human beings, and occasionally to pet animals. It is used with defining and non-defining relative clauses:

*I'm sure there'd be a lot more people **who**'d be better qualified than myself.* (defining)

*We'll ask Dick, **who**'s the oldest in the family, just to say a few words.* (non-defining)

*That's the dog **who** bit Tom.*
(defining; referring to an animal)

In all three examples, *who* stands for the subject of the relative clause:

*I'm sure there'd be a lot more people **who**'d be better qualified than myself.*
(I'm sure there'd be a lot more people. Those people would be better qualified than myself.)

*We'll ask Dick, **who**'s the oldest in the family, just to say a few words.*
(We'll ask Dick. Dick's the oldest in the family.)

*That's the dog **who** bit Tom.*
(That's the dog. The dog bit Tom.)

In most styles, except very formal ones, *who* may also refer to the object of the relative clause:

*She's the sister of a good friend of mine **who** we visited in Oxford before coming to you.*

*It was from a woman **who** I know slightly.*

When *who* refers to the complement of a preposition, the preposition is placed at the end of the relative clause, and not immediately before *who*:

*I met Bill's mate Rob, **who** I went to school **with**; Bill's in prison now.*
(~~I met Bill's mate Rob, with who I went to school; Bill's in prison now.~~)

→ **317d *Whom***

Collective human nouns (e.g. *cabinet, committee, government, group, panel, police, team* → 182a) tend to be used with *who* when followed by plural concord and *which* when followed by singular concord. *Who* with plural concord tends to be used when the members of the groups are seen as individuals; *which* with singular concord tends to be used when the group is seen as a whole:

- Plural concord (group seen as individuals):

  *The reports then go to a panel **who decide** what action to take.*

  *At the very beginning I had some sympathy for the police, **who were** so convinced they had found their man.*

[*World Cup* here refers to the football championship]
The Monaco midfielder, a key member of the Scotland team ***who face*** *Latvia in a crucial final World Cup qualifier …*

- Singular concord (group seen as single body):

Ignoring immigrants excludes a social group ***which*** *already* ***plays*** *an important role in social and economic development.*

The Disasters Emergency Committee, ***which coordinates*** *overseas crisis appeals, raised £3 million for the Bangladesh cyclone appeal.*

[referring to the hypocrisy of governments supporting conservation of natural resources while continuing to increase the use of them]
The same charge of hypocrisy is levelled at the British government, ***which says*** *we must find more oil yet use less.*

Who is not used for inanimate reference:

This is a problem ***which*** *occurs regularly.*
(~~This is a problem who occurs regularly.~~)

Whom 317d

Whom, which was traditionally used to refer to the human object of a relative clause or complement of a preposition, is now confined to very formal styles and mostly to writing. It is used with both defining and non-defining relative clauses:

Was she another of the ex-soldiers ***whom*** *Dennison had recruited from the army?*
(defining; formal, literary style)

It appeared she had struggled with her attacker, ***whom*** *she almost certainly knew.*
(non-defining; formal journalism)

Whom is used more extensively (but still only in formal styles and mostly in writing) when it refers to the complement of a preposition, and is always used when the preposition is placed immediately before the relative pronoun:

She taught piano and had three daughters, ***about whom*** *she worried incessantly.*
(~~She taught piano, and had three daughters, about who she worried incessantly.~~)

I soon discovered that she was thirty-one, had three boys aged nine, eleven and fourteen, whose father was a Norwegian ***from whom*** *she was now separated.*

There was also a bunch of Claire's friends ***whom*** *Cory had yet to be introduced to.*

Whom is many times more frequent in writing than in speech.

Which 317e

Which is used to refer to a non-human subject or object of a relative clause. It is used with both defining and non-defining clauses:

He dialled <u>*a number*</u> ***which*** *was answered immediately at the other end.*
(defining; referring to the subject of the relative clause)

*He had given them a number **which** they could call, day or night, if they needed him.* (defining; referring to the object of the relative clause)

*And I remember sailing out of Dublin Bay, **which** is a beautiful, beautiful bay with the Hill of Howth on one side.*
(non-defining)

→ **317c** ***Who*** for error warning

Which can refer to the complement of a preposition, and the preposition may be placed at the end of the relative clause (more informal) or immediately before the relative pronoun (more formal):

*She taught at the school **which** my nieces went **to**.*

*Why did he keep asking questions **to which** you could not possibly be expected to know the answer?*

Sentential relative clauses are always introduced by *which*:

*We've been told not to tell him because he doesn't know yet, **which** is really stupid.*

That 317f

In a wide range of informal styles, *that* is used instead of *who/whom* or *which* in defining relative clauses. It is used for reference to either a subject or an object.

In all of these examples of defining relative clauses from sections **317a–317e** above, *that* can be used.

Examples of *that* in defining relative clauses

example	alternative with *that*
*The guy **who** shouted must have been on about the seventh floor.*	*The guy **that** shouted must have been on about the seventh floor.* (refers to the subject)
*This is the problem **which** we're having at the moment.*	*This is the problem **that** we're having at the moment.* (refers to the object)
*He dialled a number **which** was answered immediately at the other end.*	*He dialled a number **that** was answered immediately at the other end.*
*Was she another of the ex-soldiers **whom** Dennison had recruited from the army?*	*Was she another of the ex-soldiers **that** Dennison had recruited from the army?*
*He had given them a number **which** they could call, day or night, if they needed him.*	*He had given them a number **that** they could call, day or night, if they needed him.*
*She taught at the school **which** my nieces went to.*	*She taught at the school **that** my nieces went to.*
*I'm sure there'd be a lot more people **who**'d be better qualified than myself.*	*I'm sure there'd be a lot more people **that**'d be better qualified than myself.*
*That's the dog **who** bit Tom.*	*That's the dog **that** bit Tom.*
*She's the sister of a good friend of mine **who** we visited in Oxford before coming to you.*	*She's the sister of a good friend of mine **that** we visited in Oxford before coming to you.*
*It was from a woman **who** I know slightly.*	*It was from a woman **that** I know slightly.*
*This is a problem **which** occurs regularly.*	*This is a problem **that** occurs regularly.*

→ **317c** ***Who*** for error warning

That does not normally introduce non-defining relative clauses, except in informal spoken usage:

[referring to a man arrested for football hooliganism]
*Mr Collinson, **who** has never been in any kind of trouble, had not been to an England football international before.*
(~~Mr Collinson, that has never been in any kind of trouble, had not been to an England football international before.~~)

*The biggest tourist event in Lincoln is the Christmas market, **which** takes place over four days in the castle and cathedral grounds.*
(preferred to: ... that takes place over four days ...)

*And as you know, the meeting, **that** we'd never wanted anyway, was just foisted on us.*
(informal spoken)

That may refer to the complement of a preposition, but not when the preposition is placed immediately before the relative pronoun:

*The other girl **that** I told you **about** also lives in Bristol.*

*I've got some exercises **that** you can practise **with**.*

*It was like a dream **from which** I feared I would wake at any moment.*
(~~It was like a dream from that I feared I would wake at any moment.~~)

Whose 317g

When the relative pronoun stands for a possessive determiner, *whose* is used in defining and non-defining clauses:

*They've moved now, the people **whose** car it was.*
(it was the people's car)

*We've got a Spanish friend **whose** family have an orange orchard.*

[*a theatre sister* is a nurse who works in a hospital operating theatre]
*A theatre sister, **whose** blood group was the same as mine, bravely volunteered.*

Whose is mostly used for possession by humans and animals, but in more formal styles it can also be used for things:

*He couldn't shake away the idea that she had survived a catastrophe, **whose** details he was unable to imagine because her life had been so different.*
(the details of the catastrophe)

An alternative to *whose* in more formal styles is determiner + noun + *of which*:

*He couldn't shake away the idea that she had survived a catastrophe, **the** details **of which** he was unable to imagine because her life had been so different.*

*He wrote one novel, **the** title **of which** I've forgotten.*
(or, less formal: He wrote one novel, whose title I've forgotten.)

Zero relative pronoun 317h

Referring to the object

In informal styles and especially in spoken language, a defining relative clause referring to the object of the clause may occur without any relative pronoun:

That's a job I could never do.
(understood: a job which/that I could never do.)

A: *Who was present at this Sunday lunch?*
B: *Oh, some people we didn't even know.*
(understood: some people that/who/whom we didn't even know.)

As complement of a preposition

Zero relative pronoun can also occur as the complement of a preposition, but only when the preposition is placed at the end of the relative clause:

Is this the car Fiona was talking about?
(understood: Is this the car that/which Fiona was talking about?)
(or, more formal: Is this the car about which Fiona was talking?)
(But not: ~~Is this the car about Fiona was talking?~~)

[showing someone an old photograph in which they appear]
Huh, there's you in the back garden of the second house we lived in.
(understood: … the second house that/which we lived in.)

When the relative pronoun is the complement of a preposition, the preposition and relative pronoun may both be omitted in informal styles:

That seems to me a sensible moment to make that decision.
(understood: … a sensible moment at which to make that decision.)

Referring to the subject

In informal speech, zero relative pronoun may occur with reference to the subject of a defining or non-defining relative clause. This happens particularly with existential *there* constructions:

There was a train came by every morning about half-past eight.
(understood: There was a train which/that came by every morning …)

A: *There's quite a lot of colour photocopying needs doing.*
B: *Er, right, when do you want it for?*
A: *Today if possible.*
(understood: … colour photocopying which/that needs doing.)

There was this strange guy, Harry Foster, was President of the company. He was tall and thin.
(understood: …Harry Foster, who was President of …)

Occasionally in informal speech a subject relative pronoun and an immediately following auxiliary verb may both be omitted:

[talking about the activities of mysterious neighbours]
Yeah, they do seem to be dragging stuff about. It's really weird. There seems to be more stuff come out than gone in.
(understood: … more stuff that/which has come out than stuff which/that has gone in.)

→ 539 **Glossary** for any unfamiliar terms

Non-defining relative clauses

Zero relative pronoun does not occur with non-defining relative clauses:

The lost-property office, which is on the floor below, is closed until next Tuesday.

(~~The lost-property office, is on the floor below, is closed until next Tuesday.~~)

Punctuation and intonation of relative clauses 317i

Punctuation

Defining relative clauses are not usually marked with commas:

*Rosie knew he was a person **that** handled trouble casually.*

(~~Rosie knew he was a person, that handled trouble casually.~~)

*But then the person **who** owned it decided they didn't want to rent it until April.*

(~~But then the person, who owned it, decided ...~~)

Non-defining relative clauses are normally separated off in writing by commas:

[about food additives, which have official European codes beginning with E-]
*Tartaric acid, **which** is just made from grapes, is sometimes listed as E334.*

*The fields could be protected by hedges and trees, **which** could also be used to produce fruit and nuts.*

*Tim Waites, **who** was hosting the evening, did his best to draw attention away from the two of them.*

Sentential relative clauses are also marked off by a comma:

*At the end of the day that gentleman finished up dead, **which** is very sad.*

Intonation

In speech, especially in more careful and formal speech, non-defining relative clauses are typically separated by breath pauses at the points where commas would normally be placed in writing. There may also be a drop to a lower pitch level for the non-defining clause:

[university lecture]

normal pitch level	**lowered pitch level**	**normal pitch level**
X-rays have been around for a long time, over a hundred years, and the plain radiograph [breath pause]	***which** we'll be looking at today* [breath pause]	*in part at least really hasn't changed that much over the last hundred years.*

Sentential relative clauses may be preceded by a breath pause or a slightly longer pause in speech.

Non-finite relative clauses 317j

Many of the same principles which apply to finite defining and non-defining relative clauses apply to their non-finite equivalents. However, with non-finite relative clauses, the zero relative pronoun is used:

The woman sitting next to Marian is her sister.
(defining: specifies which woman)
(~~The woman who sitting next to Marian is her sister.~~)

Each cell will continue to divide to form a human composed of millions of cells.

There's food to be served and drinks to be poured.

Preliminary investigations indicate that some, if not all, of the clients' money, believed to total £6 million, has instead found its way into unquoted companies and property purchases.
(non-defining: adds relevant information about the money)

In the case of *-ing* and *-ed* clauses, non-finite relative clauses only occur when the subject of the non-tensed verb is the same referent as the head noun:

The man I'm looking for has dark hair.
(~~The man looking for has dark hair.~~ *Man* is object, so the relative clause cannot be non-finite *-ing*)

Relative *-ed* clauses correspond to passive voice finite equivalents:

The company she sold has made millions.
('The company sold has made millions' is possible but can only be related to its passive finite equivalent by ellipsis: The company which was sold has made millions.)

-ing clauses are not just reduced forms of their equivalent progressive finite forms. Verbs which are normally not used in progressive aspect may be used in non-finite relative *-ing* clauses:

Half a mile later, they reached what appeared to be a derelict complex consisting of half a dozen buildings.
(Half a mile later, they reached what appeared to be a derelict complex ~~which was consisting of half a dozen buildings.~~)

To-infinitive clauses may be used if the noun is subject or if it is the complement of a preposition in the non-finite clause:

The person to answer any questions about computers is Tania.
(*the person* is subject of *answer*)

Obviously the person to sit next to at a dinner party is the witty, charming and attractive one.
(*the person* is the complement of the preposition *(next) to*)

There is often a choice between an active *to*-infinitive clause and a passive one. Sometimes the difference in meaning is hardly noticeable. With existential *there is/are*, the difference is often negligible:

***There are** all those apples to peel.*
(There are all those apples to be peeled.)

With other constructions, especially where quantifiers occur, the passive is less common:

We've got a lot of cooking to do.
(less likely: We've got a lot of cooking to be done.)

I have an essay to write for tomorrow morning.
(less likely: I have an essay to be written for tomorrow morning.)

In general, the active voice versions emphasise activity, while the passive voice versions emphasise the existence or absence of something.

CLAUSES AND NOUN PHRASES IN APPOSITION 318

The placing of elements with identical reference next to each other is called apposition:

| My cousin | Mary | worked at that school.
(the two noun phrases, *my cousin* and *Mary* refer to the same person)

Most typically the adjacent elements are noun phrases:

| My friend | Jim | works there.
(defining)

| Susan |, | a friend of mine |, has just moved here from Liverpool.
(non-defining)

A clause may also be in apposition to a noun phrase:

| Her answer |, | that she had forgotten to set her alarm clock |, was not a convincing excuse.

→ **173 Noun phrases occurring together** (in apposition)

Adjuncts

Adjuncts

INTRODUCTION 319

The adjunct is the fifth major clause function, the other four being subject, verb, object and complement. Adjuncts modify, comment on or expand in some way the meaning of the clause in terms of manner, place, time, frequency, reason, intensity, etc. Adjuncts are never obligatory items in a clause.

TYPES OF ADJUNCT 320

The adjunct in a clause may be realised by an adverb phrase, a prepositional phrase, or (less frequently) a noun phrase.

- Adjunct realised by an adverb phrase:

  adjunct subject verb complement
  Luckily | *the weather* | *was* | *very nice.*

  subject verb object adjunct
  I | *met* | *Prince Charles* | ***fairly recently.***

- Adjunct realised by a prepositional phrase:

  adjunct subject verb complement
  After that | *I* | *felt* | *really bad.*

  subject verb object adjunct
  They | *were having* | *a conversation* | ***in the background.***

Adverb phrases and prepositional phrases are both commonly used as adjuncts, and may often paraphrase each other in meaning:

I'm going to have to drive ***very carefully.***

Even where records are available, they have to be interpreted ***with care.***

- Adjunct realised by a noun phrase:

  subject verb object adjunct
  We | *'re celebrating* | *our silver wedding* | ***this year.***

Adjuncts may also be compared to adverbial clauses. In this grammar book, adverbial clauses are treated as elements of the sentence structure, rather than as adjuncts in the clause structure. However, the meanings of adverbial clauses are often similar to the meanings of adjuncts:

She wrote to me ***when she arrived in Oxford****.*
(adverbial clause)

She wrote to me ***upon her arrival in Oxford****.*
(same meaning realised as prepositional phrase adjunct)

→ **304–318 Clause combination**

TYPES OF MEANING 321

There are a number of different types of meaning that adjuncts typically express.

Examples of important general types of meaning expressed by adjuncts

manner 326	refers to how something happens	*A robin was singing* ***beautifully*** *from a garden tree.* *You're going to have to encourage your children to think about this* ***in a serious way****.*
place 326	refers to where something happens	*Have you got all your family* ***locally****?* *There's a shortage of housing* ***in the neighbourhood****.*
time 326	refers to when something happens	*I've had some really weird dreams* ***lately****.* *I retired* ***last May****.*
duration 327	refers to length of time over which something happens	*We met her at your wedding* ***very briefly****.* *Well, Pat said to me, 'Go out and you can leave the house* ***for good****!'*
definite frequency 328	states how often something happens using specific time expressions	*She gets paid* ***monthly****.* *They meet* ***every three weeks*** *and they discuss things.*
indefinite frequency 328	states how often something happens using non-specific time expressions	*She phones me* ***quite often****.* *We bumped into each other* ***from time to time****.*
reason 329	states why	*I told him off* ***for all the mess on the floor****.* *Going to the USA is cheap at the moment* ***because of the exchange rate****.*

continued overleaf

continued

purpose **329**	states a goal or purpose	*I went to the café* ***for a quick coffee.*** *You might think I'm exaggerating* ***for the purpose of this story.***
degree and intensity **330**	refers to how much, to what degree something happens	***Largely*** *they looked after themselves.* *That seems to be working, and does seem to be helping* ***to a certain extent.***
focusing **331**	focuses on or specifies an entity	*He* ***specifically*** *asked to meet with me alone.* *Wildlife which lives alongside well-used paths becomes accustomed to the presence of people. This applies* ***in particular*** *to birds.*
modal **332**	expresses degrees of truth, possibility, necessity, etc.	***Probably*** *the most famous desert plant is the cactus.* *Medical evidence at the post mortem revealed* ***without doubt*** *that Mrs Marline had died through an overdose of the drug.*
evaluative **333**	judges or comments on the event, gives the speaker's opinion	A: *Did Charlie do anything?* B: *No he didn't actually,* ***amazingly.*** ***With luck*** *we should be finished by five-thirty.*
viewpoint **334**	expresses the perspective or standpoint from which the speaker sees things	***Personally*** *I don't want to carry on with what I'm doing for ever.* *It's a disgrace,* ***to my mind.***
linking **335**	links and relates clauses and sentences to one another	*So he dropped his hand from her shoulder. And* ***moreover*** *left her side.* *In 1990, girls accounted for fully two thirds of the children globally without access to schools.* ***In addition,*** *more than two thirds of the children who drop out of school every year in developing countries are girls.*

There is some overlap in the types of meaning, and some adjuncts can be classified in different ways, according to their context of use:

It has changed ***a lot.***
(to a great degree)

We plan to go away ***a lot*** *you see. For weekends and things.*
(frequently)

So we sent Joe up the street to go and find out what was happening. ***Meanwhile*** *Maria was in her bedroom, looking out of the window.*
(time: at the same time)

[about a women's golf tournament in Britain]
Total prize money for the week – to be shared among the players – is £150,000, with £25,000 as the top prize; ***meanwhile*** *in the States you're playing for up to $700,000 a time. So what have the Americans got that we haven't?*
(used for expressing comparisons and contrasts)

POSITION OF ADJUNCTS 322

There are three positions that adjuncts are typically used in: end, front and mid position.

End position is considered the most neutral position for most common adjuncts of manner, place and time, and is by far the most common position for such adjuncts in everyday conversational language:

- End position:

  I've had a lot of funny dreams ***lately****.*
  (neutral position for manner, place and time adjuncts)

- Front position:

  Yesterday *I didn't eat my lunch.*
  (*Yesterday* is given greater emphasis in front position)

- Mid position:

  We ***usually*** *eat around seven o'clock.*
  (between subject and verb: typical position for common adjuncts of indefinite frequency)

END POSITION 323

End position means after any object or predicative complement:

They don't have the right attitude ***in this country****.*

I've been very tired ***lately****.*

Adjuncts do not normally come between a verb and an object:

They started to build the road ***in 1981****.*
(~~They started to build in 1981 the road.~~)

He had to pass the shop ***on his way****.*
(~~He had to pass on his way the shop.~~)

In written and spoken journalistic style, however, adjuncts are sometimes found between verb and object, especially with reporting verbs:

Mr Ford announced ***yesterday*** *his resignation from the party.*

The same applies in general to predicative complements. Adjuncts follow them:

[tennis player talking about pre-match nerves]
You'd become nervous ***before the match.***
(~~You'd become before the match nervous.~~)

However, complements of the verb *be* may be preceded by adverbs of indefinite frequency:

He's ***always*** *happy.*

FRONT POSITION 324

Front position means that the adjunct is the first item in the clause structure:

In the job description *it says you'll get paid a basic car allowance.*

A front-position adjunct comes after a conjunction:

He looked tired but ***nevertheless*** *managed a smile as he caught sight of his two employees and walked over to join them.*
(~~nevertheless but managed a smile …~~)

Front position for adjuncts which normally occupy mid or end position gives greater emphasis to the adjunct:

In the garden *they grew all the food they needed.*
(adjunct of place, normally found in end position)

Quite often *I don't have any breakfast at all.*
(adjunct of indefinite frequency, normally found in mid position)

MID POSITION 325

Mid position means between the subject and verb. However, the exact position varies depending on whether auxiliary or modal verbs are used, and on the type of adjunct:

I ***usually*** *stay at a hotel near the airport.*
(between subject and verb)

I've ***never*** *had a holiday like it in my life.*
(following the first auxiliary/modal verb)

Indeed in the past two months central banks have been ***modestly*** *selling dollars to check the currency's rise.*
(following the last auxiliary verb)

*Well I **certainly** would join if I could afford it.*
(emphatic: preceding a stressed first auxiliary or modal verb)

Mid position and auxiliary/modal verbs 325a

Mid position normally means between subject and lexical verb or between an auxiliary/modal verb and a lexical verb.

If there is more than one auxiliary verb or a combination of modal and auxiliary verbs, then the adjunct normally comes after the first auxiliary verb (**aux1**) or after the modal verb:

aux1 adjunct aux2 main verb
*We | 've | **always** | been | striving | to improve the service.*

modal adjunct aux main verb
*He | should | **really** | have | resigned.*

However, for adjuncts of degree and for other adjuncts which modify the lexical verb rather than the whole clause, mid position is immediately before the lexical verb, following all modal and auxiliary verbs:

*We have been **totally** rejected and we didn't expect that.*

[the parliament of the Isle of Man, a region of the UK, debated a maritime disaster near the island in its Parliament, *the Tynwald*]
*The parliament, known as the Tynwald, held a meeting at which unanimous approval was given for the operation to return the bodies of the crew to their families 'so that funerals can be held and so that the pain of their losses may be, **in some degree**, eased'.*

*Save the Children has been **actively** supporting farmers cultivating fields along the Shabelle River Belet Weyne district since 1992.*

Instead of coming after the first auxiliary or after a modal verb, mid-position adjuncts can be placed before for extra emphasis:

*I **honestly** don't know.*
(compare neutral (or unmarked) position after the first modal or auxiliary verb: I don't honestly know.)

*I **probably** could have said if I'd wanted to see it.*

In speech, pre-auxiliary/pre-modal position is particularly the case when the auxiliary/modal is stressed:

*I **never** have worked out which is which.*

*They know that they **definitely** are going to work.*

*I **really** will have to try harder next time.*

Mid-position adjuncts can sometimes occur after a modal verb followed by an auxiliary verb, or after a second auxiliary verb (instead of the more normal position after the first one). This is common in spoken language when the second verb is contracted:

I think she would've ***probably*** *married him.*

They might've ***actually*** *had to alter the text. I don't know.*

[*the AA* is the Automobile Association, a club for motorists]
She's been working for the AA since she left school, she's been ***just*** *working, she loves it.*

Mid position and clause type 325b

In interrogative clauses, mid-position adjuncts follow the subject:

Did you ***seriously*** *think about ringing up Gwen?*
(~~Did seriously you think ...?~~)

In emphatic and negative imperatives, the adjunct usually comes between *do/don't* and the verb:

Do ***always*** *remember that we only have one opportunity to clinch it.*

Don't ***just*** *say 'I'm going to include that' unless you can justify it.*

Mid position and *be, do* and *have* 325c

It is necessary to distinguish between the auxiliary uses of *be*, *do*, and *have* and their uses as lexical verbs with regard to the placing of adjunct elements in mid position (see the table below).

When *be*, *do* and *have* are used as auxiliaries, the adjunct is placed in mid position, after the auxiliary.

When *be* is a lexical verb, the adjunct is placed after the verb.

When *do* and *have* are lexical verbs, the adjunct is placed in mid position between subject and verb.

Positions of *be, do* and *have* as auxiliaries and as lexical verbs

	as auxiliary	as lexical verb
be	*I'm* ***often*** *accused of being too strict.*	*He's* ***often*** *in a bad mood.*
do	*We don't* ***usually*** *get back here till about one o'clock.*	*I* ***always*** *do it because I want to make sure they've got what they want.*
have	*You've* ***hardly*** *eaten anything.*	*We* ***usually*** *have tea for breakfast and coffee later.*

Mid position in tags and reduced clauses 325d

In speech, when modal and auxiliary verbs and lexical verb *be* are used in tags or in reduced clauses, the adjunct typically comes before the modal/auxiliary/*be*:

A: *I hope they'll disappear.*
B: *I think they* ***probably*** *will.*

A: *Do you celebrate the New Year too?*
B: *Yeah we **usually** do.*

*I'm not unhappy. I **never** have been.*
(preferred to: I've never been.)

A: *It's not the same.*
B: *No it **never** is.*
(preferred to: No it's never.)

*I thought it was glass. **Probably** is.*
(ellipsis of subject: *It* probably is.)

However, extra emphasis can be placed on the adjunct by placing it after the modal/auxiliary:

A: *Does the bus stop there?*
B: *Well it doesn't **usually** but you could ask him to.*

*I was worried I was going to lose the money and I did **almost**.*

In informal speech an adjunct belonging to the main clause may occasionally follow the tag, almost as an afterthought:

*We won't rush dear, will we **tomorrow**?*

*Spanish is more widely used, isn't it, **outside of Europe**?*

MANNER, PLACE AND TIME 326

Positions 326a

Most frequently, manner, place and time adjuncts are used in end or front position. End position is considered the most neutral (unmarked) position, but front position is also frequent, and a little more emphatic:

place | time
He played the piano | ***in the village hall*** | ***one night***.

The factors which determine choice of position have to do with the topical development of the text and the cohesive linking of clauses, as well as the length of the adjunct. They may be used in front position to emphasise them. This is especially common with time adjuncts:

*Oh **tomorrow morning**, er, we're going to get up about eleven.*
(tomorrow is a special, different morning)

***Thirty-one years** we've been together.*
(the number of years is important)

***Up near the church** there was an old tree.*
(helps to orient the listener)

Without a car *you'll never get there.*
(emphasises the problem of being carless)

A man in a white coat was making a drill a bit longer. ***Near him*** *there stood an intriguing railway carriage.*

In this last example, typical of literary style, the adjunct is brought to the front of the sentence to link it topically with something important in the sentence before (the man in the white coat).

→ **473c Adjuncts**

Manner, place and time adjuncts can also be used in mid position to emphasise them. The emphasis is even stronger than when they are used in front position. Mid position is particularly common in formal written texts and journalistic and literary styles:

[about Mark Knopfler, the rock musician]
He has, ***in other ways****, become an elder statesman of his profession.*

Paul Parker ***yesterday*** *chose to join Manchester United.*

I couldn't stop thinking about the noise of the waterfall. It was a noise that would never stop. It would always be roaring, even now it was, ***in the middle of the night, all the days and all the nights****, shattering itself down the sides of the crevasse.*

More than one adjunct in end position 326b

Where there is more than one adjunct in end position, the most neutral (unmarked) order is manner – place – time.

Examples of more than one adjunct in end position

clause	manner (how?)	place (where?)	time (when?)
We were working		*in the garden*	*all morning.*
She played	*magnificently*		*the second time.*
An 18-year-old teenager was arrested		*in Cyprus*	*yesterday.*
She died	*peacefully*	*in Hartlepool General Hospital*	*on Sunday.*
A group of women protested	*angrily*	*outside the parliament building*	*yesterday.*

Although the last two examples show that it is possible to have all three types of adjunct in the same clause, this is rare in informal spoken language and is associated with more formal registers such as journalism and formal writing.

More than one adjunct of the same type 326c

If there is more than one adjunct of the same meaning-class, there is usually a choice of order, with more emphasis falling on the last adjunct.

Manner

1 *We survived* | *quite well* | *without one* |.

Or: **2** *We survived* | *without one* | *quite well* |.

However, the order in **1** is more common, with prepositional phrases (especially longer ones) coming after shorter adjuncts:

I just wanted to live my life | *quietly* |, | *independently* | *and* | *with the minimum of disruption* |.

Place

1 *You'll see the station* | *just round the corner* | *next to the library* |.

Or: **2** *You'll see the station* | *next to the library* | *just round the corner* |.

The order in **1**, with the more general location followed by the more specific location, is more common.

Time

1 *I'll see you* | *at six o'clock* | *on Wednesday* |.

Or: **2** *I'll see you* | *on Wednesday* | *at six o'clock* |.

With time adjuncts there is little difference between the two orders, but the second adjunct is felt to carry greater emphasis.

Topical linking of clauses and sentences 326d

Combinations of manner, place and time adjuncts in front position are flexible, and the order may vary, often depending on topical links between clauses and sentences:

[*rubbering* refers to the sound of the rubber tyres of a car on the road]
Only the odd car rubbering by in the boulevard below and the hum of the air-conditioning disturbed my sleep. | *In the morning* |, | *at an international newspaper stand* |, *I met my first Moroccan friend, Muhammad.*

Here the choice of time adjunct (*in the morning*) before place adjunct (*at an international newspaper stand*) is appropriate because of the contrast between the two sentences (night/sleep, and morning).

In 1979 Mogador bought the house known as the Creek overlooking the Orwell estuary near Ipswich, where the family had been holidaying for some years. | *There* |, | *following William's death and her own 70th birthday* |, *Hetta decided to organise an open-air performance of 'A Midsummer Night's Dream' for June 21, 1986.*

Here the choice of place adjunct (*there*) before time adjunct (*following William's death and her own 70th birthday*) is appropriate because of the topic of place which is continued from the first to the second sentence.

→ **539 Glossary** for any unfamiliar terms

DURATION 327

Duration adjuncts, expressing how long an event lasts, are normally used in end or front position. End position is the more neutral:

She's been going out with her current boyfriend ***for three years****.*

Throughout history*, all commanders have known that no victory is complete until the chief of the opposing side has been killed, captured or fled.*

They may be found less frequently in other positions, in more formal styles:

The church has ***throughout the ages*** *given a moral lead to society.*

Bruckner showed, ***throughout his life****, an attitude of deference, if not abasement, towards established authority.*
(between verb and object; characteristic of journalistic and literary styles)

DEFINITE AND INDEFINITE FREQUENCY 328

Definite frequency

Adjuncts of definite frequency most typically occupy end position:

The temperature is checked ***twice daily****.*

The electoral register is compiled ***every October 10th****.*

They also occur in front position, for greater emphasis or for reasons of topical linking. They do not normally occupy mid position:

Every day *she spends hours on her personal fitness programme, which includes gym sessions, aerobics and swimming.*
(~~She every day spends hours on her personal fitness programme, …~~)

Four times a year *I get a magazine from them, which I never read.*
(~~I four times a year get a magazine from them, …~~)

Indefinite frequency

Adjuncts of indefinite frequency most typically occupy mid position when they take the form of adverb phrases:

They ***quite often*** *ask about you.*

It ***usually*** *turns out that way.*

Common adverbs of indefinite frequency include:

always	*never*	*regularly*
frequently	*occasionally*	*seldom*
generally	*often*	*sometimes*
hardly ever	*rarely*	*usually*

Prepositional adjuncts and longer adjuncts in general expressing indefinite frequency are normally used in front or end position:

> ***Every now and again*** *they would get her to fill in these forms for them.*
> (preferred to: They every now and again would get her to fill in these forms for them.)
>
> *I see her* ***from time to time****.*
> (~~I from time to time see her.~~)
>
> *I've been to Paris* ***many a time****.*
> (preferred to: I've many a time been to Paris.)

Formal written styles may sometimes have longer indefinite frequency adjuncts in mid position:

> [talking of aristocrats and their choice of servants (*retainers*)]
> *Many aristocrats preferred personal retainers who were* ***more often than not*** *recruited from suspect sectors of society.*
> (formal written)

For emphasis, indefinite frequency adjuncts can be used in front or end position. End position is much more common in spoken language:

> ***Sometimes*** *we would start teasing him.*
>
> ***Usually*** *it's a matter of discussing things till we reach agreement.*
>
> *The decisions judges make in court cases, well it's unbelievable* ***sometimes****.*
>
> *We don't get a candidate for my party except at General Elections* ***usually****.*

REASON AND PURPOSE 329

Reason and purpose adjuncts typically occupy end or, less frequently, front position:

> *Pay negotiations are due to begin next month,* ***with the aim of agreeing a two-year deal from January****.*
>
> *Cycling is forbidden on the canal path* ***for reasons of safety and security****.*
>
> ***Because of all the confusion****, I didn't tell them until the next morning.*

Occasionally, in more formal styles, they may occupy mid position:

> *Social workers have to make extremely difficult decisions in cases where all the facts,* ***for reasons of privacy****, cannot possibly be revealed.*

DEGREE AND INTENSITY 330

Degree and intensity adjuncts express the degree, extent or intensity of an event. They most typically modify the lexical verb rather than the whole clause, and therefore come immediately before the lexical verb, after modal or auxiliary verbs, especially when they take the form of adverb phrases:

*I **really** enjoyed that party.*

*Sorry, I've **completely** forgotten where I got up to.*

*Although he wouldn't have been **directly** blamed if anything went wrong, it wouldn't have done his flourishing career any good.*

They may also occur in end position:

[*Conservative* here refers to the British Conservative Party; *disenfranchised* means having no power to vote]
*There's such a big Conservative majority we're disenfranchised **completely**.*

*I take your point **entirely**.*

*The stories have to be treated as allegories **almost***.*

* *Almost* in end position is very rare in formal written language.

Degree/intensifying adverbs such as *entirely*, *almost* and *completely* are not normally used in front position:

*I **almost** got killed.*
(~~Almost I got killed.~~)

*I've **completely** forgotten where I was.*
(~~Completely I've forgotten where I was.~~)

When *really* and *actually* come in front or end position, they tend to have a modal meaning ('as a matter of fact'/ 'the truth is') rather than an intensifying meaning, and comment on the whole clause:

A: *How does that make you feel?*
B: ***Really** it's sickening.*
(compare: It's really sickening.)

***Actually** a friend of mine was there.*
(compare: A friend of mine was actually there – emphasising the unexpectedness of the action)

Longer degree adverbs normally occupy end or front position:

*Only a country with a profound identity crisis could pervert history **to such an extent**.*

***To some extent** the problem has already been solved.*

*The government, arguing that nobody should be treated as a refugee in their own country, provided little comfort – calculating that this would encourage them to disperse. It worked **up to a point**.*

FOCUSING 331

Focusing adjuncts specify or focus upon an event in some way. They occur in all positions, but tend to be used immediately before or after the clause element they are focusing upon:

*The key to Cuba's distant past is found in the area known as Oriente and, **in particular**, the city of Baracoa.*

*I don't think I need it **specifically**.*

*But it is **above all** a family matter and in taking my decision, I've given priority to family considerations.*

MODAL 332

Modal adjuncts judge events in terms of the speaker's view of the probability of things being or happening in a particular way. They indicate how things appear to the speaker, and the speaker's view of the necessity of things. In this respect, they parallel the meanings of the modal verbs (→ 379).

Modal adjuncts frequently occupy mid position, especially when they consist of adverb phrases:

*He **definitely** needs six more months.*

*That couldn't **possibly** happen.*

*It isn't something that we **necessarily** have to spend all our time doing.*

*He **obviously** didn't recognise you.*

They may also be found in front position:

***Apparently** he had a terrible childhood.*

***Obviously** I'm going to need a lot of training to start with.*

***Probably** 'The Sun' is the most popular newspaper.*

Modal adjuncts may also occur in end position, especially in informal speech:

*Without you, they wouldn't have a job, **necessarily**.*

*You know which one I mean, **probably**.*

[tennis player speaking]
*I don't normally get uptight but in key situations with people I'm supposed to beat, **possibly**.*

As with other types of mid-position adjunct, longer modal adjuncts are more likely to be used in front or end position, especially in spoken language:

__In all probability__, local opposition to such a proposal would be overwhelming.

I knew __without a shadow of a doubt__ that something supernatural had happened.
(preferred to: I without a shadow of a doubt knew that …)

You have to register by the end of the month, __to the best of my knowledge__.

EVALUATIVE 333

Evaluation is an important type of adjunct meaning. It is possible to emphasise that the adjunct is expressing an opinion, comment, or judgement of an action (rather than a description of the way it is done) by putting it in mid position:

The most you can __sensibly__ do is forget it.
(speaker's opinion that it is sensible)

He __wisely__ decided to keep it to himself till he got back.
(speaker's opinion that it was wise of him)

In end position, such adjuncts can have quite a different emphasis, with the possibility of a more objective interpretation as an adjunct of manner:

She believed she had acted __sensibly__.

Evaluative adjuncts are rather rare in positions other than mid, but they can occur elsewhere:

__Appropriately__, he was wearing a long black coat.

Just like that, a common spoken evaluative adjunct, usually occurs in end position:

[*just like that* means 'abruptly, with no formalities or hedging']
I was literally asked if I fancied doing it, __just like that__.

VIEWPOINT 334

Viewpoint adjuncts express the personal perspective from which the speaker views an event or a subject or topic. They may occur in all positions, but certain positions are more frequent than others.

They are very often found in front and mid position:

__Quite honestly__, I think we need more representation.

__In fairness__, he did say that he'd tried and spoken to local people.

__Quite frankly__, I don't think there are any advantages.

I ***personally*** *feel that within our department the change was introduced too quickly.*

It's something I've not, ***in all honesty****, thought about.*

Viewpoint adjuncts can be used in end position for emphasis. End position is much more common in spoken language than in written:

I'd rather not have gone to Holland, ***personally****.*

We were entitled to use the material, ***quite frankly****.*

Viewpoint adjuncts that specify or restrict the topic in some way most typically come in front position:

Also, ***culturally****, if you can speak the language you tend to be better off.*
(from the perspective/point of view of culture)

Architecturally*, it was just fantastic.*

A: *So* ***from a management point of view****, then, it's your problem.*
B: *It's my problem.*

Historically*, such movements have had little impact on society.*

They may also occur in other positions:

The question is: given that this must, ***constitutionally****, be his final term as president – what does he have to campaign for now?*

Religious believers have ***historically*** *been responsible for many political reforms.*

We were building up a good act, ***musically****.*

How did it affect you ***in terms of everyday life****?*

LINKING 335

Linking adjuncts normally occupy front position:

[health visitor speaking to patient]
We arranged for you to be seen again in three months. ***Consequently****, as arranged, you were seen on the 17th of July.*

Linking adjuncts follow conjunctions:

English is obviously important, but ***at the same time*** *it's important to learn another language to broaden your horizons.*

Linking adjuncts are also found in mid position, especially in more formal speech and writing:

[university seminar]
France doesn't need Africa and is ***therefore*** *trying to move away into other areas.*

[*Hal* is the name of a computer in the science-fiction film *2001, A Space Odyssey*]
*Computers are there to help, and that should be all. Engineers may not want to put machines like Hal into space any more, but according to Mr Hammond, most of Hal's powers can **nevertheless** be matched by computers today.*

Linking adjuncts may occur in end position, especially in informal contexts:

[students discussing the 'upgrading' process from one degree course to a higher one]
*A report by Professor Logan would be okay. The formal upgrading is important for us, **however**.*

[*The Quality Team* is a group which monitors quality of performance at the workplace]
*I very rarely use The Quality Team and I'm not popular **because of that**.*

*Comparisons may be unavoidable. They are odious, **nevertheless**.*

Linking in written and spoken English **335a**

Some linking adjuncts are particularly associated with written or spoken styles and particular positions in those styles. For example, *on the contrary* is very rare in informal conversation. In written English it is more common and usually occurs in front (or much less frequently in mid) position:

*He had no private understanding with Mr X. **On the contrary**, he knew very little of him.*

On the other hand occurs frequently in both spoken and written usage. But the concessive adjunct *then again* (always in front position) is much more frequent in spoken than in written language:

[speakers are discussing training in the use of a new computer program; *Arrow* is a software supply company]

A: *We've hopefully got some people from Arrow who might be able to help a bit.*
B: *But **then again**, if you're interested in computers, er, it's very easy to learn quickly.*

Other linking adjuncts more common in written than in spoken usage include:

accordingly *furthermore* *therefore*

as a consequence *in the event*

duly *moreover*

Other linking adjuncts more common in spoken than in written usage include:

as I say

because of that

in the end

what's more

→ **108 Discourse markers: organising the discourse**

INVERSION 336

Inversion after negative adjuncts 336a

Adjuncts of negative meaning (including negative frequency) which are normally found in mid position cause the subject and modal/auxiliary verb (or copular verb *be*) to be inverted when they are used in front position. This is normally a feature only of very formal and literary styles, but does occasionally occur in conversation:

> ***Never*** *could she understand how he cared.*
>
> ***Rarely*** *did anyone declare the true size of his property.*
>
> ***Not only*** *is it a remarkable book, it is also a highly successful one.*
>
> ***Not one day this week*** *have I been able to do any work on it.*
> (conversation)

Other expressions of this type include:

hardly	*on no occasion*	*under no circumstances*
*little**	*scarcely*	
on no account	*seldom*	

(*in contexts such as: *Little did I realise that I was being deceived.*)

Inversion after place adjuncts 336b

Particularly in very formal and literary styles, inversion of subject and lexical verb may occur after a front-placed adjunct denoting location:

> ***In the corner*** *stood another man of the law, by his isolation and beribboned uniform clearly one of a higher rank.*
>
> ***Out of the dark, away to my right,*** *came the roar of a pneumatic drill.*

This does occur occasionally in informal speech, especially with frequent expressions such as *here comes* and *there goes*:

> ***Here comes*** *the bus.*
>
> ***There goes*** *the phone.*
> (often said when a phone starts to ring)
>
> [telling a story about a crime and the arrival of a police helicopter]
> ***Out comes*** *the helicopter, hovering over everybody's house, waking everybody up.*

 45 ***Here, there***

Inversion after linking adjuncts 336c

Linking adjuncts such as *first, next, now, then* which organise lists and sequences of events may be followed by inversion of subject and verb in very formal and literary styles:

[a report on public opinion-poll findings]
*[Health care] is still the most important problem in most people's eyes, but only 27 per cent now put it top of the list of issues that will influence their vote. **Next** comes unemployment – 25 per cent rate it most important, 4 per cent down.*

*It began with iced melon. **Then** followed roast chicken.*

Inversion with direct speech reporting clauses 336d

In literary style, sometimes the reporting verb and subject are inverted. In these cases the adjunct comes in end position:

*'Cut it off short' said the father **rashly**.*
(~~… said rashly the father./… rashly said the father.~~)

Split infinitives 337

Many language purists believe that split infinitives are wrong or bad style. Split infinitives are where an adjunct (usually an adverb phrase) is inserted between *to* and the verb (e.g. *I want **to carefully check** everything*). In fact, in spoken English split infinitives are very common and pass unnoticed, though they are often thought inappropriate in writing:

*So if you'd like **to perhaps continue** …*

*It's very common **to actually not like** the Birmingham accent isn't it? People tend **to automatically laugh** at it.*

Present time

Present time

INTRODUCTION 338

Present time is seen either as the moment of speaking or writing, or as 'time around now', or as the more general, permanent time relating to truths and general facts.

References to present time are most typically indicated in the verb phrase through the simple and progressive forms of the present tense.

Forms of the present tense

form	structure	examples
present simple	present tense forms of lexical verbs or of auxiliary *do*	*I/you/we/they* ***eat*** *three meals a day.* *He/she/it/one* ***eats*** *three meals a day.* *I* ***don't*** *eat three meals a day.* ***Does*** *she eat three meals a day?*
present progressive	present tense forms of *be* + lexical verb in *-ing* form	*I* ***am eating*** *right now.* *He/she/it/one* ***is eating*** *right now.* *We/you/they* ***are eating*** *right now.*

The present tense is the most common way of referring to present time, and in this chapter (338–345) we deal principally with the present simple and present progressive. Past tense forms may occasionally refer to present time, often for reasons of politeness or indirectness. These and the perfect forms (present perfect simple and progressive, formed with *have* and the *-ed* participle) are dealt with in **346–360 Past time**.

PRESENT TIME REFERENCES WITH THE PRESENT SIMPLE 339

General truths and facts 339a

The present simple can be used to refer to a general or permanent state of affairs, or facts which are considered true at the present time:

My daughter ***lives*** *in Berlin.*
(compare: 'My daughter is living in Berlin', which would suggest a less permanent situation)

She's Swedish. She ***comes*** *from Stockholm.*
(a permanent fact about her nationality)
(~~She's coming from Stockholm.~~)

My brother's ***coming*** *from Wales.*
(this cannot be a statement of my brother's origin/nationality, and can only mean that he is in the process of travelling or has arranged to travel from Wales to where the speaker is)

*I **want** a change. I've been in this job for almost twenty years.*

*I just **love** Thai curries.*

[from a recruitment leaflet for the Friends of the Earth environmental campaign]
*By joining us, you **make** your voice heard and **help** us to continue working. The Earth **needs** all the friends it can get.*

The present simple is also used to convey general truths and permanent facts about the world:

*2 plus 2 **makes** 4.*

*A boundless warm river, some 80 kilometres wide and 500 metres deep, the Gulf Stream **passes** into the colder waters of the western Atlantic. There it **spreads** into four main currents and gradually **loses** momentum.*
(~~the Gulf Stream is passing ... there it is spreading ...~~)

A work of art or the activities of an artist from the past may be referred to in the present simple, to emphasise their continued existence, relevance and availability at the present time:

*Jane Austen **allows** us to see within the minds not only of her heroines but of many other characters as well.*

*It is, however, perhaps in the 55th Sonnet that Shakespeare **gives** to this idea its fullest expression.*

Plot summaries, book blurbs and reviews of novels, plays, etc. also use the present simple:

[plot summary on the back cover of a novel]
*One morning, Rebecca **wakes** up and **realises** she has turned into the wrong person.*

Regular and habitual events 339b

Regular or habitual events are usually referred to in the present simple:

*We always **have** breakfast at around eight o'clock.*
(~~We're always having breakfast at around eight o'clock.~~)

*I **get** up before six o'clock every day.*

[this advertisement for running shoes is aimed at people who run regularly for fitness]
SATELLITE. *You **play**, you **lift**, you **train**, you **run**. And you **wear** the Reebok Satellite, a lightweight cross training shoe with running profile.*

Immediate reactions 339c

The present simple can be used to talk about feelings and reactions experienced at the moment of speaking:

*That **looks** too risky.*

*It **tastes** very bitter. Are you sure it's chocolate?*

It can also be used to describe immediate perceptions and feelings:

*Quick! Open the car window! I **feel** sick!*

[child to parent trying to comb the child's unruly hair]
*Ow, mummy! That **hurts**!*

Immediate communication 339d

The present simple is used in commentaries on sports events and on public ceremonies. Commentators use the form to describe what they can see immediately before them, especially if it forms a sequence of actions which are completed as the commentator speaks:

[football match commentary]
*Shearer to Gillespie … Gillespie **beats** his man on the outside and **moves** forward.*

A similar use occurs in demonstrations and in instructions:

[a plumber is showing a friend how to mend a tap which is leaking]
*You **put** the washer on first, then the metal ring and then you **tighten** the screw.*

Mental process verbs 339e

Verbs such as *hear, know, reckon, see, suppose, think, understand*, are most typically used in the present simple, not the progressive:

*I **hear** you went to see the rugby match.*
(~~I'm hearing you went to see the rugby match.~~)

*My mum **reckons** it's because he's stressed out.*

*I **see** what you mean.*

*I **think** he's lost a bit of weight actually.*

Progressive uses of these verbs usually have a slightly different meaning.

Think in present progressive often means 'consider' or 'incline towards an opinion':

*I'**m thinking** of the neighbours really.*

*She'**s thinking** of moving to London.*

*I'**m thinking** more like, you know, the middle of July.*

See in the present progressive tends to mean 'meet with' or 'have a romantic relationship with':

*I'm sorry, he's busy. He**'s seeing** a client at the moment.*

*She**'s seeing** some guy she works with.*

Speech act verbs 339f

The present simple is used with speech act verbs. These are verbs which explicitly label the speaker's communicative intention in the performance of speech acts (e.g. promising, denying, apologising, demanding):

*I won't forget this time, I **promise**.*
(~~I won't forget this time, I'm promising.~~)

*I **swear** I saw tears in his eyes.*
(~~I'm swearing I saw tears in his eyes.~~)

*I **agree** dangerous drivers should be put in prison rather than fined.*

*I **name** this ship Beatrice II.*

In a similar way, the present simple is used in formal statements and in business or legal communications:

*We **enclose** our cheque for £2,300 in settlement of invoice no. 10878.*

*I **write** to inform you that you have been successful in your application to join the service.*
('I'm writing to inform you …' would be less formal)

THE PRESENT PROGRESSIVE 340

Events in progress at the time of speaking 340a

The present progressive is used to refer to events which are in progress or happening at the moment of speaking.

Compare:

[someone on the telephone whilst being given directions]
*Well er, **I'm looking** across the road now and all I can see is a chemist's shop.*

*I **look** at catalogues. I always read so many catalogues on the train.*
(a regular event, but not necessarily happening at the moment of speaking)

Compare:

*Why **is** he **smiling** like that? It all looks a bit suspicious.*

*She's changed the way she **smiles**, hasn't she?*
(reference to her general behaviour, not necessarily what she is doing at the moment)

The present progressive is also used to refer to things which are taking place or which are true around the moment of speaking, though they may be only temporary:

They ***are travelling*** *through Italy at the moment.*

*She****'s having*** *a bad time right now.*
(her life is difficult at the moment)

Repeated events in temporary contexts 340b

The present progressive is also used to describe actions which are repeated or regular, but are either temporary or may be judged to be temporary:

*She****'s seeing*** *him quite a bit at the moment.*
(she's meeting him regularly)

Is *she still* ***swimming*** *three times a week?*
(implies she has recently started swimming three times a week; compare: 'Does she still swim three times a week?', which implies she has always swum three times a week)

The present progressive is also used to describe regular actions in relation to a particular time or a specified event, especially where those events interrupt things already in progress (⇢ **348a** to compare the similar use of the past progressive):

I'm *always* ***having*** *a shower when the newspaper comes.*
(I have always already started my shower when the paper arrives; compare 'I always have a shower after a swim', where having the shower follows on from swimming.)

*He won't answer the phone when he****'s working*** *at the computer.*
(... when his work at the computer is already in progress)

Processes of change 340c

The present progressive is used to refer to gradual processes of change:

He's been in hospital for three weeks but ***is improving*** *steadily.*

*They're building a new by-pass. It'll be good for the town but it****'s taking*** *ages to finish.*

With adverbs of indefinite frequency 340d

The present progressive is often used with indefinite frequency adverbs such as *always*, *constantly*, *continually* and *forever* to describe events which are regular but not planned, and often undesired:

I'm always losing *my car keys. I really must get one of those massive big key rings.*

I'm constantly telling *the children not to go in there.*

*She****'s forever doing*** *homework.*

Verbs rarely used in the present progressive 340e

Some verbs in English are only rarely used in the present progressive. These include:

- verbs which describe mental states and processes such as *believe, know, think, understand* (→ 339e above)
- verbs which describe responses of the senses such as *smell, taste*
- verbs expressing emotional responses such as *admire, adore, detest, hate, like, respect*
- verbs which describe an ongoing process such as *have to, need, want*
- speech act verbs such as *appreciate, deny, promise, swear* (→ 339f above)
- verbs describing permanent qualities or characteristics such as *consist, contain, hold, last, take*

The + sign indicates an interrupted turn which continues at the next + sign
[in the kitchen, cooking]
A: *This **consists** of walnuts, garlic butter+*
B: *It **smells** nice.*
A: *+and that's about it really.*

*We **need** rain. The garden is so dry.*

*I **promise** I'll be there on time next time.*

[to a waiter]
*Er, **does** this dish **contain** meat?*
(~~Is this dish containing meat?~~)

However, when used to describe a current process at the moment of speaking, or to give extra emphasis to the ongoing nature of the event, these verbs may occur in the present progressive:

*What **are** you **thinking**?*
(What thoughts are passing through your mind at this moment?; compare 'What do you think?', which usually means 'What is your opinion?')

***I'm understanding** things better now, since I started going to the lectures.*
(emphasises 'understanding' as a developing process; compare 'I understand', which treats understanding as an achieved state)

[whilst preparing and tasting food]
***I'm tasting** something very bitter on my tongue at the moment.*
(there is a kind of tentativeness here; compare 'it tastes bitter')

*The job for life has become a fantasy. Most people **are having to** take more responsibility for their own careers and for what they do.*

*The whole match is being played at too slow a pace. It**'s needing** a goal.*

*Can't you hear what I'm saying? I **am promising** to marry you.*

The verb *be* in the present progressive 340f

When the copular verb *be* is used in the present progressive with an adjectival complement, it refers to the current actions or behaviour of the subject rather than referring to a quality or attribute of the subject:

I think she ***is being*** *awfully broadminded and tolerant here.*
(she is acting in a broadminded and tolerant way; compare 'I think she is broadminded', which would be an expression of a general opinion about her character)

*Stop it! You****'re being*** *silly.*
('You're silly' would suggest a more general evaluation of the person's character)

INDIRECTNESS AND POLITENESS 341

The present progressive is often used to make a request, enquiry or statement of opinion more indirect, often out of politeness:

[a muffin is a kind of cake]
Are *you* ***wanting*** *a muffin, Peter?*
(less direct than 'Do you want ...?')

I'm wondering *when I could come and pick up the calendars that I ordered from you at the beginning of October.*
(less direct than 'I wonder when I could ...')

*We****'re hoping*** *that it will have some practical benefits.*
(less direct than 'We hope that it ...')

In these cases, the past simple, and even more politely, the past progressive, may also be used with present time reference:

Did *you* ***want/were*** *you* ***wanting*** *a muffin, Peter?*

I ***wondered/was wondering*** *when I could come and pick up the calendars that I ordered from you at the beginning of October.*

We ***hoped/were hoping*** *that it would have some practical benefits.*

THE PRESENT SIMPLE AND PROGRESSIVE: SUMMARY 342

The present simple sees time in terms of facts, truths, generalities and permanent states of affairs. The present progressive sees time more in terms of its unfolding at the moment of speaking, and observes actions and events from within, as ongoing, in progress:

I ***love*** *Dublin.*

This is a wonderful plant. It ***flowers*** *all summer.*

It's ***raining*** *now.*

We're ***making*** *progress.*

Sometimes the differences may not be great, and may only suggest more of a sense or possibility of permanence in the case of the simple form and a sense or possibility of being only temporary in the progressive:

We ***live*** *in a small village.*

I ***feel*** *more confident these days.*
(focus is on facts, suggesting the possibility of greater permanence)

*We****'re living*** *in a small village.*

I'm feeling *more confident these days.*
(focus is on present situation, with less focus on permanence)

PRESENT TIME REFERENCES WITH THE PAST TENSE 343

As seen in **341** above, for reasons of indirectness and politeness, the past simple and the past progressive may sometimes be used with present-time reference, especially with verbs such as *be, hope, look for, think, want, wonder*:

[on the phone to train timetable enquiries]
Actually I ***wanted*** *to check if there's a twenty-five-past train.*

[at a cosmetics counter in a store, enquiring about face protection products; A is the customer]
A: *What's the best kind?*
B: *Probably just a very light liquid.*
A: *Right. I* ***was looking for*** *one for the cold weather, you know.*

[customer in a travel agent's]
We ***were wondering*** *about going to Amsterdam. We* ***were wanting*** *to stay in tents or in a caravan or in a bed and breakfast, to sort of see what the different prices* ***were****.*

[dry cleaner's store: customer (B) is leaving a jacket for cleaning]
A: *Right. What* ***was*** *the name please?*
B: *Smith.*

Be is not used in the past tense form in this way to comment on the immediate situation:

[dinner guest to host, at the moment of tasting a fish dish]
A: *Mm. This fish* ***is*** *delicious.*
B: *Thank you. I'm glad you like it.*
(~~This fish was delicious.~~)

Note also the expression *It's time* .... When used with a finite clause, the verb is in the past simple form:

It's time you ***got*** *up.*
(~~It's time you get up~~.)

It's time that we ***did*** *something about it.*

WILL REFERRING TO GENERAL TRUTHS OR USED FOR POLITENESS 344

Will can be used to refer to generally accepted truths and to what we might always expect to happen:

I suppose most people ***will prefer*** *to own their home.*

*In the evening he****'ll sit*** *all night watching TV.*

Will can sometimes be used to soften a directive or to make it more polite:

I'm sorry but ***I'll*** *have to ask you to sit in the Waiting Room for a few minutes.* (compare the more direct: I'm sorry but I have to ask you to sit in the Waiting Room ...)

Will *you turn the TV down please. I'm on the phone.*

→ also **387** ***Will***

THE SUBJUNCTIVE 345

In formal and literary styles, present references to unfulfilled actions or events may be in the subjunctive mood after verbs such as *demand, insist, recommend, require, stipulate*. The subjunctive mood uses the base form of the verb for all persons (i.e. no final -*s* on third person singular; → **159e**):

The Head of Security has ***demanded*** *that the guard* ***resign****.*

I ***insist*** *that she* ***do*** *these things herself.*

It is ***recommended*** *that they* ***repay*** *the amount stolen in full within one year.*

Past time

Past time

INTRODUCTION 346

Past time is seen as time before the moment of speaking or writing, or as 'time around a point before the moment of speaking'.

References to past time are most typically indicated in the verb phrase through the simple and progressive forms of the past tense.

Forms of the past tense

form	structure	examples
past simple	past tense forms of lexical verbs or of auxiliary *do*	*I/you/he/she/it/one/we/they* ***worked*** *eight hours a day.* *We* ***didn't*** *work eight hours a day.* ***Did*** *he work eight hours a day?*
past progressive	past tense forms of *be* + lexical verb in *-ing* form	*I he/she/it* ***was*** *work****ing*** *when it happened.* *We/you/they* ***were*** *work****ing*** *when it happened.*

The past tense is the most common way of referring to past time and in this chapter (346–360) we deal with the past simple and past progressive forms. Past tense forms may also occasionally refer to present time, often for reasons of politeness or indirectness.

The perfect forms (present perfect and past perfect, simple and progressive) refer to events in time from a point in the past up to the moment of speaking/writing (present perfect), or events in time from one point in the past up to another, later, point in the past (past perfect).

Forms of the present perfect and past perfect

form	structure	examples
present perfect simple	present tense forms of *have* + *-ed* participle	*I/you/we/they* ***have*** *work****ed*** *hard.* *He/she/it/one* ***has*** *work****ed*** *hard.* *We* ***haven't*** *work****ed*** *hard.* ***Has*** *he work****ed*** *hard?*
past perfect simple	past tense forms of *have* + *-ed* participle	*I/you/we/they* ***had*** *work****ed*** *hard.* *He/she/it* ***had*** *work****ed*** *hard.*
present perfect progressive	present tense forms of *have* + *been* + lexical verb in *-ing* form	*I/you/we/they* ***have been*** *work****ing*** *hard.* *He/she/it/one* ***has been*** *work****ing*** *hard.* *We* ***haven't been*** *work****ing*** *hard.* ***Has*** *he been work****ing*** *hard?*
past perfect progressive	past tense forms of *have* + *been* + lexical verb in *-ing* form	*I/you/he/she/it/we/they* ***had been*** *work****ing*** *hard.* *We* ***hadn't been*** *work****ing*** *hard.* ***Had*** *he been work****ing*** *hard?*

Modal *would* and semi-modal *used to* are also used for past time reference (→ 402 *Used to* and *would*).

THE PAST SIMPLE 347

Definite time reference 347a

References to definite past time clearly separated from the moment of speaking are normally made using the past simple. The most common type of reference to the past is through definite time adjuncts and definite time adverbial clauses:

__Did__ you __watch__ that film yesterday?

He __went__ at the end of November.

My grandfather __died__ about four weeks ago.

When I was a lad, __I lived__ on a farm.

She __came__ through for a coffee after she'd finished cooking.

With such definite past references, the present perfect is not normally used:

My grandfather __died__ about four weeks ago.
(~~My grandfather has died about four weeks ago.~~)

When I was a lad, __I lived__ on a farm.
(~~When I was a lad, I have lived on a farm.~~)

Definite time adjuncts 347b

Common definite time adjuncts that indicate a clear break between the past and present time include:

*a year/two weeks/five minutes/*etc. *ago*

at two o'clock/half past three, etc.

earlier today/this month, etc.

in the spring/summer, etc.

last night/week/month/year, etc.

on Monday/Wednesday, etc.

the other day/week

yesterday

(→ examples at **347a** above)

→ **359a** on past simple with temporal subordinators (e.g. *when*) in complex sentences

The past simple without explicit time markers 347c

Often there is no explicit time marker, but definite past time may be implied either by the situation of speaking or writing, or by assumptions of shared and general knowledge. In such cases, the past simple may be used:

Charles Dickens __wrote__ 'Great Expectations' in instalments.
(we know that Dickens lived and died a long time ago, separated from the present)

Do you know Fiona? Because I __went__ to school with her.
(the speaker's schooldays were long ago, in a time separated from the moment of speaking)

***Did** you **receive** my fax?*
(the speaker is looking back to the point of time when he sent the fax as separated in his mind from the present; compare 'Have you received my fax?', where the speaker is considering the event in terms of the present moment)

Events and states 347d

The past simple may be used for single events or habitual events or states in the past.

- Single events:

  *He **suffered** a head wound, for which he **went** to hospital and **received** ten stitches.*

  *And then she **went** out and she **phoned** my brother.*

- Habitual events:

  [*hung out in* means 'spent time in']
  *He **visited** the opera regularly and mostly **hung** out in local cafés.*

  *We **did** a lot of acting at school.*

- States:

  *She **looked** a bit upset.*

  *Where **were** you? I've been worried sick.*

Where more than one event is reported, a time sequence is normally assumed. This can be shown by changing the word order in the sentence:

event 1 event 2
*Then she **went out** and she **phoned** my brother.*

event 1 event 2
*Then she **phoned** my brother and she **went out**.*

If the real sequence of events is different from the word order of the sentence, then this must be indicated explicitly (e.g. by a temporal conjunction):

event 2 event 1
*She **identified** herself when she **answered** the phone.*
(she answered the phone first, then identified herself)

However, events may also be understood as simultaneous:

*I wasn't satisfied so I **wrote** to them and **complained**.*
(the writing of the letter and the complaining were one and the same thing)

When the past simple is used to refer to habitual events, the meaning is similar to *used to*:

*We **did** a lot of acting at school.*
(or: We used to do a lot of acting at school.)

→ **402 *Used to* and *would***

THE PAST PROGRESSIVE 348

Events in progress 348a

The past progressive may refer generally to events in progress around a particular time in the past. It may highlight the temporary nature of events:

*Where I **was living** in Leicester six months ago, I had a massive room. It was too big really.*

*I **was working** last night.*

*Fourteen hours later, we **were entering** Kingston Harbour.*
(compare: Fourteen hours later we entered Kingston Harbour. The past simple emphasises the whole event, from start to finish; the past progressive emphasises the event as being in progress but unfinished at the time referred to)

Background events 348b

The past progressive may refer to past-time events occurring as a background to other events which interrupt them.

The events which occur in the foreground are usually in the past simple:

background **foreground**
*She was here once, and I **was baking** a cake. And she **said**, 'Can I help you?'*

*Two builders **were working** on our house when it **was being built**, and a ghost **passed** them on the stairs, and they **refused** to come back and finish the building. It **terrified** them.*

→ **347d The past simple** on sequences of events

Reasons and contexts for events 348c

The past progressive is often used to give a reason or context for an event:

*Her husband **was doing** a PhD at the university, and that's how I came to meet him.*

A: *I rang you yesterday but there was no answer.*
B: *I **was gardening**.*

Ongoing and repeated events 348d

The past progressive may refer to ongoing or repeated events in the past. There is often a suggestion that the situation was temporary or subject to change:

A: *She only had a very small income which I gave her each week and that **was coming** out of my overdraft.*
B: *I see.*
A: *But the bank were only prepared to support me up to a point.*

The past progressive may occur with adverbs such as *always*, *constantly*, to describe repeated unplanned (or undesired) events:

*People **were always warning** me that my success wouldn't last.*

*I **wasn't constantly collapsing** in floods of tears, but I was in quite a bad way.*

⇢ 340d The present progressive with adverbs of indefinite frequency

⇢ 359b Temporal subordinators and the past progressive

⇢ 492d The past progressive in speech representation

The past progressive and definite time 348e

The past progressive can be used to refer to definite past time, usually to emphasise the extended nature of an event:

*I **was talking** to Mark last night.*

*We **were working** in the garden all day yesterday.*

THE PAST PROGRESSIVE VERSUS THE PAST SIMPLE 349

Often there is little difference between the past progressive and the past simple, except that the past progressive suggests that the events may be seen more as background or of secondary importance, or their temporary nature may be more emphasised:

*Being an eye clinic, it **was dealing** with a very high proportion of elderly people.* (or: Being an eye clinic, it dealt with a very high proportion ...)

[describing an archaeological dig]
*And scattered throughout a lot of the area he dug, he found iron slag, so, you know, they **were making** quite a lot of stuff. Phase one, under the bank he found some crucibles and crucibles were used in bronze working. In the earlier phase at least they **were making** bronze implements as well.*
(or: ... so, you know, they made quite a lot of stuff. ... In the earlier phase at least they made bronze implements as well.)

VERBS NOT NORMALLY USED IN THE PAST PROGRESSIVE 350

Verbs which rarely occur in the present progressive (⇢ 340e) are similarly rarely used in the past progressive, and the past simple is generally preferred. These include:

believe	*contain*	*hate*
consist	*dislike*	*have to*

know
like
mean
smell
taste
think
understand
want

Breakfast ***consisted*** *of a mug of tea and a piece of fruit pudding each.*

You ***didn't have to*** *explain it to me. I* ***knew*** *what you* ***meant****.*
(~~You weren't having to explain it to me. I was knowing what you were meaning.~~)

The room still ***smelt*** *of smoke from the last occupant's cigarettes.*

However, as with the present tense usage, the past progressive may occasionally be used to emphasise an ongoing or unfolding process in the past, though this happens much less frequently than in the present tense:

We had a pleasant ride back. I ***was liking*** *James more and more and he was very attentive to me, showing very clearly how much he enjoyed my visits to his home.*

Emma had been worrying for some time that she was going to crash her meagre budget with all the minicabs and taxis she ***was having to*** *use.*

THE PRESENT PERFECT 351

Time up to now 351a

The present perfect (simple and progressive) is used to refer to events taking place in a past time-frame that connects with the present:

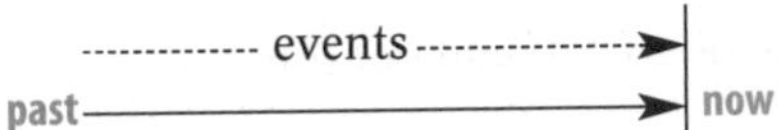

So, what's ***been happening since the last time we met****?*
(from that moment till now)

In fact, alligators ***have killed*** *only eight people in Florida* ***in the last half-century****.*
(in the fifty years up to the time of writing)

The present perfect progressive can place greater emphasis on the duration of an event up to the present moment and can indicate an uninterrupted action:

I've been waiting *for you for over an hour.*

With time adjuncts

The time-frame may be indicated explicitly by an adjunct indicating 'time-up-to-now'. Such expressions include:

before

*during/in the last x minutes/hours/ weeks/years/*etc.

in my life

lately

over the last x months/years

recently

so far

this week/month/year/century

to date

today

up to/till/until now

*During the last 20 years there **has been** a big change from wooden to plastic window frames in many houses.*

*We **have** quite recently **made** some important structural changes to our Editorial Department.*

*I know **I've lost** a lot of weight this week.*

*To date, the families of at least 900 of these children **have been found**.*

With no time adjunct

The time-frame may be implied or understood, without any explicit time adjunct:

*Local authorities **have warned** that they will be forced to sack teachers if the Government refuses to fund next year's pay settlement.*
(understood: during recent days/weeks, during the time of the present debate/crisis)

***I've been working** and am working at Amsterdam University, on several projects.*
(understood: from some point in the past, up to and including now)

***Have** you **phoned** your sister?*
(from the point when you said you were going to do it up to this moment in time; if the speaker had said 'Did you phone your sister?', there is a greater expectation from the speaker that the phone call should have taken place or did take place)

The first time

Note that the expression *this is the first time* ... when referring to an immediate event is normally used with the present perfect, not the present simple or progressive:

[one passenger to another during a flight]
*Is this **the first time** you**'ve flown** on British Airways?*
(~~Is this the first time you fly on British Airways?~~)

'Is this the first time you're flying on British Airways?' is likely to be heard as a reference to the future, i.e. 'You've bought a British Airways ticket; will it be your first flight with them?'

The present perfect or the past simple

Some time adjuncts can be used with either the present perfect or the past simple, depending upon the speaker's/writer's perspective. These include:

already	*once*	*this morning/week/*etc.
before	*recently*	*today*

With this group of adjuncts, if the events are considered as happening at a definite point in the past, then the past simple is used:

The house ***was sold*** *recently.*
(speaker is thinking of a definite point in the past when the house sale took place)

I ***rang*** *him this morning.*
(said after midday, when 'this morning' has finished)

[referring to the day at work]
Did *you* ***see*** *everybody you wanted to see today?*
(speaker considers 'today' finished as a work day)

If the events are seen as connected to or relevant to the moment of speaking or writing, then the present perfect is used:

[loudspeaker announcement on a train]
To all passengers who ***have*** *recently* ***joined*** *this service. My name is Chris and I'm your chief steward.*
(speaker focuses on the fact that the passengers are on the train now)

I've been *busy this morning.*
(said during the morning)

I haven't asked her yet. I ***haven't seen*** *her today.*
(speaker considers 'today' to be still current)

For and *since* — 351b

For and *since* both commonly introduce time expressions which can refer to 'time up to now' and which are used with the present perfect.

For refers to periods of time, *since* refers to a previous point in time:

We've ***had*** *that TV set* ***for fifteen years.***
(~~We've had that TV set since fifteen years.~~)

I've been *awake* ***since half past four this morning.***

Expressions with *for* can also refer to periods of time separated from now, when the period referred to has come to an end or lies in the past, in which case the past tense is used:

A: *I* ***lived*** *in Sweden* ***for five years.***
B: *When was that?*
A: *Oh* ***in the 1970s.***

✪ *Since* is not used with the present simple or progressive when referring to 'time up to now':

We've ***lived/been living*** *in the village since 1987.*
(~~We live/are living in the village since 1987.~~)

Now-relevance 351c

A basic use of the present perfect is when the speaker considers an event to be still important or relevant in some way to the moment of speaking:

Well, we were here in the house, and the neighbour came in and said, 'There's something going on up the street. I think someone ***has stabbed*** *someone.'*
(a newsworthy event that is very important to the speaker)

A: *I don't remember seeing any cigarette adverts on TV, do you?* ***Have they been banned****?*
B: *Yeah. They were banned, oh, years and years ago.*
(a possible explanation for the speaker's present understanding)

It's too dangerous to touch. I think somebody ***has been tampering*** *with it.*
(the effects of someone interfering with it are visible now)

The present perfect indicates that the speaker chooses to mark the event as important/relevant to now, or may wish to stress that the event happened very recently. Compare:

*That's probably why I'm so tired, because I****'ve been chattering*** *to people I don't really know.*

That's probably why I'm so tired, because I ***was chattering*** *to people I don't really know.*

The difference here may be an emphasis on how recently the chattering took place, but both versions may also refer to the same event, with no difference in time reference.

THE PRESENT PERFECT SIMPLE VERSUS THE PRESENT PERFECT PROGRESSIVE 352

Completed and punctual events 352a

The simple form of the present perfect can emphasise completion of an event when used with verbs denoting actions or events:

Advertising agency FCB ***has carried out*** *extensive research on how people in short-term contracts feel about their jobs.*

The progressive form is not normally used with punctual verbs such as *start, stop, finish*, which refer to actions that are completed at a single point in time:

My mobile phone ***has started*** *working again.*
(~~My mobile phone has been starting working again.~~)

Have *you* ***finished*** *eating?*

The progressive form is not used to refer to single, completed actions or punctual events:

Essex County Council ***has approved*** *expenditure of £50,000 on the project this year.*
(~~Essex County Council has been approving expenditure of £50,000 on the project this year.~~)

*Now the government **has admitted** it has been able to collect only half of the taxes planned.*

Events in the past still continuing 352b

The progressive form is often used for events which started in the past and are still continuing, or which have stopped, but whose effects are still continuing:

*She**'s been working** for the company for years, hasn't she?*

*Maybe they can see I**'ve been crying**.*
(the tears or the effects are still visible; 'Maybe they can see I've cried' would not allow the possibility that the crying was still continuing right up to the present moment)

***Have** you **been watching** 'The Lonely Planet'?*
(the TV programme, *The Lonely Planet*, is still continuing each week, and people continue to watch it)

References to things which have been true for very long periods of time often prefer the simple form:

*A church **has stood** on this site since the twelfth century.*
(preferred to: has been standing)

References to events closed and completed at some indefinite point in the past prefer the simple form:

A: *Do you know 'A Tale of Two Cities'?*
B: *I **have read** it, but I don't remember much about it.*
(not: ~~I have been reading it …~~)
('I've been reading *A Tale of Two Cities*' might mean that the speaker had not finished it but was still reading it, though not necessarily at the moment of speaking. It could also suggest that the speaker had finished the novel but had been kept occupied by it: 'I've been reading *A Tale of Two Cities*, that's why you haven't seen me all week. I had to write an essay on it.')

The difference between the present perfect simple and the present perfect progressive may sometimes be between an emphasis on the event itself as a progressive, extended activity (progressive form), compared with the results of the event, or some other, secondary reference to the event (simple form). Both forms may refer to completed events:

[looking out of the window]
*It**'s been raining**.*
(the rain has stopped)

*In sub-Saharan Africa … the rate of decline in infant mortality **has slowed** noticeably: a child's risk of dying before reaching the age of five is higher than anywhere else in the world.*
(the slowing of the rate may or may not have stopped; what is important are the results)

⇢ 539 **Glossary** for any unfamiliar terms

Sometimes there is little difference between the two forms:

*He's **lived/been living** there for years and years.*

*I've **felt/been feeling** better since I started taking those tablets.*

The only difference here is that the simple form may suggest the possibility of permanence, while the progressive form may suggest a more temporary state of affairs.

When the frequency of a repeated action or event is stated, the simple form is preferred:

*That's **happened** to Lydia several times this morning.*
(~~That's been happening to Lydia several times this morning.~~)

→ 342 to compare the present simple

Mental process and sense verbs 352c

Some verbs are rarely used in the progressive form. These include verbs of mental process (*know, like*) and sense verbs (*smell, taste*):

*I've **known** Anne at least forty-odd years, I would think.*
(~~I've been knowing Anne ...~~)

*The water's always **tasted** metallic to me.*

Repeated or extended events which are felt to be developing, ongoing or perhaps temporary may occasionally lead to the use of progressive for such verbs:

*The water's definitely **been tasting** better since we bought the filter.*

THE PRESENT PERFECT AND DEFINITE PAST TIME 353

In spoken and written journalistic styles, the present perfect is sometimes used to stress the current relevance of events, even though definite past time adjuncts may be present:

[speaker is speaking in 1998, i.e. not 'the early 1990s']
*We've **lost** so much of our manufacturing industry in the 1980s and early 1990s.*

*A man **has been arrested** last night and will appear in court tomorrow.*

THE PRESENT PERFECT AS A FRAME FOR PAST TIME EVENTS 354

The present perfect is often used initially to provide an overall frame for the reporting of past events, in spoken and written narratives and reports. The present perfect verb often provides a headline or statement of a newsworthy event, followed by a series of verbs in the past tense reporting the details:

*Poisonous black widow spiders **have invaded** Britain by plane. They **stowed away** in crates of ammunition flown from America to RAF Welford, Berks. A US airman at the base near Newbury **captured** one of the spiders in a jar after it **crawled out** of a crate.*

*I've **been going** to the weight-watchers but, wait till you hear this, I **went** first time and I'd lost three and a half pounds, and I **went** last week and I'd lost half a pound, so I **went** down to the fish shop and **got** fish and chips. I **was** so disgusted!*

THE PAST PERFECT 355

Time up to 'then' 355a

Just as the present perfect refers to a time-frame leading up to the moment of speaking (351a), so the past perfect refers to a time-frame leading up to a point in the past. The present perfect refers to 'time up to now'; the past perfect refers to 'time up to then':

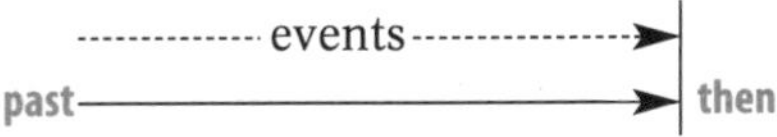

*That was in 1938. I left in June with the children for a new home in Oxford, where my mother **had bought** a house. My father **had died** in 1936.*

This can be illustrated as:

time before 'then'	'then' (= 1938)
	I left in June
*... my mother **had bought** a house*	
*... my father **had died***	

*The au pairs always used to call her Cruella. She was terrible. Her husband **had died** of cancer two years previously so I could see why she had a problem.*
(two years before the events the speaker is recounting)

[speaker is talking about his tennis coach]
*At my club there was Frank Parsons, who **had coached** similar boys my age.*
(during a time before the time he coached the speaker)

*As she sat eating in the caged silence, she thought of all the thousands of meals George must have had here, alone, in all these years. Did he ever cook himself something good? What **had he been thinking** all those silent weekends and evenings on his own?*
(the thoughts he had in the time before she sat there thinking of him)

Reported clauses 355b

The past perfect is very frequent in reported clauses where the reporting verb is in the past:

*Linda kept me informed and she said that her husband **had moved** back in. They**'d got** back together again. She**'d got** pregnant.*

*The police told me that he**'d done** it very often.*

Reporting verbs include verbs of perception:

*I noticed he **had hurt** his leg.*

*He saw that she **had been** able to cure herself.*

References to changed states 355c

The past perfect is often used to refer to situations which were true but which have been or are to be changed. In such cases, *had* is often stressed in speech:

[telephone conversation between travel agent (A) and customer (B)]
A: *And you want to go London Hong Kong.*
B: *That's right.*
A: *On the ... what date do you wish to travel now?*
B: *I **had booked** on the third. But erm ...*
A: *On the third.*
B: *Should be on the second. And this is the flight number.*

*I **had planned** to work till I was sixty but I can't any more.*

*At the moment Sarah is quite interested in tourism, anything to do with tourism. So it looks like she will leave school and go on to something like this. I **had hoped** she'd carry on for a bit longer.*

The past perfect in conditional clauses 355d

The past perfect must be used when there is past reference in a hypothetical conditional clause with *if*:

*I'd have been killed **if I'd been caught** down there.*
(I would have been killed if I had been caught ...)

*Well, even **if you'd come** home tonight, you'd have been upset anyway.*
(... if you had come home, you would have been upset ...)

The past perfect is not used in the main clause in a hypothetical conditional sentence:

*If I **had had** more time I **would have been** in touch earlier.*
(~~If I had had more time I had been in touch earlier.~~)

THE PAST PERFECT AND THE PAST SIMPLE 356

Sometimes the past perfect may be necessary to resolve possible misunderstanding or ambiguity as regards the sequence of events and the semantic relationship between them:

*They all left the room when she **recited** her poem.*
(suggests they all left the moment she started reciting)

*They all left the room when she**'d recited** her poem.*
(suggests they left after she'd finished reciting)

The past simple often suggests a more immediate causal link between two events, compared with the past perfect:

__When__ he __opened__ his desk, he discovered a dead bird.
(stresses the immediate result, rather than 'When he had opened his desk …')

__When__ he__'d opened__ his third present, he looked at the roller skates and smiled.
(not such an immediate or direct relationship; the roller skates may not have been in the third present)

THE PAST PERFECT SIMPLE VERSUS THE PAST PERFECT PROGRESSIVE 357

The principles for choosing between the past perfect simple and progressive are the same as those which operate between the present perfect simple and progressive (··➤ 352):

We__'d been playing__ five minutes when you turned up.
(ongoing event continuing up to that point in the past)

After their departure Edith noticed the small white card lying on the mantelpiece. She __had been meaning__ to tell her brother about it, he had a right to know, but their behaviour __had put__ everything else out of her mind.
('had been meaning …' refers to an extended event going on around that time; 'had put' refers to a single, completed event that occurred during that time)

And Thursday night I was so cold, and I__'d been sneezing__ a lot and __blowing__ my nose, and I thought it was my hay fever.
(repeated events during the time up to then)

[talking about a man who had tried, unsuccessfully, to make an old clock work again]
And he went away on holiday and everything, and when he got back the other people that worked in there said as soon as he__'d gone__ it __had started__ working.
(single, completed events)

··➤ **448–459 Condition**

TIME-FRAMES: SUMMARY 358

The past tense forms refer to a time-frame that is in some way separated from the present; there is a break between the completion of the event and the present moment. This break may be explicitly stated by an expression of definite past time (e.g. *yesterday, last week, in 1975*) or may be implicit, or indicated somewhere in the context.

The past tense forms may be contrasted with the present perfect forms, which are used to refer to events in a time-frame that is still connected to the present moment, or to events which the speaker considers to be still current or relevant to the present moment.

The basic difference between the speaker's perception of time as past or as extending until now, and the choice of past tense or present perfect forms can be expressed thus:

Past tense forms

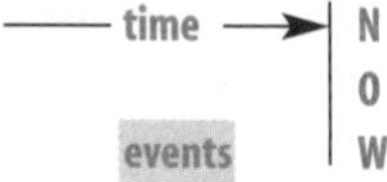

*I **posted** your letter.*

*We **were working** in the garden all day yesterday.*

Present perfect forms

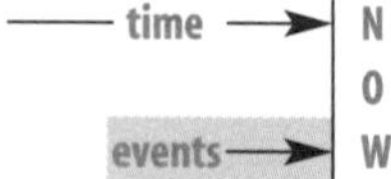

*I**'ve posted** your letter.*

*She**'s been feeling** unwell for the last few days.*

Past perfect forms

A speaker may also refer to a time-frame in the past and to events from an earlier past that are linked in some way to that time-frame. In these cases, the past perfect forms may be used. This relationship may be represented thus:

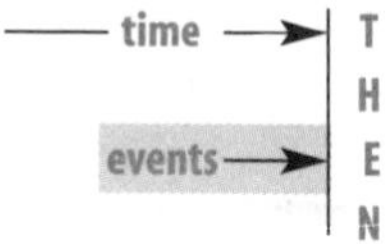

*I **had already told** Margaret, so the news came as no surprise to her.*

*He said he **had met** me before, but could not remember where.*

TENSE CHOICE IN COMPLEX SENTENCES 359

Temporal subordinators (e.g. *when*) and the past simple 359a

Temporal subordinators such as *after, as soon as, before, once, until, when* and *while* can refer to definite points and periods of time in the past separated from the moment of speaking. In such cases, the subordinators are used with the past simple:

*As soon as I **got** home, I phoned my sister.*

*Once the initial shock **was** over, Mr Coldman had to settle into his new role.*

[speaker is recounting a fainting attack]
*When I **woke** up, I didn't know where I was.*

Temporal subordinators and the past progressive 359b

The temporal subordinators *as*, *when* and *while* (or less frequently *whilst*) are often used with the past progressive to indicate background events:

*I read the letter on the Underground as I **was coming** into town.*

*He mentioned it to Janet when he **was making** a cup of tea.*

*My friend Rachel came round while I **was sorting** things out.*

While/whilst may connect two clauses in the past progressive, to indicate simultaneous or parallel events:

*They **were messing around** most of the time enjoying themselves while I **was looking after** the children.*

Temporal subordinators and the present perfect 359c

Temporal subordinators such as *after*, *as soon as*, *before*, *once*, *until*, *when* can refer to finished events at points and periods of time in the future as seen from the present moment. In such cases they occur with the present perfect simple:

*Tell me after I**'ve eaten** my dinner, because I want to enjoy it.*

*I'm going to start revising as soon as I**'ve done** this project.*

*Once I**'ve become** more familiar with the territory, maybe I'll be able to find things for myself.*

*Shall I give you a ring when I**'ve sorted** the invoice out?*
(~~Shall I give you a ring when I will have sorted the invoice out?~~)

The same subordinators may also refer to past events completed at the moment of speaking, or to past events still relevant at the time of speaking/writing, especially when such events are seen as generally true. Such references also occur with the present perfect simple:

*Once you**'ve bought** a house, you start falling into trap after trap, you know, mortgage and bills, and buying things for the house, and things that'll make it comfortable, and what have you.*

*You're put into a medical ward after you**'ve been treated** in the coronary care unit.*

*When I**'ve been** out to buy something and I see the price, it shocks me that things are so expensive.*

Temporal subordinators and the past perfect 359d

Some time expressions occur with either the past simple or the past perfect, and it is usually the choice of whether the information is considered background or 'foreground' that determines the choice, **not** the fact that something happened before something else. Items in this category include *after, as soon as, before, until, when*:

*She came through for a coffee after she'**d finished** cooking.*
('after she finished cooking' would also have been correct, but with greater foregrounding of the subordinate clause than the version with the past perfect)

*It ended up with her having to go back on the Saturday so that my son could come as soon as she'**d gone**.*
('as soon as she went' would also be correct, but with a different, more immediate emphasis)

The construction *after having* + *-ed* participle is infrequent. *After* + *-ing* form is more common, even in writing:

*And **after having worked** very closely with Michael Blake for so many years and **having had** so many people I think actually believing that he was a member of the Press staff, it's very nice finally to be able to welcome him as a real member of the Press staff.*
(infrequent: formal public speech)

*I feel a bit better **after lying down** for a bit.*
(more frequent than: after having lain down)

Perfect infinitive clauses 359e

A perfect infinitive clause can be used for events which did take place:

*I am sorry for the Formans. **To have worked** so hard and then to have that done to them overnight!*
(they did work hard)

It may also refer to events that have not taken place:

[*Millie* is a cat]
*But this time the button was too close to the wall. **To have activated** it, Millie would have needed to use her paw like a finger.*
(in this case, the following clause (*would have needed*) indicates that the event was hypothetical; compare: To activate it, Millie would need to use her paw ... etc., where the possibility of activating the button is still open)

PRESENT TENSE REFERENCES TO PAST TIME 360

The present simple for dramatic effect 360a

For stylistic reasons, the present simple is often used for true and fictional past events in narratives to create a sense of immediacy, and to suggest that past events are unfolding at the moment of speaking or writing.

Story-tellers frequently shift from one tense to another. This use of the present tense is often called the historic present:

[a woman is telling a story about a laser light show she went to in a theatre]
A: *In the beginning there* ***was*** *darkness, and we* ***hear*** *this scraping sound, and you* ***see*** *this little coloured pattern, the coloured pattern* ***gets*** *bigger and bigger and bigger.*
B: *What* ***was*** *this projected by? A movie projector or a video?*

[from the novel 'Twenty Years a Growing', by Maurice O'Sullivan]
I ***felt*** *a prod in my shoulder. 'The bus is coming,'* ***said*** *George. She* ***comes*** *across with a loud grating noise. The crowd* ***moves*** *towards her, myself and my companion among them. She* ***moves*** *away rapidly.*

The present progressive for narrative build-up 360b

When a story builds towards a peak or climax, especially in spoken story-telling, the verb form may change to the present progressive to describe the background to the main event(s) or to dramatise an ongoing event:

And he walked right up in the pitch blackness, on the top edge of this crane. ***We're all sitting*** *there, and the police turned up, and he said, 'What's going on, boys?'*

I said, 'There's been a pigeon in here eating my sandwiches and I had to throw a few things at it'. She used to have the windows wide open, you know, winter, summer, everything. So, anyway, ***I'm telling her off*** *for all this mess on the floor, I went to pick the tail up, some of the bits the other side of the bed, and as I got up* ***I'm looking*** *straight into this pigeon's eyes.*

News headlines 360c

News headlines (both spoken and written) often report (recent) past events in the present simple.

TIDAL WAVE ***HITS*** *PAPUA NEW GUINEA*

PRIME MINISTER ***SAYS*** *TRAFFIC MUST BE CURBED*

Such headlines may refer either to a subsequent present perfect time-frame (e.g. 'A tidal wave has hit Papua New Guinea') or to a definite past time-frame (e.g. 'A tidal wave hit Papua New Guinea late last night').

→ 539 Glossary for any unfamiliar terms

Present tense references to historical events 360d

In lists or descriptions of important historical events, the present simple is often used to refer to definite past time:

1939
15 March: Germany ***invades*** *Czechoslovakia. Hitler* ***claims*** *that German troops were invited to 'keep order'.*
31 March: Britain and France ***offer*** *a guarantee to defend Poland from a German attack. Similar assurances* ***are given*** *to Greece and Romania.*

[from a TV football commentary]
2003 Arsenal ***sign*** *Antonio Reyes. 2004 Man United* ***sign*** *Wayne Rooney. It's just tit for tat, isn't it?*

Speech-reporting verbs 360e

Reports with extended relevance

When a speech report refers to something said in the past that is always true or always relevant, the present simple is often used for the reporting verb:

[speaker reports verbal instructions she received from the owner of a portable baby's bed as to how to assemble it]
She ***says*** *you've got to twist these round and it makes them solid or something.*

Her earliest memory, she ***tells*** *me, is of her father returning from the First World War.*

→ **492b The present simple** in **Speech representation**

Hear, *tell* and *understand* as reporting verbs are also often used in the present simple tense, to report or to query newsworthy past events:

What's all this I ***hear*** *about you attacking Barbara?*

Jane ***tells*** *me you've not been too well since you got back from holiday.*

[customer (A) and check-out assistant in a store; *Switch* is a kind of charge-card]
A: *I* ***understand*** *you're taking Switch soon.*
B: *We're taking Switch now.*
A: *Oh.*
(somebody told me, or I read it somewhere)

→ **339e Mental process verbs**

Direct speech reports in spoken narratives

In informal spoken narratives recounting definite past time events, direct speech reports often have a reporting verb in the present simple. Speakers may alternate between present and past tenses, but usually reserve the present tense for quoting speech that is in some way important in the story:

> *And somebody saw her and she* ***said****, 'Ooh Mrs Naylor,' she* ***said****, 'Have you sent your little girl to school?' she* ***says****. 'Yes,' she* ***says****. 'Well she's on Grange Street sat on top of a load of coal, throwing it!'*

Speakers may add an *-s* ending to the present tense verb, even for first person subjects:

> *He* ***says****, 'You almost killed me there you know.' I* ***said****, 'Why?' He* ***says****, 'You know who those two men were?' I* ***says****, 'No I didn't.' And he* ***told*** *me.*
> (this is non-standard usage, but becoming increasingly frequent)

→ also **501e Use of *I says, go, be* and *be like*** in **Speech representation**

Future time

Future time

INTRODUCTION 361

There is no future tense ending for English verbs as there is in other languages, but English has several widely used ways of referring to future time. The most common forms are:

*We'**re going to** buy a new camera.*
(*be going to* + infinitive)

*She'**s coming** next Thursday.*
(the present progressive form)

*I'**ll** be home about eight.*
(*shall/will*)

*My flight **leaves** in two hours' time.*
(the present simple form)

*The government **is to** introduce a new funding system for universities.*
(*be to* + infinitive)

*We'**re about to** have dinner.*
(*be about to* + infinitive)

References to the future can depend on how much evidence there is for future statements. It is often not possible to refer to the future with complete certainty, even though some future events and actions are inevitable. Sometimes, therefore, choices of form depend on how definite or certain the speaker wants to sound. For this reason, a number of the ways of referring to the future involve modal verbs. The most common verb used is *will*.

→ **377–407 Modality**

BE GOING TO AND THE PRESENT PROGRESSIVE 362

Be going to and the present progressive are commonly used for referring to future plans, decisions and arrangements. Sometimes either form can be used, sometimes there are contrasts in meaning between them, and sometimes one form is preferred. *Be going to* is more frequent in spoken and informal contexts.

In general, *be going to* and the present progressive can both be used to refer to future events when there is greater involvement on the part of the speaker in the decision-making process:

*What **are you going to drink**?*
*What **are you drinking**?*

***I'm going to have** a drink with Jill after the film.*
***I'm having** a drink with Jill after the film.*

*She**'s not going to borrow** my car.*
*She**'s not borrowing** my car.*

*Karen**'s going to arrive** tomorrow. I couldn't put her off.*
*Karen**'s arriving tomorrow**. I couldn't put her off.*

Be going to usually indicates that a decision has been made and that the event will take place soon, but that all the necessary plans have not yet been made. *Be going to* stresses the subjective view of the speaker:

*We**'re going to** pave over the front garden when we get round to it, so we can park off the road.*

***I'm going to** ask him to marry me.*

The present progressive usually indicates that a decision has been made and that arrangements are probably in place or have been made:

***I'm starting** a new job next week.*
(typically means I have agreed terms and a starting date)

*I shall actually be leaving earlier than expected. **I'm flying** on Friday.*
(I have booked the flight and made all the arrangements)

The present progressive is not used when a prediction is made based on present evidence:

*It's gone really dark. It**'s going to** rain any minute.*
(~~It's raining any minute.~~)

[said to a little child who has just received a gift of money]
*You**'re going to** lose that money if you don't put it in your pocket.*
(~~You're losing that money …~~)

Will may be used in such cases (→ 363).

BE GOING TO AND *WILL* 363

Be going to and *will* can both be used to make predictions based on present evidence or the present situation:

*Hurry up or we**'re going to** be late!*
(or: Hurry up or we'll be late!)

Normally, *be going to* is used when there is some outside evidence for what is said or when the statement can be clearly interpreted:

*Rumiko **is going to** have a new baby.*
(outside evidence)

*He**'s going to** burn that toast.*
(it can be seen)

Will/shall is preferred when evidence is not so obvious or is less immediately relevant and when judgements or opinions have to be relied on:

*The baby **will** have black hair.*
(statement based on the speaker's judgement/knowledge)

*Don't let him cook. He**'ll** even burn the toast.*
(evidence is less obvious, but the speaker knows that the person mentioned cannot cook)

*I'm sure that we **shall** have a good discussion.*
(based on the speaker's judgement)

Will may be used to state absolute certainties about the future:

*My birthday **will** fall on a Tuesday in 2007.*

There are contrasts in formality between *will* and *be going to*. In general, *will* is more formal. The following example shows a switch of formality from *will* to *be going to*:

[TV weather forecast]
*Temperatures **will** be below freezing … and it**'s going to** be icy on those country roads, so do take care if you're driving.*

The following example shows a speaker change from *be going to* (informal, in this case *gonna*) to *will* (more formal):

[to friend, while looking at a menu]
***I'm gonna** have fried mushrooms, you like mushrooms don't you?*

[shortly afterwards, to the waiter]
*I**'ll** have deep fried mushrooms with … erm … an old timer burger.*

When the future reference is based on decisions, plans and intentions, *be going to* is used:

*She**'s** already **going to** buy some new shoes; she can't have the coat as well.*
(~~She will already buy some new shoes …; she can't have the coat as well.~~)

*I didn't realise you**'re going to** apply for the job too.*
(… that you plan/intend/have decided to apply)

GONNA 364

Gonna (pronounced /ˈgənə/) is an informal alternative to *going to* in most informal spoken contexts (see the example in 363 above). It is the normal way in which *going to* is pronounced at normal speeds; *going to* is therefore often represented in writing as *gonna*:

*It's not **gonna** take two minutes. Then we'll have finished.*

*What are you **gonna** do with them?*

INDEPENDENT *'LL* 365

There are contexts involving decisions and arrangements where *'ll* is normally the only choice. In such cases *'ll* is best not seen as a contraction of either *will* or *shall*; it may be seen as an independent form.

As an independent form, *'ll* is often used to indicate an instantaneous personal decision:

*There's a garage. We**'ll** just stop and get some petrol.*
(~~There's a garage. We shall/will just stop and get some petrol.~~)

[speaker A has just poured herself some water]
A: *Anyone else want some?*
B: ***I'll** have a drop, yes. Thanks.*

Independent *'ll* is also used for indicating informal decisions or arrangements where *will* or *shall* would sound too direct or imposing:

*Okay. That's it then. We**'ll** meet next week, I suppose.*

[*Asda* is the name of a supermarket chain]
*Then we**'ll** get a bus to Bridgford, the boys**'ll** get off near Asda and we**'ll** all walk to the school.*

WILL/SHALL: INTENTION AND VOLITION 366

When a speaker wants to make their will or intention clear, then *will* or *shall* is normally used:

*I **will** not do it. You can't make me.*

*I promise I **will** not be beaten.*

*'I **shall** be at the station to meet you,' she said. 'Friday week.'*

A: *Don't forget the party. You **will** come, won't you?*
B: *I certainly **will**. I wouldn't miss it, would I?*

*I **will** definitely stop smoking. I really **will**.*

WILL VERSUS *SHALL* 367

Will may be used for all persons, but *shall* often occurs with *I* and *we*. *Will* is generally less formal when used with *I* and *we*:

A: *Right. Have a nice weekend.*
B: *I **shall** try. You too.*
A: *Okay then. Bye bye sweetheart.*

*We **shall** find some other work for you to do.*

Shall also has a specialised legal usage for stating rules, laws, legal provisions, etc. In such cases, it often occurs with third person subjects:

*The insured **shall** remain the sole owner of the vehicle.*

WILL/SHALL IN REQUESTS, OFFERS, ETC. 368

Will/'ll is often used to make offers of future action. In such cases the present simple is not used:

*Oh, that looks heavy. **I'll** carry it for you.*
(~~That looks heavy. I carry it for you.~~)

Shall is frequently used to make first person suggestions regarding future actions:

***Shall** I close the door?*

***Shall** we go out for a meal with them for their anniversary?*

Note that *will* is becoming more frequent in such cases.

→ 388 ***Shall***

→ **408–423 Speech acts**

THE PRESENT SIMPLE 369

References to fixed events in the future (e.g. schedules, timetables and firm arrangements) are often made using the present simple:

The = sign indicates an utterance which is cut short
[two people exchanging information about their respective travel arrangements]
A: *So you're going on the …?*
B: *Twentieth. On the twentieth. And then I **come back**=*
A: *November the twelfth.*
B: *Yeah. Cos I **leave** on the eleventh but I **do come** overnight so I should be back here on the twelfth.*

THE FUTURE PERFECT SIMPLE 370

The future perfect simple is formed with *will/shall* + *have* + *-ed* participle. It is used when there is reference to something that is seen as already completed before a certain time.

Future time adverbials are normally required to complete the meaning:

*Send a fax to the hotel. He'**ll have left** home by now.*

*In January I **will have been** at the company for twenty years.*

*Do you think you**'ll have heard** about the job by tomorrow?*

THE FUTURE PROGRESSIVE 371

The future progressive is formed with *will/shall + be + -ing*. It is used when there is reference to something that will be in progress at some specified or understood time in the future:

*Next week **I'll be swimming** every day in the Caribbean.*

***I'll be having** a word with him when he returns.*

*She**'ll be starting** school soon, I suppose.*

*Don't worry. **I'll be waiting** for you at the station.*

The future progressive is also used to refer to events which are due to happen and which may result in other events taking place or make other events possible:

***I'll be seeing** the boss tomorrow morning. Do you want me to mention the promotion?*

The future progressive can also be used to soften questions about the future and make them more polite:

***Will** you **be coming back** on Friday night or Saturday morning?*

THE FUTURE PERFECT PROGRESSIVE 372

The future perfect progressive is formed with *will/shall + have + been + -ing*. It indicates that an event will be in progress at a particular time in the future and additionally highlights the duration of the event.

Time or duration adverbials are usually needed to show the time-frame:

*By six o'clock they **will have been meeting** for almost ten hours.*

*Next January the captain **will have been playing** for the club for twenty years.*

FUTURE IN THE PAST 373

References to events in the past which were still in the future from the point of view of the speaker normally use past tense verb forms:

*He **was coming** until this afternoon and then he changed his mind.*
(it was his plan/intention for the future until this afternoon)

*Last time we met, your wife **was going to** learn Japanese.*
(refers to an earlier point in time when the listener's wife said 'I'm going to learn Japanese', or something similar)

Would/should is used in such cases instead of *will/shall*:

*Joseph looked at the building where he **would** work for the next six months.*

*I knew then that I **should** never see him again.*
(or less formal: … that I would never see him again.)

FUTURE REFERENCE IN SUBORDINATE CLAUSES 374

In subordinate clauses with future reference introduced by subordinators such as *as, before, if, once, unless, until, when*, the present tense is used, not *shall/will*:

[giving someone directions]
*As you**'re coming** into the village, you'll see a pub in front of you. Turn right there.*

[tennis player speaking]
*If I **win** this set, it will be a great result.*
(~~If I will win this set, it will be a great result.~~)

*So what are you going to do when you **get** back?*
(~~So what are you going to do when you will get back?~~)

In reported clauses involving verbs such as *ask, insist, request, suggest*, and after conditional subordinators such as *if, lest, on condition that*, subjunctive mood (involving the base form of the verb, → 159e) may occur in formal contexts to refer to unfulfilled future events in the past:

*They suggested he **contact** a different person.*

*Indeed so great was the press of people around us, that I gripped my brother's arm lest he **be** trampled underfoot.*

OTHER MODAL VERBS AND FUTURE REFERENCE 375

Other modal verbs are also often used with future reference:

*There **might** be a student demo next week against the rise in fees.*

*Do you think you **may** go camping again this summer?*

***Can** you cope with the kids this afternoon?*

*She **could** arrive tonight, we're not sure.*

*You **must** come here tomorrow at ten o'clock.*

→ **377–407 Modality**

OTHER FORMS FOR REFERRING TO THE FUTURE 376

Other forms can be used to refer to future events, particularly if they are to happen in the near future.

Be to

Be to may be used for future reference in the context of obligations, requirements, formal decisions, etc. *Be to* structures are common with conditional clauses:

It's a very big problem. What ***am*** *I* ***to*** *say to them?*

*If we****'re to*** *get there by five, we should get a move on.*

*If Tom****'s to*** *go and live with his mother, then his sister should too.*

Be to for giving instructions, orders or commands is rare in informal conversation:

*You****'re to*** *do your homework and to do it neatly this time.*

*She****'s*** *not* ***to*** *come back late.*

Be to is common in specific styles such as newspaper headlines and news reports. In headlines it often occurs in an ellipted form:

Pupils ***to*** *sit new national exams.*
(Pupils are to sit new national exams.)

[headline about laws to control gun ownership. *MP* = Member of the British Parliament]
Police ***to*** *challenge MPs on guns.*
(The police are to challenge MPs on guns.)

The government ***is to*** *introduce legislation to restrict immigration.*

Be about to and other forms

The following forms enable reference to future events treated as occurring immediately or in the near future. The forms are mainly used in more formal contexts:

*He****'s about to*** *resign.*

They ***are on the point of*** *issuing a statement.*

People ***are on the verge of*** *despair.*

*Is that the flight that****'s due to*** *arrive at 22.25?*

*We****'re certain to*** *run out of time. I think we should postpone the meeting.*

*It****'s sure to*** *rain. Let's postpone the match.*

England ***are likely to*** *lose their next match against Spain.*

*They****'re supposed to*** *meet us at the station.*

He ***is obliged to*** *be there.*

→ **404 Other modal expressions with *be***, where these are dealt with separately

Modality

Modality

INTRODUCTION 377

This chapter (377–407) describes the main modal forms and meanings. The emphasis is on the core modal verbs but the chapter is also concerned with other items which carry a modal meaning.

The term 'modality' refers to a speaker's or a writer's attitude towards, or point of view about, a state of the world. In particular, modals are used to say whether something is real or true, or whether it is the subject of speculation rather than definite knowledge. For example, *Charles is at home now* is a statement of what is believed to be true, and indicates a high degree of certainty on the part of the speaker; *Charles may be at home now*, on the other hand, is more speculative and an assessment of possibility rather than a statement of fact. *Charles should be at home now* can be either a statement of what is probably true or a statement of what is desirable or necessary. All of these statements, even the simple, neutral statement of fact, can be said to carry modality, in other words the speaker's point of view.

Modal items, especially the modal verbs, also play a very important part in the expression of politeness and formality in English.

MODAL FORMS 378

The most significant expression of modality is by means of modal verbs. The core modal verbs are: *can, could, may, might, will, shall, would, should, must.*

There is also a set of semi-modal verbs. These verbs behave in similar ways to core modal verbs but share some characteristics with lexical verbs. The semi-modal verbs are: *dare, need, ought to, used to.*

This chapter also describes other expressions of modality apart from the modal and semi-modal verbs. For example we consider the role of other verbs which can express modal meanings (e.g. *hope, manage, suppose, seem, wish, want*) and modal phrases which have become grammaticalised (e.g. *had better, be meant to, be obliged to, be supposed to*). The chapter also refers to expressions of modality by means of adjectives, adverbs and nouns.

TYPES OF MEANING 379

There are two main types of modal meaning.

One meaning is to do with certainty, probability and possibility, with an assessment of potential facts and with deductions or predictions based on the assessment:

*I **might** see you later.*
(it is possible, not certain)

I'll *see you tomorrow.*
(speaker is certain)

The other meaning involves getting things done or trying to control the course of events. Modals used in this way express degrees of obligation and whether or not something is necessary, desirable, permitted or forbidden. This use also refers to volition, people's will to do or not do things, and to their ability to do things:

You ***may*** *go now.*
(speaker grants permission)

I ***must*** *be careful what I say.*
(speaker expresses necessity/obligation)

Liz ***can*** *work right through the night without getting tired.*
(speaker refers to ability)

Often, the same modal form can be used with different meanings, depending on context:

I don't know. You ***may*** *be right.*
(possibility: It is possible you are right.)

[spoken instruction to students taking a timed examination]
You ***may*** *start now.*
(permission: You are allowed to start now.)

Could *it be the other one that's causing the problem?*
(possibility: Is it possible that the other one is causing the problem?)

Could *we come and see it on Saturday?*
(permission: request for permission to come)

CORE MODAL VERBS 380

General formal properties of modal verbs 380a

The forms of modal verbs differ from the forms of other types of verb in significant ways. Modal verbs have only one form and do not inflect for person or number.

Modal verbs do not have infinitive forms, either with *to* or without. Modal verbs have no *-ing* form and no *-ed* participle form and therefore lack progressive and perfect forms:

I'd like to be able to speak Japanese.
(~~I'd like to can speak Japanese.~~)

Modal verbs are placed first in the verb phrase and are followed by a verb in the base form. The next verb may be a lexical verb or an auxiliary verb (*be*, *do*, *have*) or the substitute verb *do*, but cannot be another modal verb:

We ***might stay*** *an extra night.*

We ***should be leaving*** *soon.*

*It **might have got** lost in the post.*

A: *We **can stick** these in the letterbox tonight.*
B: *We **could do**, yeah.*
(followed by substitute *do*)

Modal verbs cannot be used as lexical verbs:

*I **must go** to bed.*
(~~I must to bed.~~)

*I **can speak** Italian.*
(or: I know Italian.)
(Not: ~~I can Italian.~~)

Modal verbs can only stand alone when the lexical verb is understood:

A: *Karen might have his number.*
B: *Yes, she **might**.*
(understood: she might have his number)

Modal verbs cannot indicate voice or aspect, though they may precede constructions with passive voice and/or progressive/perfect aspect:

*I think Jim **could** have been offended.*

*I don't know when we'**ll** be arriving yet.*

*We **should** have thought of that earlier.*

*He **might** have been expecting it.*

Modal verbs and tenses 380b

Some of the core modal verbs historically represent present and past tense forms which are no longer in one-to-one contrast as tenses.

Historical tense forms of modal verbs

historical present tense forms	historical past tense forms
can	*could*
may	*might*
shall	*should*
will	*would*

The historical present tense forms are not used to refer to the past; however, all of the forms may refer to either present or future time. In general, the historical past tense forms are used to express greater tentativeness, distance and politeness.

Interrogatives 380c

The interrogative with modal verbs is formed by inverting the subject and modal verb. Auxiliary *do* is not used:

> ***Can they*** *repair it?*
> (~~Do they can repair it?~~)
>
> ***Will your mother*** *be offended?*

Negative forms of modal verbs 380d

The negatives of modal verbs are formed by adding *not/'nt* (➝ 380e) after the modal verb. Auxiliary *do* is not used:

> *I* ***can't*** *understand what she's saying.*
> (~~I don't can understand what she's saying.~~)
> (~~I not can understand what she's saying.~~)
>
> *I just* ***could not*** *bear even talking to him.*

Contracted forms of modal verbs 380e

Subject-verb contraction

Subject-verb contraction is only possible with *shall* and *will* (which become *'ll*), and *would* (which becomes *'d*):

> *They**'ll** always be successful.*
>
> *I**'ll** let you know what's going to happen.*
> (I shall/I will let you know …)
>
> *He**'d** be very cross if I told him.*

Negative form contraction

Modal verbs are often used in contracted negative forms (sometimes causing a change in the form of the verb).

Uncontracted and contracted negative forms of modal verbs

modal verb	uncontracted negative	contracted negative
can	*cannot*	*can't*
could	*could not*	*couldn't*
may	*may not*	*mayn't* (very rare)
might	*might not*	*mightn't*
will	*will not*	*'ll not, won't*
shall	*shall not*	*'ll not, shan't*
would	*would not*	*'d not, wouldn't*
should	*should not*	*shouldn't*
must	*must not*	*mustn't*

➝ 387 ***Will*** and 390 ***Would***

CAN 381

Uses

Can is the most frequent modal verb. It has a number of meanings; its most frequent uses are for permission and ability.

Permission

Can is frequently used to seek permission, give permission or, in the negative, to forbid:

*You **can** borrow the car but be careful.*

*Students **can** hand in essays at any time before midday on February 3rd.*

A: ***Can** I smoke in here?*
B: *No, I'm sorry you **can't**.*

[adult to a very small child who has just picked up a glass]
*No. You **can't** have that. You might break it.*

Ability

A very frequent use of *can* is to indicate ability. This is particularly so with verbs of perception such as *hear* and *see* and with mental process verbs such as *follow* (in the sense of 'understand'), *guess, imagine, picture, understand*:

*You **can hear** the atmosphere in the stadium.*

***Can** you **see** the post office on the corner?*

*I **can guess** what you're thinking right now.*

*I **can** just **imagine** how surprised they looked.*

*Liz **can work** right through the night.*

General truths

Can is used in statements about events and states which are true or which are usually the case:

*Steel **can** resist very high temperatures.*

*It **can** rain quite a lot in Ireland in August.*

*Thai **can** be a very difficult language for Westerners to pronounce.*

Could is not normally used for general or current truths with present time reference:

*The verb 'help' **can** be used with or without infinitive 'to'.*
(stating a fact about English grammar)
(~~The verb 'help' could be used with or without infinitive 'to'.~~)

*Tommy **can** be really irritating at times. I don't think he realises.*
(the speaker believes this is true)
(~~Tommy could be really irritating at times. I don't think he realises.~~)

Could is used in such contexts only in reference to past time:

Liam ***could*** *be so stubborn, but at the end of the day, he was a good colleague.*

→ 382 for the use of *could* as the past tense of *can*

Possibility

Can is used to indicate or assess logical possibilities:

How ***can*** *they be there already? They only left ten minutes ago.*

That ***can't*** *be right.*

→ 384 *Can, could* and *may*

COULD 382

Uses

Could has a number of meanings. The most frequent uses are for possibility/probability and for making suggestions, and as the past tense of *can*.

Probability

One of the main uses of *could* is for assessments of possibility or weak probability:

I think that ***could*** *be the answer to the problem.*

We ***could*** *all be having holidays on the moon within thirty years.*

[in a shop; A is the assistant]
A: *We don't give refunds without a receipt I'm afraid.*
B: *Really?*
A: *Yeah.*
B: *All right. That* ***could*** *be tricky.*

Suggestions

Could is often used in making suggestions:

A: *I* ***could*** *just cook dinner tonight and then you* ***could*** *cook it some other night and, you know, reciprocate.*
B: *Alright. Okay.*

Permission

Could is used to ask for permission:

Could *I talk to you for a moment?*

Criticism

Could have + -ed participle is often used to express disapproval or criticism:

You ***could have told*** *me. Why did you keep it all to yourself?*

The expression *how could you* is often used to indicate disapproval or to issue a reproach:

> ***How could you*** *forget that we're going out to dinner tonight?*
>
> *'You have quite ruined our day.* ***How could you****?' she sobbed. '****How could you****?'*

Past tense of *can*

Could is used as the past tense form of *can* when clauses with *can* are reported as past events:

> *In tennis I wasn't that good but I knew I* ***could*** *get better.*
> (at the time, the speaker thought 'I know I can get better')
> (~~In tennis I wasn't that good but I knew I can get better.~~)
>
> *When I was a kid I* ***couldn't*** *swim at all. I only learnt when I was thirty.*
>
> *They said we* ***could*** *do whatever we wanted.*
>
> *We* ***could*** *hear that dog barking all through the night.*

However, when actual achievements are indicated, *was/were able to*, not *could*, is preferred in past affirmative clauses. The negative forms *couldn't* or *wasn't/ weren't able to* are both used to indicate non-achievement:

> *The thieves escaped but the police* ***were able to*** *arrest them later that evening.*
> (~~The thieves escaped but the police could arrest them later that evening.~~)
>
> [talking about a live concert by the Beatles in the 1960s]
> *Sharon and I* ***were able to*** *get special seats but we* ***couldn't*** *hear a thing. The screaming was just something else. There were kids fainting, and being taken out, everything.*
>
> *She* ***was not able to*** *move on her own.*
> (or: She couldn't move on her own.)

MAY 383

Uses

May is used with a number of meanings.

Permission

May is used to ask for, grant and refuse permission:

> ***May*** *I see that?*
> (possible responses: Yes, you may./No, you may not.)

Probability

May is used to refer to weak probability:

> [talking about a delivery]
> *There's a bank holiday in between, so it* ***may*** *or* ***may not*** *get to you by the end of that week.*

General truths

May is used in formal written English to describe things which are likely to occur or which normally do occur. In this sense it is a more formal equivalent of *can*:

Frog spawn ***may*** *be found in river beds at that time of year.*
(is typically/normally found)

→ **146b Hedging: modality** in **Grammar and academic English**

Concession

May often has a concessive meaning, especially when accompanied by *well* and/or followed by *but*:

[talking about dunlins, a small sea-bird]
A few ***may well*** *have nested in Britain,* ***but*** *the vast majority would have flown in from their breeding grounds in the far north around arctic shores.*

I ***may*** *be in danger of stating the obvious,* ***but*** *I shall state it anyhow.*

Stalin ***may*** *be long since dead,* ***but*** *Stalinism is not.*

Good wishes and curses

May is used in formal expressions of good wishes and in formal curses:

[speech at a wedding, addressing the newly-married couple]
May *you both have a long and happy married life together.*

May *you rot in hell!*

→ also **385** ***Might***; **384** ***Can, could*** **and** ***may***; **386** ***Could, may*** **and** ***might***

→ **408–423 Speech acts**

CAN, COULD AND *MAY* 384

Probability

When assessing probabilities, *can* refers to what the speaker believes to be a fact or to be usually the case. *Could* and *may* refer to possible events. Compare:

It ***can*** *be very cold in Stockholm, so take a big coat.*
(this is a known fact)

It ***could/may*** *be very cold in Stockholm, so take a big coat.*
(it is possible that it will be cold in Stockholm when you are there)

Could and *may* rather than *can* are used to speculate about whether something is true or possible:

A: *Where's Julia?*
B: *She* ***could*** *be in the garden.*
(or: She may be in the garden.)
(~~She can be in the garden.~~)

It ***could*** *rain this afternoon.*
(~~It can rain this afternoon.~~)

Permission

Can, *could* and *may* are all used to seek permission. *Could* is usually heard as more formal and polite than *can*, and *may* is the most formal/polite of the three:

> ***Can*** *I use your phone?*
>
> ***Could*** *I use your phone?*
> (more formal/polite)
>
> ***May*** *I use your phone?*
> (even more formal/polite)

→ **385 *Might***

In giving permission, *can* and *may*, but not *could*, are used; *may* is more formal/polite than *can*, and much less frequent:

> [in a clothes shop; A is the customer]
> A: *Can I try a shirt on as well?*
> B: *You* ***can****, sir, yes.*
> (~~You could, sir, yes.~~)
>
> *'You* ***may*** *go now,' she said.*
>
> [to a child]
> *You* ***can*** *watch TV for an hour, then off to bed.*
> (~~You could watch TV for an hour, then off to bed.~~)

Requests

A wide range of requests and directives are made with *can* and *could* (but not *may*). As with seeking permission, *could* is more polite than *can*:

> ***Can*** *you spell that for me please.*
>
> ***Could*** *you give me a ring if you can't make it, Bob.*
>
> [adult to child]
> ***Could*** *you just shut up for a minute!*

→ also **416 Requests** in **Speech acts**

MIGHT 385

Uses

Might has a number of meanings. In general, it is a more indirect and tentative alternative to *may*. Its most frequent uses are for expressing probability; its uses referring to permission are mostly formal and much less frequent.

Probability

The most frequent uses of *might* are for referring to probability:

> A: *So I'm going to buy a digital camera.*
> B: *Yeah.*
> A: *And I* ***might*** *buy a video camera as well.*

Permission

When used to refer to permission, *might* is very formal and infrequent:

__Might__ I speak to Mrs Lutterworth?

Past tense of *may*

Might is used as the past form of *may* in indirect reports:

When they reached the shore road, she said to him, 'Mother __may__ be expecting you.'

The probable indirect report of this sentence would be:

She said that mother __might__ be expecting him.

Suggestions

Might is also used to issue advice or suggestions politely or indirectly, especially when used together with *like* or *want*:

[university tutor recommending a book to a student]
I won't go any further with it now but you __might__ like to take a copy of it out with you. It elaborates on a number of the claims that Wade makes. And I do recommend that you look at the book.

→ **414e Declaratives with *may as well* and *might (just) as well*** in **Speech acts**

COULD, MAY AND *MIGHT* 386

Could, *may* and *might* are all used to express degrees of certainty. *May* expresses a slightly greater degree of certainty than *could*, and tends to be used in more formal contexts. *Might* is more tentative than *may* or *could*:

He __may__ also find some graduate school course that he can do.
(expresses slightly greater likelihood than *could*)

[referring to the single European currency, the Euro]
Staying outside the single currency __could__ be detrimental to the UK.

It __might__ take us months to find the right person.

WILL 387

Uses

Will has a number of uses, the most frequent being those used to refer to future time and prediction.

Future time

One of the principal functions of *will* is to refer to future time, since English does not have a separate, inflected future tense (→ **361–376 Future time**):

[talking of a plan to redesign an urban area]
Cars __will__ be banned. Coaches, bikes, wheelchairs and pedestrians __will__ be catered for; drivers __will__ not be welcome.

*The referendum **will** take place on June 23rd.*

*I'**ll** be sixty-five in a few years' time and I'**ll** be retiring.*

Will is used for first, second and third person subjects to refer to future time. (→ also **388 *Shall***)

Predictions

Will is used to make predictions about the future or deductions about a present situation from the available evidence:

*I think we'**ll** do it but it **won't** be easy.*

*If she gets the right grades, she'**ll** go to university.*

*That'**ll** be Jim at the door.*
(deduction about the present situation: it is very likely that the person knocking/ringing at the door is Jim)

Will is used to make general predictions about things that always happen:

*Dry twigs **will** burn easily.*

*A dog **will** growl when it's angry or frightened.*

Habitual events

Will is used to refer to habitual events:

*On a Friday night we'**ll** get a take-away and we'**ll** just relax.*

Intentions and offers

Will is used to express intentions or decisions. The present simple form is not used in such situations:

[in a photo shop; A is the assistant]
A: *I'm afraid they won't be ready till three o'clock.*
B: *Okay. Er, I'**ll** come back at three.*
(intention/decision to act)
(~~Okay. I come back at three.~~)

Will is used to express degrees of willingness to do something, and is often used to make offers. The present simple form is not used in such situations:

*I'**ll** carry that for you.*
(~~I carry that for you.~~)

*I **won't** lend him any money. Why should I?*
(~~I don't lend him any money.~~)

Requests and invitations

Requests and invitations are often made with *will*:

***Will** you pass me that newspaper please?*

***Will** you join us for a drink after the concert?*

A rarer, more formal use of *won't* occurs in polite requests and invitations:

The manager will be here in a minute. ***Won't*** *you take a seat, Mr Parker?*

Directives

Strong directives can be issued using *will* in the interrogative:

[parent to child]
Will you *sit down and just be quiet!*

A rarer use of *will* is in declarative clauses which command someone to do something or insist that they do something:

[adult to a child who is refusing to pick up an object she has thrown on the floor]
You ***will*** *pick it up and you****'ll*** *pick it up now!*

You ***will*** *ring me as soon as you get there,* ***won't*** *you?*

Disapproval

Will is often used in a disapproving way to refer to persistent actions of oneself or of others. In this usage *will* is often stressed:

He ***will*** *leave that door open every time he goes through!*
(more emphatic than: He leaves that door open every time he goes through.)

Oh, I ***will*** *keep banging my elbow on that shelf.*

Responding

Will may be used to refer to inanimate objects and how they respond or fail to respond to human intervention:

A: *This window* ***won't*** *open.*
B: *I know. It's been stuck ever since we painted it.*

Will *this printer do double-sided copies?*

[talking about a computer]
It ***won't*** *let me save the file with a different name.*

→ **344 *Will* referring to general truths or used for politeness**

SHALL 388

Uses

Shall has two main meanings; one refers to future intentions, the other is concerned with offers and advice.

Predictions and intentions

Shall is used instead of *will* with first person subjects in rather formal contexts to make predictions and to announce intentions or decisions. It is much less frequent than *will*:

While she's here, we ***shall*** *never be able to put the past behind us.*

I ***shall*** *always be grateful for what he did on that day.*
(less formal: I will/I'll always be grateful …)

'I don't want anyone with me. I ***shall*** *do this on my own,' Bless said, and he hurried out of the room.*

Shall not/shan't is even rarer, but does occur in formal contexts to make predictions and announce intentions or decisions:

I ***shan't*** *be here for much more than half an hour.*

Directives

Shall is also used to issue directives but this use is very formal and rare:

[notice in an aircraft cabin]
This curtain ***shall*** *be left open during takeoff and landing.*

'You ***shall*** *be punished,' said Mrs Marline. 'You* ***shall*** *go to your room and stay there without a light when it is dark.'*

Making offers and seeking advice

Shall in first person interrogatives is much more frequent than other uses of *shall* and is common in the making of offers and suggestions, and in seeking advice:

So as soon as Bob comes back, Ken, ***shall*** *I give you a ring?*

Shall *we go and have a walk in the garden?*

A: *What* ***shall*** *I do? Come in first thing in the morning then?*
B: *Mm, that's probably the best thing, yeah.*

WILL, SHALL AND 'LL 389

Will is almost ten times more frequent than *shall* in spoken and written texts taken together. The contracted form *'ll* is almost three times more frequent than the full forms *will* and *shall* taken together.

Shall is, in general, not very frequent, but is twice as common in spoken texts as in written texts because of the use of *shall I/we* to make suggestions or to seek advice.

Although *shall I/we* is the normal form for making suggestions, in informal conversation *will I/we* also sometimes occurs instead:

[a couple, A and B, are organising food for a dinner party]
A: ***Will*** *I bring out the salads?*
B: *No. But, erm, is this fish cooked?*

→ also **363** and **365** for discussion of the use of *'ll* and for comparisons between *will* and *be going to*

WOULD 390

Uses

Would has many meanings. A number of its uses refer to past time. It is also used in conditional sentences, and as a hedge to soften statements and requests.

Past time 390a

Reported clauses

Would can function as the past tense of *will* in reported clauses:

*I knew that **would** cause a problem.*
(report of a thought or statement: I know that will cause a problem.)

Future-in-the-past

Would can refer to future-in-the-past, when the speaker looks forward in time from a point in the past:

*Her funny crooked smile and short bouncy hair inspired him with exciting ideas of friendship. Perhaps one day he **would** summon the courage to speak to her, see how things went.*

Habitual actions

Would can refer to typical habitual actions and events in the past and often occurs in narratives:

*We stayed in an inn which had been built by a film company when they had made a film in the area. Every morning, the waiters **would** come down the long verandah, followed by two small but very active monkeys, and leave us a tray of coffee, rolls and tropical fruit. The fruit looked divine, but I never tasted any of it. The monkeys **would** sit there staring, and I couldn't resist their eyes begging for food. The waiters **would** return, collect the tray and the monkeys **would** follow them to the next room and do it all over again.*

In this meaning, *would* is similar to *used to*, but tends to occur in more formal contexts.

→ **402 *Used to* and *would***

Volition

Would may be used to refer to volition in past time situations:

*Patsy was so kind. She **would** always help when we needed her.*

*I did ask him, but he **wouldn't** give me an answer.*

Responding

Would (especially the negative *wouldn't*) can refer in past time contexts to how inanimate things responded or failed to respond to human intervention:

*It was a freezing cold morning and the car **wouldn't** start.*

Other uses 390b

Conditional sentences

Would is common in the main clause of hypothetical conditional sentences:

*If I had to leave, I **would** probably go to India.*

[talking about a flat the speaker was considering renting]
*D'you know what I mean? If it had another little room, it **would** have been quite nice.*

Hedging

Would is often used with verbs such as *advise, imagine, recommend, say, suggest, think* as a softener or hedge:

A: *I **would imagine** actually it's still cold because it's still quite windy isn't it?*
B: *Yeah.*

[shop assistant to customer who is buying a bed]
*I **would** always **recommend** a slightly softer bed than a harder one.*

[advising a friend choosing a jacket in a shop]
***I'd say** get the bigger one.*

*The total would be about £260, I **would think**.*

Requests

Would is frequent in requests. It is a more polite or indirect form of *will*:

***Would** you give me a call this evening?*

*I want you to have a look at this, if you **would**.*

WILL AND *WOULD* 391

Would functions as a more formal or polite alternative to *will* in requests:

***Would** you excuse me just one second?*
(heard as more polite than: Will you excuse me just one second?)

***Would** you look after my seat for me please?*

Will and *would* can both refer to willingness, with *would* functioning in past time contexts:

*Josh says he'**ll** do it for you.*

*When he was at home, his mother **wouldn't** allow him to go out anywhere and do anything.*

However, *would* is not used to refer to someone's willingness to do something on a specific occasion in a past time context:

*I suggested she came on her own, and she finally **agreed to it**.*
(~~I suggested she came on her own, and she finally would.~~)

SHOULD 392

Uses

Should has a number of meanings. It can refer to things that are likely or possible, but it is more frequently used to refer to things that are desirable, and to give advice and make suggestions. It is also used in conditional sentences.

What is desirable

The most frequent uses of *should* are to indicate what the speaker considers to be the ideal or desired state of affairs:

*He **should** have been here at five and he's not here yet.*

*She **should** be wearing glasses.*

[complaining about the inadequacies of the English national school inspection system]
A: *I think there **should** be some kind of system, Mary.*
B: *Yes. Oh I agree.*
A: *I think the authorities **should** do it and there **should** be, you know, guidelines from a central place.*
B: *Uh huh.*
A: *Erm, and er, it **should** be done thoroughly.*
B: *Yes.*

What is likely or possible

Another frequent use of *should* is where speakers indicate what they think is likely to occur:

[answerphone message]
*Hello. Er, this is a message for Helen Mitchell. It's Frampton College, Allchester. Erm your evening class tonight has had to be cancelled because the lecturer's ill but it **should** be back to normal next week. Thank you.*

[a teacher talking about the school day]
A: *Tomorrow I've got a lot of sport. Cos I've got games in the morning then I've got swimming for four lessons.*
B: *It **should** be a pleasant day then.*
A: *Mm.*

Should can also be used in a more general way to refer to 'possible worlds' or events which might possibly happen:

*It seems unfair that you **should** have to do all the driving. Let me drive.*

*Why **should** anyone object to her getting the job?*

Surprise

Should is also used for events which did happen but to which the speaker reacts with surprise or disbelief:

*I'm sorry that he **should** be so upset by what I said.*

*I'm amazed that he **should** have done something so stupid.*

Suggestions

Should is very common in advice-giving and in making suggestions:

*You **should** tell him straight what you think.*

*We **should** leave it till tomorrow, don't you think.*

Thanking

Shouldn't have is used conventionally to express gratitude for gifts:

> [email message after the receipt of a gift CD]
> *Thanks so much for the CD. You really* ***shouldn't have.***

Conditional sentences

Should occurs in hypothetical conditional clauses with *if* in formal contexts, expressing tentative possibilities:

> *Some people carry a card which says that* ***if*** *they* ***should*** *be killed in an accident, they are willing for their organs to be used for transplantation.*

> ***If*** *you* ***should*** *need anything else, do just let me know.*

Should also occurs with subject-verb inversion as an alternative to *if* in more formal contexts to refer to hypothetical situations:

> [giving someone a mobile phone number]
> *I'll be contactable on this number* ***should*** *you need me.*

> [referring to a request to Cambridge City Council for building planning permission by the University of Cambridge]
> *Cambridge City Council has specified that it will not permit further development of the teaching facilities without related student housing.* ***Should*** *the Cromwell Road plan be rejected, the University fears that students may end up living in unsuitable residences paying higher rents than students elsewhere.*

→ 399 ***Ought to*** **and** ***should***

SHOULD AND *WOULD* 393

Should occurs as a more formal alternative to *would* with first person subjects in hypothetical clauses, in future-in-the-past clauses and in clauses where *would* can occur as a softener or hedge:

> [referring to the pleasures of living in a country cottage, despite the disadvantages]
> *I had been there long enough to see the disadvantages, but even if they had been doubled or trebled, I* ***should*** *still have been of the same opinion.*

> *She was aware of our feelings for each other and she guessed we* ***should*** *like to be alone.*

> *Things change, especially in your field, I* ***should*** *imagine.*

MUST 394

Must has a number of meanings. It is used for different strengths of obligation, from polite invitations to laws. It is also frequently used to express deduction.

Deduction

The use of *must* to express a deduction is particularly common, especially to express reactions in spoken contexts:

*I'm twenty-eight, so she **must** be twenty-seven.*

A: *There was a power-cut on the London Underground.*
B: *That **must** have been terrible. Er, I read about that. Yeah.*

Obligation and invitations

Must expressing obligation is quite strong, but it is also used to express polite invitations:

*You **must** get those done by tomorrow.*

*I told her she **must** keep her door locked at all times.*

A: *You **must** come down and have a meal with us sometime.*
B: *Yeah.*
(polite invitation)

Rules and laws

Must and *must not* often occur in public signs and notices indicating laws, rules and prohibitions:

[airline website information]
*All passengers **must** present valid photo identification at check-in for all flights.*

[public notice at a railway station]
*Passengers **must not** cross the line.*

Reproaches

Must in the interrogative form is used to issue reproaches and often expresses a feeling of exasperation on the part of the speaker:

***Must** you have that music so loud?*

*Why **must** people always park right across our exit?*

Tense and time references with *must* 394a

Must has no past form.

Obligation

Obligation in the past is expressed by *had to*:

[someone talking about their childhood home]
*We didn't have water inside, we **had to** go to an outside pump to pump the water to the house.*
(~~We didn't have water inside, we must go to an outside pump ...~~)

References to obligations which will or may occur at a given point in the future are made with the future forms of *have to* rather than *must*:

*Maybe one day he **will have to** accept the inevitable truth.*

*If he turns up after midnight, then he'**ll have to** eat whatever he can find in the fridge.*

Must can be used to express the future-in-the-past, and occurs in reported clauses in formal contexts:

She had little appetite for the food on the tray, but she knew that she ***must*** *eat something or else she would faint with hunger.*

Deduction

The perfect form *must have* always refers to deduction, not obligation:

I ***must have*** *been on the phone.*
(it is likely/probable that I was on the phone)

Negative of *must* 394b

Obligation: *must not* and *need not*

Must not is used to forbid something. *Need not* or the negative forms of *have (got) to* or the negative of the lexical verb *need to* are used to express an absence of obligation:

[parent to child]
A: *Samantha?*
B: *What?*
A: *You* ***must not*** *leave stuff like this under the sofa!*
(forbidding something)

[pharmacist advising a customer about a medical product]
This ***needn't*** *be kept in the fridge.*
(there is no obligation or necessity to keep this in the fridge; 'This must not be kept in the fridge' would mean it is forbidden/wrong/dangerous to keep it in the fridge)

[speaker B is a pensioner who enjoys free bus travel]
A: *The bus is going to be about £1.*
B: *Well I* ***don't have to*** *pay.*
(~~Well I mustn't pay.~~)

We should have a general discussion at this stage. Er, we ***don't need to*** *reach any final decisions.*

→ **397** ***Need*** and **403d** ***Have to, have got to***

Deduction

The negative of *must* when denying or negating logical deductions or conclusions is *can't/cannot*:

[speakers are measuring distances on a map]
A: *There's no way that's thirty miles.*
B: *That* ***can't*** *be right. No it isn't.*
A: *Maybe the scale's wrong.*
B: *Mm,* ***must*** *be.*

Mustn't is also used to express negative deductions, especially in more informal spoken contexts:

[talking about time sheets to record work done]
*But she said 'Oh you **mustn't** have filled it in because I haven't got any record of you working those two shifts.' But I'm sure I did. I'm sure I filled it in but now I can't remember.*
(or: You can't have filled it in because ...)

SEMI-MODAL VERBS 395

The semi-modal verbs are: *dare, need, ought to* and *used to*. (*Dare* and *need* are also lexical verbs.)

These verbs are also sometimes called 'non-typical' or 'marginal' modal verbs. In some ways they behave grammatically like lexical verbs; in some ways they behave grammatically like the core modal verbs:

*I **dare not** tell her what's happened.*
(as with core modal verbs, negative formed without auxiliary *do*)

*Marie **didn't dare** say anything to them.*
(as with lexical verbs, negative formed with auxiliary *do*)

*We **ought to** wash this tray, **oughtn't we**?*
(unlike core modal verbs, followed by *to*; like core modals, can be used in a tag question)

Often the different behaviour marks a difference between formal and informal styles:

*I've learnt to become open-minded. I **didn't used to** be.*
(negative formed with auxiliary *do*; the most common negative form of *used to* in general contexts)

*There is something rather secretive about Lucian at times. He **used not to** be like that. He was such a frank sort of boy, if you know what I mean.*
(negative formed without auxiliary *do*, but only usually found in formal styles)

DARE 396

Dare as a semi-modal occurs frequently in negative and interrogative clauses. When used as a semi-modal, it is followed by the infinitive without *to*:

*I **daren't** ring Linda again.*

*She **dare not** ask her mother to lend her money.*

***Dare** we write to them and complain?*

The negative of semi-modal *dare* may occur as *dare not/daren't* or may be formed with auxiliary *do*:

*I **dare not** go in there because goodness knows what's in there.*

*His eyes were all swollen up and everything, so he **didn't dare** go out.*

Semi-modal *dare* is usually not inflected for person or tense. When *dare* is used as a lexical verb, it may be followed by a *to*-infinitive and it may be inflected. The non-inflected past form is rare and rather formal:

[expressing strong disapproval of someone's criticism]
*And she **dare** criticise the running of the Centre!*

*I think they all feel the same but nobody ever **dares to** say it, you know.*

*She **dared to** hope that she had seen the last of him.*

*He was such a terrifying man; no one **dare** contradict him.*
(rare and formal)

NEED 397

Semi-modal *need* most commonly occurs in the negative declarative, to indicate absence of obligation:

*She **needn't** take the exam if she doesn't want to.*

*At least the spare time on his hands could be good fun. He'd please himself and no one else. His tie could hang loose all the time. He **need not** wear a tie. He **need not** wear a suit. That was the uniform of servitude. He **need not** hasten through the city streets, his coffee hardly drunk, to be at work on time.*

Affirmative declaratives with semi-modal *need* are much rarer and are associated with formal styles and contexts. There is almost always some element of negation in the clause, even if the verb phrase is affirmative:

*No one else **need** see what he was doing either.*

*If we feel wisdom itself is lost, we **need** only enter a library.*
(we need not do more than enter a library)

Interrogatives with semi-modal *need* are very rare and are associated with formal styles and contexts:

[*She* here refers to a fishing boat which sank while at sea]
*She was most likely run down by a larger ship which never stopped. Fishing is dangerous – er, but **need** it be this dangerous?*

Semi-modal *need* has no past tense equivalent, and the lexical verbs *didn't need to* or *didn't have to* are used to express absence of obligation in the past:

*I got better quite quickly and I **didn't need to** go back to the hospital.*

*She'd done half the course the year before so she **didn't have to** go to all the lectures.*

Semi-modal *need* can be used with a future-in-the-past meaning:

*I was locked out but I knew I **needn't** panic because Laura would be home at five.*

Needn't have + *-ed* participle is used to refer to events which happened but which the speaker considers were unnecessary:

*I **needn't have bought** so much food now that Suzie won't be with us for dinner.*
(speaker did buy food but now considers it was unnecessary)

Semi-modal *need* and lexical verb *need* 397a

The meanings of semi-modal *need* and the lexical verb *need* often overlap and lexical verb *need* can often be used as an alternative to semi-modal *need*:

*Fishing is dangerous – but **need** it be this dangerous?*
(or: *Fishing is dangerous – but **does it need to** be this dangerous?*)

[lecturer to students]
*There is an intimate link between the presence of the virus in these cells and the production of the tumour. We **needn't** take the figures down here, erm, but what this shows is the second transforming virus, which is hepatitis B virus.*
(or: *We **don't need to** take the figures down …*)

The full lexical verb *to need*, not the semi-modal *need*, must be used when the verb complement is a noun phrase or noun-phrase equivalent (e.g. an *-ing* clause):

*You **don't need** an invitation.*
(~~*You needn't an invitation.*~~)

*The hedge **doesn't need** cutting.*
(~~*The hedge needn't cutting.*~~)

OUGHT TO 398

Uses

The meanings of *ought to* are similar to the meanings of *should*.

What is desirable

Ought to is used to refer to ideal or desired states of affairs. It is very similar to *should*, but is far less frequent:

*I really **ought to** go outside and get some fresh air for a bit.*

*You **ought to** put more money into your pension fund.*

A: *Well that isn't good enough. You **ought to** complain.*
B: *I don't like complaining.*

→ 539 **Glossary** for any unfamiliar terms

What is likely

Less frequently, *ought to* is used, again in a similar way to *should*, to state what is likely or probable:

*I think it **ought to** take about three hours, if the traffic is not too bad.*

[lecturer advising a student on which authors to read]
*Er, look at Brinton and if necessary go to Rowland's book. But I think Brinton **ought to** be able to give you the information.*

Interrogative

Interrogatives with *ought to* are rare, and confined mostly to formal styles:

*Who do you think it is? **Ought** we **to** call the police?*

Negative

The negative of *ought to* is *ought not to* or *oughtn't to*, but both are infrequent, especially in informal spoken language:

[speaker is talking about whether meetings at work are useful or not]
*If I don't feel the same when I come away as I did before I went, then I **ought not to** have gone.*

Oughtn't is generally only found in question tags:

*I ought to photocopy this, **oughtn't** I?*

An even rarer form of the negative, found only in formal styles, is not followed by *to*:

*She **ought not have felt** either surprise or offence at the discovery that Emma showed Jag her letters, but she could not ignore the fact that she felt both and felt them sharply.*

To is also omitted in question tags:

A: *This picture ought to be hung somewhere, **oughtn't it**?*
B: *Yeah.*
A: *Erm. Don't know where though.*

Past form

Ought to has no past form. The perfect construction *ought to have* + *-ed* participle is used to refer back to states of affairs which were desirable at points in the past:

*We probably **ought to have talked** about it ages ago.*

In informal conversation, question tags may occur with auxiliary *did* following clauses with *ought to have*:

*They **ought to have** told you, **didn't** they?*

OUGHT TO AND *SHOULD* 399

Should is much more frequent than *ought to*, in referring to both what is desirable and what is likely.

Tags for clauses with *ought to* often occur with *should*, instead of *ought*:

*There **ought** to be criteria, **shouldn't** there?*

*It **oughtn't** to have been like that really, **should** it?*

Interrogatives and negatives with *ought to* are rare; *should* is generally preferred instead:

***Should** we have this window open again now or not?*
(preferred to: Ought we to have this window open ...?)

*It's a tax form to say I'm a student and I **shouldn't** be paying tax.*
(preferred to: ... I'm a student and I oughtn't/ought not to be paying tax.)

USED TO 400

Used to refers to past habitual behaviour or states of affairs in the past which are no longer true:

A: *She's very tall isn't she?*
B: *Yes, she **used to** do ballet.*
(she did ballet but no longer does it)

*There **used to** be a railway going through the village but it was closed in the 1960s.*

Negative

The negative of *used to* is most typically *didn't use(d) to*. In more formal styles, *used not to* occurs. The contracted form *usedn't to* may occasionally occur, but is very rare:

[talking of a married couple who grew to dislike each other over the years]
*When he went home she was nasty and fed up and he said sometimes she never even looked up when he went in and yet they **didn't used to** be like that. But they grew to be like that.*

*She **used not to** be so censorious of others' behaviour but her own betrayal had, she thought, seared her more than she understood.*

The alternatives *didn't used to/didn't use to* both occur as written representations of the negative with *didn't*, though in speech it is often impossible to hear a difference and the most likely pronunciation is /dɪdn(t) ˈjuːstə/.

Interrogative

The interrogative of *used to* has two forms; the more common form is with auxiliary *did*. The alternative form involves subject-verb inversion, and is very rare:

> ***Did you used to** have ambitions when you were younger for the future?*

> A: ***Didn't** that big building on the corner **used to** be a cinema?*
> B: *Yes it was, years ago.*

> *It looks different. **Used it to** be like that?*
> (very rare)

Emphatic

Emphatic *did* may occur with *used to*. The construction may be represented in writing as *did used to* or *did use to*:

> A: *Do you stay up to celebrate the New Year?*
> B: *When me and my sisters used to get together before I got married we **did used to** celebrate it, with my sisters.*

> *She **did use to** cuddle me, my mother, not passionately, like Aunt Eileen did.*

Tags

When a tag follows a clause with *used to*, it is normally constructed with auxiliary *did*:

> *You **used to** work in Manchester, **didn't you**?*

> *I **used to** go there every year, **I did**, when I was younger.*

Used to, be used to and expressions of typicality 401

Used to and *be used to* are different.

Used to refers to habits and states which happened or were true in the past but are no longer the case. *Used to* only has one form, and cannot refer to the present or future:

> *I **used to** swim every morning before work.*
> (refers to a past habit which is no longer the case)

Be used to refers to how familiar something is for someone; it can occur in different tense forms. *Be used to* is followed by a noun phrase or a verb in the *-ing* form or a clausal complement:

> *She**'s not used to** the new system yet.*
> (she's not familiar with it)

> [said by someone driving a big car for the first time]
> ***I'm not used to driving** such a big car.*
> (I am not familiar with driving such a big car./I do not have experience of driving such a big car.)
> (~~I'm not used to drive such a big car.~~)

> *I **was used to** **getting** all my meals cooked for me.*
> (getting my meals cooked for me was a familiar/normal experience)
> (compare: 'I used to get all my meals cooked for me', which would simply mean that this was true in the past but is not true any more)

> ***I'm not really used to** how they do it in America.*

To express habits or things which are normal and typical, in the present, past or future, the simple forms of the present or past tense are used, or adverbs such as *usually*, *normally*, *typically*. Such meanings are not expressed by the verb *use* in the present tense.

> *I **usually** have tea and toast for breakfast.*
> (~~I use to have tea and toast for breakfast.~~)
>
> *He **normally** comes round at about half past one.*
> ('He used to come round at about half past one' would mean that is what happened in the past)
>
> *I **swam** three or four times a week when I was working in Bristol.*
> (or: I usually/normally swam three or four times a week.)
> ('I used to swim three or four times a week' would emphasise that I no longer do it)

USED TO AND *WOULD* 402

Used to and *would* both refer to habitual actions and events in the past:

> *Sandra **used to** come down here and watch me bake cakes. And she **used to** find it quite fascinating. She wanted to bake them herself but she never really knew how. And her grandmother always **used to** bake cakes and she **would** go and watch you know.*

However, with *would*, it is necessary to have an already established past time-frame. The past time-frame is often established by a previous occurrence of *used to* (as in the example above) or by time adverbial expressions (e.g. *years ago*, *when I was a child*):

> ***When I was a kid** we**'d** always go to my aunt's house in the holidays.*

Would is not used to refer to states in the past which are no longer true:

> *Our village hall **used to** be a school years ago.*
> (~~Our village hall would be a school years ago.~~)
>
> [pointing to a house]
> A: *See that cottage on the right?*
> B: *Yeah.*
> A: *I **used to** live there.*
> (~~I would live there.~~)

OTHER MODAL VERB PHRASES 403

Some common idiomatic verb phrases carry modal meanings. These include *be to*, *be going to*, *had better*, *have (got) to* and *would rather*. These verbs have no non-tensed forms and cannot be preceded by other modal verbs or auxiliary verbs (except for *have to* without *got*; → **403d**):

> *She **was to** have met a gentleman friend at Southampton. He did not show up.*
> (*be to*, referring to a fixed or pre-decided event)

*I thought I **had better** warn you now. Before you get too hopeful.*
(*had better*, referring to a desired or preferable course of action)

***I've got to** photocopy these stories.*
(*have got to*, referring to an obligation)

***I'd rather** you came at three-thirty instead of four, if you could.*
(*would rather*, referring to a preferred state of affairs)

Be to 403a

Uses

Be to is rare in informal conversation, and only occurs in rather formal spoken contexts such as meetings. It is used for directives, and to talk about events in the future which are fixed, desirable or hypothetical.

Directives

Be to can be used to express orders and instructions:

*The orders **are to** be carried out without delay.*
(must be carried out)

[sign on a door]
*This door **is to** remain locked at all times.*

[business meeting; speaker A is announcing agreed actions]
A: *Rob **is to** look at it and Ann Pascoe **to** look at it and formal comments to be collated and sent back to David.*
B: *And one month for that.*
A: *Er, yeah.*
B: *I think that's safest.*

In the negative, *be to* can be used to prohibit or forbid something:

*He **is not to** be disturbed, Jackie instructed. He is sleeping. Let him sleep. He **is to** see **no one**.*
(He must not be disturbed.)

[parent scolding a small child]
*Come here! You**'re not to** do that!*

Fixed events

Be to is used to refer to fixed or pre-decided events, or things destined to happen:

*The first opera ever to be staged in England **is to** be recreated to celebrate its 300th anniversary.*

[about planned changes to telephone charges]
*International calls **are to** cost an average 10 per cent less – up to 20 per cent cheaper in some cases.*
(this has been decided/is destined to happen)

[about someone who died just after retiring from work]
*He'd hoped to travel and see the world in his retirement but it **wasn't to** be.*
(was not destined to happen)

What is desirable
Be to is used to refer to necessary or desired states of affairs:

Children need access to a healthy diet if they ***are to*** *achieve their full potential, whether physically or mentally.*
(... if it is desirable/considered necessary that they achieve, or if it is the goal that they achieve ...)

[university literature seminar]
The text is fiction, and ***is to*** *be read as such.*

Hypothetical future
The subjunctive form *were to* (and its more informal alternative *was to*, used with singular subjects) can be used to refer to a hypothetical future:

I'd hate it if anything ***were to*** *happen to them.*
(or: I'd hate it if anything happened to them/if anything should happen to them.)

I suppose if I ***was to*** *be honest, I'd have to say no to it.*
(more informal)

→ **159e** on **subjunctive *were***

Be going to 403b

Be going to may be used to make firm predictions based on evidence at the time of speaking:

[looking at a very cloudy, dark sky]
It's ***going to*** *rain any minute now.*

I don't think there's ***going to*** *be any problem at all.*

They rang me to say it ***was going to*** *cost £300, so I decided not to do it.*

In this meaning, it is very similar to the predictive meaning of *will*. However, *be going to* is not used when predictions or announcements about the future are hypothetical and remote from present reality:

*If we win the lottery, we'****ll*** *buy a big house in Italy.*
('If we win the lottery, we're going to buy a big house in Italy' suggests there is a reasonable chance or hope of winning)

*If you're looking for good restaurants in Waltisham, you'****re going to*** *be disappointed.*
(*going to* suggests the listener may indeed be expecting to find good restaurants)

Had better 403c

Had better refers to desirable or advisable actions in particular situations. It is particularly common in spoken language and is normally contracted to *'d better* in informal contexts. The verb form is always *had*, not *have*:

[the phone rings]
A: ***I'd better** answer that.*
B: *Okay.*

[looking at the clock]
*If that's the right time, we**'d better** hurry.*
(~~We have better hurry.~~)

Had better is not used to refer to general obligations or requirements. In such cases, *have to* is used instead:

*You **have to** get good exam grades to get into university.*
(~~You'd better get good exam grades to get into university.~~)

Had better is not used to express preferences:

A: *Would you like a coffee?*
B: ***I'd better** just have a cold soft drink. I won't be able to sleep otherwise.*
(this means: it is advisable/desirable that I have a soft drink; it does not mean 'I'd prefer a soft drink')

The negative of *had better* is *had better not*. It can be used to advise or to warn:

*We**'d better not** stay too late tonight. We've got to be up at six tomorrow morning.*

*You**'d better not** tell Rachel. She'll be scandalised.*

The interrogative of *had better* is formed by inversion of subject and *had*:

*Shall I phone through or **had I better** write?*

Negative interrogatives are much more common than affirmative ones:

***Hadn't you better** warn them?*

Occasionally, *had best* may occur as an alternative to *had better*:

*She **had best** talk to their lawyers before saying too much.*

*I thought perhaps it was me, perhaps I'd been a bit rude, you know. So I thought I**'d best** apologise really.*

Have to, have got to 403d

Uses

Have (got) to has similar meanings to *must*, referring to obligation and deductions. The most frequent uses are for obligation.

Obligation

Have to and the less formal *have got to* are used to refer to obligations which come from outside of the speaker. *Have got to* is far more frequent in spoken language than *have to*:

> [talking about working hours]
> *I **have to** be in at six every morning.*
>
> *I'll be back in a minute. I**'ve** just **got to** make a phone call.*
>
> *We**'ve got to** stay over a Saturday night to get the cheap flight.*
>
> ***Have** you **got to** get up early tomorrow?*

Have got to does not have a non-tensed form and may not be preceded by other modals or auxiliary verbs. *Have to*, without *got*, may be used in a variety of forms:

> *I may be free. **I'll have to** check my diary.*
> (~~I'll have got to check my diary.~~)
>
> ***Do** we **have to** go down to Devon on Tuesday?*
> (~~Do we have got to go down to Devon on Tuesday?~~)
>
> *People want to use technology without **having to** be aware of it, which is still a major problem for the Web experience as a whole.*
> (~~People want to use technology without having got to be aware of it, …~~)

When future obligations and arrangements are already fixed and agreed, the present tense of *have (got) to* is preferred, rather than *will have to*:

> ***I've got to** go to the dentist at half past ten tomorrow.*
> (an arrangement/obligation already fixed)
>
> *I've chipped a bit off one of my teeth. **I'll have to** go to the dentist.*
> (obligation which will be fulfilled in the future; no arrangement is yet made)

Interrogative

The interrogative of *have got to* is formed by subject-verb inversion:

> ***Have you got to** do it all again?*

The interrogative of *have to* is formed most commonly with auxiliary *do* or, less commonly, in formal contexts, by subject-verb inversion:

> ***Do I have to** pay the deposit immediately?*
>
> A: *When **have you to** meet them?*
> B: *Eleven o'clock.*

Negative

The negative of *have got to* is formed by adding *not* after *have*:

*I **haven't got to** go till five.*

The negative of *have to* is normally formed with auxiliary *do*. In rare cases, especially in formal contexts, it may occur as *have/had not to* or *haven't/hadn't to*:

*It **doesn't have to** look so perfect.*

*He **had not to** wait many minutes, however, for he soon heard her dress rustling in the hall, followed by a soft closing of the door.*
(formal, literary style)

Deductions

Have (got) to is also used, though less frequently, to make deductions or draw logical conclusions. In this meaning it is similar to *must*:

[looking for a particular house]
*He said a white house next to the village shop. Er, this **has got to** be it.*
(or: This must be it.)

[telling a story about getting on the wrong train]
*So I said, 'Maureen, this one'll be our train,' and of course it **had to** be the wrong one. So we got off at the next stop.*
(predictably, it was the wrong one)

Have (got) to and *must* 403e

Must generally refers to obligations which originate from the speaker, and is often used to express a sense of obligation or necessity, or a directive aimed at the speaker or the listener. *Have (got) to* is generally more associated with external obligations, originating from outside of the speaker:

*I **must** buy a camera.*
(directive to oneself)

*I **have to** go back to the hospital for a scan next week.*
(external obligation)

The negatives *must not* and *don't have to/haven't got to* are quite different. *Must not* expresses prohibition or a negative directive; *don't have to/haven't got to* expresses an absence of obligation:

*You **mustn't** tell anybody what I've just told you, okay?*

*I **mustn't** forget to buy stamps when I'm in town.*

*You **don't have to** have insurance, but you would be wise to buy some.*

*I **haven't got to** go to Oxford next week. They've cancelled the meeting.*

→ **394b** for the negative of *must*

Don't have to can occasionally be used to reproach someone or to tell them not to do something. In this usage, it is less direct than *must not*:

You ***don't have to*** *shout!*
(Stop shouting.)

To make logical deductions, both *must* and *have (got) to* may be used (⇢ **394** and **403d**). *Must* is more frequent than *have to* in this meaning.

Would rather **403f**

Would rather says that one state of affairs is preferable to another. In both its full form and the contracted form, *'d rather*, it occurs most commonly with *I*. *Would rather* has two different constructions.

Same subject

When the subject is the same person in both clauses, *would rather* is followed by a verb in the base form:

I'd rather be *a waiter than a barman.*

*He felt he****'d rather do*** *something useful than sit about.*

Would rather is not used with an *-ing* form or a *to*-infinitive:

[speaking of a jacket with two buttons]
I didn't know it had two buttons, you know. ***I'd rather have*** *three.*
(~~I'd rather having/to have three.~~)

I'd rather stay *here than* ***travel*** *any further tonight.*
(~~I'd rather to stay here than to travel any further tonight.~~)

References to the past may be expressed with *would rather* plus a perfect infinitive form:

The people ***would rather have died*** *than let the old-style conservatives back into power again.*

The negative is formed by adding *not* after *rather*:

A: *If you get a job anyway, you'll probably get a car won't you?*
B: *Yeah. Well, I don't know. I****'d rather not*** *have a car.*
A: *Oh, what, environmental pollution?*
B: *Yeah.*

I'd rather not *say what I really think about him.*

Different subjects

Would rather may also be followed by a clause containing a different subject. In this case, *would rather* is followed by a finite clause with the verb in past subjunctive form (⇢ **159e**):

*I****'d rather*** *she* ***came*** *on Tuesday than Monday.*

*I****'d rather*** *it* ***were*** *this way.*

The negative occurs in the finite clause, not attached to *would rather*:

I'd rather you didn't say anything about it at all.
(~~I'd rather not you said anything about it at all.~~)

In very informal usage, an object pronoun + infinitive without *to* construction may occur:

***I'd rather him tell** her the news than me.*
(more formal equivalent: I'd rather he told her the news than me.)

Reduced responses
Would rather not is frequently used in reduced responses:

A: *Do you want to go with Charlie?*
B: ***I'd rather not**, if you don't mind.*

With *much*
Would rather may be intensified with *much*:

***I'd much rather** be at home than here.*

Declining requests
Would rather not or *would rather* + a negative reduced finite clause are often used to decline invitations or requests:

A: *Will you have another cup of coffee?*
B: ***I'd rather not**, if you don't mind. It keeps me awake.*

A: *Would it be okay if he left his things here?*
B: *Well **I'd rather he didn't**. Er, there's not much room.*

Would sooner and *would just as soon* 403g

A less frequent alternative form of *would rather* is *would sooner*:

*I don't really want to spend my holidays with the family. **I'd sooner** be with friends.*

An even less frequent alternative form is *would just as soon*:

*If it's okay with you, Lee, **I'd just as soon** leave now. I'm not very hungry any more.*

OTHER MODAL EXPRESSIONS WITH *BE* 404

A range of expressions with *be* have modal meanings. These include:

be about to	*be due to*	*be supposed to*
be able to	*be likely to/that*	*be sure to*
be bound to	*be meant to*	
be certain to	*be obliged to*	

*She's obviously very upset so she**'s bound to** say that.*

***Aren't** they **meant to** be at the restaurant by now?*

*There **was supposed to** be a sale here yesterday.*

The most important of these are dealt with in **404a–404h**.

Be about to 404a

Be about to refers to things which are arranged or destined to happen very soon after the time of speaking:

[public announcement from the buffet car on a train]
*We would like to advise all passengers that the third and final sitting of breakfast **is** now **about to** start. Any further passengers who require breakfast, you are advised to take your seats in the restaurant car now.*

Be about to frequently occurs with *just*:

*We**'re just about to** go and have something to eat. Would you like to join us?*

The negative of *be about to* may refer to things which are not destined to happen, but it also less frequently has the meaning of 'not prepared to/not willing to':

*Don't worry, **I'm not about to** break down into floods of tears. I've cried enough for Rick. It's time for me to get on with my life.*

*Mrs Green was seen to pale and it was clear that she **was not about to** open the envelope in the presence of witnesses.*
(was not prepared/willing to open the envelope)

Be able to 404b

Be able to often means the same as *can* when referring to abilities (⇢ **381**), but it is much less common. It is often used in situations where *can* is not grammatically possible:

*I might not **be able to** get an eyesight test for tomorrow.*
(~~I might not can get an eyesight test for tomorrow.~~)

*Will you **be able to** carry that big box all on your own?*

[giving directions]
***Can** you see that white building down there? It's just next to that.*
(preferred to: Are you able to see that white building ...?)

The negative of *be able to* is formed with *not* or (more formally) with *unable*:

[university science lecture]
*The virus **is no longer able to** attach to a target cell. It**'s** therefore **not able to** cause an infection.*

*We have**n't been able to** contact her, I'm afraid.*

*Did anybody ask you why you **were unable to** attend?*

Be bound to 404c

Be bound to means 'be very certain to', and expresses strong predictions or inevitability:

You'll have to remind me to bring that book. ***I'm bound to*** *forget otherwise.*

She had to go through two lots of X-rays. It ***was bound to*** *be painful for her.*

The negative of *be bound to* for making predictions is *be bound not to*, but it is very rare:

[predicting the result of a sports competition between England and Scotland; *scrape a win* means win by a narrow margin; *two legs* means two separate events; *stroll it* means win easily]
England will probably scrape a win over two legs, but they will not stroll it and ***it's bound not to*** *be pretty.*

Be bound to also less frequently has a meaning of 'be obliged to'; the negative form *not bound to* usually means 'not obliged to/not committed to':

I'm bound to *admit that there could be serious problems.*

I'm not bound to *deliver a lecture on my family affairs, I have not undertaken to do it, and I'm not going to do it.*

Be due to 404d

Be due to refers to things which are fixed or destined to happen within or at a determined or known time after the time of speaking:

Britain's second child prison ***is due to*** *open next month.*

I'm due to *retire next year.*

The negative of *be due to* is formed with *not* attached to *be*:

She had only just settled a £136 bill for the last quarter and ***was not due to*** *receive another one until mid-October.*

Be likely to/that 404e

Be likely to/that means that something is probable:

A: *When* ***are*** *you* ***likely to*** *hear about the Chicago job?*
B: *I haven't been for the interview yet.*
A: *Oh. Right.*

A: *I'm in every afternoon.*
B: *All right.*
A: *The only time* ***I'm likely to*** *be out is say between ten and twelve.*

Accidents ***are likely to*** *happen, of course.*

Be likely is normally used with a preparatory *it* subject when followed by a *that*-clause:

[text about global warming]
***It is** also **likely that** global rainfall patterns will shift away from the subtropical areas towards higher latitudes, so disrupting present agricultural patterns.*

Preparatory *it* is not used with the *to*-infinitive construction:

***I'm likely to** be out most of tomorrow.*
(~~It's likely for me to be out most of tomorrow.~~)

The negative of *be likely to/that* is formed either with *not* or, in more formal contexts, with *unlikely*:

[doctor reassuring a patient about possible side-effects of a medication]
*In fact they're not very common but they're recorded, and I can't say whether it'll happen to you or not. Statistically they**'re not likely to** happen to you.*

*Then we should say goodbye to the people with whom we were travelling and it **was unlikely that** we should see any of them again.*

*This opportunity **is unlikely to** occur again.*

Be likely is often used comparatively, with *more, most, less* and *least*:

[*Blockbuster* is a chain of video rental shops]
A: *We**'re more likely to** get what we want at Blockbuster cos er they've got like fifteen thousand of every film, don't they.*
B: *Oh yeah.*

A: *So if you practise deep breathing exercises you**'re less likely to** get a chest infection. Is that right?*
B: *Yes.*

Other verbs with modal meanings, such as *seem* and *look*, can be used instead of *be* with *likely to/that*:

*This year, pre-tax profits **seem likely to** fall to £165 million or less before recovering next year.*

[referring to the European single currency, the Euro]
*There seemed plenty of time for EU member governments to rein in inflation and put fiscal houses in order before the single currency was launched. It also **seemed likely that** only seven or eight countries would join initially.*

[weather forecast]
*The south of England **looks likely to** escape today's wintry showers.*

→ **539 Glossary** for any unfamiliar terms

Be meant to 404f

Be meant to refers to things which are destined, or generally accepted to be true:

*I thought we were going to marry each other, but it **wasn't meant to** be.*
(it was not destined to happen)

[talking about ghosts]
A: *Animals are more sensitive aren't they? Bob's dog has a fit when the ghost comes out. It goes and hides under the bed. Or has a massive barking fit. Animals **are meant to** be able to see them before humans can.*
B: *Yeah.*
(it is generally accepted that animals can see them before humans can)

Be meant to can also refer to what is desirable, necessary or intended:

*We**'re meant to** reply before the end of the month.*
(it is desired or necessary)

[university lecturer explaining a difficult poem in a literature class]
*It's intentionally fragmented. It **is meant to** be difficult. Everything you're doing **is meant to** be difficult. It's suggesting something about the difficulty of modern living, in the sense that it's all fragmented. The poem's fragmented but life has become fragmented as well.*
(it is intended to be difficult)

*We were back here two hours before we **were meant to** be.*

The negative is *not meant to*. It typically means 'not supposed to/not intended to':

*It was **not meant to** be a criticism.*

Be obliged to 404g

Be obliged to normally refers to obligations originating outside of the speaker. It occurs mostly in formal contexts:

*Washington, spacious and green, is a cosmopolitan and pleasing city. People still come here because they **are obliged to**; they stay on because they have come to love the place.*

*When you're on a pedestrian crossing, the driver**'s** legally **obliged to** stop.*

The negative form *not obliged to* means that something is not necessary or obligatory:

*You **are not obliged to** answer.*

The negative form *obliged not to* means that something must not be done/is prohibited:

*You **are obliged not to** inform anyone of this decision.*

Be supposed to 404h

Be supposed to refers to what is planned or expected to happen, or to duties and obligations:

*Ben's **supposed to** be here at half past ten.*
(it is planned or expected)

*They didn't give me a tax code. As a casual employee **I'm supposed to** have a casual-employee tax code.*
(referring to a duty or an obligation)

In the negative, *be supposed to* can refer to things which are prohibited or unadvisable. The negative form is *not supposed to*:

*You**'re not supposed to** put the coffee-pot in the dishwasher.*

Be supposed to can also refer to what is generally believed to be true:

***Isn't** dark chocolate **supposed to** be good for you?*

OTHER VERBS WITH MODAL USES 405

Expressing possibility, etc. 405a

Other common verbs which express modal meanings of possibility and likelihood, especially with a first person singular subject, include:

appear	*guess*	*seem*
believe	*know*	*sound*
expect	*look*	*suppose*
feel	*promise*	*tend*
gather	*reckon*	*think*

*I **gather** she may be back Sunday.*
(I believe it is true, based on what I have been told)

*I **guess** the bus service isn't too good, is it?*
(I suppose/it is likely that …)

*The final next week **promises** to be an exciting match.*
(is likely to be/has the potential to be)

*Anyway, I **reckon** I'd better be going.*
(I think …)

*She **seems** to be quite clever for her age.*
(it is reasonable to believe that from the evidence)

*It doesn't make any sense at all, Diane. It **sounds** a load of rubbish.*
(typically refers to what someone has said or written: conclusion based on the evidence)

Appear, *feel*, *look*, *seem* and *sound* occur frequently with dummy *it* as subject:

*It **appears** there was a technical fault.*

*It **feels** as if they're all criticising me.*

*It **looks** like you didn't get very much sleep last night.*

*It **seems** as if you put these papers in the wrong order.*

*It **sounds** as if she's going to retire soon.*

Tend to is increasingly heard in everyday spoken language to refer to what is typically true or to habitual actions:

[hairdresser asking customer how she likes to have her hair]
*Do you **tend** to like to have it forward like that, swept over, with a bit down, like that?*

*I **tend** to like to save my money and spend it when I go to London.*

There is considerable flexibility in the complementation patterns allowed with these verbs, though there are restrictions, sometimes determined by degrees of formality.

Typical complementation patterns

+ *to*-infinitive	(*to* sb) + *that*-clause	+ *like* + clause (informal)	+ *as if* + clause
*It **appears to be** an error.*	*It **appears that** I have some apologising to do.*		[describing a new audio system] *It makes the music **appear as if** it's coming from behind you.*
	*They **feel that** they have caused a lot of trouble.*	*He **felt like** he was coming into his own house as a guest.*	***I feel as if** I ought to say something to her.*
*The police **look to have** lost control of the crowd.*		*It **looks like** we'll need another day to get through everything.*	*It **looks as if** he's lost something.*
*They **seem to have** caused a lot of trouble.*	*It **seems (to me) that** they need a lesson in politeness.*	*It **seems like** you were right all along.*	*It **seems as if** everything is going wrong.*
	*It **sounds to me that** the sort of theology you're describing is one in which religion is getting out of the churches and into people's homes.*	*It **sounds like** we should think again.*	*It **sounds as if** we're getting a pay rise after all.*

Expressing obligation, etc. 405b

Other common verbs which express modal meanings of obligation, necessity, etc. include:

allow	*involve*	*permit*
demand	*let*	*prohibit*
entail	*make*	*require*
forbid	*mean*	*want*
force	*necessitate*	

Living so far from work ***means*** *gett****ing*** *up really early and driving for an hour.*
(makes it necessary to get up early; always followed by *-ing* or a noun)

All these evaluations and appraisals just ***mean*** *more paperwork for us and more bureaucracy.*

The weather has ***necessitated*** *a change in plans.*
(formal)

[university lecturer in an applied linguistics class; the first four skills are reading, writing, speaking and listening]
The fifth skill is the skill of thinking, processing, negotiating with the language. The skill that ***requires*** *the student, the reader, to go beyond the referential meaning and bring his or her own meaning to the text.*

Force and *make* are often used in the passive, with meanings referring to actions made obligatory by external agents:

*It's not much of a holiday if you****'re forced to*** *walk two miles every morning for breakfast … but I suppose it keeps you fit.*

I remember swimming lessons at school when we ***were*** *all* ***made to*** *jump into a freezing cold outside swimming pool.*

A–Z 51 ***Make***, where the uses with and without *to* are described

Want + *to*-infinitive is used in informal contexts with a modal meaning of *should/ought to* or *need*:

[talking about how important it is that young people both plan for the future and train for the future too]
At that age you need to think of both things. You ***want to be*** *looking ahead and you* ***want to be*** *improving your skills as well.*

[preparing a drink for a party]
Put some more sugar in. It doesn't ***want to taste*** *bitter.*

[post-office assistant, taking a package from a customer; *first class* is a fast, more expensive system of delivery]
That one ***wants to go*** *first class. Right.*

Want + *-ing* is used in informal contexts with a meaning similar to *need*:

*My hair **wants** cutt**ing**.*

*The whole living room really **wants** redecorat**ing**.*

MODAL NOUNS, ADJECTIVES AND ADVERBS 406

Several nouns, adjectives and adverbs can express modal meanings. These include:

clear(ly)	*likelihood/likely*	*supposed(ly)*
definite(ly)	*obvious(ly)*	*sure(ly)*
doubtless	*seeming(ly)*	*undoubted(ly)*

Sometimes the same meaning can be expressed in all three word classes:

Nouns, adjectives and adverbs with modal meanings

noun	adjective	adverb
appearance	*apparent*	*apparently*
certainty	*certain*	*certainly*
evidence	*evident*	*evidently*
inevitability	*inevitable*	*inevitably*
necessity	*necessary*	*necessarily*
possibility	*possible*	*possibly*
probability	*probable*	*probably*

*He took aim and fired, but it was a difficult shot with no **certainty** of success.*

*There was no **evidence** that he had been there or done any work.*

*The most **likely** outcome will be a compromise.*

*There's not **necessarily** only one way of doing these things.*

*Would it be **possible** for me to have a copy of the document?*

*I can **probably** finish the repair work by Friday, if that's all right.*

A less frequent use of *likely* (but one which is quite common in North American English) is as an adverb:

*A heavy week for economic data will **likely** keep trading cautious.*

FOR CERTAIN, FOR DEFINITE, FOR SURE 407

The expressions *for certain*, *for definite* and *for sure* are also frequently used. *For definite* and *for sure* are especially common in informal speech. *For certain* usually occurs with the verb *know*:

A: *Did he say **for definite** whether he's coming next week?*
B: *I'm not sure. I'll ask him again.*

*After a journey like that, I won't be flying in a two-seater plane again, that's **for sure**.*

*Do you **know for certain** that the bus is at ten?*

Speech acts

Speech acts

INTRODUCTION 408

This chapter (408–423) is concerned with interpersonal meanings of grammar, that is, how language enables us to get things done by ourselves or by others.

The term speech act refers to what the speaker or writer is doing in uttering a particular form of words. For example, an imperative form such as *Come here!* usually has the meaning of directing the listener to act in a certain way, and a clause such as *Can you pass me that book?* is likely to be a request to someone actually to pass the book, rather than an enquiry about the person's physical ability. Speech acts are concerned with the speaker's intention rather than the content-meaning of the utterance.

In everyday written and spoken interactions, common speech acts occur such as informing, directing, questioning, requesting, exemplifying, offering, apologising, complaining, suggesting, promising, permitting, forbidding, predicting and so on.

Speech acts may be divided into five broad types:

- Constatives:

  The speaker asserts something about the truth of a proposition, associated with acts such as: affirming, claiming, concluding, denying, exclaiming, maintaining, predicting, stating beliefs.

- Directives:

  The speaker intends to make the hearer act in a particular way, associated with acts such as: advising, asking, challenging, commanding, daring, forbidding, insisting, instructing, permitting, prohibiting, questioning, requesting, suggesting, warning.

- Commissives:

  The speaker commits to a course of action, associated with acts such as: guaranteeing, offering, inviting, promising, vowing, undertaking.

- Expressives (or acknowledgements):

  The speaker expresses an attitude or reaction concerning a state of affairs, associated with acts such as: apologising, appreciating, complimenting, condemning, congratulating, regretting, thanking, welcoming.

- Declarations:

  The speaker performs the speech act solely by making the utterance, for example: *I pronounce you man and wife*; *I declare this meeting closed*; *I name this ship x*.

This chapter focuses particularly on directives and commissives, as these are the speech acts in which grammatical choices figure most prominently, especially involving modal verbs and clause types (e.g. declarative versus interrogative).

The chapter describes how the clause structure contributes to different kinds of speech act (such as statements, questions, directives, etc.) (→ **410**). We also consider the role of modal verbs in constructing speech acts such as requesting (*Would you hold this for me?*), offering (*I'll carry that for you*), promising (*I'll buy you one for your birthday*), suggesting (*We could stay in a bed-and-breakfast place*), permitting (*You can stay up till ten o'clock*), and so on (→ **411–420**).

There are also verbs, referred to as speech act verbs, which a speaker can use to label a speech act explicitly (*I **promise** you I'll be there*; *He **denied** that he was involved in any way*) (→ **422**). When these are used actually to perform the speech act (e.g. *I apologise*), they are called performative verbs (→ **422a**).

The way speech acts are realised also involves politeness and the efforts speakers make to avoid loss of face, or dignity, for themselves and their interlocutors. For instance, a speaker who says *I **was wondering** if I **could** have a word with you?* will be heard as less direct, more polite and less imposing than one who says *I **wonder** if I **can** have a word with you*, which in turn is more polite and less imposing than someone who says *I **want to** have a word with you*. Tense and aspect choices are therefore also implicated in speech acts (→ **423**).

On the larger scale, speakers need to perform functions such as opening conversations, closing them, making sure they get their turn to speak, and so on. These are referred to in passing in this chapter (→ **423d**) and are dealt with in greater detail in **104–122 From discourse to social contexts**.

Speech acts can only be interpreted in context, and so it is often necessary to use quite long examples to illustrate how particular acts are realised, especially in face-to-face conversation, where speech acts such as requests, invitations, advice, etc. have to be carefully negotiated between speakers and listeners and are not necessarily realised in one phrase or clause.

Although we also exemplify speech acts in written texts, and although there are a potentially huge number of possible speech acts which could be discussed, our emphasis in this chapter will be on the performance of the most common, everyday, frequent speech acts which occur in spoken contexts, using grammatical resources. We focus particularly on those speech acts which are interactive, involving getting others to act in a particular way.

Typical speech acts which occur in academic contexts are covered in **140–154 Grammar and academic English**.

WAYS OF REALISING SPEECH ACTS 409

Principally, speech acts are realised using the following resources:

- formulaic utterances (fixed expressions conventionally associated with particular speech acts): greetings such as *Hi*, *Goodbye*; expressions of reaction to events such as *Congratulations*, *Gosh!*, *Sorry*, *Excuse me*, *Pardon*.
- explicit lexical items (speech-act verbs or speech-act nouns) to perform or to label the speech act: *I **pronounce** you man and wife*; *My **advice** is not to use olive oil.*

- syntax (e.g. clause types, tense and aspect choices): *Was I surprised!* as an exclamation; ***Did** you want to say something?* as a polite invitation to someone to take the speaking turn.
- modal constructions (typically modal verbs): ***Can** I get you a drink?* uttered as an offer; *You **must** be patient* as a directive.
- prosodic means: a declarative clause plus rising intonation may indicate a question rather than a statement, e.g. A: *You'll be arriving late?* B: *Yes.*

CLAUSE TYPES AND SPEECH ACTS 410

The chapter **Clause types (290–303)** described the basic types of clause. The clause types most directly correspond to common speech acts as shown in the table below.

Typical correspondences between clause types and speech acts

clause type	typical speech act	examples
declarative	statement	*He works in Barsham.*
interrogative	question	*How long did it take?*
imperative	directive	*Put it all in a pile here.*
exclamative	exclamation	*How nice you look!*

However, such a direct correspondence is not always the case, and the clause types, especially declarative and interrogative, are used to perform other speech acts too, as shown in the table below.

Other possible correspondences between clause types and speech acts

clause type	possible speech acts	examples
declarative	question	A: *So you're going to be here about quarter past?* B: *Yeah quarter past, twenty past, yeah.*
	command	*You sit there.*
	offer	*I'll hold that for you.*
	exclamation	*There's a rat!*
interrogative	command	*Will you be quiet!*
	request	*Could you carry this for me?*
	intensified statement, or exclamation	*Was I embarrassed when I realised what had happened!* (I'm telling you I *was* embarrassed)
imperative	warning about a particular course of action	*Do that again and I'm going to smack you.*
	offer	*Have a banana.*

Declarative clauses functioning as questions 410a

A declarative clause may function in context as a question. Although these are less frequent than interrogative questions, a common type of declarative question is when a speaker checks an assumption or inference drawn from the ongoing conversation. Initial *so* and/or final *then* are common in such questions:

[speaker A is recounting how an elderly relative has found a good place to live in her old age]
A: *It's a little terraced house. And sort of very old fashioned but spotlessly clean and very cosy.*
B: *Oh well.*
A: *New kitchen new what not.*
B: *Yeah.*
A: *And a thousand and something a month.*
B: *Yeah.* ***So you're pleased****?*
A: *Oh I'm relieved. Yes. Yes.*

A: ***So you had a good day at work then****?*
B: *Yes it was all right.*

The declarative question may also be used as a comprehension check:

[speaker A is on the phone to a printing company to check on the progress of a print job]
A: *I'm ringing just to see if everything was okay with the job when Dave got it opened up and printing out and everything.*
B: *Ah. No, he said this morning there were some fonts missing, Chris.*
A: ***There were some fonts missing****?*
B: *Yes.*

→ **430 Declarative questions** on the intonation of declarative questions

Modal verbs and interrogative clauses as directives 410b

Because the bare imperative is considered extremely forceful and in many cases impolite in English, many directive speech acts (commands, instructions, requests, etc.) involve interrogative clauses and modal verbs:

Will you *look at your handouts, now, please.*

Can you *shut that door?*

These will be dealt with more fully in **412–413**.

Interrogative clauses as exclamations 410c

Occasionally, clauses with affirmative or negative interrogative structure can also be used as exclamations:

[speaker is recounting a long and problematic journey]
Oh God, ***was I*** *exhausted by the time I got home!*

[looking at a small child]
Gosh! ***Hasn't she grown!***

Sometimes life played cruel tricks ... ***Didn't it just!***

Imperative clauses as offers and invitations 410d

Friendly offers and invitations, which are commissive speech acts (→ **417–419**), often occur in the imperative form:

A: ***Have*** *another drink.*
B: *Oh, no thanks, I've had enough thanks.*

A: ***Come*** *and see us some time if you're in the area.*
B: *Mm, yeah, that'd be nice. I will.*

MODAL EXPRESSIONS AND SPEECH ACTS 411

When modal expressions concerned with necessity, obligation, permission, etc. (→ **377–407 Modality**) are used in declarative and interrogative clauses, they often function as directives (realising speech acts such as commanding, instructing, suggesting, advising, warning, requesting) and commissives (promising, offering, inviting).

The modal verbs *can/could, will/would, shall/should, may/might, must, ought to* are used frequently in this way:

[swimming instructor to learner]
You ***shouldn't*** *be looking at me Joseph, you* ***should*** *be looking out of the window.*
(*should* is heard as a directive: the swimmer must do what the instructor says)

Could *you just hang on a second, Joan?*
(*could* is heard as a directive; Joan can hardly refuse to do what the speaker asks)

Here, ***I'll*** *carry that for you.*
(*'ll* is heard as an offer)

*We'**ll*** *get it done for you by Friday, no problem.*
(*'ll* is heard as a promise)

It is not just which modal verb is used but which clause type it occurs in that affects the speech act being performed. In the subsequent sections on modal verbs (**412–420**), declarative and interrogative uses are distinguished as the speech acts they signal may vary.

Each type of speech act is described in terms of its modal verb choices and its occurrence in declarative and interrogative clauses.

MODALITY AND DIRECTIVES (COMMANDS, REQUESTS, ADVICE) 412

Directives are speech acts where the speaker intends the listener to act in a particular way.

In sections **413–416**, we divide directives into the more direct type (commands, instructions) on the one hand and the more indirect type (warnings, requests, advice, suggestions, permissions) on the other hand, and we look at the way modal verbs are used to realise such acts.

COMMANDS, INSTRUCTIONS 413

Commands and instructions are speech acts which are intended to make the receiver act in a particular way. The person who performs the speech act usually needs to have authority to issue the command or instruction for the act to be recognised by the receiver.

Declaratives with *can* 413a

Declarative structures with *can* are occasionally used in polite commands and instructions:

[in the kitchen, to a guest holding a used plate]
***You can** just leave that on the draining board. I'll wash it later.*
(note the inclusion of softener *just*)

[travel agent (A) issuing tickets to a customer (B)]
A: *That's lovely. I've actually debited your credit card.*
B: *Mm mm.*
A: *The price of it is one twenty four by two, and sixty two pounds for the little boy. So in total that's three hundred and ten pounds. And it's been debited as a telephone order. **If you can** just keep your receipt and check it against your statement.*
B: *Okay.*
(note the non-conditional polite use of *if*, which further softens the instruction)

Declaratives with *must* 413b

Must occurs in commands and instructions in declarative clauses:

[teacher (A) to class]
A: ***You must** be clear of what the right answer is. Because you're gonna mark some of these answers.*
B: *Do we write the answers in the book sir?*
A: *Yeah you can put your answer in the book.*

[instructions to sales personnel at a training session]
This part of the selling process is directed towards finding out about your client and completing the client questionnaire. With all clients ***you must*** *attempt to complete all relevant areas of the questionnaire. This includes gathering hard facts, date of birth, marital status, dependants, hobbies and so on.*

[university tutor to student, discussing how long she will have to study to get her PhD]
I think ***you must*** *aim for three years.*
(note the softener *I think*)

Must in directives is very strong in English, and should be used with care, especially in contexts such as suggesting and advising. It is normally only used in directives by people in positions of power and authority, and even then may be softened (e.g. the university tutor's use of *I think* in the example above).

Declaratives with *will* and *shall* 413c

Declaratives with *will* occur in commands in very formal styles, but are rare in everyday conversation:

'You can't come in here. Who asked you in? ***You will*** *please leave, this minute.' We protested, naturally, …*

Declaratives with *shall* occur in very formal contexts, and in archaic, literary styles to express commands:

*'Arthur, you must repent!' cried I, in a frenzy of desperation, throwing my arms around him and burying my face in his bosom. '**You shall** say you are sorry for what you have done!'*
'Well, well, I am.'

There Fanny, ***you shall*** *carry that parcel for me – take great care of it – do not let it fall; it is a cream cheese, just like the excellent one we had at dinner.*

You're going to and *would you like to* 413d

Declarative form *you're going to/gonna* and interrogative form *would you like to* also occasionally occur as commands:

[swimming instructor to learners]
Legs nice and straight. No knees popping out of the water. And ***you're gonna*** *look at that window for me. I don't want anybody looking at me. Or here. You're looking up. Right. Are you ready, crocodiles? Off you go.*

[teacher to student]
Would you like to *tell the rest of the class your own definition of what a tower block is?*

Interrogatives with *can*, *could*, *will* and *would* 413e

One way to make a directive softer or more polite is to use an interrogative structure with *can*, *could*, *will* or *would* rather than an imperative. Such interrogatives are very frequent, and even people in power and authority (e.g. superiors at the workplace) regularly soften commands and instructions in this way.

In general, *will* is heard as most direct, with *can*, *could* and *would* being heard as progressively less direct/more polite:

[mother to very small child who picks up a knife at the table]
***Will you** put that down darling. That's dangerous, that is.*

[adult carer to child]
*Be careful David. No! **Can you** go and take that somewhere else please because you're going to break something aren't you?*

[chiropractor (A) examining a patient (B)]
A: *And how have you been Nigel? All right?*
B: *Well not too bad.*
A: ***Could you** raise your left leg.*
B: *Ooh.*
A: *And your right leg.*
B: *Very difficult.*
(compare the more direct: Raise your left leg.)

[chairperson at business meeting]
*Shall we just look at one or two documents that you've already looked at please, **would you** go to page twenty-nine.*

WARNINGS, ADVICE, SUGGESTIONS 414

Warnings are speech acts in which the speaker states the possible negative outcome of a particular course of action for the listener. The listener may choose to heed or not heed the warning.

Advice is a speech act where the speaker expresses their view of how the listener or others ought best to act to solve a problem or achieve a goal. The listener may choose to heed or not heed the advice.

Suggestions are speech acts where the speaker proposes a course of action for the listener or others, which may include the speaker. The listener may choose to take up or not take up the suggestion.

Declaratives with *can, could, may* and *might* 414a

Can, could

Can and *could* in declarative clauses can be used to make suggestions. *Could* is generally heard as less forceful than *can* and is much more frequent. Tags often also occur:

[speakers are discussing possibilities for making framed pictures as craft items to sell]
A: ***You can*** *make little designs.*
B: ***We can*** *do like little designs to put in them* ***can't we.***
C: *Mm.*
B: *And sell them off as like individual little pictures.*

[speakers are discussing the problems of camping out, and the possibility their tents could be stolen while they were away from them; *wanna* represents the informal spoken form of 'want to']
A: *We don't wanna have to pack them up every time we go out.*
B: ***We could*** *stay in a hotel.*
A: *Mm.*

[speakers are planning how to organise a set of personal accounts]
A: *We need a register for deposits.*
B: ***You could*** *have four columns.* ***You could*** *have 'opening' 'deposit' 'withdrawal' 'closing'.*

Could always is often used in making suggestions in everyday conversation:

[speakers are discussing the need to have a guide book for a trip they are planning; *Lonely Planet* is a popular series of guide books]
A: *So we need to look at if there's a sort of basic thing about different regions.*
B: *Most probably get this from the libraries. You should have that in your Birmingham library. We've got it in Manchester.*
A: *Mm. Yeah. I'll go and get it out tomorrow.*
B: *Or* ***you could always*** *get Lonely Planet, Japan.*
A: *Yeah. Buy it.*
B: *Yeah you could.*

May

May is used in advice-giving and suggestions, most typically in the formulaic expressions *may as well* (→ **414e**), *may (well) find (that), may want/wish to*:

Travellers intending to fly from Canada are likely to find that, with less competition on these routes … fares are somewhat higher than they are for flights wholly within the US. ***You may well find that*** *it's worth the effort to get to a US city first, and fly on to California from there.*

[advice to language teachers in a teaching manual]
Give students ten minutes or so to prepare and practise their conversations. Don't let them make them too long. If they come up with amusing dialogues, ***you may want*** *to let them perform for the class.*

Might

Might is also used in advice and suggestions, particularly in the routine expression *you might want to*:

> [during a university linguistics class, where students are analysing English sentences; B is the tutor]
> A: *Erm, there's a difficult sentence here.*
> B: *I think there's an argument for thinking that's part of the verb phrase. But* ***you might*** *look at that.*

> [interviewer (A), recording an interview, addressing interviewee (B)]
> A: ***You might want to*** *move your chair a little bit closer.*
> B: *Right.*

> [advising an applicant for an educational course]
> A: *The only other person I think that* ***you might want to*** *come and talk to is Patricia Matthews. Now Patricia Matthews is our finance officer. So she deals with anything to do with grants or awards. And* ***you might want to*** *come and talk to her about what are realistic options in terms of funding this course.*
> B: *Right.*
> A: *And it's just a question of ringing the college, making an appointment and coming to talk to Margaret.*
> B: *Right.*

Negative interrogatives with *can* and *could* 414b

Can't/can not and *couldn't/could not* often occur in suggestions and advice-giving:

> [talking about a houseplant with glossy leaves]
> A: *A nightmare to clean, because the leaves will fall off. They're cactuses, those ones. Like, where you get all the dust.*
> B: ***Can't you*** *get some sprays like anti-dust sprays?*
> A: *Oh yeah I could do.*
> B: *Or* ***can't you*** *just spray it with water?*

> [A is complaining about travel arrangements made on his behalf by his employer; *BA* means the airline, British Airways]
> A: *Stupid really. I'd rather go economy class on BA. Get there faster.*
> B: *Yeah. Well did you not say that to them?* ***Can you not*** *organise your own travel a bit?*
> A: *Not to get there, because I said about coming back that I'd go any way possible. Economy class or anything. But they wouldn't let me. So now I still have to come back on a different flight than Tom. First class.*

[A notices how B's jumper has become prematurely faded]
A: *I've just noticed. Do you know what's happened to your jumper? Have you seen it?*
B: *That always happens to my jumpers.*
A: *That's dreadful though.* ***Could you not*** *send it back?*
B: *Send it back.*
A: *Yeah. Brand new isn't it?*
B: *I've only washed it once.*
A: *I'd send it back.*
B: *Would you?*
A: *Mm.*
B: *Would you really?*
A: *Mm. That shouldn't happen for years.*

Declaratives with *must* 414c

Must occurs in warnings and strong advice-giving contexts:

[A is a health visitor; speaker B has been unwell]
A: *Oh how are you? Better?*
B: *A bit better than, what was it? Last week.*
A: *Yes but you seem to be losing weight rapidly.*
B: *Well, I can only eat certain things.*
A: *I mean* ***you must*** *take care.*

A: *I can give you some oven cleaner. But the problem with it is* ***you must*** *make sure you get all of it off. And* ***they mustn't*** *use it while you're doing it because it's very strong. Don't get it on your hands either. It's really very very strong. And* ***you must*** *make sure it all washes off before they use it again.*
B: *Okay.*

Must is considerably stronger and more forceful than *should* or *could* in advice-giving contexts and is less frequent in everyday conversational contexts.

Declaratives with *should* 414d

Declaratives with *should* occur in warnings, advice and suggestions:

A: *You know* ***you should*** *never open one of these like that don't you?*
B: *Mm.*
A: *Cos someone lost their eye.*
B: *Mm.*
A: *It never ever occurred to me till I saw that programme about the number of people who've lost eyes and things.*

[speaker A is advising an out-of-work artist (B) on the best place to look for jobs]
A: *But London, I think **you should** try London.*
B: *Mm. I think you're probably right.*
A: *London's definitely the place.*
B: *I think though they would understand what I'm trying to do much more.*
A: *Mm.*

[speakers are disturbed by a beeping noise]
A: *It's the smoke alarm that's beeping. **We should** put a new battery in.*
B: *Yeah.*

[speakers are discussing a woman who has problems with her ex-partner, who keeps returning to her home despite having been told never to come back]
A: *Maybe **she should** double lock the doors.*
B: *Yeah.*

Declaratives with *may as well* and *might (just) as well* 414e

May as well and *might (just) as well* are commonly used for making suggestions in everyday conversation. *Might (just) as well* is more frequent. It is used to suggest what the speaker considers the easiest/most logical course of action:

[speaker A is about to go to the counter in a café to buy a glass of orange juice for B]
A: *Do you want ice?*
B: *Er, no I'm fine.*
A: *You sure.*
B: *Yep. That's grand.*
A: *I'm quite happy to go. I'll take that. **I may as well** take the tray back anyway.*

[speakers are discussing whether to rent a video for home viewing]
A: *They're about three quid a day to rent though, aren't they?*
B: *Mm, that's true. Yeah.*
A: ***We might as well** go to the cinema.*

A: ***You might as well** fill all the details you've got down on that front page.*
B: *Mm.*

Declaratives with *ought to* 414f

Many occurrences of *ought to* in everyday conversation are associated with suggestions and advice:

A: *Er, I think **we ought to** turn these radiators down you know.*
B: *Do you?*
C: *It is roasting hot in here isn't it.*
A: *Yeah.*

[speaker is recounting difficulties with the Health Service, concerning appointments for treatment that were repeatedly cancelled]

A: *They were amazed how many times it was cancelled and how many times I got there and didn't have physiotherapy as well.*

B: *Mm. And was there anybody there that you felt you could've spoken to?*

A: *No because I'm not the kind of person that really complains. And it was just starting to get more and more and I was getting more and more annoyed and each time I came back on the ambulance the ambulance staff were saying, 'Well this isn't good enough,* ***you ought to*** *complain.' I said, 'I just don't like complaining.'*

You want to 414g

You want to is used in informal contexts to make suggestions and to give advice:

[speaker A is complaining about poor sound-proofing in their terraced house]

A: *I realise that they can hear everything through that wall.*

B: *Oh dear.*

A: *Cos I heard Michael cough once and it was like he was sitting next to me and I thought, 'Oh my God, I mean, what can he hear?'*

B: ***You want to*** *sound-proof your room with egg boxes.*

A: *Well. No. You live in a terrace. It's a hazard of life isn't it?*

B: *Yeah. Yeah. That's true.*

(Note also the use of *want* following *may* and *might*, → **414a** above)

→ also **421a** ***What about, what if, how about***

A–Z **75** ***Want***

Had better 414h

Had better (not) is used to give warnings and strong advice:

A: ***You'd better*** *move your car Pete cos I'm sure somebody's gonna nip in and steal that trailer. They're terrible thieves of trailers.*

B: *Oh right.*

[*lights* here refers to car headlights]

You've left your lights on. ***You'd better*** *go and turn them off.*

A: ***You'd better*** *get an early night if you're going to be up early.*

B: *Mm.*

You'd better not *post that letter.*

✪ *Had better* is quite a strong expression, used when the speaker thinks there will be negative consequences if the desired action is not taken; it is not appropriate when making ordinary suggestions or recommendations:

I recommend you go to the Tokyo Tower in Shibaura. If you go to the top of the tower you will see a view of most of Tokyo. At night go to Aoyama where you can find many nice restaurants.

(~~At night you'd better go to Aoyama where you can find many nice restaurants.~~)

PERMISSIONS, PROHIBITIONS 415

Permissions are concerned with requesting and granting freedom for someone to act in a particular way.

Prohibitions deny freedom of action.

Declaratives with *can* and *may* 415a

Declaratives with *can* and *may* are used to give permission. *May* is more formal than *can*, and is rare in everyday conversation for giving permission:

*She asked if she could come and stay so I said 'Of course **you can**.'*

*Mum says **you can** eat as much fruit as you want.*

*You acknowledge that the material and content contained within the Website and the Services is for your personal use only and that **you may** download such material and content onto only one computer hard drive for such purpose.*

Interrogatives with *can, could, may* and *might* 415b

Can, could, may and *might* are all used to ask for permission to do something.

Can I is the least formal and most direct, *could I* is more formal and less direct, and *may I* is the most formal and least direct of the three. *May I* to ask permission is infrequent in informal conversation. *Might I* is very formal and rare:

A: *I haven't read the complete thing at all. I've just I've kind of flicked through it and read bits and pieces.*
B: [reads the title] *'The Teaching of Languages in Linguistics'. **Can I** borrow it for a week or so? And then I'll give it back to you then.*
A: *Yeah. Sure. Absolutely.*

A: ***Could we** have this room for the next hour?*
B: *Yes, you can. Don't forget to lock it though when you've finished.*
(note the positive reply: 'Yes, you can', not 'Yes, you could', which would suggest hesitation, or perhaps that there is a problem: 'Yes you could, but it may be too small for you')

*She glanced around the kitchen, reluctant to move farther into the apartment, coming up with one more item of business to delay it a few minutes. '**May I** use your phone, Christopher? I'd like to call the shop.'*
'Sure.'

*'**Might I** speak to Mrs Lutterworth?' said Willow.*
'I am not sure that she's in. Who is it who wants her?'
'My name is Woodruffe, Cressida Woodruffe. I'm a writer and I'm doing some research for a novel about an architect.'

→ 539 **Glossary** for any unfamiliar terms

Negative forms of *can, must* and *may* in prohibitions 415c

Prohibiting or forbidding something may be realised with *can't, mustn't* or (more formally) *may not*:

[speaker A is talking about learning how to use a computer]
A: *I'm finding it fascinating, cos, like I say, I knew nothing about computers. I've played on games consoles but that's it. I knew nothing about it. But of course, these computers, they tell you everything, you know, they're totally idiot-proof. You know, 'No,* ***you can't*** *do that! Press something else!' you know. So I like that. You see it's teaching me as I'm going along.*
B: *Mm.*

The + sign indicates an interrupted turn which continues at the next + sign
[friends chatting]
A: *Everybody says every time you pass the railwaymen on the track+*
B: *They're not doing anything.*
A: *+they're standing there.*
B: *Right.*
A: *Because when the train is passing* ***they can't*** *be doing anything.*
C: *They can't, no. That's right. Yeah.*
A: *Cos the law says they've got to stand in the tunnel.*
D: *But everyone always says 'looking at them they never do any work. Look at them all chatting'.* [laughs]
A: ***You mustn't*** *be within eight foot of the train.*
B: *Ah.*

[in the classroom: teacher (A) and young pupils]
A: *Now, this is what you can do if you want to. You may do some maths if you want to. You may do your language work if you want to. If you don't want to do either of those things and you are keen on writing a story, you may write a story.*
B: *Miss, I've written a story.*
A: *Right.* [to another pupil] *No* ***you may not*** *draw a picture. This has got to do with work.*

Negative forms of *shall* and *will* in prohibitions 415d

Shall not occurs in very formal/literary contexts in acts of forbidding or prohibition. It is rare in such acts:

*'****He shall*** *not go,' she said slowly, one word at a time. 'Do you hear me? Cromwell is not going to the front.'*
'He has to. He is an officer of the King, he must do as he is ordered.'

Will not is also very formal. It is more frequent than *shall not*:

Then the judge folded his arms and began to speak rapidly, staring down at Frank. 'I hereby grant the exclusion order, in the name of Frank Little and Eleanor Little. You will give an undertaking to leave the jurisdiction within seventy-two hours. ***You will not*** *return to the jurisdiction for a period of three months. Thereafter* ***you will not*** *return to the jurisdiction without prior notification to the Ministerio del Interior in writing. You will surrender your visa to the clerk of the court immediately.* ***You will not*** *approach any embassy, consulate or honorary consulate of the Popular Republic of Nicaragua for the purpose of obtaining a visa for a period of three months.'*

Would you mind and *do you mind* 415e

Would you mind and *do you mind* are most commonly followed by *if* when permission is being requested. With *would you mind* the tense in the *if*-clause may be past (more formal) or present (more informal):

A: ***Do you mind if*** *I take my shoes off?*
B: *No.*

Would you mind if *one of our representatives comes and gives you a free demonstration?*

[referring to the tape-recorder being used to record the conversation]
Would you mind if *I* ***turned*** *this off just for a few minutes?*

Note that the appropriate reply to give permission is *no*, not *yes*. *Mind* means 'object', so saying *no* means 'I do not object to what you wish to do'.

A: *Do you mind if I sit here?*
B: ***No, not at all.*** *Please do.*

Less frequently, an object pronoun or noun phrase and a verb in the *-ing* form may follow *mind*:

Would you mind *us com**ing** too?*

Do you mind *me sitt**ing** in on the interview?*

Do you mind *this towel be**ing** used?*

In formal contexts, a possessive pronoun may be used instead of an object pronoun:

*'**Do you mind** my smok**ing**?' he asked. 'Oh, not at all, sir.'*

The *do*-construction with object pronoun and *-ing* form may be used to check that something is permitted or acceptable which is already happening or has already happened:

Do you mind me *com**ing** round?*
(could be spoken when the person is already at the place referred to)

→ **539 Glossary** for any unfamiliar terms

Turn-taking and asking for permission to speak 415f

A very frequent context for asking for permission or leave to do something in conversation is connected with turn-taking (asking if one can speak, asking a question, mentioning something, commenting on something, etc.). Very often, asking 'permission' to speak is a mere formality and the speaker speaks anyway. The request for leave to speak simply acts as a preface or softener to the taking of the turn by the speaker, or an apology for interrupting, etc. This is particularly so in more formal contexts such as meetings and interviews. *Can, could, may* and *might* often occur in these contexts:

[journalists' production meeting]
A: *Erm **can I ask a question.** With Susan's package is it possible to have a news clip as well? Cos it's in the morning.*
B: *Okay. Yeah. Yeah. Don't see why not. Yeah.*
A: *Lovely.*
B: *Okay.*

[formal meeting]
A: *I think it would have to be some time this week.*
B: *Yes. Right.*
C: *Chairman, **could I also mention** that the county council has a conference centre down in Redwood, which I think is probably bigger than this particular room, and may well also have catering facilities.*

[final question in a semi-formal research interview]
A: *And erm **may I ask** who lives in the house with you?*
B: *Yes. My husband and my youngest son.*
A: *Right. Right. Thank you. Right.*
B: *So my other sons are all away in various parts of the country.*
A: *Right. Well thank you very much indeed for talking to me about this.*
B: *Pleasure. Pleasure. Yes.*

Might I is also used to ask leave to speak or just as a preface to taking the speaking turn, but it is rare and sounds rather formal or dated:

[speaker B is an elderly speaker]
A: *His mother was a character but ... she was not nice. Not nice but she had a strong character.*
B: *Mm. This reminds me.*
A: *Mm?*
B: ***Might I just say this**, darling, 'cos I've just remembered. I'll forget. We have a video of the last programme of the Churchill series which a friend in London very kindly made for us because we were out with her mother and couldn't see it.*
A: *Mm.*

REQUESTS 416

Requests are speech acts where the speaker desires a particular course of action from the listener, but where, unlike commands, the listener has a far greater choice whether to act in the way indicated. Requests and commands occasionally overlap, as a command may be softened by making it seem more like a request.

Interrogatives with *can, could, will* and *would* 416a

Interrogatives with *can*, *could*, *will* and *would* are very common in requests. *Could* is generally heard as more polite than *can*, and *would* is heard as more polite than *will*:

A: ***Can you*** *do a receipt in the name of Mrs M.A. Peters, please?*
B: *What name?*
A: *Mrs M.A. Peters.*
B: [writes]

[in a car; passenger to driver]
A: ***Can you*** *drop me off at the garage on Long Road?*
B: *Yeah, sure.*

The + sign indicates an interrupted turn which continues at the next + sign
[on the phone]
A: *Before you move on+*
B: *Yeah?*
A: *+is my watch anywhere in your house?*
B: *Er, I haven't seen it but I haven't really looked for it.*
A: ***Could you*** *have a look?*
B: *What, now?*
A: *Well er where are you speaking?*
B: *In the kitchen.*
A: *Are you on your mobile?*
B: *Yeah.*
A: ***Can you*** *go and see whether it's in those jeans?*
B: *Ah, jeans. Where are they then?*
A: *They're hanging up on the rail.*
B: *Oh okay.*

A: ***Will you*** *get me a glass of water?*
B: *Yeah.*
A: *Thanks.*

[talking of a 'haunted' house]
The thing is, right, this woman had lived there before us called Sue and she lived there for eight years. And she said that the best way to control the ghost was to talk to it and just say 'Look. Look. ***Would you*** *please be quiet, I'm trying to sleep.'*

Negative declaratives with *couldn't* and *wouldn't* 416b

You couldn't and *you wouldn't* occur in polite requests, often followed by an affirmative tag. These forms often suggest a request that is non-routine in the context:

A: *Erm,* ***you couldn't*** *find a copy of 'Hamlet',* ***could you****, Ann?*
B: *Mm?*
A: *Oh sorry. Oh there's one, look. I can see it.*
(compare: 'Could you find a copy …', which would probably be heard as a more routine request)

[speakers are trying to calculate bank interest on a sum of money]
A: *It doesn't tell you how you calculate it.* ***You wouldn't*** *ring Roland and ask?*
B: *Yeah.*

→ **539 Glossary** for any unfamiliar terms

Declaratives with *might* 416c

The declarative use of *might* in requests occurs in formal styles, but is rare in everyday conversation:

> *Tim decided to keep up the pressure. '**You might** tell me what this son of yours is like. I mean, does he look like a Waites? Or does he take after his mother?'*

Would you like to 416d

Would you like to is also used to request someone to do something. It is less forceful than *will you* or *would you*:

> [adult carer to child]
> A: *Have you finished? What did you have in there?*
> B: *Juice.*
> A: *Juice. Not fizzy juice.*
> B: *No.*
> A: *All right darling just leave it there. You're not allowed to leave anything on the table either. There. **Would you like to** go and play with your toys now? Right, you can eat those bits and no more. And then you go and play with your toys.*

Want 416e

Want in the interrogative occurs occasionally in polite directives or requests. It is frequently followed by *just*, which softens the directive:

> [speakers are assembling a piece of flat-pack furniture]
> A: ***Do you want** to **just** bang gently on this side here.*
> B: *There?*
> A: *Yeah.* [B hammers lightly on the furniture] *That's it.*

Would you mind and *do you mind* 416f

Would you mind and *do you mind* are used in polite requests. Most occurrences of *would you mind* in conversation are in requests:

> [A and family are eating on their terrace; B, a guest, arrives]
> A: ***Would you mind** eating out here with us?*
> B: ***No**, good heavens, **no**.*

> ***Do you mind** speaking up, cos we can't hear you.*

Note how speaker B answers *no*, not *yes* in the first example. This is the normal, polite answer to requests with *mind* (*to mind* means 'to object', thus: No, I have no objection to, or problem with, your request.). → 415e above

Note the use of the *-ing* form, not the infinitive:

> ***Would you mind moving** your car?*
> (~~Would you mind to move your car?~~)

A–Z 53 *Mind*

MODALITY AND COMMISSIVES (OFFERS, INVITATIONS, PROMISES) 417

Commissives are speech acts where the speaker commits to a course of action; they are typically associated with offering, inviting, promising, etc.

In sections **418–420**, we look at the way modal verbs are used to realise such acts.

OFFERS 418

Offers are speech acts in which the speaker volunteers to do something beneficial for the listener (or a third party) or give something to the listener (or a third party). The listener may accept or reject the offer. Offers may be offers to do something or offers of physical things (e.g. food, drink).

Declaratives with *can* and *could* 418a

Can and *could* in declarative form may be used to make offers:

A: *Do you know Liverpool Airport at all?*
B: *Never been.*
A: *No? **I can** get directions for you. That's not a problem.*
B: *Right.*

A: *I was just wondering if I set my alarm and get up …*
B: ***I could** wake you up at eight if you wanted.*
A: *I was thinking if you were coming in at, like, about half ten or something, you could make sure I was up by then. But I think eight's a little, a bit excessive.*

Interrogatives with *can*, *could* and *may* 418b

Can, *could* and *may* also occur in interrogative form in offers. *Could* is more polite and indirect than *can*, and *may* is the most polite/indirect:

A: ***Can I** get you a cold drink?*
B: *That would be nice, thanks.*

A: *Jim's arriving at six and I'm waiting for a call from Janet.*
B: ***Could one of us** pick him up for you?*
A: *Well, that'd be very kind of you.*
B: *Mm. No problem.*

***May I** get you something? A coffee perhaps?*

Declaratives with *'ll* 418c

Declaratives with *'ll* are commonly used in offers to do something. A tag with *shall I/will I* may accompany the offer:

[in a coffee bar, speaker B is about to go to the counter to buy drinks]
A: ***I'll** come and give you a hand, **shall I**?*
B: *Yeah.*

A: *Sorry, what was the number?*
B: *You don't know the number?* ***I'll** check it now for you.*
A: *Oh right. Thanks.*

✪ Note the use of *I'll check it now for you*, not ~~*I check it now for you*~~. The present simple form is not used to offer to do something.

The contraction *I'll/we'll* is different from *I will/we will* or *I shall/we shall*. The full forms with *will* and *shall* are not normally used to make offers. They usually express a declaration or decision that the speaker has decided or is determined or is promising to do something, and are more common in rather formal contexts:

I fear I am too old for you, but believe me ***I will** take more care of you than would many a man of your own age.* ***I will** protect and cherish you with all my strength –* ***I will** indeed!*

***I shall** introduce her, of course, very particularly to my brother and sister when they come to us. I am sure they will like her extremely.*

Offers involving a third party may be made using *'ll* (or the full form *will*):

[speaker B is carrying a heavy suitcase]
A: ***Nick'll** carry that for you.*
B: *Oh thanks.*

Interrogatives with *shall* and *will* 418d

Shall I is frequently used when the speaker is offering to do something or suggesting a course of action involving the speaker:

A: ***Shall I** make you a drink, would you like a tea or coffee?*
B: *Erm, black coffee please.*
A: *Black coffee.*
B: *No milk no sugar. That'd be wonderful.*
A: *Right.*

[adult to children]
A: *All right. Let's read a story. How should we do it?* ***Shall I** sit in the middle of you? Yeah?* ***Shall I** sit in between you so you can both look at the story together? Is that all right?* ***How about if I** sit in between you?*
B: *Mm.*
(note here also: *How about if* ..., which is also used for making suggestions. → 421a ***What about, what if, how about*** below)

***Shall we** eat out tonight?*

Will I is used in several British and Irish English dialects (ones where *shall* is rarely used, e.g. Scottish, Welsh) in offers to do something:

[friends together in an informal group]
A: ***Will I** take a group photograph?*
B: *No. It won't come out.* [laughter]
A: *Oh, I think I should yeah.*
C: *Yeah.*

Do you want, will you have and *would you like* 418e

Do you want, will you have and *would you like* are all used to offer physical things, especially food and drink. *Will you have* is more polite than *do you want*, and *would you like is* the most polite:

A: *Jake, **do you want** some fruit or anything now? Have some fruit, have a banana or a tangerine or something. Jake, what **would you like**? Apple? **Would you like** a banana?*
B: *Yes please.*

A: ***Would you like** some soup?*
B: *Mm, please.*

A: ***Will you have** a cup of coffee?*
B: *No thanks, no I'm alright.*

Would you like to can also be used in a way which involves the speaker more directly in an offer to do something, by adding a first person pronoun:

[customer (A) and travel agent (B)]
A: *Is there the child's discount for that one?*
B: ***Would you like me to** check on a full costing for you now?*
A: *Yes please.*
(compare: Shall I check on a full costing?/Would you like a full costing?)

Negative *don't you want, wouldn't you like* and *won't you have* 418f

The negative forms, *don't you want, wouldn't you like* and *won't you have* also occur in the context of offering things, but far less frequently than their affirmative forms. They occur mostly when the speaker thinks the listener does not want something or may be holding back (perhaps out of politeness) from accepting something:

[at the dinner table; speaker A is the hostess, B is a guest]
A: *Want some water? **Don't you want** any bread?*
B: *No, thanks.*

Won't you have also occurs in more formal contexts to make polite offers, again particularly in contexts of food and drink:

*An hour later, one of the veterans brought in a simmering samovar and a teapot. 'Maksim Maksimych,' I called from the window, '**won't you have** some tea?'*
'Thanks, I don't want any particularly'.

INVITATIONS 419

Invitations are concerned with offering someone an opportunity to do or share something (usually pleasurable) with the speaker. The listener may accept or reject the invitation.

Would you like to 419a

Would you like to is often used to give invitations:

Katrina looked at him. 'I've got the tickets. You've met Gloria and Sophie, they're coming. ***Would you like to*** *come too?' The opera? He had never been. Opera had never appealed to him.*

A: ***Would you like to*** *come to dinner on Friday night?*
B: *Oh, I'd love to, yeah.*
(note the typical polite/friendly reply with *love to*)

Do you want to 419b

Do you want to is also used for invitations. It is less formal than *would you like to*:

[A and B are discussing plays which are on at London theatres; '*Antony and Cleopatra*' is a play by Shakespeare]
A: *And when's 'Antony and Cleopatra'? Monday?*
B: *We're going Monday.*
A: *Excellent.*
B: ***Do you want to*** *come?*
A: *I can't cos of work.*

You must and you'll have to 419c

You must and *you'll have to* are often used to give non-specific invitations:

A: *And* ***you must*** *come down to Barr at some stage or another.*
B: *It would be nice actually. I'd like to.*
A: *You know, for a weekend.*
B: *It would be good.*
A: *Or even a day or two.*
B: *Yeah. Yeah. I might do that.*
A: *You know. You should.*
B: *Yeah.*
A: *Just give me a ring, cos I won't mind.*
B: *Yeah.*
A: *Go out for dinner or something as well.*
B: *Perfect. That's great. Yeah.*
(note the typical friendly, positive reply to a non-specific invitation: *it would be nice/good*)

A: ***You'll have to*** *come round for a coffee.*
B: *Yeah.*

PROMISES, UNDERTAKINGS 420

Promises and undertakings are concerned with committing oneself to a particular course of action which the listener usually believes will happen. If the course of action is not followed, it will constitute a breaking of the promise.

Will, shall and *'ll* 420a

Promises and undertakings are most commonly realised by *'ll* and *will*:

*Can you lend me twenty pounds? **I'll** pay you back when I get to the bank.*

[speakers are deciding what to give family members as birthday presents]
A: *I haven't thought of anything for Raymond actually.*
B: *He's a bit complicated.*
A: ***I'll** give him fifty pounds towards his computer.*

*So see you Thursday. Don't worry, I **will** be there.*

Very rarely, *shall* occurs with *you*, but only in contexts such as promises and warnings, and only in very formal contexts:

*'When the war's over, **you shall** have clean water,' Esther promised.*

The present simple form is not used to make promises and undertakings. This includes clauses which are the object of speech act verbs such as *guarantee*, *promise*, *undertake*:

***I'll** give you a call about seven o'clock.*
(~~I give you a call about seven o'clock.~~)

[teacher in a computer class addressing pupils]
*Apologies to those of you working on spreadsheets. I haven't managed to mark any of your work as yet but **I promise I'll** have it back to you by next week.*
(~~I promise I have it back to you by next week.~~)

The speech act verbs (*guarantee*, *promise*, etc.) are in the present simple in such contexts.

NON-MODAL EXPRESSIONS AND SPEECH ACTS 421

What about, what if, how about 421a

What about, *what if* and *how about* may all be used to make suggestions or give advice or make offers. They are common in everyday conversation:

*A lot of people went to the meeting and said, 'Why don't you, if you're going to have all these extra concerts and it's going to allow seven more thousand people into the ground, **what about** putting double glazing in cos of the noise?' And they wouldn't.*
(suggestion)

[deciding where to place the cooker in a new kitchen]
A: *It's going to become a little bit dangerous here.*
B: [indicating a different place] *Yeah well **what if** we had it here?*
A: *Er, well, yeah.*
(suggestion)

[house guest to host just before dinner]
A: ***What if*** *I set the table?*
B: *Oh, thanks, yes, that'd be nice.*
(offer)

[informal student meeting: deciding times to meet again]
A: *I'm available at eleven but if it goes on past, like, twelve, I've got a tutorial at twelve so er …*
B: *No it wouldn't go past twelve.*
A: *Well that's alright then.*
B: *Right.* ***How about*** *Thursday at twelve then?*
C: *We've got a class then.*
D: *Yeah everyone's got …*
B: *Anybody want to do Thursday at nine?*
(suggestion)

In informal contexts, *how's about* occurs as an alternative to *how about*:

A: *I'll fit it around your schedule.*
B: *Oh that's very kind of you.*
A: *Erm* ***how's about*** *kind of half eight-ish?*
B: *Yeah.*
A: *Yeah.*

All three expressions realise other important functions too. *How about* (and to a lesser extent *what about*) is frequently used to invite someone to speak or comment, or to reciprocate a speaking turn. They are also used to raise new topics of conversation or to shift the topic to a different sub-topic:

A: *It was very interesting doing it.*
B: *It was all right was it. Yeah. Yeah. How did everybody else feel?* ***Lucy, how about*** *you?*
C: *Er, well, the same really.*

A: *Are you Norwich born and bred?*
B: *Yeah I am.* ***What about*** *you? Where were you born?*
A: *No I'm from Kent but I've lived in Wales.*

A: *I think there should be stronger government regulations to make the industry reduce the risks to the public because they are admitting there are risks.*
B: *Right.*
A: *So there should be some. That's my point of view.*
B: *But* ***how about*** *the argument that industry knows its operations better than anyone else?*

What if is also used to hypothesise or to imagine possible situations:

[friends chatting, dreaming of winning the national lottery]
A: *What do you think is a reasonable amount that you'd like to win?*
B: *A couple of million.*
C: *Enough to do you till you die.* [laughs]
A: *Planning ahead are we?* [laughs]
B: *Well that's a good amount* [laughs] *isn't it.*
A: *Mm.*
B: *But* ***what if*** *you have a short life?*
C: *Then you write a big will.* [laughs]

Why don't and *why not* 421b

Why don't

Most occurrences of *why don't* are concerned with making suggestions. Other less frequent uses include asking for reasons and issuing invitations and directives:

[friends talking about a university course which has a language-learning requirement; *TEFL* here means a qualification in teaching English as a foreign language]
A: *If I do it over two years, then I'll have to learn Russian. I'll have to do Russian.*
B: *You know, you did the English stuff,* ***why don't you*** *go and teach English in Russia. I've seen loads of jobs in the newspaper and some of them you don't need TEFL for.*
A: *Yeah. I could do.*
(suggestion)

The + sign indicates an interrupted turn which continues at the next utterance.
[discussing the best time to go away for a holiday]
A: *We would have that cottage which was right on the beach. So I mean we were thinking of going next weekend but it's+*
B: *Really?*
A: *+it's just the problem of this work thing. He goes to Brazil next Tuesday. So if I took off like the Monday, Tuesday, I wouldn't know what was going on.*
B: *Well* ***why don't you*** *wait until February or March.*
A: *Well, we're waiting now till Barney gets back cos he rang us the other day. He's coming back.*
B: *Oh Barney.*
A: *Yeah he's coming back for just a few weeks.*
B: *Oh great.*
(suggestion)

[speaker A is a university academic; B is an ex-student who is looking for occasional work]
A: *I could give you jobs to do in the library for me and you could save me hours and hours of work.*
B: *I'd really like to be still doing stuff like that actually. Cos I really miss that.*
A: *Well **why don't you** come up some time.*
B: *Well I will, yes.*
C: *That's a marvellous idea.*
B: *Yeah.*
A: *Come up in the spring when it's at its loveliest.*
(invitation)

***Why don't you** just shut up for a moment and listen to me!*
(directive)

Why don't in making suggestions is also followed frequently by *I* and *we*, and, less frequently, by references to third parties:

***Why don't I** make us a nice cup of tea. We'll all feel better then.*

A: *Yeah. Well, look, use your lunch hour to find your way around.*
B: *By the time I've found my way around the place I'll be starving and my lunch hour will be gone.*
A: *Well **why don't I** make you lunch then. I'll make you some sandwiches then.*
B: *We could use that meat.*
A: *Yeah.*
B: *Yeah.*

A: *So I said to Sarah **why don't we** come to New York with you for your first week?*
B: *Sounds good.*
A: *I think that's what we're going to do.*
B: *Mm. Oh well that'll be all right won't it?*
A: *Yeah.*

[speaking on the phone]
*You'd think it'd be cheaper to get a little van. ... Oh. ... Well wouldn't it be worth suggesting to Gary at some stage **why don't they** get a small van so ... Oh right. Mm still seems stupid.*

Why not

Why not is also used to make suggestions. It differs from *why don't you* in that the suggestion is often a more general one, not necessarily directly aimed at the listener. It is common in advertising and promotional contexts, where the addressee is non-specific:

[local radio programme: promoting educational training courses]
*If this is you and you'd like to get back into education and get on a course **why not** go along to Fast Forward. They can help you with your training needs your child care and your travel and they can also provide the support you need if you're not confident about going back to learning.*

[public meeting to decide how best to run a local theatre and to encourage more people to go to it]

A: *Here's a simple suggestion.* ***Why don't you*** *move the facilities from the stage door club down to the foyer bar so that a load of people can go in there. You'd change the general atmosphere of the foyer bar.*

B: *Yeah. Simple. Ambience.*

A: *I think there's nothing, Chairman, that £150,000 wouldn't do.*

B: *Well,* ***why not*** *go outside for funding? So, marketing exercise once again.*

Although *why don't you* can be used to ask a question, *why not* is not normally used to ask a question:

[B has been talking about cooking and how he never uses salt]

A: ***Why don't you*** *use salt?*

B: *Well, they say it's bad for your heart.*

(a genuine question as to why B chooses not to use salt)

Why not *use salt?*

(normally heard as a suggestion)

SPEECH ACT VERBS (*AGREE, INSIST, PROMISE*) 422

Speech act verbs are verbs which a speaker can use to explicitly label a speech act. These include verbs such as *advise, allow, apologise, ask, demand, deny, (dis)agree, forbid, insist, object, order, permit, predict, promise, state, suggest.*

Performative verbs 422a

When these verbs are used to perform the speech act (i.e. in their performative function), they occur with a first person subject and present simple tense form:

I ***name*** *this ship 'Fearless'.*

(~~*I am naming this ship 'Fearless'.*~~)

A: *You're a bit late.*

B: *I* ***apologise****.*

Many of the common functions associated with the modal verbs can also be realised by explicit use of speech act verbs. Speech act verbs are more frequent in formal contexts:

'Just what are you going to do about this?' Pearson yelled at them. ***'I demand*** *you arrest them all.'*

(compare: Arrest them all!/You must arrest them all.)

[speakers are cleaning out a cupboard]

A: *Er,* ***I suggest*** *we take everything out and just look at it, decide whether we want it. And if we really don't want it then just chuck it if we don't know.*

B: *Okay. But we've got a bit of a space problem.*

A: *That's true.*

(compare: We could/should take everything out./How/what about taking/what if we take everything out.)

[meringues are a type of sweet confectionery]
Now who's for more tea? ***I insist*** *on you sampling some of Bessie's meringues.*
(compare: You must sample some of Bessie's meringues.)

As soon as she comes back, ***I promise*** *I'll ask her.*
(compare: As soon as she comes back, I'll ask her.)

A speech act verb may not necessarily correspond one-to-one with the speech act being performed. For example, verbs such as *suggest* and *promise* can be used to issue directives. The exact interpretation depends on context:

I promise *you you'll regret it later if you don't study now.*
(I warn you that you'll regret it)

Speech act verbs and politeness 422b

In general, in conversation, in situations where threats to the listener's dignity and self-esteem are high, speakers avoid explicit labelling of speech acts. Verbs such as *disagree, forbid, refuse, reproach, accuse* in unmodified form are rare as performative speech act verbs; most typically they occur to report speech acts, or are softened and modified in some way. For instance, the clause *I disagree with you* only occurs once (in a formal discussion at a meeting) in a 15-million-word sample of spoken English.

Examples with *disagree* show how speakers are careful to avoid direct challenges to the listener's face. Many utterances express disagreement with a non-present third party, or with a proposition or argument, thereby making the act of disagreement more impersonal. Others downtone or hedge the disagreement:

I would disagree *a huge amount.*
(use of modal verb as hedge)

Well I completely ***disagree with that****.*
(disagreeing with an idea or proposition rather than with the speaker)

But what I ***disagree with, well to a degree****, is that at school they don't teach them the basics any more.*
(downtoning the disagreement)

I, I would have to, I'd have to disagree *with my colleague here.*
(modal verb hedge plus suggestion of the act not being the speaker's preferred response)

I hate to disagree *with you, Peter.*
(expressing reluctance at having to disagree)

These same principles of modification apply to other speech act verbs (e.g. *I* ***hate to complain****, but …; I* ***would ask*** *you to make less noise; I'm sorry but I* ***have to object*** *to what you're proposing; I* ***regret to inform*** *you that …; I* ***must admit*** *that …; I* ***would insist*** *that …*).

Reporting verbs 422c

Speech act verbs are frequent in reports of speech acts. They may be more neutral reporting acts involving verbs such as *say*, *tell*, *ask*, or more evaluative reports involving verbs such as *complain*, *moan*, *mumble*:

'You all right, Crom?'
'Ooh, God, of course I'm not all right,' he ***moaned****. 'I've never felt so ill in my life. I think I'm going to die.'*

'... by the time he realises he's walked into a trap, it'll be too late for him to do anything about it.'
'I only wish I could be there to see it,' Dennison ***sneered****, and watched Amaya cross to the door.*

→ also **489 Reporting verbs** and **499 Reporting verbs and speech acts**

POLITENESS 423

Many of the examples of speech acts in sections 413–421 have displayed aspects of politeness and indirectness (e.g. *would you mind ... -ing*), while others are more forceful and direct (e.g. imperatives).

Politeness serves to protect the self-esteem and dignity of the speaker and listener, and to prevent speakers imposing on listeners or forcing them to act against their will. It is an important aspect of interpersonal meaning, and enables communication to proceed harmoniously.

Modal verbs often hedge or soften the force of a speech act which may threaten the listener's dignity or self-esteem. Past forms such as *could* instead of *can*, or *would* instead of *will*, or *might* instead of *may*, or *wanted* instead of *want*, can also soften speech acts and contribute to politeness. In sections 423a–423e we summarise the use of tense and aspect for politeness and also consider some other forms which soften or hedge speech acts.

Tense and aspect 423a

Past tense

Past tense forms can make a speech act more polite:

A: ***I wondered*** *if you****'d*** *help me out in the garden, perhaps, like, if it's still nice when you come home from school?*
B: *Yeah.*
(compare the more direct: I wonder if you will help me ...)

A: *How* ***did you want*** *to pay?*
B: *I'll pay cash.*
(compare the more direct: How do you want to pay?)

[store assistant taking customer's personal details to order goods]
What ***was*** *the name and address please?*

Progressive aspect

Progressive aspect can also contribute to soften the directness of a speech act, and may combine with past tense to make an utterance doubly hedged:

A: *Anybody here?*
B: *Mary. But no Sandra no Lisa. Not yet anyhow.*
A: ***I was hoping** Sandra's not in cos Roger says to me when he went, you know, he was standing there, he says to me, 'It'll have to be Thursday at half past ten.' Well Sandra says that she couldn't make it half past ten Thursday, so he had to come yesterday. So **I'm wondering** if either of them are here. Or if Sandra's here. Mind you, it's more likely to be Sandra than Lisa cos Lisa's usually here at half seven.*
B: *I was going to say, the blinds were still closed and I didn't see Sandra's car at all.*

Perfect aspect

Perfect aspect may also occur in a softening/hedging function:

A: ***I've been wanting** to ask you if you'd help me write a research proposal.*
B: *Sure. No problem.*

[at a formal meeting]
A: *The first thing I want to do is just obviously say thanks for filling in all those exercises you did for me, the sorting things. And I say we had all the others through in the post. So your second one will probably be waiting for me when I get back Margaret. And thanks for bringing the other ones back today. I just wanted to get your impressions, how you'd found doing the two exercises. Erm, **had you found** them okay to do? Or?*
B: *Yeah. Interesting.*
A: *They were okay, were they?*
C: *Yeah.*
(compare: Did you find them okay to do?)

Negation 423b

Boosting

Negative (most typically interrogative) forms can often boost a speech act (make it more forceful) and say that the speaker thinks the listener really should act in a particular way:

*My son said, 'I don't think she's very well daddy. I think she's, she's ill, **don't you think you should** go in and see what's happening?' I said, 'No, I, I don't think so, I think her husband will take care of that.'*
(compare: Do you think you should go in ...)

***Can't you** turn that music down!*

Hedging/downtoning

Negation can also have the opposite effect to boosting, i.e. it can hedge or downtone a speech act. This occurs in a number of formulaic declarative structures with verbs such as *have, know, suppose*:

A: ***You don't have*** *Jane Carey's email address by any chance?*
B: *Yeah, sure.*

The + sign indicates an interrupted turn which continues at the next utterance
A: ***I don't suppose*** *you've brought the saw back?*
B: *Have I still got it?*
A: *Yes.*
B: *Oh yeah I took it last weekend.*
A: *You borrowed it and brought it back+*
B: *Yeah yeah.*
A: *+and then you took it again.*

You don't know *what time the shop opens, do you?*

Other syntactic features of politeness 423c

In many of the examples in sections 413–421, speakers make their speech acts more polite by using a variety of prefaces and other devices. Speech acts such as questions, requests, invitations, suggestions, can be softened or made more polite by using reporting structures:

Hope, think, wonder, to soften questions

Reporting structures with *hope, think* and *wonder* are commonly used to soften questions and requests:

I was hoping *I could speak to Roger.*
(this seems to be a way of enquiring if Roger is in)

[*Michael* is a small child]
A: *Deana,* **do you think** *you could watch Michael please?*
B: *Yes.*
(compare: Deana, could you …?)

I'm wondering *if either of them are here.*
(the speaker is asking: Are either of them here?)

Modal expression + *ask* to soften commands, requests and questions

A modal expression + *ask* is used to soften a request or question. *Ask* is not used in this way without a modal or hedging expression:

A: ***Can I ask*** *you to sign that and then the banker's order.*
B: *Yes.* [signs]
(~~I ask you to sign that …~~)

A: *Mrs Smith,* **could I ask** *for your date of birth as well please.*
B: *Yes, twenty-three, seven, forty-five.*
A: *And your occupation?*
B: *Housewife.*

Prefaces to speech acts 423d

Speakers often delay or preface the performing of a speech act. A lead-in remark or question (a preface) may occur before the speech act itself. This is particularly so in the case of speech acts which impose on the listener or possibly put the listener in the position of having to refuse, etc., such as invitations, requests, advice, commands.

Speakers also use a wide variety of expressions to hedge or soften speech acts. These include modifiers such as *a bit*, the use of *if*, the use of informal lexis (e.g. *pop in* instead of *visit/call on*, *a wee favour* instead of *a (small) favour*), adverbs such as *ideally*, *possibly*, *maybe*, *just*, the *-ish* suffix, and a range of fixed expressions such as *let's say*, *perhaps you could see your way to …*, *if it's/that's okay with you*, *if you like*, *if it's all the same with you*, *sorry to bother you*:

A: ***Are you doing anything Sunday?***
B: *No.*
A: *I **might pop in** on Sunday with the boys **if that suits you**?*
B: *Yes. Yes.*
(note the preface: the listener is given the chance to say she is busy before the speaker suggests she will visit her; note also the softener *might*, the informal verb *pop in*, which suggests a brief, unimposing, informal visit, and *if that suits you*)

[beginning a phone call; *fire away* means 'start talking']
A: ***Is this a good time to talk?***
B: *Yes, fine, no problem. Fire away.*

A: *Are you free **a bit** later on this afternoon, **probably around about** threeish **possibly**? No, erm any time any other time later on today? No? What about early**ish** on Monday. I'm free early**ish** on Monday. **What about, is it a big hassle** you getting in for nine?*
B: *No.*
A: *No, okay.*
(note how speaker A negotiates his way gradually towards the potentially imposing request to B to come in at 9am on Monday morning; note the softening effect of the suffix *-ish* and the approximators *a bit*, *around* and *about*, and the use of the hedges *probably* and *possibly*)

*Thursday we're gonna do a major evaluation task with text books you haven't seen before, new ones. Do one of those before Thursday and give it to me then. I'll give you some feedback straightaway. **Ideally if** you could do different ones and we could put them together in a **little** folder and photocopy them, and you're gonna have examples of different types.*

[university tutor (A) to student]
A: *Do you want to **just** come in and start because Claire's cancelled her appointment, **if that's okay with you**?*
B: *Oh that's okay.*

[message on an answerphone]
Hi Louise. It's Rick. ***Sorry to bother you this late****. Erm* ***I was wondering if*** *tomorrow, and if it is portable,* ***whether or not*** *you could bring in that office chair you wanted to give away.*

Please **423e**

Please is used more to soften directives in English than its equivalent in some other languages.

Compare the bare imperatives with their more polite realisations:

Come in.
Please *come in.*

Pass me the phone book.
Pass me the phone book, ***please****.*

Give me a call on the number I've just given you.
Please *give me a call on the number I've just given you.*

In interrogative directives, *please* is most typically used in end position:

[guest has just been served a cup of coffee]
Can I have some sugar, ***please****?*
(preferred to: Please can I have some sugar?)

However, children often use *please* in front position in such contexts:

[child at table]
Please *can I have more bread?*

Please is especially frequent in requests during service encounters in shops, restaurants, etc., and is used by both customers/clients and servers, even though the customer/client may consider themselves more important than the server:

[customer (A) to waiter (B) in a restaurant]
A: *Can I have the bill,* ***please****?*
B: *You want the bill?*
A: *Thank you.*

[renewing an insurance policy over the telephone]
A: *Okay and what's your first initial Mrs Leach?*
B: *G.*
A: *And your occupation* ***please****?*
B: *Housewife.*
A: *And your date of birth* ***please****?*
B: *Twenty four, eleven, forty-nine.*
A: *All right, okay.*

Yes please is often used in response to offers:
A: *Would you like some more coffee?*
B: ***Yes please****.*

→ 539 Glossary for any unfamiliar terms

Questions

Questions

INTRODUCTION 424

Questions are broadly defined as utterances which require a verbal response from the addressee. There are a number of types (→ 425–425e), constructed using a variety of structural patterns (→ 426–432). Some types are more central or prototypical questions, while others are less prototypical and function differently.

Questions may range from forms involving imperatives, to simple interrogatives, interrogatives with modal verbs, indirect interrogatives, declaratives and reduced questions, all of which have different pragmatic functions in terms of formality, politeness, directness, dependence on immediate context, projections of degrees of shared knowledge, etc.

Examples of questions and typical contexts:

Tell me what you want for dinner.
(imperative; informal)

Are you tired?
(simple interrogative; neutral)

Ready?
(reduced question; informal, highly context dependent)

Would you be George, by any chance?
(modalised; polite, low assumption of shared knowledge)

Can I ask if you know what this is?
(question with preface and modal verb; polite)

A: *So you got here early?*
B: *Yes.*
(declarative; high assumption of shared knowledge)

This chapter (424–433) describes the various question types, and the main question forms, starting with the most prototypical ones. It excludes interrogatives functioning as directives, which are dealt with in **413e Interrogatives with *can*, *could*, *will* and *would*** in **Speech acts**.

QUESTION TYPES 425

Five broad structural and functional aspects of questions can be used to characterise the central and more marginal question types. These are:

1. whether the question is a complete clause or not
2. whether it has an interrogative structure
3. whether it elicits a verbal reply
4. whether it elicits information or not
5. whether it elicits new information, not known to the questioner.

Complete and reduced forms 425a

Prototypical questions are complete clauses:

Are you ready?

When are you going to Manchester?

Other types of question may be reduced clauses, phrases, or single words:

A: ***You hungry****?*
B: *Mm, a bit.*

A: *So I'd go to London if I were you.*
B: ***And what about Leeds****?*
A: *Oh hang on. Yeah. Yeah. That would be nearer.*

A: *I'm very nervous.*
B: ***Why****?*
A: *Cos I've never done anything like this before.*

Interrogative form 425b

Prototypical questions have interrogative form:

Do you want one?

Are you nervous?

Would you prefer Spain or Portugal?

What do you want?

Who was looking for me?

→ **292 Interrogative clauses** for the structure of interrogative clauses

Many questions do not have interrogative structure, and may be declarative or imperative in form. Intonation and context indicate that the utterance is to be heard as a question:

A: ***So you like the people round there****?*
B: *Oh yes.*

A: ***Tell me what time you're arriving again****?*
B: *It'll probably be around six, or six-thirty.*

Eliciting a verbal reply 425c

Most questions desire and get a verbal reply from the addressee. However, one type, the rhetorical question, simply raises a question in the recipient's mind or is a question which the asker, not the recipient, answers:

We all know that, statistically, we've got more chance of winning the lottery jackpot than of dying in a plane crash, so ***why is it that the more I fly, the less I want to****? It's not a question of safety.*

Even the National Union of Students, which has vociferously campaigned for free university education, has now formally recognised that student debt is a way of life. At its recent conference it voted in favour of backing a system of loans. ***So who is going to provide those loans in the future?***

Eliciting information 425d

Prototypical questions seek information of some kind from the addressee. However, many questions do not do this. One type which does not is the rhetorical question (→ **149 Imperatives and rhetorical questions**). Another, quite common, type is when what appears to be a question is functioning as a request or command, where a response in the form of action is required rather than an informative reply:

Denise, could you pass me my chocolate?
(Denise reacts by passing it; she does not say 'Yes, I could')

Will you stop messing about?

→ **408–423 Speech Acts**

Exclamatives may also share characteristics of questions (e.g. interrogative structure), but do not necessarily demand any informative reply from the listener:

[opening a present]
I'm going to open it cos I don't know what it is. Costa Rica. Coffee beans are they? Coffee beans. ***Oh isn't that nice!***

→ **410c**

Eliciting new information 425e

Prototypical questions seek information which the asker does not know. Other question types may not do this. Some questions simply seek confirmation of something the speaker already knows:

I got very moody, didn't I?

Display questions (questions to which the questioner already knows the answer) are common in contexts such as classrooms, quiz shows and other tests of knowledge, and media interviews. The purpose of a display question is to put knowledge or information on public display. In the classroom, this is an important way of transmitting and testing knowledge for teachers and pupils/students.

In situations where display questions are used, such as classrooms and quizzes, the questioner follows up the answer by stating whether it is the desired/correct answer or not (in green in the example):

[tutor (A) and students (B, C) in a university law seminar]
A: *Right. Now,* ***what about this reasonableness test? What criteria do the courts take into account?***
B: *What is reasonably expected of the parties at the time they made the contract.*

A: *Well Section Eleven says 'We look at whether it was reasonable to incorporate the term'. So we do look at the time of the contract.* ***But what specific criteria do they take into account?***
B: *Is it, erm, bargaining power?*
A: *They certainly look at bargaining power. There's no doubt.* ***But what else?***
C: *Erm, insurance?*
A: *They look at who's the best insurer.*

In display questions in media interviews (e.g. a TV interview with a politician), the questioner typically does not follow up in this way, and listeners are left to make their own evaluation of the answer.

YES-NO QUESTIONS 426

Yes-no questions are one of the most common question forms. The reply either affirms or negates the proposition of the question. The reply may simply be *yes* or *no*, or *yes/no* plus some sort of elaboration, or simply an implied *yes* or *no*. Variants of *yes* and *no* in informal spoken language include *yeah*, *mm*, *okay*, *yep*, and *nah*, *nope*:

A: *Is that all right?*
B: ***Yeah.***
A: *Are you sure?*
B: ***Yes.***

A: *Are there any shops nearby?*
B: ***Yes.*** *Shops,* ***yes.*** *The village centre is about a hundred metres away I should say. And there's a shop across the road as well.*

[in a camera shop; *a cable release* is a cable which enables the camera to be operated from a distance]
A: *I've got a Nikon F70 and I wanted a cable release for it.*
B: *Erm, is it the remote one?*
A: ***Mm.*** *Believe so.*

A: *There's a nice yachting centre at West Ranby.*
B: *Oh is there?*
A: ***Yep, yep.***

A: *Would you like to hear the CD?*
B: ***Okay.***

A: *Can you remember which company it was?*
B: ***No.***

[trying to identify a travel brochure]
A: *Was it a white cover?*
B: ***No, no,*** *it was something like that holiday one there. Brown, and it had holidays to Prague and Vienna, it had holidays to Bulgaria, it was Eastern Europe, I expect.*

A: *Are you coming round for coffee tomorrow?*
B: ***Erm, I'm here on my own.***
A: *Oh are you.*
B: *So I can't get round. Unless you want to call here.*
(implied *no*)

The reply to a *yes-no* question may consist of an affirmative or negative response tag instead of *yes* or *no*:

A: *Did you break it?*
B: ***I did.*** *I pressed the yellow button.*

A: *Did you say 'I told you so?'*
B: ***I didn't. I didn't.*** *A gentleman never does that sort of thing* [laughs].

The reply may contain repeated elements of the question which imply a *yes* or *no*:

A: *Are you rushing about again?*
B: *I'm always rushing about, I really am.*
(implied *yes*)

Yes-no questions in informal conversation may end with *or* ..., which has the effect of reducing any suggestion of pre-judgement of the answer on the part of the asker. This use of *or* ... may be compared to question tags (→ **300** and **431**):

A: *Did you go into hospital immediately* ***or*** *...?*
B: *I did.*

A: *Did you reply to the letter when you got it at all* ***or*** *...?*
B: *No.*

→ **292a** for the structure of *yes-no* questions

Phonetic reduction and ellipsis in *yes-no* questions 426a

Phonetic reduction of *do* and *did* may occur in informal speech:

D'you *want a biscuit?*
(/dʒuː/ = do you)

D'you *get home all right last night?*
(/dʒuː/ = did you)

Often, especially in informal spoken contexts, it is not necessary to include all the clause elements in the question: subjects and auxiliary verbs, or lexical verb *be*, may not need to be present as references will be obvious to the speaker and listener(s):

A: ***You want*** *some more bread, Nick?*
B: *Yes please.*
(without auxiliary *do*)

[teacher, to students]
There should be three sheets coming down. You should have three by the time you've finished. Okay. ***Everybody got*** *three sheets?*
(without auxiliary *has*)

Finished*?*
(without auxiliary *have* or subject *you*)

A: ***Ready****?*
B: *Yeah, in a minute.*
(without lexical verb *be* or subject *you*)

→ **94c Interrogatives with no auxiliary or subject**

→ **429a** on intonation and *yes-no* questions

WH-QUESTIONS 427

Questions with *what, when, where, which, who(m), whose, why, how* request specific information about something, and the circumstances surrounding actions and events (e.g. time, manner, place).

The anticipated response to such questions is not *yes* or *no*, but information which provides the missing content of the *wh*-word:

[discussing a new type of cooking grill]

A: *And* ***what*** *did this machinery cost you?*

B: *Five hundred and fifty pounds.*

A: ***Where*** *is your farm?*

B: *Right at the bottom of the lane.*

Whose *turn is it to wash up?*

How *are you feeling?*

Emphatic *wh*-questions 427a

A *wh*-question may include an emphatic *do*-auxiliary. In speech, the auxiliary is stressed. Such questions often occur in contexts where the asker feels they have not been given information they wanted or expected.

Non-emphatic *wh*-questions do not use auxiliary *do* when the *wh*-word is the subject. Emphatic *wh*-questions involve *do*-auxiliary even when the *wh*-word is the subject of the verb:

Who wants *coffee?*
(non-emphatic)
(~~Who does want coffee?~~)

What did happen *in the end?*
(emphatic)

A: *There was hardly anybody there.*
B: *Oh really?* ***Who did turn up****?*
(emphatic)

Wh-questions involving *what, who, why, when, where* and *how* (but normally not *whom* or *whose*) can also be emphasised by the use of *on earth*, or, even more emphatically, by using *the devil/the hell/the heck/in heaven's name* after the *wh*-word. The latter group should be used with care, and may cause offence, though *the heck* is rather mild and less likely to cause offence:

What on earth *are you doing?*

Oh, ***what the hell*** *does he want?*

Why on earth *did it take so long?*

How the heck *did you come to do that?*

Phonetic reduction and ellipsis in *wh*-questions 427b

Some phonetic reduction of auxiliary *do* may take place in *wh*-questions in informal speech:

Where ***d'you*** *work?*
(/dʒuː/ = do you)

A: *Where* ***d'you*** *buy that?*
B: *In Barcelona.*
(/dʒuː/ = did you)

In informal speech, occasionally, auxiliary verbs may not need to be present where the meaning is obvious:

A: *And Peter goes, like, '****What you*** *talking about?' I thought that was weird.*
B: *Yeah.*
(understood: What are you talking about?)

Where you *going tonight? Anywhere special?*

A *wh*-question may be declarative in form, especially if the speaker is checking information already given or checking on a particular detail:

A: *So what do you do?* ***You kind of arrive at what time****?*
B: *Twelve o'clock or something.*
(compare the more formal: (At) what time do you arrive?)

A: *So you just send it through the post?*
B: *Yeah.*
A: ***And you address it to who****?*
B: *Just the Manager.*
(compare the more formal: And who do you address it to?, or most formal: And to whom do you address it?)

→ **429b** on intonation and *wh*-questions

ALTERNATIVE QUESTIONS 428

Alternative questions give the answerer a choice between two or more items contained in the question which are linked by *or*. Alternative questions may be *yes-no* interrogatives or *wh*-interrogatives:

[waiter to customer, as the customer is about to be shown to a table]
A: *Would you like* ***smoking or non-smoking****?*
B: *Smoking please.*

A: ***How*** *do you want to go to London,* ***by coach or rail or are you driving****?*
B: *Erm, oh, rail would be better.*

An alternative question may offer the recipient the choice of one or all of the alternatives:

A: *Do you want* ***tea or coffee****?*
B: *I'd prefer a cup of coffee thank you.*
A: ***Sugar or milk****?*
B: *Sugar and milk.*
(choose one of tea or coffee/choose sugar, or milk, or both)

Alternative questions are often asked in reduced form in informal speech, with just the alternatives being present:

[A is a swimming instructor, B is a pupil]
A: *Right then, all go and swim whichever stroke you want to swim for two lengths. When the first two get back to the side the next two are gonna do a nice jump in and race. Swim back to the side. Then the next two are gonna jump in.*
B: ***Length or width****?*
A: *Width.*
(*gonna* = informal 'going to')

[waiter to customer in a restaurant]
A: ***Any tea or coffee****?*
B: *Can I have some tea please.*

An alternative question does not normally produce *yes* or *no* as a reply, but *no* can occur to emphatically negate one of the alternatives:

A: *Are you actually somebody who's working at the university* ***or*** *are you a student?*
B: *Oh* ***no****. I'm working there.*
(I'm emphatically not a student)

[talking about a tourist trip to the Grand Canyon in the USA, starting from Las Vegas]
A: *Do they pick you up from Las Vegas* ***or*** *do you drive there?*
B: *Oh* ***no****. You leave from Las Vegas.*
A: *In a helicopter?*
B: *Yeah.*

→ **429c** on intonation and alternative questions

QUESTIONS AND INTONATION 429

Note: the intonation for the examples here may be heard on the accompanying CD.

Yes-no questions 429a

Yes-no questions most typically have a simple rising intonation (↗) or a complex fall-rising intonation (↘↗). Fall-rising intonation projects a greater assumption of a shared perspective and/or that the addressee will agree with the proposition of the question:

A: *There's a bank machine in the other terminal.*
B: *Oh, right.* ***Is it far from here****?*
(open question; no assumption whether it is near or far)

[listening to music]
A: *It's a great CD.*
B: *Yeah.* ***D'you want to borrow it****? I can leave it with you.*
A: *Mm, thanks. Yeah, can I?*
(projecting an assumption that the listener may like to borrow it)

Are you angry with me?
(speaker probably suspects the listener is angry)

Falling intonation can occur with *yes-no* questions, especially when they are follow-up questions in a series of such questions:

A: ***D'you want some soup****?*
B: *No thanks. I'm not very hungry.*
A: ***Would you like some cheese and biscuits****?*
B: *Mm, no, no thanks.*
A: ***D'you want a cup of tea then****?*
B: *Okay. Thanks.*

Wh-questions 429b

Wh-questions most typically have falling intonation:

Well whose fault is it then?

Why do you need to see me?

Wh-questions which seek to check or clarify information already given may have rising or fall-rising intonation:

Who did you say was coming?
(please tell me again)

What was his name again?

Alternative questions 429c

Alternative questions most typically have a rising intonation on each alternative (↗↗), a rise followed by a fall (↗↘), a fall-rise followed by a fall (↘↗↘), or a rise followed by a fall-rise (↗↘↗).

Examples of intonation with alternative questions

type	example	typical context
↗↗	*Could you go and work in France or Italy?*	both alternatives are held up for equal consideration by the speaker, and the answer could be *yes* to both
↗↘	*Was it a CD-ROM or a DVD?*	both alternatives are possible: only one of them can be the right one
↘↗↘	*Are you hungry or do you want to eat later?*	both alternatives are possible: there is a possible assumption that the listener is hungry

Alternative questions with more than two alternatives can have more complex intonation choices:

Would you like tea or coffee or water?
(suggests the listener may choose any of the three or none of the three; could also be three fall-rises)

Do you want a sandwich or a roll or something sweet?
(suggests a contrast between savoury food as a set and sweet food)

DECLARATIVE QUESTIONS 430

Not all *yes-no* questions have interrogative form, and a declarative clause may function in context as a question:

A: ***You're Philip****?*
B: *Yes, that's me.*

The intonation is typically rising (↗) (asking for confirmation) or falling (↘) (strongly assuming something):

B: ***You're busy all day****?*
A: *Yeah.*

A: *So* ***you're going to be here about quarter past****?*
B: *Yeah quarter past, twenty past, yeah.*
A: *That's fine.*

If a listener repeats a speaker's utterance as a request for confirmation, it may have rising intonation and be heard as a question:

A: *I've got her number.*
B: ***You've got her number****?*
A: *Yeah.*

The repeated utterance may also have a falling intonation and be heard as expressing a doubt, which the speaker may also interpret as questioning:

A: *I've got her number.*
B: ***You've got her number**?*
A: *Yeah.*

TAG QUESTIONS 431

A tag after a declarative clause can form a question.

Tag questions are highly interactive in that they may constrain the range of possible or desired responses from the addressee. Some patterns are more constraining than others.

Types of tag question

type	clause + tag polarity	falling tone ↘	falling or rising tone: ↘ or ↗	constrained or desired answer
1	affirm. + neg.	*They've **been** affected by it,*	***haven't** they?*	agreement with *yes* (*Yes, they have.*)
2	affirm. + affirm.	*He's **gone** back,*	***has** he?*	agreement with *yes* (*Yes, he has.*)
3	neg. + affirm.	*She **never talked** to anybody,*	***did** she?*	agreement with *no* (*No, she didn't.*)
4	affirm. + neg.	*You've **worked** hard,*	***haven't** you?*	anticipated agreement with *yes* (*Yes, I have.*) but open to challenge with *no* (*No, I haven't.*)
5	neg. + affirm.	*He **didn't get** it,*	***did** he?*	anticipated agreement with *no* (*No, he didn't.*) but open to challenge with *yes* (*Yes, he did.*)

Types **1** and **2** contain an affirmative statement by the speaker in the main clause, and an expectation of a *yes*-answer as confirmation in the tag.

Type **3** contains a negative statement by the speaker in the main clause, and an expectation of a *no*-answer as confirmation in the tag.

Type **4** contains an affirmative statement by the speaker in the main clause, and a more neutral possibility (i.e. of a *yes*- or a *no*-answer) in the tag.

Type **5** contains a negative statement by the speaker in the main clause, and a more neutral possibility (i.e. of a *yes*- or a *no*-answer) in the tag.

→ **300 Question tags** for a full account of the structures and patterns found in tag questions

→ also **100 Follow-up questions**

ECHO AND CHECKING QUESTIONS 432

Echo questions repeat part of the previous speaker's utterance, usually because some part of it has not been fully understood. They often have declarative word order and a *wh*-word at the end of the clause:

A: *Steve was singing with the group.*
B: ***Who*** *was singing, sorry?* (stressed)
A: *Steve, Steve Jones.*
B: *Oh.*

A: *He's called Oliver.*
B: *He's called* ***what****?*
A: *Oliver.*

A: *The map is in the rucksack.*
B: *In the* ***what****, sorry?*
A: *The rucksack.*

In spoken language, an interrogative-form self-checking question may interrupt an utterance in order to focus on specific information or to show uncertainty or hesitation, or to ask for confirmation:

I was talking to, oh, ***who was it****, that that guy from Edinburgh.*

[travel agent to customer]
Well, I've got you on the flights that you required, i.e. coming back on the, ***what was it****, the twentieth.*

→ also **100 Follow-up questions**

INTERPERSONAL ASPECTS OF QUESTIONS 433

Questions may be very direct and may threaten the dignity or face of the addressee. To avoid such threats and to signal politeness, questions may be prefaced with hedging expressions or other signals of politeness:

Can I ask you *how old Fiona is?*

Could you tell me *where the nearest toilet is?*

[student to university tutor]
I have a question*. Does the word-count for the assignment include the appendix?*

The use of bare *no* as a reply to a *yes-no* question may be considered impolite or inappropriate, and in most cases, *no* is accompanied by an expansion, explanation or justification:

A: *Would you like to live in London?*
B: ***No****, I don't think I could stand all the noise and pollution.*

Where the respondent feels they cannot answer a *yes-no* question with a straightforward affirmative or negative answer, the discourse marker *well* is often used to signal a shift in the desired or anticipated question-answer sequence:

A: *Do you live in Bristol?*
B: ***Well**, near Bristol.*
(B feels he cannot answer with just *yes* or *no*, and shifts the anticipated sequence)

Oh may be used to preface a reply, especially to indicate a range of emotive reactions to the question, in the form of enthusiasm, surprise, shock, etc.:

A: *Would you like a receipt?*
B: ***Oh**, yes, please! Got to have one of those.*

A: *Do you feel you've had a good treatment all of the times that you've been to the doctor's?*
B: ***Oh** definitely. Yes.*
C: *We think we've got wonderful doctors.*

A: *I always go to a party on Hallowe'en you know, just in the village hall.*
B: *Is it fancy dress and all that?*
A: ***Oh** no! You're joking aren't you?*

Oh may also be used to express a polite hesitation or a need for thinking time, or to preface an undesired reply which may be face-threatening to the asker:

A: *What do you pay for beef in the supermarket, a kilogram?*
B: ***Oh** I don't know.*

[in a restaurant; A is the waiter, B is a customer]
A: *Are you ready to order the second course as well, or not?*
B: ***Oh**, can we do that later?*
A: *Yes, certainly.*

Absolutely, *certainly* and *definitely* frequently occur as interpersonally engaged alternatives to bare *yes* or *no* (if followed by *not*) or together with *yes* or *no*:

A: *Do you think that's a good idea?*
B: ***Absolutely**.*
A: *Okay.*

A: *Shall I leave my coat here?*
B: ***Yeah certainly**.*
A: *Is that all right?*
B: *Yeah. Yeah.*
A: *Thanks.*

A: *You didn't find them uninventive or dull?*
B: ***No, definitely not**.*

→ **248 Adverbs used as short responses** for further examples of such usage

A-Z **56 *Of course*; 57 *Oh***

→ also **95 Response tokens; 101 Two-step questions and responses**

Negation

Negation

INTRODUCTION 434

When a speaker or writer makes a negative statement, they normally say that something cannot be the case or is not true or is not happening. Clauses, phrases and words can be made negative. *No* and *not* are the core negative words in English, but there are many other words that signal negation.

Primary negative words in English are:

neither	*none*	*nothing*
never	*no one*	*nowhere*
no	*nor*	
nobody	*not*	

Other secondary forms that are used to form negative or quasi-negative statements include:

few	*little*	*scarcely*
hardly	*rarely*	*seldom*

The following affixes are also most commonly used for negation:

prefixes: *de-, dis-, il-/im-/in-/ir-, mis-, non-, un-*

suffix: *-less*

In this chapter (434–447) clause negation is described first, followed by sections on negative words, then we consider negation as a discourse feature. Several individual negative words are treated in greater detail in A–Z entries.

Negation is more common in spoken than in written language. One of the main reasons for this is that in spoken, face-to-face interaction there are communicative risks in being too assertive; for example, asserting too much and too definitely can be impolite. *I'm sure* can sound very assertive whereas *I'm not sure* can keep options and channels of communication open. Using negatives allows a speaker to remain non-committal.

A–Z 44 ***Hardly***; 50 ***Little, a little; few, a few***

CLAUSE NEGATION 435

Negative declaratives 435a

Negative declarative clauses are formed by using *not* after a modal or auxiliary verb, or after the copular verb *be*:

Native speakers ***may not*** *be aware of the history of their language.*

George ***has not*** *been here recently.*

Julia ***was not*** *happy about travelling alone at night.*

Can + *not* is normally written as one word, *cannot*.

In informal contexts, the contracted form *n't* can be attached to modal and auxiliary verbs and copular verb *be*, written without a space. *Am* and *may* are not used with contracted *n't*:

You ***mustn't*** *shout.*

We ***hadn't*** *met before.*

My gloves ***aren't*** *warm enough for this weather.*

I'm not *sure.*
(~~I amn't sure~~)

She ***may not*** *have arrived yet.*
(~~She mayn't have arrived yet~~.)

Exceptions which require a special spelling and pronunciation are: *can't* (cannot), *shan't* (shall not) and *won't* (will not).

→ also **380e Contracted forms of modal verbs** for further examples of negative contractions with modal verbs and **233b Negative forms and auxiliary verbs** for negative contractions with auxiliary verbs and copular verb *be*

If there is no modal or auxiliary verb or copular verb *be*, auxiliary *do* is used with *not* to form the negative. The contracted forms *don't* (for *do not*), *doesn't* (for *does not*) and *didn't* (for *did not*) are used in informal contexts:

I ***do not believe*** *a word he says.*

It ***did not occur*** *to her that she was in any danger.*

They go into town during the week but they ***don't*** *usually* ***bother*** *at weekends.*

His brother ***doesn't like*** *fish.*

We ***didn't see*** *the notice until yesterday.*

With the verb *be* (both as a lexical verb and as an auxiliary), there is a choice of contracted negative form in the present tense between forms with *isn't/aren't* and forms with *'s not/'re not*. In informal spoken contexts, when the subject is a pronoun, the preference is overwhelmingly for the forms with *'s not/'re not*. When the subject is a lexical noun phrase, the choice is more open, but with a strong preference for the *isn't/aren't* forms:

*She**'s not** here today.*
(pronoun subject + *'s not/'re not*: most frequent preferred form)

*They **aren't** going to change the format of these big meetings.*
(pronoun subject + *isn't/aren't*: far less frequent)

*The plans **aren't** settled yet, he was saying.*
(lexical noun phrase + *isn't/aren't*: preferred form)

*The handle**'s not** very good, it's loose.*
(lexical noun phrase + *'s not/'re not*: less frequent)

Negative interrogatives 435b

Negative interrogatives typically function as questions seeking agreement or confirmation. They have a contracted *n't* negative. The word order is: modal/auxiliary verb + *n't* + subject + lexical verb. If copular *be* is used, the word order is *be* + *n't* + subject:

***Shouldn't** the government do more to increase productivity?*
(speaker thinks the government should do more and seeks agreement)

***Haven't** you got a knife and fork?*
(speaker sees that the listener apparently has no knife and fork and seeks confirmation)

***Isn't** this coat yours?*

Uncontracted negative questions have the word order: modal/auxiliary verb + subject + *not* + lexical verb. If copular *be* is used, the order is *be* + subject + *not*. Such questions sound very formal:

***Might** we **not** consider those less fortunate than ourselves?*

***Did** you **not** feel offended by her comment?*

***Is** she **not** an acquaintance of yours?*

Negative interrogatives and speech acts 435c

Negative interrogatives can be used to make polite offers and suggestions:

*Would**n't** you like some more salad?*

*Is**n't** this a good point to end the meeting?*

Negative interrogatives with the forms *won't you* and *couldn't you* can be used to make requests:

***Won't you** lend me your bike? I promise you I'll look after it.*

***Couldn't you** postpone your meeting until next Thursday?*

***Couldn't she** give us a lift into town?*

→ 539 **Glossary** for any unfamiliar terms

Negative interrogatives with *can't you* are often used in directives:

> ***Can't you*** *hurry up!*
>
> ***Can't you*** *do something about it!*

→ also **408–423 Speech acts** for further examples of the speech act functions of negative interrogatives

Negative imperatives 435d

Second person imperatives are made negative by the forms *don't/do not* plus a lexical verb:

> ***Don't*** *be silly.*
>
> ***Don't*** *expect to learn how to drive in a few weeks.*

Do not is a more formal alternative:

> ***Do not*** *cross until the green light shows.*

Don't + *you* also occurs in imperatives in informal contexts:

> ***Don't you*** *try to do that.*
>
> ***Don't you*** *worry. We'll do that for you.*

Imperatives may also be formed with a negative subject:

> ***Nobody*** *move!*

Negative imperatives may also occur with *never/not ever*:

> ***Never*** *forget who your real friends are.*
>
> ***Don't ever*** *do that again.*

First person negative imperatives are formed with *let's not* and *don't let's*. More formal alternatives are *let us not*, and *don't let us*:

> ***Let's not*** *get too carried away.*
>
> ***Don't let's*** *panic. We've got another few weeks to decide.*
>
> ***Let us not*** *forget the victims of this awful crime.*
> (more formal)
>
> ***Don't let us*** *be severe,* ***don't let us*** *be in a hurry to condemn him.*
> (more formal)

Very rarely, in mock formal styles, the full form of the lexical verb + *not* may occur:

> [said by a husband to his wife who has just phoned to say that the car has broken down and that she is stranded by the roadside]
> ***Worry not!*** *Your knight-in-shining-armour will soon be with you.*

Negative subjunctive 435e

The subjunctive mood is rare in English, but it occasionally occurs following verbs such as *insist*, *recommend*, *suggest*, expressions of necessity such as *it is important/essential that*, and conditional subordinators such as *if*, *lest*, *on condition that*, *unless*. The negative is formed with *not* plus the base form of the verb:

He had tried to call her during the week, but she had ***insisted*** *that he* ***not call*** *her at home and there was no other number he could try.*

Her father had had a slight stroke and the doctors ***recommended*** *that he* ***not travel***.

[TV presenter introducing a woman who has agreed to a secret interview]
She agreed to be filmed ***on condition that*** *we* ***not show*** *her face.*

NEGATION AND TAGS 436

Question tags which follow a negative main clause are affirmative:

You're not *on the same course as me,* ***are you****?*
(~~*You're not on the same course as me, aren't you?*~~)

He mustn't *do that,* ***must he****?*

They didn't *like Manchester,* ***did they****?*

It's not *too late to pop over,* ***is it****?*

Question tags which follow an affirmative main clause may be negative or affirmative, depending on whether the speaker thinks the answer is probably *yes* (affirmative + negative) or whether the speaker makes no assumption about whether the answer is *yes* or *no* (affirmative + affirmative). The intonation of a negative tag, whether rising or falling, also affects interpretation (··➤ 431):

They just ***gave*** *the whole class a warning,* ***didn't*** *they?*

He ***has*** *a house in Wales,* ***doesn't*** *he?*

*She****'s*** *a colleague of yours,* ***is*** *she?*

You ***got*** *here early,* ***did*** *you?*

Negative statement tags and negative tails (··➤ 97b) may follow a negative declarative main clause in informal spoken language:

*I****'m not*** *at all hungry,* ***I'm not****.*

He's just ***not*** *the right person for the job,* ***Joe isn't****.*

An affirmative tag follows an affirmative or negative imperative. The tag is usually formed with *will* for second person imperatives and *shall* for first person imperatives:

__Be__ quiet, __will you__!

Do__n't__ put the rubbish out yet, __will you__.

Let's __not__ argue, __shall we__.

A negative tag following an affirmative imperative is rather formal:

__Come__ again tomorrow, __won't__ you.

Exclamative clauses can also have negative tags which function to seek confirmation:

What a storm that was, __wasn't it__!

How lovely to be going home, __isn't it__!

➜ **300 Question tags** and **98 Questions and tags** for further description of the formation of question tags and other tags

A–Z **69 *Right, rightly*** for *right* as a tag

NEGATION AND MENTAL PROCESS VERBS (*BELIEVE, THINK*) 437

When mental process verbs such as *believe, imagine, suppose, think* are used to express uncertainty, it is more usual for the negation to be placed on these verbs rather than on the complement clause:

We __don't imagine__ there are sufficient funds to expand the business this year.
(preferred to: We imagine there are not sufficient funds …)

I __don't think__ dinner's ready yet.
(preferred to: I think dinner's not ready yet.)

Exceptions are the verbs *hope* and *wish*, where the negation is placed in the complement clause:

I __hope__ you __aren't__ going to make a mess in the kitchen.
(~~I don't hope you're going to make a mess in the kitchen.~~)

We're __hoping__ England __don't__ lose their first match against Norway.

I __wish__ he __wouldn't__ make so much fuss.

When mental process verbs are used in affirmative short replies, *so* is added:

Will Tim be at the party?
I'm afraid so.
I guess so.
I hope so.
I think so.
I suppose so.

If the reply is negative, there are different patterns. *Not* is used with *be afraid, guess, hope*. With *think*, the usual form is *I don't think so*; *I think not* is a more formal alternative. With *suppose*, both forms are possible:

Will Tim be at the party?
I'm afraid ***not***.
I guess ***not***.
I hope ***not***.
I ***don't*** *think* **so**./*I think* ***not***.
I ***don't*** *suppose* **so**./*I suppose* ***not***.

NEGATIVE CLAUSES WITH *ANY, ANYONE, ANYTHING, ANYWHERE*, ETC. 438

Words such as *some, somebody, someone, something, somewhere* are not normally used following *not*. *Any, anybody, anyone, anything, anywhere* are used instead:

There is ***some*** *room at the front of the train.*
*There is****n't any*** *room at the front of the train.*
(~~There isn't some room at the front of the train.~~)

There's ***someone*** *in the garden.*
*There is****n't anyone*** *in the garden.*
(~~There isn't someone in the garden.~~)

I've found ***somewhere*** *to stay tonight.*
I've ***not*** *found* ***anywhere*** *to stay tonight.*
(~~I've not found somewhere to stay tonight.~~)

Following verbs with a negative meaning such as *decline* or *refuse*, *anything* is preferred to *something*:

I ***refused*** *to have* ***anything*** *to do with him.*
(~~I refused to have something to do with him.~~)

After affirmative verbs *no* is used, and with negated verbs *any* is used. Compare the following two sentences, both of which mean the opposite of *We had some money*:

We had ***no*** *money.*

*We did****n't*** *have* ***any*** *money.*

Although these sentences both mean the same, the structure with *not … any* is normally preferred in informal contexts. The structure with *no* is more emphatic and more associated with formal contexts.

Double negatives and usage 438a

Words such as *never, nobody, no one, nothing, nowhere* have a negative meaning and do not require a negative verb form:

The company ***never*** *told the new staff that they needed a password.*
(~~The company didn't never tell the new staff that they needed a password.~~)

*When I got there, there was **nobody** in the park.*
(~~When I got there, there wasn't nobody in the park.~~)

However, in many non-standard dialects of English, double and multiple negatives are frequent with words such as *never, nobody, nothing* and *nowhere*:

*I **didn't** see **nobody nowhere**.*

Double and multiple negatives are used, especially in spoken English, in order to create emphasis. Traditional grammar books prohibit them, and the use of double negatives with words such as *never, nobody, nothing* and *nowhere* is a very sensitive issue. Learners of English are advised not to use them.

However, a kind of emphatic double negative often occurs in reinforcing statement tags (→ 436 above; → also 97b) and in end-position reporting clauses with verbs such as *imagine, suppose, think*. In everyday speech these are accepted as standard:

*You're **not** going near the paper-shop, I **don't** suppose?*

A: *We **won't** be allowed in, I **shouldn't** think.*
B: ***Not** without an invitation we **won't**.*

[deciding where to place a temporary bed]
*It should fit there, because it's **not** that big I **don't** think.*

→ See also 119 for the use of double negatives in many dialects of English

NOT IN NON-FINITE AND ELLIPTED CLAUSES 439

The negative *not* is placed before the verb phrase in non-finite clauses. Such structures are common in formal, written styles:

***Not** having a strong enough defence, the team let in four goals at the end of the second half.*

*I wrote the address down, so as **not** to forget it.*

In informal spoken English, *not* often follows the infinitive *to*. Such 'split infinitives' are considered bad style in writing by many people, but they are common in speech:

*It took a lot of self-control to **not** hit him.*

Sometimes verb phrases can be subject to ellipsis (→ 94 Situational ellipsis). *Not* can be used to negate the understood element(s):

*Come early in the morning, but **not** too early though.*
(Come early in the morning but do not come too early though.)

*The CD's playing okay but **not** with the right sound quality.*
(The CD's playing okay but it is not playing with the right sound quality.)

It's a powerful car though **not** *as expensive on petrol as you'd think.*
(It's a powerful car though it is not as expensive on petrol as you'd think.)

NEGATIVE PREFIXES AND SUFFIXES 440

Words can be made negative in English by the use of prefixes.

The main negative prefixes

prefix	examples
a-	*amoral*
de-	*deforestation*
dis-	*dissatisfaction*
il-	*illegally*
im-	*immodest; immature*
in-	*inhuman*
ir-	*irregular; irresponsible*
no-	*no-go; no-win*
non-	*non-conformist; non-believer*
un-	*unhappy; unimportant*

Many negative words are adjectives that are formed from nouns + the suffix *-less*:

careless *endless* *pointless*
childless *harmless* *useless*
doubtless *homeless* *worthless*

Words and phrases of negative or adverse meaning when negated with *not* can often convey a positive meaning:

That pasta's **not** *too* **bad***.*
(it's quite good)

[said during a car journey]
We're **not far away** *now. We'll soon be there.*

→ also **261 Prefixes** and **262 Suffixes** for further discussion

NO 441

In spoken English, *no* is most frequently used as a response to *yes-no* questions, as a response agreeing with a negative assertion, or as an interjection:

A: *Are you ready yet?*
B: **No***. Not yet. Can you give me another couple of minutes?*

A: *The system doesn't take account of people's individual circumstances.*
B: **No***. That's right.*

No*, don't move! I want to take a photo of you two together.*

No + noun is not the same as *not a* + noun, unless the noun has a gradable meaning:

> *A whale is **not a** fish.*
> (~~A whale is no fish.~~)
> (*fish* is non-gradable: it is either a fish or not; it cannot be 'more of a fish' than another animal)
>
> *When it comes to computers, er, I'm **no expert**.*
> (gradable: one person can be more of an expert than another person)
>
> *He's **no fool**, is he?*

No is also a degree adverb. It premodifies comparative adjectives, adverbs and determiners:

> *The second performance was **no better than** the first.*
>
> *She had been fishing **no more than** three or four times in her life.*
>
> *There were **no less than** four hundred people in the audience.*

Similar meanings can be conveyed with a negation of a verb + *any*:

> *The second performance was**n't any better than** the first.*

In some fixed expressions, *no* negates a following noun, adjective or adverb:

> ***It's no good** phoning Arthur, he won't be at home yet.*
> (~~It's not good phoning Arthur, …~~)
>
> A: *What's that woman Nancy's second name?*
> B: *I **have no idea**.*
>
> *It's **no use** phoning. He won't be there.*
>
> A: *Could we change our dinner-date to Friday?*
> B: *Yes. **No problem**.*

NONE, NONE OF 442

None is a pronoun. It is more emphatic than *not any*:

> *The weather forecast predicted showers all afternoon but there were **none**.*
> (more emphatic than: The weather forecast predicted showers all afternoon but there weren't any.)

None of is a quantifier and is used with pronouns and noun phrases introduced by a determiner:

> ***None of us** had much money in those days.*
>
> ***None of my dogs** are ever allowed upstairs.*
>
> ***None of the book** is about phonetics.*

With plural noun phrases, *not one of* is a more emphatic alternative to *none of*:

__Not one of these children__ has been to a dentist in the last five years.

NOTHING, NO ONE, NOBODY 443

The pronouns *nothing, no one* (also written *no-one*) and *nobody* are more emphatic than the parallel structures *not … anything/anyone/anybody*. Compare:

I did __nothing__ at all yesterday.

I did__n't__ do __anything__ at all yesterday.

Not … anything and *not … anyone/anybody* are the neutral choices and are therefore used more often than *nothing* and *no one/nobody*, which are used in more emphatic contexts:

I have__n't__ heard __anything__ from Marie for ages.

Don't ask me what's happening. I know __nothing__.

Do__n't__ tell __anyone__ I'm coming. I want it to be a surprise.

I can think of __no one__ who sings as beautifully as Lisa.

It's a big, big secret for the moment. Tell __nobody__.

Nobody is a variant of *no one* but, although the two forms mean the same, there is a difference in the way they are used. In spoken language, *nobody* is far more frequent than *no one*. In written texts, *no one* is much more frequent than *nobody*.

Nobody and *no one* can be used as emphatic alternatives to *not … anybody/not anyone*:

We knew __nobody__ when we first came to London.
(or: We knew no one when we first came to London.)
(both are more emphatic than: We didn't know anybody when we first came to London.)

Nobody and *no one*, rather than *not anybody/not anyone* are used as the subject of a clause:

We need engineers but __nobody__ wants to learn how to be one.
(preferred to: … but not anybody wants to learn how to be one.)

You can describe the past, but __no one__ can predict the future.

Nothing, no one and *nobody* can be followed by *but*, the whole phrase having the meaning of 'only':

They must tell the truth and __nothing but__ the truth.
(… and only the truth)

__No one but__ the head of the company himself should meet the delegation at the airport.
(Only the head of the company …)

NEVER, NOWHERE 444

In negative statements *not* ... *ever* and *not* ... *anywhere* are normally preferred. *Never* and *nowhere* are more emphatic alternatives:

*I have**n't ever** eaten clams.*
(less emphatic than: I've never eaten clams.)

*I'd **never** lie to you, you know that.*
(emphatic)

*Have you seen my keys? I **can't** find them **anywhere**.*
(preferred to: ... I can find them nowhere.)

*There's **nowhere** to sit, is there?*

Never sometimes occurs in marked mid positions for extra emphasis:

***It never was** very clear to me why she resigned.*
(marked position between subject and lexical verb *be*)

A: *Janet got divorced last month.*
B: *Really? She never said a word!*
A: *Well **they never did** get on together.*
(marked position before first auxiliary verb)

Further emphasis for *never* is provided by *ever*:

*They **never ever** go out, do they?*

→ **336a** for subject-verb inversion after negative adverbs such as ***hardly***, ***never***, ***rarely***, ***scarcely***, ***seldom***

NEITHER, NEITHER OF, NEITHER ... NOR, NOT ... OR/NOR, NOT ... NEITHER/NOR 445

Neither

Neither can be used on its own in replies to refer to two alternatives which have already been mentioned:

A: *Does that mean they're going to win or lose?*
B: ***Neither**. We think they'll probably draw.*

Neither is also used as a determiner before singular countable nouns. It allows a negative statement to be made about two things at the same time:

***Neither** party has shown any real commitment to improving the environment.*

***Neither** parent should be held responsible for what happened.*

Neither of

Neither of is used with pronouns and plural countable nouns preceded by a determiner. Traditional grammar books state that it is followed by a singular verb, but a plural verb is also common, especially in informal speech:

> ***Neither of*** *the two choices* ***leaves*** *us in any doubt.*
>
> ***Neither of*** *them* ***was*** *able to get to sleep because of the noise outside their window.*
>
> ***Neither of*** *the teachers* ***were*** *present at the meeting.*

Neither ... nor

Neither ... nor function as a correlative coordinator (··➤ 308). They are used to link two or more alternatives:

> ***Neither*** *the American company* ***nor*** *its British subsidiary have prepared for the takeover.*
>
> *It's* ***neither*** *possible* ***nor*** *likely that they will succeed.*

A similar meaning is expressed by *either ... or* plus a negative verb:

> *They didn't have* ***either*** *still* ***or*** *sparkling water, so I just got tap water.*
> (or: They had neither still nor sparkling water, so I just got tap water.)

When two or more clauses are coordinated, there is subject-verb inversion in the clause introduced by *nor*. Coordination with subject-verb inversion is associated with formal styles:

> *They can* ***neither*** *understand practical causes,* ***nor*** *are they sympathetic to the relationship between theory and practice.*

Nor ... nor can occur after *neither*:

> *He stood like a statue. He* ***neither*** *spoke* ***nor*** *moved.* ***Nor*** *did he appear to be listening to what was happening around him.*

Not ... or/nor

Alternatives introduced by *not* can be linked with either *or* or *nor*. *Nor* is more emphatic than *or* and less common:

> *It is****n't*** *good* ***or*** *bad. It's just pretty mediocre.*
>
> *She was* ***not*** *annoyed* ***or*** *offended. In fact she seemed completely indifferent.*
>
> *It is* ***not*** *sweet* ***nor*** *sour, but something in between.*

Not ... neither/nor

If a coordinated clause follows a negative clause, *neither* or *nor* can be used to make the subsequent clause negative. In such cases the verb and subject are inverted:

> *This is* ***not*** *your best set of exam results by any means but* ***neither*** *is it your worst.*

A: *I **don't** think their products are particularly reliable.*
B: ***Neither** do I.*
(or: Nor do I.)

*The cottage has **no** central heating, **nor** does it have a proper boiler.*

HARDLY, RARELY, SCARCELY, SELDOM, ETC. 446

Adverbs such as *barely, hardly, rarely, scarcely, seldom* have quasi-negative meanings. They are used without *not*:

*They could **hardly** believe their eyes.*
('They couldn't hardly believe their eyes' and similar sentences may occur, but are considered non-standard)

*Examiners are only **rarely** generous in such circumstances.*

*The results felt **scarcely** worth celebrating.*

*The committee only very **seldom** makes such awards.*

***Scarcely** anyone turned up, did they?*
(~~Scarcely no one turned up.~~)

Little and *few* function in a similar way:

*They go out very **little** these days.*

*There's **little** point in asking him, is there?*

***Few** would disagree with the party, I suppose.*

*There were very **few** people at the cricket match.*

Note also that *little* and *few* are marked (more emphatic) when compared to non-assertive equivalents *not much* and *not many*:

*He does**n't** have **much** time for relaxation.*
(non-assertive)

*He has **little** time for relaxation.*
(marked)

*She did**n't** have **many** opportunities while working for the previous company.*
(non-assertive)

*She had **few** opportunities while working for the previous company.*
(marked)

→ **336a** for subject-verb inversion after negative adverbs such as ***hardly, never, rarely, scarcely, seldom***

A-Z **50 *Little, a little, few, a few***

NEGATION AND DISCOURSE 447

Intensifying negation 447a

At all is the most common intensifier of negative items:

*You've **hardly** eaten anything **at all**.*

*Are there **no** tickets **at all** left?*

*They were running the economy **without** any control **at all** from the International Monetary Fund.*

*There's just **nowhere at all** where you can get decent coffee in this town.*

 12 *All*

Whatsoever, which is used after *no, no one, none* and *nothing*, has a similar meaning to *at all* but is more emphatic. *Whatsoever* can be used to intensify any negative noun phrase:

*I want **no** interruptions **whatsoever** during this meeting. And **no one whatsoever** is to know about it.*

A: *Have you no juice in the fridge?*
B: ***None whatsoever**.*

Not a bit, a little bit, in the least, the least bit are also used to intensify negatives:

*The students **weren't a bit** interested in having extra classes in the evening.*

*I **didn't** find his remarks amusing **in the least**.*

*The doctors **weren't the least bit** worried about his health.*

 27 *Bit, a bit (of)*

Intensified negation can also be used as a mark of politeness:

A: *Would it disturb you if I use your phone?*
B: *Not **in the least**.*

Not and hedging 447b

In negative clauses, *not* is often accompanied by *actually, necessarily, really* or *very* in order to soften the force of the negative and to sound more polite or tentative:

*Her acting was**n't actually** convincing, was it?*

*Sorry, but I do**n't really** feel like going out tonight.*

*I'm **not very** familiar with this type of printer. Can you help me?*

Other words such as *absolutely*, *altogether*, *entirely* are used in the same way, although they are more formal:

*I'm **not altogether** sure whether we should support him for election.*

*The shopkeepers are **not entirely** against the idea of twenty-four-hour shopping.*

These structures are often used as short hedged replies:

A: *Did you mind not being invited?*
B: ***Not really**, no. I didn't.*

A: *I suppose you've made up your mind to buy the roses?*
B: *No, **not necessarily**.*

Repeated negation and affirmative statements 447c

Two or more negative statements can be used to make a forceful affirmative statement:

[said by a retired actor who is being asked if his day is now boring and difficult to fill]
*I do**n't** do anything I do**n't** want to do.*
(more forceful than: I only do things that I want to do.)

[a brand name of a margarine-spread product which claims to taste no different from butter]
*I Ca**n't** Believe It's **Not** Butter.*

***None of** the countries have **no** proper hygiene regulations.*
(All of the countries have at least some proper hygiene regulations.)

Double negation and hedging 447d

Double negation involving *not* plus a negative-affixed word (→ 440 above) commonly occurs in more formal styles of English such as academic writing. It enables speakers and writers to express ideas cautiously:

*The government is **not** blame**less** as regards the recent rise in unemployment.*

*This is a **not un**interesting essay.*

*Unfortunately, it is **not im**possible that at least one third of Shakespeare's sonnets were written by Sidney.*

*It is **not un**usual for people to see the film three or four times.*

Double negation as a hedging or distancing device may take the form of two negative elements in a phrase, clause or sentence:

***Not** a day passes when he does **not** remember being the cause of her unhappiness.*
(Every day he remembers being the cause of her unhappiness.)

[A is commenting on the unwillingness of B to go to a hotel which they both know suffers regular electricity power failures]
A: *So you went to the hotel in the end?*
B: *Yes but **not without** a powerful torch.*
(Yes, but with a powerful torch.)

With the verb *surprise*, two negative verb phrases in sequence can also be used to hedge an opinion or other expression of stance:

*I should**n't** be surprised if he did**n't** retire soon.*
(I think he'll retire soon.)

A–Z 44 *Hardly*

Condition

Condition

INTRODUCTION 448

Conditions deal with imagined situations: some are possible, some are unlikely, some are impossible. The speaker/writer imagines that something can or cannot happen or have happened, and then compares that situation with possible consequences or outcomes, or offers further logical conclusions about the situation.

Conditionality is conveyed chiefly by means of conditional clauses. Conditional clauses are most typically introduced by the subordinating conjunction *if*:

conditional clause **main clause**
If *it rains,* | *we're going to stay in the house.*

Differences in tense and modality are important to a possible or imagined situation. In the conditional clause, tense choices express different types of potential event; in the main clause, modal verbs are used to indicate the unfulfilled outcome of those events.

Examples of conditional sentences

conditional clause: possible situation	main clause: possible outcome	comments
If *they* ***promote*** *her,* (present tense)	*she'****ll*** *get a big pay rise.* (*will/shall*)	there is a possibility that the event will happen
If *I* ***had*** *the money,* (past tense)	*I'****d*** *go on a round-the-world cruise.* (*would/should*)	the event is unlikely and is purely hypothetical
If *he* ***had gone*** *there,* (past perfect)	*he* ***might have*** *enjoy****ed*** *it.* (*might have* + *-ed* participle)	the event is impossible; it did not happen

Conditional clauses can be formed with other conjunctions than *if*: for example, *as long as, unless* (→ 454–456). For the first part of this chapter (449–453) examples are confined to clauses with *if*.

Conditional clauses typically precede main clauses but may also follow them:

conditional clause **main clause**
If *I don't hear from you,* | *I'll assume the meeting is still on for tomorrow morning.*

main clause **conditional clause**
We can manage | ***if*** *you let us know in time.*

If may also occur in substitute structures:

Are you coming? ***If so****, can you get ready quickly?*
(with clause-substitute *so*)

If you want to join us, give me a ring. ***If not****, then see you next week.*

Some conditional clauses are used to impose conditions by the speaker/writer on the listener/reader or on the situation. These include clauses introduced by subordinators such as *as/so long as, only if, on condition that, providing/provided (that)*:

A: *Can I borrow this dictionary?*
B: *Yeah.* ***So long as*** *you don't hold on to it.*

He was released from prison ***on condition that*** *he went into exile.*

THE FIRST, SECOND AND THIRD CONDITIONALS 449

The most commonly described conditional clauses are often known as the first, second and third conditionals. They have the following structures.

The first conditional

The structure of the first conditional is: *if* + present simple tense + modal verb with future reference (e.g. *will/shall/may*).

In the first conditional, a speaker or writer predicts a likely result in the future if the condition is fulfilled. There must be at least some chance of the condition being fulfilled:

If *Sally* ***comes*** *too, there'****ll be*** *five of us.*

We ***won't*** *have enough time* ***if*** *we* ***want*** *to do some shopping too.*

> *Will* and *shall* are used in the main clause, not the *if*-clause:
>
> *If he* ***moves*** *to Manchester, he* ***will*** *have to sell his house in Bristol.*
> (~~If he will move to Manchester, he will have to sell his house in Bristol.~~)

The second conditional

The structure of the second conditional is: *if* + simple past tense + modal verb with future-in-the-past reference (e.g. *would/could/might*).

In the second conditional, a speaker or writer responds to a possible or hypothetical situation by indicating a possible outcome. The speaker or writer states that the condition must be fulfilled for the present or future to be different:

If *I* ***knew*** *what you wanted, maybe I* ***could help*** *you.*

I ***would do*** *a computer course* ***if*** *I* ***had*** *the time.*

The third conditional

The structure of the third conditional is: *if* + past perfect tense + modal verb with future-in-the-past reference (e.g. *would/could/might*) + *have* + *-ed* participle.

In the third conditional, the speaker's or writer's attitude to an imagined past situation is described. Here the speaker or writer is talking about a past event which did not happen, and therefore things are different from how they might have been:

If *I* ***had seen*** *you walking, I* ***could have offered*** *you a lift.*

Tessa ***would have been*** *furious* ***if*** *she* ***had heard*** *him say that.*

Many conditional clauses occur in these structures, but there are also several other possible structures.

REAL CONDITIONALS 450

It can also be helpful to describe conditional clauses by the degree to which they refer to real or unreal situations. Real situations are things that are true, have happened, generally happen or are likely to happen. Unreal situations are things that are untrue or are imagined, have not happened and are only remotely likely to happen. Unreal situations are the basis of the second and third conditionals (··❯ 449 above).

In conditional clauses which refer to real situations, tenses are normally used in the same way as in other kinds of sentence. Present tenses are used to talk about present and future events as well as about general truths and facts, and past tenses are used to talk about past events:

> ***If** you **want to** learn the guitar, you really **need** to practise for at least a couple of hours a day.*
> (for any person who does in fact want to learn)
>
> ***If** I **criticised** her unfairly, then I always **apologised**.*
> (it did sometimes happen that I criticised her, and I did apologise)

A wide variety of patterns occur with real conditionals. Some examples of common patterns are given here:

- present simple *if*-clause and present simple main clause:

  ***If** steel **is** exposed to air and water, it **resists** rust for a considerable length of time.*

  ***If** I **feel** like some exercise, I **take** the dog for a walk.*

- *be going to if*-clause and *be going to* main clause:

  ***If** you**'re going to** buy a house, then you**'re going to** need a lot of money.*

- present simple *if*-clause and modal verb in main clause:

  ***If** you **have** toothache as bad as that, you **must** go to a dentist today.*

  ***If** that**'s** on the disk, we **should** have it on our system.*

- present simple *if*-clause and present progressive main clause:

  ***If** they **think** I'm going to retire quietly, then they**'re making** a big mistake.*

  *They **are breaking** the law **if** they **give** you that information.*

- present progressive *if*-clause and present progressive main clause:

  ***If** you**'re getting** backache all the time, then you**'re not sitting** properly.*

- present progressive *if*-clause and present simple main clause:

  ***If** you**'re suffering** from hay-fever, you **need** one of these sprays.*

- past simple *if*-clause and past simple main clause:

  ***If** I **missed** the last train, I just **stayed** over with friends.*
  (*if* here is synonymous with *when*)

- past simple *if*-clause and present perfect main clause:

  If *you* ***ate*** *too much over the holidays, then it's no surprise you****'ve put*** *on weight.*
  (you did eat too much and you have put on weight)

- past perfect *if*-clause and past simple main clause:

  If *they****'d missed*** *something out or* ***had got*** *it wrong, she* ***showed*** *them how to correct it.*
  (*if* here is synonymous with *when*)

- past progressive *if*-clause and past simple main clause:

  They always ***took*** *the dog with them* ***if*** *they* ***were going*** *anywhere.*

MAIN CLAUSES 451

Although main clauses in *if*-sentences are most typically declarative, it is also possible for interrogative and imperative clauses to occur.

- *if*-clause and interrogative main clause:

  If *you want to speak to him,* ***why don't you just give him a ring****?*

  Would you tell everyone, ***if*** *you won a huge amount of money on the lottery?*

  If *you'd lost your keys,* ***what would you do****?*

- *if*-clause and imperative main clause:

  If *you get bad migraines,* ***try*** *a homeopathic cure.*

MODAL VERBS IN CONDITIONAL CLAUSES 452

Modal verbs (most typically *will* or *would*) may occur in conditional clauses if they have a meaning of willingness or prediction, or where it is important to mark politeness:

If *you****'ll*** *wait a minute, I'll fetch the porter to help you.*

If *you* ***would*** *all follow me, I'll show you to your rooms.*

If *you* ***would*** *have allowed them more time, I still think they would have done better.*
(if you had been willing to allow them more time)

I'll take care of the tea and coffee, ***if*** *it****'ll*** *help to get things done quicker.*
(if the assumption is true/valid that things will get done quicker)

I'll do it for you, ***if*** *you* ***could*** *just wait a minute.*

Should can be used in a conditional clause where it has the meaning of 'happen to'/'chance to'. *Should* suggests that the speaker thinks the possibility is remote:

If you ***should*** *run into Peter, tell him to call me.*

OTHER CONDITIONAL CLAUSES WITH *IF* 453

If it were not for

If it were/was not (had not been) for + noun phrase refers to hypothetical situations and actions:

> ***If it weren't for*** *the police, I think those burglars would have got away with even more.*
> (if the police had not arrived/intervened)

If he were to

If + noun phrase + *was/were to* + verb (base form) also refers to hypothetical situations and actions (with a singular subject, *was to* is less formal than *were to*):

> ***If I was to say*** *to you 'Barcelona', what would you think of?*

> ***If the headteacher were to resign****, it would be a disaster for the school.*

> *The garden's really special.* ***If Rick and Joan were to sell*** *the house, people would be queuing up to buy it.*

Only if

Only if is used to impose conditions:

> *You can go* ***only if*** *you are back by midnight.*

Only may be separated from *if*, with *only* in the main clause:

> *They'll* ***only*** *let you check in* ***if*** *you've got a passport or photo ID.*

Even if

Even if may be used as an emphatic form of *if*:

> ***Even if*** *you flew business class, it would still be an exhausting journey.*

If only

If only is used to express a wish that things could be different. It refers to an unreal condition. The clause often occurs without an accompanying main clause:

> ***If only*** *we could get to a warmer country in the winter.*
> (I wish we could get to a warmer country in the winter.)

If in ellipted and non-finite clauses

If also appears in ellipted and non-finite clauses in more formal contexts:

> ***If wet****, the match will be played on the indoor courts.*
> (ellipted conditional clause)

> ***If paying by direct debit****, please make sure that you notify your bank at least one month in advance.*
> (non-finite conditional clause)

If and *when*

If and *when* are not the same. In unreal conditionals, only *if*, not *when*, may be used. *When* is used to refer to something the speaker knows will happen at some point in time:

> ***If*** *we win the lottery, we'll give up our jobs and fly to the Caribbean.*
> (speaker does not know the event will happen)

> ***When*** *Georgina comes in, tell her I want to speak to her.*
> (speaker knows Georgina is coming)

→ **539 Glossary** for any unfamiliar terms

UNLESS AND *IF ... NOT* 454

Unless has a meaning of 'if ... not' or 'except if'. *Unless* and *if ... not*, and *unless* and *except if* are often, but not always, interchangeable. *Unless* can only normally refer to things which have not happened or did not happen or probably won't happen:

__Unless__ you __can__ reduce the weight of that case, I'm afraid you won't be allowed on the flight.
(or: If you can't reduce the weight of that case, I'm afraid you won't be allowed on the flight.)

Come over tomorrow afternoon around five, __unless__ my secretary __contacts__ you.
(or: Come over tomorrow afternoon around five, except if my secretary contacts you.)

I always think Dave would be happier __if__ he __didn't__ work so hard.
(*unless* cannot be used, since Dave does in fact work hard)
(~~I always think Dave would be happier unless he worked so hard.~~)

[speakers are talking about plants in their garden which they covered to protect them from a severe frost which occurred]
A: *__If__ we __hadn't__ covered them, they'd have been ruined.*
B: *Yes, I think they'd have been dead by now.*
(*unless* cannot be used, since the speakers did in fact cover the plants)

Unless is used, especially in spoken English, to introduce an additional comment or afterthought:

We don't have anyone to captain the team, now Tina's resigned – __unless__ you're interested, of course.

A: *Do you want to take a break now?*
B: *Yeah, right.*
A: *__Unless__ you want to go on for another half an hour or so?*

WH-CONDITIONAL CLAUSES 455

Clauses introduced by *whatever, whenever, however, whoever, whichever* can introduce conditions which always seem to obtain and cannot seem to be changed:

__Whatever__ she says, don't believe it.

__Whenever__ the team loses, they are miserable for the rest of the weekend.

__However__ late they arrive, how can we find the time to meet them?

Whether ... or and *whether ... or not* can be used to link two different conditions which the speaker regards as having the same likely outcome:

__Whether__ we drive __or__ go by train, it will still take about four hours.

I don't think it'll make any difference __whether__ Jake comes with us __or not__.

OTHER CONDITIONAL EXPRESSIONS 456

The other subordinating conjunctions listed here operate in a similar way to *if*: the conditional clause typically contains a non-modal verb in the present or the past tense, while modal verbs usually occur in the main clause.

Providing, provided that

Providing is more frequent in spoken language; *provided that* is more frequent in writing. Both may be used for real and unreal conditions:

A: *But presumably you've got some sort of senior citizen's fare?*
B: *Yes, **providing** you've got a railcard.*

*This article may be freely distributed **provided that** our copyright is fully acknowledged.*

On condition that, in the event that, in the event of + noun phrase

On condition that and *in the event that/in the event of* are much more frequent in formal written contexts than in informal spoken contexts. They may be used for real and unreal conditions:

[from a leaflet published by an anti-smoking campaign]
*Many surgeons offer patients an operation only **on condition that** they give up smoking – and often find that the ensuing improvement makes surgery unnecessary.*

***In the event that** the plane lands on water, life-jackets are located under every seat.*

***In the event of** a sudden loss of cabin pressure, oxygen masks will be lowered automatically from the panel above your seat.*

As long as, so long as

As long as and *so long as* occur frequently in informal spoken contexts. They may both be used for real and unreal conditions:

***As long as** you promise to be back by 6, you can borrow the car.*

***As long as** it doesn't rain, we'll have a great time.*

*I'm always fine **as long as** I can get about six or seven hours of sleep.*

*But I won't mind too much **so long as** she's coming back.*

Suppose (that), supposing, assuming

Suppose (that), *supposing* and *assuming* can be used to imagine unreal conditions:

A: *You just have to say yes.*
B: *But **suppose** you're not sure? **Suppose** you have to decide later? **Suppose** you feel you have to go but don't really want to?*

***Assuming** we don't sell the house, we can still move next spring. There are always more buyers in the spring.*

Supposing and *assuming* do not impose conditions:

This article may be distributed ***if*** *our logo is shown.*
(or: ***provided that*** *our logo is shown.*)
(or: ***on condition that*** *our logo is shown.*)
(or: ***as (so) long as*** *our logo is shown.*)
(but not: ~~**supposing/assuming**~~ our logo is shown.)

But for

But for is a fixed expression meaning 'if it were not for'. It is used in more formal contexts and is followed by a noun phrase:

But for *Sunita, we'd all have got lost ages ago.*

He would have gone to university ***but for*** *the fact that his parents were poor and couldn't afford it.*
(~~He would have gone to university but for (that) his parents were poor and could not afford it~~.)

Otherwise

Otherwise can be used to express an outcome which is likely if a condition is not met. It may introduce the clause which indicates the outcome or, especially in informal spoken language, it may come in end position:

I won't tell Brenda, ***otherwise*** *she'll be furious.*
(If I tell Brenda, she'll be furious.)

Take the umbrella. You'll get soaked ***otherwise****.*
(If you do not take the umbrella, you'll get soaked.)

In case, in case of

In case has a meaning of *because x might be/happen* or *because there is a risk of x*:

I'll take these shoes with me ***in case*** *it rains.*
(I will take the shoes whether it rains or not, because there is a risk of rain)
(compare: 'I'll take these shoes with me if it rains.' i.e. 'I will not take the shoes if it does not rain.')

In case is frequently premodified by *just*, indicating that the speaker thinks the outcome is unlikely:

I'll give you the address to give Paul, ***just in case*** *you bump into him.*

In case may, in very formal and literary contexts, be followed by the subjunctive form *were to* (→ **159e**):

Urquhart had taken the precaution of taking down the details from Simon's driving licence, just ***in case*** *he* ***were to*** *continue to cause trouble and needed to be tracked down.*
(more typical: ... just in case he continued to cause trouble ...)

The phrase *in case of* + noun phrase carries a slightly different conditional meaning. It has negative connotations and is used for real conditions in formal contexts such as warning notices:

> ***In case of*** *fire, do not use the lift.*
> (Only if/when there is a fire …)

> ✪ *In case of* is not used with an *-ing* form:
>
> ***In case of*** *a breakdown, call this number.*
> (~~In case of breaking down, call this number.~~)

Lest

Lest is used in very formal and literary contexts, and is a formal alternative to *in case*. It is used to indicate that an action is done in order to prevent a possible negative outcome. It is followed by *should* or, even more formally, by a subjunctive form (→ **159e**):

> *She threw on a jacket and walked quickly out, head down into her collar,* ***lest*** *anyone* ***should*** *later be able to recognise her.*

> ***Lest*** *she* ***appear*** *over-familiar, she nodded and turned away.*

What if …?

What if …? is used to imagine unreal situations and to pose questions about their possible outcomes:

> ***What if*** *she doesn't turn up? What shall we do?*

> A: ***What if*** *we'd waited and left later? We'd have missed the flight with all that traffic.*
> B: *Yes, you're right.*

No conditional subordinator

Conditions can also be conveyed without any overt conditional subordinator, often using *and*, especially in informal spoken language:

> *We'd better not be late. They'll leave without us.*
> (They'll leave without us if we're late.)

> [parent to misbehaving child]
> *Do that again* ***and*** *I'll get very angry.*
> (If you do that again, I'll get very angry.)

> *Buy three CDs* ***and*** *get one free.*
> (If you buy three CDs, …)

LINKING WITH *THEN* 457

Then is often used to link a main clause following a conditional to add emphasis:

> [from an Oxford City Council tourist brochure]
> ***If*** *you are visiting Oxford,* ***then*** *why not take the opportunity to visit The Oxford Story – a museum of Oxford life down the ages?*

If she had prepared better for the interview, ***then*** *she would have got the job.*

As long as *it's okay with you,* ***then*** *I'll stay till Monday.*

Unless *you've got certain qualifications,* ***then*** *you can't get a contract.*

CONDITIONAL CLAUSES AND FORMALITY 458

Conditions can be expressed at different levels of formality. More formal structures sometimes involve inversion and the omission of conjunctions such as *if*:

[extract from a letter concerning an application to join a Health and Fitness Club]
Were you *to apply before the 15th of September, you would still be given a preferential discount.*

Inversion instead of using *if* is normally only possible in the case of the verb forms *had, should* and subjunctive *were* (i.e. *were* used for all persons, singular and plural:

Had they *not been so uncooperative, I might have forgiven them and not complained.*

Should you *wish to visit the factory and to inspect the plant, the best time for our management team would be in the early evening.*

Were it *not for help from a psychologist, she might have been a lot more unwell by now.*
(~~Was it not for help from a psychologist, she might have been ...~~)

After *if*, the subjunctive forms *were* and *be* are sometimes used in second conditional sentences in very formal contexts (→ 159e). *Were* is used in hypothetical conditionals, *be* tends to be used more in real conditionals:

If *there* ***were*** *any reason to doubt his word, we would ask him to resign.*

I am delighted to see you again, even ***if*** *it* ***be*** *under such tragic circumstances.*

In most informal contexts, indicative forms of *be* are preferred, except for the semi-fixed expression *if I were you*:

If *she* ***was*** *to sell her place now, she'd probably make a big profit.*
(preferred to: If she were to sell ...)

If I were you*, I'd book a taxi the night before.*

IF AND POLITENESS 459

If-clauses do not always mark conditions; they can be used to issue polite directives, especially in spoken contexts, where the *if*-clause often stands alone and typically involves a modal verb:

[a headteacher speaking to a group of parents before a meeting begins]
***If** I could just have your attention for a moment please. Thank you.*

[request to a friend to hold a computer cable which will be attached to a printer]
***If** you'd just like to hold this for me.*

[extract from a letter from an insurance company]
***If** you would like to return your insurance certificate to us, we will issue a new certificate for your vehicle within three working days.*

Other common expressions involving *if* include *if I may say so*, *if it'll help*, *if you see what I mean*, *if that's all right with you*, *if I may put it like this*, *if it's not rude to ask*, *if you don't mind*. These expressions add a tone of politeness, and function to soften statements and questions:

*You've still got an awful lot of work to do on this, **if I may say so**.*

***If it's not rude to ask**, how old are you?*

*Could you move to the other room, please, **if you don't mind**.*

Comparison

Comparison

Comparative forms compare one entity or process with another. The most common comparative forms are adjectives and adverbs used with the suffix *-er* or premodified by *more*. The object of the comparison is most commonly introduced with *than*.

Comparison involves both morphological patterns in the form of endings, and syntax in the form of comparative clauses.

Comparatives often say that two things are different in quality or quantity or that something becomes different by changing over time:

Your dog might be fat but our dog is ***lazier****, I'm sure.*

In fact, I think that this school has a ***brighter*** *future* ***than*** *the private school has.*

It's getting ***hotter*** *and* ***hotter****.*

Comparatives also say that two things are of the same quality and quantity. A common structure used to indicate this function is *as ... as*:

Geoff is ***as*** *overweight* ***as*** *his wife.*

Leeds has almost ***as*** *many coffee bars* ***as*** *London.*

Superlative forms involve comparison by singling out one thing as having a unique quality. A superlative defines a specific member of a set. An adjective or adverb with an *-est* ending or which is premodified by *most* is a common marker of a superlative form:

Taipei has the ***tallest*** *building in the world.*
(Taipei has the building which is taller than all the other buildings in the world)

I've got four daughters. They are all small but Chloë is the ***smallest****.*

Tiger Woods is definitely the ***most improved*** *golfer in the year 2000.*

Comparison can indicate choices and preferences:

Bob'll have salad ***rather than*** *chips. He's trying to lose weight.*

Comparative forms also allow attitudes to be expressed. The comparative form sometimes refers to an assumed norm. For instance, in the following examples it is normal to assume that people have one house and that ice cream is delicious:

Jill now has ***as*** *many* ***as*** *five houses.*

Italian ice cream is always the ***most delicious****.*

[slower ski slopes are not as dangerous]
*Don't you think it'll be dangerous for Bill to ski on the **faster** slopes?*

ONE-SYLLABLE ADJECTIVES 461

One-syllable adjectives normally form comparatives and superlatives with *-er* and *-est*.

Examples of the comparative and superlative of one-syllable adjectives

adjective	comparative	superlative
cold	*colder*	*coldest*
strong	*stronger*	*strongest*
fine	*finer*	*finest*
rich	*richer*	*richest*
big	*bigger*	*biggest*
thin	*thinner*	*thinnest*

✪ *More* and *most* are not normally used before one-syllable adjectives:

*She is two years **older** than her sister.*
(~~She is two years more old than her sister.~~)

*The **strongest** businesses in the region have also contracted in the last six months.*
(~~The most strong businesses in the region …~~)

*That's the **fattest** pigeon I've ever seen.*

In informal contexts, *more* and *most* can be used with some short adjectives, often when followed by *than*. When spoken, the stress normally falls on the word *more*:

*It's **more** cold in the North **than** it is in the South.*

*She looked **more** thin today **than** I've ever seen her.*

More and *most* do have to be used with the single-syllable adjectives *apt*, *real*, *right* and *wrong*:

*He made what he was teaching seem **more real**, didn't he?*
(~~He made what he was teaching seem realer, didn't he~~?)

*You couldn't be **more wrong**.*
(~~You couldn't be wronger.~~)

TWO-SYLLABLE ADJECTIVES 462

Two-syllable adjectives which end in *-er*, *-le* or *-ow* can have comparatives and superlatives either with *-er* and *-est* or with *more* and *most*. Such adjectives include *able, clever, hollow, narrow, simple*:

*Peter is the **cleverer** brother.*
(or: Peter is the more clever brother.)

*The **simplest** approach is often the best approach.*
(or: The most simple approach is often the best approach.)

The comparative and superlative forms of two-syllable adjectives ending in *-y* are spelled *-ier*, *-iest*. Among the most frequent are: *angry, busy, clumsy, easy, friendly, funny, happy, lovely, lucky, pretty, silly, windy*.

Examples of the comparative and superlative of two-syllable adjectives ending in *-y*

adjective	comparative	superlative
friendly	*friendlier*	*friendliest*
lucky	*luckier*	*luckiest*
angry	*angrier*	*angriest*

*Be careful! He's **clumsier** than you think.*

*It's been one of the **windiest** days on record, with gusts reaching 100 miles per hour.*

MULTI-SYLLABLE ADJECTIVES 463

Multi-syllable adjectives form their comparative and superlative with *more* and *most*:

*He is **more interesting** than his brother.*
(~~He is interestinger than his brother.~~)

*The **most intelligent** solution would be to do nothing.*
(~~The intelligentest solution would be to do nothing.~~)

Some negatively prefixed forms are exceptions. They can take either *more* and *most* or *-er* and *-est*:

*She's one of the **untidier** guests.*
(or: She's one of the more untidy guests.)

*Yesterday was the **unpleasantest** day of my life.*
(or: Yesterday was the most unpleasant day of my life.)

IRREGULAR ADJECTIVES (*BAD, GOOD, ILL, WELL*) 464

Some very frequent adjectives have irregular comparative and superlative forms.

Examples of the comparative and superlative of irregular adjectives

adjective	comparative	superlative
good	*better*	*best*
well	*better*	*best*
bad	*worse*	*worst*
ill	*worse*	*worst*
old	*older/elder*	*oldest/eldest*
far	*farther/further*	*farthest/furthest*
little	*smaller*	*smallest/littlest*

The weather in Scotland was ***better*** *than we thought.*

Compared with the other teams in the division, they have had the ***worst*** *results.*

He was ill last week; this week he is ***worse****.*

The same applies to the use of these words in compound adjectives:

It's always advisable to book with the ***best-known*** *company.*

Don't you think she is ***better-looking*** *than her sister?*

That was one of the ***worst-organised*** *trips I've ever been on.*

Older/elder; farther/further

Note that when talking about members of a family, *elder/eldest* may be used. In other contexts *older/oldest* are used:

Janet is my ***elder*** *sister but Mary is the* ***eldest****.*

Their ***eldest daughter*** *has just won a swimming scholarship to an American university.*
(preferred to: Their oldest daughter …)

The cathedral is the ***oldest*** *in Northern Europe.*
(~~The cathedral is the eldest in Northern Europe.~~)

Elder may not be used with *than*:

My sister's ***older*** *than me.*
(~~My sister's elder than me.~~)

There is no difference in meaning between *farther* and *further* when both refer to distances. However, only *further* is used when the meaning is 'extra' or 'additional':

I just can't walk any ***farther****.*

The ***furthest*** *road is sometimes the best road to take.*

For ***further*** *information, see your Weekend magazine supplement this Saturday.*
(~~For farther information see …~~)

COMPARATIVE AND SUPERLATIVE ADVERBS 465

Short adverbs normally have comparative and superlative forms with *-er* and *-est*. The most common examples are: *early, fast, hard, high, late, long, loud, low, near, soon*:

Isn't it possible for them to come ***earlier****?*

Who jumped ***highest*** *in last year's Olympics?*

They said they couldn't finish the job ***sooner*** *than midday.*

Adverbs with two or more syllables form the comparative and superlative with *more* and *most*:

This book explains things a bit ***more comprehensively*** *than the other one.*

The new hotel is the ***most elegantly*** *designed building in the city.*

The adverbs *well* and *badly* have the same comparative and superlative forms as the adjectives *good* (*better, best*) and *bad* (*worse, worst*):

The whole team excelled themselves but Jane performed ***better*** *than I expected.*

We all sang badly but I sang ***worst*** *of all.*

COMPARATIVES 466

Than 466a

Than is used to introduce the second element in a comparative structure:

London is ***less*** *crowded* ***than*** *Paris.*

Don't you think the painting looks ***better*** *in the kitchen* ***than*** *it does in the front room?*

In the winter, I think hot drinks are ***better*** *for you* ***than*** *cold drinks.*

It was ***warmer*** *yesterday* ***than*** *today.*

He is much ***more*** *intelligent* ***than*** *he looks.*

She goes there ***more*** *often* ***than*** *I used to.*

These days Jim buys ***more*** *things for Anna* ***than*** *Bill buys for his daughter.*

That is not used to introduce the second element of a comparison:

She seems thinner ***than*** *she was the last time I saw her.*
(~~She seems thinner that she was the last time I saw her.~~)

When *than* is followed by a personal pronoun acting as the head of a noun phrase, the object forms (*me, him, her, us*, etc.) are used:

My sister is prettier ***than me****.*
(or: My sister is prettier than I am.)
(~~My sister is prettier than I.~~)

While she is training, they'll all have better-paid jobs ***than her****, won't they?*
(or: While she is training, they'll all have better-paid jobs than she has, won't they?)
(~~While she is training, they'll all have better-paid jobs than she, won't they?~~)

Rather than stresses one element of a comparison to the exclusion of the other (→ also **471g** below):

I'd say he was incompetent ***rather than*** *ignorant.*
(I'd say he was incompetent, not ignorant.)

They should buy experience ***rather than*** *youth and energy if they want to progress as a team.*
(They should buy experience, not youth and energy ...)

Comparative meanings 466b

A comparative form relates one entity to another. If a person says *I feel better today*, they are comparing their present state with how they felt before, which may have been 'not well/bad', rather than 'well/good':

Their house is ***smaller*** *than ours.*
(both houses may be big, or both may be small, depending on context)

The use of *even* makes the meaning of the quality being compared inherent rather than relative:

You're there for a semester. It's not just three months. It may be ***even longer*** *than that.*
(speaker considers a semester, i.e. six months, to be a long time)

Still and *yet* are more formal alternatives to *even*:

The last lap of the race was ***still*** *more exciting.*

Yet *more perplexing was the loss of £200 from the main company office.*

Even and *still* are often used in end position, especially in spoken contexts:

They played badly didn't they, ***worse*** *than last week* ***even****.*

The journey home was ***more boring still****.*

Traditional grammar books indicate that when two entities are compared, only the comparative form (*-er* or *more*) can be used. However, in informal spoken contexts the comparative and the superlative form are both used, with a general preference for the superlative:

Both brothers are very bright but Paul is ***the brightest****.*
(or, more formal: Both brothers are very bright but Paul is the brighter.)

*Which of these two photos do you think is **the best**? I need one for the passport form.*
(preferred to: Which of these two photos do you think is the better?)

In more formal contexts, *the* + comparative + *of* may be used:

*The **more relaxed of** the candidates didn't in fact get the job.*
(less formal: The more relaxed candidate didn't in fact get the job.)

Promotional texts often use comparatives rather than superlatives to evaluate products. The comparison is often implicit with other members of the class of entities:

[review of a new car model; *toss in* means 'add in']
*The Shelta is a **more refined**, **keener**-handling car that's a **more restful** motorway mile-eater. And you can toss in the bonus of **greater** exclusivity.*

Premodification of comparatives 466c

A lot, far, much
To indicate a much greater degree on the scale of comparison, premodifiying adverbs such as *a lot, far, much* and *somewhat* are used. The most informal and commonly used in speech is *a lot*:

*Joan's been **a lot happier** since she moved to London, hasn't she?*

*The film was actually **far more entertaining** than the review suggested.*

*No one mentioned that I would get **much less money** and would have to work **somewhat harder**.*

A bit, rather, slightly
To indicate a small degree on the scale of comparison, items like *a bit, rather, slightly* are used. The most informal of these is *a bit*, which is very common in conversation:

*I think the coast is probably **a bit cooler** at this time of the year.*

*I think we're **rather more broadminded** nowadays, certainly in comparison to the last generation.*

*It's only **slightly less humid** here than in Sri Lanka.*

A–Z 27 *Bit, a bit (of)*

Not (all) that much
Not (all) that much is used with a comparative adjective ending in *-er* to mean 'not as much as expected or indicated'. In all cases, the omission of *all* is optional, especially in informal contexts:

*The ferry is**n't all that much** cheaper.*

*She's **not that much older** than him, just a few years.*

539 **Glossary** for any unfamiliar terms

More than, less than

More than and *less than* are both used before adjectives as alternatives to *very* and *not very*:

*They are **more than satisfied** with the pay rise they have received.*
(very satisfied)

*Her tutor was **less than happy** with the examination results.*
(not very happy)

No, not any

No + comparative and *not any* + comparative can be used to indicate a limit to the scale of a comparison:

*Some of the roses in the garden were **no bigger** than small coins.*

*Three of the children were **not any older** than six or seven.*
(an equivalent alternative is: Three of the children were as young as six or seven.)

Fixed phrases

A number of fixed phrases are used to indicate the extent (or otherwise) of the difference between the degrees being compared. These include:

all the better	*any the wiser*	*any the worse*
all the more	*none the wiser*	*no worse*
		none the worse

*She is **all the better** for seeing him again.*

*The film was **all the more** impressive because the ending left the mystery unexplained.*

*There's no point telling him. He won't be **any the wiser** even if he knew the truth.*

*They seem to be **none the worse** for having been interviewed by the police.*

COMPARISONS OF SIMILARITY 467

As … as 467a

When comparisons of degree are made between things which are similar or the same, then the comparative clause structure *as* + adjective/adverb + *as* + phrase or clause is frequently used:

*Is the Sultan of Brunei **as** rich **as** the Queen of England?*

*They are **as** keen to join in **as** we are.*

*Property in Guanzhou isn't **as** expensive **as** in Hong Kong.*

*Because of the currents, they had swum out **as** far **as** they dared.*

*He doesn't smoke **as** much **as** he used to.*

The negative of *as … as* may be *not as … as*, or *not so … as*. The form *not as … as* is by far the more frequent:

*This new dentist is **not as** good **as** my old one.*

*It's **not as** cold **as** it was yesterday.*

*The second quiz was **not so** easy **as** the first.*

*These two extremes are **not so** contradictory **as** they might seem.*
(or: These two extremes are not as contradictory as they might seem.)

When used with attributive adjectives in a noun phrase introduced by the indefinite article *a/an*, the word order is *as/not as/not so* + adjective + *a/an* + noun + *as*:

*It was **as happy a marriage as** anyone could ever dream of.*

*It's **not as difficult a task as** I thought.*

*It turned out to be **not so big a room as** they said it was.*

 37 *Ever*

The same, similar 467b

The same as or *the same* + noun phrase + *as* are used to say whether things are identical:

*Most shopping malls are not **the same as** the ones back home in Chicago.*

*That woman over there has just bought **the same** video recorder **as** ours.*

*They're both wearing **the same** jacket **as** my husband.*

Similar means 'sharing many characteristics but not identical'. It is followed by *to*:

*Your garden is **similar to** ours, long and narrow.*

*What he's done is **similar to** what we're trying to do.*

Than is not used with *same* or *similar*, because *than* indicates a difference:

*Her Walkman is **the same as** the one I used to have.*
(~~Her Walkman is the same than the one I used to have.~~)

*Your kitchen is **similar to** ours.*
(~~Your kitchen is similar than ours.~~)

Same may be intensified using the following adverbs:

almost	*more or less*	*precisely*
exactly	*much*	*roughly*
just	*nearly*	

*Your jacket's **exactly the same** as mine.*

*We did **more or less the same** as we always do, just toured round and stayed in bed-and-breakfast places.*

539 **Glossary** for any unfamiliar terms

Very and *exact* may also intensify *same*, but they are used **after** *the*:

*They bought **the very same** DVD player as we did without realising it.*
(or: They bought the exact same DVD player ...)

Like 467c

Like is used as a preposition and as a conjunction (but ⇢ **471f** below) to indicate similarity:

*Your dog's **like** mine. He'll eat anything.*

*Are you going to France again, **like** you did last year?*

The following adverbs are commonly used to modify *like*:

a bit	*just*	*somewhat*
a little	*quite* (meaning 'somewhat')	*very*
exactly		

*Your ideas sound just **a little like** our ideas.*

*It feels **just like** a new car.*

*His nature is **quite like** my father's.*

Note that sentences with *look*, *seem* and *sound* may sometimes not be true comparisons but may be hedged modal forms:

[identifying a coat among a pile of coats]
*That looks **like** mine.*
(could mean either: 'It appears similar to mine.' or 'It probably is mine.')

*That sounds **like** Steve's car.*
(could mean either: 'That car sounds similar to Steve's car.' or 'That probably is Steve's car.')

A–Z **49 *Like***

SUPERLATIVES 468

General 468a

Superlative adjectives are used to compare an entity with a whole group of which they are assumed to be a part:

*Nepal has the world's **highest** mountain.*

*Japan is the second **richest** country in the world.*

*In the 1980s Jack Nicklaus was the **best** golfer in the world.*

When a superlative is used with *the* to refer to something or somebody in a group, a prepositional phrase is often used to identify the group:

*Henry was **the tallest** of them all.*

*She was **the fastest worker** on the staff.*

Note the use of *in*, not *of*, when places are mentioned:

*Ben Nevis is the **highest** mountain **in** Scotland.*
(~~Ben Nevis is the highest mountain of Scotland.~~)

Superlative forms also occur in a range of common prepositional phrases:

*She's not been **in the best of health** this winter.*

*The storm was **at its worst** at 2 a.m.*

*Valencia were not **at their best** in the first half but things improved later in the game.*

Note the non-superlative use of *most*, meaning 'very'/'extremely', which may occur with the indefinite article *a*:

*That really is **most** kind of you.*
(~~That really is kindest of you.~~)

*The group has completed the exercise **most** imaginatively and above all **most** accurately.*

*It was **a most interesting** lecture.*

Use of *the* 468b

The is obligatory before superlative adjectives used attributively:

*It's **the most interesting** novel I've read in a long time.*
(~~It's most interesting novel I've read in a long time.~~)

*She's not **the most approachable** person, first thing in the morning.*
(~~She's not most approachable person, first thing in the morning.~~)

When a superlative adjective is used predicatively in expressions which define an entity, *the* is obligatory:

*His brother is quite tall but Henry is **the tallest** of them all.*
(~~His brother is quite tall but Henry is tallest of them all.~~)

The is optional before predicative adjectives in a *wh*-clause or in adverbial uses of the superlative:

*Let's see who's **(the) quickest** at answering these questions.*

*It depends on what's **(the) best** for you personally.*

*Patsy arrived **(the) earliest**.*

The + superlative adjective + *of* is also used, particularly before indefinite nouns. The structure is rather formal:

> ***The best of** ideas happen when you are not thinking.*
>
> *In New York even **the cheapest of** apartments is not affordable.*

The is optional with superlative adverbs modifying verb phrases:

> *A lot of students work hard but mature students generally work **(the) hardest**.*

The is used with superlative adverbs if the adverb modifies an adjective:

> *It is one of **the most beautifully** structured pieces of music.*

Intensifying superlatives 468c

Imaginable, possible, etc.

In more formal contexts, superlatives can be complemented by adjectives such as *conceivable, imaginable, possible, thinkable,* etc., in the structure superlative adjective + noun head + complement:

> *It's the **most beautiful** landscape **imaginable**.*

Superlative adjective complements of this kind can alternatively precede the noun head:

> *The travelling conditions were designed to inflict the **greatest possible** suffering.*

By far, easily, much, quite, etc.

The emphatic expressions *by far, easily, much, quite* (meaning 'absolutely'), and *simply* may premodify expressions with *the* + superlative:

> ***By far the biggest** island in Scilly is St Mary's.*
>
> *They were **easily the best** vegetables in the competition.*
>
> *We scaled many minor cliff faces during the expedition, but this was **much the most dangerous**.*
>
> *It was **quite the most significant** event in recent Greek history.*

Very

Very is used to emphasise superlatives with *best, worst, first* and *last*:

> *This is the **very best** choice you will ever have.*
>
> *We had to wait for ages. We were the **very last** in the queue.*

The absolute

The absolute may also be used to intensify a superlative adjective:

> *It was **the absolute biggest** ice cream I'd ever seen.*
>
> *Yes, after 25 years of successful development of the North Sea, our expertise is some of the best, if not **the absolute best**, in the world.*

COMPARISONS OVER TIME 469

Comparatives and superlatives are often used to compare things at different times:

*She looks **healthier** than the last time we saw her.*

*They are **more optimistic** than they were about the direction of the economy.*

*It was the **best** summer holiday I'd had in five years.*

In order to say that there is gradual or progressive change, either the comparative adjective or adverb can be repeated or the phrase *more and more* can premodify an adjective or adverb:

*She's hardly eating and just getting **thinner** and **thinner**.*

*I can't follow him. He's become **more and more** incoherent.*

*The team started to play **more and more** aggressively.*

In more formal uses, the adverb modifier *increasingly* is used for similar purposes:

*We are more optimistic, a little wealthier and enjoy the conviction that things are changing for the better and that the worst is somehow behind us in an **increasingly** distant past.*

Ever is often used with comparative constructions with *than* and *as ... as*:

*The students scored **more** passes **than ever** this year, and the exams were **as** tough **as ever**.*

Ever and *yet* can be used as the complement of a superlative construction to indicate a time dimension. *Ever* may occur immediately following a superlative adjective or after the noun. *Yet* normally follows the noun:

*It was **the biggest ever** demonstration of loyalty to the governing party.*

*That was **my most difficult** moment **ever**.*

*In tonight's game the team face **their stiffest** test **yet**.*

COMPARISON AND OTHER WORD CLASSES 470

The determiners (and their pronoun equivalents) *little*, *many* and *much* are used in their comparative and superlative forms to make comparisons. They have irregular comparative and superlative forms.

Comparative and superlative forms of determiners/pronouns

determiner/pronoun	comparative	superlative
little	*less*	*least*
many, much	*more*	*most*

*It's **less exciting** than the first book.*

*That's the margarine that has **the least fat content**.*

→ 539 **Glossary** for any unfamiliar terms

*They haven't got **much** but I'm afraid they can't offer you **more**.*

*There's **more milk** in the fridge.*

*Which of you could come and help us? Who's got **the most spare time**?*

→ also **190 Determiners and pronouns**

More and *less* 470a

More and *less* can be used with all the major phrase classes:

- Noun phrases:

  *They will go on strike unless they are offered **more** money.*

  *People seem to have **less** money to spend nowadays.*

- Verb phrases:

  *Leeds attack **more** than Milan but their defence will see them through.*

  *It rains **less** here than in the west.*

- Adjective phrases:

  *Their house is **more** spacious than ours.*

  *I'm **less** keen on seeing Oxford than London.*

- Adverb phrases:

  *The garage over the road does repairs **more** quickly.*

  *He seemed to answer the questions **less** honestly than the other witness.*

- Prepositional phrases:

  *The problem lies **more** in her attitude than in her ability.*

  *I have **less** in common with my cousins than with some of my colleagues at work.*

More of and *less of* can be used to modify countable nouns which are gradable (i.e. which can be measured on a scale):

*I'm afraid she's being **more of** a hindrance than a help.*

*I'm **less of** an expert than you are.*

Less is used with singular non-count nouns. It is often followed by *than*:

*Now I have **less** time **than** her to do jobs around the house.*

*I think I'm getting old. I have a lot **less** energy **than** I used to.*

Increasingly, in a wide range of spoken and written contexts, *less* is used with plural countable nouns:

*If there were **less than** six students in the class, they cancelled it.*
(or: If there were fewer than six students in the class, they cancelled it.)

Most and *least* 470b

Most and *least*, like *more* and *less*, can be used with all major phrase classes:

- Noun phrases:

  Whoever has ***most*** *money can pay now and we can pay it back later.*

  We had the ***least*** *work to do of any of the groups.*

- Verb phrases:

  Restaurants and taxis – that's where we spent the ***most****.*

  I wouldn't like to say who works ***least*** *in that family, no one seems to have a proper job.*

- Adjective phrases:

  They're the ***most*** *delicious chocolates I've ever tasted.*

  She seemed to be the ***least*** *anxious of all.*

- Adverb phrases:

  Of all of them, she worked the ***most*** *intensely.*

  I think she spoke the ***least*** *sincerely of all the women.*

- Prepositional phrases:
  In the case of prepositional phrases, *mostly*, not *most* is used, and has the meaning of 'more than in any other case':

  The damage was ***mostly*** *to the side of the car.*

  This action provoked a storm of international criticism, ***not least*** *from the United States.*

→ **190 Determiners and pronouns** for *less* and *least* as determiners

COMPARATIVE CLAUSES 471

General 471a

Comparative clauses are clauses which express the second part of a comparison of degree. Comparative clauses (in bold type in the examples) are frequently introduced by *as*, *than*, or *which/that*. They function as complements of comparative expressions (in green in the examples):

The garden wasn't as big ***as I had imagined it would be****.*

The interview was the same ***as I'd experienced several times before****.*

He's worked here longer ***than I have****.*

In Malaysia we lived in a bigger house ***than we could ever afford in Britain****.*

It was the ugliest dog ***that I'd ever seen.***

The weather wasn't so bad ***that it spoiled the holiday.***

Clauses with *as* 471b

As (or *just as*) is used in comparative clauses as a conjunction:

Do they drive on the left in Australia, **as** *we do?*

English uses modal verbs to refer to future times, **just as** *other languages use verb endings.*

Subject-verb inversion may occur after *as* with modal and auxiliary verbs, copular *be* and substitute *do*. In such inverted clauses, *just* is not used with *as*:

I only wanted to help, ***as would anyone have done.***

He was a train driver, ***as was his father*** *before him.*

[talking about a new computer]
It's got two USB connections, ***as did the old one*** *in fact.*

In informal contexts, *like* is frequently used instead of *as* (→ **471f** below):

Is he having a New Year's party, **like** *he did last year?*

Clauses with *as if* and *as though* 471c

As if and *as though* can introduce clauses operating as the second element in comparisons of similarity. They may be used in finite, or, in more formal contexts, non-finite clauses:

He took a deep breath before he spoke, **as if** *to keep himself calm.*

What's the matter? You're acting **as if** *you're in pain.*

He looked round the table **as if** *daring anyone to smile.*
(non-finite; more formal)

When I resigned from my job, I felt **as though** *a weight had been lifted from my shoulders.*

Chantal looked uncomfortable, **as though** *forced to consider the matter for the first time.*
(non-finite; more formal)

She stood up **as though** *to leave.*

Ellipted clauses with adjectival complements are common with *as if* and *as though* in more formal contexts:

She just sat there, ***as if totally unaware*** *of what was happening.*

He took off his glasses and began to polish them ***as though afraid*** *of showing some emotion.*

Clauses with *so, too, enough* 471d

Comparative clauses with *so* + adjective/adverb + *as*, *too* + adjective/adverb, and adjective + *enough* are followed by non-finite clauses with the *to*-infinitive:

*Would anyone be **so** irresponsible **as** to drink and drive after a party like that?*

*They are just **too** upset to speak about it.*

*He was driving **too** slowly to have had any chance of getting there before us.*

*If anyone is stupid **enough** to withdraw now, they'll lose all their money.*

When *too* is used with an attributive adjective in a noun phrase introduced by the indefinite article *a/an*, the word order is *too* + adjective + *a/an* + noun:

*It's **too big a job** to finish in one day.*

Clauses with *the same* 471e

The same as may introduce comparative clauses of equality:

*We're going to Spain for our holidays, **the same as** we always do.*

A comparative clause may follow when *the same* premodifies a noun. The comparative clause may be introduced by *as* or by a relative pronoun (*who/which/that/zero relative*, etc.):

*He gave **the same** reason **as** you did.*

*That's **the same** woman **who** I saw the other day.*

*It's **the same** switch **that** broke the last time.*

In informal use, when *same* is used in front position, *the* can be omitted:

A: *What did you have to drink?*
B: ***Same as** I always do. Tea.*

Clauses with *like* 471f

Like can also be used to express similarity or identity either as a conjunction or as a preposition. Traditional grammar books warn that only *as* can be used as a conjunction and not *like*, but its use as a conjunction is widespread, especially in spoken English. It is generally regarded as a less formal alternative to *as*:

*But bees, even on chilly mornings, are capable of making a cold start. They shiver just **as** we do to warm our muscles.*
(formal, written)

*Do you go to Giorgio's every Friday, **like** we do?*
(informal, spoken)

A–Z **49 *Like***

Clauses with *rather than* 471g

Rather than is normally used to stress one element of a comparison to the exclusion of the other. It is typically followed by a verb in the same non-tensed form as the verb with which the comparison is made:

I always prefer ***getting*** *up early in the morning* ***rather than lying*** *in bed reading the papers.*

The editor has decided to ***cut*** *the paragraph* ***rather than rewrite*** *it.*
(also possible: '… rather than to rewrite it.' or '… rather than rewriting it.')

Rather than is often fronted to emphasise the comparison. When fronted in this way, the *-ing* form or the base form, but normally not the *to*-infinitive form, is used:

Rather than complain *all the time, he decided to change to another hotel.*
(or: Rather than complaining all the time, he decided to change to another hotel.)
(~~Rather than to complain all the time, he decided to change to another hotel.~~)

Clauses with superlatives 471h

Both finite and non-finite clauses may follow superlatives. The non-finite clauses have a similar function to relative clauses (··✤ 317j):

That's one of ***the best*** *films I've ever seen.*

She's ***the youngest*** *swimmer to qualify for the Olympics.*

They were ***the fittest*** *team finishing the course.*

Double *the* + comparative 471i

Two comparative clauses preceded by *the more* (or *the less*, or a combination of both) are used to say that one situation, event or action results from another. The entities compared are normally fronted:

The more *I swim,* ***the more*** *energetic I feel.*

The less *I work,* ***the less*** *I feel like working.*

The more *I read it,* ***the less*** *impressed I am.*

The same structure can be used to coordinate noun phrases. The entities compared are normally fronted:

The less *effort they put in,* ***the more*** *money they earned. It was very unfair, really.*

Similar structures are used involving *the* + comparative adjective/adverb. Again, the entities compared are fronted:

The sooner *we finish,* ***the earlier*** *we can go home.*

The more *important she became,* ***the less*** *we saw each other.*

··✤ **473b Predicative complement** in **Word order and focus** on subject-verb inversion after expressions of comparison in fronted complements

Word order and focus

Word order and focus

INTRODUCTION 472

Word order in this chapter is principally concerned with how the elements of the clause (subject, verb, object, complement, adjunct) are arranged. Word order choices also affect phrases, and the chapters on phrase classes (155–257) specify the patterns of word order found in noun, verb, adjective, adverb and prepositional phrases.

Theme and rheme

Clauses may be considered as having two parts in relation to how information is arranged within them: the theme (or topic) and the rheme (or comment). The theme/topic is typically the starting point of the clause, who or what the clause is 'about'. The rheme/comment is the main part of the message, the important information given about that topic. In the sentence:

theme/topic	rheme/comment
Sue	| *is starting a new job on Monday.*

the clause is 'about' Sue, and the new or important information is that she is starting a new job on Monday. In English, the theme/topic is located in the beginning of the clause (and is most typically the subject), while the rheme/comment occupies the latter part of the clause after the subject.

The end of the clause is important in English, as that is where the most 'weight' falls in terms of the focus on new information, sometimes referred to as endweight.

Marked and unmarked word order

Unmarked word order refers to the normal, most typical sequence of elements. For example, the unmarked word order for a declarative clause with an object is s–v–o, where s is the subject, v is the verb and o is the object. In English, the word order o–s–v is marked (possible but far less typical):

S V O
He loves football.
(unmarked, normal word order: the subject, *he*, is the theme)

O S V
That furniture we bought years ago, this lot is more recent.
(marked word order: *that furniture* is the theme, rather than *we*)

Marked (untypical) word order may be used to create various kinds of focus, that is, special emphasis on particular elements for a variety of purposes.

The basic rules for clause and sentence structures (→ 269–337) describe how to build unmarked sentences. However, in connected discourse, other choices have to be made concerning such things as introducing new topics, distinguishing between new and old information, linking events in particular ways, flagging or highlighting the importance of something, foregrounding some things and backgrounding others, all of which may have implications for choices of word order.

Simple word order choices

Some choices of word order simply rearrange elements without any other grammatical changes. These include fronting and the use of headers and tails.

Fronting involves moving objects, complements and adjuncts to front position in the clause, which, in unmarked word order, is typically occupied by the subject:

object
That bowl *we got in Italy. The other one's from Spain, I think.*
(fronting of the object in order to focus on a contrast between the two bowls)

adjunct
First thing tomorrow morning *we'll have to check all the plants for frost damage.*
(fronting of the adjunct to emphasise when the task must be done)

The creation of headers and tails (→ 96, 97 and 474), is another way of putting extra focus on selected entities.

In the case of fronting, the elements remain fully integrated within the clause. In the case of headers and tails, elements of the clause are placed outside of the clause structure, either immediately before the first clause element or after all other elements in the clause. This is a particular phenomenon of spoken grammar:

header S V O adjunct
That brown chair, we bought ***that*** *years and years ago.*
(header: gives extra focus to *that brown chair*)

S V complement tail
They*'re awful people, my neighbours.*
(tail: gives extra focus to the subject)

Choices of structure

Some choices of word order involve choosing between alternative structures, for example choosing whether to use an indirect object or a prepositional complement with verbs such as *give* or *bring*, or choosing whether to use active or passive voice:

[talking about birthdays and activities associated with them]
Do you send birthday ***cards*** *to your friends?*

The new, important information here, which would be phonologically stressed, is *to your friends*. Birthdays and things associated with birthdays are already the topic of conversation; they are 'old' or 'shared' information. *Do you send your friends birthday cards?*, using an indirect and direct object, is also possible and correct, but would have suggested a focus on birthday cards as 'new', 'non-shared' information.

Some choices of word order involve more complex grammatical structures and choices, for example embedded clauses or cleft sentences:

It was on Sunday I first noticed I had a rash.
(cleft sentence enabling emphasis on 'on Sunday')

So ***what you really want*** *is a hotel that's got the facilities for the children, isn't it?*
(*wh*-cleft enabling extra focus on the complement 'a hotel that's got …')

→ 539 **Glossary** for any unfamiliar terms

That they thought they could use the computers without permission ***is hard to believe.***
(*that*-clause as subject enabling extra focus on the object of 'believe')

FRONTING 473

Direct objects 473a

A direct object may be fronted, that is, made the theme (or 'thematised') in a declarative clause, especially in spoken language; this occurs most typically when the speaker wishes to contrast things. Phonologically, the fronted object (bold in the examples below) is typically stressed:

[speaker is talking about the early days of computers, and how he bought one type after another and occasionally upgraded the power]

O S V
And then we bought an Impact, and ***that*** *we couldn't get upgraded.*
(the 'Impact' is contrasted with other computers which the speaker upgraded)

O S V
I must admit, ***my favourite books*** *I do read over and over.*
(here there is an implicit contrast with other books which the speaker would not read over and over)

[talking about pipes a plumber is working on; contrasting different ones]
O S V
He's got those disconnected, but ***that one*** *he's still got connected.*

Objects of prepositional verbs and phrasal verbs may also be fronted:

The other list *we can look at later.*

[wife talking about how she and her husband share the work in their garden]
I do the flowers; ***the vegetables*** *he looks after.*

Object fronting can also occur in interrogatives in informal speech, but this is not very common:

[speaker is looking over someone's shoulder while they are cooking]
O aux S V
Soup *are you making? Wow, lovely!*

Predicative complements 473b

Subject predicative complements are often fronted for extra focus or for contrast. This may occur in declaratives and in interrogatives.

In informal spoken language, fronted noun subject complements are more common than fronted adjective subject complements:

[looking at a photo of an old car]
complement S V
Mm, ***my very first car****, that was.*

C modal S V
***Jack**, could it have been?*
(fronted noun complement)

C S V
***Ambitious** it may be, but when a club sells 20,000 season tickets and makes £3.3 million during the summer, it knows it is back in the big league.*
(fronted adjective complement)

Fronted complements which are expressions of comparison may be followed by subject-verb inversion, especially in more formal written styles:

[from a text about the Maastricht Agreement signed in 1992 by 12 member states establishing the European Union]
*Maastricht was not a triumph for any Government, although each of the Governments present claimed it as one. **Least of all** was it a triumph for the British Prime Minister.*

*Children make a substantial contribution to the social, economic and cultural life of their families, communities, and even to national economies. These contributions are rarely recorded by official statistics and are usually ignored when policy decisions are made. **Equally unnoticed** is the unpaid 'work' that children do around the home, in the fields, or at institutions of learning.*

[discussing a conference on debt and international development]
*The conference was helpful in aiding my understanding of the great mass of information that I am faced with in my volunteer role. But **much more important for me** was to be exposed to the experience of people working with the poor in the Third World whose suffering results from debt.*

Object predicative complements may also occasionally be fronted:

A: *Down our end in Victoria Street there was a bookmaker they used to call Ray, and he had just one arm. '**Ray the Bookie**' we used to call him.*
B: *Yeah. I can remember him.*

Adjuncts 473c

Adjuncts may be fronted for emphasis or contrast:

***Ten years** we've lived here.*

***Without my glasses** I can't see a thing.*

When adjuncts of negative meaning (e.g. *never, not once, rarely, seldom*) are fronted for emphasis, they are followed by subject-verb inversion:

***Not once** did she thank me.*
(~~not once thanked she me.~~)

***Seldom** had we witnessed such bad behaviour.*

→ **319–337 Adjuncts**

In rather formal styles, inversion may occur after initial *thus*, and after expressions such as *in this way*, *for this reason*:

[at the time of writing, Mr Blair was the British Prime Minister, and Mr Campbell was his press secretary, with whom he had a very close working relationship]
***Thus** does Mr Blair find himself ever more closely closeted with Mr Campbell.*

→ **324 Front position** in **Adjuncts** for a full account of fronting of adjuncts

Verbs 473d

A lexical verb with an accompanying complement or adjunct may sometimes be fronted for purposes of focusing on some other element of the verb phrase:

[British Prime Minister Tony Blair, speaking when newly elected in 1997]
*The British people are a great people. There is no greater honour than to serve them, and **serve them** we will.*
(creates strong endweight on *will*, since it must be phonologically stressed in final position)

***Sitting in the garden** I've been, all morning.*

Occasionally, an auxiliary/modal verb and a lexical verb may both be fronted. This typically occurs in spoken language:

*Why didn't you phone your mother? **Been really panicking** she has.*

HEADERS AND TAILS 474

Headers and tails stand outside of the normal subject – verb – object – complement – adjunct clause structure. They typically occur in informal spoken language.

Headers

Headers usually take the form of an initial noun phrase which refers to the same entity as a later pronoun. They are used to focus on an entity, or to highlight contrasts:

***Paul**, in this job that **he**'s got now, when he goes into the office, he's never quite sure where he's going to be sent.*
(Paul is the speaker's new topic or entity focused on)

***Edward**, **he**'s always the first person to complain.*

Headers may also occur with interrogative clauses:

***That key**, did you put **it** there or did I?*

Headers may involve more than one extra noun phrase used initially, to take the listener step-by-step from familiar entities to the new entity the speaker wishes to focus on or say something about:

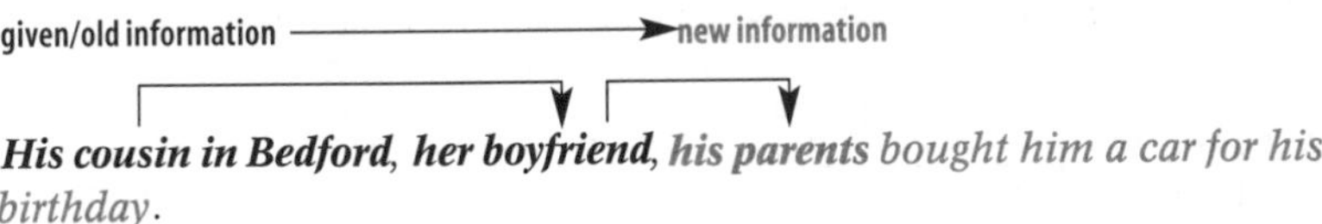

His cousin in Bedford, her boyfriend, his parents *bought him a car for his birthday.*

Tails

Tails involve noun phrases used at the end of the clause, referring to the same person or thing as a previous pronoun in the clause. Such word order is typically used to highlight judgment, comment or evaluation rather than mere statement of fact:

*And **he**'s quite a comic, **the fellow**, you know.*

***It**'s really nicely done out, **this place**, all wooden.*

The tail may involve a demonstrative pronoun rather than a full noun phrase:

***It**'s a speciality, **that**.*

***It**'s driving me crazy, **this**.*

→ **96 Headers; 97 Tails**

STRUCTURAL OPTIONS 475

Indirect object versus prepositional complement 475a

In expressing the recipient or beneficiary of an action, there is often a choice between an indirect object or a prepositional complement.

Unmarked word order is indirect object (IO) + direct object (DO):

*Did you give him **the money**?* (him = IO, the money = DO)

If the recipient/beneficiary is to receive more focus, it can be expressed as a prepositional complement (PC) and placed at the end of the clause, giving it endweight:

[speaker B has just given speaker A a present]
A: *Oh, you didn't have to do that!*
B: *I bought **a present** for Rhonda as well.* (a present = DO, for Rhonda = PC)
(*Rhonda* is the new, important information here; 'presents' are old, given information)

*The plans were revised about 1974 but they still gave **a disproportionate focus** to France.* (a disproportionate focus = DO, to France = PC)

Where two pronouns are involved, a prepositional complement is often preferred:

DO PC
She wrote her name and address on the card and gave ***it*** *to me.*
(or: ... and gave me it./... and gave it me.)

DO PC
I think my mother gave ***them*** *to them.*
(preferred to: ... gave them them.)

Delexical expressions, using verbs such as *do, get, give, make, take* enable a verb-type meaning to be expressed in a following noun object. In expressions where the verb *give* is used delexically, IO + DO is preferred to DO + PC:

IO DO
Well, I gave them ***a song.***
(I sang)
(~~I gave a song to them.~~)

IO DO
The doctor gave him ***a quick examination.***
(examined him)
(~~The doctor gave a quick examination to him.~~)

Prepositional complements may be fronted, especially in formal styles, creating endweight on the direct object:

PC
To his wife he gave ***a pearl necklace.***

Indirect objects are not normally fronted:

IO
I gave Liam ***the wrong postcode.***
(~~Liam I gave the wrong postcode.~~)

Active versus passive voice 475b

Unmarked active voice word order places the subject first, since the subject is typically the theme (who or what the clause is 'about'). Passive voice enables the speaker either to omit reference to the agent/doer altogether (unless the agent is required by the verb) or to place the agent/doer in a prepositional phrase after the verb and thus create focus on it:

I ***was admitted*** *to hospital.*
(focus is on the rheme, my being admitted to hospital; compare: 'The hospital admitted me', where *the hospital* would be unmarked subject/theme, thus losing its focus)

I was just coming home and five minutes after I left this friend I was with, he ***was attacked*** *by two men.*
(the rheme includes the agents – *two men*)

He ***got arrested***.
(focus on the event of his arrest; there is no need to explicitly mention the agent, understood as probably the police; compare: 'He was arrested by a huge, ugly police officer', with focus on the agent)

The audio-lingual method of teaching ***was imposed*** *upon us.*
(no one is named or blamed for the event)

The hotel ***was owned*** *by the Greek Church, wasn't it?*
(obligatory agent phrase with the verb *own*; but compare: 'The Greek Church owned the hotel', where *the Greek Church* loses its special focus)

→ also **480, 484, 485** in **The passive** for pseudo-passives with *have*

Cleft sentences (*It was David who called.*) 475c

A cleft sentence is one where a single message has been split/divided (or 'cleft') into two clauses. Cleft sentences with *it* allow different clause elements to be brought into focus. In a typical *it*-cleft structure, the focus is on the final element of the *it*-clause (in green in the examples below), with the subsequent *wh*-clause (underlined in the examples) reiterating given or previously known information:

[talking of someone whose job it is to evict people from houses for unpaid rents, mortgages, etc.; the dwellings are 'repossessed' by the bank or other lender]
He was telling me he was called in for a repossession this week. ***It was*** *an elderly lady <u>who had this house</u> and they'd sent her umpteen letters and appeals and she'd ignored the lot.*
(focus on the subject, *an elderly lady*; 'who had this house' is given/old information in the context of house possession)

[talking about waiting for an eye operation]
A: *I talked it over with my optician then went to my doctor and got a reference to the hospital which would be about March and he warned me that it would be about six months.*
B: *So* ***it was*** *in March <u>that you went</u>?*
(focus on the adjunct *in March*; 'going (to the hospital)' is already given/old information in the context)

I doubt people would have as many pets because ***it's*** *usually the children <u>who say 'Mum can I have a pet?'</u>.*

I've always had morning stiffness, I accept that's part of my life. By the time I've had my pills for two hours in the morning, the stiffness eases and I'd sooner have a bit of stiffness than I'd have the pain. ***It's*** *the pain <u>I can't cope with</u>.*
(focus on the object of the prepositional verb 'cope with': *the pain*)

Wh-cleft sentences (*What we need is a hammer.*) 475d

What …

Wh-cleft sentences are most often introduced by *what*. *Wh*-cleft structures shift the focus to the end of the clause. The information in the *wh*-clause (bold in the examples below) is typically old or given in the context, while the copular complement (in green in the examples) contains the new, important information:

[speakers are discussing speaker B's banking needs]
A: ***What you need*** *is a telephone bank account.*
B: *Mm.*
(focus on the object; the listener's state of 'need' is already given; the telephone bank account is the new, important information)

[speakers are talking of someone they dislike]
A: *It never happens really that I get angry with people er but I did with him last night and I had to go for a walk to calm down.*
B: *Well* ***what gets me*** *is the way he spends his time being sexist and unpleasant.*
(focus on *the way he spends* …)

The *wh*-cleft construction may itself receive end-focus by occupying the complement slot in the main clause:

[university literature tutorial about the writer Samuel Beckett and a critic who has written about Beckett's work, Martin Eslin]
A: *You aren't just saying Eslin is occupying a philosophically untenable position therefore I'm occupying one which is tenable.*
B: *No that's* ***what I don't want to say.***
A: *That's* ***what you don't want to say.***
B: *But I think that's* ***what James thought I wanted to say.***
C: *Yeah. What you're saying is Eslin is occupying a philosophically untenable position and also has misread Beckett.*

How …, where …

Wh-clefts with a *what*-clause as subject are far more frequent than *wh*-cleft sentences introduced by *why, where, how*, etc. as subject. One reason for this is that the meanings of *why, where, who, when* and *how* are often expressed by nouns such as *the person, the place, the way*, used in front position to create the same kind of focus on the complement of the main verb:

Well, ***the way*** *I see it going is that the European Union will expand to include not only Lithuania but also other former Soviet Republics.*
(or: How I see it going is that …)

The place where *I've been is where they train local midwives.*
(or: Where I've been is where they …)

The reason *it wasn't sorted out earlier was because they were short of staff.*
(or: Why it wasn't sorted out earlier was because …)

The person *you need to talk to is the manager.*
(preferred to: Who you need to talk to is the manager.)

***The day** we wanted to travel was a Monday, but it was all booked up.*
(more frequent than: When we wanted to travel was a Monday, ...)

However, when the *wh*-cleft clause is in complement position, *wh*-clauses are often used:

[an elderly man, speaker A, is recounting how he was an apprentice railway wagon-maker as a young man]
A: *And, of course, I gradually built up then to until I got the main overall jobs, and by the time I was twenty-one, of course, I was considered a full wagon repairer.*
B: *Twenty-one was **when you finished your apprenticeship**.*
A: *Yes, that's right.*

What ... + clause
The *wh*-cleft may serve as a marker highlighting a whole clause or a longer stretch of discourse instead of focusing on one clause element. This is especially common in spoken language:

[speaker B is asking for advice about pensions and insurance, on the telephone]
A: *Would you like me to get one of the advisers to give you a call sometime? And they can go over with you basically what pensions are available to you and what life insurance.*
B: *That would be good yeah.*
A: *Okay that's fine. **What I'll do** is I'll take all your details from you.*
B: *Uh-huh.*
A: *And then we'll send it out to your closest branch and they give you a call in the next few days.*

[talking about arriving late for an interview for a teaching post]
*But by the time I got to that school I thought, well, nothing else can possibly go worse than this. And I went in and I got met at the front gate. And **what happened** was I'd arrived so late that I'd missed the tour round the school which I'd had previously when I'd been up. And I got there the time that I was due to see the headmistress. So I went straight to see the headmistress, went in and apologised for being late.*

This .../that ... + clause
A clause introduced by *this* or *that* with a *wh*-cleft complement can also serve a similar purpose. *This* clauses generally point forward, *that* clauses generally point back in the text:

*So **this** is what we'll do. Firstly, introduce the speakers.*

*So if you want to stay warm in winter all you do is you wear, instead of wearing one thick layer of clothes, you wear lots and lots of layers of clothes. They may be thin but lots of, lots of layers and what they'll do is they'll trap air between them and **that**'s what will keep you warm.*
(in this example, several types of focusing structure occur together; note also the construction with *all*: *all you do is* ...)

⇢ 539 **Glossary** for any unfamiliar terms

What I did …

In spoken language, the connecting copular verb is often omitted:

> ***What I did**, I bought the medium size and they said I can take it back if it doesn't fit.*

> ***What happened**, I drove through one of those speed cameras and I wasn't concentrating.*

The thing, one thing, something 475e

Initial constructions with *the*, *a*, *something* plus a relative clause can be used to create focus on subsequent clause elements in a similar way to other cleft constructions. These constructions occur typically in informal contexts:

> ***The thing I was struck by** was their complacency.*
> (similar to: What I was struck by was their complacency.)

> ***One thing she's been doing recently** is buying white shoes to decorate them for people.*

> ***Something you might like to look at** is the sequence of events in the story.*

 74 *Thing, stuff*

Anticipatory *it* 475f

Anticipatory *it* often enables a subject to appear at the end of the clause, thus producing end-focus:

> ***It** amazes me how open and honest the staff are.*

> A: *Beatrice says that it's hard to insure antiques because, you know …*
> B: ***It**'s hard to put a value on it all for that, isn't it?*
> A: *Yeah.*

> *It says that you've got to pay certain legal fees if you leave. You know, we were thinking **it** was wrong paying £25 a week.*

474 above to compare tails with *it*

Extra focus on fronted time adjuncts may be created with *it is/was not until, it is/was only when*:

> ***It's not until** we lift the carpet in our bedroom that we'll know what we've got to deal with.*
> (compare: 'Until we lift the carpet in our bedroom, we won't know …', or 'We won't know what we've got to deal with until we lift …')

> ***It was only when** he mentioned that he lived in Cambridge that I knew who he was.*

Existential *there* 475g

Existential *there* makes possible an optional (and often preferred) variant of clauses with an indefinite subject. The pattern enables focus to be placed on the subject by locating it in the rheme of the clause instead of its usual position as the theme:

[talking about visiting a house with a view to buying it]
We drove past it one time and ***there*** *was a woman standing outside, she said, 'Oh what do you want?' I said, 'Oh, well, we've come to see the house.'*

With verbs other than *be*, the *there* construction is confined to formal/literary styles:

A few days after that meeting with Lucian, ***there came*** *the letter.*

All signs of the market had vanished and in its place in front of the squat town hall, ***there stood*** *only a platform.*

Raising (*It was hard to understand.*) 475h

There are often different structural options available with adjectives such as *certain, difficult, easy, hard, impossible, likely, sure*, verbs such as *appear, look, seem*, and mental process verbs in the passive such as *be considered, be estimated, be found*.

Adjectives such as *difficult, easy, hard, impossible* most typically take an infinitive-clause complement and most frequently occur with anticipatory *it*:

It *was* ***impossible*** *to say hello to everyone.*

It'*s not* ***easy*** *to ride a monocycle.*

The infinitive complement may, however, occur as the subject of the clause or as a 'raised subject', to create different types of focus:

- Infinitive clause as subject:

  To summarise our work ***is impossible.***

  To find a shop open so early in the morning ***isn't going to be easy.***

- Infinitive clause as 'object-raised-to-subject':

  In practice, however, this distinction is ***impossible to make.***
  (*this distinction* is the object of *make* but becomes the grammatical subject of the clause)

  Jina's quite ***difficult to understand.***
  (Jina, the object of *understand*, becomes the subject of the clause)

→ 539 **Glossary** for any unfamiliar terms

Verbs such as *appear, look, seem* present various structural options, which include raising:

He always ***seems*** *to come at some unlucky moment.*
(subject-to-subject raising: *he* is the subject of *come* and is chosen as the subject of *seem*; compare the anticipatory *it* alternative: 'It always seems (that) he comes at some unlucky moment.')

It ***seems*** *that nobody does anything.*
(anticipatory *it* as subject; *nobody* is the subject of *does*; compare: 'Nobody seems to do anything.')

That ***looks*** *to be the right place.*
(subject-to-subject raising; compare: 'It looks as if that is the right place.')

Mental process verbs in the passive such as *be considered, be estimated, be observed* and verbs reporting research results such as *be discovered, be found* also present raising options, especially in formal and academic styles:

Overall, the scheme ***was found*** *to produce clear benefits on an individual level, largely in terms of teachers' revised perceptions and attitudes.*
(subject-to-subject raising: *the scheme* is subject of *produce* and subject of *was found*)

On analysis of the women's diets, it ***was found*** *that all the women in the control group consumed a minimum of 500 ml of cows' milk daily.*
(anticipatory *it* as subject; compare subject-to-subject raising alternative: 'All the women in the control group were found to consume ...')

[text about the relationship between brain hemispheres and left- and right-handedness in humans]
The proportion of right hemisphere speakers ***was estimated*** *to be about 9.27 per cent of the population irrespective of handedness.*
(subject-to-subject raising; compare anticipatory *it* alternative: 'It was estimated that the proportion of ...')

Pseudo-intransitive constructions (*Fish cooks quickly.*) 475i

Verbs which are normally used transitively are sometimes used intransitively in clauses where the real recipient/beneficiary of the action becomes the grammatical subject (→ **475h** above to compare raising), and where the agent is not mentioned. This gives endweight to the verb (and any accompanying complement/adjunct).

Verbs used in this way include:

clean	*iron*	*print*
close	*keep*	*read*
cook	*open*	*sell*
drive	*pack*	*store*
fold (up)	*photograph*	*wash (up)*

*The base of the bed is still in the dining room, they can't get it up the stairs although **it folds up**, you know, it's standing like this in the dining room.*

A: *I like your outfit you had on on Sunday.*
B: *Frank bought it last year for my birthday.*
A: *I thought maybe you'd got it while you were abroad.*
B: *No, no, he bought it from a woman, a friend, she makes them and she knitted it. Well, she knew my size so ...*
A: *Yeah.*
B: *And **it washes up lovely**.*

[looking at a photograph of a woman called Helen]
***Helen photographs** really well doesn't she?*

→ also **283a Pseudo-intransitive construction** in **Verb complementation**

Nominalisation and adjectivalisation 475j

An option which is often chosen in academic and more formal styles is to use a noun-form of a verb as subject in order to turn the verb into the theme and to give extra focus to the rheme.

Nominalisation may be seen as the opposite of clefting (→ **475c, above**) in that two clauses are condensed into one. The nominalised clause (bold in the examples below) typically represents old, background or given information, and the complement (in green in the examples) represents new, important information:

***The capture of the suspected terrorists** is a major breakthrough for the authorities.*
(compare: The suspected terrorists have been captured, and this is a major breakthrough for the authorities.)

[about ex-US President Richard Nixon, whose presidency fell after the Watergate crisis]
*Ironically, **his insistence on taping all White House conversations to ease the writing of his future memoirs** was to be the major stumbling block to his surviving the crisis.*
(compare: He insisted on taping ... and this was the major stumbling block ...)

Adjective forms of verbs along with their complements may also function in a similar way to rearrange or condense information in the clause:

*She seemed most **insistent** that we should know it.*
(compare: She really insisted that we should know it.)

*I am very **desirous** to serve a friend.*
(compare: I very much desire to serve a friend.)

→ also **142 Nominalisation** in **Grammar and academic English** and **175 Formation of nouns (nominalisation)**

The passive

The passive

INTRODUCTION 476

Choice of voice (active or passive) is one of several ways of organising the content of clauses.

The active voice is the most frequent form, typically chosen to state something about the agent of an action (i.e. who does what). The agent is expressed as the grammatical subject and normally initiates the action:

Ken *took that photograph.*

Ken is here the grammatical subject and also the agent of the action. *Ken* is also the starting point or theme of the message (→ 472). *Took that photograph* is the rheme; it describes the action, what the speaker wants to say about *Ken*.

If a passive voice is chosen, the starting point of the message is the person or thing that is the affected participant of the action:

Those houses *were built by John Walton.*

Here *those houses* are the starting point or theme of the message. *Those houses* becomes the grammatical subject of the clause. What is said about the houses here includes information about the agent (the person who built them, *John Walton*). In this case the agent is expressed in the prepositional phrase *by John Walton*.

Finite forms

Various forms of the passive exist (→ 478–480 below). The most typical is the passive with *be*:

I ***was approached*** *and asked to go along.*

No crime ***has been committed****.*

We ***were rung up*** *by one of those consumer survey companies.*

New features ***are being added*** *to the machines all the time.*

Other forms share some characteristics with passive forms and are called pseudo-passive forms. They are based on *get* and *have* and are more common in spoken language. They are similar to true passives with *be* in that the grammatical subject is typically the recipient, rather than the agent, of the action. However, they differ from true passives in the functions they perform and the contexts in which they are used, especially with regard to the degree of involvement of the recipient in initiating the action, as can be seen in the table below (→ also 479 and 480):

The village ***is getting*** *more and more* ***built up****.*

She ***had*** *her car* ***stolen****.*

In spoken language, the *get*-passive is especially common:

*He **got thrown out** of a restaurant in town.*

*I wrote a letter to a newspaper and it **got published**.*

Non-finite forms

Passive and pseudo-passive structures also occur in non-finite clauses:

*I was grateful for the privacy and **to be allowed** to give in to the sadness that enveloped me.*

***Having been diagnosed** with cancer, I consulted both my acupuncturist, who was also a medical doctor, and my nutritionist.*

*I assume the matter **to have been filed** in the appropriate records.*

***Organised** by the Norwegian Trade Union movement, the festivities were attended by representatives from the church and state.*

*Do you remember Joan's son's wife **getting killed** at Mayheath?*
(*get*-passive)

[talking about a baby]
*As soon as you pick her up, though, she shuts up. She doesn't like **having her nappy changed**.*
(*have*-passive)

Passives may be seen as on a gradient from most typical, central passives to pseudo-passives and purely adjectival constructions. Agents and recipients of actions and events may be represented in a wide range of ways.

Examples of passives, pseudo-passives, and related constructions

example	comments
*He **was killed** in the war.*	central *be*-passive
*They **got arrested**.*	central *get*-passive
*He **got himself promoted** to manager.*	reflexive *get*-passive (recipient more actively involved)
*We **had some trees taken down**.*	*have*-pseudo-passive (causative: beneficiary of the action initiated the action)
*They **had their garden furniture stolen** last year.*	*have*-pseudo-passive (non-causative: beneficiary of the action did not initiate the action)
*I **got my car serviced** in that garage once.*	*get*-pseudo-passive (causative: beneficiary of the action initiated the action)
*I'll **get you set up** on the computer and then you can work away on your own.*	*get*-pseudo-passive (describes a process initiated by someone who may or may not be the agent)
***I'm quite fascinated** by what you say.*	semi-passive (like passive but also like adjectival construction: may be modified like an adjective)
*He's **totally obsessed** with astrology.*	more adjectival; prepositional complement has no active agent role
*The tape seems to have **got stuck**.*	resultative; describes a state resulting from an agentless process
*The handle**'s broken**.*	adjectival; describes a state

VERB COMPLEMENTATION AND PASSIVE VOICE 477

Only transitive clauses and certain clauses where the verb has a prepositional phrase complement may be made passive. Other active-voice clauses may not be made passive:

Active: *Someone* ***stole the car.***
(monotransitive: direct object)
Passive: *The car was stolen.*

Active: *Someone* ***gave him a warning.***
(ditransitive: direct and indirect object)
Passive 1: *He was given a warning.*
Passive 2: *A warning was given to him.*

Active: *Someone* ***broke into their car.***
(verb + prepositional phrase complement)
Passive: *Their car was broken into.*

Passives are not formed from copular verbs:

*She****'s*** *a teacher.*
(~~A teacher is been by her.~~)

Carol ***seems*** *right for the job.*
(~~The job is seemed right by Carol.~~)

Paula ***became*** *a nurse.*
(~~A nurse was become by Paula.~~)

THE *BE*-PASSIVE: FORMATION 478

The *be*-passive is formed by making the object of an action or event the grammatical subject of the clause and by using auxiliary *be* + the *-ed* participle (***ed*-p**) of the verb.

The agent may be realised as a prepositional phrase, most typically with *by* (→ 481 below):

	subject	verb	object
Active:	*A police patrol*	*spotted*	***a suspicious vehicle.***

	subject	*be* + *ed*-p	agent phrase
Passive:	***A suspicious vehicle***	*was spotted*	*by a police patrol.*

Be-passives are different from lexical verb *be* plus *-ed* form adjectives, which cannot normally have an agent phrase, and which may have particular prepositional structures following them:

I'm ***worried about*** *my mother.*
(*-ed* form adjective)
(~~I'm worried by my mother.~~)

Most people ***are worried by the thought of what a surgeon's going to do.***
(passive clause)

They're just ***tired of*** *each other.*
(~~They're just tired by each other.~~)

The table below gives examples of *be*-passive structures (in green) in different tense-aspect combinations. The passive elements are realised in the final *be*-auxiliary and the *-ed* participle (in bold). The examples marked with an asterisk (*) represent very rare types.

Examples of *be*-passive structures

tense-aspect form	example
present simple	*They **are sold** in three sizes.*
present progressive	*The house is **being sold**.*
past simple	*Alison and Jane **weren't asked** for their views.*
past progressive	*Did you feel as if you were **being ignored**?*
present perfect simple	*Has her father **been told**?*
present perfect progressive	*He has been **being watched** by the police for about three weeks.**
past perfect simple	*I saw at once how it had **been done**.*
past perfect progressive	*The town had already been **being visited** by three coaches full of tourists.**
modal simple	*The top can **be left** on.*
modal progressive	*They'll be **being interviewed** when we're in our meeting.*
modal perfect simple	*He fears that a man may have **been hanged** because of his carelessness.*
modal perfect progressive	*The house might have been **being watched** while we were away, before they burgled it.**

THE *GET*-PASSIVE: FORMATION 479

The *get*-passive is formed with *get* + the *-ed* participle of the verb. As with *be*, a range of tense-aspect forms is possible, though in fact a narrower range of forms actually occurs. These are the most frequent:

Do you know how much lawyers ***get paid*** *for an hour, the best ones?*

[reference to a company receiving a fine for safety violations]
*They**'re getting fined** by the Health and Safety Executive.*

All of a sudden they ***got raided*** *by the police.*

[student talking about upcoming hectic social timetable]
I've got invited *to the school ball as well.*

We found some parcels that ***had got pushed*** *into the corner.*

They ***may have got mixed up*** *the first time we used them.*

Reflexive structures occur with *get*-passives when the recipient of an action/event is felt to share at least some of the role of agent:

*She **got herself locked out**.*
(it was an accident, but partly her fault; compare: 'She got locked out', which was not her fault)

A *get*-passive structure similar to the pseudo-passive with *have* occurs occasionally in informal spoken language. The construction enables a person affected by an action or event to be made the grammatical subject:

[talking of strict customs searches at airports]
*I **got my belt searched** once when I went to Sweden.*
(non-causative; similar to: I had my belt searched/my belt was searched …)

*I'll **get you sorted out** with some boots for the walk, cos it'll be muddy.*
(causative: I myself will give you the boots or I'll find someone else to give them to you)

Prepositional phrases expressing an agent, although they do occur with *get*-passives, are far rarer than with *be*-passives:

*She **got arrested** by the Austrian police.*

PSEUDO-PASSIVES WITH *HAVE*: FORMATION 480

Pseudo-passives with *have* are formed with *have* + an object + the *-ed* participle of the verb (***ed*-p**):

have object ed-p
*Hilary **had her luggage searched** at the airport.*

*Did we tell you about the incident with the next door neighbour who**'d had his car kicked**?*

*We **had the house painted** last year.*

[complaining about someone who receives social security benefits and who refused a job]
*Now that man **should have his benefits stopped** because there was a job for £400 a week and he said no.*

The pseudo-passive word order *have* + object + *-ed* participle is different from that of active present and past perfect verb phrases:

*I **had** my hair **cut** the day before the wedding.*
('I had cut my hair the day before the wedding' would mean I did it myself)

***Do** they **have** their car **serviced** regularly?*
('Have they serviced their car regularly?' would suggest they normally do it themselves)

539 Glossary for any unfamiliar terms

AGENT PHRASES 481

Agent phrases most typically begin with *by*:

I was sort of adopted ***by a wonderful family****.*

Pollution in cities is also caused ***by cars, lorries, big buses, trains****.*

Other prepositions are used when the grammatical subject of the equivalent active clause is not the true active agent of an event. This often occurs with stative verbs:

The instructions are included ***on a separate sheet****.*
(active equivalent: 'This sheet includes the instructions.'; the sheet is not the true active agent – the agent is the person who included the instructions)

Clothes are sold ***in supermarkets*** *these days.*
(active equivalent: 'Supermarkets sell clothes these days.'; the true agent of the selling is 'companies' – supermarkets are the places where the clothes are sold)

I got covered ***in mud*** *when I fell.*

PASSIVES WITHOUT AN AGENT PHRASE 482

General 482a

Passives frequently occur without an agent phrase and are called agentless passives. There are a number of reasons why such a choice might be made. The entity responsible for an action may not be known or may not be considered relevant, or may simply be obvious.

The agentless passive enables focus to fall on the process. What is or is not done, or what happens, is important:

Swimming in the lake ***is prohibited****.*

The interview ***is being televised*** *tonight.*

The town ***was rebuilt*** *after the war.*

Five of us ***were sacked*** *for no reason.*

Applications ***should be received*** *by Friday June 23rd.*

Taxes ***will have to be put up*** *again.*

It was agreed *that no action needed to be taken.*

There were *twenty people* ***arrested****.*

Get-passives occur more frequently with no agent phrase than *be*-passives:

She's been a bit nervous ever since we ***got burgled****.*

He ***got conscripted*** *into the army and had to go to Belgium.*

Reference to the agent(s) may be omitted in order to deflect possible criticism, because it may be embarrassing/inappropriate to mention the agent, or because it may be necessary to omit such reference:

I'm sorry. It seems that your forms ***got mislaid***.

I've been told *that she is unreliable.*

Students ***will be penalised*** *for late submission of assignments.*

We would like a new approach ***to be worked out***.

Detached/impersonal styles 482b

Agentless passives are conventionally used in impersonal speaking and writing styles (e.g. academic and technical language) when processes are the focus of attention:

Heat ***was applied*** *until the mixture came to the boil.*

The central heating system ***has to be*** *regularly* ***maintained***.

Vitamin tablets ***should be taken*** *daily.*

Such impersonal uses often involve reporting verbs such as *believe, consider, find, say, think*:

What is poverty? Much of the debate centres on what level of income ***is considered*** *to be the poverty level.*

[scientific text about birds: *young* here means 'young birds']
Losses of eggs and young ***were found*** *to be relatively constant throughout the season, even though their numbers increased dramatically for a short time.*

Anticipatory *it* 482c

Anticipatory *it* makes forward reference to a complement clause, and may be used to express impersonal agency:

The German reply was exactly what the Austrian government had wanted. ***It was decided*** *to issue an ultimatum to the Serbian government, framed in a manner that would be likely to provoke war.*

It has been argued *that rights are inevitably relative to each culture.*

Existential *there* 482d

Existential *there* allows an indefinite subject to be placed later in a passive clause. This has the effect of creating greater focus on the passive subject:

There were *hundreds* ***killed*** *in the earthquake.*
(Note the word order. ~~There were killed hundreds in the earthquake.~~)

I did complain, but ***there was*** *no action* ***taken*** *at the time.*

539 **Glossary** for any unfamiliar terms

Functions of the *get*-passive

483

The *get*-passive is used in more informal contexts and is more common in spoken than in written English. It is only used with dynamic verbs (verbs denoting actions or events rather than states):

A headmaster **got stabbed** *a few weeks ago. What is the world coming to?*
(dynamic verb)

The standard unit of mass used by all scientists **is kept** *at the International Bureau of Weights and Measures at Sèvres, near Paris, France.*
(non-dynamic verb: ~~The standard unit of mass used by all scientists gets kept at the International Bureau of Weights and Measures ...~~)

The *get*-passive enables a clear distinction to be made between a dynamic event and a state or situation:

The fence **got damaged***.*
(dynamic event)

The fence **was damaged***.*
(not clear if it is a state or a dynamic event)

The *get*-passive places a little more emphasis on the grammatical subject or the entities involved. For this reason it is often used to recount newsworthy events. The actions/events most typically do not benefit the entity described and the form is often used when a situation is judged to be problematic in some way:

[speaker who once worked for a tobacco company]
Well actually I **got sacked** *because I was purposely trying to disrupt the business cos I hate smoking so much.*

A: *My interview was supposed to be on the fifteenth and then it* **got moved** *to the nineteenth.*
B: *Oh no.*
A: *And then guess what Martin.*
B: *What?*
A: *It* **got cancelled** *at five to eleven on the nineteenth.*

The *get*-passive is not used exclusively in negative or problematic contexts, and positive newsworthy events are also (though less often) described using the *get*-passive:

Liam **got promoted** *again. He's now the sales and marketing director.*

[tennis player talking]
I **got picked** *for the county so I played county matches.*

When a reflexive construction is used with the *get*-passive, it often indicates the involvement or responsibility of the grammatical subject:

Somehow the key **got itself jammed** *in the door.*
(speaker 'blames' the key)

For all his power, you see, Dr Primo Nebiolo has never succeeded in **getting himself elected** *to the International Olympic Committee.*

The *get*-passive is informal. In the following examples the *get*-passive sentences would be more likely to be used in informal contexts. The *be*-passive equivalents sound more detached and neutral:

He damaged the picture and ***got sued*** *by the owners, who said that it had lessened its value.*
(He damaged the picture and was sued by the owners, who said that it had lessened its value.)

That town ***got*** *really badly* ***hit*** *by an earth tremor.*
(That town was really badly hit by an earth tremor.)

FUNCTIONS OF PSEUDO-PASSIVES WITH *HAVE* 484

The *have*-pseudo-passive most typically enables a person affected by an action or event to be made the grammatical subject, thereby making that person the starting point for the message:

They ***had*** *their keys* ***stolen****.*

He ***had*** *his window* ***smashed****.*

Other alternatives make different participants the theme of the sentence:

Someone stole their keys.

Their keys were/got stolen.

The meaning may be causative or non-causative:

I don't mind paying to go to the dentist or to ***have*** *my eyes* ***checked****.*
(causative: I make it happen)

My friend round the corner recently ***had*** *his video* ***stolen****.*
(non-causative: it was not his intention or aim)

In the case of some verbs which take an object plus prepositional complement, the *have*-pseudo-passive compensates for the lack of a *be*-passive and enables the affected participant to become the theme:

I've ***had some ideas suggested to me****, but I need time to think.*
(or: Some ideas have been suggested to me …)
(~~I've been suggested some ideas …~~)

We'll ***have that explained to us*** *all over again at the next meeting, I'll bet.*
(or: That will be explained to us all over again …)
(~~We'll be explained that all over again …~~)

✪ The meaning of the *have*-pseudo-passive is not the same as the perfect aspect form of the verb:

*Oh, you**'ve had your hair cut**. It looks nice.*
(someone, a hairdresser, cut your hair; 'Oh, you've cut your hair' would mean you did it yourself)

GET- AND *HAVE*-PSEUDO-PASSIVES 485

Get-pseudo-passives and *have*-pseudo-passives can often both be used to express causative and non-causative meanings. The *have*-passive is more formal than the *get*-passive:

*We **got** our car radio **stolen** twice on holiday.*
(or: We had our car radio stolen twice on holiday.)

*They**'ll have had** the phone **connected** by now.*
(or: They'll have got the phone connected by now.)

*I **have** my hair **done** about once a month.*
(or: I get my hair done about once a month.)

VERBS USUALLY ONLY FOUND IN THE PASSIVE 486

Some verbs are most typically used in the passive rather than the active voice. These include:

be born	*be populated*	*be strewn*
be deemed	*be stranded*	*be taken aback*

***Were you born** in Bristol, Mary?*
(used in the past tense: ~~Are you born in Bristol, Mary?~~)

*They **were deemed** unsuitable as foster-parents.*

*They **were taken aback** by the violence of the film's ending.*

DESERVE, NEED, REQUIRE, WANT WITH A PASSIVE MEANING 487

Deserve, *need*, *require* and *want* can be followed by an active *-ing* form structure although the grammatical subject is the affected participant of the process denoted by the verb, thus creating a meaning similar to a passive voice structure:

*The picture's dark, very dark. It **needs restoring**.*
(similar to: It should be restored.)

*Your jacket **wants cleaning**.*
(similar to: It should be cleaned.)

→ also **475b Active versus passive voice** in **Word order and focus**

A–Z **75 *Want***

Speech representation

Speech representation

INTRODUCTION 488

Representations of speech are ways of reporting one's own or another person's speech. Speech reports are normally divided into direct and indirect reports.

Direct reports

A direct report consists of a reporting clause and a reported clause. The reporting clause contains a verb indicating speech, such as *ask, demand, say, shout, tell*. The reported clause represents or attempts to recreate the exact words someone used, as they occurred at the moment of speaking, with the same pronouns, tenses, clause types, etc. which the original speaker used. The reported clause is separated by punctuation from the reporting clause, usually by means of commas and speech marks (normally single or double inverted commas):

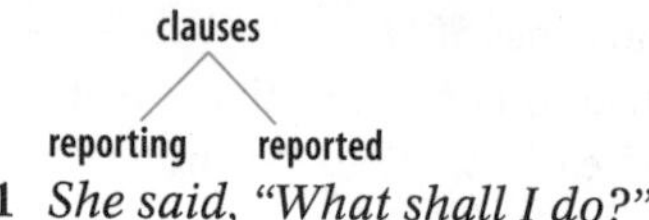

1 *She said, "What shall I do?"*

clauses

reported reporting

2 *"Where are you going?" he asked.*

Indirect reports

An indirect report consists of a reporting clause, plus a reported clause which is more fully integrated as the object of the reporting verb and not usually separated by punctuation. The reported clause has a form which reflects the speech act of the original utterance.

The reported clause may be a *that*-clause (reporting a statement), a *wh*-clause (reporting a *wh*-question or exclamation), a clause with *if* or *whether* (reporting a polar question) or an infinitive clause (reporting a directive):

- Reporting statements:

  ***She informed me that** she used to know my mother and was on friendly terms with half a dozen of my aunts.*

  ***I told him** I hadn't seen it.*
  (*that*-clause with zero-*that*)

- Reporting *wh*-questions and exclamations:

  ***Miguel told me what** happened at the farmhouse tonight.*

  ***She asked who** we'd been talking to.*

  ***She remarked what** a beautiful house it was.*

- Reporting polar (*yes-no*) and alternative questions:

  *Pointing at my forehead, he asked **if** I had been fighting.*

  *She took his hand and asked **whether** he had slept.*

  *I asked her **if** she was full-time or just part-time.*

- Reporting directives:

  A: *I told you **to phone** her up.*
  B: *I know. Er, sorry, I forgot.*

  *The doctor ordered him **to rest** for at least a month.*

When someone's words are reported indirectly, pronouns, tenses, clause types, etc. change to reflect the situation of the current report in relation to the original moment of speaking of the words reported.

Example **1** above (*She said, "What shall I do?"*) would typically be made into an indirect report as in **1a**:

1a *She asked what she should do.*

- *I* has now become *she*, as the speaker is reporting the words of a female third person.
- *Shall* has become *should* to reflect the time lapse since the words were uttered.
- The interrogative clause has become declarative as the clause is now an indirect report and is no longer a direct question.
- *Said* has become *asked* as a question is being reported.

Example **2** above (*"Where are you going?" he asked.*) would typically be made into an indirect report as in **2a**, with similar changes to the grammar of pronouns, tenses and clause types:

2a *He asked where I was/we were/they were going.*

Other ways of reporting

In direct speech, the report represents or attempts to recreate or give the illusion of the original speaker's exact words. In indirect speech reports, the report is not necessarily meant to be a recreation of someone's exact words; it may function just to report the content of what they said.

Speech reports, both direct and indirect, are most commonly made with reporting clauses containing verbs such as *ask*, *say* and *tell* with a reported clause. There are also other, more indirect ways in which people's speech can be reported, by using nouns such as *argument*, *comment*, *complaint*, *observation*, *remark* to refer to someone's words, or by quoting them, especially the words of famous people:

*I didn't like his **comment** that we were spending too much money.*

*Well their biggest **complaint** was that the room was too small.*

***To quote** Shakespeare: "All the world's a stage, and all the men and women merely players."*

Speech reports may be reports of real, past speech events or they may be hypothetical or be reports of things people will say or intend to say:

*If he asks me to do it again, I think **I'll just say**, "No. Do it yourself."*

***We should ask them** what day they can deliver the fridge and things.*

REPORTING VERBS 489

Say in its past tense form *said* is by far the most frequent reporting verb in direct reports, especially in everyday spoken language:

*I **said**, 'Gran, I was only doing this while I was waiting for the kettle to boil.'*

'So you're too busy for me,' he **said**. *'I feared it had come to that.'*

Say and *tell* are also by far the most frequent reporting verbs in indirect reports in everyday spoken language:

*And after a moment he **said** that he had been in the valley for forty-seven years.*

*Mrs Johnson **told** her that Robert was part of a consortium.*

Ask is used frequently in informal conversation for indirect reports, but not for direct reports:

*They **asked** me what I thought about the food.*

The use of *ask* in direct reports is mostly confined to written fictional styles:

*'Will you not tell me the truth now?' he **asked**.*

Say versus *tell* 489a

Say and *tell* function differently in speech reports. *Tell* focuses on the content or message of what was said:

*She **told** him they were going on holiday.*
(focus on the information)

Say focuses more on the words someone said:

*'Hello,' she **said**.*
(~~'Hello,' she told me.~~)

Say can introduce direct reports. *Tell* is not normally used in this way:

*He **said**, 'I'm not paying £50 for that.'*
(~~He told me, 'I'm not paying £50 for that.'~~)

Say and *tell* have different rules of complementation. *Say* is used with an optional prepositional complement and an object (which is the reported clause). *Tell* normally has an indirect object, along with a direct object (which is the reported clause):

*I **said to her**, 'When I'm ready I'll tell you.'*

*She **said** she didn't know anything about it.*
(or: She told me she didn't know anything about it.)
(~~She told she didn't know anything about it.~~)

*And then they **told us** we had to do it.*
(or: And then they said we had to do it.)
(~~And then they told we had to do it.~~)

Say is not used with an indirect object to refer to the person addressed:

***I said to her**, 'When I'm ready I'll tell you.'*
(~~I said her, 'When I'm ready I'll tell you.'~~)

They told me I'd have to wait.
(or: They said I'd have to wait.)
(~~They said me I'd have to wait.~~)

Generally, *tell* but not *say* is used with an infinitive clause to report directives:

*The man from Foreign Affairs had **told** her **to prepare for the worst**.*

But in informal spoken contexts, *say* may also be used with an infinitive clause to report a directive:

*I phoned up the hospital and they **said to go down**.*

PUNCTUATION 490

Punctuation and direct speech 490a

A variety of punctuation conventions exist for direct speech reports. Direct speech may be enclosed in single or double inverted commas:

'I want to do it,' Anna said.

"Not always," replied Bobby.

As seen in these examples, a comma is used at the end of the direct speech, before the closing speech marks. A comma is also used when the reporting clause comes first. The speech marks close after the final full stop:

Anna said hastily, 'She doesn't mean to be patronizing.'

The direct speech normally begins with a capital letter. Where a reported sentence is interrupted (e.g. by a reporting clause or a discourse marker), the continuation of the report does not have a capital letter:

'Okay, come on Pat,' she said, 'let's go and have some tea.'

A colon may also be used to separate the reporting and reported clause, especially in quotations (e.g. in academic articles, journalism, quoting famous people):

He said: 'If we want to maintain our global role, we must be a leading player in Europe.'

Subscript inverted commas („... .") and the symbols «...» are not used in English to indicate direct speech:

I said, "Oh it's very kind of you."
(Not: I said, „Oh it's very kind of you." / « Oh it's very kind of you »)

→ **506f Direct speech** in **Appendix: Punctuation** for further details concerning punctuation of direct speech

Punctuation and indirect speech 490b

In indirect speech, the reporting clause is not separated from the reported clause by a comma when the reporting clause is first:

The lorry driver simply said that it was meat and bone meal from another delivery.
(~~The lorry driver simply said, that it was meat and bone meal ...~~)
(~~The lorry driver simply said that, it was meat and bone meal ...~~)

When the reporting clause is in end position, a comma is used to separate the clauses:

[referring to a picture]
It had been painted with love, he said.

Indirect reports of questions do not have question marks:

So people complained and asked him why we were waiting.
(~~... and asked him why we were waiting?~~)

REPORTING AND REPORTED CLAUSES 491

Position of the reporting clause 491a

A reported speech sentence typically consists of a reporting clause and one or more reported clauses (→ 488, above). The reporting clause most typically comes before or after the reported clause.

Examples of reporting clause before reported clause

reporting clause	reported clause
I said,	*'No, no, no, it's Sunday.'*
She told him	*(that) they were going on holiday.*
He asked,	*'What can I tempt you with?'*

Examples of reported clause before reporting clause

reported clause	reporting clause
'Oh it's been a real disaster!'	*she said.*
'Why wasn't I told?'	*she asked.*

In direct speech reports in informal spoken language, the reporting clause most frequently comes first. In literary fiction, the reporting clause most frequently comes after the reported clause. Reporting clauses may also interrupt the reported clause; this type is most frequent in written fictional styles:

- Before:

***He said**, 'They've double-booked you for a wedding reception.'*

- Interrupting:
  'What's happened?' ***Nicole demanded****. 'Please, I've got to know.'*
- After:
  'Have you found Michelle?' ***she asked anxiously****.*

In indirect speech reports, the reporting clause normally occurs before the reported clause:

A: ***I told you*** *that Ernie, her husband, died.*
B: *Yes.*

Less frequently, the reporting clause may occur after the reported clause.

He wasn't going to see Louise leave school, ***he said****.*

He was in the middle of an enforced career change, ***he said****.*

TENSE AND ASPECT IN REPORTING VERBS 492

The past simple 492a

When the report refers to a single past occasion of speech as a concluded event, the reporting verb is usually in the past simple tense. This form is by far the most frequent, in both spoken and written contexts:

'Well,' ***he said****, 'you're not 21.'*

They said *that was exactly what they wanted.*

The present simple 492b

In indirect speech reports, if the reported speech is seen as always true or relevant, or likely to be said on any given occasion, the present simple may be used with the reporting verb:

He went to a lady doctor in there. ***He says*** *she's very nice.*
(he would probably always say that if asked)

But when ***she says*** *water sports, what does she mean?*
(every time she says that word, not just one occasion)

→ 360 The present simple for dramatic effect

The present progressive 492c

In indirect speech, if the speech reported represents someone's current position or opinion (which might possibly change), then the present progressive can be used:

He's saying *it was a Head Office decision but did he know prior to that?*
(that is his current position on the matter)

→ 360b The present progressive for narrative build-up

The past progressive 492d

The past progressive is frequent in indirect reports in spoken language. It is used to focus on a new topic or to emphasise an important bit of news or information which the speaker has heard first-hand. It takes the focus away from the actual words reported and puts it on the content:

*Jenny **was saying** that five mortar bombs have been found at Heathrow Airport.*

*Don **was telling** me the Magdeburg students have lectures at seven o'clock in the morning.*

*He **was suggesting** I should travel.*

Reports of newsworthy items that the speaker has read about also often occur with the past progressive:

[Tony Blair was the British Prime Minister at the time of speaking]
*I **was reading** in the paper that Blair's going to the Caribbean for his holidays.*

VIEWPOINT: TIME AND PLACE REFERENCES 493

Deictic expressions (*now, here*) 493a

Ways of pointing to time (e.g. tenses, and words such as *today*, *ago*), place (e.g. *here*, *this shop*) and persons (*I*, *you*) at the moment of speaking are called deictic expressions. Deictic meanings are relative to where the speakers are and when they are speaking. Such meanings may undergo changes in indirect reports to reflect the viewpoint of the person reporting the words spoken (since the person reporting is frequently in a different time and place from the original situation and reporting someone else's words).

For example, the question *'Will you be coming here tomorrow, Jane?'* may be reported indirectly in a variety of ways, depending on where and when the report is made, and by whom. An illustration of some of the many possible changes to deictic reference are given in the table below.

Examples of changes to deictic reference (original question: 'Will you be coming here tomorrow, Jane?')

indirect reports	explanation
*I asked Jane if **she will** be **coming here tomorrow**.*	reporter is the same person and is at the same place where the original question was asked, and 'tomorrow' has not yet come
*I asked Jane if **she would** be **going there the next day**.*	reporter is the same person but is at a different place from where the original question was asked, and 'tomorrow' has gone
***He/she** asked Jane if **she would** be **going there the next day**.*	reporter is a different person and is at a different place from where the original question was asked, and 'tomorrow' has gone
***He/she** asked **me** if **I'll** be **coming here tomorrow**.*	reporter is Jane herself. She is at the same place where she was originally asked the question, and 'tomorrow' has not yet come

Tense backshift 493b

When the indirect report is perceived as referring to the past, the tense in the reported clause usually changes to a past form of the tense of the original speech. This process is known as tense backshift.

Examples of tense backshift

direct report	original tense form	indirect report	backshifted tense form
'Robert ***is*** *part of a consortium,' Mrs Johnson said to her.*	present simple	*Mrs Johnson told her that Robert* ***was*** *part of a consortium.*	past simple
*He said, 'I'****m*** *just* ***leaving*** *for the airport.'*	present progressive	*He said he* ***was*** *just* ***leaving*** *for the airport.*	past progressive
*She said, 'We'****ve lived*** *here fifteen years and we'****ve*** *never met him.'*	present perfect	*She said they* ***had lived*** *there fifteen years and they* ***had*** *never* ***met*** *him.*	past perfect
'I ***will go****,' he said.*	'future' *will*	*He said he* ***would go****.*	'future-in-the-past' *would*

For some tense-aspect forms, there may be no change between direct and indirect speech.

Examples of no change in tense

direct report	tense form	indirect report	tense form
He said, 'I ***was thinking*** *of getting my mum one for her birthday.'*	past progressive	*He said he* ***was thinking*** *of getting his mum one for her birthday.*	same
*She said, 'We'****d wanted*** *to go there for years.'*	past perfect	*She said they'****d wanted*** *to go there for years.*	same

The past progressive may change to the past perfect progressive if the speaker perceives the event as relating to a past before the moment of the direct speech.

Example of past progressive changing to past perfect progressive

direct report	tense	indirect report	backshifted tense form
He said, 'I ***was thinking*** *of getting my mum one for her birthday.'*	past progressive	*He said he* ***had been thinking*** *of getting his mum one for her birthday.*	past perfect progressive

When the report refers to something treated as still relevant, or still true, or as yet unfulfilled, the verb may not necessarily shift to the past:

*I've just talked to Barbara and she said she'****s taking*** *it on Monday.*
(Barbara probably said, 'I'm taking it on Monday.')

*He said he'****s going to do*** *military service.*
(he probably said, 'I'm going to do military service.')

Why ***is*** *Joanna angry? About what? You said she'****s*** *angry about a party.*

··➝ 539 Glossary for any unfamiliar terms

Backshift and modal verbs 493c

Backshift changes to modal verbs are more complex.

Must

Must usually changes to *had to*, especially when reference is made to an accomplished past event. However, if the event is still unaccomplished (i.e. the future-in-the-past), *must* may be retained in the indirect report.

***Must* in indirect reports**

direct report	indirect report
*'We **must** replace the cooker.'*	*She said they **had to** replace the cooker.
	She said they **would have to replace the cooker.
*'I **must** read it.'*	He said he **must** read it. (future-in-the-past)

* The form with *had to* may refer to an unfulfilled obligation or a fulfilled one.
** The form with *would have to* can only refer to an unfulfilled obligation.

Shall

Shall with first person subject (and its short form *'ll*) changes to *would* in reports of statements, but changes to *should* when questions are reported.

***Shall* in indirect reports**

direct report	indirect report
*'I'm not even certain this year whether I **shall** bother.'*	*He said he wasn't even certain this year whether he **would** bother.*
*'**Shall** I try it?'*	*She asked if she **should** try it.*

Can

Can changes to *could*.

***Can* in indirect reports**

direct report	indirect report
*'I **can** do it on Monday.'*	*She said she **could** do it on Monday.*

Other modal verbs

Could, might, should, would, ought to and *used to* do not change.

Other modal verbs in indirect reports

direct report	indirect report
*'I **could** come here seven nights a week.'*	*He said he **could** come here seven nights a week.*
*'I **might** need that money.'*	*She said she **might** need that money.*
*'Everybody **should** have a copy.'*	*He said everybody **should** have a copy.*
*'I **would** like a refund if possible.'*	*She said she **would** like a refund if possible.*
*'They **ought to** get an accountant to sort it out.'*	*He said they **ought to** get an accountant to sort it out.*
*'I **used to** take the dogs for a walk on the path there.'*	*He said he **used to** take the dogs for a walk on the path there.*

In the case of *could, might, should, would* and *ought to*, backshift does not require a shift to the perfect infinitive of the lexical verb. Such a change, if made, may produce a different meaning. Compare:

*She said she **would like** a refund.*
(report of what she wished for at the moment of speaking but had not yet received)

*She said she **would have liked** a refund.*
(understood: but they didn't give her one; report of what she had wished for but she did not in fact get it)

Personal pronouns 493d

References to people using personal pronouns in indirect reports depend on whether the person reporting the speech and the person(s) whose speech is reported are the same or different.

Examples of personal pronouns in indirect reports

direct report	indirect report
*'I'm spending the day in Glasgow with a school friend,' **she** said.*	***She** said **she** was spending the day in Glasgow with a school friend.* (reporting someone else's words)
*'**You** can use the cotton dressing gown as a nice tablecloth if **you** don't want to wear it,' **I** said to her.*	***I** told **her she** could use the cotton dressing gown as a nice tablecloth if **she** didn't want to wear it.* (reporting one's own words)
*'**I** have been in the valley for forty-seven years,' **he** said.*	***He** said that **he** had been in the valley for forty-seven years.* (reporting someone else's words)
*'**I**'ll mention it,' **I** said.*	***I** said **I'**d mention it.* (reporting one's own words)

⇢ also the table in **493a**

REPORTS OF STATEMENTS 494

That is often omitted in the reported clause, especially in informal contexts:

*She said (**that**) she was going to Majorca on a walking holiday.*

*I suggested (**that**) she actually invites a group of people back.*

When the report is the complement of the noun-form of a reporting verb, it is normal to include *that*:

*And what about the suggestion **that George might get an earlier appointment**?*

Occasionally, especially in less formal spoken language, *that* may be omitted after a reporting noun:

*There's a hint **the government's going to change its policy on house-building**.*

REPORTS OF QUESTIONS 495

Reports of polar (*yes-no*) and alternative questions 495a

When a *yes-no* question or an alternative question (a question involving a choice of *x* or *y*) is reported indirectly, *if* or *whether* is used with a declarative clause structure. In all the examples in the table below, *if* and *whether* can be used with no change in meaning.

Examples of reported *yes-no* and alternative questions

direct report	indirect report
'Will you work as a co-editor with us?'	*They asked me **if** I would work as a co-editor with them.*
'Will you be able to do it?'	*I asked him **whether** he would be able to do it.*
'Should I come over in the near future?'	*Jules just phoned me wondering **whether** she should come over in the near future.*
(possible question that was never asked) *'Do you want to stay overnight?'*	*I'm glad they didn't ask me **if** I wanted to stay overnight.*

Whether is preferred when *or not* immediately follows:

*Yeah, but they haven't stated **whether or not** it will be accepted.*
(preferred to: ... stated if or not)

However, when *or not* comes at the end, either *if* or *whether* can be used:

*She asked **if/whether** we had registered **or not**.*

In informal spoken style, a direct interrogative clause may occur instead of *if/whether*:

[speaker is talking of an experience while staying in hospital]
*You know the sweetener, I asked one of the cleaners **could she get me something** because it was on a very bad day and she had to ring down for permission for somebody else to get one.*

*At what point should we ask **have they got any rooms**?*

Reports of *wh*-questions 495b

When a *wh*-question is reported indirectly, the word order is normally declarative rather than interrogative:

*So I asked him **what** the arrangements were.*
(~~So I asked him what were the arrangements.~~)

*I phoned up the hospital and asked **who** I should address the letter to.*
(~~... who should I address the letter to~~)

In informal spoken style, interrogative word order is sometimes used:

*I asked him **where** was he going but he wouldn't say.*
(instead of: I asked him where he was going ...)

VOICE IN THE REPORTING CLAUSE 496

Most reporting verbs are active voice, but passive voice is also frequent in indirect reports, especially indirect reports with *ask* and *tell*:

My husband ***had been told*** *at the hospital that they were short-staffed.*

They ***should have been asked*** *if it had cost them money to get there.*

Passive voice is much less frequent in the reporting clause in direct reports, but it does occur (as *be-* and *get-*passive) in complement clauses of reporting nouns:

A question I'm often asked *is, 'Why do we need a pronouncing dictionary?'*

One question we often get asked *is, 'Do the crew sleep on board?'*

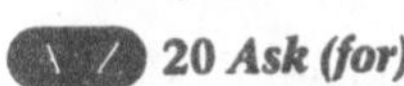
20 ***Ask (for)***

SPEECH REPORTS INTRODUCED BY NOUNS 497

Speech reports may be introduced by nouns. Nouns used in this way include:

accusation	*complaint*	*point*
advice	*concern*	*remark*
answer	*denial*	*response*
argument	*excuse*	*statement*
assertion	*explanation*	*suggestion*
claim	*news*	
comment	*observation*	

The noun may be the subject of a clause with *be*, with the reported clause as complement. Such reports may be direct or indirect:

A: *I mean if they didn't insist on that, would we bother?*
B: *Yeah.*
A: *And* ***the answer's*** *probably,* ***'No, we wouldn't.'***

Two weeks ago Senator John D Rockefeller of West Virginia abruptly abandoned his exploratory campaign for the Democratic nomination. ***His explanation was that he didn't have time to mount an effective bid***

The report may be the complement of the reporting noun:

The excuse that the computer was down *was a bit weak.*

I had a place next to my father, and ***the news*** *came down* ***that war had broken out***

I did make ***a suggestion as to whether I should increase the price of the property***

The report may simply be an expansion or elaboration of the reporting noun in a separate clause:

[electrical engineering university tutorial]
Well again we come back to ***the point that we made earlier****: are you actually plotting it against T, you know have you had to plot it against T or against something else?*

QUOTING AND ATTRIBUTING 498

The speech of others, especially of famous people, and proverbs and conventional sayings may be quoted, in order to support arguments, to invoke particular emotions, etc. Different structures may occur:

[Tony Blair was the British Prime Minister at the time of speaking]
To quote *Tony Blair, 'Education, education, education'.*
(verb infinitive)

Dr Fanshaw has this, ***I quote****, 'miracle cream' that he gives to all his ladies to reduce the stretch marks, and it really does work.*
(present simple tense)

As *the old proverb* ***says****, 'There's no smoke without fire.'*
(present simple tense)

As *she* ***put it****, 'I thought my time was up.'*
(past simple tense)

Speech may also be attributed to others by the use of expressions such as *according to X, so X says/said*, or more vaguely or obliquely with adverbs such as *allegedly, apparently, evidently* and expressions such as *or so I was/have been told, I've heard (that), they say/'re saying*. These expressions are particularly frequent in everyday conversation. Impersonal passive-voice expressions such as *it is said (that)/it is reported (that), it has been claimed/suggested/proposed (that)* are more frequent in formal (especially academic) texts (→ 502b, below):

A: *We're not getting copies.*
B: *Well* ***according to Gillian*** *you are.*

He happened to be an archer, ***or so he said.***

I was told that *I look nineteen.*

They say *it's a bad road, an accident black-spot.*

In ironic contexts, speakers often use the expression *quote-unquote* to refer obliquely to what is or has often been said in similar situations:

[ironic reference to a lifeguard's considerable legal responsibility when working with children]
A: *Is Sarah all right with them?*
B: *Yeah. Because she's a qualified lifeguard so she's been with the teachers. She's okay to cover them,* ***quote-unquote.***

REPORTING VERBS AND SPEECH ACTS 499

Speech acts (the communicative functions performed by utterances, ··➝ 408–423) are often indicated by the choice of reporting verb.

The reporting verb may represent the reported clause as performing a specific speech act. Verbs that are frequently used in this way include:

add	*confirm*	*offer*
admit	*continue*	*order*
advise	*deny*	*plead*
agree	*disclose*	*point out*
announce	*explain*	*protest*
argue	*hint*	*repeat*
assert	*inform*	*reveal*
beg	*interrupt*	*state*
claim	*intervene*	*suggest*
comment	*maintain*	*threaten*
complain	*note*	*warn*
confess	*observe*	

These verbs are most frequently used to introduce indirect reports:

*'I'll call Janice,' Sylvia **offered**.*

*'There's that photo of Michelle you keep on your desk,' Carole **suggested**.*

*I **pointed out** yesterday that sales so far this year are down.*

A: *Did they complain?*
B: *No, no. We **warned** them we were doing it in advance.*

REPORTS IN SPEECH AND WRITING 500

Subject-verb inversion 500a

In written direct speech reports, the subject and verb in the reporting clause may be inverted. This occurs particularly in literary writing and in journalism. It is very rare in informal speech:

*'And have we found a tenant for that charming room upstairs?' **asked Mr Perkins**.*

*'This is certainly someone the city wants to celebrate,' **said a spokesman for the city council**.*

This kind of inversion is even less frequent when the reporting clause comes before the reported clause, but does occur in written journalism:

> ***Says a spokesman cagily**: 'Pamela is away on holiday at the moment.'*

Reports of questions and answers 500b

In direct speech reports in formal written styles, a question is normally reported with a verb such as *ask, demand, enquire*, but in informal spoken language, questions are often reported with *say*:

> *'What happened?' the policeman **demanded**.*
> (written)

> *He **said**, 'Are you going to catch the bus home?' I **said**, 'Yeah.' He **said**, 'Are you paying?'*
> (spoken)

> *I **said**, 'D'you know anyone here?'*

Similarly, an answer to a question is often reported with verbs such as *answer* and *reply* in formal written style:

> *'Has the chaplain informed the family yet?'*
> *'No,' Captain Anderson **answered**.*

Reply is often used in this way in literary style:

> *'Am I allowed back into the kitchen yet?'*
> *'No,' she **replied** with a grin.*

In informal spoken language, *reply* is normally only used to refer to written answers to letters and other written communications, and *say* is preferred for reporting answers:

> *'What do you mean?' she said. 'Well,' I **said**, 'I don't know the whole story yet.'*
> (spoken)

Verbs used in formal written styles to report questions and answers include:

answer	*enquire/inquire*	*reply*
ask	*query*	*respond*
demand	*question*	*wonder*

> *'Didn't your surveillance team see anything?' Graham **demanded**.*

> *Remembering I hadn't a receipt for the luggage transported by Melchett's chauffeur, I **enquired** if it was to hand.*

> *'Who is it?' Smylie **queried**.*

The use of such verbs for direct speech in informal spoken language is extremely rare, except for *ask*:

> *Then they **asked** him, 'Did you mean this?' and he said, 'No, I just wrote it as a joke.'*

Representing vocal and emotional characteristics 500c

In written fictional styles, the reporting verb often indicates characteristics of the way something was said (e.g. whether it was shouted or whispered), or something about the emotional state of the original speaker (e.g. that they were angry or excited). Using reporting verbs in this way in informal speech is extremely rare.

Verbs of this type include:

bark	*moan*	*shout*
bellow	*mumble*	*shriek*
call (out)	*murmur*	*sigh*
coax	*mutter*	*snap*
cry	*retort*	*stammer*
groan	*roar*	*stutter*
growl	*rumble*	*whisper*
grumble	*shoot back*	*yell*

> *'What fun!' **cried** Camilla.*
>
> *'Amen,' **rumbled** the men in answer.*
>
> *'Turn on the meter,' I **sighed**.*
>
> *'No one dies here,' **snapped** Aunt Agatha.*

Adjuncts and reporting verbs 500d

It is also common in written literary style for adjuncts to modify the reporting verb in order to indicate contextual features of the reported clause:

> *'I don't know what this country is coming to,' she stated **firmly**.*
>
> *'Not much harm done,' she added **reassuringly**.*
>
> *'I guess I'll have to be looking after your mother now,' he added **with a kind of feeble cheerfulness**.*
>
> *I was **politely** informed that he had left the building.*

Free direct and free indirect speech and thought 500e

Literary style often omits the reporting clause, when it is clear who is speaking and in what order. This is known as free direct speech:

> *His teeth slid out as he stared me in the face.*
> *'Where? Where?'*
> *'I don't know. You tell me.'*

Free direct speech occurs in informal spoken contexts, especially in extended reports and narratives where blends of different types of speech representation are common:

A: *So we'd been wandering round in the morning doing the usual thing, came back and had lunch and* ***I said****, 'What would you like to do this afternoon, Doris?'* ***She said****, 'Oh, Annie, let's go to bingo.' Now bingo is never ever my cup of tea, but seeing that I was supposed to be, with her…*
B: *Supporting her yeah.*
A: *Exactly. I had to fall in with her.* ***All right then, Doris, where do we go now to bingo?*** *'I don't know,'* ***she said****, 'but we'll find out.'*

Literary style also permits indirect speech reporting, or the indirect reporting of inner speech or thoughts, with no explicit reporting verb. This is known as free indirect speech:

Julie got up. She looked determined. ***She would go to Brighton after all.***
(implied: She said/thought, 'I'll go to Brighton after all.')

REPORTS IN CONVERSATION 501

Direct versus indirect reports 501a

Speech representation in everyday informal conversation often mixes direct and indirect reports, especially in extended informal spoken reports and narratives; different reporting verbs, in different tenses, are often used side by side (indirect reports within direct reports are in green):

A: ***I said****, "I'll try and get a game of squash on Wednesday," and he was going about ten.* ***Said****, "I'll try and get a court."* ***I said****, "If I get a court we'll play, if I don't we won't bother."*
B: *Yeah.*
A: ***I said****, "I'll ring you on Wednesday and* ***say*** *if I've got one." So I rang him on Wednesday and* ***he said****, "Oh I couldn't get a court on Monday so I booked one at the university."* ***I said****, "I've organised other things. Like I've made other plans now."* ***He said****, "Well I cancelled things to play squash tonight."* ***I said****, "Well I told you on Monday.* ***I said****, 'Don't book one. If I don't get one I'll ring you on the Wednesday and* ***tell you*** *if I've got one or not'." And* ***he says****, "So you're letting me down then."*
B: *Mm.*
A: *And* ***I went****, "No not really. I've just got other things here." "So you're letting me down."* ***I said****, "No I'm not."* ***He says****, "You are. You're letting me down. Tell me. Are you letting me down?"* ***I said****, "If you wanna put it like that all right I'm letting you down."*
B: *Yeah.*
A: *Anyway what kind of attitude is that?*
B: *Oh, he's a complete idiot.*

[teachers talking about class discipline problems]
A: ***I told him*** *to go out.* ***I said****, "Go out and listen. Go on. Leave this classroom."*
B: *Did he go?*
A: *Yeah, it was excellent.*

Topics, openings and closings 501b

Self-reports and reports of what other participants in the conversation have said are often used in spoken language to repeat a point already made, to signal a desire to open or close a topic, or to return to an earlier topic, perhaps after a diversion or interruption.

Opening or changing a topic

For signalling a desire to open a new topic or change the topic, past progressive reporting verbs are often used:

The + sign indicates an interrupted turn which continues at the next + sign
[speakers have been talking about a forthcoming trip to New York]
A: *So where are you staying?*
B: *Erm I think it's Thirty-eighth Street. It's just a couple of blocks south of Time Square.*
A: *Yeah. Yeah.*
B: *So it should be okay+*
A: *Yeah.*
B: *+shouldn't it.*
A: *Erm Mark* ***was saying*** *he's been in Exeter and Swansea this week on a course.*
B: *Who Mark?*
A: *Yeah. He's with a chap who used to work in the health service in Edinburgh.*

Repeating a point or closing a topic

For repeating points already made, and for signalling the desire to close a topic, *as I say* and *as you say* are the most frequent forms:

[A has been telling B about a village that was destroyed by an earthquake]
A: *It was 1909 I think.*
B: *Mm.*
A: *And it was actually destroyed.*
B: *Mm, oh really?*
A: *And they rebuilt it again, this small village.*
B: *Mm.*
A: *But* ***as I say*** *it was very very interesting.*

Well ***as you say****, it's difficult to know what you might do next.*

Resuming a topic

For resuming or returning to an earlier or interrupted topic, *as I was saying* and *as you were saying* are frequently used:

[speaker at a company sales conference]
Those forms I mentioned in the last session, the market-specific forms. Oops! Oops! We've lost the microphone. At least part of it. Anyway. Er, yeah. ***As I was saying****, those two forms are on the table in front of you, so you can take those.*

→ **539 Glossary** for any unfamiliar terms

Checking, recapping and summarising 501c

In spoken language, indirect reported speech can serve as a memory or comprehension check. The most frequent forms are *did you say* and *you say*:

***Did you say**, Maggie, you'd read something by Lessing before?*

A: *Have you used that twice, **did you say**?*
B: *I've sort of used it twice, yeah.*

A: *Mrs Collett is a brilliant headteacher.*
B: ***You say** there's 36 people in your class?*
A: *Yeah.*

Progressive reporting verbs are common when speakers are checking agreement or mutual understanding of what is or was said:

*If **you're saying** we should do the whole thing, it'll take six months.*

*I think **we were saying** at this point that there'd be no need to repeat it.*

Speakers often recap or produce summaries of what was said, or repeat earlier speech. Simple and progressive forms of reporting verbs may occur:

[Margaret, called away temporarily from an informal business meeting, returns]
***We were just saying**, Margaret, we haven't left enough time to revise all the components.*
(*just* is particularly common with this type of report)

***Like we said** yesterday, it's all a bit hypothetical.*
(or, more formally: As we said yesterday, ...)

Dramatisation and narrative 501d

In narratives, especially spoken ones, the verb may occur in forms other than the past simple. This dramatises the speech report, making it more vivid.

The past progressive is used to emphasise an ongoing or repeated event, or simply to dramatise the reported speech:

*He went in to the supermarket and he was singing down the aisles and **he was saying**, 'Come on everybody,' you know, 'join in.'*

*Then it really surprised me how **she was saying**, 'Oh, take this fifty pence,' and **I was thinking**, gosh, did she really pay you for it?*

Extra dramatisation can be created by using the historic present tense (i.e. present simple form, but with past reference). This often occurs alongside the past simple:

*So I go back to Doris and she **says**, 'All right, Annie, will the bingo be starting soon? I can't see any chairs and tables.' 'No,' I **said**, 'we're in the wrong place.'*
(some speakers of English may consider this form non-standard)

Even greater dramatisation can be produced by using the present progressive with the reporting verb, with the possibility of shifting from the historic present (simple form) to progressive at particularly important moments in the narrative:

> [speaker is talking about Britain's National Lottery; a 'tenner' is ten pounds sterling]
> *He **says**, 'Oh no, I've won a tenner twice,' and **I'm saying**, 'When?' you know, 'You didn't tell me!'*

Use of *I says*, *go*, *be* and *be like* 501e

I says and the use of *go*, *be* and *be like* to dramatise direct speech are considered by many people to be non-standard and grammatically unacceptable. However, they are widespread and normal within major social varieties of British English (→ 84).

Although many would consider it a grammatically unacceptable form, *I says* is very common as a dramatising reporting clause in informal speech:

> [narrating an incident where the speaker feels he was overcharged for a film for his camera]
> A: *I called in, they charged £9.99 for the same film.* [tuts] ***I says** 'You're overcharging for that film you know.' So he says, 'Oh that's what the price says.' **I says**, 'I won't come here again you know.'*
> B: *Yes. Yeah.*
> A: *'You won't get me in here again.' It's only because I was in a bit of a hurry.*

In very informal spoken language, *go*, *be* and *be like* may be used to report direct speech. They are often accompanied by dramatising body-language or a change in the speaker's voice to suggest a dramatic re-creation of the original speech.

Such usage is often considered non-standard and bad style. However, it occurs in a wide range of informal conversations, especially among younger speakers.

Go, *be* and *be like* may be further dramatised by the use of the present simple form:

> *I was embarrassed and when we were out and I had a dress on, **she went**, 'Look at her legs, she's got hairy legs.'*
>
> ***He goes**, 'It will cost you 75 quid.' And **I'm**, you know, 'We can't afford that!'*
>
> *He keeps coming and trying to kiss me and **I'm like**, 'Go away! Go away!'*
>
> ***I was like**, 'Oh, thank God for that!' you know.*

Go also occurs in progressive aspect:

> *There were like magazines flying all over my room and **I'm going**, 'Oh I can't get up. Can't get up.'*

In very informal contexts, first person *I* may occur with third person *goes*. This is likely to be considered incorrect and unacceptable usage by many people:

> [talking about looking after someone's dog for the day]
> *She said, 'You've got a little friend to look after tomorrow.' And **I goes**, 'Has he got four legs?' She said, 'Yes.'*

A–Z 49 *Like*

Use of discourse markers in direct reports 501f

Direct reports often contain discourse markers such as *erm*, *oh*, *well*, which may or may not have been part of the original utterance:

*When we first moved into the house we had a cup of tea. You know, they made us that horrible herbal tea stuff. And then of course we had to sit in the living room. And they were just saying, '**Oh well** what are you doing today?' Like that. And my mum and dad said, '**Oh** I think we'll just **you know** do a little bit of food shopping.'*

[*a work placement* is when a person, typically a student, works somewhere without pay for a short time to gain experience]
*About two or three weeks ago I phoned them up and said, 'Can I do a work placement?' And they said, '**Well**, fax us a letter saying when.' So I did.*

SPEECH REPORTS IN SPECIFIC REGISTERS 502

Newspaper headlines 502a

Newspaper headlines have developed special conventions for reporting speech not normally found elsewhere. A typical convention is an indirect report with the reporting clause in end position, and an ellipted passive reporting verb:

*STAND UP TO SCHOOL BULLIES, **TEACHERS TOLD***
(teachers have been told)

Inversion of subject and verb in reporting verbs in end position may occur, with or without inverted commas:

*BROCCOLI MAY PREVENT CANCER, **SAY U.S. DOCTORS***

Unattributed quotations also occur:

[*NHS* = British National Health Service]
*RECORD SHORTAGE OF NURSES **'COULD THREATEN NHS CARE'***
(it is not clear who spoke the words *could threaten NHS care*)

Impersonal reports in formal registers 502b

Formal styles such as journalism and academic English often use impersonal constructions to report and quote other people's words. These include passive voice constructions and constructions with *it*:

***Someone** once said that there's nothing as old as yesterday's news.*

*Many royal watchers predicted then that Isabel's chances of becoming Queen of Spain had been dashed by the embarrassing affair, and **it was said that** Felipe's mother, Queen Sofia, was particularly keen to bring an early end to the romance.*
(we are not told who said this)

***It is claimed that** any small retailer who wants to cut prices is threatened with the withdrawal of supply.*

→ **146d Hedging and impersonal constructions** in **Grammar and academic English**

Appendices
Glossary
Bibliography
Index

Appendices

Appendix: Word clusters and grammar

Appendix: Punctuation

Appendix: English spelling

Appendix: Numbers

Appendix: Word clusters and grammar

INTRODUCTION 503

Language use is very repetitive. Words cluster together, those clusters of words repeat themselves time and time again, and some of the most frequently repeated clusters reveal grammatical regularities. However, the most frequently repeated clusters often lack grammatical completeness, in the sense that they are not complete phrases or clauses. They merit special consideration outside of the normal structural rules as described in the rest of this grammar book, since they perform important basic functions in everyday usage.

In this conversational extract, clusters of words which occur with high frequency in the spoken corpus used in the preparation of this book are shown in bold, with adjacent clusters separated by /:

> [a tennis player is talking about his match tactics]
> ***I think***, *erm, when I'm on court sometimes* ***there's / a lot of things*** *that* ***kind of*** *determine how I play.* ***If I'm*** *tired* ***I might*** *shout* ***and that sort of thing***. *Erm,* ***I think***, *I prepare better* ***you know***. *Er, like, before,* ***you know*** *er, maybe I wouldn't push myself* ***like that / you know*** *but now, erm, I'll go on court, right, with the game plan, erm, and I'll use that as, like, the base of what* ***I'm going to*** *do* ***and then*** *if that's not working then obviously I've got to,* ***kind of***, *I've still* ***got to / try and*** *stick with it because* ***I know*** *er,* ***I know*** *that* ***that's what / I've got to*** *do. But if the guy is,* ***you know***, *finding it quite easy to cope with, or I,* ***kind of like***, *break down or it's,* ***kind of***, *five four* ***or something / and I'm*** *doing the right thing* ***but I'm*** *not doing quite well enough,* ***I might / try and*** *change* ***a couple of things / here and there***. *Erm,* ***I might*** *er* ***try and*** *put* ***a bit more*** *pressure on the guy if er he's serving and it's fifteen thirty,* ***and then / I might*** *stand over* ***a bit more***, */* ***so I / try and*** *invite him to hit it to my forehand,* ***that sort of thing***.

All informal conversations contain a high number of such clusters, and many of the clusters occur more frequently than some of the common, everyday single words. Clusters also occur in written texts; however, the most common clusters differ between written and spoken texts. It can be argued that clusters such as those highlighted are retrieved from memory as whole units; they are formulaic, and are very possibly not assembled afresh each time they are used. They make an important contribution to fluency. The language use of native speakers and expert users always contains a high number of such clusters, especially in speech.

The 20 most frequent co-occurring pairs of words (two-word clusters) in the spoken texts in the corpus used in this grammar book are shown in the table below. Hesitant speech, recasts and exact repetitions, which often occur in unplanned speech, such as *and–and*, or *you–you–you* are excluded from the tables. Contractions such as *don't* and *it's* are not counted as separate words.

Two-word clusters in spoken texts

1	*you know*	11	*I was*
2	*I mean*	12	*on the*
3	*I think*	13	*and then*
4	*in the*	14	*to be*
5	*it was*	15	*if you*
6	*I don't*	16	*don't know*
7	*of the*	17	*to the*
8	*and I*	18	*at the*
9	*sort of*	19	*have to*
10	*do you*	20	*you can*

All of these pairs occur more than 5,000 times in the spoken corpus, the top seven occur more than 10,000 times and *you know* occurs more than 28,000 times.

In the case of three-word clusters, the top 20 clusters all occur more than 1,000 times, and *I don't know* occurs more than 5,000 times.

Three-word clusters in spoken texts

1	*I don't know*	11	*you want to*
2	*a lot of*	12	*you know what*
3	*I mean I*	13	*do you know*
4	*I don't think*	14	*a bit of*
5	*do you think*	15	*I think it's*
6	*do you want*	16	*but I mean*
7	*one of the*	17	*and it was*
8	*you have to*	18	*a couple of*
9	*it was a*	19	*you know the*
10	*you know I*	20	*what do you*

These clusters reveal how patterns are repeated time and time again in conversation, even though they may be fragmentary and grammatically incomplete. The same applies to writing, though the patterns are in many cases different and the overall frequency of the top clusters is lower.

Two-word clusters in written texts

1	*of the*	11	*he was*
2	*in the*	12	*in a*
3	*to the*	13	*with the*
4	*on the*	14	*of a*
5	*it was*	15	*by the*
6	*at the*	16	*was a*
7	*and the*	17	*she was*
8	*to be*	18	*I was*
9	*for the*	19	*had been*
10	*from the*	20	*with a*

Three-word clusters in written texts

1	*one of the*	11	*it would be*
2	*out of the*	12	*in front of*
3	*it was a*	13	*it was the*
4	*there was a*	14	*some of the*
5	*the end of*	15	*I don't know*
6	*a lot of*	16	*on to the*
7	*there was no*	17	*part of the*
8	*as well as*	18	*be able to*
9	*end of the*	19	*the rest of*
10	*to be a*	20	*the first time*

When we come to four-word clusters, all the clusters occur less than 1,000 times and there are considerably fewer of them.

Four-word clusters in spoken texts

1	*you know what I*	11	*I thought it was*
2	*know what I mean*	12	*I don't want to*
3	*I don't know what*	13	*you know I mean*
4	*do you want to*	14	*that sort of thing*
5	*do you know what*	15	*I don't know how*
6	*I don't know if*	16	*if you want to*
7	*a bit of a*	17	*well I don't know*
8	*I think it was*	18	*I was going to*
9	*I don't know whether*	19	*have a look at*
10	*what do you think*	20	*you don't have to*

Four-word clusters in written texts

1	*the end of the*	11	*per cent of the*
2	*at the end of*	12	*one of the most*
3	*for the first time*	13	*the side of the*
4	*the rest of the*	14	*the edge of the*
5	*in the middle of*	15	*the middle of the*
6	*at the same time*	16	*in front of the*
7	*the back of the*	17	*I don't want to*
8	*at the top of*	18	*for a long time*
9	*the top of the*	19	*is one of the*
10	*the bottom of the*	20	*on the other hand*

The tables below show the top 20 five-word spoken and written clusters.

Five-word clusters in spoken texts

1	*you know what I mean*	8	*this that and the other*
2	*at the end of the*	9	*I know what you mean*
3	*do you know what I*	10	*all the rest of it*
4	*the end of the day*	11	*and all that sort of*
5	*do you want me to*	12	*I was going to say*
6	*in the middle of the*	13	*and all the rest of*
7	*I mean I don't know*	14	*and that sort of thing*

15	*I don't know what it*	18	*to be honest with you*
16	*all that sort of thing*	19	*an hour and a half*
17	*do you want to go*	20	*it's a bit of a*

Five-word clusters in written texts

1	*at the end of the*	11	*the other end of the*
2	*by the end of the*	12	*at the bottom of the*
3	*for the first time in*	13	*the rest of the world*
4	*at the top of the*	14	*for the first time since*
5	*at the back of the*	15	*had nothing to do with*
6	*on the other side of*	16	*at the foot of the*
7	*in the centre of the*	17	*in and out of the*
8	*the end of the day*	18	*in the direction of the*
9	*for the rest of the*	19	*is one of the most*
10	*the middle of the night*	20	*the end of the year*

Although there are four- and five-word clusters, and even six-word clusters (*do you know what I mean*, *from the point of view of*), the most frequent clusters consist of two and three words. It is also clear that there is often a relationship between shorter and longer clusters as the longer cluster can be an extension of the shorter cluster. The figures below show the total number of occurrences for each size of cluster, up to six words in length, occurring 20 or more times in a spoken and written corpus of five million words each.

Distribution of clusters occurring 20 or more times in spoken texts

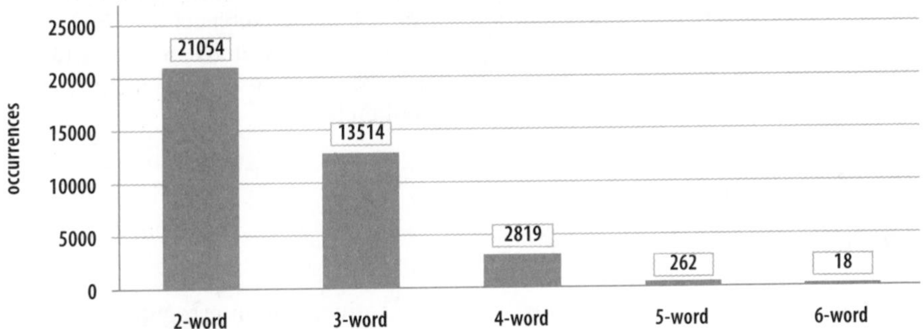

Distribution of clusters occurring 20 or more times in written texts

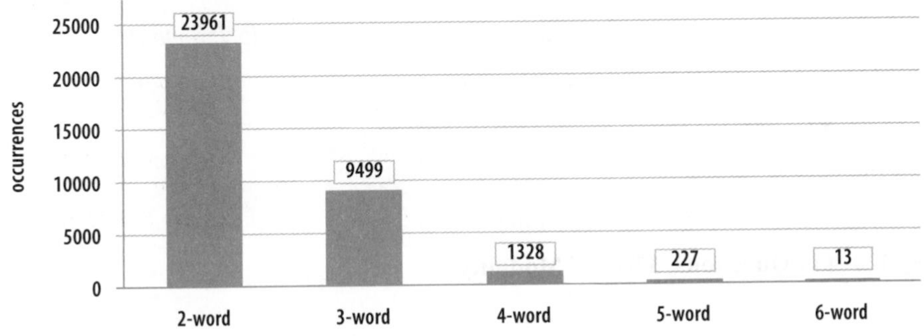

539 **Glossary** for any unfamiliar terms

COMMON TYPES OF CLUSTER 504

Preposition + article 504a

The most frequent two-word clusters are prepositions followed by articles, such as *at the*, *in the*, *of the*, *on the*, *of a*, *with a*. These are particularly frequent in written texts:

*He studied **at the** Royal Academy of Dramatic Art, London.*

*My father's birthday is **on the** fifth.*

*It can be danced either solo, **with a** partner, or in a group.*

Some three-word prepositional patterns with articles are also very frequent, especially *on to the* and *out of the*:

*Screw the top tight **on to the** bottle.*

*We were never allowed **out of the** school.*

→ **250–257 Prepositions and prepositional phrases**

Subject + verb 504b

Various combinations of pronoun subjects and verbs appear among the most frequent clusters. These are particularly common in spoken texts. They include subject + lexical verb patterns (*you know*, *I think*, *I mean*), subjects with *be* (which may occur as an auxiliary verb or a copular verb, e.g. *it was*, *I was*) and subjects with other auxiliary verbs and modal verbs (e.g. *I don't*, *you can*). Interrogative *do you* is also very frequent in spoken texts:

***I was** working so desperately hard.*

***You can** carry on if you want.*

***Do you** want a chocolate?*

Three-word subject and verb clusters include negatives, and interrogatives with *do* and *what*:

I don't know	*you have to*	*do you think*
I don't think	*you want to*	*do you want*
it would be	*do you know*	*what do you*

***I don't know** what time it starts.*

***You have to** choose.*

***Do you think** things are different now?*

→ **424–433 Questions; 377–407 Modality**

Subject + verb with complement items 504c

The three-, four- and five-word clusters in the spoken texts also show frequent occurrences of subject–verb patterns followed by the beginning of a complement structure (such words as *what, how, if, whether*). These include:

I mean I	*I don't know if*	*do you know what I*
you know what	*I don't know what*	*do you want me to*
you don't have to	*I don't know whether*	

***You know what** it's like when you've got a family.*

***You don't have to** pay if you're a student.*

*If it was my kid, **I don't know what** I'd do.*

··❯ **304–318 Clause combination**

Noun phrase + *of* 504d

A number of high-frequency three-, four- and five-word clusters centre round a noun phrase + *of*, where *of* is the first element of the complement. In the longer clusters, a further element of the complement (typically *the*) occurs. A number of these noun phrases function as the complements of prepositions.

Especially in the written texts, this type is dominated by expressions which often denote a metaphorical location and time:

a bit of	*the side of the*	*at the bottom of the*
a couple of	*at the end of*	*at the foot of the*
a lot of	*at the top of*	*at the top of the*
part of the	*in front of the*	*by the end of the*
the end of (the)	*in the middle of (the)*	*in the direction of the*
the rest of (the)	*the back of the*	*on the other side of*

*You'll have **a lot of** fun with it.*

*She gathered up **the rest of the** plates, turned and walked towards Claudette.*

*She stood silent **in the middle of the** room, looking at him intently.*

*Jake stood **at the top of the** stairs and turned round.*

··❯ **167–175 The noun phrase**

 **55 *Of***

Other types 504e

Other, less frequent, types of cluster occur. These include:

- Verb infinitives (with and without *to*), e.g. *to be (a), be able to*:

  *I used **to be a** bus driver.*

  *We should **be able to** say what we want, shouldn't we?*

- Conjunction + noun-phrase element, adverb or subject + verb, e.g. *and I, and the, if you, and then, but I mean, and it was*:

  ***If you** play well and you lose, it's tough.*

  *It's not the most wonderful area, **but I mean** it was okay.*

→ **304–318 Clause combination**

- Grammatically complete prepositional expressions, especially those of time; these occur with particularly high frequency in the written texts, and include:

at the moment	*in the morning*	*for a long time*
at the time	*at the same time*	*on the other hand*
in the end	*for the first time*	

  ***For the first time** she tried to imagine herself in that situation.*

  *After the meal, she sat **for a long time** at the window.*

  ***On the other hand**, nothing was impossible.*

→ **250–257 Prepositions and prepositional phrases**

FUNCTIONS OF CLUSTERS 505

Relations of time and place 505a

Some of the most frequent clusters, especially in the written texts, express relations of time and place, particularly through prepositional expressions:

*I'll see you **in the** morning.*

*There was nobody **on the** beaches.*

*She sat on **the edge of the** bed, dialled the number for the Police Department ...*

*He was waiting at **the bottom of the** stairs.*

***In the middle of the** night a noise woke Henry.*

→ **242–249 Adverbs and adverb phrases; 319–337 Adjuncts**

Other prepositional relations 505b

High-frequency preposition-based clusters such as *of a/the, to the, with a/the, by the, for the* express a variety of basic relations such as possession, agency, purpose, goal, direction. These prepositional clusters are most frequent in the written texts:

*The amount of rainfall is measured **with a** rain gauge.*

*In 1912 he was arrested, and some of his work was destroyed **by the** police.*

*It was a surprise **for the** kids.*

Interpersonal functions 505c

One central aspect of clusters, especially in the spoken texts, is how they reflect the interpersonal meanings (meanings which build and consolidate personal and social relations) created between speakers and listeners, and between writers and readers.

The high-frequency clauses and clause-fragments in the spoken clusters show how speakers are constantly monitoring the state of shared versus new knowledge, or assumptions about common ground between themselves and their listeners, and how speakers can hedge their assertions and express degrees of certainty about the world. This is reflected in the high frequency of clusters based round the verbs *know*, *mean* and *think*, together with their extensions, such as the following:

you know	*do you know what (I)*	*I mean*
I don't know	*I know what you mean*	*I think*
you know what (I)	*you know what I mean*	*I don't think*
you know I mean		*do you think*
I don't know what (it)		

***I don't know what** he's going to do.*

*I find French so hard, **you know what I mean**?*

***Do you think** you're going to carry on doing what you're doing now?*

***I don't think** it does any harm for different people to be involved.*

Vague language 505d

Among the most frequent spoken clusters, a number of items enable speakers to refer vaguely to things without having to be explicit. This may be because it is often impossible to be precise, or, more typically, because speakers can assume that their listeners will understand what they are referring to because they have experiences and viewpoints in common, or they share cultural reference points. These items include:

kind of	*sort of thing*	*(and) that sort of thing*
sort of	*this and that*	*this, that and the other*
and stuff	*(or) something like that*	*(and) all that sort of thing*
and things	*(and) things like that*	*(and) all the rest of it*
and so on		

*She **kind of** keeps herself hidden away, doesn't she?*

*I mean we have towels and toothbrushes **and so on**.*

[tennis player talking about how some players considered winning to be the only important thing and would do anything to win]
I thought at the time, you know, they must just be concentrating on winning at all costs ***sort of thing****, you know. And there was a lot of cheating* ***and all that sort of thing*** *and so yeah I'd say they were focused on winning.*

And the first time was, I think, February ***or something like that****.*

→ **103a Vague language**

Linking functions 505e

A number of clusters function to link clauses or sentences. In the spoken texts, the most frequent clusters centre round the conjunctions *and* and *but*, while longer linking clusters tend to be more frequent in the written texts. Linking items include:

and I/the/then	*at the time*	*in the first place*
and I said	*but I mean*	*on the other hand*
and it was	*but it was*	*as a result of (the)*
as well as	*at the same time*	*but at the same time*

The kitchen's okay ***but I mean*** *it'd be nice if you had comfy chairs in there.*

She wanted to turn around and run back to her room – run up the stairs and slam the door behind her. ***At the same time*** *she wanted to tell them, tell them everything.*

In the first place*, she persisted in disbelieving the whole of the matter; secondly, she was very sure that Mr Collins had been taken in.*

As a result of the *fuel shortage, Cuba has become a nation of cyclists.*

→ **335 Linking** in **Adjuncts**

Turn-taking 505f

A number of the common clusters in the spoken texts function to hand the speaking turn over to the listener or in some way demand a response from the listener, even if the response is just a minimal, back-channel response. These include *(do) (you) know what I mean?*, interrogative fragments such as *do you think …?*, *do you want to …?*, *what do you …?*, and common tags such as *… do you?*, *… shall I?*, *… was it?*, *… don't you think?*:

A: *We have to have it because the law says we have to,* ***do you know what I mean****?*
B: *Yeah.*

A: *Now do you all see the view here? It's quite beautiful,* ***don't you think****?*
B: *Mhm.*

A: *I'll make some lunch,* ***shall I****?*
B: *Mm, yes, please.*

I was going to say features as a preface to a turn, drawing attention to what the speaker is about to say, or to repeat or reinforce someone else's turn:

A: *What time does it start? Three?*
B: *No half past.*
A: *Oh.*
B: *We can't expect to be there on time though.*
A: ***I was going to say**, well you wouldn't want to be there on time.*

Clusters in academic English 505g

Academic language possesses a large number of recurring clusters which have become a conventional part of academic style, in speech and in writing. These include:

such as	*the importance of*	*at the same time*
for example	*the nature of*	*the way in which*
make sure that	*likely to be*	*in the course of*
in terms of	*the use of*	*one of the things*
the fact that	*a (wide) range of*	*in the case of*
in other words	*has to do with*	*a large number of*
and so on	*take a look at*	*you can see that*
in order to	*in the same way*	*if you look at the*
a variety of	*it turns out that*	*there are a number of*

[university literature seminar]
*I suppose we've also touched on **the fact that** for modern readers works can raise questions which perhaps they didn't raise for their original readers.*

*I then show how **the nature of** observations leads to the structure of theories.*

*It consisted of two main subsamples designed to span **a wide range of** age and experience for both males and females.*

[seminar discussing business law]
*If I sell to one of you, are you a consumer? Not unless you're acting **in the course of** a business.*

→ **140–154 Grammar and academic English**

Appendix: Punctuation

INTRODUCTION 506

Punctuation exists in order to indicate the boundaries of grammatical units and to indicate grammatical information that is marked in spoken language by means of intonation, pitch, etc. Punctuation consists of both rules and conventions. Punctuation rules have to be followed; but punctuation conventions give writers greater freedom and allow choices.

There are many ways in which written text can be punctuated. The major punctuation marks are full stops, question marks, commas, exclamation marks, colons, semi-colons, apostrophes and dashes. The most frequent forms are the full stop ('period' in American English) and the comma.

Common punctuation marks: symbols and typographic conventions 506a

. = full stop, period (US English), dot, (decimal) point
, = comma
: = colon
; = semi-colon
? = question mark
! = exclamation mark
– = dash
' = apostrophe (as in *Jim's*, *don't*)
"..." = quotation marks, double quotes
'...' = single quotes
- = hyphen (when used to separate words)
* = asterisk
& = *and*
@ = *at* (in email addresses: jane34@opennet.com)
/ = forward slash (as in website addresses)
\ = backwards slash or backslash
% = per cent, percentage
(...) = (round) brackets
(= open bracket
) = close bracket
[...] = square brackets
{...} = chain brackets
<...> = diamond brackets
London = underline
London = bold (on first letter)
London = italics
6.7 = *six point seven*
3.4 = *three point four*

Capitals and full stops 506b

A capital (sometimes called upper case) letter marks the beginning of a sentence. A full stop marks the end of a sentence:

I went to the shops. I was surprised they were open. But I'd forgotten about late opening times.

The ASEAN summit is to be held in Jakarta this year. Last year it was held in Singapore.

Capital letters

Capital letters are also used for proper nouns. Proper nouns include personal names (including titles before names), nationalities and languages, days of the week and months of the year, seasons, public holidays, geographical locations:

Jack Dawson'll meet them at King's Cross railway station.

Sir James and Lady Wilson are holidaying in Antigua and St Kitts.

Can you speak Spanish?

I suggest we meet on Monday.

What are you doing at New Year?

Capital letters are also used for titles of books, magazines, newspapers, etc. The capitals normally apply only to content words, not grammatical words:

'Pride and Prejudice' is easily my favourite novel by Jane Austen.

They are performing Beethoven's 'Eroica' symphony.

'The Times' has the best Sunday colour supplement, don't you think?

→ **84 Proper names** in **The noun phrase**

Full stops

In addition to closing sentences, full stops are also sometimes used to indicate sentences that are not grammatically independent. These sentences are sometimes called sentence fragments or simply orthographic sentences. They can involve ellipsis but single words are also common, especially in advertisements, in dialogue involving responses and in writing which seeks to create a dramatic effect:

Our airline now flies you to Majorca. Daily. And to Barcelona. Five times a week.

A: *They've decided to ban him for three matches.*
B: *Really. That's awful.*

A: *So it's okay if she's out till after midnight.*
B: *As long as she gets a taxi back.*

What must she be feeling now? Deep anxiety. Loneliness. Despair.

Conventions change. Full stops used to be common after addresses or after dates in letters but are now much less commonly used. It is, however, a rule that they are not used after the name that ends a letter:

[typical address and date from a business letter]

Duffield Engineering
Netherfield Court
Longstone Road
Ableton
SH5 5TW

15 July 2002

Dear Supplier,

Note that a comma is normally placed after the name of the addressee (→ **506d** below).

Full stops are used in initials for personal names, though increasingly they are omitted:

J.D. Power

Richard A. Johnston, Managing Director

A I Briggs

Full stops are also used after abbreviations. This practice is, however, becoming less common:

The Microbiological Society
The annual lecture will be given by David James M.A. and will take place in Saint George's Hall at 7 p.m. on Tues. Dec. 13th.
R.S.V.P. to Prof. Lionel Jackson

NB.
(take note, from Latin 'nota bene'; N.B. is also possible)

Cf.
(compare, from the Latin, 'confer')

Norwegian territories have been prohibited for the U.K. fishing industry for a number of years now.
(also possible: ... for the UK fishing industry)

Where abbreviations are curtailed words (words with the end cut off), they take a full stop. For example, *Addr.* (*address*), *Arr.* (*arrival*), *Prof.* (*professor*) and *etc.* (*etcetera*). Where abbreviations of words include the last letter of the word, they do not require a full stop:

St = Street (also 'Saint' as in St John)
Rd = Road
Ltd = Limited (company)
Dr = Doctor

A full stop is not used for common sets of initials or for acronyms (where the initials are pronounced as a word):

Millions of pounds have been invested in the NHS in recent years.
(NHS = National Health Service; not: N.H.S.)

The BBC's coverage of the events has been exemplary.
(not: B.B.C.)

AIDS affects people in over three quarters of the countries of the world.
(not: A.I.D.S.)

Full stops are not used in newspaper headlines, in headings and sub-headings in books, magazines and newspapers or in the titles of books and other works:

Family Lost In Fishing Boat Mystery

Economics and Business Management: Part one: Personnel management

Losing Your Way In Losing Weight

Computers For Fun: A Book For The Whole Family

Question marks and exclamation marks 506c

Question marks

When question marks are used, full stops are not used at the end of the sentence:

How many times can we afford to change our family car?

Question marks are also used in order to make clear that a declarative sentence should be heard as a question. On the other hand, questions that are indirect requests to do something do not normally take a question mark:

I wonder if you can help me?

Karen, can you pass that chair over here.

Exclamation marks

Exclamation marks are used for exclamatives and after interjections:

What a nice coat!

Wow! Really?

Gosh! Does it cost that much?

Exclamation marks are used more in informal writing. One exclamation mark is the norm but occasionally more than one may be used for emphasis:

Will you all please be quiet!

Oh no!!! I don't believe it!

Exclamation marks are not normally used with imperative clauses unless the writer wishes to emphasise that a directive was or may have been shouted:

Don't get yourself too involved with the day-to-day management.

Let's get going or we're gonna be late.

Stop! Push the door this way!

→ **539 Glossary** for any unfamiliar terms

Commas 506d

Separating main clauses

Commas are used to mark clause boundaries. Main clauses separated by *and* or *or* or *but* are not normally separated by commas, although commas may be used between clauses which do not have the same subject. American English uses commas before *and*, *but* and *or* more frequently than British English:

*They **were** friendly and **invited** us back to their flat.*
(same subject)

*Students these days **leave** with large debts and **have to** repay loans.*
(same subject)

It was a restaurant a good distance from the city centre, but we decided it was worth making such a long journey.
(different subjects)

Separating main and subordinate clauses

Normally commas are used if the subordinate clause comes before the main clause. Subordinate clauses can be separated by a comma from a preceding main clause, especially when the relation between them might be obscured because the clauses are long. But it is not obligatory, particularly in short sentences.
Compare:

***If you get stuck,** come back and see me.*

*Come back and see me **if you get stuck.***

***As long as she takes the examination,** we will overlook the problems with her attendance.*

We can get there for around six if there are no problems with the traffic on the motorway.

or

We can get there for around six, if there are no problems with the traffic on the motorway.

Subordinate or comment clauses that provide additional information or that elaborate information given in the main clause are punctuated with commas:

*It doesn't suit you, **to be honest.***

*You do need to use a microphone to be heard, **if I may say so.***

***To tell you the truth,** I thought she was wrong.*

With relative clauses

Commas are also used to mark non-defining relative and non-defining non-finite clauses. Such clauses normally add to, amplify or evaluate information concerning a noun or noun phrase:

*The tablets, **which began to take effect after about twenty minutes,** soon brought the fever under control.*

Barcelona, ***where the first conference was held,*** *has changed out of all recognition.*

The visiting supporters, ***treated like criminals by the local police,*** *were grateful to leave the country when the competition was over.*

The severe turbulence, ***lasting as it did for more than an hour,*** *caused several passengers to be quite ill.*

→ also **317i Punctuation and intonation of relative clauses**

Defining relative and defining non-finite clauses do not add to or amplify a statement. They postmodify a noun and specify or define properties associated with the noun. Such clauses are **not** punctuated by a comma:

The people ***who caused most trouble*** *have left the area.*
(~~The people, who caused most trouble, have left the area.~~)

The town house ***which they had bought*** *was let out to tenants within a matter of days.*

The best pictures ***to buy in Cuba*** *are always by the street artists.*

The city braced itself for the storms ***caused by a cyclone in the Pacific.***

Embedded clauses, however long and complex, that function as the subject of the main clause, are not marked off by commas:

The decisions ***about congestion parking that have been pushed through by the City Council without proper consultation*** *are now beginning to cause even more problems for motorists.*

What we've always been short of is soup bowls.
(~~What we've always been short of, is soup bowls.~~)

Similarly, non-defining clauses in apposition are punctuated by commas, whereas defining clauses in apposition are not punctuated. The most common form of apposition involves nouns and noun phrases but non-restrictive apposition can also refer back to an earlier part of the clause:

His brother, ***the one who lives in Osaka,*** *has just set up his own book importing business.*
(~~His brother the one who lives in Osaka, has just set up his own book importing business.~~)

The London Eye, ***a revolving wheel on the banks of the Thames,*** *gives excellent views across the whole city and has attracted many visitors.*

People were beginning to put money into savings accounts, ***an early indication of economic uncertainty.***

My sister's daughter ***Nora*** *and her daughter* ***Rita*** *and the boys are all living close by.*
(defining noun phrase in apposition)

The group leader, ***a man in his eighties,*** *went swimming twice a day.*
(non-defining noun phrase in apposition)

With adjectives

Commas are used between adjectives in attributive and predicative positions. A comma is not normally used before an adjective followed by *and*:

The town was ***cold, dark and inhospitable.***

It was an ***energetic, competitive and committed*** *performance and the team deserved its victory.*

This is the ***lightweight, portable and wireless*** *version.*

With lists

Commas are used to separate items in a list, except for a final item preceded by *and*. In American English, however, the norm is to have a comma before *and* in a list:

They bought a rail pass and visited ***Rome, Milan, Venice and Verona.***

She spent the whole week ***watching videos, listening to CDs, reading detective novels and writing postcards to friends.***

They've got ***apples, pears, bananas, and peaches.***
(American English preferred form)

With adjuncts

Commas play an important part in punctuating adjuncts, most markedly when they provide a comment or linking function. In such cases the comma often coincides with a pause in speech:

It was, ***however,*** *the best decision taken at that point in the company.*

Unfortunately, *the proposal was turned down without any explanation.*

Have you had any contact with Karin, ***by the way****?*

The economic gloom continued through the post-war period; ***on the other hand,*** *employment prospects were beginning to improve.*

With tags and responses

Tags and *yes-no* responses are separated by commas:

He is going to be there, ***isn't he****?*

I'm thirsty, ***I am.***

Yes, *thank you. I'd be delighted to accept.*

With vocatives, discourse markers and interjections

Vocatives, discourse markers and interjections are also punctuated with commas:

Open the door for them, ***Jake,*** *can you. Thanks.*

The trouble is, ***doctor,*** *I've stopped taking the prescription.*

Ros, *can you get me a paper while you're out.*

Well, *what do you suppose they did about it?*

Oh, so, *you'll be off in about an hour,* ***then****?*

In reporting speech

Commas are used to indicate that direct speech is following or has just occurred. When the direct speech is first, the comma comes before the closing of the quotation marks:

He said, "Now it's time for big changes."

"I'm too old for that kind of thing," she said with a broad grin.

→ also **506f** below

Commas are not used in reporting structures after *that*, *what* and *where* even though stress and a consequent pause may fall on the verb immediately preceding *that*:

Everyone knew that she wouldn't pass the exam.
(~~Everyone knew, that she wouldn't pass the exam.~~)

Certain fixed expressions with *say* do not have a comma or quotation mark:

***Say hi** to Jim for me.*

*I'm really sorry but I'm afraid I have to **say no** to your kind offer.*

In letters

In letters, forms of address and signing off are marked by commas:

Dear David, (addressing the recipient of the letter)

Thank you for your letter of Feb. 14th.

...

Yours sincerely, (signing off at the end of the letter)

Jill Paton

Colons and semi-colons 506e

Colons are used to introduce lists, to indicate a sub-title or to indicate a subdivision of a topic:

There are three main arguments for the withdrawal of the troops: military, economic and, above all, ethical.

The History of Britain: A Personal View

Colons may also be used to mark a clause in which reasons or explanations are given:

We decided against buying the DVD player: it wasn't lightweight enough to take on holiday with us.

Semi-colons are sometimes used to separate items included in a sequence or list:

The facility has a number of features: a cinema; two meeting rooms; a fast-food café; a small gymnasium.

Semi-colons may also be used instead of full stops to separate two main clauses. In such cases the clauses remain grammatically separate but are linked in meaning. Semi-colons are not frequently used in contemporary English. Full stops and commas are much more common:

Some cats sleep during the night; most cats are active during the dark.

Bangkok is the capital city; Chiang Mai is the main tourist destination.

Direct speech 506f

In direct speech, a reconstruction of the actual words somebody has spoken or written are indicated. Direct speech is normally enclosed within a pair of single or double quotation marks, though single quotation marks are becoming more widespread. Direct speech begins with a capital letter:

She said, "Who do you think you are?"

The reporting clause can appear in three different positions. Note the position of commas and full stops:

The course tutor said to us, 'Don't waste your time in your first term here.'
(quotation mark after comma introducing speech and after full stop)

'Don't waste your time in your first term here,' the course tutor said to us.
(comma before closing quotation mark)

'Don't waste your time', the course tutor said to us, 'in your first term here.'
(commas separating intervening reporting clause)

For direct speech inside direct speech, either single quotation marks inside double or double quotation marks inside single may be used. Note that quotation marks in English are superscript, not subscript plus superscript, as in some languages. That is, they are marked '...' or "...":

David said, 'He was getting really cross and kept shouting "Get out!".'

"It was getting really tense," she said, "and everybody was yelling 'Why don't you go home?'"

Question marks normally occur inside the quotation marks unless the question is part of the reporting clause:

'Don't you know the way then?' they asked.

So after all that, did she really say 'I plan to resign'?

Occasionally, colons may be used to introduce direct speech. This is common in dramatic transcripts or when a particularly long section of direct speech is marked. Note also that in film and play scripts, quotation marks are not used:

Polonius: *What do you read my Lord?*
Hamlet: *Words, words, words.*

The company secretary then turned to me and said: 'The results of this company are better than in any time in the past five years and we object most strongly to the negative reporting we have received in some parts of the media'.

→ also **490a Punctuation and direct speech; 490b Punctuation and indirect speech**

Citations 506g

It is sometimes necessary to highlight individual words. This citation or special mention may be punctuated in a number of ways. (In order to highlight the italics, complete examples in this section (506g) are not, as elsewhere in the book, italicised.)

The citation may be underlined or in italics or placed within quotation marks. Definitions or translations are usually in single quotation marks:

Boot has several different meanings in English. And when it refers to storage space in the rear of a motor car, it is 'trunk' in American English.

The *marguerite* or 'common daisy' is cultivated in a variety of different colours.

Weltanschauung means a 'view of the world', formed from the German noun *Welt* (meaning 'world') and the verb *anschauen* (meaning 'to look at').

Single quotation marks are sometimes used to draw attention to a word, or to indicate an unusual use of a word, or to suggest that the writer wants to be distanced from the word in some way. In such cases the writer intends that the word or phrase should be taken in a non-literal or non-obvious sense:

The bus broke down twice and, as far as I am concerned, I won't be using the city 'transport' system again.

[newspaper headline]
PM 'ANGERED' BY OPPOSITION ATTACK

Titles of books, newspapers, magazines, videos or CDs also qualify as a special form of citation. Such mentions are usually punctuated by italics or underlining. Articles or chapters within books or titles of short stories are normally punctuated by single quotation marks:

There's a report all about it in *The Times* today.

[*Hello!* is a magazine dedicated to pictures of celebrities]
Hello! has some really good pictures of the wedding.

The best-argued chapter in the book is the one on 'Arab Unity since 1956'.

[*Moby* is a musician who released a CD called *18*]
Moby's *18* has eighteen tracks. The most moving one is 'Harbour'.

A character in a novel or play which has the same name is not highlighted but the title of the work is:

Othello was manipulated as much by what Iago didn't say as by what he did say.

Othello is one of Shakespeare's most complex psychological tragedies.

Apostrophes 506h

Apostrophes are used for three main purposes: to mark letters that have been omitted in contracted forms; to mark possessive forms of nouns and pronouns; and to mark special plurals.

Common contractions include:

it's = it is	*where's = where is, where has*
I'd = I would/had	*what's = what is, what has*
can't = cannot	*how's = how is, how has*
who's = who is, who has	

Apostrophes with nouns are used before and after the possessive -*s* ending. The main rules are:

1 For a singular noun, use 's:

*the cat: The cat**'s** milk is in the fridge.*

*the student: The student**'s** views are most important.*

*Laura: Laura**'s** brothers are all younger than her.*

*year: This year**'s** fashion show is in Turin.*

2 For a plural noun which does not end in -*s*, use *'s*:

*his men: His men**'s** obsession with football is out of hand.*

*the police: The police**'s** actions cannot be supported.*

3 For a plural noun which ends in -*s*, use *s'*:

*your colleagues: Your colleague**s'** decisions must be respected.*

*his dogs: His dog**s'** kennels need cleaning out.*

*two hours: Two hour**s'** walk is too far at our age.*

4 The apostrophe *'s* is also added to names ending in -*s*. However, many writers prefer simply to add an apostrophe mark after the final -*s*, especially to names which have more than one syllable:

Dickens's novels	or	*Dickens' novels* (more common)
Socrates's writings	or	*Socrates' writings* (more common)
Keats's poetry	or	*Keats' poetry* (more common)

5 An apostrophe is added to first names ending in -*s*:

*Angu**s's** offer had to be turned down.*

*In my opinion, Iri**s's** car is too dangerous to go on the road.*

*The service is at St Augustu**s's** church at midday.*

6 The apostrophe *'s* is also added to whole phrases. In compound nouns the *'s* is added after the final noun:

*The people next door***'s** *dog is a nuisance.*

*You might have guessed. Richard and Pat***'s** *new car is French.*

*It's my brother-in-law***'s** *fault.*
(~~**brother's-in-law**~~).

7 In fixed expressions such as *for goodness' sake* or *for appearance' sake*, a single apostrophe is added, though it is becoming optional.

8 Possessives can also be used without a following noun. If the reference is clear, the noun is not normally needed. When referring to people's names or when people's houses are meant, the apostrophe is retained:

*Don't forget I'm going to the doctor***'s** *after work.*

*I'm staying over at Jack***'s** *this evening. Okay?*

*I think we'd better go over to my mother***'s** *before dinner.*

Apostrophes can be used when referring to firms, shops and businesses. But the rule is in flux and many shops drop the apostrophe in their names. The use of the apostrophe in reference to decades is also in flux:

*I'm going over to Blue***'s** *for coffee.*

[name of a supermarket chain]
*He bought his TV at Sainsbury***'s**.

[name of a chain selling pharmaceutical products]
Are you getting the prescription at Boots?

Was that band really on tour in the 1960s?
(1960's can also be found, even though it is **not** a possessive but a plural: nineteen sixties)

The apostrophe *'s* also occurs with particular indefinite pronouns: for example, *one* and compounds ending in *-one* or *-body*. When combined with *else*, the apostrophe *'s* is added to *else*:

*One***'s** *responsibility is to one***'s** *family.*

*Is this somebody***'s** *jacket?*

*It's all right. It's nobody***'s** *fault.*

*This must be someone else***'s** *room.*

The indefinite pronoun *other* has the same forms as nouns. The singular adds *'s* to 'other', while the plural adds an apostrophe after the plural *-s* ending:

*You two are always sharing each other***'s** *secrets.*

*This is your room. The others***'** *rooms are across the hall there.*

539 **Glossary** for any unfamiliar terms

Possessive pronouns ending in -*s* do not have an apostrophe:

That was theirs.

Which keys are yours?

Whose book is this?
(~~Who's book is this?~~)

The apostrophe is not used with the impersonal possessive pronoun *its*. *It's* means 'it is':

The cart had lost one of ***its*** *wheels.*
(~~The cart had lost one of it's wheels.~~)

Possessive noun phrases with *of* normally retain the apostrophe form which would occur if they preceded a noun:

That's another cat ***of*** *Nell****'s****, isn't it? She had over twenty at the last count.*
(Nell's cat)

I'd like you to meet Bill. Bill is a partner ***of*** *my father****'s****.*
(my father's partner)

Dashes and other punctuation marks 506i

Dashes are more common in informal writing. They can be used in similar ways to commas. Both single and multiple dashes may be used:

Our Head of Finance – who often loses his temper about travel expenses – was the calmest in the room. I couldn't believe it!

Just to let you know we've just got back from Mallorca --- we really loved it.

Brackets have a similar function to dashes. They can also function as a punctuation of what are presented as afterthoughts:

We were up late most nights (not working, of course!) and so never really got up till after midday.

Hyphens are a form of dash and can be used within modifiers:

a twelve-year-old girl
(compare: she's twelve years old)

Forward slashes are common in internet addresses and to act as an 'and/or' marker in academic references:

You can find more information on www.bbc.co.uk/sport.

Jenkins 1991/1997 has given three reasons for this state of affairs.

→ also **156 Punctuation** in **Grammar and academic English** for further guidance on punctuation conventions in academic writing.

→ also **256 Compounds** and **266 Hyphenation** for further examples of word compounds and hyphens

Numerals and punctuation 506j

Full stops are less commonly used in dates. Other punctuation conventions such as forward slashes or dashes are becoming more common:

Date of birth: 12.7.1981
(also possible: 12/7/1981 or 12-7-1981)

Note that American usage reverses the day and the month so that July 12th 1981 is written:

7-12-1981 or *7/12/1981* or *7.12.1981*

Abbreviations used in science and technology follow an international system in which full stops are not used:

NCl (chemical symbol for sodium chloride)

H_2O (chemical symbol for water)

kg (*kilograms*)

200w bulbs (*200 watt electric light bulbs*)

Punctuation of weights and measures and of numbers follows the same rules:

2kg (*2 kilograms*)

3yds and 3ins = 1m (*3 yards and 3 inches = one metre*)

5m dollars (*5 million dollars*)

Punctuation of times can involve full stops or colons:

I'll be there at 4.30.
(or 4:30)

Commas are used in numbers to indicate units of thousands and millions. Full stops are used to indicate decimal points:

7,340
(*seven thousand three hundred and forty*)

13,987,460
(*thirteen million nine hundred and eighty seven thousand four hundred and sixty*)

3.5
(*three point five*)

7.8
(*seven point eight*)

➜ also **512–525 Appendix: Numbers**

Appendix: English spelling

This appendix introduces some of the most basic spelling rules in British English, with a panel showing some differences between British and American spelling. It makes reference to the structure of words discussed in **258–268 Word structure and word formation** but can also be read independently.

SPELLING AND PREFIXES 507

When there is a prefix, letters are not normally added or taken away:

un + sure = unsure

un + necessary = unnecessary

dis + obey = disobey

dis + similar = dissimilar

mis + read = misread

mis + rule = misrule

over + hear = overhear

under + spend = underspend

in + humane = inhumane

in + sane = insane

in + secure = insecure

il-, im-, ir-

When the first letter of a word is *l*, *m*, *p*, or *r*, the prefix *in-* is regularly changed to *il-*, *im-* or *ir-*. For example: *in* becomes *il-* before *l*; *in* becomes *im-* before *m* or *p*; *in* becomes *ir-* before *r*:

-il	*-im*	*-ir*
illegible	*immoral*	*irreparable*
illegal	*immeasurable*	*irreplaceable*
illiberal	*impartial*	*irrepressible*
illiterate	*impossible*	*irresolute*
illogical	*imprudent*	*irresponsible*

SPELLING AND SUFFIXES 508

There are two kinds of suffix.

A suffix can be attached to the end of a base form to create a new word. This process typically changes the word class:

noun suffixes: *act**ion***, *train**ee***, *free**dom***, *arriv**al***

adjective suffixes: *inform**al***, *home**less***, *grate**ful***

verb suffixes: *simpl**ify***, *dark**en***, *international**ise***

adverb suffixes: *quick**ly***, *home**ward(s)***, *clock**wise***

However, inflectional suffixes express grammatical meanings and do not change the class of the word. For example, *-ed* is added to *paint* to produce the past tense *painted*. The spelling rules for suffixes below apply also to inflections. ⇢ also **262 Suffixes** in **Word structure and word formation**

Rule 1: consonant is doubled before a suffix 508a

Consonants doubled

The final consonant of a word is often doubled when a suffix beginning with a vowel is added. Examples of such suffixes are: *-ed*, *-er*, *-est*, *-ing*.

The rule applies in the case of the following single consonants: *b*, *d*, *g*, *l*, *m*, *n*, *p*, *r*, *t*:

rub + ed = rubbed

red + ish = reddish

big + er = bigger

travel+ er = traveller

slim + ing = slimming

sin + er = sinner

drop + ed = dropped

war + ing = warring

fit + ing = fitting

If the suffix is added to a word with more than one syllable, consonant doubling follows a stressed syllable:

*re**fer** + ed = referred*

*o**mit** + ing = omitting*

*sub**mit** + ing = submitting*

*oc**cur** + ence = occurrence*

*up**set** + ing = upsetting*

Compare, however, the word *visit*, where the stress is on the first syllable:

> ***vis**it = visiting*
> (~~visitting~~)

Note too that in each case the vowel before the last consonant is a short vowel.

Consonants not doubled

The final consonant is not doubled before a suffix:

- if the word ends in two written consonants (*export–exported, find–finding, insert–inserting, insist–insisted, lift–lifted, persist–persistence*)
- if there are two written vowels (*meeting, rained, beaten, trainer, repeated*)
- if the stress is not on the last syllable of the word to which the suffix is added (*de**liv**er–delivered, de**vel**op–developing* (~~developping~~), ***o**pen–opener*)

Irregular forms and exceptions

Some monosyllabic words ending in *-s* are irregular and the *s* may be doubled or not (*busses/buses, gasses/gases*). In a few polysyllabic words ending in *-s*, the *s* may also be doubled, even though the final syllable before the suffix is unstressed (either ***bi**ased* or ***bi**assed*, either ***fo**cusing* or ***fo**cussing*). There is a preference for the forms with a single *s*, and those with double *s* are relatively rare.

Some words with more than two syllables, several of them words ending in *-l*, have a double consonant even though the last syllable is not stressed (***mar**vellous, **mo**delling, **tra**veller, **e**qualled, **han**dicapped, **pro**grammed*).

Words ending in a final *-c* change to *-ck* before a suffix; this mainly involves the suffixes *-ed, -er, -ing* (*mimic–mimicking, panic–panicking, picnic–picnicked, traffic–trafficked*).

Note, however, the single consonant spelling in American English of *worshiper, kidnaper, traveling*.

Rule 2: dropping the final *-e* — 508b

When a suffix beginning with a vowel is added to a word ending in *-e*, the *e* is usually dropped:

hope + ing = hoping	*invite + ation = invitation*
debate + ed = debated	*note + able = notable*
fame + ous = famous	*approve + al = approval*
love + able = lovable	

There are exceptions to this rule. For example, where the *e* is kept before a vowel:

- the *e* in *dyeing* (from *dye*) and *singeing* (from *singe*) is kept in order to differentiate them from similar words *dying* (from *die*) and *singing* (from *sing*)
- the *e* in *ce* and *ge* before a suffix beginning with *a* or *o* is kept to preserve the /s/ and /dʒ/ sounds (*replaceable, noticeable, peaceable, knowledgeable, advantageous, courageous*)

However, the *e* is not dropped before a suffix beginning with a consonant, such as *-ful*, *-less*, *-ly* (*forceful*, *blameless*, *widely*).

Exceptions occur when the *e* is dropped before a consonant (*argue–argument*, *awe–awful*, *due–duly*, *noble–nobly*, *true–truly*, *whole–wholly*).

Additionally, some words have alternative forms with or without an *e* (*abridgment/abridgement*, *acknowledgment/acknowledgement*, and *judgment/judgement*).

Rule 3: plurals of nouns and *-s* forms of verbs 508c

There are rules for the plurals of regular nouns and the *-s* forms of regular verbs.

General rule: add *s* (*week–weeks*, *speak–speaks*, *eye–eyes*, *bring–brings*, *summer–summers*, *define–defines*).

If the ending is pronounced as a separate syllable, *es* is added:

noun plurals	verb *-s* forms
church–churches	*fetch–fetches*
fox–foxes	*fizz–fizzes*
bush–bushes	*rush–rushes*

However, if a word already ends in an *-e*, an *s* is added (*base–bases*, *lose–loses*, *judge–judges*, *face–faces*).

If the word ends in a consonant plus *-y*, *y* changes to *i* and the suffix *es* is added:

noun plurals	verb *-s* forms
worry–worries	*marry–marries*
fly–flies	*try–tries*

Some words ending in *-o*, require *es*:

noun plurals	noun plurals and verb *-s* forms
buffalo–buffaloes	*echo–echoes*
cargo–cargoes	*embargo–embargoes*
hero–heroes	*go–goes* [*go* here = attempt]
potato–potatoes	*torpedo–torpedoes*
tomato–tomatoes	*veto–vetoes*

Some of the words in this group have a less common alternative form in *-s* (*video–videos*, *radio–radios*).

For some nouns ending in *-f* or *-fe*, the plural is formed by changing the *f* or *fe* to *ves* (*thief–thieves*, *loaf–loaves*, *wife–wives*, *half–halves*).

Rule 4: changing *y* to *i* 508d

When a suffix is added to a word ending in a consonant plus *-y*, the *y* normally changes to *i*:

easy + *ly* = *easily*
happy + *ly* = *happily*
amplify + *er* = *amplifier*
beauty + *ful* = *beautiful*
reply + *ed* = *replied*
spy + *s* = *spies*
hurry + *s* = *hurries*
mystery + *ous* = *mysterious*
fury + *ous* = *furious*
busy + *ness* = *business*
empty + *ness* = *emptiness*
amplify + *cation* = *amplification*

There are, however, exceptions where the *y* is kept after a consonant:

- a few words of one syllable keep the *y* before a suffix (*dryness, shyness, slyness*)
- the *y* is kept before *-ing* (*studying, applying*)
- the *y* is kept before *-'s* (*the spy's name, July's weather*)

The *y* is kept in most words that end in a vowel + *-y*:

buy + *er* = *buyer*
destroy + *s* = *destroys*
enjoy + *ment* = *enjoyment*
grey + *ish* = *greyish*
play + *ful* = *playful*
try + *ing* = *trying*

Exceptions occur where the *y* after a vowel is changed to *i* (*day–daily, pay–paid*).

Rule 5: spelling of verb forms: *-ed* forms 508e

The past tense and *-ed* participle are the same in regular verbs. The following are the spelling rules for regular verbs:

General rule: add *ed* (*play–played, load–loaded, mail–mailed, echo–echoed*).

If the word ends in *-e*, a *d* is added (*agree–agreed, note–noted, save–saved, tie–tied*).

If the word ends in a consonant plus *-y*, the *y* is changed to *i* before *-ed* (*cry–cried, dry–dried, imply–implied, reply–replied*).

There are three exceptions, where the *y* is changed to *i* after a vowel and just *d* is added (*lay–laid, pay–paid, say–said*).

The rules for doubling a single consonant before *-ed* are as described above at **508a**. For example (*beg–begged, enter–entered, float–floated, prefer–preferred*).

Rule 6: spelling of verb forms: *-ing* forms 508f

General rule: add *ing* (*cash–cashing, go–going, hurry–hurrying, play–playing*).

If the word ends in *-e*, *e* is dropped before *-ing* (*lose–losing, judge–judging, save–saving, write–writing*).

But if the word ends in *-ee*, *-oe* or *-ye*, the *e* is kept:

see–seeing	*hoe–hoeing*
agree–agreeing	*dye–dyeing* (compare: *die/dying*)

If the word ends in *-ie*, the *i* is changed to *y* and the *e* is dropped before the *-ing* (*die–dying, lie–lying, tie–tying*).

See Rule 1 (508a above) for doubling a single consonant before *-ing*.

Rule 7: the suffix *-ally* 508g

The suffix *-ally* is added to adjectives ending in *-ic* to form adverbs (*basic–basically, emphatic–emphatically, realistic–realistically, tragic–tragically*). Exception: *publicly*.

SPELLING AND SHORT AND LONG VOWELS 509

Doubling 509a

The vowels *a, e, i, o, u* have long and short pronunciations. Thus there is a long vowel *a* in the word *mast* and a short vowel *a* in the word *mat*.

When a long vowel is followed by a single consonant plus a vowel, the consonant is **not** doubled when a suffix is added (*scene–scenic, enthuse–enthusiasm, skate–skating, wide–widen, hope–hopeful*).

Doubling of consonants, where it occurs, enables words with similar forms to be differentiated (*diner, dinner*; *later, latter*).

Addition of final *e* to indicate long vowel 509b

A final silent *e* is used to indicate that the preceding stressed written vowel is long:

long vowel	short vowel
hate, fate	*hat, fat*
theme, impede	*them, moped*
dine, bite	*din, bit*

There are some common exceptions, where the preceding vowel does not have the regular pronunciation (*have*; *there, where*; *were*; *come, done, love, none, one, some*; *gone*; *live* (as a verb), *give*).

The general rule applies also in the sequence vowel + consonant + *-le*. Hence, in *gable* the vowel *a* is long whereas in *gabble* it is short. Further examples of the long vowel in this position are: *able, fable, ladle, bible, cycle, idle, trifle, noble*. Exception: *label*.

539 Glossary for any unfamiliar terms

SPELLING CHECKS 510

One word or two? 510a

Some sound pairs are spelt either as one or as two words, depending on the meaning intended:

one word	two words	one word	two words
already	*all ready*	*however*	*how ever*
altogether	*all together*	*into*	*in to*
always	*all ways*	*maybe*	*may be*
anybody	*any body*	*nobody*	*no body*
anyway	*any way*	*someone*	*some one*
awhile	*a while*	*somebody*	*some body*
everyone	*every one*	*whatever*	*what ever*
everybody	*every body*	*whoever*	*who ever*

i before *e* except after *c* 510b

If in doubt about *ie* or *ei* when the sound of the vowel is as in *brief*, spell it *ie*; but after *c*, spell it *ei*:

ie		ei after c
brief	*thief*	*ceiling*
belief	*achieve*	*conceive*
believe	*field*	*conceit*
diesel	*niece*	*deceive*
relief	*priest*	*receipt*
relieve	*siege*	*perceive*

Exceptions for spelling *ie*:

- *financier, species*
- words in which *y* has changed to *i* end in *-ies* even after *c* (*prophecies, democracies*).

In most words that do not have the pronunciation as in *brief*, the usual order is *e* before *i*: for example, *neighbour, weigh, reign, leisure*. The most common exception is *friend*.

British and American English spelling 511

Some words are spelled differently in American English and British English.

For example:

British English	American English
centre	*center*
cheque	*check*
colour	*color*
defence	*defense*
labour	*labor*
theatre	*theater*
programme	*program*

Variants

There are several variants with *-ise* or *-ize*, *-isation* or *-ization* . Both variants are acceptable, though the spelling with *s* is perhaps more common in British English (*criticise–criticize, colonisation–colonization*).

The following words, and words formed from them, should be spelled with *ise* in British English:

advertise
advise
arise
chastise
comprise
compromise
despise
devise
disguise
enterprise
exercise
franchise
improvise
merchandise
revise
supervise
surmise
surprise
televise

Appendix: Numbers

ORDINAL AND CARDINAL NUMBERS 512

The conventional abbreviations for ordinal numbers are as follows. The suffix may be written as superscript (1st) or as normal script (1st):

first	*1st/1st*
second	*2nd/2nd*
third	*3rd*
fourth	*4th*
fifth	*5th*
sixth	*6th*
seventh	*7th*
eighth	*8th*
ninth	*9th*
tenth	*10th*
sixteenth	*16th*
thirty third	*33rd*
twenty fifth	*25th/25th*
seventy first	*71st*

In handwriting, *seven* is typically written as *7*, but may also be written as 7. *Four* is most commonly handwritten as 4 but may also be written as *4*.

A hyphen is used to separate tens and units (*twenty-four, six hundred and forty-nine*).

Both cardinal numbers and ordinal numbers are common with titles of books and films and for referring to chapters and parts of documents. After the noun, a cardinal number is used. Both cardinal and ordinal numbers are normally acceptable, though the cardinal number is more informal:

*I think the reference is in Book **7** of 'Paradise Lost'.*
(or: the seventh book)

*The play didn't get started until the **third** act.*
(or: Act 3)

*I will return to these questions in the **ninth** chapter.*
(or: chapter 9)

The definite article is not used when cardinal numbers occur after the noun:

I will return to these questions in chapter 9.
(~~I will return to these questions in the chapter 9.~~)

See figure 9 below.
(~~See the figure 9 below.~~)

Turn to page 28.

Ordinal numbers are used with the names of kings and queens and aristocrats:

*He is **the fourth** Earl of Gloucester.*
(~~He is Earl 4 of Gloucester.~~)

*King Henry **VII**/King Henry **the Seventh***
(~~King Henry Seven~~)

FRACTIONS AND DECIMALS 513

Simple fractions are normally said in the following ways:

$^{1}/_{2}$	*a half*
$^{1}/_{4}$	*a quarter*
$^{1}/_{5}$	*a/one fifth*
$^{3}/_{8}$	*three eighths*
$^{2}/_{3}$	*two thirds*
$^{13}/_{14}$	*thirteen fourteenths*
$^{3}/_{4}$ *hour*	*three quarters of an hour*
$^{3}/_{10}$ *mile*	*three tenths of a mile*

Decimals are normally said and written as follows:

0.245 *nought point two four five*
(in American English normally *zero point two four five*)
(~~nought point two hundred and forty five~~)

4.7 *four point seven*

More complex fractions can be expressed by using the word *over*:

$^{423}/_{500}$ *four hundred and twenty three **over** five hundred*

Singular and plural with fractions and decimals 513a

With fractions and decimals below 1, *of a* + singular noun is commonly used:

$^{2}/_{5}$ *k* *two fifths **of a kilogram***

*That's almost **three quarters of a** pint of milk that she's drunk.*

0.8cm *(nought) point eight **of a centimetre***

When the decimals are below 1, they can also be followed by a plural noun:

0.255cm *nought point two five five* ***centimetres***

Fractions and decimals over 1 are normally followed directly by a plural noun:

two and a quarter ***hours***
(~~two and a quarter hour~~)

I'll have four and a half ***bags****, please.*
(~~I'll have four and a half bag, please.~~)

2.7 ***millimetres***
(~~2.7 millimetre~~)

Note that after fractions and amounts, singular verbs are normally used:

8 kilometres **is** *about 5 miles.*

Note also the structure *a … and a half*:

We've been waiting for delivery now for about ***a month and a half.***

PERCENTAGES 514

Percentages are written with a special symbol % and are spoken as *per cent*:

Sales tax is added to all items. The current rate is ***17.5%.***
(seventeen point five per cent)

Interest rates reached an all-time low last month when banks and building societies reduced mortgage rates by ***one half per cent*** *to* ***4.75%.***
(four point seven five per cent)

Note that in the previous sentence it is also possible to say *half a per cent* or *(a) half of one per cent.*

TELEPHONE NUMBERS 515

Each figure in a telephone number is commonly indicated separately. Speakers tend to pause after groups of three or four figures. When the same figure comes twice, either it can be said twice or the word 'double' can be used:

9807 6933
nine eight oh seven, six nine ***double three***
or: *nine eight zero seven, six nine* ***three three***

→ **524 Spoken forms of *0***

USES OF *AND* 516

And is commonly used before the tens in a number:

310
three hundred ***and*** *ten* (or *three ten*)

5,642
five thousand, six hundred ***and*** *forty-two*

However, *and* can be omitted in measurements that contain two different units. *And* can be used before the smaller unit, but it is usually omitted:

*two hours (**and**) ten minutes*

*two metres (**and**) thirty centimetres*

USES OF COMMAS 517

In writing, commas are normally used to divide large numbers into groups of three figures, usually in order to indicate the thousands and the millions. Full stops are not used in this way:

5,139
(~~5.139~~)

8,577,184

Commas may be omitted from four-figure numbers. They are not used in dates:

7,934
(or: 7934)

the year ***1738***

➝ **519 Round numbers and dates** below

A AND *ONE* 518

It is possible to say *a hundred* or *one hundred*, *a thousand* or *one thousand*, *a million* or *one million*. When *one* is used, it is more formal:

I want to live for a hundred years.
(~~I want to live for hundred years.~~)

[on a formal notice]
The membership fee for the Club is ***one*** *thousand pounds a year.*

A can only be used at the beginning of a number:

a/one *hundred*

three thousand ***one*** *hundred*
(~~three thousand a hundred~~)

A thousand can be used alone, and may be followed by *and*, but *a* is not normally used before a number of hundreds:

__a/one__ thousand

__a/one__ thousand and forty-nine

__one__ thousand, six hundred and two
(more natural than: a thousand, six hundred and two)

A or *one* are used with measurement words:

__a/one__ kilometre
(but: one kilometre six hundred metres)

__an/one__ hour and thirteen minutes
(but: one hour thirteen minutes)

__a/one__ pound
(but: one pound twenty-five)

ROUND NUMBERS AND DATES 519

The phrases *eleven hundred*, *twelve hundred* are often used instead of *one thousand one hundred*, etc. The form with *hundred* is especially preferred in American English. It is most common with round numbers between 1,100 and 1,900:

They only paid __eleven hundred pounds__ for the whole holiday.

It all cost __twenty eight hundred__ dollars.
(preferred American form)

This form is used in historical dates. *Hundred* is omitted in informal contexts:

Shakespeare was born in __fifteen sixty four__. (1564)

It was built in __seventeen (hundred and) twenty-nine__. (1729) (more formal)

When speaking, it is normal for the numbers to be pronounced in full. In writing, numerical figures are normally preferred to written numbers.

Decades are commonly written as follows (usually without an apostrophe, but may also occur with an apostrophe):

The __1980s__ were years when money became a key word.

BRITISH POUNDS STERLING 520

There are *100 pence* in a British pound. Sums of money are named as follows:

1p	*one penny* (informal *one p* or *a penny*)
10p	*ten pence* (informal *ten p*)
£5.45	*five pounds forty-five (pence)* or *five pounds __and__ forty-five pence* (more formal)

Pound is often used informally as a plural:

They charged me nine __pound__ fifty for parking.

Singular forms are used in premodifying expressions like *a five-**pound** note* (see above). However, *pence* is often used instead of *penny* (*a five **pence** coin*; *a twenty-six **pence** stamp*).

MEASURING AREAS 521

The most typical form is to say, for example, that a room is *twelve feet **by** fifteen feet*, or that a garden is *thirty metres **by** forty-eight metres.*

A room *twelve feet by twelve feet* can be called *twelve **feet square***; the total area is *144 **square feet**.*

SPOKEN CALCULATIONS 522

Common ways of saying calculations in British English are:

2 + 2 = 4	*Two and two is/are four.* (informal) *Two plus two equals/is four.* (formal)
9 – 4 = 5	*Four from nine is/leaves five.* (informal) *Nine take away four is/leaves five.* (informal) *Nine minus four equals/is five.* (formal)
5 × 4 = 20	*Five fours are twenty.* (informal) *Five times four is twenty.* (informal) *Five multiplied by four equals/is twenty.* (formal)
15 ÷ 3 = 5	*Three(s) into fifteen goes five (times).* (informal) *Fifteen divided by three equals/is five.* (formal)

ROMAN NUMERALS 523

Roman numerals (*I, II, III, IV*, etc.) are not common in modern English, but they are still used in a few cases – for example the names of kings and queens, page numbers in the introductions to some books, the numbers of paragraphs in some documents, the numbers of questions in some examinations, the figures on some clock faces, and occasionally the names of centuries.

The Roman numerals normally used are as follows (large Roman and small Roman):

1	*I*	*i*	10	*X*	*x*	40	*XL*	*xl*
2	*II*	*ii*	11	*XI*	*xi*	45	*XLV*	*xlv*
3	*III*	*iii*	12	*XII*	*xii*	50	*L*	*l*
4	*IV*	*iv*	13	*XIII*	*xiii*	60	*LX*	*lx*
5	*V*	*v*	14	*XIV*	*xiv*	90	*XC*	*xc*
6	*VI*	*vi*	19	*XIX*	*xix*	100	*C*	*c*
7	*VII*	*vii*	20	*XX*	*xx*	500	*D*	
8	*VIII*	*viii*	21	*XXI*	*xxi*	1000	*M*	
9	*IX*	*ix*	30	*XXX*	*xxx*	1998	*MCMXCVIII*	

It was built in the time of ***Henry V****.*

For details, see Introduction ***page ix****.*

Do ***question (vi)*** *or* ***question (vii)****, but not both.*

a fine ***XVIII-century*** *English walnut chest of drawers*

Spoken forms of *0* 524

0 is usually said as *nought* in decimal numbers where it occurs before the decimal point:

0.455 litres
(*nought point four five five litres*)

American English prefers *zero*, and this is becoming more common in British English too:

0.885 centimetres
(*zero point eight eight five centimetres*)

0 is typically said as *oh* where it occurs after a decimal point and in a wide range of numbers such as telephone numbers, addresses, years:

7.05 seconds
(*seven point oh five*)

She lives at 205 Hills Avenue.
(*two oh five*)

His phone number is 470503.
(*four seven oh five oh three*)

She was born in 1908.
(*nineteen oh eight*)

Car registration number Y205 CNA
(*two oh/zero five*)

In giving the scores of sports games, other words are used:

- football:

  Valencia lost 1–0.
  (*one nil*)

- tennis:

  Klisters leads Williams 40–0 in the first game of the second set.
  (*forty love*)

- American team sports:

  [American football]
  The Seattle Sea Hawks beat the Cincinnati Reds 7–0.
  (*seven nothing* or *seven to nothing* or *seven zip* – 'zip' is informal American English)

  [baseball]
  Miami Hurricances 7, Northern Colorado Bears 0

In measurements of temperature, *zero* is more common but *nought* is possible:

Zero degrees Celsius is thirty-two degrees Fahrenheit.

Singular forms with plural meanings 525

After an expression of number, *dozen, hundred, thousand, million* and *billion* have no final -*s*, and *of* is not used:

five hundred *pounds*
hundreds of *pounds*

several thousand *times*
It cost ***thousands****.*

a few million *years*
millions of *years*

Singular forms are used as modifiers before nouns in plural measuring expressions:

*a five-****pound*** *note* — *a three-****mile*** *walk*

*six two-****hour*** *lessons* — *a three-****month****-old baby*

*a four-****foot****-deep hole* — *a six-****foot****-tall man*

In an informal style, *foot* is often used instead of *feet*, especially with reference to people's height:

My father's just over six ***foot*** *two.*

539 Glossary for any unfamiliar terms

Appendix: Referring to the time

TELLING THE TIME 526

There are two common ways of saying what the time is:

6.05 *five past six* or *six (oh) five*
6.10 *ten past six* or *six ten*
6.15 *(a) quarter past six* or *six fifteen*
6.20 *twenty past six* or *six twenty*
6.25 *twenty-five past six* or *six twenty-five*
6.30 *half past six* or *six thirty*
6.35 *twenty-five to seven* or *six thirty-five*
6.40 *twenty to seven* or *six forty*
6.45 *(a) quarter to seven* or *six forty-five*
6.50 *ten to seven* or *six fifty*
6.55 *five to seven* or *six fifty-five*
7.00 *seven o'clock*

Most speakers prefer to say *minutes past/to* for times between the five minute divisions (*seven* ***minutes*** *past six, four* ***minutes*** *to seven*).

In informal speech, *past* is often dropped from *half past*:

Okay, see you at ***half four.***
(4.30 **not** 3.30)

If the hour is understood, then just *half past* or *quarter to* are used in informal speech:

Hurry up. We've got to be there at ***quarter to.***

The expression *o'clock* is only used at the hour:

The first meeting is at ***seven (o'clock).***

Wake me at ***ten past six.***
(~~Wake me at ten past six o'clock.~~)

O'clock is often omitted in informal contexts when referring to the hour:

The concert starts at ***seven.***

In American English, and increasingly in internet communication, colons are used to mark clock time (*3:40, 10:05, 13:25*).

The twenty-four-hour clock 526a

The twenty-four-hour clock is used mainly in transport timetables and official announcements. In everyday conversation, people usually use the twelve-hour clock:

[reading a rail timetable]
The last train leaves at ***22.20****.*
(twenty-two twenty)

Check-in time is ***a quarter past six in the morning****.*
(preferred form in informal contexts)

[public announcement at a railway station]
The train about to leave from platform 13 is the ***fourteen forty-five*** *departure for Manchester.*

When using the twenty-four-hour clock, times on the hour are normally pronounced as follows:

The flight will depart at ***seventeen hundred hours****.*
(17.00)

In public announcements, the following pronunciations of numbers are common:

The ***oh nine hundred*** *service is delayed and will now depart at* ***oh nine fifteen****.*
(09.00 and 09.15)

Times can be indicated by using *in the morning/afternoon/evening*. In a more formal style, *am* (Latin *ante meridiem* = 'before midday') and *pm* (*post meridiem* = 'after midday') are used:

09.00 = *nine o'clock in the morning* or *nine am*

21.00 = *nine o'clock in the evening* or *nine pm*

Note that punctuation is normally omitted in *am* and *pm.*

12.00 can mean at midnight or at midday. This is commonly distinguished by reference to *12.00 noon* and *12.00 midnight* (spoken as *twelve noon* and *twelve midnight*).

Appendix: Units of measurement

NON-METRIC MEASURES 527

Metric measurement units are increasingly used in the United Kingdom, but non-metric measures are also still widely used, especially by older people who still use the older system of imperial units such as pounds, feet and gallons. Below are some of the common terms along with their approximate values in the metric system. Some of the units have the same names but mean different quantities in the UK and the USA. The international system of metric measurements is not commonly used in the USA.

Approximate values of non-metric units 527a

Units of length and distance and their abbreviations

1 inch (in) = 2.5 centimetres (cm)

1 foot (ft) = 30 cm

1 yard (yd) = 90 cm

5 miles (m) = 8 kilometres (km)

Inches and feet are sometimes indicated in writing with ' for feet and " for inches:

The living room is 9'8" by 15'6".
(nine feet eight inches by fifteen feet six inches)

Units of area

11 square feet = 1 square metre (or *1 sq metre,* or *1m*^{2})

5 acres = 2 hectares

1 square mile = 2.6 square km

1 square inch = 6.4516 cm^2

Units of weight

1 ounce (oz) = 28 g

1 pound (lb) = 450 g

14 pounds = (Br) 1 stone = 6.4 kg

1 ton = (Br) *1 tonne =* (Am) *0.9 tonnes*

Units of volume and capacity

1 cubic centimetre (cc) = 0.0610 cubic inch (cu in)

There are 8 pints in a gallon:

	British	American
1 pint (pt)	*0.6 litres*	*0.5 litres*
1 gallon (gall)	*4.5 litres*	*3.8 litres*

Units of temperature

Except in the USA, temperatures are now more commonly given in degrees Celsius (°C, sometimes called *centigrade*) than degrees Fahrenheit (°F):

	°F	°C
ice	32	0
warm room	70	20
hot day	85	30
body temperature	98	37
boiling water	212	100

Usage 527b

Personal weight and height

British English speakers usually measure their personal weight in stones and pounds. American English speakers just use pounds. *Stone* is not commonly used in the plural. The word *pounds* is typically omitted in informal contexts:

*I weigh eight **stone** six.*
(~~I weigh eight stones six.~~)

*He's overweight. He needs to lose a couple of **stone**.*

Personal height is measured in feet and inches, with the word *inches* usually omitted in informal contexts. *Foot* is normally preferred to *feet* (→ 525):

*I'm **five foot eleven**.*

Height

The height of buildings and other structures, tall plants and trees, altitude and elevation above sea level are typically measured in feet (but increasingly in metres for elevation above sea level):

*We are now flying at an altitude of 28,000 **feet**.*

*That tree was only about four **feet** tall when we planted it.*

Distance

Distance can also be measured in feet, but longer distances along the ground are measured in yards and miles:

*I was standing about six **feet** away from the Prime Minister.*

*The car park's straight on, about 500 **yards** on the right.*

*From here to the airport is about 35 **miles**.*

Appendix: Nationalities, countries and regions

INTRODUCTION 528

Referring to a nation or region and its affairs normally requires four words:

- The name of the country or region:

  Sweden, Japan, France, Venezuela, Asia

- The adjective:

  Swedish, Japanese, French, Venezuelan, Asian

- The singular noun used for a person from the country or region:

  a Swede, a Japanese, a Frenchman/woman, a Venezuelan, an Asian

- The plural expression *the* ... used for the population as a whole:

  the Swedes, the Japanese, the French, the Venezuelans, the Asians

The name of a national language is commonly the same as the national adjective. In this case the words are nouns and may be modified by adjectives. The definite article *the* is not used, nor is the word *language*:

> *Do you speak **Hungarian**?*
> (~~Do you speak the Hungarian?~~)
> (~~Do you speak Hungarian language?~~)
>
> ***Thai** is not easy to learn.*
>
> *She speaks fluent **English**.*

The singular noun is normally the same as the adjective (e.g. *Japanese, Moroccan*), and the plural expression is the same as the adjective + *-s* (e.g. *the Moroccans*).

All words of this kind (including adjectives) begin with capital letters:

> *He has a degree in American literature.*
> (~~He has a degree in american literature.~~)

Examples of countries and regions, and associated adjectives and nouns 528a

country/region	adjective	person	population
America/USA	*American*	*an American*	*the Americans*
Belgium	*Belgian*	*a Belgian*	*the Belgians*
Brazil	*Brazilian*	*a Brazilian*	*the Brazilians*
China	*Chinese*	*a Chinese*	*the Chinese*
The Congo	*Congolese*	*a Congolese*	*the Congolese*
Europe	*European*	*a European*	*the Europeans*
Greece	*Greek*	*a Greek*	*the Greeks*
Hungary	*Hungarian*	*a Hungarian*	*the Hungarians*
Iraq	*Iraqi*	*an Iraqi*	*the Iraqis*
Israel	*Israeli*	*an Israeli*	*the Israelis*
Italy	*Italian*	*an Italian*	*the Italians*
Kenya	*Kenyan*	*a Kenyan*	*the Kenyans*
Morocco	*Moroccan*	*a Moroccan*	*the Moroccans*
Norway	*Norwegian*	*a Norwegian*	*the Norwegians*
Portugal	*Portuguese*	*a Portuguese*	*the Portuguese*
Russia	*Russian*	*a Russian*	*the Russians*
Switzerland	*Swiss*	*a Swiss*	*the Swiss*
Thailand	*Thai*	*a Thai*	*the Thais*

Some main exceptions 528b

country/region	adjective	person	population
Britain	*British*	*a British man/ woman/person* (more formally: *a Briton*)	*the British*
Denmark	*Danish*	*a Dane*	*the Danes*
England	*English*	*an Englishman woman/person*	*the English*
Finland	*Finnish*	*a Finn*	*the Finns*
France	*French*	*a Frenchman/ woman/person*	*the French*
Holland/ The Netherlands	*Dutch*	*a Dutchwoman/ man/person*	*the Dutch*
Ireland	*Irish*	*an Irishman/ woman/person*	*the Irish*
New Zealand	*New Zealand*	*a New Zealander*	*the New Zealanders*
Poland	*Polish*	*a Pole*	*the Poles*
Scotland	*Scottish*	*a Scot*	*the Scots*
Spain	*Spanish*	*a Spaniard*	*the Spanish*
Sweden	*Swedish*	*a Swede*	*the Swedes*
Turkey	*Turkish*	*a Turk*	*the Turks*
Wales	*Welsh*	*a Welshman/ woman/person*	*the Welsh*

→ **539 Glossary** for any unfamiliar terms

Notes

1 *English* referring to population is not the same as *British*; it is not used for Scottish or Welsh or Northern Irish people.

2 The word *Briton* is unusual except in newspaper headlines (*TWELVE BRITONS INJURED IN COACH COLLISION*). The noun *Brit* (*the Brits*) is sometimes used informally. Most British people call themselves *Scottish*, *Welsh* or *English*.

3 *(Great) Britain* refers to the landmass of England, Scotland and Wales. *The United Kingdom* (or *the UK*) refers to England, Scotland, Wales and the six counties of Northern Ireland. Some people from Northern Ireland refer to themselves as *British* in the context of *the United Kingdom of Britain and Northern Ireland*. However, everyone from Northern Ireland has the right to Irish nationality and can hold an Irish passport. *Irish* also refers to citizens of the Irish Republic.

4 The Scots themselves prefer the adjective *Scots* and it also occurs in the compounds *Scotsman/Scotswoman*. The adjective *Scotch* is normally only used to refer to food and drink from Scotland (*Scotch broth*, *Scotch egg*).

5 Although *America* and *American* are the normal English words for the United States, its citizens and affairs, people from other parts of the north and south American continent may object to this use. It is sometimes avoided for these reasons. It is more usual to say: *She's a US citizen*; *I've got some US dollars to change*.

6 *Arabic* is used for the language spoken in Arab countries; in other cases, the normal adjective is *Arab*. *Arabian* is used in a few fixed expressions and place names (e.g. *Saudi **Arabian***, the ***Arabian** Sea*).

7 The mostly monosyllabic non-compound words listed above under person (*Dane*, *Spaniard*) are normally avoided when referring to a woman (*a Danish woman*, *a Spanish woman* are preferred).

Appendix: Irregular verbs

INTRODUCTION 529

With some irregular verbs, there is a choice of past form and *-ed* participle.

Table of irregular verbs 529a

base form	past form	*-ed* participle
arise	*arose*	*arisen*
awake	*awoke*	*awoken*
bear	*bore*	*borne*
beat	*beat*	*beaten*
become	*became*	*become*
begin	*began*	*begun*
bend	*bent*	*bent*
bet	*bet*	*bet*
bind	*bound*	*bound*
bite	*bit*	*bitten*
bleed	*bled*	*bled*
blow	*blew*	*blown*
break	*broke*	*broken*
breed	*bred*	*bred*
bring	*brought*	*brought*
build	*built*	*built*
burst	*burst*	*burst*
burn	*burnt/burned*	*burnt/burned*
buy	*bought*	*bought*
cast	*cast*	*cast*
catch	*caught*	*caught*
choose	*chose*	*chosen*
cling	*clung*	*clung*
come	*came*	*come*

base form	past form	*-ed* participle
cost	*cost*	*cost*
creep	*crept*	*crept*
cut	*cut*	*cut*
deal	*dealt*	*dealt*
dig	*dug*	*dug*
draw	*drew*	*drawn*
dream	*dreamt/dreamed*	*dreamt/dreamed*
drink	*drank*	*drunk*
drive	*drove*	*driven*
eat	*ate*	*eaten*
fall	*fell*	*fallen*
feed	*fed*	*fed*
feel	*felt*	*felt*
fight	*fought*	*fought*
find	*found*	*found*
flee	*fled*	*fled*
fling	*flung*	*flung*
fly	*flew*	*flown*
forbear	*forbore*	*forborne*
forbid	*forbade*	*forbidden*
forget	*forgot*	*forgotten*
forgive	*forgave*	*forgiven*
forsake	*forsook*	*forsaken*
forswear	*forswore*	*forsworn*
freeze	*froze*	*frozen*
get	*got*	*got*
give	*gave*	*given*
go	*went*	*gone*
grind	*ground*	*ground*
grow	*grew*	*grown*
hear	*heard*	*heard*
hide	*hid*	*hidden*
hit	*hit*	*hit*

base form	past form	*-ed* participle
hold	*held*	*held*
hurt	*hurt*	*hurt*
keep	*kept*	*kept*
know	*knew*	*known*
lay	*laid*	*laid*
lead	*led*	*led*
lean	*leant/leaned*	*leant/leaned*
leave	*left*	*left*
lend	*lent*	*lent*
let	*let*	*let*
light	*lit/lighted*	*lit/lighted*
lose	*lost*	*lost*
make	*made*	*made*
mean	*meant*	*meant*
meet	*met*	*met*
mislay	*mislaid*	*mislaid*
mislead	*misled*	*misled*
pay	*paid*	*paid*
put	*put*	*put*
quit	*quit*	*quit*
read (/riːd/)	*read* (/red/)	*read* (/red/)
rend	*rent*	*rent*
ride	*rode*	*ridden*
ring	*rang*	*rung*
rise	*rose*	*risen*
run	*ran*	*run*
saw	*sawed*	*sawn*
say	*said*	*said*
see	*saw*	*seen*
seek	*sought*	*sought*
sell	*sold*	*sold*
send	*sent*	*sent*
set	*set*	*set*

→ **539 Glossary** for any unfamiliar terms

base form	past form	*-ed* participle
sew	*sewed*	*sewn*
shake	*shook*	*shaken*
shed	*shed*	*shed*
shine	*shone*	*shone*
shoe	*shod*	*shod*
shoot	*shot*	*shot*
show	*showed*	*shown*
shrink	*shrank*	*shrunk*
shut	*shut*	*shut*
sing	*sang*	*sung*
sink	*sank*	*sunk*
sit	*sat*	*sat*
slay	*slew*	*slain*
sleep	*slept*	*slept*
slide	*slid*	*slid*
sling	*slung*	*slung*
slink	*slunk*	*slunk*
sow	*sowed*	*sown*
speak	*spoke*	*spoken*
spend	*spent*	*spent*
spin	*spun*	*spun*
spill	*spilt/spilled*	*spilt/spilled*
spread	*spread*	*spread*
speed	*sped*	*sped*
spring	*sprang*	*sprung*
stand	*stood*	*stood*
steal	*stole*	*stolen*
stick	*stuck*	*stuck*
sting	*stung*	*stung*
stink	*stank*	*stunk*
strew	*strewed*	*strewn*
stride	*strode*	*stridden*
strike	*struck*	*struck*

base form	past form	*-ed* participle
string	*strung*	*strung*
strive	*strove*	*striven*
swear	*swore*	*sworn*
sweep	*swept*	*swept*
swim	*swam*	*swum*
swing	*swung*	*swung*
take	*took*	*taken*
teach	*taught*	*taught*
tear	*tore*	*torn*
tell	*told*	*told*
think	*thought*	*thought*
throw	*threw*	*thrown*
thrust	*thrust*	*thrust*
tread	*trod*	*trodden*
understand	*understood*	*understood*
wake	*woke*	*woken*
wear	*wore*	*worn*
weep	*wept*	*wept*
win	*won*	*won*
wind	*wound*	*wound*
wring	*wrung*	*wrung*
write	*wrote*	*written*

→ 539 **Glossary** for any unfamiliar terms

Appendix: North American English grammar

INTRODUCTION 530

The basic grammar of English speech and writing as used in North America is, in almost all respects, the same as that in use across the islands of Britain and Ireland. What marks American English out as different from the European variety are mostly differences in pronunciation, spelling and vocabulary. Written grammar displays fewer differences between American and British usage than spoken grammar. However, North America is a vast continent which is home to many different regional and social dialects of English, often reflected in distinct spoken grammatical usage; we cannot hope to cover all this diversity within the limits of one book. Across the islands of Britain and Ireland there are also differences in usage, but this grammar has focussed on what is shared among the widest range of speakers. This appendix therefore discusses those aspects of standard North American spoken usage which are notably different from the spoken description as presented in this book. The differences are usually differences of degree rather than of kind: there seem to be very few forms that are the exclusive domain of one variety, but there are often quite striking differences in frequency of use of everyday items between the varieties. It must also be noted that American influence on the grammar of Britain and Ireland is considerable, and changes in usage can often be attributed to the influence of American popular culture, for example the use of *like* as a marker of direct speech reporting (→ 501e and A–Z 49 *Like*). For convenience, the spoken grammar presented in the main chapters of this book will be referred to as BrE, and references to standard North American English will be abbreviated to AmE. The spoken North American segment of the Cambridge International Corpus (CIC) was consulted in the preparation of this appendix.

MODAL VERBS AND OTHER MODAL EXPRESSIONS 531

Some modal verbs and other modal expressions are more frequent in BrE than AmE, and vice-versa.

Shall 531a

Although quite frequent in BrE, *shall* is relatively infrequent in AmE. BrE usage allows *shall* in first person declaratives about the future:

*I **shall** be in the office till five thirty.* (BrE)

AmE prefers *will* or *be going to* in such situations. However, AmE does allow *shall* in first person interrogatives, especially those functioning as suggestions and in semi-fixed expressions such as *How shall I say it?*:

*Let's try to use words that are in the dictionary next time, **shall we**?* (AmE)

[talking about whether to go to the cinema to see films or to wait till they are available on video]
You know, and you have to start thinking about, is it, is it worth spending the money to go see it, or ***shall*** *I just wait?*
(AmE)

Frequency of *shall* (per 1 million words) in spoken AmE and BrE

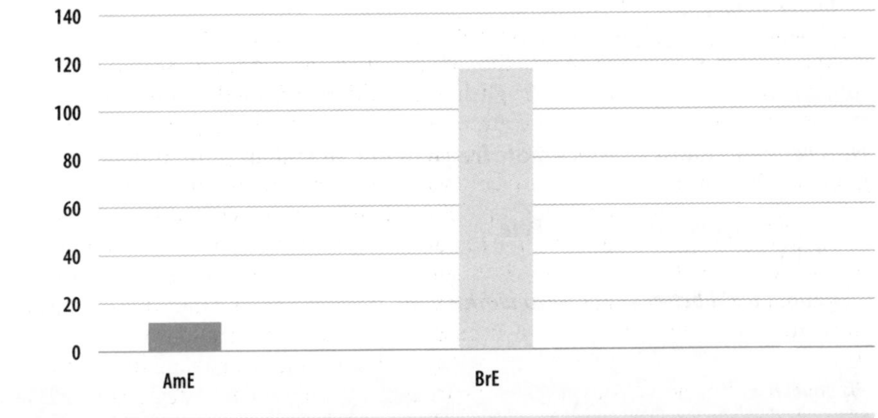

Must 531b

Must is overall much more frequent in BrE than in AmE. Although obligation and predictive meanings occur in both varieties, the majority of uses of *must* in AmE are predictive, and AmE tends to prefer *have to* for expressing obligation:

Something ***must****'ve been on her mind.* (AmE)

Everybody says I don't need to lose weight, but I feel I ***must****.* (AmE)

Frequency of *must* (per 1 million words) in spoken AmE and BrE

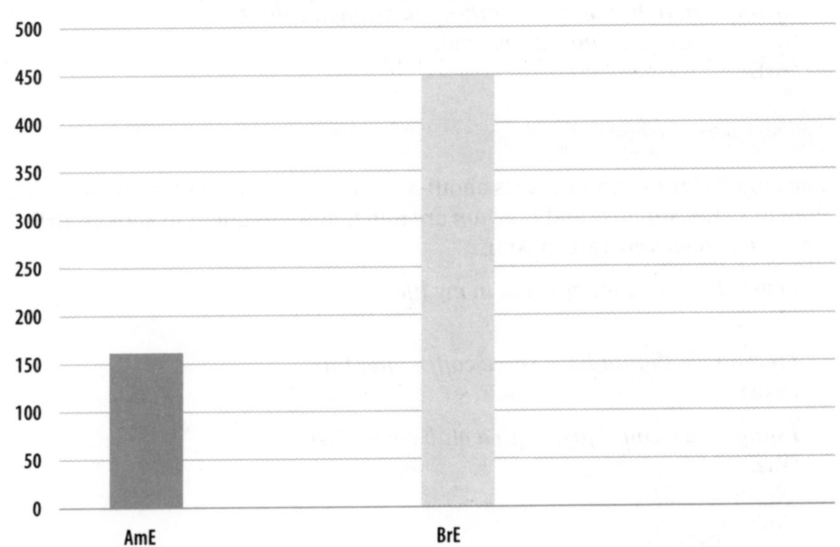

Have got to and *have to* 531c

Modal *have got* to is almost twice as frequent in spoken BrE compared with AmE. *Have to* (without *got*) is 50% more frequent in AmE than in BrE:

I've got to go and meet my mum for lunch.
(preferred spoken form BrE)

I have to meet my advisor at one.
(preferred spoken form AmE)

Had better 531d

Had better is almost six times more frequent in BrE than in AmE, though it is used in both varieties:

*You'**d better** move your car, Pete.*
(BrE)

*I guess we'**d better** get back to work.*
(AmE)

Be going to 531e

Be going to (and the contracted form *gonna*) is often used in direction-giving in AmE, which is not a characteristic use in BrE, which typically uses imperatives (with and without *you*), and present or future forms with *will*:

*You'**re gonna** go two blocks and then you'**re gonna** see a big white building.*
(AmE)

A: ***Come** to T-junction, **turn** left. **Go** down there about half a mile, **you come** to a right turn with a pub on the corner.*
B: *Yep.*
A: ***You turn** right there, that **takes** you straight into it.*
B: *Right lovely. Thank you very much.*
(BrE)

I guess, I suppose, I reckon 531f

The modal expression *I guess* is about 30 times more frequent in spoken AmE than in BrE. *I suppose* and *I reckon* are much more frequent in spoken BrE. *I reckon* is relatively rare in AmE:

***I guess** I create a lot of stress in my life.*
(AmE)

***I reckon** we should have some coffee after this.*
(BrE)

***I suppose** we could just go to a club somewhere.*
(BrE)

OTHER VERBS 532

Be 532a

With the verb *be*, although both types of negated form exist in BrE and AmE, there is a stronger preference in AmE for the negated forms with *not* in both the present and the past tense (e.g. *is/'s not, were not*), rather than the contracted forms *isn't, aren't, wasn't* and *weren't*. *Isn't*, in particular, is many times more frequent in BrE than in AmE:

*Tim **isn't** working there anymore.*
(BrE)

*Joe**'s not** coming back anymore.*
(preferred AmE form)

Have and *have got* 532b

The present tense form of *have* with *got* used for possession is more than twice as frequent in spoken BrE as in AmE:

***I've got** one sister and one brother.*
(BrE)

***I have** a cousin who never married.*
(AmE)

Go (and) 532c

The AmE equivalent to informal BrE *go and* + infinitive without *to* occurs often without *and*:

*Where's your towel? Is it in the drawer? **Go and see** if you can find it.*
(BrE)

*I actually hadn't heard anything about it, and some friends called up and said do you want to **go see** this movie, and, and they said it starred Meryl Streep and Mel Brooks.*
(AmE)

Get 532d

In AmE, *get* has an *-ed* participle form *gotten*, which is not used in BrE:

*I mean, as poverty has **gotten** worse, as, you know, education has **gotten** worse, as there's been more single-parent families, as there's been more homelessness, there's been more crime.*
(AmE)

A frequent use of *get* (followed by a verb in *to*-infinitive form) in AmE is to refer to achievements. This usage occurs in BrE but is much rarer:

That's great advice. I'm so glad ***I got to talk*** *to you.*
(AmE)

A: *It was a lot of fun.* ***I got to see*** *Arkansas. I* ***got to see*** *that country.*
B: *Yeah.*
A: *It was really green down there.*
B: *No kidding.*
(AmE)

[talking about an actress, a friend of speaker A's, who was offered film work]
A: *The thing is she couldn't have turned it down because she hadn't done any work for two years so she had to.*
B: *Oh yeah absolutely.*
A: *And* ***she got to film*** *on location in Majorca.*
(BrE)

Fit 532e

In AmE, the past tense of *fit* is most often *fit*, while standard BrE prefers *fitted*:

Jennifer says she never really ***fit*** *in, and that made it easy for the other teachers to be suspicious of her.*
(AmE)
(preferred BrE form: *fitted in*)

I found a pair of boots that ***fitted*** *me and they weren't too bad-looking either.*
(BrE)

Learn, burn, dream, etc. 532f

Verbs such as *burn, dream, lean, learn, smell, spell, spill* often allow a past tense and *-ed* participle ending of either *-ed* (*learned, spilled*) or *-t* (*learnt, spilt*). AmE overwhelmingly prefers the *-ed* ending:

One night I had a bad dream. I ***dreamt*** *that someone was trying to attack me.*
(BrE)

[discussing changing British dietary habits]
Well, in my grandma's day and age they would never have ***dreamed*** *of eating a curry, would they?*
(BrE)

When I was a boy, I ***dreamed*** *of playing football.*
(AmE)

Other verbs 532g

Some other verbs display irregular past forms in AmE which are not used in BrE, for example *dove* as the past tense of *dive* (BrE *dived*), and *pled* as the past tense of *plead* (BrE *pleaded*):

He ***pled*** *guilty to avoid the death penalty.*
(AmE)

The eagle just folded his wings, folded his legs, ***dove*** *right down and crashed right into the guy and almost killed him.*
(AmE)

TAGS AND TAILS 533

Interrogative tags (→ 300, 431) are around four times more frequent in BrE than in AmE, but a wide range of interrogative tags occur in both varieties:

He's brilliant, ***isn't he****?*
(BrE)

They weren't reading, ***were they****?*
(AmE)

In informal contexts, AmE speakers often use an interrogative copy tag with rising intonation in responses denoting surprise or emotional involvement, which is not common in BrE:

A: *I changed schools three times.*
B: ***You did****?*
A: *In one year.*
B: *Wow. Wow.*
(AmE; BrE prefers *Did you?* here, with fall-rise or rising intonation)

A: *You know what guys? One of my big weaknesses is bags. I love bags. I don't know why.*
B: ***You do****?*
A: *Yeah.*
(AmE; BrE preferred form: *Do you?*)

BrE often adds substitute *do* to reduced clauses with modal verbs, especially in tag responses. AmE uses the modal verb only:

[*Riverjazz* is a jazz club]
A: *Do you want to go to Riverjazz tonight?*
B: *Do I have to?*
A: *No.*
B: *Are you going?*
A: ***I might do****.*
(BrE)

A: *So uh what do you think you'll do for your twenty-first birthday? Are you gonna go to a party or anything?*
B: *No. Yeah. Yeah.* ***I might.*** *I mean … Yeah. Maybe.*
(AmE)

Affirmative copy tags occur in both varieties but are much rarer in AmE than in BrE:

I think it's really funny that they live together, ***I do.***
(BrE)

[talking about car mechanics]
A: *That's hard work.*
B: *It is.*
A: *I think they earn their money,* ***I do.***
(AmE)

The universal tag, *right?* is almost four times more frequent in AmE than in BrE:

You lived in Canada, though, ***right?***
(AmE)

I was hoping we could change this one, ***right?***
(BrE)

Tails are considerably less common in AmE than in BrE, but they do occur in informal spoken AmE:

[talking of a US Senator; name disguised here]
He*'s a scary guy, that* ***Dan Boland.***
(AmE)

The last car we had was a Grand Prix which, … huh, never again! ***That*** *was a nightmare,* ***that one.***
(AmE)

ADVERBS, ADJECTIVES 534

Really, real 534a

In informal spoken AmE, *really* as a modifier of adjectives and other adverbs is often used without the *-ly* ending, in its adjective form. This is sometimes considered non-standard by traditionalists:

They were ***real*** *nice to us. The President of the company took us and showed us around.*
(AmE)

We all get along ***real*** *well.*
(AmE)

Well, good 534b

Similarly, *good* is often used in informal spoken AmE where BrE requires *well*. However, the AmE form is increasingly heard in BrE:

*Well I made it through college you know just cramming before the test kind of thing but I always did **good** so I never had a problem with that part.*
(AmE)

A: *Hi, how're you doing?*
B: *I'm **good**.*
(AmE)

Likely 534c

Spoken AmE allows the use of *likely* as an adverb (in the same way as *probably*, *possibly*, etc.) or as an adjective. In BrE, *likely* is usually only an adjective:

[discussing the US economy]
*So I think we created the conditions which will **likely** allow us to have a much longer recovery than you would have otherwise expected.*
(AmE; BrE preferred form: *which are likely to allow us* ... *which will probably allow us* ...)

*The more things you have to remember, the more you're **likely** to forget.*
(AmE; adjectival use, also typical of BrE)

THE PRESENT PERFECT 535

The frequency of use of the present perfect form is different in BrE and AmE, with a tendency to use it less in AmE. AmE often allows the past simple in situations which demand the present perfect in BrE:

[at a hotel; speakers have recently checked in]
A: *Where's the main pool at?*
B: *It's in the other side of the hotel.*
A: *Oh. Is it bigger than this?*
B: ***We didn't get that far yet*** [laughs].
(AmE; BrE would prefer: *We haven't got that far yet.*)

[discussing how much money speaker B is allowed to take out of a cash machine each day]
A: *How much can you get out of here?*
B: *Three hundred.*
A: *So you'd have three hundred? You've got three hundred you can get out right now?*
B: *Yeah.*
A: *But **you already got some out**. So you can do three hundred a day. **You already took out some today**. How much did you take out?*
B: *A hundred. I can only take another two hundred.*
(AmE; *already* typically accompanied by perfect aspect in similar situations in BrE)

CONCORD 536

There is a tendency in spoken AmE to prefer singular verb concord with collective nouns such as *government, team, group, rest*, etc., whereas BrE is more flexible in allowing singular or plural verbs:

By and large ***the government does*** *a good job.*
(AmE preferred form)

A: ***The government are*** *making a profit.*
B: *No,* ***the government aren't****. It's the private enterprise.*
(BrE; allows greater flexibility of use of plural verb)

[talking about American football]
While he was with the team, the ***rest*** *of the team* ***was*** *pretty poor so you couldn't really tell if it was just him or the team and I always just assumed that he was too good for the rest of the team.*
(AmE; BrE likely to prefer *the rest of the team were pretty poor* ...)

PREPOSITIONAL USAGE 537

There are some differences in prepositional usage between BrE and AmE, especially in time expressions:

I've been stranded in my house for days on end. I get to go out ***at the weekend*** *and that's it.* [laughs] *That's my life.*
(preferred BrE)

[talking about TV viewing habits]
During the week I don't have much time, and I spend a lot of time with my daughter ***on the weekend*** *and she lives a way away.*
(preferred AmE)

AmE allows *in + time period* after negatives with greater flexibility than BrE:

I haven't played basketball ***in two years****.*
(AmE; BrE preferred form: *for two years*)

AmE uses *through* in many situations where BrE uses *to* or *till* in references to the end points of time periods:

[*dress-down-Fridays* refers to the practice of allowing employees to come to work in informal dress on Fridays]
It started with dress-down-Fridays, which was a couple of years ago. Now it's really Monday ***through*** *Friday.*
(AmE)

[at a travel agent's]
You can use that ticket on any train except ones that depart Monday ***to*** *Friday before nine.*
(BrE)

AmE uses *on* with street names, whereas BrE prefers *in*:

A: *She lives* ***on*** *Third Street and I lived* ***on*** *Third Street but we lived between different avenues.*
B: *Hmm. Okay.*
(AmE)

I think she was born ***in*** *Leonora Street and then moved to Castle Street.*
(BrE)

EXCLAMATIVE EXPRESSIONS 538

AmE uses some exclamative and intensifying expressions which are not common in BrE. These include *geez, goddam, oh my gosh*:

But I went in there one day and I had cream-of-chicken soup. It was the best tasting ***goddamn*** *stuff I'd ever eaten in my life.*
(AmE)

[talking about hot weather; 80 degrees Fahrenheit = approximately 27 degrees Celsius]
A: *It's been eighty degrees here.*
B: ***Oh my gosh!***
(AmE)

→ **539 Glossary** for any unfamiliar terms

Acronym A type of abbreviation where the initial letters of two or more words are combined to produce consonant and vowel sequences that can be pronounced as words (*RAM*: **r**andom **a**ccess **m**emory; *NATO*: **N**orth **A**tlantic **T**reaty **O**rganisation).

Active The most common and unmarked form of voice. The grammatical subject and the agent/doer of the action are one and the same (*The thief had stolen all my money.*). In contrast, the passive voice is formed with subject + *be* + *-ed* participle, followed by an optional '*by*-phrase'. The recipient of the action is the grammatical subject; the *by*-phrase indicates the agent/doer. A passive construction gives less prominence to the agent (*All my money had been stolen (by the thief).*).

Adjective, adjective phrase Describes the qualities, features or states attributed to a noun or pronoun (*a **nice** room, a **happy** girl, she's **beautiful***).

A phrase with an adjective functioning as the head is an adjective phrase (*Are you **willing** to volunteer?*). An adjective phrase can have an attributive function (used before a noun: *It has a **smooth** texture.*) or a predicative function (used after a verb: *That film was **very strange**.*).

→ **Discontinuous adjective phrase**

Adjunct An optional element in a clause which modifies, comments on or expands the circumstances of an action or event in terms of such entities as time, place, manner, degree, intensity, reason, frequency. An adjunct can occupy different positions and can be realised by an adverb phrase, a prepositional phrase or, less frequently, a noun phrase or adverbial clause.

prep phrase — adv phrase
***In the summer** we **very often** make our own ice cream.*

→ **Linking adjunct**

Adverb, adverb phrase Indicates the time, place, manner, degree, frequency, duration, viewpoint, etc. of an event, action or process. It is mostly realised by the *-ly* suffix added to an adjective (*beautifully, fortunately, angrily, actually*).

A phrase with an adverb functioning as the head is called an adverb phrase (*The lecturer spoke very **clearly**.*). Adverb phrases can modify verbs, adjectives, other adverbs and whole clauses.

Adverbial, adverbial clause Any word, phrase or clause that functions like an adverb.

Adverbial clauses are clauses which act as modifiers to a main clause:

*Tell me **after I've eaten my dinner**.* (time)

*Drive carefully **because it is snowing**.* (reason)

→ **Modification**

Affirmative A grammatical construction with positive polarity that has an assertive meaning. Affirmative contrasts with negative:

I have done my homework. (affirmative)

I haven't done my homework. (negative)

Affix A syllable or group of syllables which are added to the beginning or end of a word to make a new word. Affixes added to the beginning of a word are prefixes. Affixes added to the end of a word are suffixes. In the adjective ***un**work**able*** there are two affixes, *un-* (prefix) and *-able* (suffix).

Agent, agency Refers to the performer or 'doer' of an action. In *the little girl tidied up the playroom*, 'the little girl' is the agent. In a passive clause, the agent may be indicated by the noun phrase that follows the optional *by*-phrase (*The government is criticised by **everybody**.*).

➝ Active

Agreement ➝ Concord

Anaphora (adjective = **anaphoric**) A process whereby one word or phrase points backwards to another and marks the relationship between what is being said and what has been said. The reference can normally only be located in the preceding context:

*Janet took the paper. **She** wrote a phone number on **it**.*
(*She* refers anaphorically to *Janet*; *it* refers anaphorically to *the paper*)

Anaphora is contrasted with cataphora.

➝ Endophora; Exophora

Antecedent The unit of word(s) to which a following word refers back. In ***Janet** took the paper. **She** wrote a phone number on it.*, *Janet* is the antecedent of *she*.

➝ Anaphora

Anticipatory structure Refers to structures that make forward reference to produce an end-focus:

***It** amazes me how open and honest the staff are.*
(anticipatory *it* enables the end-focus to be placed on the subject)

***It's not** until we lift the carpet in our bedroom **that we'll know what we've got to deal with**.*
(anticipatory *it* enables the end-focus to be placed on the time adjunct)

***It can, of course, be argued** that the bank has been lucky in its timing.*
(anticipatory *it* enables the end-focus to be placed on the complement clause)

Antonymy Refers to the most common type of gradable adjectives which occur as pairs of opposites denoting the upper and lower parts of an open-ended scale (*tall–short, hot–cold, heavy–light, good–bad*).

Apposition A relationship between two linguistic elements (usually noun phrases) which have identical reference:

***My boss**, **the woman in green**, used to work in Beijing.*
(my boss = the woman in green)

Aspect Indicates the speaker's perspective on time as indicated in a verb phrase, particularly whether an action is treated as finished or is still in progress or still relevant to the moment of speaking. English has two aspects: perfect and progressive (sometimes known as continuous).

⇢ **Perfect; Progressive**

Assertion Is associated with both positive and negative clauses (*he is in financial difficulties*; *that is just not true*). Assertions convey the truth of the communication.

Attributive Refers to the role of an adjective phrase as a modifier before a noun (*she had a* ***huge*** *suitcase*). The attributive function is in contrast with the predicative function (*her suitcase was* ***huge***).

⇢ **Predicative**

Auxiliary Refers to a closed set of verbs (*be*, *do* and *have*) that are usually followed by a lexical verb. They typically help to denote grammatical contrasts of aspect, voice, polarity and clause type (e.g. interrogative):

He ***was*** *working over there.*

I ***don't*** *like garlic.*

Have *you been home?*

Back channelling Verbal and non-verbal vocal devices used to provide feedback and other supportive responses between speakers, normally as a way to encourage the speaker to continue. Vocalisations, words and phrases such as *mm*, *uhum*, *yeah*, *right* are typical back-channelling devices.

Backgrounding A device used to make something less important. For example, nominalised forms (⇢ **Nominalisation**) can be used to conceal or purposefully make less important a cause or an agent. Backgrounding is contrasted with foregrounding:

The ***closure*** *of the factory caused 200 workers to lose their jobs.*
(agent backgrounded)

Meteorcorp closed the factory and 200 workers lost their jobs.
(agent 'Meteorcorp' foregrounded)

⇢ **Foregrounding**

Backshift Refers to the process when there is a shift of tense. For example, when an indirect report is perceived as referring to the past, the tense in the reported clause usually changes to a past form of the tense of the direct report:

'Robert ***is*** *part of a consortium,' Mrs Johnson said to her.*
Mrs Johnson told her that Robert ***was*** *part of a consortium.*
(present simple → past simple)

'I ***will go****,' he said.*
He said he ***would go****.*
('future' *will* → 'future-in-the-past' *would*)

*'I **can do** it on Monday.'*
*She said she **could do** it on Monday.*
(modal verb *can* ➛ modal verb *could*)

Base form The form of verb used to mark the present tense form (*People always **look** at me.*) and the infinitive with or without *to* (*Let me **look**.*).

Base is also a term that refers to the form of a word which cannot be broken down into further grammatical parts and where an affix can be added:

works = ***work*** (base) + *-s* (inflection)

playful = ***play*** (base) + *-ful* (suffix)

unusual = ***usual*** (base) + *un-* (prefix)

➝ **Word formation**

Blend A type of abbreviation in which parts of existing words are combined to form a new word: (*smog* = blend of ***sm**oke* and *f**og***; *heliport* = blend of ***heli**copter* and *air**port***).

Boosting A technique used to express a claim or viewpoint more assertively. Boosting is principally realised through a range of adverbial and prepositional constructions (*certainly, inevitably, unquestionably, definitely, emphatically, without doubt*) and modal and related expressions (*must, for sure/for certain, it is/was clear/obvious/indisputable/*etc. *that* …):

*Yet utilities and transport **unquestionably** provide a service rather than a commodity.*

*In the early nineteenth century this was **without doubt** true of much of the Nord region and the Normandy textile area.*

Case A grammatical category that marks the function of a noun or pronoun, for example as subject (also known as nominative case: *the boy, he, I, who*), object (also known as accusative case: *him, me, whom*) or genitive (also known as possessive: *the boy's, his, mine, whose*).

Cataphora (adjective = **cataphoric**) A process where a word or a phrase points forward to another and marks the relationship between what is being said and what is about to be said:

***It**'s delicious, that cake.*
(*It* refers forward to *that cake*)

Cataphora is contrasted with anaphora.

➝ **Endophora; Exophora**

Catenative A verb phrase which includes a verb such as *appear to, come to, fail to, get to, happen to, manage to, seem to* or *tend to* followed by a lexical verb. It expresses modal and aspectual meanings:

*Do you **happen to know** Suzie's number?*

*We **seem to have been** this way before.*

➝ **541 Index** for individual terms not in the Glossary

Causative Refers to the meaning of making something happen. For instance, *get*-pseudo-passives and *have*-pseudo-passives can be used to express causative and non-causative meanings:

I think I'm going to ***get*** *my ears* ***pierced.***
(causative: to make it happen)

We ***had*** *our house* ***broken*** *into while we were at the wedding.*
(non-causative: it was not our intention or aim)

Class (open class, closed class) Refers to a group of words which have similar functions. Word classes are divided into open classes and closed classes. Open classes include lexical words such as nouns (*dinner, place, Francis*), verbs (*meet, drive, go, pick*), adjectives (*old, angry, helpful*), and adverbs (*quickly, carefully, fast*) which admit new words. Closed classes have limited membership. They include function words such as pronouns (*it, he, who, anybody, one*), determiners (*a, the, that, some, each, several*), modal verbs (*may, could, must*), auxiliary verbs (*be, have, do*), conjunctions (*and, but, if, unless*) and prepositions (*in, at, of, by, with*). They do not admit new words.

Clause A grammatical construction that expresses the relationship between processes, participants and circumstances in actions, states or events. Clauses are constituents of sentences. Most typically, a clause consists of a subject (S), a verb (V), and any other required elements such as an object (O), a predicative complement (C), or an adjunct (A):

S V C
She | is | a friend of mine.

S V O A
I | will post | the letter | today.

The basic types of clause are declarative, interrogative, imperative and exclamative.

An embedded clause functions as a constituent phrase in a larger unit. For example, it may be a relative clause (*The points* ***that I'm talking about*** *are similar.*), or a nominal clause (***Building your own house*** *is cheaper.*).

→ **Embedding**

Cleft A cleft structure involves recasting a normal sentence pattern to give focus to a particular topic. The pattern is *it* + *be* + focus + clause. *Catherine plays tennis* can be recast into:

➛ *It is tennis that Catherine plays.*
(focus on the sport)

➛ *It is Catherine who plays tennis.*
(focus on the person)

→ **Pseudo-cleft**

Clipping Denotes a type of abbreviation where a word is shortened with one or more syllables omitted or 'clipped'. Proper names for people are commonly clipped (*ad* = *advertisement, advert*; *lab* = *laboratory*; *medic* = *medical student, doctor*; *Liz* = *Elizabeth*).

Cluster Refers to unitary or fragmentary and grammatically incomplete structures, usually in patterns of two, three or more words, that repeatedly occur. Clusters are usually retrieved from memory as whole units and contribute to fluency. They help to indicate relations of time and place (*I'll see you **in the** morning.*), perform interpersonal functions (*I find French so hard, **you know what I mean**?*) and linking functions (*Going by train's okay **but I mean** I'd prefer it if we could find a flight.*), and mark turn-taking, etc. (A: *I'll make some lunch, **shall I**?* B: *Mm, yes, please.*).

Coherence Refers to the relationships which link the meanings of utterances so that they are perceived as a text rather than as a random, unconnected sequence. The interpretation of coherence can be best derived from the speakers' shared knowledge and understanding of the speech acts being performed:

Husband: *The baby's crying.*
(husband requests wife to perform an action – attend to the baby)
Wife: *I'm on the phone.*
(wife states reason why she cannot comply with the request)
Husband: *Okay. I'll go.*
(husband undertakes to perform action)

Cohesion Refers to the grammatical and/or lexical links that mark relationships between clauses or across larger units of text. Conjunction, ellipsis, reference, repetition, substitution, etc. play a role in cohesion.

Collective noun A type of noun referring to a group of people, animals or things (*family, gang, committee, crowd, cattle, fleet*).

Collocation Refers to how lexical words co-occur regularly and in a restricted way.

typical collocations	untypical collocations
blonde hair	*blonde car*
lean meat	*slim meat*
perform a play	*perform a meeting*

Comment Comment refers to the main part of the message which indicates the important information about the topic. A comment is typically associated with the predicate in a clause:

topic comment
Sue ***is starting a new job on Monday.***

'Theme' is also a term used to describe the topic or starting point for a message. 'Rheme' then refers to the information about the theme:

theme rheme
Beijing ***has been chosen as the site for the Olympic Games.***

→ **541 Index** for individual terms not in the Glossary

Comparative, comparison The comparative is the form of a gradable adjective or adverb which is used to compare the different degree of qualities, properties, states, conditions, relations, etc. between two entities. The comparative is realised by the suffix *-er*, or by the use of *more*:

*Africa is **bigger** than Europe.*

*It is **more difficult** to get into a famous university **than** a little-known one.*

Complement, complementation A word or phrase which is required to complete the meaning of another word or phrase:

*A rise **in interest rates** is inevitable.*

*The claim **that he was innocently involved** was not accepted by the judge.*

Complementation is the process of completing the meaning of an item. For example, the complementation requirement for the verb *put* is that it must normally include an object and a phrase indicating location:

O prepositional phrase
*She put **the book** | **on the shelf**.*

A predicative complement is a phrase which completes a clause with verbs such as *be, become, look, taste*:

*She's **away**.*

*He became **a teacher**.*

*That looks **very nice**.*

→ **Transitive complementation**

Complex verb phrase A phrase which includes a combination of different elements with the lexical verb:

*I **do like** pizza.*
(auxiliary + lexical verb)

*We**'ve talked** about that.*
(perfect + lexical verb)

*We**'re being fooled**.*
(progressive + passive + lexical verb)

*I **might be seeing** Bob.*
(modal + progressive + lexical verb)

*It**'s been being repaired** for ages.*
(perfect + passive + progressive + lexical verb)

A complex verb phrase indicates person, number, tense (except in modal verbs), aspect, voice and mood.

→ **Verb phrase**

Compound Compounding is a word-formation process which refers to two or more words linking together to produce a form which creates a new, single unit of meaning. Compounds are found in all word classes: Nouns (*pop-group*, *car park*), adjectives (*heartbreaking*, *homesick*), verbs (*babysit*, *dry-clean*), prepositions (*into*, *onto*).

Compound sentences are sentences with two or more main clauses: ***He should have been here at five*** *and* ***he's not here yet***, *but* ***he'll come***.

Concord (or agreement) Subject-verb concord refers to the agreement between the verb and subject in a finite clause with respect to number and person:

It *takes ages to get there.*
(present tense, plus third person singular subject requires -*s* on a lexical verb)

Concordance A computer technique that allows searches to be conducted in a corpus for specific target words or phrases in their original textual environments. The most standard concordance type is called KWIC display (Key Word in Context), which highlights the chosen keyword in the centre of a line of words with its surrounding context on each side (→ **3d** for an example)

→ **Corpus**

Conditional clause A clause that expresses a condition or hypothesis about a situation. It is typically introduced by the subordinating conjunction *if*, and other conjunctions such as *unless*, *as soon as*:

If they promote her, *she'll get a big pay rise.*

Unless you try, *you'll never do it.*

Conjunction (another term for connector) Refers to items used to mark logical relationships between words, phrases, clauses and sentences. There are two types of conjunction: coordinating and subordinating. Coordinating conjunctions (or coordinators) (*and*, *but*, *or*) join linguistic units with equal grammatical status:

Mary felt ill ***and*** *could not go to school.*

Subordinating conjunctions (or subordinators) (*although, after, as, because, before, since, when*) indicate the semantic relationship between a subordinate clause and a main clause:

main | subordinate
He failed the exam | ***although*** *he worked hard.*

Connector, connective

→ **Conjunction**

Continuous

→ **Progressive**

Contraction, contracted forms A phonologically reduced or simplified form attached to the preceding word: *I've* is a contracted form of *I have, haven't* is contracted from *have not, isn't* is contracted from *is not*.

→ **Phonetics**

Conversion A process of word formation which involves a change in the functioning of a word from one word class to another without adding an affix:

*The film is an absolute **must** for all lovers of Westerns.*
(conversion from verb to noun)

*Can we **microwave** it?*
(conversion from noun to verb)

Coordination, coordinator Expresses a relation between linguistic units that are of equal grammatical status. Coordinators such as *and, but,* are used to link coordinated constructions:

*Kay **and** Stuart got married last week.*

Coordination is a principal way in which clauses are combined to form sentences:

*Jim brought me here **but** Phil's taking me home.*

Correlative coordinators refer to conjunctions such as *either ... or* or *neither ... nor*:

*I'll **either** phone **or** email him about it.*

Copula(r) verb Verbs such as *be, become, feel, remain, seem, smell, taste* that describe the states of people and things. A copular verb is used to link the subject and the complement of a clause:

*I **was** very excited.*

*It **seems** strange, doesn't it really?*

*It **smells** a bit funny.*

Copy tag

⇢ Tag

Core modal verb These are *can, could, may, might, will, shall, would, should, must,* which are used to express various kinds of modal meaning, mainly referring to degrees of certainty and degrees of obligation. Modal verbs have only one form and do not indicate person, number, voice or aspect. They are placed first in the verb phrase and are followed by a verb (either an auxiliary verb or a lexical verb) in the base form:

*I **might** see you later.*
(speaker denotes a possibility, but not with certainty)

*I **must** phone her to find out how long she's staying.*
(speaker states an obligation or necessity)

⇢ Modality; Modal expressions; Semi-modal verb

Corpus A large collection of written text or transcribed speech which is stored and processed by computer so as to serve as a basis for linguistic analysis and description.

Correlative

⇢ Coordination, coordinator

Count (or countable) A grammatical distinction of nouns that refers to objects, people, animals and abstract entities that are treated as easily counted (*a cat/two cats, one egg/three eggs*).

Count nouns are contrasted with non-count (or uncountable) nouns.

Declarative A clause type that is typically associated with statements to make assertions and convey information. The word order in declarative clauses is subject + verb + x, where x is any other element present (e.g. object or complement):

subject	verb	x
She	*works*	*in publishing.*
I	*saw*	*him in the distance.*

Defining relative clause (or restrictive relative clause) A relative clause which defines or restricts the meaning of the head noun:

The guy *who shouted must have been on about the seventh floor.*
(defines *the guy*; specifies which guy is being referred to)

It is contrasted with a non-defining relative clause.

In this grammar book the terms defining and non-defining are used in preference to restrictive/non-restrictive.

··➔ **Postmodification**

Definite article Refers to determiner *the* which is used with a noun to define and specify entities projected as known to speaker/writer and listener/reader. It is contrasted with the indefinite article (*a/an*):

The *university is closed today.*

I'll try to put you through to ***the*** *right department.*

Degree adverb

··➔ **Adverb**

Deixis (adjective = **deictic**) A term for words or expressions that depend for their interpretation on the immediate external situation in which they are uttered. Deictic words are orientational features and are typically realised by determiners (*a, the, this, that, these, those*), adverbs (*here, there*), personal pronouns (*I, you, them*):

Could ***we*** *just move* ***that*** *into* ***this*** *corner* ***here****?*

Delexical verb Delexical verbs refer to common verbs (*do, give, have, make, take*) that combine with nouns to describe an action. The lexical meanings expressed by the verbs become weak (***do*** *some listening,* ***have*** *a swim,* ***take*** *a walk*). In such constructions, the nouns are referred to as deverbal nouns.

Demonstrative Grammatical term for the items *this, that, these, those*. The demonstrative specifies whether the referent is close or distant in relation to the speaker:

***This** is not correct.*

*I'd like to have **these** not **those**.*

*Shall I put **that** into **this** box over here?*

Deontic A characteristic of modality which involves the use of a modal verb to mark necessity, permission or obligation:

*You **may** go now.*
(permission)

*I **must** be careful what I say.*
(necessity/obligation)

In this book, terms such as necessity and obligation are used in preference to deontic.

⇢ **Epistemic; Modality**

Dependent clause Dependent clauses cannot stand alone, but depend on another sentence constituent, typically a main clause. Subordinate clauses and embedded clauses are dependent.

⇢ **Main clause**

Derivation A main process of word formation by which one word is formed ('derived') from another, most commonly by adding affixes to base forms. This brings about a change of meaning (*-able* indicates that something is possible; *mid-* indicates the middle part of something) and/or grammatical class (***mid**night, **un**fortunate, **re**do, read**able**, play**ful**, hope**less***).

Determiner Item which indicates the kind of reference a noun phrase has. Determiners include words like *a, the, some, my, his, each, those, which, several* which express a range of meanings including definite/indefinite (***the** dining room, **a** ruler*), possessive (***my** study, **their** children*), demonstrative (***this** box, **that** man, **these** teenagers*), quantifier (***some** milk, **every** citizen*), and numeral (***two** soldiers, the **second** birth*).

Deverbal noun

⇢ **Delexical verb**

Diminutive A form with an affix which has the meaning of 'small' or 'little'. A diminutive is used either literally or as a term of endearment (*-let*: *leaflet, booklet*; *-ling*: *duckling, darling*; *mini-*: *mini-cab, mini-skirt*; *-y*: *Johnny, doggy*),

Directive

⇢ **Imperative**

Direct object Refers to the noun phrase indicating the entity directly affected by an action:

S V O
I | *cut* | ***my finger.***

⇢ **Object; Indirect object**

Direct speech Refers to a reconstruction of the exact words a speaker has said, usually involving quotation marks and without making any grammatical changes. Actual utterance: *'Keep quiet!'* Direct speech: *The teacher said, 'Keep quiet!'*

Direct speech is contrasted with indirect speech.

Discontinuous adjective phrase Refers to an adjective phrase which is split into two parts, with one part pre-head and the other post-head:

pre-head post-head
He is | ***as*** | ***tall*** | ***as his father.***

Discourse Any naturally occurring stretch of language, spoken or written. Some linguists use the term to distinguish speech from writing, in which 'discourse' is used to refer to speech, and 'text' is used for writing.

Discourse marker A lexical category made up of words (*well, right*), phrases (*at the end of the day*), or clauses (*to be precise*). Discourse markers function to organise and monitor an ongoing discourse, most commonly in speech, by marking boundaries between one topic and the next (*so, right*), by indicating openings (*well, right*) and closure and pre-closure (*okay*) of topics, by indicating topic changes (*well*) or by bringing a conclusion to the discourse (*anyway, so*). They also function to mark the state of knowledge between participants (*you know, you see, I mean*).

Disjunct An adverbial expression which indicates the speaker's viewpoint towards or evaluation of what is said (*oddly, personally, fortunately, frankly, indeed*). Syntactically, it is less integrated in the clause structure and may modify the whole sentence or utterance:

What was more, ***oddly****, he seemed to have bought enough for two.*
(evaluative)

Personally*, I don't think she's capable of doing the job.*
(viewpoint)

Ditransitive A term for verbs that are used with two objects to complete the meaning. In *My mother* ***made*** | *me* | *a cake.* | , *made* is ditransitive, with a direct object *a cake* and an indirect object *me*. Other verbs used ditransitively include *promise* (*I* ***promised*** | *the kids* | *a treat.* |) and *give* (*I* ***gave*** | *the beggar* | *some money.* |).

Downtoner A downtoner is a sub-class of intensifier that is used to mark a lessening effect on a particular aspect of meaning. This is achieved by adverbs such as *barely, hardly, partially, slightly*:

Her heartbeat was ***slightly*** *erratic.*

⇢ **Intensifier**

Dummy

⇢ **Subject**

Dynamic verb A verb which primarily expresses activity (*drink, eat, play, work*), process (*change, deteriorate, grow*) and bodily sensation (*ache, feel, hurt*). A dynamic verb can be used in the progressive aspect (*My dad is watching TV.*) and in the imperative (*Stop it!*).

Dynamic verbs are contrasted with stative verbs.

Ellipsis The non-use of words or phrases whose meanings are understood or implied between speakers and hearers, or are recoverable from the immediate text or context. In spoken English, ellipsis is a linguistic indicator of informality:

Right … what next?
(*What* ***is/will be/could happen/etc.*** *next?* verb understood)

Mud on my shirt!
(***There's/I've got*** *mud on my shirt!* subject and verb understood)

Embedding, embedded Refers to the use of a phrase or clause as a constituent of a higher level phrase or clause:

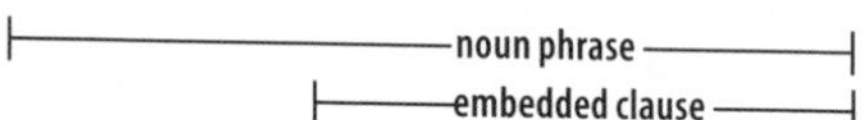

The man who ***you spoke to on the phone*** *is my uncle.*

⇢ **Clause; Subordinate clause**

Empty *it* Occurs when *it* is used as an empty pronoun, a 'dummy' subject form in anticipatory structures. Empty *it* does not refer to any specific object or entity:

It*'s very hot today, isn't it?*
(empty *it* as reference to weather)

It*'s getting late.*
(empty *it* as reference to situation)

⇢ **Anticipatory structure**

Endophora (adjective = **endophoric**) A term meaning reference to people, places, things and ideas within a text. Endophoric references are of two types: anaphoric (pointing backward to something mentioned earlier in the text) and cataphoric (pointing forward to something mentioned later in the text).

⇢ **Exophora**

Endweight Indicates where the most weight falls in terms of the focus on new information. In English, endweight is typically at the end of a clause.

⇢ **Focus; Fronting**

Epistemic A characteristic of modality concerned with the speaker's judgement about the certainty, probability or possibility of something. It involves an assessment of potential facts:

I ***might*** *see you later.*
(it is possible, not certain)

I'll see you tomorrow.
(speaker is certain)

In this book, terms such as probability and possibility are used in preference to epistemic.

→ **Deontic; Modality**

Exclamation mark A form of punctuation which is used after an exclamative clause or when a sentence expresses emotive force (*How nice! Well done! I don't believe it!*).

Exclamative A phrase or a clause type that expresses the speaker's reaction of surprise, shock or strong impression. Exclamatives usually consist of phrases with *what* and *how* followed by a subject + verb construction. In writing, they are punctuated with an exclamation mark (!):

What *a nuisance!*

How *lovely you are!*

→ **Interjection**

Existential *there* Contains an indefinite subject which does not refer to any object or entity:

There *were a lot of people in the town centre.*

There*'s something I want to talk to you about.*

Sentence patterns with existential *there* enable a focus to be placed on the subject by locating it in the rheme (→ **Comment**) of the clause:

We drove past one time and ***there*** ***was a woman standing outside.***

Exophora (adjective = **exophoric**) A term meaning reference to the situation outside of the text:

[on a public sign]
This exit *must be kept clear at all times.*

Exophora is contrasted with anaphora and cataphora.

→ **Endophora**

Filler Refers to vocalisations (*er, erm, um, mm*) or words that are used to fill gaps in conversations. A filler can mark hesitation, a shift in topic (***Okay***, ***erm***, *let's move on.*), or can indicate the speaker's online process of thinking and planning (***Well***, *of course,* ***erm***, *I think we should take our time before taking any action.*).

Finite A finite clause contains a verb which signals a choice of tense (a tensed verb). It typically has a subject, and can be a main or subordinate clause:

He ***lives*** *on his own.*
(present tense)

Finite is contrasted with non-finite.

→ **Non-finite**

→ **541 Index** for individual terms not in the Glossary

Fixed expression A term for routinised and pre-formulated expressions. Fixed expressions have a varying degree of fixity (*at the end of the day, as far as I am concerned, once and for all, how do you do?*).

Focus Enables special emphasis to be placed on particular elements of a clause through the use of fronting, headers and tails, cleft sentences, etc. for purposes such as introducing new topics, distinguishing between new and old information, foregrounding and backgrounding things:

That bowl *we got in Italy. The other one's from Spain, I think.*
(fronting of the object to show a contrast between the two bowls)

That brown chair*, we bought that years and years ago.*
(header gives extra focus to *that brown chair*)

He's quite a comic ***that fellow****.*
(tail gives extra focus to the subject *he*)

It was on Sunday *I first noticed I had a rash.*
(cleft sentence gives extra focus to *on Sunday*)

→ **Backgrounding; Cleft; Fronting; Foregrounding; Header; Raised subject; Tail**

Foregrounding Refers to grammatical structures used to highlight some important information in a discourse:

Perhaps ***what is most important is*** *the origin of such ideas.*
(the *wh*-cleft structure signals that this is a key sentence in what follows)

→ **Backgrounding; Fronting**

Formal A term associated with variation in speech or writing style in which choices of pronunciation, grammar and vocabulary are made which express a polite distance between participants, as in formal situations such as debates and official ceremonies:

I should like to extend my warm welcome to all guests tonight.
(compare the more informal: *I want to welcome you all here tonight.*)

Free direct and indirect speech Free direct speech refers to a reconstruction of the exact words a speaker has said without a reporting clause. It is common in literary style and in informal spoken contexts when it is clear who is speaking:

They looked at each other knowingly.
'Okay?'
'Right, I'll come with you.'

Free indirect speech refers to a reconstruction of the words or thoughts of a speaker conveyed in a reported clause without a reporting verb. This is common in literary style:

David moved slowly and thoughtfully. ***He would not be deterred.***
(implied: He said/thought, 'I won't be deterred.')

→ **Direct speech**

Fronting Refers to the front-placing of words or phrases in a clause or sentence which gives extra prominence to the items thus placed:

I really would like to see ***Berlin.***
(object in neutral position, after the verb)

Berlin *I really would like to see.*
(object fronted for greater prominence)

➝ **Focus; Header; Tail; Topic**

Gender A grammatical distinction in which words are marked for masculine, feminine or neuter. Only pronouns and possessive determiners are marked grammatically for gender (*he, him, she, it, his, hers*). However, English does occasionally distinguish gender in nouns for male or female people or animals (*She's a famous* ***actress****, isn't she?*).

Generic, generic pronoun A term used for a class of entities rather than a specific member of a class:

Leopards *are dangerous animals.*
(all leopards)

You *never know what the future will bring.*
(generic *you*: all humans)

Genitive A case that denotes a possessive relationship with another noun phrase in a sentence. It is realised by an *of*-phrase (*the headteacher* ***of*** *the school*), or by adding *'s* to singular nouns (*Lily****'s*** *toys, the woman****'s*** *husband*) and *s'* for plural nouns ending with *-s* (*the Teacher****s'*** *Union, the girl****s'*** *room*).

Gerund A word derived from a verb form which ends in *-ing* and is used as a noun. It is also referred to as a verbal noun or *-ing* noun:

Smoking *is hazardous to health.*

No ***eating*** *or* ***drinking*** *in the library.*

Gradable Refers to adjectives or adverbs which can be set on a scale of 'more' or 'less' in terms of their qualities, properties, states, conditions, relations, etc. (*good, small, easily, nicely*). Gradable adjectives and adverbs can be premodified by degree adverbs (*That's an* ***extremely*** *good camera.*) and can take the comparative and superlative inflections (*small****er****, small****est***), or be preceded by *more* or *most* (*more easily, most superior*).

Gradable is contrasted with non-gradable.

➝ **Non-gradable**

Head, headword Refers to the central element of a phrase. The accompanying constituents in the phrase have a grammatical relationship with the head: *a new* ***home*** *for the children* (noun head), ***in*** *the country* (preposition head), *very* ***nice*** (adjective head), *rather* ***slowly*** (adverb head).

Header Headers are a type of fronting which serve an orienting function in spoken utterances. They involve placing a noun phrase or a clausal construction at the front of a clause, followed by one or more pronouns which refer back to the noun phrase. A header indicates the main topic of the clause:

That leather coat, *it looks really nice on you.*

Walking into that room, *it brought back a lot of memories.*

Headers are contrasted with tails. The terms 'left dislocation' and 'pre-posed' are sometimes used to refer to headers.

Hedging A linguistic strategy used to avoid sounding too authoritative or direct. This can be achieved through negation, through short hedged replies, or by using expressions such as *kind of, sort of, probably, actually, really*:

*Sorry, but I do**n't really** feel like going out tonight.*

A: *I suppose you've made up your mind to buy the roses?*
B: *No, **not necessarily**.*

→ **Softening**

Historic present tense The use of present tense form for past reference. This occurs particularly in narratives, stories or jokes, usually for purposes of dramatising important events:

*Emma, this friend of mine, brought these photographs out of the family through the years and he**'s looking** at them, and he said 'Oh!'*

*Then suddenly he **picks** up the book and **tears** it into pieces. It was amazing, I couldn't believe it.*

Homograph, homophone, homonym These terms describe relationships of similarity between words. Homographs are words which have the same spelling (sometimes with different pronunciations) but different meanings:

saw (noun and past tense verb); *row* (/rəʊ/ and /raʊ/)

Homophones are words which have the same pronunciation but different meanings:

meat–meet, flour–flower, bare–bear

Homonyms are unrelated words which share the same pronunciation and spelling:

rose (flower and past tense of verb *rise*)

bank (river bank and financial institution)

mole (mark on a person's skin and small animal)

Honorific Words such as *sir* or *madam*. They are often respectful and deferential.

Hypercorrect A term used to describe excessive care in the production of speech or writing in order to sound educated and native-like which can lead to over-generalisation of rules:

The chips smell nice.
(hypercorrect: ~~The chips smell nicely.~~)

Imperative A clause type which is typically associated with directives, commands, orders, instructions, etc. It consists of the base form of the verb, typically with no overt subject, + any other required elements:

***Get** some kitchen paper, quick!*

***Sign** here, please.*

Indefinite article, indefinite pronoun Indefinite article refers to the determiner *a/an* that is used to express an indefinite meaning:

*Give me **a** pen, please.*

*I went for **an** eye test.*

An indefinite pronoun is a pronoun that expresses a non-specific or non-definite meaning (*someone, anybody, everything, many, one, more, all*).

Indicative A form of clause mood which expresses the factual or 'indicative' meaning of stating or questioning. It is the most frequent form and involves all the choices of person, tense, number, aspect, modality and voice (*It**'s** a nice day. **Are** we **going** out?*).

Indicative is contrasted with imperative and subjunctive.

Indirect interrogative clause Refers to the use of *wh*-clause, a clause with *if/whether* or a nominal clause as object in a sentence. In order to avoid being too assertive or threatening, a direct interrogative is not used:

*Tell me **what you want for dinner**.*

*Could I possibly ask **why you're unable to attend**?*

*I asked **whether she wanted to stay** overnight.*

Indirect object Refers to the indirect recipient or beneficiary of an action which has a direct recipient. An indirect object (IO) always co-occurs with a direct object (DO):

S	V	IO	DO
The teacher	*gave*	***the pupils***	*some homework.*

→ **Direct object; Object**

Indirect speech (or reported speech) A reconstruction of the words of a speaker conveyed in a reported clause, accompanied by a reporting clause with verbs such as *tell, say, reply, suggest, mention*. For example, direct speech *He said, 'I am unhappy.'* contrasts with indirect speech *He told me/said that he was unhappy*.

Infinitive The non-tensed form of a verb that usually combines with *to* (*It's time for me **to order now**.*). It can also occur without *to* (also known as the 'bare infinitive') (*I may **see** you tomorrow; let me **help***).

Inflection A process of word formation in which items are added to the base form of a word to express grammatical meanings. For example: the *-s* on *dogs* indicates plural; the past form *drank* contrasts with the present *drink*; the *-est* on *cleverest* indicates the superlative form.

→ **541 Index** for individual terms not in the Glossary

Informal A term associated with variation in speech or writing style in which a more relaxed and colloquial choice of pronunciation, grammar and vocabulary is made, projecting a closer relationship among participants:

I got into Oxford on law.
(informal)

I was accepted by Oxford University to study law.
(formal)

-*ing* form A non-tensed verb form which is made by adding *-ing* to the base form, and is used with auxiliary *be* to form progressive aspect (***I was doing** some work for Sally.*). It also occurs in non-finite clauses (*Please listen carefully to all the options before **making** your choice.*), and functions as a noun-like form sometimes called the gerund (***Smoking** is not allowed; I'm tired of **shouting**.*).

Intensifier An adverb which strengthens, intensifies or focuses on a particular aspect of the meaning of an item. Intensifiers are often subdivided into amplifiers (*very, really, completely, extremely*) and downtoners (*partially, hardly, barely, slightly*):

*I was **extremely** annoyed.*

Interjection A term for exclamatory words or expressive vocalisations used to express emotional reactions such as surprise, shock, delight (*crikey, gosh, hooray, oh, ouch, wow*):

***Gosh**! That's quick.*

***Ouch**, that hurts!*

→ **Exclamative**

Interrogative A clause type that is typically associated with questions. The normal word order is auxiliary/modal verb + subject + verb + x, where x is any other element present (e.g. object/predicative complement):

***Do you need** any help at all?*

*Where **did you have** your hair done?*

→ **Indirect interrogative clause**

Intonation Use of variation in pitch, loudness, rhythm and syllable length associated with different types of meaning. For example, in *wh*-questions, the intonation is typically a falling tone (↘) on the most important syllable:

*When are you **lea**↘*ving?*

Intransitive Refers to the use of verbs without any other items being necessary to complete their meaning, for example, verbs such as *appear, begin, die, go, laugh, rain, happen*):

*The old man **died**.*

*We all **laughed**.*

Inversion A reversal of the usual sequence of constituents. For example, in an interrogative clause, the subject and auxiliary/modal verb are inverted (***Are we** going to have a party?*).

Irregular verb Refers to the form of verb which has a variety of types of ending and internal change applied to the base form. Irregular verbs are similar to regular verbs in making their *-s* form and *-ing* participle (*speaks, speaking; meets, meeting; takes, taking; swims, swimming*). But almost all irregular verbs are irregular in their past form and *-ed* participle (*spoke, spoken; met, met; took, taken; swam, swum*).

Left dislocation

→ **Header**

Lexeme Refers to the underlying forms of words which can only belong to one word class. For example, the word *water* has a similar meaning when used as a noun (*I drank the **water**.*) and when used as a verb (*I must **water** the plants.*) but it is a different lexeme in each case. Forms such as *water, waters, watering* and *watered* are grammatically distinct forms of the same lexeme, the verb *water*.

Lexical Concerned with vocabulary rather than grammar, and concerned with content meaning rather than grammatical meaning. Nouns, adjectives, adverbs and most verbs are lexical items. Modal and auxiliary verbs, prepositions, pronouns, etc. are treated as grammatical, not lexical, items.

Linking adjunct A single word or phrase which explicitly indicates the semantic relationship between two clauses, sentences or paragraphs. The semantic relations that are signalled by linking adjuncts include: additive (*also, above all*); resultative (*so, therefore*); contrastive (*rather, on the contrary*); inference (*then, in that case*); time (*eventually, then*); concessive (*anyway, though*); summative (*overall, in short*); listing (*firstly, lastly*); and meta-textual (*namely, so to speak*).

Locative, locative complement Refers to a prepositional phrase which locates the object in terms of place or time. A locative complement occurs after certain verbs of placement and direction such as *bring, drive, lay, lead, put, show, stand, take*:

verb | object | locative complement

*Edith | led | her | **through her own front door**.*

verb | object | locative complement

*Did you | put | your stuff | **in our bedroom**?*

Main clause (another term for independent clause) This is a clause that can form a sentence on its own. It must have a tensed verb (a verb indicating tense):

I went to speak to them.
(one main clause as whole sentence)

***I like ice cream** but **I don't like yoghurt**.*
(main clause + main clause)

*After you have returned home, **please give me a ring**.*
(subordinate clause + main clause)

Marked Refers to an untypical use of something.

Marked word order in English refers to word order which is untypical; for example, the word order O-S-V is marked:

O S V
That furniture we bought years ago, this lot is more recent.
(marked word order: *that furniture* is the theme, rather than *we*)

Marked word order is used to create various kinds of focus on particular elements for a variety of purposes.

When a grammatical or semantic structure is distinguished by a contrast between widespread, normal regional/social varieties of British English and less widespread ones, it is referred to as regionally or socially marked (e.g. the use of *ain't*).

Marked stress refers to the use of extra force in pronunciation or in intonation to make words or syllables sound louder or more emphatic.

Middle construction

→ **Pseudo-intransitive**

Modal expression Refers to expressions that carry modal meanings apart from the modal and semi-modal verbs. These include:

- verbs (e.g. *allow, demand, hope, let, make, seem, want, wish*):

  *She **seems** to be quite clever for her age.*

- grammaticalised modal phrases (e.g. *be going to, be meant to, be obliged to, be supposed to, had better*):

  *I thought I **had better** warn you now.*

- modal adjectives, adverbs and nouns (e.g. *certain(ly), definite(ly), possible, probability, supposedly*):

  *Would it be **possible** for me to have a copy of the document?*

Modality Refers to a speaker's or a writer's attitude towards, or point of view about, a state of the world. It is centrally concerned with the expression of certainty, volition, possibility and obligation. Core modal verbs (*can, could, may, might, will, shall, would, should, must*) and semi-modals (*dare, need, ought to, used to*) are the principal way in which modal meanings are expressed.

→ **Core modal verb; Semi-modal verb**

Modification A term used to refer to the structural dependence of one grammatical unit on another in which the meaning of the head of a phrase is affected by words that are used to indicate qualities and attributes of the head. For example, in the noun phrase *those **big** boxes **in the garage***, both *big* and *in the garage* modify *boxes*, performing premodification and postmodification, respectively.

Mono-transitive Refers to verbs that require an object. In *I* ***took*** *the last piece of bread, took* is a mono-transitive verb, with its direct object *the last piece of bread*. The direct object is typically a noun phrase, but it may also be a clause, as in *You always* ***know*** *what I'm thinking*.

➜ **Transitive verb**

Mood A grammatical category relating to the speaker's or writer's attitude to express a factual, non-factual or directive meaning through the verb. The three moods distinguished are indicative (*She* ***enjoys*** *her new job.*), imperative (***Enjoy*** *your meal!*) and subjunctive (*We insist that he* ***enjoy*** *the meal first before making his speech.*).

➜ **Imperative; Indicative; Subjunctive**

Morpheme A morpheme is the smallest unit of meaning in a word. Some words consist of just one morpheme (*help*), some consist of several (*unhelpful* consists of three morphemes: the base form *help*, the prefix *un-* and the suffix *-ful*).

Morphology Morphology is the study of the internal structure of words, and includes the study of base forms, affixes, compounding, derivation, etc.

Multi-word verb A lexical verb which may be combined with one or two particles to function as a verb with a unitary meaning. There are three kinds of multi-word verb. Phrasal verbs have adverb particles (*sit down, go away, get off, give in*). Prepositional verbs take a preposition (*go against, call on, look after*), and phrasal-prepositional verbs take both an adverb and a preposition (*look forward to, look down on, catch up with, put up with*).

Negation Refers to a grammatical construction with negative polarity. Negation can be formed through affixes (***un****healthy*, ***ir****responsible*, ***non****-existent*, *care****less***), and through negative words like *not, no, neither, never, no one, nobody, none*:

George has ***not*** *been here recently.*

A: *Are****n't*** *you ready yet?*
B: ***No. Not*** *yet.*

Negation is contrasted with affirmative meanings which have positive polarity.

Nominal clause A clause type that fulfils a noun-like function (e.g. an object):

nominal clause | complement
Writing novels | *is* | *not easy.*

subject verb nominal clause
I | *know* | ***what you mean.***

➜ **Nominalisation**

Nominalisation Involves forming a noun from other parts of speech, most commonly from verbs or adjectives (*flying* ➝ *flight, bright* ➝ *brightness, long* ➝ *length, industrial* ➝ *industrialisation*).

The nominalised form offers the possibility of a more formal expression of the equivalent verb or adjective meaning:

I was dazzled by the ***extremely bright*** *lights.*

I was dazzled by ***the extreme brightness*** *of the lights.*

➜ **541 Index** for individual terms not in the Glossary

Nominative

⇢ **Case**

Non-count (or uncountable) A grammatical distinction of nouns which denote things that are treated as indivisible wholes, for instance, materials and liquids, states of mind, conditions, topics, processes and substances (*water, cheese, music, information, sand, love*). With non-count nouns there is no contrast in number between singular and plural:

They gave us some ***information****.*
(~~They gave us some informations.~~)

Non-defining relative clause (or non-restrictive relative clause) This is a clause that describes or gives additional information to the head noun in a noun phrase. A non-defining clause usually begins with a relative pronoun *who, whom, which, whose*, and is marked off by a comma in writing:

Have you ever heard of ***Guy Preston****, who had a hit song with 'Loving Ways'?*
(describes or gives extra information about Guy Preston)

Non-defining relative clauses are contrasted with defining relative clauses.

⇢ **Postmodification**

Non-finite Non-finite clauses contain a verb which does not indicate tense, for example, an infinitive (*We queued up early so as* ***to get*** *a good seat.*), an *-ed* participle (*You should read the parts* ***highlighted*** *in yellow.*) or an *-ing* form (***Coming*** *round the corner, we spotted the old house.*).

⇢ **Finite**

Non-gradable Refers to adjectives or adverbs that cannot be graded on a scale of 'more' or 'less' in terms of the property they describe (*dead/alive, male/female, truly, main, married*). Non-gradable adjectives and adverbs cannot take the comparative or superlative inflection, nor can they be preceded or premodified by words like *more, most, quite, rather, so, very* (*more male, rather dead, very truly, very married* are not possible).

Non-gradable is contrasted with gradable.

⇢ **Gradable**

Non-restrictive relative clause

⇢ **Non-defining relative clause**

Non-standard A term that refers to the use of grammar, vocabulary and pronunciation that does not conform to the norms used by educated native speakers of the standard variety. An example is the use of *ain't* as a negative contraction in speech:

I know something. That ***ain't*** *the answer.*
(standard form: *isn't*)

Non-tensed Any verb form which does not indicate present or past tense, e.g. the *-ing* form or the infinitive.

Non-tensed is contrasted with tensed.

Noun (proper, common, concrete, abstract), noun phrase Refers to words which denote classes and categories of things in the world, including people, animals, inanimate things, places, events, qualities and states (*accident, cat, club, competition*).

A noun phrase has a noun or pronoun as its head. Noun phrases can act as the subject (S), object (O) or predicative complement (C) of a clause:

S O
*My **father** used to play the **piano**.*

C
*You're a good **friend**.*

Nouns can be divided into proper nouns and common nouns. Proper nouns give names to people and things (*Tony Blair, Greece, Oxfam*). Nouns which are not proper nouns are common nouns (*table, boy, heat*).

Concrete nouns refer to physical entities that can be observed and measured (*cat, garage, soldier*). Abstract nouns refer to abstractions that cannot be observed and measured (*competition, conscience*).

→ **Collective noun**

Number A grammatical distinction which contrasts singular and plural in nouns (*story–stories*), pronouns (*I–we*), determiners (*this–these*) and verbs (*he works hard–they work hard*).

Object Refers to a clause element that follows the verb, and includes both direct (bold in the examples) and indirect (in green) objects. Objects indicate the direct and indirect recipients of actions. Objects are made up of noun phrases (*I like **that restaurant**. Joe gave me **a present**.*).

Orthography A term that deals with the writing system in a language: the distinctive written symbols and their possible combinations.

Participle The non-tensed forms of verbs ending in *-ing* (*working, joining, trying*) and *-ed* (*worked, joined, tried*) are called the *-ing* and *-ed* participles. In irregular verbs, the *-ed* participles display variant forms (*burnt, swollen, taught, taken, gone*).

Particle Refers to a small group of words mostly made up of adverbs and prepositions. They are closely linked to verbs to form multi-word verbs (*sit **down**, go **away**, go **astray**, look **forward** to, look **down** on*). Other particles include *not*, and *to* used with an infinitive.

Partitive A quantifying expression used before a non-count noun to specify the units, parts and collections of things (***a pair of** trousers, **a piece of** paper, **a bunch of** roses, **four slices of** ham*).

→ **Quantifier**

Part of speech Another term for word class, referring to the linguistic units that realise sentence elements.

→ **Class**

→ **541 Index** for individual terms not in the Glossary

Passive

→ **Active**

Perfect A type of aspect that gives information about a speaker's perspective on the relationship of events to the moment of speaking or to some other point in time. It is realised by auxiliary *have* + *-ed* participle of a lexical verb.

The present perfect relates events or states taking place in the past to a present time orientation:

*I've **made** a lot of friends since I moved here.*

The past perfect relates situations or events anterior to a time of orientation in the past:

*She **had been** unhappy for years and so decided to join the slimming class.*

Performative A term that refers to a type of utterance that performs a speech act simply by saying it (*I name this ship 'Victory'*; *I apologise*).

Person A grammatical category which indicates the choice of personal reference and number. Three kinds of contrast exist: first person (which includes the speaker/writer, e.g. *I, my, we, our*), second person (which refers to the addressee, e.g. *you, yours*), and third person (which refers to a third party, e.g. *he, she, it, they, him, her, its*). These distinctions apply to personal, possessive and reflexive determiners and pronouns.

Phatic Communication where participants are less concerned to convey information than to build a relationship or to make social contact; for example, talking about the weather is phatic in several cultures.

Phonetics, phonology Phonetics is concerned with the study of physical properties of speech sounds in a language, and the actual articulation or production of speech sounds. Phonology is the study of the sound system in a language.

Phrasal verb, phrasal-prepositional verb

→ **Multi-word verb**

Phrase A word or group of words which form grammatical units such as noun phrase, verb phrase or adjective phrase. Phrases are the constituents of clauses.

Pitch Refers to the way in which speakers vary their sound level. Pitch movement is denoted by a rising or falling tone as a result of the vibration of the vocal cord.

→ **Intonation**

Plural A grammatical category in number that refers to more than one, in the case of nouns (*tables, computers*), verbs (*they come*), pronouns (*we, they*), etc.

→ **Singular**

Polarity (adjective = **polar**) A term used to mark affirmative/negative contrasts in a clause:

The children are lovely.
(affirmative)

*They **don't** do it during the summer.*
(negative)

Polar (or *yes-no*) questions demand the answer *yes* or *no*:

Are you a teacher?
(yes or no?)

Position (front, mid, end) Refers to the 'location' of a grammatical element in a clause. The three possible positions are front, mid and end positions. For example, adjuncts can occupy a variety of positions in a clause:

***In the morning** we had to pretend nothing happened.*
(front position)

*We **sometimes** go to Rochester.*
(mid position)

*That young guy seems to deliver the post **quite often these days**.*
(end position)

Objects and predicative complements have slightly less flexibility and occasionally occur in less typical positions for reasons of emphasis.

Compared with written English, positioning in spoken conversation is generally more flexible (*Are my keys in the door **still**?/Are my keys **still** in the door?*).

Focus

Possessive A word or part of a word that describes possession: possessive determiner (*my, your, his, her, its, our, their*); possessive pronoun (*mine, yours, his, hers, ours, theirs*); genitive (*cow**'s** milk, men**'s** jacket*); the *of* construction (*the rules **of** the school, a student **of** this class*).

Post-head Refers to the dependent elements that come after the head in a phrase. They can be complements and postmodifiers. Complements complete the meaning of the head and they precede postmodifiers:

head | post-head complement
*a | rise | **in interest rates***

head | post-head complement
*She was too | tired | **to work**.*

head | post head complement | postmodifier
*Students | **of astronomy** | **at Cambridge** all get very high grades.*

Complement, complementation; Modification

Postmodification, postmodifier A term used to refer to the modification which occurs after the head word in a phrase:

noun | postmodifier
*The children | **who are playing in the playground** | live down the street.*

adverb | postmodifier
*Luckily | **enough**, | I had a spare key.*

Pragmatics (adjective = **pragmatic**) The study of communication in relation to the intended meanings of particular utterances within particular situations. For instance, *It is cold here.* is typically heard as a statement of fact; however, depending on the intention of the speaker and the context of the utterance, it can be a complaint, a challenge or a request to shut a window.

→ **Speech act**

Predicate, predicative The part of a clause which elaborates what the subject is, does or experiences. It consists of the verb and its object or complement:

subject predicate
Susan | ***won the race.***

Predicative refers to a clause element that occurs in the predicate:

predicative adj
The old lady is | ***very nice.***

predicative subject complement
These books are | ***encyclopaedias.***

Prefix An affix that is attached to the beginning of a base form to create a new word (***mis****understanding*, ***post****-war*, ***re****check*, ***un****happy*, ***anti****-social*).

→ **Derivation; Word formation**

Pre-head Refers to the dependent elements that come before the head in a phrase. In the noun phrase, they can be determiners and premodifiers. Determiners indicate the type of reference for the whole noun phrase and they come before premodifiers:

|——pre-head——| head
det premodifier
some | ***baked*** | *potatoes*

|——pre-head——| head
det premodifier
all | ***university*** | *students*

→ **Modification**

Premodification, premodifier A term used to refer to the modification which occurs before the head word in a phrase. Modifiers which occur before the head are premodifiers (*a* ***different*** *bus*, ***rather*** *good*, ***very*** *quickly*, ***right*** *on the edge*).

Pre-posed, post-posed

→ **Header; Tail**

Preposition, prepositional phrase, preposition stranding Class of word used to express relationships between two events, things or people in terms of time (***at*** *2 o'clock*), space (***to*** *the school*) and other abstract relations (*the capital city* ***of*** *Brazil*). Prepositions can occur as single words (*about, at, by, into*) or in pairs (*out of, next to, as for*).

A phrase with a preposition as the head followed by a complement is called a prepositional phrase (*I'll come* ***with*** *you*.).

Preposition stranding occurs when the preposition is separated from its complement and placed at the end of the clause:

complement preposition
What *was she referring* ***to***?

Preposition stranding

➔ **Preposition**

Present perfect Used to relate events or states taking place in the past to a present time orientation. It has simple and progressive forms:

*We****'ve had*** *that TV set for fifteen years.*
(fifteen years ago till now)

*So, what****'s been happening*** *since the last time we met?*
(from that moment till now)

The simple form is used to emphasise completed and punctual events:

Advertising agency FCB ***has carried out*** *extensive research on how people on short-term contracts feel about their jobs.*

The present perfect progressive can place greater emphasis on the duration of an event up to the present moment to indicate an uninterrupted action:

I've been waiting *for you for over an hour.*

Proform Proforms function to substitute for the object, complement, adjunct, or the whole clause in a sentence. For instance, definite pronouns (*he, this, those*) or indefinite pronouns (*one, all, none*), auxiliary verbs (*do, have*), or adverbs (*so, similarly*) can be used as proforms:

A: *Oh those cakes look lovely.*
B: ***They do****, don't they?*
(***they*** is a proform for *those cakes*; ***do*** is a proform for *look lovely*)

➔ **Ellipsis; Substitution**

Progressive (or continuous) A grammatical aspect which sees time in terms of its unfolding at the moment of speaking, and observes actions and events as incomplete, in progress or developing. It is realised by auxiliary verb *be* and the *-ing* form of a lexical verb:

We ***are leaving*** *now.*

They ***are travelling*** *through Italy at the moment.*

In this grammar book the term progressive is used in preference to continuous.

Pronoun An item used to substitute for the references to entities which lexical noun phrases indicate:

Your boxes of photos have been delivered. ***They****'re in the kitchen.*
(they = your boxes of photos)

The main sub-classifications include personal (*he, you*), possessive (*his, yours*), reflexive (*himself, yourselves*), reciprocal (*each other, one another*), relative (*who, which, that*), interrogative (*who, what, which*), demonstrative (*this, these, that, those*), and indefinite (*some, none*).

➔ **541 Index** for individual terms not in the Glossary

Proposition The topic and comment in a clause together constitute a proposition:

topic comment
We | baked some potatoes in the fire.

Prosody (adjective = **prosodic**) Refers to variations in spoken features such as stress, rhythm, intonation, voice quality, pitch, loudness, tempo, pauses.

Prototypical Shows that a category or representation is the most typical, usual, or characteristic. For example, prototypical questions have interrogative form and function to elicit information.

Pseudo-cleft A grammatical structure which allows end focus to be placed on the clause element. Pseudo-cleft sentences are most often introduced by a *what*-clause which provides old or given information, while the copular complement contains the new, important information:

What we need *is a hammer.*

What you want *is a telephone bank account.*

→ Cleft

Pseudo-intransitive (or middle construction) Refers to the use of verbs intransitively which are normally used transitively in clauses (*clean, close, cook, drive, iron, photograph, read*). In this construction, the agent is not mentioned and the recipient/beneficiary of the action becomes the grammatical subject. This gives endweight to the verb (and any accompanying complement/adjunct):

Fish ***cooks*** *quickly.*

Helen ***photographs*** *really well, doesn't she?*

→ Transitive

Pseudo-passive Structures based on *get* and *have* which are more common in spoken language. Pseudo-passives are similar to true passives in that the grammatical subject is typically the recipient, rather than the agent/doer, of the action:

They ***got deported.***

She ***had her car damaged.***

→ Causative; Passive

Punctuation This involves conventions such as the comma (,), colon (:), semi-colon (;), full-stop (.), hyphen (-), question mark (?), exclamation mark (!), quotation marks (' '), dashes (–), parentheses ( ). Punctuation functions to separate grammatical units and paragraphs in written language, and to specify particular properties of units through quotation marks, italics, initial capitals, bold face, etc.

Quantifier A word or phrase used before a noun to express a positive or negative contrast in quantity. There are closed and open classes of quantifiers.

Closed class: *all, some, many, much, few, little, several, enough*, etc.

Open class: *a lot of, plenty of, large amounts of, a bottle of, two loaves of*, etc.

··➝ **Partitive**

Question (*yes-no*, *wh-*, alternative, follow-up, echo, display, two-step) An utterance (most typically in interrogative form) which requires a verbal response from the addressee.

Yes-no questions ask if something is true, and require a response of *yes* or *no*:

A: ***Are you ready***?
B: *Yes/no.*

Wh-questions are introduced by words such as *who, what, why*, and require information to be given in the response:

A: ***What time are you leaving***?
B: *Six o'clock.*

Alternative questions present options for the respondent to choose from:

A: ***Would you like tea or coffee***?
B: *Er, tea, please.*

Follow-up questions serve to request further specification. They usually appear as short questions with *wh*-words:

A: *I've done lots of work.*
B: ***Have you***? ***Like what***?
A: *Like writing a first draft of my essay.*

Echo questions seek confirmation or clarification of what has been said by repeating part of the speaker's utterance. They often have a declarative word order and an end-position *wh*-word:

A: *Pay attention to this!*
B: ***Pay attention to what***?

Display questions seek confirmation of something the speaker already knows, with the purpose of putting knowledge or information on public display. Display questions are common in contexts such as classrooms, quiz shows and other tests of knowledge:

Teacher: ***What is the capital of France***?
Pupil: *Paris.*

Two-step questions involve a two-stage process in which one question may act as a preface for another question:

A: ***Are you going to the match tonight***?
B: *Yeah, I am.*
A: ***Do you mind if I tag along***?

Raised subject Refers to the placing of items as subjects of their clauses in order to create different types of focus. Very often adjectives (*easy, difficult, hard, likely, certain, impossible*), verbs (*seem, appear, look*) and mental process verbs in the passive (*be found, be considered, be estimated*) are involved:

***To summarise our work** is impossible.*
(*to summarise our work*, the complement of *impossible*, is raised as the subject)

***Jina**'s quite difficult to understand.*
(*Jina*, the object of *understand*, is raised as the subject)

***It** seems that nobody does anything.*
(anticipatory *it* is raised as the subject)

→ Focus; Subject

Rank-shifting Refers to the phenomenon where an item associated with a higher rank in the grammar shifts to a lower rank. In the sentence *Two people I know have gone there.*, the clause *I know* modifies the head noun *people*, and is a constituent (an embedded clause) of a subject noun phrase which is of a lower grammatical rank.

Recipient of action Refers to the person or thing that is the affected participant of an action. In the passive sentence ***Those houses** were built by John Walton.*, *those houses* is the recipient of action as well as the grammatical subject. The agent is indicated by the *by*-phrase *by John Walton*.

In *get*- and *have*-pseudo-passive constructions, the grammatical subject is typically the recipient, rather than the agent, of the action (***The thief** got arrested. **Mary** had her watch stolen.*).

→ Pseudo-passive

Reciprocal, reciprocal verb, reciprocal pronoun A term that expresses a two-way relationship. A reciprocal use of a verb suggests that the coordinated subjects are doing the same thing to each other (*meet, divorce, kiss, separate, fight*):

*Frank and Diane **met** in 1979.*

A reciprocal pronoun refers to a mutual relationship between people or things:

*They hate **each other/one another**.*

Reduced clause, reduced question Reduced clauses refer to incomplete clause structures where verbs are ellipted:

A: *Has he eaten the cauliflower?*
B: ***Not all of it.*** (reduced clause)

Reduced questions refer to interrogative clauses where verbs are ellipted.

A: ***You hungry**?* (reduced question)
B: *Mm, a bit.*

They occur in very informal, highly context-dependent situations, especially when meaning is very clear.

→ Ellipsis

Reduplicative compound, reduplication A form of compound which involves identical or near identical or rhyming bases. Reduplicative compounds are often very informal in usage and are used in talk by or with children (*goody-goody, tick-tock* (clock), *bow-wow* (dog), *easy-peasy*).

Reference, referent, referring expression Terms used to indicate how speakers and writers refer to people, places, things and ideas. The broad distinctions are endophoric (reference to situation within the text) and exophoric (reference to situation outside the text). Endophoric references are divided into anaphoric and cataphoric. The referent is the entities referred to:

referent — referring expression

The children *looked tired. They had been travelling all day.*

referent — referring expression

They arrived at ***the resort****. Here at last was a place they could relax.*

→ **Anaphora; Cataphora; Endophora; Exophora**

Reflexive A construction that contains a verb with a reflexive pronoun object, or a reflexive pronoun complement of a preposition where the referent of the complement is the same as that of the subject:

Shall I serve ***myself****?*

Did you hurt ***yourself****?*

He kept it all for ***himself****.*

Reformulation Some discourse markers can signal reformulations or alternative expressions, indicating that the speaker has not selected the most appropriate way of expressing things and is refining what they say with a more apt word or phrase. Among such markers are: *I mean, so to speak, to put it another way*.

Register Refers to the style of speaking or writing that is used in particular fields of discourse or particular social contexts (e.g. academic writing, journalism, advertising, legal, science and literary conventions).

Regular verb Refers to the form of verb which simply adds inflections to the base form without any change (base form: *cough*; present form: *cough*; *-s* form: *cough****s***; *-ing* form: *cough****ing***; past form: *cough****ed***; *-ed* participle: *cough****ed***).

Relative clause Relative clauses are of two main kinds:

- embedded clauses used to postmodify noun heads (*The book* ***that I want*** *is not available in the library*.)
- sentential relative clauses: *which*-clauses referring to a whole sentence or stretch of discourse (*She's always out when I call,* ***which is very inconvenient****.*)

Normally they are preceded by a relative pronoun.

→ **Defining relative clause; Non-defining relative clause**

Relative pronoun Refers to words (*who, whom, whose, which, that*) which introduce a relative clause:

*The lady **who** runs this shop has just moved.*

*The book **that** I am reading is fascinating.*

Sometimes the relative pronoun can be omitted, referred to as a zero relative pronoun.

Reporting clause, reported clause A reporting clause introduces someone's speech or thoughts (***Nick said**, 'Hello.'*) The speech or thought itself is contained in the reported clause (*She said **she was leaving**.*).

Request A form of speech act where the speaker desires a particular course of action from the listener, and the listener has a choice whether to act in the way indicated. For example, it can be realised by *can/could, will/would, would you like to, would you mind* in interrogatives:

A: ***Will you** get me a glass of water?*
B: *Yeah.*

***Would you** take this letter to the post for me?*

Response token Word or phrase used to acknowledge what a speaker says, and to indicate on the part of the listener interest or engagement in what is being said. Response tokens include minimal response tokens (sounds or words like *oh, mm, yeah, okay, no*), and non-minimal response tokens, which are frequently made up of adjectives and adverbs or short phrases or clauses (*great, exactly, very good, that's true*).

Restrictive relative clause

→ **Defining relative clause**

Rheme

→ **Comment**

Rhetorical question An interrogative clause used for rhetorical effect, posing a question to which the reader or listener is not expected to give an informative verbal response (*Who knows where I'll be next year?*).

Right dislocation

→ **Tail**

Semantics Refers to the study of meaning, which includes the meanings of words and the meanings of larger semantic units, e.g. sentences.

Semi-modal verb A kind of marginal modal verb (*dare, need, ought to, used to*) which expresses modal meanings. They behave like core modal verbs which do not take auxiliary *do* in the negative (***I dare not** tell her what's happened.*). But they also behave like lexical verbs as they allow an auxiliary to precede them (*Marie **didn't dare** say anything to them.*).

→ **Core modal verb; Modality**

Sentence The largest independent unit of grammar. It consists of at least one main clause. In writing, sentence boundaries are defined by an initial capital letter and a full stop, an exclamation mark or a question mark at the end. Sentences are composed of clauses.

Simple aspect Simple aspect is in contrast with progressive aspect. Simple aspect involves base and inflected forms of verbs (*she sings, they ran, we have eaten, he'll leave*); progressive aspect involves the use of *be* + *-ing* with a verb (*she's singing, they were running, we have been eating, he'll be leaving*).

Singular The most common form of nouns (*table, computer*), verbs (*she cries*), pronouns (*he, she, it*), etc. It denotes only one in number. Singular contrasts with plural.

Softening The effect of mitigating, or weakening, the force of what is written or said to make a speech act more polite or less assertive. For example, the use of tense and aspect (past tense, progressive or perfect aspect), lexical verbs (*reckon, wonder, hope, think*) and modal verbs (*may, should, can, could*) can help to achieve this effect:

*I **wondered** if you**'d** help me out in the garden.*

*I **was hoping** they were not here.*

*I **reckon** that's what you **should** do.*
(compare: That is what you must do.)

⇢ **Hedging**

Speech act Refers to the speaker's intention rather than the propositional meaning (content) of the utterance. The sentence *I am hot.* has the propositional meaning of a sensation of increased temperature by the speaker, but it may be heard as a complaint, or a request or order to someone to open a window. Common speech acts in everyday situations include informing, directing, complaining, exemplifying, offering, apologising, promising, permitting.

Speech reporting, speech representation A term for reporting one's own or another person's speech by using a reporting clause (*he said, I replied, they asked*). The accompanying speech, thought or writing is called the reported clause and can be either direct or indirect speech.

Speech representation

⇢ **Speech reporting**

Split infinitive Refers to the use of an adverb or other item between *to* and the infinitive form of the verb (*I want you to* ***seriously*** *consider his resignation.*). Some people have objections to this usage on stylistic grounds.

Stance Refers to a speaker's or writer's attitude towards the proposition of an utterance. Among the expressions which commonly signal stance are: *admittedly, basically, frankly, if you ask me, obviously, sadly, to be honest.*

Standard A term used to refer to the most prestigious variety of the language based on the spoken and written norms adopted by educated native speakers in domains such as the mass media, foreign language teaching, dictionary compilation and similar institutionalised uses. Linguistic forms which deviate from this norm are viewed as non-standard.

Statement A sentence which conveys information, makes assertions, and describes actions, feelings, or a state of affairs. A statement is most typically a declarative clause (*He works in Barsham.*). Statements are contrasted with questions.

Stative verb, state verb A verb that describes a state or situation, in which no obvious action takes place. A stative verb cannot normally be used with the progressive aspect:

He hates me.
(~~He is hating me.~~)

I believe you.

→ **Dynamic verb**

Stem Refers to the form of a word to which prefixes and suffixes are attached (*re**duce**, un**trace**able, **snow**y, **capt**ive*).

Stranded preposition

→ **Preposition**

Sub-class Refers to elements of a class of word. For example, gradable and non-gradable adjectives are sub-classes of adjectives.

→ **Class**

Subject, dummy subject Identifies the doer or agent of an action, a state or an event, in the form of either a noun phrase or a nominal clause. It usually precedes the verb in a declarative clause and determines the person and number of the verb (***My mother** works there.*).

Dummy subject refers to the use of *it* or *there* as a non-referential pronoun which fills the required subject position:

***It** is good to be here.*
(~~Is good to be here.~~)

***There**'s a cat walking across the garden.*

→ **Empty *it***

Subjunctive A form of mood which expresses wished for or desired states, after verbs such as *insist, demand, recommend, require, stipulate*. It is realised by the base form of the verb for all persons, with no inflections. It is associated with very formal styles (*I insist that she* **do** *these things herself.*).

Subordinate clause A dependent clause that cannot form a sentence on its own, and is usually linked to a main clause by a subordinating conjunction such as *although, because, before, for, that, when*. A subordinate clause may be finite or non-finite (*I spoke to her **before** she left.*).

Subordinator Another term for subordinating conjunction.

→ **Subordinate clause**

Substitution A term used to refer to the use of a proform to substitute a previously mentioned entity. It is a device for brevity to avoid repetition. Substitution can occur at phrasal and clausal levels:

Peter has bought a new jacket and Sam has bought ***one*** *too.*

Cambridge is the most prestigious university in the UK. People say ***so***.

Suffix An affix that is attached to the end of a base form to create a new word. This process typically changes the word class: noun suffixes (*act**ion**, train**ee**, free**dom**, arriv**al***); adjective suffixes (*inform**al**, home**less**, grate**ful***); verb suffixes (*simpl**ify**, dark**en**, internationa**lise***); adverb suffixes (*quick**ly**, home**ward(s)**, clock**wise***).

Superlative The form of a gradable adjective or adverb which is used to specify the most or the least of qualities, properties, states, conditions, relations, etc. among entities. The superlative is realised by the suffix *-est*, or use of *(the) most*:

*Of all of them, Tom is **cleverest**.*

*Tom is **the tallest** boy in class.*

*Tom is **the most handsome** boy in class.*

Suppletion Refers to a word which completely changes its shape in its inflected forms (*good, better, best*).

Swearing A form of taboo language that is considered to be rude or blasphemous. People use swear words to express strong feelings like annoyance, frustration and anger.

Syntax Concerns the rules that govern the arrangement of words in phrases, clauses and sentences, i.e. the study of the structure of sentences.

Taboo language Contains swearing or other types of words or phrases which carry an intensifying and often negative comment on people and events. They are discouraged in a society owing to their offensive or embarrassing nature.

Tag, tag question, fixed tag, copy tag A type of clause without a lexical verb. It normally consists of an auxiliary verb, a modal verb, or the verb *be* and a subject pronoun; it shows concord with the main-clause subject. Tags occur very frequently in spoken English.

A tag question consists of a tag after a declarative clause which changes the clause into a question or request for confirmation. It may have affirmative or negative polarity:

*She's a teacher, **isn't she**?*

*We've never been to Stockholm, **have we**?*

A fixed tag involves items such as *(all) right, okay, yeah, eh, don't you think?* at the end of a declarative clause. It functions to check that a statement has been understood:

*So we're meeting at 7 outside the pizza place, **okay**?*

*Let's stop talking in circles, **right**?*

A copy tag has the same polarity and subject-verb word order after a declarative clause. It functions to make emphatic statements, frequently in evaluative contexts:

affirmative affirmative
*She**'s** lovely, **she is**.*

negative negative
*It's **not** very good, **that one isn't**.*

541 **Index** for individual terms not in the Glossary

Tail Refers to the word or phrase that occurs at the end of a clause through which a speaker clarifies, strengthens, extends or emphasises a preceding topic entity. Tails are a common feature of informal spoken English:

He*'s quite a comic* ***that fellow****.*

They *do tend to go cold, don't they,* ***pasta****.*

The terms 'right dislocation' and 'post-posed' are also sometimes used to refer to tails.

Tense A grammatical category to indicate the relationship between the form of the verb and the time reference of an event or action. English has two tenses, present and past:

The players ***practise*** *every day.*
(present tense)

They ***had*** *a football match yesterday.*
(past tense)

➝ **Historic present tense**

Tensed The form of a verb which indicates present or past tense:

He ***loves*** *fish.*

They ***worked*** *hard.*

I ***was*** *thinking about you.*

It is contrasted with non-tensed.

Text A stretch of language, either in speech or in writing, that is semantically and pragmatically coherent in its real-world context. A text can range from just one word (e.g. a SLOW sign on the road) to a sequence of utterances or sentences in a speech, a letter, a novel, etc.

➝ **Coherence; Discourse**

Theme

➝ **Comment**

Time (past, present, future) A non-linguistic concept which refers to the past, the present and the future. Time can be expressed by tense, through a change of verb forms. Time is also related to aspect, which represents speakers' perspectives on time in relation to events.

Present time denotes time reference for actions, events or states at the moment of speaking or writing, or at 'time around now'.

Past time denotes time reference for actions, events or states before the time of speaking or writing.

Future time denotes time reference for future actions, events or states. There is no future tense ending for English verbs; future time is mainly expressed by *shall/will, be going to,* present progressive form, *be about to, be to,* etc.

Tone unit Refers to the minimal unit of communication with at least one intonation contour that ends in a rising or falling tone. Tone units typically appear as clauses, but they can also be phrases or single words:

***ME**?*

***ANY**way.*

*I'm **LOO**king for a **PEN**cil.*

***ARE**'nt you **REA**dy?*

Topic Refers to the main subject matter a speaker or writer wants to talk about. The topic is most typically associated with the grammatical subject.

→ Comment

Transitive complementation, transitive oblique Transitive complementation refers to the type of complementation a transitive verb requires to complete its meaning. This can be single complementation or dual complementation:

*I **spotted** a taxi.*
(single complementation: the speaker must say what they spotted)

*He **put** it in the rubbish bin.*
(dual complementation: the speaker must say *what* was put and *where* it was put)

Transitive oblique refers to a type of ditransitive complementation (direct object + prepositional complement with *to*) in which the recipient of the direct object is obliquely put into focus. Transitive verbs associated with this usage are *bring, give, grant, hand, leave, send, owe,* etc.:

	direct object	transitive oblique prep complement
She sent	*a letter*	***to Ivy Bolton.***

Transitive verb The use of a verb with one or two objects to complete its meaning when used in the active voice. Verbs such as *ask, bring, carry, find, get, give, love, make, use,* are typically used transitively:

*I **love** carrots.*

*My mother **gives** | me | pocket money | every week.*

Turn A basic unit of conversation. Speakers take turns to speak, and a turn ends when the speaker changes. A turn may be very short or very long:

Assistant: *There you go. There's your ticket. And your accommodation there. Insurance, and just some general information.* (turn 1)
Customer: *Excellent. Right.* (turn 2)

Uncountable

→ Noun; Non-count noun

Unmarked

→ Marked

→ **541 Index** for individual terms not in the Glossary

Utterance Refers to a communicative unit in speech that is both communicatively and pragmatically complete. An utterance may consist of single words, phrases, clauses or clause combinations spoken in context. There are four utterances in the following example:

1 A: *But he's trying to send us an email and I'm having some trouble with the computer you see.*
2 B: *Right.*
3 A: *You know.*
4 B: *Yeah.*

The term 'utterance' is contrasted with 'sentence' in written language.

Vague language Words or phrases with very general meanings (*thing, stuff, or whatever, sort of, or something, or anything*) which deliberately refer to people and things in a non specific, imprecise way. Purposefully vague language is very common in informal spoken language:

Does he think I'm stupid ***or something****?*

She's ***sort of*** *interested.*

→ **Softening**

Verb In a clause, the verb is an obligatory and the most central element. It denotes actions, events, processes and states. Verbs are either regular (*cough, coughs, coughing, coughed*) or irregular (*speak, speaks, spoke, speaking, spoken*). There are three main grammatical classes of verb: lexical (*walk, love, put, cook*), auxiliary (*do, be, have*) and modal (*can, must, will*). Lexical and auxiliary verbs indicate contrasts of tense, person and number:

She ***walks*** *too quickly for me.*
(lexical verb *walks* in present tense, agreement in person and number with subject *she*)

He ***has*** *been a good friend.*
(auxiliary verb *has*, agreement of tense, person and number)

We ***must*** *get there early.*
(modal *must*: no inflection for tense, person or number)

Verb phrase A phrase with a lexical verb as its head:

I ***asked*** *you.*

We should have ***phoned*** *you.*

A verb phrase introduces the predicate part of a clause, indicates the clause type, and shows contrasts in tense, aspect, voice and mood.

→ **Complex verb phrase**

Vocative A noun phrase used to directly address the listener or reader, normally in the form of a personal name, title or term of endearment:

Paul*, can you help us?*

This is for you, ***daddy****.*

Voice Gives information about the roles of different participants (agent or recipient) in an event. Voice may be active or passive. Voice changes the semantic relationship between the grammatical subject and object of a verb.
Active voice: *My sister cooked the meal.*
(grammatical subject as doer/agent)

Passive voice: *The meal was cooked by my sister.*
(grammatical subject as recipient of the action)

Volitional Expresses a meaning of willingness, usually by means of modal verbs such as *will* or *would* in offers and requests:

*I would be grateful if you **would** lend me a pound.*

***Wh*-clause** A declarative clause that is introduced by question words *who(m), whose, what, when, where, which, why* or *how*. A *wh*-clause is often used as a direct object after verbs such as *advise, ask, inform, remind, show* and *tell* and in cleft sentences:

*I asked him **why he came**.*
(as direct object)

*Could you please advise me **what I should do**.*
(as direct object)

*It was an elderly lady **who had this house**.*
(in cleft sentence)

***Wh*-cleft** A *wh*-cleft contains given information but shifts the focus of a clause to the end to indicate new and important information. This is especially common in spoken language:

given information / new, important information
*So **what you really want** is a hotel that's got the facilities for the children, isn't it?*

given information / new, important information
***What I'll do** is I'll take all your details from you.*

→ Cleft; Pseudo-cleft

Wh-question

→ Question

Word The basic linguistic unit which relates the grammar of a language to its vocabulary. Words can be categorised into lexical and grammatical words. Lexical words (most of the vocabulary of a language) belong to open systems, where new words are frequently added. Grammatical words (e.g. determiners, conjunctions, prepositions) belong to closed systems, with new items only rarely being formed. Words are bounded by spaces in writing.

→ Class

Word class

→ Class

→ **541 Index** for individual terms not in the Glossary

Word formation Refers to the process of the creation of words and new forms of existing words. There are three main types of word formation:

- derivation: forming words by adding prefixes and suffixes
- compounding: combining words to form units of meaning (*car + park = car park, down + load = download*)
- conversion (*a **text** ➛ to **text***: noun ➛ verb)

Other minor word formation processes include:

- acronym: use of initial letters of a set of words pronounced as a word (*AIDS – acquired immune deficiency syndrome*)
- blending: combining parts of existing words to form a new word (***sm**oke + **fog** = smog; **br**eakfast + **lunch** = brunch*)
- clipping: reducing the number of syllables from a word (*ad – advertisement, lab – laboratory*)

Word order The sequential arrangement of words in a sentence, for example, subject – verb – object word order in declarative clauses:

S V O
Babies like milk.

A change in the word order normally indicates a change in function.

➛ **Fronting; Header; Tail; Topic**

***Yes-no* question**

➛ **Question**

Zero (zero plural, zero article, zero relative pronoun) A zero plural has the same form in both singular and plural. This happens in some animal nouns (*sheep, salmon, fish, deer, cattle*), certain numerals (*three hundred, ten thousand, two dozen*), etc.

A zero article refers to the use of no article or other determiner before a noun (*I like **coffee**; **dinner** is served*).

A zero relative pronoun refers to the non-use of a relative pronoun in a relative clause (*That woman* [zero relative] *I met last week could probably help you.*).

CANCODE PUBLICATIONS (1994–2006)

Publications by the authors and their co-researchers based round the five-million-word CANCODE spoken corpus. These publications have fed into the construction of the present grammar. (CANCODE = Cambridge and Nottingham Corpus of Discourse in English.) The following items have all been or are about to be published as part of the CANCODE project.

Adolphs, S. and Carter, R.A. (2003) 'Corpus stylistics: point of view and semantic prosodies in *To the Lighthouse*', *Poetica* 58: 7–20

Carter, R.A. (1997) *Investigating English Discourse: Language, literacy and literature*, London: Routledge

Carter, R.A. (1997) 'Grammar, the spoken language and ELT', in Hill, D.A. (ed) *Milan 95: English Language Teaching*, Rome: The British Council: 26–32

Carter, R.A. (1997) 'Speaking Englishes, speaking cultures, using CANCODE', *Prospect* 12 (2): 4–11

Carter, R.A. (1998) 'Orders of reality: CANCODE, communication and culture', *ELT Journal* 52 (1): 43–56

Carter, R.A. (1999) 'Common language: corpus, creativity and cognition', *Language and Literature* 8 (3): 1–21

Carter, R.A. (1999) 'Standard grammars, standard Englishes: some educational implications', in Bex, A.R. and Watts, R. (eds) *Standard English: The Continuing Debate*, London: Routledge

Carter, R.A. (2002) 'Spoken English, grammar and the classroom' in Hughes, R. (ed) *At Full Stretch: Spoken English and the National Curriculum*, London: Qualifications and Curriculum Authority. Published at http://www.qca.org.uk

Carter, R.A. (2002) 'Recognising creativity', *IH Journal of Language and Development*, 13: 9–14

Carter, R.A. (2004) 'Spoken Grammar', in Coffin, C., Hewings, A. and O'Halloran, K. (eds) *Applying English Grammar: Functional and Corpus Approaches* (London: Edward Arnold), 35–49

Carter, R.A. (2004) *Language and Creativity: The Art of Common Talk London*: Routledge

Carter, R.A. and Adolphs, S. (2003) 'Creativity and a corpus of spoken English', in Goodman, S., Lillis, T., Maybin, J. and Mercer, N. (eds) *Language, Literacy and Education: A Reader*, Stoke-on-Trent: Trentham Books: 247–262

Carter, R.A. and Adolphs, S. (2003) 'And she's like 'it's terrible like': spoken discourse, grammar and corpus analysis', *International Journal of English Studies* 2003, 3 (1): 45–57

Carter, R.A. and Schmitt, N. (2004) 'Formulaic sequences in action: An introduction' in Schmitt, N. (ed.) *Formulaic Sequences*, Amsterdam: John Benjamins: 1–22

Carter, R.A. and McCarthy, M.J. (1995) 'Grammar and the spoken language', *Applied Linguistics* 16 (2): 141–158

Carter, R.A. and McCarthy, M.J. (1995) 'Discourse and creativity: bridging the gap between language and literature', in Cook, G. and Seidlhofer, B. (eds) *Principle and Practice in Applied Linguistics*, Oxford: Oxford University Press: 303–321

Carter, R.A. and McCarthy, M.J. (1997) *Exploring Spoken English*, Cambridge: Cambridge University Press

Carter, R.A. and McCarthy, M.J. (1997) 'Written and spoken vocabulary', in Schmitt, N. and McCarthy, M.J. (eds) *Vocabulary: Description, Acquisition, Pedagogy*, Cambridge: Cambridge University Press, 20–39

Carter, R.A. and McCarthy, M.J. (1999) 'The English *get*-passive in spoken discourse: description and implications for an interpersonal grammar', *English Language and Linguistics*, 3 (1): 41–58

Carter, R.A. and McCarthy, M.J. (2001) 'Size isn't everything: spoken English, corpus and the classroom', in *Research Issues, TESOL Quarterly* (July, 2001): 337–340

Carter, R.A. and McCarthy, M.J. (2001) 'Designing the discourse syllabus', in Hall, D. and Hewings, A. (eds) *Innovation in English Language Teaching*, London: Routledge: 55–63

Carter, R.A. and McCarthy, M.J. (2004) 'Talking, creating: interactional language, creativity and context', *Applied Linguistics*, 25 (1): 62–88

Carter, R.A. and McCarthy, M.J. (2004) 'If you ever hear a native speaker, please let us know!' in A. Pulverness (ed) *IATEFL 2003 Brighton Conference Selections*, Kent: IATEFL: 116–23

Carter, R.A. and McCarthy, M.J. (2006) *Cambridge Grammar of English: A comprehensive guide to spoken and written grammar and usage*. Cambridge: Cambridge University Press

Carter, R.A., Hughes, R. and McCarthy, M.J. (1998) 'Telling tails: grammar, the spoken language and materials development', in Tomlinson, B. (ed) *Materials Development in L2 Teaching*, Cambridge: Cambridge University Press: 45–68

Carter, R.A., Hughes, R. and McCarthy, M.J. (2000) *Exploring Grammar in Context*, Cambridge: Cambridge University Press

Carter, R.A. and White, J. (2004) (eds) *Introducing The Grammar of Talk*, London: Qualifications and Curriculum Authority

Fung, L. and Carter, R.A. (2005) *Discourse Markers and Spoken English: Native and Non-native Use in Pedagogic Settings*. m/s School of English Studies, University of Nottingham

Hughes, R., Carter, R.A. and McCarthy, M.J. (1995) 'Discourse context as a predictor of grammatical choice', in Graddol, D. and Thomas, S. (eds) *Language in a Changing Europe*, Clevedon: BAAL/Multilingual Matters: 47–54

Hughes, R. and McCarthy, M.J. (1998) 'From sentence to grammar: discourse grammar and English language teaching', *TESOL Quarterly*, 32 (2): 263–87

McCarthy, M.J. (1994) 'What should we teach about the spoken language?', *Australian Review of Applied Linguistics*, 2: 104–20

McCarthy, M.J. (1994) 'Vocabulary and the spoken language', in Longo H.P. (ed) *Atti del seminario internazionale di studi sul lessico*, Bologna: Clueb: 119–30

McCarthy, M.J. (1995) 'Conversation and literature: tense and aspect', in Payne, J. (ed.) *Linguistic Approaches to Literature*, Birmingham/University of Birmingham: English Language Research: 58–73

McCarthy, M.J. (1998) *Spoken Language and Applied Linguistics*, Cambridge: Cambridge University Press

McCarthy, M.J. (1998) 'Taming the spoken language: genre theory and pedagogy', *The Language Teacher*, 22 (9) 21–23

McCarthy, M.J. (1998) 'Talking their heads off: the everyday conversation of everyday people', *SELL* 0:107–128

McCarthy, M.J. (1999) 'What constitutes a basic vocabulary for spoken communication?' *SELL* 1: 233–249

McCarthy, M.J. (1999) 'What is a basic spoken vocabulary?', *FELT Newsletter*, 1999, 1 (4): 7–9

McCarthy, M.J. (1999) 'Turning numbers into thoughts: making sense of language corpora technology and observing language', *The Language Teacher* 23 (6): 25–7

McCarthy, M.J. (2000) 'Captive audiences: the discourse of close contact service encounters', in Coupland, J. (ed) *Small Talk*, London: Pearson: 84–109

McCarthy, M.J. (2001) 'Discourse' in Carter, R.A and Nunan, D. (eds) *Teaching English to Speakers of Other Languages*, Cambridge: Cambridge University Press: 48–55

McCarthy, M.J. (2001) *Issues in Applied Linguistics*, Cambridge: Cambridge University Press

McCarthy, M.J. (2002) 'What is an advanced vocabulary?' *SELL* 3: 149–163. Reprinted in Tan, M. (ed.) *Corpus Studies in Language Education*, Bangkok: IELE Press: 15–29

McCarthy, M.J. (2002) 'Good listenership made plain: British and American non-minimal response tokens in everyday conversation', in Biber, D., Fitzpatrick S. and Reppen, R. (eds) *Using Corpora to Explore Linguistic Variation*, Amsterdam: John Benjamins: 49–71

McCarthy, M.J. (2003) 'Talking back: 'small' interactional response tokens in everyday conversation' in Coupland, J. (ed.) Special issue of *Research on Language and Social Interaction* on 'Small Talk', 36 (1): 33-63

McCarthy, M.J. (2004) 'Lessons from the analysis of chunks', *The Language Teacher* 28 (7): 9–12

McCarthy, M.J. (2005) 'Fluency and confluence: what fluent speakers do', *The Language Teacher* 29 (6): 26–28

McCarthy, M.J. and Carter, R.A. (1994) *Language as Discourse: Perspectives for language teaching*, Harlow: Longman

McCarthy, M.J. and Carter, R.A. (1995) 'Spoken grammar: what is it and how do we teach it?', *ELT Journal* 49 (3): 207–218

McCarthy, M.J. and Carter, R.A. (1997) 'Grammar, tails and affect: constructing expressive choices in discourse', *Text* 17 (3): 231–252

McCarthy, M.J. and Carter, R.A. (2000) 'Feeding back: non-minimal response tokens in everyday English conversation', in Heffer, C. and Sauntson, H. (eds) *Words in Context: a tribute to John Sinclair on his retirement*, Birmingham: ELR Discourse Monograph 18: 263–283

McCarthy, M.J. and Carter, R.A. (2001) 'Ten criteria for a spoken grammar', in Hinkel, E. and Fotos, S. (eds) *New Perspectives on Grammar Teaching in Second Language Classrooms*, Mahwah, N.J.: Lawrence Erlbaum Associates: 51–75

McCarthy, M.J. and Carter, R.A. (2002) 'From conversation to corpus: a dual analysis of a broadcast political interview', in Sánchez-Macarro, A. (ed.) *Windows on the World: media discourse in English*, Valencia: University of Valencia Press: 15–39

McCarthy, M.J. and Carter, R.A. (2002) '*This, that and the other*. Multi-word clusters in spoken English as visible patterns of interaction', TEANGA (2002) (Yearbook of the Irish Association for Applied Linguistics) 21: 30–52

McCarthy, M.J. and Carter, R.A. (2004) 'There's millions of them': hyperbole in everyday conversation', *Journal of Pragmatics* 36: 149–184

McCarthy, M.J. and Handford, M. (2004) 'Invisible to us': A preliminary corpus-based study of spoken business English. In Connor, U. and Upton, T. (eds) *Discourse in the Professions. Perspectives from Corpus Linguistics.* Amsterdam: John Benjamins: 167–201

McCarthy, M.J. and O'Dell, F. (1999) *English Vocabulary in Use* (elementary level), Cambridge: Cambridge University Press

McCarthy, M.J. and O'Dell, F. (2002) *English Vocabulary in Use* (advanced level), Cambridge: Cambridge University Press

McCarthy, M.J. and O'Dell, F. (2002) *English Idioms in Use* (upper intermediate level), Cambridge: Cambridge University Press

McCarthy, M.J. and O'Dell, F. (2003) *English Phrasal Verbs in Use* (intermediate level), Cambridge: Cambridge University Press

McCarthy, M.J. and O'Dell, F. (2005) *English Collocations in Use*, Cambridge: Cambridge University Press

McCarthy, M.J. and O'Keeffe, A. (2003). 'What's in a name? Vocatives in casual conversations and radio phone-in calls', in Meyer, C. and Leistyna, P. (eds), *Corpus Analysis: language structure and language use*, Amsterdam: Rodopi: 153–185

McCarthy, M.J., Matthiessen, C. and Slade, D. (2001) 'Discourse Analysis', in Schmitt, N. (ed) *An Introduction to Applied Linguistics*, London: Arnold: 55–73

McCarthy, M.J. and Slade, D. (in press) 'Extending our understanding of spoken discourse', in Cummins, J. and Davison, C. *Kluwer Handbook on English Language Teaching*, Dordrecht: Kluwer Academic Publishers

McCarthy, M.J. and Spöttl, C. (2003) 'Formulaic utterances in the multi-lingual context' in Cenoz, J., Jessner, U. & Hufeisen, B. (eds) *The Multilingual Lexicon*, Dordrecht: Kluwer: 133–151

McCarthy, M.J. and Spöttl, C. (2004) 'Comparing the knowledge of formulaic sequences across L1, L2, L3 and L4' in Schmitt, N. (ed.) *Formulaic Sequences*, Amsterdam: John Benjamins: 191–225

McCarthy, M.J. and Tao, H. (2001) 'Understanding non-restrictive *which*-clauses in spoken English, which is not an easy thing', *Language Sciences* 23: 651–677

McCarthy, M.J. and Walsh, S. (2003) 'Discourse', in Nunan D. (ed) *Practical English Language Teaching*, New York: McGraw-Hill: 173–195

Stanfield, C. (1996) 'English as she is spoke' (conversation with CANCODE researcher Jean Hudson), *Cambridge Language Reference News* 2: 2

Index

Note: the numbers are section numbers, not page numbers.

B

C

D

E

F

G

H

M

N

O

P

Q

R

S

T

U

V

W

Y

Z